Lecture Notes in Artificial Intelligence   5291

Edited by R. Goebel, J. Siekmann, and W. Wahlster

Subseries of Lecture Notes in Computer Science

T0238834

Sergio Greco   Thomas Lukasiewicz (Eds.)

Scalable Uncertainty Management

Second International Conference, SUM 2008
Naples, Italy, October 1-3, 2008
Proceedings

 Springer

Series Editors

Randy Goebel, University of Alberta, Edmonton, Canada
Jörg Siekmann, University of Saarland, Saarbrücken, Germany
Wolfgang Wahlster, DFKI and University of Saarland, Saarbrücken, Germany

Volume Editors

Sergio Greco
Università della Calabria, DEIS
Via P. Bucci, cubo 42c, 87036 Rende, CS, Italy
E-mail: greco@deis.unical.it

Thomas Lukasiewicz
University of Oxford, Computing Laboratory
Wolfson Building, Parks Road, Oxford OX1 3QD, UK
E-mail: thomas.lukasiewicz@comlab.ox.ac.uk

Library of Congress Control Number: 2008935559

CR Subject Classification (1998): I.2, F.4.1

LNCS Sublibrary: SL 7 – Artificial Intelligence

ISSN 0302-9743
ISBN 978-3-540-87992-3 Springer Berlin Heidelberg New York

This work is subject to copyright. All rights are reserved, whether the whole or part of the material is
concerned, specifically the rights of translation, reprinting, re-use of illustrations, recitation, broadcasting,
reproduction on microfilms or in any other way, and storage in data banks. Duplication of this publication
or parts thereof is permitted only under the provisions of the German Copyright Law of September 9, 1965,
in its current version, and permission for use must always be obtained from Springer. Violations are liable
to prosecution under the German Copyright Law.

Springer is a part of Springer Science+Business Media

springer.com

© Springer-Verlag Berlin Heidelberg 2008

Typesetting: Camera-ready by author, data conversion by Scientific Publishing Services, Chennai, India
Printed on acid-free paper   SPIN: 12533572   06/3180   5 4 3 2 1 0

Preface

Originally, managing uncertainty and inconsistency has especially been explored in the field of artificial intelligence. During recent years, particularly with the availability of massive amounts of data in different repositories and the possibility of integrating and exploiting these data, technologies for managing uncertainty and inconsistency have started to play a key role in databases and the Web. Some of the most prominent of these technologies are probably the ranking algorithms behind Web search engines. Techniques for handling uncertainty and inconsistency are expected to play a similarly important role in the Semantic Web.

The annual International Conference on Scalable Uncertainty Management (SUM) has grown out of this very large interest on managing uncertainty and inconsistency in databases, the Web, the Semantic Web, and artificial intelligence. The conference aims at bringing together all those interested in the management of large volumes of uncertainty and inconsistency in these areas. The First International Conference on Scalable Uncertainty Management (SUM 2007) was held in Washington DC, USA, October 10–12, 2007.

This volume contains the papers presented at the Second International Conference on Scalable Uncertainty Management (SUM 2008), which was held in Naples, Italy, October 1–3, 2008. It contains 27 technical papers, which were selected out of 42 submitted papers in a rigorous reviewing process, where each paper was reviewed by at least three Program Committee members. The volume also contains extended abstracts of the three invited tutorials/talks.

We wish to thank all authors who submitted papers and all conference participants for fruitful discussions. We are grateful to Jan Chomicki, Prabhakar Raghavan, and Dan Suciu for their invited tutorials/talks at the conference. We would like to thank the Program Committee members and external referees for their timely expertise in carefully reviewing the submissions. Special thanks also to Antonio Picariello and his team from the University of Naples "Federico II" for the organization of the conference and wonderful days in Naples. Many thanks also to the developers of the EasyChair Conference System, which we used for the reviewing process and the preparation of this volume.

October 2008

Sergio Greco
Thomas Lukasiewicz

Organization

SUM 2008 was organized by the University of Naples "Federico II".

General Chair

Antonio Picariello · · · · · · · · · University of Naples "Federico II", Italy

Program Chairs

Sergio Greco · · · · · · · · · University of Calabria, Italy
Thomas Lukasiewicz · · · · · · · · · Oxford University, UK

Program Committee

Chitta Baral · · · · · · · · · Arizona State University, USA
Leopoldo Bertossi · · · · · · · · · Carleton University, Canada
Bir Bhanu · · · · · · · · · University of California-Riverside, USA
Fabio Gagliardi Cozman · · · · · · · · · University of Sao Paulo, Brazil
Luc de Raedt · · · · · · · · · K.U. Leuven, Belgium
Michael I. Dekhtyar · · · · · · · · · Tver State University, Russia
Debabrata Dey · · · · · · · · · University of Washington, USA
Jürgen Dix · · · · · · · · · TU Clausthal, Germany
Francesco M. Donini · · · · · · · · · University of Tuscia, Italy
Didier Dubois · · · · · · · · · IRIT, France
Thomas Eiter · · · · · · · · · TU Vienna, Austria
Nicola Fanizzi · · · · · · · · · University of Bari, Italy
Filippo Furfaro · · · · · · · · · University of Calabria, Italy
Avigdor Gal · · · · · · · · · Technion, Israel
John Grant · · · · · · · · · Towson University, USA
Pascal Hitzler · · · · · · · · · University of Karlsruhe, Germany
Eyke Hüllermeier · · · · · · · · · University of Marburg, Germany
Edward Hung · · · · · · · · · Hong Kong Polytechnic University
Anthony Hunter · · · · · · · · · University College London, UK
T.S. Jayram · · · · · · · · · IBM Almaden Research Center, USA
Gabriele Kern-Isberner · · · · · · · · · University of Dortmund, Germany
Christoph Koch · · · · · · · · · Cornell University, USA
Laks V.S. Lakshmanan · · · · · · · · · University of British Columbia, Canada
Mounia Lalmas · · · · · · · · · Queen Mary, University of London, UK
Kathryn Blackmond Laskey · · · · · · · · · George Mason University, USA
Nicola Leone · · · · · · · · · University of Calabria, Italy
Weiru Liu · · · · · · · · · Queen's University Belfast, UK

Serafin Moral   University of Granada, Spain
Simon Parsons   City University of New York, USA
Gabriella Pasi   University of Milan, Italy
Michael Pittarelli   State University of New York, USA
Henri Prade   IRIT, France
Andrea Pugliese   University of Calabria, Italy
Emad Saad   Abu Dhabi University, UAE
Domenico Saccà   ICAR-CNR, Italy
Maria Luisa Sapino   University of Turin, Italy
Umberto Straccia   ISTI-CNR, Italy
Heiner Stuckenschmidt   University of Mannheim, Germany
V.S. Subrahmanian   University of Maryland, USA
Maurice van Keulen   University of Twente, The Netherlands
Peter Vojtáš   Charles University, Czech Republic
Nic Wilson   University College Cork, Ireland
Carlo Zaniolo   UCLA, USA

External Referees

Fabrizio Angiulli   Antonia Azzini   Tristan Behrens
Mario Cataldi   Carmela Comito   Claudia d'Amato
Célia Da Costa Pereira   Ander de Keijzer   Nicola Di Mauro
Sander Evers   Stefano Ferilli   Michael Fink
Sergio Flesca   Gianluigi Folino   Giovambattista Ianni
Thomas Krennwallner   Gianluca Lax   Massimiliano Mazzeo
Cristian Molinaro   Luigi Palopoli   Francesco Ricca
Giorgio Terracina   Martijn van Otterlo

Local Organization

Immacolata Acunzo
Flora Amato
Vincenzo Moscato
Antonio Penta

Sponsoring Institutions

This conference was partially supported by the Department of Electronics, Informatics, and Systems (DEIS) of the University of Calabria and by the Institute of High Performance Computing and Networking (ICAR) of the Italian National Research Council (CNR).

Table of Contents

Consistent Query Answering: The First Ten Years*

Jan Chomicki

Dept. of Computer Science and Engineering
University at Buffalo
Buffalo, NY 14260-2000
chomicki@cse.buffalo.edu

Usually, the data in a database instance is supposed to be *consistent* and satisfy the database integrity constraints. However, it is quite common for the two to diverge. The data may fail to satisfy the constraints for various reasons: it may be erroneous, out of date, or come from mutually inconsistent sources.

In order to deal with inconsistency in a flexible manner, database research and practice have developed different approaches: prevention (usual constraint enforcement), active rules, isolation of inconsistent data, exceptions etc.

A separate class of responses to inconsistency is based on the notion of *repair*: a consistent instance minimally different from the original one. Such repairs can be *materialized* [1] or *virtual*. *Virtual repairing*, which is usually called *consistent query answering* (CQA) [2], does not change the database but rather returns query answers true in all repairs (*consistent* query answers).

Note the similarity of the notion of consistent query answers to that of *sure* or *certain* answers studied in the context of incomplete databases [3,4]. The area of consistent query answering has been surveyed in [5,6,7].

In this tutorial, we present a comprehensive survey of CQA, focusing on the following issues:

Formal semantics. Many different notions of repair have been identified, using different repair dimensions that include:

- Tuple- vs. attribute-based repairs: tuple-based repairs [2,8,9,10] are constructed using tuple insertions and/or deletions, while attribute-based repairs [11,12,13] allow the modification of individual attribute values.
- Set vs. cardinality repairs: in the first case it is the set of operations that is minimized [2], and in the second, the cardinality of the set [10].

Computational approaches. Three main computational approaches to CQA have been proposed. In *query rewriting* [2,14,15], the given query is rewritten independently of the database to return only consistent answers. Alternatively, a space-efficient representation of all repairs may be constructed and used to compute consistent answers [16]. Finally, repairs may be specified using logic programs [17,18,19,9] and consistent query answers computed using logic programming systems like dlv [20]. All of those approaches have been implemented in prototype systems.

---

* Research supported by NSF grant IIS-0119186.

S. Greco and T. Lukasiewicz (Eds.): SUM 2008, LNAI 5291, pp. 1–3, 2008.
© Springer-Verlag Berlin Heidelberg 2008

Computational complexity analysis. Clearly, the complexity of CQA depends on the classes of queries and constraints under consideration, as well as on the repair semantics. This issue has been extensively studied [21,8,22,14,10,23].

Future directions. Future work should lead, among others, to practical applications of CQA, tighter relationship with data integration and cleaning, further refinement of the computational approaches, and a better understanding of the scope of applicability of different repair semantics. New classes of queries and integrity constraints [24,25] should also be considered.

Most of the work on CQA has focused on the relational model but proposals for XML databases exist too [26,27]. Despite a variety of notions of repair, consistent query answers are usually defined as answers true in every repair.

References

1. Embury, S.M., Brandt, S.M., Robinson, J.S., Sutherland, I., Bisby, F.A., Gray, W.A., Jones, A.C., White, R.J.: Adapting Integrity Enforcement Techniques for Data Reconciliation. Information Systems 26(8), 657–689 (2001)
2. Arenas, M., Bertossi, L., Chomicki, J.: Consistent Query Answers in Inconsistent Databases. In: ACM Symposium on Principles of Database Systems (PODS), pp. 68–79 (1999)
3. Lipski Jr., W.: On Semantic Issues Connected with Incomplete Information Databases. ACM Transactions on Database Systems 4(3), 262–296 (1979)
4. Fagin, R., Kolaitis, P.G., Miller, R.J., Popa, L.: Data Exchange: Semantics and Query Answering. In: Calvanese, D., Lenzerini, M., Motwani, R. (eds.) ICDT 2003. LNCS, vol. 2572, pp. 207–224. Springer, Heidelberg (2002)
5. Bertossi, L., Chomicki, J.: Query Answering in Inconsistent Databases. In: Chomicki, J., van der Meyden, R., Saake, G. (eds.) Logics for Emerging Applications of Databases, pp. 43–83. Springer, Heidelberg (2003)
6. Bertossi, L.: Consistent Query Answering in Databases. SIGMOD Record 35(2) (June 2006)
7. Chomicki, J.: Consistent Query Answering: Five Easy Pieces. In: Schwentick, T., Suciu, D. (eds.) ICDT 2007. LNCS, vol. 4353, pp. 1–17. Springer, Heidelberg (2006)
8. Calì, A., Lembo, D., Rosati, R.: On the Decidability and Complexity of Query Answering over Inconsistent and Incomplete Databases. In: ACM Symposium on Principles of Database Systems (PODS), pp. 260–271 (2003)
9. Greco, G., Greco, S., Zumpano, E.: A Logical Framework for Querying and Repairing Inconsistent Databases. IEEE Transactions on Knowledge and Data Engineering 15(6), 1389–1408 (2003)
10. Lopatenko, A., Bertossi, L.: Complexity of Consistent Query Answering in Databases under Cardinality-Based and Incremental Repair Semantics. In: Schwentick, T., Suciu, D. (eds.) ICDT 2007. LNCS, vol. 4353, pp. 179–193. Springer, Heidelberg (2006)
11. Wijsen, J.: Database Repairing Using Updates. ACM Transactions on Database Systems 30(3), 722–768 (2005)
12. Bohannon, P., Flaster, M., Fan, W., Rastogi, R.: A Cost-Based Model and Effective Heuristic for Repairing Constraints by Value Modification. In: ACM SIGMOD International Conference on Management of Data, pp. 143–154 (2005)

13. Bertossi, L., Bravo, L., Franconi, E., Lopatenko, A.: The Complexity and Approximation of Fixing Numerical Attributes in Databases under Integrity Constraints. Information Systems 33(4-5), 407–434 (2008)
14. Fuxman, A., Miller, R.J.: First-Order Query Rewriting for Inconsistent Databases. Journal of Computer and System Sciences 73(4), 610–635 (2007)
15. Wijsen, J.: On the Consistent Rewriting of Conjunctive Queries Under Primary Key Constraints. In: Arenas, M., Schwartzbach, M.I. (eds.) DBPL 2007. LNCS, vol. 4797, pp. 112–126. Springer, Heidelberg (2007)
16. Chomicki, J., Marcinkowski, J., Staworko, S.: Computing Consistent Query Answers Using Conflict Hypergraphs. In: International Conference on Information and Knowledge Management (CIKM), pp. 417–426. ACM Press, New York (2004)
17. Arenas, M., Bertossi, L., Chomicki, J.: Answer Sets for Consistent Query Answering in Inconsistent Databases. Theory and Practice of Logic Programming 3(4–5), 393–424 (2003)
18. Barcelo, P., Bertossi, L.: Logic Programs for Querying Inconsistent Databases. In: Dahl, V., Wadler, P. (eds.) PADL 2003. LNCS, vol. 2562, pp. 208–222. Springer, Heidelberg (2002)
19. Calì, A., Lembo, D., Rosati, R.: Query Rewriting and Answering under Constraints in Data Integration Systems. In: International Joint Conference on Artificial Intelligence (IJCAI), pp. 16–21 (2003)
20. Eiter, T., Fink, M., Greco, G., Lembo, D.: Repair Localization for Query Answering from Inconsistent Databases. ACM Transactions on Database Systems 33(2) (2008)
21. Arenas, M., Bertossi, L., Chomicki, J., He, X., Raghavan, V., Spinrad, J.: Scalar Aggregation in Inconsistent Databases. Theoretical Computer Science 296(3), 405–434 (2003)
22. Chomicki, J., Marcinkowski, J.: Minimal-Change Integrity Maintenance Using Tuple Deletions. Information and Computation 197(1-2), 90–121 (2005)
23. Staworko, S.: Declarative Inconsistency Handling in Relational and Semi-Structured Databases. PhD thesis, University at Buffalo (2007) UB CSE TR 2008-03
24. Bohannon, P., Fan, W., Geerts, F., Jia, X., Kementsietsidis, A.: Conditional Functional Dependencies for Data Cleaning. In: IEEE International Conference on Data Engineering (ICDE), pp. 746–755 (2007)
25. Flesca, S., Furfaro, F., Parisi, F.: Consistent Query Answers on Numerical Databases under Aggregate Constraints. In: Bierman, G., Koch, C. (eds.) DBPL 2005. LNCS, vol. 3774, pp. 279–294. Springer, Heidelberg (2005)
26. Flesca, S., Furfaro, F., Greco, S., Zumpano, E.: Querying and Repairing Inconsistent XML Data. In: Ngu, A.H.H., Kitsuregawa, M., Neuhold, E.J., Chung, J.-Y., Sheng, Q.Z. (eds.) WISE 2005. LNCS, vol. 3806, pp. 175–188. Springer, Heidelberg (2005)
27. Staworko, S., Chomicki, J.: Validity-Sensitive Querying of XML Databases. In: Grust, T., Höpfner, H., Illarramendi, A., Jablonski, S., Mesiti, M., Müller, S., Patranjan, P.-L., Sattler, K.-U., Spiliopoulou, M., Wijsen, J. (eds.) EDBT 2006. LNCS, vol. 4254, pp. 164–177. Springer, Heidelberg (2006)

Heavy Tails and Web Models
(Abstract)

Prabhakar Raghavan

Yahoo! Research

Abstract. The literature is rich with (re)discoveries of power law phenomena; this is especially true of observations of link and traffic behavior on the Web. We survey the origins of these phenomena and several (yet incomplete) attempts to model them. We then present a number of open problems in Web research arising from these observations.

S. Greco and T. Lukasiewicz (Eds.): SUM 2008, LNAI 5291, p. 4, 2008.
© Springer-Verlag Berlin Heidelberg 2008

Managing Probabilistic Data with MystiQ: The Can-Do, the Could-Do, and the Can't-Do*

Christopher Re and Dan Suciu

University of Washington

1 Introduction

MystiQ is a system that allows users to define a probabilistic database, then to evaluate SQL queries over this database. MystiQ is a middleware: the data itself is stored in a standard relational database system, and MystiQ is providing the probabilistic semantics. The advantage of a middleware over a re-implementation from scratch is that it can leverage the infrastructure of an existing database engine, e.g. indexes, query evaluation, query optimization, etc. Furthermore, MystiQ attempts to perform most of the probabilistic inference inside the relational database engine. MystiQ is currently available from `mystiq.cs.washington.edu`.

The MystiQ system resulted from research on probabilistic databases at the University of Washington [8, 10, 11, 13, 14, 23]. Some of these research results have been fully incorporated in MystiQ, like the query evaluation techniques that allow it to evaluate SELECT-FROM-WHERE-GROUPBY queries over large probabilistic databases: this is what MystiQ *can do*. Other results are not implemented in the system, but they could either be implemented in some future version after only minor extensions, or can be used even today by a database administrator to perform certain data management tasks manually; an example are the techniques for representing materialized views over probabilistic data. This is what MystiQ *could do*. Finally, other research results require more work before they can be implemented in a system. For example, our evaluation techniques for queries with a HAVING clause applies only to safe queries; for another example, we currently don't know of a good approach to extend safe queries and safe plans to queries with self-joins. This is what MystiQ *can't do*.

In this paper we give a gentle introduction into the MystiQ system, and describe the associated research that is used, or could be used, or is not yet ready to be used in MystiQ.

Related Work. Our research has focused primarily on SQL query evaluation and on views. Other groups have studied different aspects of probabilistic or incomplete databases. The Trio project [6, 7, 15, 29] focused on the study of lineage in incomplete databases. The MayBMS project has focused on representation problems, query language design, and query evaluation [2, 3, 4, 20]. Other

---

* Supported in part by NSF grants IIS-0415193, IIS-0627585, IIS-0513877, IIS-0428168, and a gift from Microsoft.

S. Greco and T. Lukasiewicz (Eds.): SUM 2008, LNAI 5291, pp. 5–18, 2008.
© Springer-Verlag Berlin Heidelberg 2008

groups have studied correlations in probabilistic databases [27], continuous random variables [9], and complex probabilistic models with native Monte Carlo simulations [16]. Earlier work include [5] and the ProbView system [21].

2   The Data and Query Model

2.1   Tables and Events

To use MystiQ, one must start from a relational database, created on a relational database management system; in our work we used mostly postgres or SQL Server, but any RDBMS with a JDBC conection can be used instead. Upon starting MystiQ the user needs to provide the information to connect to the database, and the name of a *configuration file* that specifies how to interpret the tables in the database as probabilistic events.

The configuration file consists of three kinds of statements:

```
STATEMENT ::= TABLE table-name(attributes)
            | CREATE EVENT event-name(attributes1)
              [CHOICE (attributes2)]
              ON table-name(prob-expression)
            | CREATE VIEW event-name AS
              SELECT ...
              FROM ...
              WHERE ...
```

The TABLE statements describe the schema of the relational database: while this is redundant, since MystiQ could obtain it directly from the database, in the current implementation MystiQ requires the schema to be given in the configuration file. Only the attribute names need to be listed, not their types.

A CREATE EVENT statement defines a probabilistic table, called *event*, from a table in the database. Here `table-name` is a relation in the database, while `event-name` is the probabilistic relation defined by this statement. The schema of the probabilistic table is the same as that of the deterministic table from which it is derived, and its semantics is a set of possible worlds: each subset of `table-name` is a possible world for `event-name`. In each possible world, `attributes1` are a key: they are called the *event key*. When present, `attributes2` are called the *choice* attributes. MystiQ requires that `attributes1` $\cup$ `attributes2` contain the primary key of `table-name`. Finally, `prob-expression` is an expression, possibly involving attributes of `table-name`, defining the marginal probability of a tuple in `event-name`.

By definition, tuples with distinct values of the event keys are independent probabilistic events, and tuples with the same event keys but distinct values choice attributes are disjoint (or exclusive) probabilistic events. Under this assumption the marginal tuple probabilities uniquely define the probability of each possible world; we refer the reader to [14] for additional details.

In the CREATE EVENT statement `table-name` can also be a probabilistic table; in that case no choice attributes are allowed. We will illustrate this in Section 4.

The CREATE VIEW statement is identical to that in SQL, except that the FROM clause may use both events and deterministic relations. We describe views in Sec. 4.

For a simple illustration, suppose we have a database or products, where the colors are uncertain:

Product:

Name	Color	Prob
Gizmo	Green	0.3
Gizmo	Blue	0.5
Gizmo	Red	0.2
Gadget	Blue	0.1
Gadget	Black	0.9

This is a standard deterministic relation, there is no probabilistic semantics yet. The attribute `Prob` represents our confidence in that product's color. In order to turn this table into a probabilistic relation, we define the configuration file:

```
TABLE Product(Name, Color, Prob)
CREATE EVENT ProductUniqueColor(Name) CHOICE(Color) ON Product(Prob)
```

In the new relation `ProductUniqueColor` is probabilistic, and `Name` is its key. Its semantics are all the possible subsets of `Product`, and each such subset has a certain probability. For example the instance[1]:

ProductUniqueColor:

Name	Color
Gizmo	Blue
Gadget	Blue

has probability $0.5*0.1 = 0.05$. There are 6 possible worlds, because `Name` must be a key.

Alternatively, we can interpret the uncertainty about the `Color` in `Product` differently, namely as saying that any product may have multiple colors, but it is uncertain which colors are present. Then we define another event:

```
CREATE EVENT ProductMultipleColors(Name, Color) ON Product(Prob)
```

Now every subset of `Product` is a possible world, and there are 32 possible worlds. The world above (with two tuples) is still a possible world, but now it has probability $(1 - 0.3)*0.5*(1 - 0.2)*0.1*(1 - 0.9) = 0.0028$.

As a last example, we can make each of the 32 possible worlds equally likely (with probability $1.0/32$) by defining the event:

---

[1] Strictly speaking `Prob` should also be an attribute of `ProductUniqueColor`, but we omit it since we only need it to define the probabilities of the possible worlds.

```
CREATE EVENT ProductUniform(Name, Color) ON Product(1.0/32)
```

In MystiQ we can define several probabilistic tables from the same deterministic table, and the system treats them as independent probabilistic tables.

2.2   Queries

MystiQ currently supports SELECT-FROM-WHERE-GROUPBY with aggregates in the SELECT clause. The FROM clause may mention both deterministic relations, and probabilistic relations. Nested queries are permitted, but these may only refer to deterministic relations (i.e. no event names). MystiQ returns a list of tuple answers together with their marginal probabilities and computes expected values for the aggregate functions (if any are present). The answers are always ranked by their marginal probabilities, and only the top k answers are returned to the user, where k is either specified in the query or is a system parameter.

We illustrate queries with three examples. The following returns all products that are not red:

```
Q1 = SELECT DISTINCT Name FROM ProductUniqueColor WHERE Color!='red'
```

The answer is:

Name	Probability
Gadget	1.0
Gizmo	0.8

Thus, the user learns that Gadget is certainly not red, since its probability is 1.0. Gizmo is not red with probability 0.8. The system returns only the marginal tuple probabilities in the answer, here 1.0 and 0.8, and does not retain any correlations between the tuples[2]: in order to retain the tuple correlations (which are needed, for example, in order to run another SQL query on the answer) one has to define a view, see Sec. 4.

The tuples are ranked in decreasing order of their probability. It is very important to rank answers when processing uncertain data, because the uncertainties will often cause many false positives in the answer. We want to return to the user the tuples with a higher probability first, and spare him the effort to examine tuples with small probabilities. MystiQ ranks the answers, and computes only the top k.

Note the importance of including DISTINCT in this query. If we run the same query without DISTINCT, then the answer is:

Name	Probability
Gadget	0.9
Gizmo	0.5
Gizmo	0.3
Gadget	0.1

---

[2] The tuples in the answer of Q1 are independent; the tuples in the answers of Q2 and Q3 are correlated in non-trivial ways.

It is much harder for the user to see here that Gadget is guaranteed to be a correct answer, or to get a sense of which are the most likely products to not be red.

For the second query, we assume to have another probabilistic table, called LikesMultipleColor, which lists for every customer, color pair the probability that the customer likes that color:

```
TABLE Customer(custID, Color, Prob)
CREATE EVENT LikesMultipleColors(custID, Color) on Customer(Prob)
```

In a possible world, a customer may like multiple colors. The query below finds all customers to which we could sell products whose colors they like:

```
Q2 = SELECT DISTINCT y.custID
     FROM  ProductUniqueColor x, LikesMultipleColors y
     WHERE x.Color = y.Color
```

Our third query illustrates aggregates, which are interpreted as expected values. The query computes for each color the number of products that have that color:

```
Q3 = SELECT Color, count(*) FROM ProductUniqueColor GROUP BY Color
```

and the answer is:

Color	Count	Probability
Black	0.9	0.9
Blue	0.6	0.55
Green	0.3	0.3
Red	0.2	0.2

3 Query Evaluation

3.1 Can Do: Safe and Unsafe Queries

MystiQ uses two algorithms for query evaluation: an efficient algorithm that works only for *safe* queries, and a more expensive algorithm that works for all queries.

First, if the query is *safe*, then MystiQ computes a safe plan and rewrites the plan into a new SQL query called the *extensive query*. It then evaluates the extensive query on the database engine. The answers of the extensive query already contain the correct probabilities, and are sorted in decreasing order of these probabilities: MystiQ simply cuts this set after the top k answers. For example, the query Q1 is safe, and the extensive query simply sums for each product the probabilities of all entries that are not red. The treatment of safe queries is fully described in [10] (this contains a system's perspective) and in [14] (this contains a complete, theoretical treatment).

Second, if the query is *unsafe* then MystiQ generates a much simpler SQL query that simply fetches and joins all relevant tuples from the database. Once these tuples are read, they are grouped by their output attributes, and MystiQ computes the probability of each output tuple using Luby and Karp's Monte Carlo simulation algorithm [23]. For example, the query Q2 is unsafe (in fact, it's data complexity is #P hard because it is essentially h_2 in [14]).

Safe queries run very fast, mostly at the same speed as a normal SQL query on a relational database. Unsafe queries, by contrast, are about two orders of magnitude slower. Thus, it is very important for MystiQ to identify if a query is safe, and run the much faster algorithm. In a trivial case, if all relations in the FROM clause are deterministic, then the query is automatically safe: this query is simply passed through to the database system. Another trivial case is when the query does not have DISTINCT or GROUP BY, then it is also safe; however, as we saw above, queries over uncertain data are likely to have the DISTINCT clause.

3.2   Can Do: Optimize

MystiQ uses two optimizations for unsafe queries. First, it tries to identify subqueries that are both safe, and whose answers consists of independent or disjoint tuples; they are called *super-safe* subqueries. These subqueries can both be evaluated with a safe plan, and their results can be used as any other probabilistic table.

The second optimization is much more important and consists of an aggressive exploitation of the top-k query answering paradigm. MystiQ attempts to perform the Monte Carlo simulation only for the top k tuples, which are the only tuples that need to be returned to the user: there are many more tuples in the answer, and restricting the simulation to only the top k results in significant performance improvement. But this is a chicken and egg problem: MystiQ doesn't know which of the candidate answer tuples are the top k until it has run the Monte Carlo simulation on all answers and ranked them by their probability. The solution to this problem is described in [23] and is called *multisimulation*.

3.3   Could Do: More Aggregates, NOT Exists

MystiQ supports only sum and count. It also supports avg, but it interprets it as the ratio of sum and count. This is not the correct semantics of avg: a correct treatment of avg is more difficult, see [17]. MystiQ *could* support min and max: they require only minor extensions to the current MystiQ system, but they are not implemented at the time of writing.

Some applications, such as management of RFID data, require SQL queries with NOT EXISTS predicates. We have investigated evaluation algorithms for queries with one level of NOT EXISTS predicates in [28], and described an evaluation algorithm that could be fully integrated in MystiQ. Our algorithm is exponential in the number of NOT EXISTS predicates; some optimizations are likely required in order to make this approach more practical.

3.4   Can't Do: Queries with a HAVING Clause, and Queries with Selfjoins

Queries with a HAVING clause are very important in decision support. For example, a manager wants to retrieve all products having at least 50 customers interested in that product. In the setting of a probabilistic database this means that we need to compute, for a given product, the probability that at least 50 customers are interested in that product. This is different from, and harder than computing the expected number of customers interested in a given product. Motivated by the need to support HAVING queries, we have studied this problem in [24]. We have described an efficient algorithm to evaluate queries with a HAVING clause, but only if its skeleton (i.e. the query obtained by removing the HAVING clause) is safe. If the query is unsafe, then we currently do not know how to evaluate a query with a HAVING clause, in similar fashion to the Monte Carlo simulation approach[3].

We say that a query has a self join if the same event name occurs twice in the FROM clause. MystiQ treats such queries automatically as unsafe queries. However, not all queries with self-joins are hard, and in fact some quite simple and natural queries with self-joins are in PTIME. Motivated by the need to extend MystiQ to handle efficiently queries with self joins, we have conducted a theoretical study in [12], and we have described a PTIME algorithm for a large class of queries with self-joins. Unfortunately, this algorithm has two limitation. First, it was developed only for probabilistic tables with independent tuples[4]: there are currently no efficient algorithms known for evaluating queries with self-joins over disjoint-independent databases. Second, the PTIME algorithm seems to be quite different from the safe plans used by MystiQ: more research is needed in order to adapt those PTIME algorithms to a query processor.

4   Views

In addition to views created on the relational database (which MystiQ treats as any regular deterministic table), MystiQ allows users to define views over events. These are an important tool in managing probabilistic data, and we discuss them here to some extend.

4.1   Can Do: Virtual Views

MystiQ allows users to define views over events; the result is a new event. For example, the view below defines an event called **Recommendations**, which contains pairs customer, product where the customer likes the product's color.

---

[3] A naive Monte Carlo algorithm can be used, but it will run in exponential time to achieve a given precision, unlike Luby and Karp's algorithms that runs in polynomial time to achieve a fixed precision.

[4] These are CREATE EVENT statements without the CHOICE clause.

```
CREATE VIEW Recommendations
    SELECT DISTINCT x.custID, y.Name
    FROM LikesMultipleColors x, ProductUniqueColor y
    WHERE x.Color = y.Color
```

Views in MystiQ have a compositional semantics when used in another SQL query. In particular this means that the correlations between the tuples in the view are accounted for. For that, MystiQ supports only virtual views, and expands the view definition when it is used in another SQL query. For example if a SQL query uses **Recommendation** in the FROM clause, then MystiQ simply expands the view definition in the query, and this is by definition compositional semantics.

Note that materializing the view makes it much harder to ensure compositional semantics. It is not sufficient to materialize **Recommendations** in a table that stores the marginal probability of each tuple, because we need to also represent somehow the correlations between tuples. By contrast, when we run a query in MystiQ we only retrieve the marginal probabilities. Thus, in MystiQ views and queries are different: views are used for their compositional semantics, while queries are used to retrieve the marginal probabilities.

Views are important in probabilistic databases for two reasons.

First, by adding views to disjoint-independent probabilistic databases one obtains a complete representation system. In notation:

Disjoint-independent-Probabilistic-DBs + Views = Complete-Representation

We proved this in [14, 22] using a simple, constructive proof that is quite useful in practice. Our result is similar to other results in the literature. For example Benjelloun et al. [7] show that a lineage system consisting essentially of DNF formulas also forms a complete representation system, and a similar result was shown by Antova et al. [3]. Our particular formulation of the result emphasizes the role of views in achieving completeness. This, we feel, is important for practical applications, since views are already used widely in data management.

We illustrate now the completeness result with a simple example. Suppose that we have a probabilistic table **ProductColorComplex** with exactly three possible worlds:

Name	Color
Gizmo	Green
Gizmo	Blue
Gadget	Black

Name	Color
Gizmo	Blue
Gadget	Black

Name	Color
Gizmo	Red
Gadget	Blue

and their probabilities are 0.2, 0.3, 0.5. Note that the tuples are no longer disjoint or independent, hence these possible worlds cannot be specified by a CREATE EVENT statement. Instead, in MystiQ the user would create the following two deterministic tables:

ProductWorld:

Name	Color	WID
Gizmo	Green	W1
Gizmo	Blue	W1
Gadget	Black	W1
Gizmo	Blue	W2
Gadget	Black	W2
Name	Color	W3
Gizmo	Red	W3
Gadget	Blue	W3

World:

WID	Prob
W1	0.2
W2	0.3
W3	0.5

then define the following events:

```
CREATE EVENT PossWorld( ) CHOICE(WID) on World(Prob)
CREATE View ProductColorComplex AS
    SELECT DISTINCT Name, Color
    FROM ProductWorld x, PossWorld y
    WHERE x.WID = y.WID
```

The possible worlds of **ProductColorComplex** are exactly the three worlds above (because the possible worlds of **PossWorld** are $\{W1\}$, $\{W2\}$, and $\{W3\}$), and their probabilities are also identical.

The second reason why views are important is that they can be used to express rules with confidences. For example, consider the following rule, derived from the Calo project [1]:

```
IsAbout(e, p) :- EmailFrom(e, u), WorksOn(u, p)   CONFIDENCE = 0.8
```

The purpose of the rule is to predict if an email is about a project. The rule says that if the email is from a user u, and u works on a project, then that email is about that project with confidence 0.8. This can be expressed in MystiQ as:

```
CREATE VIEW V AS
    SELECT DISTINCT x.Email, y.Project
    FROM EmailFrom x, WorksOn y
    WHERE x.Sender = y.Person

CREATE EVENT IsAbout(Email, Project) ON V(0.8)
```

If **EmailFrom** and **WorksOn** are deterministic tables, then **V** is also deterministic and **IsAbout** is a tuple-independent relation where each tuple has probability 0.8. If **EmailFrom** or **WorksOn** are probabilistic tables, then **V** is also a probabilistic table. The new event **IsAbout** decreases the marginal probability of each tuple by 0.8, while maintaining any correlations between the tuples in **V**.

4.2   Could Do: Representable Materialized Views

Views are as important for managing uncertain data as they are for managing traditional data. Virtual views are easy to implement, but result in poor query performance. After view expansion the new query is larger than the original query; if a query was safe, it may no longer be safe after view expansion. To improve the query performance on probabilistic views we need to materialize them. By a *materialized probabilistic view* we mean a table in a relational database that stores for each tuple its marginal probability, and represents in some way the correlations between the tuples in that relation. Lineage [7] has been developed precisely with this goal: to represent how tuples were derived and, thus, to capture all their possible correlations. However, materializing views with lineage only postpones and exacerbates the query evaluation problem. We need a technique that allows us to materialize the view and benefit from having performed the computations offline.

Motivated by this need we have studied the problem of materializing probabilistic views in [25, 26], using two approaches. The first approach was to derive automatically a full, or a partial representation of the view.

A *partial representation* of a view consists of two sets of attributes called *key attributes*, and the *choice attributes*: the set of attributes that are neither key nor choice are called *unknown attributes*. The partial representation is correct if any two tuples that have distinct values of the key attributes are independent, and any two tuples that have the same values for the key and unknown attributes and have distinct values for the choice attributes are disjoint (i.e. exclusive). In addition, when all attributes are known (i.e. are either key or choice attributes) then we say that the representation is *full*. Essentially, a fully representable view is like a probabilistic database defined by a CREATE EVENT statement, and therefore can be used during query processing without any further extensions.

We have shown that any view defined by a SQL query has a canonical partial representation, which is maximal in the sense that the sets of key and choice attributes are as large as possible. Note that any view admits a trivial representation, where all attributes are unknown, but this is useless in practice because it makes no claims about tuples being disjoint or independent. The canonical representation is the best one can get for this view definition. If a full representation exists then it is also canonical, since we cannot further increase the set of key or choice attributes.

MystiQ currently has no support for materialized views. If the view has a full representation, then the database administrator can materialize it on the database server (using MystiQ to compute the probabilities) and then define in the configuration file as a CREATE EVENT; MystiQ can then use it as a regular probabilistic table.

If the view has only a partial representation, then MystiQ could still use the materialized view to answer some queries, while for others it would have to fall back on view expansion: however this part is not implemented at the time of writing. For example the query may join two tuples in the view that agree on the key attributes, and disagree on the unknown attributes: we cannot compute the probability of the joined tuple because we don't know the correlations between these two tuples. To support such views, Mystiq would have to keep extra correlation information.

4.3   Could Do: Sufficient Lineage

Any probabilistic view can be stored faithfully by storing the complete *lineage* for each tuple in the output of the view, that is every derivation for that tuple in the database. This approach reduces the cost of processing the joins in the view, but does not reduce the complexity of the probabilistic portion of query processing, which is often the dominant cost. However, many applications can tolerate approximate query results. For example, in information extraction applications the probabilities are usually set *heuristically* and so there is very little real difference between a a tuple with probability of 0.99 and one that returns 0.995. Intuitively, to compute probabilities approximately, it is unnecessary to keep all possible derivations, just the most important ones. Figuring out which tuples are most important for a tuple, is the technical development underlying *approximate lineage* [26].

One form of approximate lineage is *sufficient lineage*, where instead of storing the complete lineage, we store only a subset of the lineage. Of course, this introduces some error in the database and so our goal is to construct such lineage to guarantee small error. An interesting property of sufficient lineage is that any conjunctive query (SFW query) returns a probability value that is a lower bound of the true probability (without approximation). Further, sufficient lineage takes up space that is orders of magnitude smaller than a complete approach, even for very low error tolerance. The reduced size enables query processing and other data exploration tasks to proceed much more efficiently. Most importantly for Mystiq, sufficient lineage is syntactically identical to standard lineage and so can be used directly.

4.4   Can't Do: Polynomial Lineage

Although sufficient lineage may provide large amounts of compression, it is often possible to get better compression ratios using *polynomial lineage*. The essential idea of polynomial lineage is to transform the lineage functions into a polynomial and then use techniques from analysis, such as Fourier transforms and Taylor series, to approximate the resulting polynomial. While we show how to use this representation to process queries, the representation of these functions is quite different than the lineage functions used in Mystiq.

5   Constraints

Database constraints are a promising technique for managing uncertain data. The hope is that by specifying application specific constraints the database administrator can reduce the set of worlds to only those that "make sense" in that particular application. A common example of constraints are key constraints: in fact the CREATE EVENT statement already incorporates one key constraint for every probabilistic table. However, multiple, overlapping constraints require significant extensions.

5.1   Could Do: Hard Constraints

A hard constraint is an assertion must hold in all possible worlds: in other words, the worlds that fail the constraint are removed from the set of possible worlds. Hard constraints are dealt with by conditioning: that is, if B is the statement that the constraint holds (on a possible world), the probability of a boolean query Q in the presence of the constraint is $P(Q|B) = P(QB)/P(B)$. This observation was used by Koch and Olteanu in [20] to incorporate hard constraints in MayBMS. The challenge in this approach is computing the constraint probabilities efficiently, i.e. $P(B)$ and $P(QB)$. In the case of functional dependencies, B is the negation of a conjunctive query; in more complicated settings it may be a more general formula. MystiQ currently does not support hard constraints.

5.2   Can't Do: Soft Constraints

A soft constraint is an assertion is increases the probability of the worlds where it holds, and decreases the probability of worlds where it doesn't hold. This semantics is especially appropriate is the constraint is learned automatically from training data. For example the machine learning module may identify a set of attributes that are a *soft key*: some violations exists, but otherwise the attributes form a key.

Motivated by the need to incorporate in MystiQ constraints learned automatically from the data, we have studied *soft key constraints* in [18]. The natural semantics for soft keys is given by a Markov Network of a special kind, where the potential of a world depends on the number of violations to the key constraint. We were especially interested in the case when multiple soft keys exists for the same table, and have defined a class of *safe* queries for a given set of soft key constraints. However, we currently don't know how to evaluate unsafe queries, nor how to extend the query evaluation algorithms to other kinds of constraints. MystiQ does not currently support soft constraints of any kind.

6   Discussions

The goal of MystiQ is to serve as proof of concept: we proved that it is possible to evaluate SQL queries on large probabilistic databases, with high performance (for safe queries), or with tolerable performance (for unsafe queries). For safe queries, the main performance bottleneck is the relational database engine, which needs to support complex, nested SQL queries: we found here that commercial database systems (like SQL Server) perform much better than free systems (like postgres). For unsafe queries, the main performance bottleneck is the inner loop of MystiQ's Monte Carlo simulation. Here we learned two lessons. The first is a project management lesson. Our initial prototype (done by the first author), which was used to report the experiments in [22], was written in C++ and deployed a number of C++ programming hacks to boost performance of the most critical Monte Carlo simulation steps: as a result the system had a very high performance. Subsequently, we used the funds from a small grant to hire a programmer and re-implement MystiQ in Java (for portability). We instructed him to emphasize features, the user interface, and completeness over performance. The initial performance of the Java code for the multisimulation was so poor that we had to replace the inner loop with our initial C++ code. This increased the performance to reasonable level, without matching that of our earlier prototype. The second lesson we learned is that the Monte Carlo simulation problem is far from being well understood. MystiQ has a friendly graphical interface that allows us to view the progress of the multisimulation and see the progress of the confidence bounds for all candidate tuples. By examining this progress it becomes quickly obvious that the top k tuples and their rankings converge much faster than the bounds given by Luby and Karp's formula [19]. While the formula is theoretically tight, observing the progress of MystiQ's multisimulation algorithm suggest that further improvements or optimizations are possible, either by stopping the current simulation earlier, or by using some other simulation algorithm.

References

1. Ambite, J.L., Chaudhri, V.K., Fikes, R., Jenkins, J., Mishra, S., Muslea, M., Uribe, T.E., Yang, G.: Design and implementation of the CALO query manager. In: AAAI (2006)
2. Antova, L., Koch, C., Olteanu, D.: 10^(10^6) worlds and beyond: Efficient representation and processing of incomplete information. In: ICDE (2007)
3. Antova, L., Koch, C., Olteanu, D.: MayBMS: Managing incomplete information with probabilistic world-set decompositions (demonstration). In: ICDE (2007)
4. Antova, L., Koch, C., Olteanu, D.: World-set decompositions: Expressiveness and efficient algorithms. In: Schwentick, T., Suciu, D. (eds.) ICDT 2007. LNCS, vol. 4353, pp. 194–208. Springer, Heidelberg (2006)
5. Barbara, D., Garcia-Molina, H., Porter, D.: The management of probabilistic data. IEEE Trans. Knowl. Data Eng. 4(5), 487–502 (1992)
6. Benjelloun, O., Das Sarma, A., Halevy, A., Widom, J.: ULDBs: Databases with uncertainty and lineage. In: VLDB, pp. 953–964 (2006)
7. Benjelloun, O., Das Sarma, A., Hayworth, C., Widom, J.: An introduction to ULDBs and the Trio system. IEEE Data Eng. Bull. 29(1), 5–16 (2006)
8. Boulos, J., Dalvi, N., Mandhani, B., Mathur, S., Re, C., Suciu, D.: Mystiq: A system for finding more answers by using probabilities. In: SIGMOD, system demo (2005)
9. Cheng, R., Prabhakar, S.: Managing uncertainty in sensor databases. SIGMOD Record 32(4), 41–46 (2003)
10. Dalvi, N., Re, C., Suciu, D.: Query evaluation on probabilistic databases. IEEE Data Engineering Bulletin 29(1), 25–31 (2006)
11. Dalvi, N., Suciu, D.: Efficient query evaluation on probabilistic databases. In: VLDB, Toronto, Canada (2004)
12. Dalvi, N., Suciu, D.: The dichotomy of conjunctive queries on probabilistic structures. In: PODS, pp. 293–302 (2007)
13. Dalvi, N., Suciu, D.: Efficient query evaluation on probabilistic databases. VLDBJ 16(4), 523–544 (2007)

14. Dalvi, N., Suciu, D.: Management of probabilistic data: Foundations and challenges. In: PODS, pp. 1–12, Beijing, China (invited talk) (2007)
15. Das Sarma, A., Benjelloun, O., Halevy, A., Widom, J.: Working models for uncertain data. In: ICDE (2006)
16. Jampani, R., Xu, F., Wu, M., Perez, L.L., Jermaine, C.M., Haas, P.J.: MCDB: a Monte Carlo approach to managing uncertain data. In: SIGMOD, pp. 687–700 (2008)
17. Jayram, T.S., Kale, S., Vee, E.: Efficient aggregation algorithms for probabilistic data. In: SODA (2007)
18. Jha, A., Rastogi, V., Suciu, D.: Evaluating queries in the presence of soft key constraints. In: PODS (2008)
19. Karp, R., Luby, M.: Monte-Carlo algorithms for enumeration and reliability problems. In: Proceedings of the annual ACM symposium on Theory of computing (1983)
20. Koch, C., Olteanu, D.: Conditioning probabilistic databases. In: VLDB (2008)
21. Lakshmanan, L., Leone, N., Ross, R., Subrahmanian, V.S.: Probview: A flexible probabilistic database system. ACM Trans. Database Syst. 22(3) (1997)
22. Re, C., Dalvi, N., Suciu, D.: Efficient Top-k query evaluation on probabilistic data (extended version). Technical Report 2006-06-05, University of Washington (2006)
23. Re, C., Dalvi, N., Suciu, D.: Efficient Top-k query evaluation on probabilistic data. In: ICDE (2007)
24. Re, C., Suciu, D.: Efficient evaluation of having queries on a probabilistic database. In: Arenas, M., Schwartzbach, M.I. (eds.) DBPL 2007. LNCS, vol. 4797, Springer, Heidelberg (2007)
25. Re, C., Suciu, D.: Materialized views in probabilistic databases for information exchange and query optimization. In: Proceedings of VLDB (2007)
26. Re, C., Suciu, D.: Approximate lineage for probabilistic databases. In: VLDB (2008)
27. Sen, P., Deshpande, A.: Representing and querying correlated tuples in probabilistic databases. In: ICDE (2007)
28. Wang, T.Y., Re, C., Suciu, D.: Implementing not exists predicates over a probabilistic database. In: Proceedings of MUD (2008)
29. Widom, J.: Trio: A system for integrated management of data, accuracy, and lineage. In: CIDR, pp. 262–276 (2005)

Frequent Itemset Mining from Databases Including One Evidential Attribute

Mohamed Anis Bach Tobji[1], Boutheina Ben Yaghlane[2], and Khaled Mellouli[2]

[1] LARODEC Laboratory, Institut Suprieur de Gestion de Tunis
[2] LARODEC Laboratory, Institut des Hautes Etudes Commerciales de Carthage

Abstract. Frequent Itemset Mining (FIM) problem has been extensively tackled in the context of perfect data. However, real applications showed that data are often imperfect (incomplete and/or uncertain) which leads to the need of FIM algorithms that process imperfect databases. In this paper we propose a new algorithm for mining frequent itemsets from databases including exactly one evidential attribute. An evidential attribute is an attribute that could have uncertain values modelled via the evidence theory, i.e., a basic belief assignment. We introduce in this paper a variant of the structure Belief Itemset Tree (BIT) for mining frequent itemsets from evidential data and we lead some experiments that showed efficiency of our mining algorithm compared to the existing ones.

1 Introduction

Most of frequent itemset mining algorithms process perfect databases ([2], [9] and [13]) and do not take into account data imperfections in real-world applications. Indeed, real-world applications suffer from data incompleteness and uncertainty. For example, medical systems that store physician diagnosis [11] or detection systems that are based on sensors [16] may generate imperfect data. That is why recently, some works focused on the problem of frequent itemset mining (FIM) from imperfect databases. In most of such works, mined data are *probabilistic* ([5] and [12]), *possibilistic* [8] or *fuzzy* ([4], [7] and [17]). In spite of *evidence theory* [14] importance, there is a lack of works on FIM from evidential databases. *Evidential databases* allow storage of uncertain data where at least one attribute could have a basic belief assignment. Evidence theory is a generalized theory for modelling data uncertainty. Thus, an algorithm that mines frequent itemsets from evidential data, could also mine frequent itemsets from probabilistic and possibilistic data. In the literature, only the works of [3] and [10] tackled FIM problem from evidential databases.

In this paper, we present an efficient algorithm for mining frequent itemsets from databases that include one evidential attribute. Our proposed algorithm, the algorithm of [10] and the one of [3] mine exactly the same frequent itemsets since the three methods are exact and based on the same uncertain FIM model, i.e., the evidential one. Our new algorithm is based on a variant of the data structure used in [10] called *belief itemset tree* (BIT) and its advantage is that the first scan of the tree allows us to generate until 50% of the final resulting set of

S. Greco and T. Lukasiewicz (Eds.): SUM 2008, LNAI 5291, pp. 19–32, 2008.
© Springer-Verlag Berlin Heidelberg 2008

frequent itemsets. Thus, the remainder of the frequent itemsets are incrementally computed which makes our method more efficient. We performed FIM operations using the three algorithms over synthetic databases and experimental results showed that our solution is more efficient than the other ones.

The remainder of the paper is organized as follows: Section 2 introduces the evidence theory. Section 3 presents the evidential databases. In section 4, we recall the problem of Association Rule Mining (ARM) in perfect databases, and then we present frequent evidential itemset mining and our algorithm in Section 5. Section 6 shows experimentation results and discusses some observations. Finally, in Section 7, we conclude our work and present some perspectives.

2   Evidence Theory

2.1   Basic Concepts

Evidence theory, also called Dempster-Shafer (DS) theory or belief function theory, was introduced in [6]. It was mathematically formalized in [14]. DS theory is often described as a generalization of the Bayesian theory since it manipulates events that are not necessarily exclusive. We present here formal concepts of this theory. Let $\Theta = \{\theta_1, \theta_2, ..., \theta_n\}$ be a finite non empty set of all elementary exhaustive and mutually exclusive events related to a given problem. Θ is called *frame of discernment* of the given problem. The *basic belief assignment* (bba) is defined on the set of all subsets of Θ, namely 2^Θ. The bba m is the function $m : 2^\Theta \rightarrow [0, 1]$ that satisfies: $m(\emptyset) = 0$ and $\sum_{X \subseteq \Theta} m(X) = 1$ The *mass function* (m) allows someone to affect a partial belief value to a subset of Θ. Thus, $m(X)$ represents belief value placed exactly in the subset X and non distributed to subsets of X. Subsets of Θ with masses strictly positive are called *focal elements* of the bba m, focal elements set is denoted by F. The triplet $\{\Theta, F, m\}$ is called a *body of evidence* and denoted by BoE. The *belief function* (*bel*) is defined and computed from the bba function m. X being an event, $bel(X)$ reflects total belief committed to X, i.e., total mass for all subsets of X.

$$bel(X) = \sum_{Y \subseteq X} m(Y)$$

The *plausibility function* (*pl*) quantifies amount of belief that could be given to a subset X of Θ. It is the sum of all masses of subsets Y that are compatible with X.

$$pl(X) = \sum_{Y \cap X \neq \emptyset} m(Y)$$

2.2   Conjunctive Rule of Combination

Let m_1 and m_2 be two bba's defined on the same frame of discernment Θ and provided by two 'independent' BoE's. The conjunctive rule of combination [15] is applicable when both sources of information (of combined bba's) are fully reliable. Conjunctive rule of combination is naturally applicable to more than two bba's.

$$m_1 \textcircled{\tiny{$\cap$}} m_2(Z) = \sum_{X,Y \subseteq \Theta : X \cap Y = Z} m_1(X) \times m_2(Y)$$

3 Evidential Database

3.1 Definition

An evidential database, also called DS database or belief database stores data that could be perfect or imperfect. It allows users to set null (missing) values and also uncertain values. Uncertainty in such database is expressed via evidence theory presented in section 2.1. An evidential database, denoted by EDB, is defined as follows: It is a database with n attributes and d lines. Each attribute i $(1 \leq i \leq n)$ has a domain D_i of discrete values. Among the n attributes, there is a one denoted by k that can store uncertain values. Each cell of the attribute k contains *evidential values* V_{kj} which is a bba defined as follows:

Definition 1 (Evidential value). *Let V_{kj} be an evidential value of attribute k and line j. V_{kj} is a BoE defined by a frame of discernment D_k, a set of focal elements F and mass function m_{kj} defined as follows:*

$$m_{kj} : 2^{D_k} \rightarrow [0, 1] \ with:$$

$$m_{kj}(\emptyset) = 0 \ and \ \sum_{x \subseteq D_k} m_{kj}(x) = 1$$

3.2 Data Imperfections

Evidential databases process different kinds of data imperfections thanks to evidence theory. Indeed, such theory represents *perfect information* when evidential value BoE includes only one focal element that is singleton with mass equal to one. For example, in the following evidential database (see table 1), the evidential attribute is C. C could have a unique and certain value such as C_3; that is a perfect information. *Probabilistic information* represented by evidential value with several focal elements that are singleton. In our database example, values of attribute C in the second line are probabilistic. *Possibilistic information* can be also represented since possibility distribution could be converted into valid BoE. In our example, values of attribute C in the first line are possibilistic with $\pi(C_1) = 0.8$ and $\pi(C_2) = 1$ (we recall that function π in possibility theory corresponds to pl in evidence one). *Missing information* corresponds to a BoE with only one focal element that includes all attribute domain D_C values with mass equal to one. For example, if the value of attribute C is missing for one line, then evidential value will be composed of only one focal element that is the whole of the set of D_C with $m(D_C) = 1$. Finally any *evidential information*

Table 1. Evidential database example

id	A	B	C
1	A_1	B_1	$C_2(0.2)$
			$\{C1, C2\}(0.8)$
2	A_2	B_1	$C_1(0.3)$
			$C_2(0.7)$
3	A_2	B_1	$\{C_1, C_2, C_3\}$
4	A_1	B_1	$C_2(0.5)$
			$\{C_1, C_3\}(0.5)$

could be represented. In our example, the value of C in the fourth line is an evidential information, that is neither perfect, nor probabilistic, nor possibilistic nor missing one.

In the next section, we recall briefly ARM problem in perfect databases before presenting the same problem in the context of imperfect databases that contain one evidential attribute.

4   Association Rule Mining from Perfect Databases

ARM problem has been introduced in [1] and has received a lot of attention thanks to its applicability in several fields. ARM problem is defined as follows: Let $I=\{i_1, i_2, \ldots, i_n\}$ be a set of n items. Let DB be a perfect database of D transactions with scheme $< tid, items >$. Each transaction is identified by a transaction identifier tid and is included in I (*items*). An association rule is $X \rightarrow Y$ with $X, Y \subseteq I$, $X \neq \emptyset$ and $X \cap Y = \emptyset$. *Support* of the association rule $X \rightarrow Y$ is the occurrence number of $Z = X \cup Y$ in DB denoted by $support(Z)$. Its *confidence* is the ratio $support(Z)/support(X)$. Given a support threshold min_{supp} and a confidence threshold $minconf$, ARM problem consists in computing association rules with supports exceeding $min_{supp}\%$ and confidences exceeding $minconf\%$. An itemset is a set of items, it is said to be *frequent* in DB if its support exceeds $min_{supp}\%$. ARM problem is divided into two subproblems:

1. Frequent itemsets generation.
2. Association rules computation from frequent itemsets.

The whole of the association rule problem is often reduced to frequent itemset mining, because once frequent itemsets are generated, association rules computation becomes a straightforward problem that is less costly compared to the first subproblem [2]. In our work we focus only on FIM step.

5   Frequent Itemset Mining from Evidential Databases

This section is an adaptation of the model of FIM from perfect databases to imperfect ones. *Item* and *itemset* notions are modified to support evidential values, *support* notion is also modified to take into account masses placed on evidential information which produces more accurate association. The preliminaries of frequent evidential itemsets mining model ([10] and [3]) are the following:

5.1   Preliminaries

Definition 2 (Evidential Item). *An evidential item denoted by iv_k is one focal element in a body of evidence V_{kj} corresponding to the evidential attribute k. Thus it is defined as a subset of D_k ($iv_k \in 2^{D_k}$).*

Example 1. In our database example (Table 1), C_1 is an item, $\{C_1, C_2\}$ too.

Definition 3 (Evidential Itemset). *An evidential itemset is a set of evidential items that correspond to different attributes domains. Formally, evidential itemset X is defined as:*

$$X \in \prod_{i \neq k} D_i \cup 2^{D_k}$$

Example 2. The itemset $A_1 A_3$ is not a valid evidential itemset because the two items correspond to the same attribute A. However, the evidential itemset $A_1 B_2 \{C_1, C_2\}$ is a valid one.

We also define inclusion operator for evidential itemsets.

Definition 4 (Evidential Itemset Inclusion). *Let X and Y be two evidential itemsets. The ith items of X and Y are respectively denoted by i_X and i_Y.*

$$X \subseteq Y \text{ if and only if: } \forall i_X \in X, i_X \subseteq i_Y$$

Example 3. The itemset $A_1 B_2 \{C_1, C_2\}$ includes the itemset $A_1 B_2 C_1$.

Now, we define the *line body of evidence* thanks to conjunctive rule of combination. A line body of evidence is computed from evidential values composing the line:

Definition 5 (Line BoE). *The frame of discernment of a line BoE is the cross product of all attributes domains denoted by $\Theta = \prod_{i \neq k} D_i \cup 2^{D_k}$. Focal elements are included in Θ, and thus vectors of the form $X = \{x_1, x_2, \ldots, x_n\}$ where $x_i \in D_i$ for $i \neq k$ and $x_k \subseteq D_k$. The mass of a vector X in a line j is computed by conjunctive rule of combination of the bba's evidential values. In this definition, we assume that perfect attributes ($i \neq k$) are evidential ones and correspond to BoEs with only one focal element having masses equal to one.*

$$m_j : \Theta \rightarrow [0, 1]$$

$$m_j(\emptyset) = 0$$

$$m_j(X) = \bigcirc_{i \leq n} m_{ij}(X) = \prod_{iv_i \in X} m_{ij}(iv_i)$$

Example 4. To illustrate this late definition, we present here the first line body of evidence in our database example (Table 1). The frame of discernment is Θ which is the cross product of all attributes domains and the frame of discernment of the whole of the bodies of evidence of the database lines. Focal elements are combinations of all evidential items in the line, and thus the *BoE* of the first line contains two focal elements $A_1 B_1 C_2$ with mass equal to 0.2 and $A_1 B_1 \{C_1, C_2\}$ with mass equal to 0.8.

Now, we introduce the notion of *evidential database body of evidence* which is induced from the line body of evidence notion since database is a set of lines.

Definition 6 (Evidential Database BoE). *Body of evidence of the evidential database EDB is defined on the frame of discernment Θ, the set of focal elements is composed of all possible evidential itemsets existing in the database and the mass function m_{EDB} is defined as follows: Let X be an evidential itemset and d be the size of EDB:*

$$m_{DB} : \Theta \to [0,1] \ with \ m_{DB}(X) = \frac{1}{d} \sum_{j=1}^{d} m_j(X)$$

Belief and Plausibility functions are naturally defined as follows:

$$Bel_{DB}(X) = \sum_{Y \subseteq X} m_{DB}(Y)$$

$$Pl_{DB}(X) = \sum_{Y \cap X \neq \emptyset} m_{DB}(Y)$$

Example 5. In our database (Table 1) the mass of the itemset $A_1 B_1 \{C_1, C_2\}$ is the sum of its line masses in the database divided by the size of the latter (equal to 4); so $m_{DB}(A_1 B_1 \{C_1, C_2\}) = 0.2$. Its belief in the database is the sum of all database masses of evidential itemsets that are included in, which are $A_1 B_1 C_2$ and $A_1 B_1 \{C_1, C_2\}$ so $Bel_{BD}(A_1 B_1 \{C_1, C_2\}) = 0.375$.

The mass of an evidential itemset X in evidential database EDB is the partial belief attributed to X. The total belief of X is the sum of masses of evidential itemsets Y included in X corresponding to belief of X in database body of evidence. Thus the support of X in EDB is simply its belief in EDB's body of evidence.

5.2   Frequent Evidential Itemset Mining Algorithm

In this section, we present our method for mining frequent itemsets from database under a support threshold denoted by min_{supp}. Let EDB be an evidential database, X be an evidential itemset and Θ be the cross product of all attribute domains. F is the set of frequent evidential itemsets in EDB under the user-defined support threshold min_{supp}. Our goal is to extract the set F that is formally defined as follows:

$$F = \{X \subseteq \Theta / support(X) \geq min_{supp}\}$$

Our algorithm proceeds in two major steps. In the first one we generate a data structure that stores the evidential database; it is a variant of the Belief Itemset Tree (BIT) introduced in [10]. Then, we scan this data structure to generate frequent evidential itemsets. These two major steps are described in detail in the following:

Construction of the Belief Itemset Tree

Belief Itemset Tree (BIT) is a data structure introduced in [10] to store an evidential database in a compressed way. A BIT contains $n + 1$ hierarchical levels. The root contains a null value, and each level contains the values of one attribute. The BIT is constructed by inserting focal elements of the database BoE one by one where each focal element corresponds to a different path. A node is labelled by an item and contains mass and belief information. Mass and belief information concern the itemset composed by all items of the path from the root until the node (item) in question.

Example 6. The following figure is the BIT corresponding to our database example. We note that we have six focal elements in our database *BoE* that are $A_1B_1C_2$, $A_1B_1\{C_1, C_2\}$, $A_2B_1C_1, A_2B_1C_2, A_2B_1\{C_1, C_2, C_3\}$ and $A_1B_1\{C_1, C_3\}$.

Note that the levels order in the BIT (B, A and C) does not correspond to the attributes order (A, B and C) given in table 1. Indeed, we provide two changes to the original construction process of the BIT in [10]. The first one consists in specifying the sequence of attributes before the construction of the BIT. Attributes are ordered ascending by the size of their domains, and the evidential attribute (in our example C) is always the last one in the sequence. In our example, we start with the attribute B because it has the smallest domain size. We choose this method to minimize as far as possible the size of our data structure and so to consume as the least as possible computer memory. In our

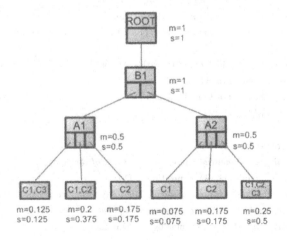

Fig. 1. BIT of our database example

Table 2. Objects and methods description

Object/Method	Description
Item	Object composed of the **label** of the item, a **mass** value and a **support** value.
Node	Object composed of two arrays. The first one, denoted by **value**, includes indexed items and the second one, denoted by **child** includes indexed nodes. It is also composed of **mass** and **support** values.
Record	Object composed of an **array** of items and the **mass** of the record in the database.
Extract(S as Set,k as Integer)	This is a function that returns the set containing all itemsets of size k included into S.
Apriori_Gen(S as Set)	It is the famous candidate generation function of Apriori [2]. It generates the set of candidates itemsets of size k from the set of frequent ones of size $k - 1$.

example, if we try to start with the attribute A instead of B, the size of the tree would be more large that in figure 1.

The second optimization consists in introducing the information support in each node. This information will be computed on the fly when inserting the database records and will speed up the frequent itemsets search in the second step of our process.

The algorithm 1 is the pseudo-code of inserting a record in the belief itemset tree. Table 2 contains a description of the objects and the methods used in the next algorithms.

Algorithm 1. *InsertRecord(in rec as record, in k as integer, in BIT as Node)*

```
01      If k < n + 1 Then /*Processing the non-last levels*/
02        If BIT.value includes rec(k) in position p Then
03          Increment BIT.value(p).mass and BIT.value(p).support by rec.mass
04        Else
05          Add the item rec(k) in BIT.value with its mass
06          Add an empty Node to BIT.child
07          Affect to p the last position of the array BIT.value /*And so, the position of rec(k)
—            in BIT.value*/
08        End if
09        InsertRecord(rec,k+1,BIT.child(p))
10      Else /*Handling an evidential value, and so a leaf of the tree*/
11        If BIT.value includes rec(k) in position p Then
12          Increment BIT.value(p).mass and BIT.value(p).support by rec.mass
13        Elsif BIT.value(k) includes items that are supersets of rec(k) Then
14          Increment supports of these items by rec(k).mass
15        End If
16        For each item i in BIT.value loop
```

17	If i is a subset of $rec(k)$ Then
18	Increment $BIT.value(p).support$ by $i.mass$
19	End If
20	End Loop
21	End

The algorithm 1 inserts only one record in the tree, to construct the whole of the belief itemset tree, we iterate the procedure *InsertRecord* for each record in the database EDB. Once we obtain the belief itemset tree, we pass to the second major step of our process which is the generation of frequent itemsets from the BIT.

Generation of Frequent Itemsets from the BIT

In this section we describe our FIM method from the data structure BIT. This operation is also performed in two steps. In the first one, we scan the BIT only one time to extract a set of maximal frequent itemsets. Indeed, we explore the whole of the paths of the tree. A path is considered as a maximal frequent itemset if we reach a node with a support less than the threshold min_{supp} (like the path $B_1 A_1$ if we assume that $min_{supp} = 0.5$) or the leaf (like the path $B_1 A_2 \{C_1, C_2, C_3\}$ for the same threshold). Then, once we have a set of maximal frequent itemsets, we generate all subsets of them, that are also frequent itemsets since support function is anti-monotone [2], i.e., if an itemset X is frequent, then all itemsets $Y \subseteq X$ are also frequent.

Example 7. Assume the support threshold $min_{supp} = 0.3$. In our BIT example, we extract maximal frequent itemsets by scanning in depth our tree. The stored paths we store are delimited either by a node with a support less than min_{supp}, either by a leaf. Thus, maximal frequent itemsets that are generated are: $B_1 A_2 \{C_1, C_2, C_3\}$, $B_1 A_2$, $B_1 A_1 \{C_1, C_2\}$ and $B_1 A_1$. In addition, all subsets of these itemsets are frequent: B_1, A_1, A_2, $\{C_1, C_2, C_3\}$, $\{C_1, C_2\}$, $B_1 \{C_1, C_2\}$, $A_2 \{C_1, C_2, C_3\}$, $B_1 \{C_1, C_2, C_3\}$ and $A_1 \{C_1, C_2\}$. Note that one scan of the BIT has allowed us to extract a significant part of the final result F of the whole of the frequent itemsets in EDB under min_{supp}.

Algorithm 2. *GenerateMax(in BIT as Node, in min_{supp} as Real, out MF as Set)*

01	For each item i in $BIT.value$ Loop
02	If $i.support >= min_{supp}$ and $BIT.child$ not Null Then
03	$GenerateMax(N.child, min_{supp}, MF)$
04	Else
05	$MF = MF \cup Path$
06	End if
07	End Loop
08	End

The algorithm 2 is the pseudo-code of the procedure that extracts maximal frequent itemsets from a belief itemset tree in the set MF.

Once the set MF (of Maximal Frequent itemsets) is extracted, we generate all subsets of the elements of MF since they are frequent too. These subsets are added to the set MF. Now, the second operation consists in completing the set MF to obtain the set F of all frequent itemsets. For this purpose, we use the same technique of [3] and [10]. But in our method, the difference is we have in memory the set MF which stores a considerable part of F. In fact, MF allows us to prune the search space and to save much time in comparison with the other two algorithms. Note that our experiments on different synthetic databases showed that MF constitutes until 50% of the final result set F while its computation is at the most 20% of the execution time of the algorithms [3] and [10].

The algorithm 3 is the pseudo-code of our main procedure that completes the set MF to obtain the set F. Figure 2 is a simplified description of the overall process of the algorithm.

Algorithm 3. *GenerateFrequent(in BIT as Node, in min_{supp} as Real, out F as Array of Set)*

```
01    GenerateMax(BIT, min_supp, MF)
02    k = 1
03    For each item i in BIT
04       If Extract(MF,1) does not include i Then
05          Compute support of i in BIT
06          If i.suport >= min_supp Then
07             F(1) = F(1) ∪ i
08          End If
09       End If
10    End Loop
11    Do While F(k) ≠ ∅ Loop
12       C = Apriori_Gen(F(k))
13       k=k+1
14       C = C \ Extract(MF, k) /*The search space is pruned here. This is the gain
--       compared to the algorithms of [3] and [10]*/
15       Compute supports of all itemsets of C in BIT
16       Remove infrequent itemsets according to min_supp from the set C
17       F(k) = C
18       C = ∅
19    Loop
20    F = F ∪ MF
21    End
```

In the next section, we present the experimentations that we led to evaluate the performance of our algorithm.

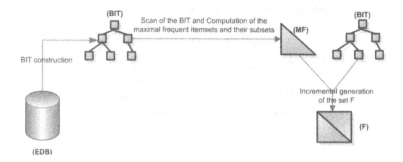

Fig. 2. A simplified description of our solution process

6   Experimentations

To assess our method performance, we implemented our proposed algorithm and the algorithms of [3] and [10] to compare them. Then we generated several synthetic databases with various values of these parameters : D (database size), I (number of items in all attributes domains), C (number of attributes) and $\%U$ (percentage of records including evidential values). We present here only tests led on the database $D = 5000, I = 800, C = 5$ and $\%U = 10$.

Figure 3 is a comparison between algorithms performances. It shows that our solution is taking a considerable advantage from the set MF computed in the first scan of the database. MF fast computation makes the second part of our process faster, since the set of candidate itemsets is significantly pruned. Note that in figure 3 our solution, the one of [3] and the one of [10] are respectively denoted by 1, 2 and 3.

To show the important contribution of the first scan, we led an experimentation on the same synthetic database to compute the percentage of generated maximal frequent itemsets (MF) in relation to the whole of the frequent itemsets (F). Table 3 presents some mining operations performed by our algorithm

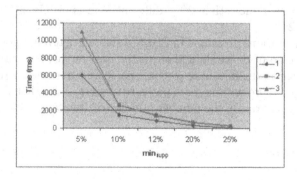

Fig. 3. Comparison between algorithms performances

Table 3. Performance of the first scan of the BIT

min_{supp}	Size ratio	Time ratio
5%	25%	3%
7%	27%	10%
10%	35%	9%
12%	50%	7%

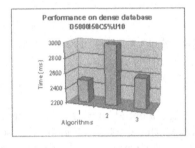 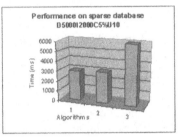

Fig. 4. Performance of the algorithms in the context of dense and sparse databases

for a range of support thresholds. For each mining operation, we compute the **size ratio** that is (size of MF)/(size of F) and also the **time ratio** that is (time of MF computation)/(time of F computation). The results show that the procedure *GenerateMax* is a main advantage in the whole of F's computation process since it generates an important part of the final result in so short time.

We also performed two experimentations to assess the behavior of our algorithm in the context of dense and sparse data. We generated two synthetic databases with the same values for $D = 5000$, $C = 5$ and $\%U = 10$ but with different values for I that are $I = 2000$ to get a sparse database and $I = 50$ to get a dense database. We recall that sparse databases contain a great number of itemsets that are scattered in the records, while dense databases contain a more little number of itemsets. For example, the search space in the first synthetic database has a size of more than 2^{2000} different itemsets while in the second one it reaches only 2^{50}.

The experimentations presented in Figure 4 showed that our algorithm is more efficient in the case of dense data than in the case of sparse data. Indeed, the BIT is more large as the database is more sparse and that makes the algorithm less efficient since there will be more paths to explore. Note that the number of paths in the BIT is exactly the number of different itemsets in the database.

7   Conclusion

In this paper we propose a frequent itemsets mining algorithm in context of databases that include exactly one evidential attribute. This kind of databases provides a large field of uncertainty expression to end-user since they allow storage of probabilistic, possibilistic, evidential information and even missing values. Our solution uses a variant of the belief itemset tree introduced in [10]. Our main contribution is the computation of an important part of the final set F of frequent itemsets (from 25% until 50%) in a little interval of time compared to the whole of the time consumed by the mining operation (from 3% until 10%). This fast computation of a considerable part of the set F gives to our solution a significant advantage and makes it more efficient than existing algorithms for mining evidential data ([3] and [10]).

Our work could be extended by *plausible* pattern mining, since mined itemsets in our model are *credible*, but we have no information about their plausibilities. In other words, it will be interesting if we compute plausibilities of frequent (credible) evidential itemsets. We can even find infrequent itemsets that are more plausible than frequent ones. A survey of this measurement will be interesting. Finally, the maintenance of frequent itemsets in imperfect databases is practically a non-explored field. Maintenance of frequent itemsets is useful in the context of dynamic databases, i.e., databases that are frequently updated. The data structure used in this algorithm is highly updatable which constitutes a good base to tackle the problem.

References

[1] Agrawal, R., Imielinski, T., Swami., A.: Mining Association Rules Between Sets of Items in Large Databases. In: Proceedings ACM SIGMOD International Conference on Management of Data, pp. 207–216 (1993)

[2] Agrawal, R., Srikant, R.: Fast Algorithms for Mining Association Rules. In: Proceedings of the 20th International Conference on Very Large Data Bases, pp. 487–499 (1994)

[3] Bach Tobji, M.-A., Ben Yaghlane, B., Mellouli, K.: A New Algorithm for Mining Frequent Itemsets from Evidential Databases. In: Proceedings of the 12th International Conference on Information Processing and Management of Uncertainty in Knowledge-Based Systems, Malaga, Spain (2008)

[4] Chen, G., Wei, Q.: Fuzzy association rules and the extended mining algorithms. Information Sciences-Informatics and Computer Science 147(1-4), 201–228 (2002)

[5] Chui, C.-K., Kao, B., Hung, E.: Mining Frequent Itemsets from Uncertain Data. In: The 11th Pacific-Asia Conference on Knowledge Discovery and Data Mining, pp. 47–58 (2007)

[6] Dempster, A.P.: Upper and Lower Probabilities Induced by a Multivalue Mapping. Annals of Mathematical Statistics 38(2), 325–339 (1967)

[7] Dubois, D., Hullermeier, E., Prade, H.: A systematic approach to the assessment of fuzzy association rules. Data Mining and Knowledge Discovery 13(2), 167–192 (2006)

[8] Djouadi, Y., Redaoui, S., Amroun, K.: Mining Association Rules under Imprecision and Vagueness: towards a Possibilistic Approach. In: Intl. Fuzzy Systems Conference, (23-26), pp. 1–6 (2007)

[9] Han, J., Pei, J., Yin, Y.: Mining Frequent Patterns without Candidate Generation. In: Proceedings of the 2000 ACM-SIGMOD International Conference on Management of Data, pp. 1–12 (2000)

[10] Hewawasam, K.K.R.G.K., Premaratne, K., Subasingha, S.P., Shyu, M.-L.: Rule Mining and Classification in Imperfect Databases. In: Proceedings of the Seventh International Conference on Information Fusion, pp. 661–668 (2005)

[11] Konias, S., Chouvarda, I., Vlahavas, I., Maglaveras, N.: A Novel Approach for Incremental Uncertainty Rule Generation from Databases with Missing Values Handling: Application to Dynamic Medical Databases. Medical Informatics and The Internet in Medicine 30(3), 211–225 (2005)

[12] Leung, C.K.-S., Carmichael, C.L., Hao, B.: Efficient Mining of Frequent Patterns from Uncertain Data. In: Proceedings of the Seventh IEEE International Conference on Data Mining, pp. 489–494 (2007)

[13] Lucchese, C., Orlando, S., Perego, R., Palmerini, P., Perego, R., Silvestri, F.: kDCI: A Multi-Strategy Algorithm for Mining Frequent Sets. In: Proceedings of the ICDM 2003 Workshop on Frequent Itemset Mining Implementations (2003)

[14] Shafer, G.: A Mathematical Theory of Evidence. Princeton University Press, Princeton (1976)

[15] Smets, P.: The Application of the Transferable Belief Model to Diagnostic Problems. Int. J. Intelligent Systems 13, 127–158 (1998)

[16] Vaughn, R.B., Farrell, J., Henning, R., Knepper, M., Fox, K.: Sensor Fusion and Automatic Vulnerability Analysis. In: Proceedings of the 4th international symposium on Information and communication technologies, pp. 230–235 (2005)

[17] Wang, X., Borgelt, C., Kruse, R.: Mining Fuzzy Frequent Item Sets. In: Proceedings of the 11th International Fuzzy Systems Association World Congress, pp. 528–533 (2005)

Evaluating Trustworthiness from Past Performances: Interval-Based Approaches*

Jonathan Ben-Naim and Henri Prade

Institut de Recherche en Informatique de Toulouse (IRIT-CNRS)
Université de Toulouse, 118 route de Narbonne
F-31062 Toulouse Cedex 9, France
{bennaim,prade}@irit.fr

Abstract. In many multi-agent systems, the user has to decide whether he (or she) sufficiently trusts a certain agent to achieve a certain goal. To help users to make such decisions, an increasing number of trust systems have been developed. By trust system, we mean a system that gathers information about an agent and evaluates its trustworthiness from this information. The aim of the present paper is to develop new trust systems that overcome limitations of existing ones. This is a challenging problem that raises questions such as: how trustworthiness may be represented, and from which information it may be estimated? We assume that a set of grades describing the past performances of the agent is given. With this common basis, two approaches are proposed. In the first one, the aim is to construct an interval that summarizes the grades. Such an interval gives a good account of the trustworthiness of the agent. We establish axioms that should be satisfied by summarizing methods, devise a particular method based on pulling, and check that it satisfies the axioms, which provides theoretical justifications for it. In the second approach, which is more briefly presented, a level of trust as the certainty that a future grade will be good, and a level of distrust as the fear that a future grade may be bad, are computed on the basis of the past grades. This approach is based on possibility theory and provides, thanks to the two levels, another view of trustworthiness, as well as summarizing intervals.

Keywords: Trust, distrust, intervals, possibility theory.

1 Introduction

In many multi-agent systems, especially in the field of e-commerce, the user has a lot of decisions to make about the agents. For example, he (or she) has to decide whether he believes that an agent is more trustworthy than another, or whether an agent is sufficiently trustworthy is the absolute sense. This is the case for example in the famous auction system Ebay. Indeed, a buyer has to compare sellers and to decide whether he sufficiently trusts them to be honest and competent. In order to help users to make such decisions, an increasing number of *trust systems* have been developed, see e.g. [SS05] for a review.

---

* The first author is supported by the French ANR-SETIN project ForTrust.

S. Greco and T. Lukasiewicz (Eds.): SUM 2008, LNAI 5291, pp. 33–46, 2008.
© Springer-Verlag Berlin Heidelberg 2008

By trust system, we mean a system composed of two parts. First, an environment in which an agent called the trustee may be put as well as a certain kind of information about it. And second, a method which (in any possible situation) constructs from this information an object giving a good account of the trustworthiness of the trustee. This object is meant to provide trustors with some help to make decisions about trustees.

For example, Ebay is equipped with a system that takes a seller, collects the grades buyers gave to him, and attributes to him a certain number of "stars" on the basis of these grades. This number indicates how reliable the seller is, and provides buyers with a new criterion for judging and comparing sellers.

The aim of the present paper is to develop new trust systems which overcome limitations of existing ones. This is a challenging problem that raises questions such as: how trustworthiness may be represented, and from which information it may be estimated? We assume that a set of grades describing the past performances of the trustee is given. By convention, the value of a grade is a real number between 0 and 1. Each grade describes how perfectly the trustee achieved some past goal. Naturally, 0 means that it did not at all achieved it, whilst 1 means on the contrary that it achieved it perfectly.

With this common basis, two approaches are proposed. In the first one, the aim is to construct a *summarizing interval*, that is, an interval which necessarily describes the past behavior of the trustee with less accuracy than the grades, but gives a good account of the essential parts of this behavior. Such an interval constitutes a concise representation of the trustworthiness of the trustee. An advantage is that it is simpler than a set of grades. Therefore, it provides a new criterion for judging and comparing trustees, that is, a trustor may use it to evaluate its trust (or distrust) in the trustee, and thus to take decisions.

First, we establish intuitive and desirable properties, called axioms, which should be satisfied by *summarizing methods*. Next, we devise a particular method based on the idea that "strong" groups of grades have the strength to pull the bounds of the interval towards themselves. And finally, we check that our method satisfies the axioms, which provides theoretical justifications for it.

In certain cases, the user needs a *trust interval* rather than a summarizing one. By trust interval, we mean an interval such that it is rational to believe (on the basis of the past grades) that the future grades will essentially fall on it. We think that we get such an interval if we take a summarizing one and add an adequate margin of error. We provide a method for constructing such a margin. It is based on the fusion of the summarizing interval and the interval $[0, 1]$.

In the second approach, which is more briefly presented, the idea is to compute a *level of trust* as the certainty (on the basis of the past grades) that a future grade will be good, and a *level of distrust* as the fear that a future grade may be bad. These two levels provide another representation of the trustworthiness of the trustee. This approach is based on possibility theory, that is, we view the grades as a basis for building an histogram, which is then transformed into a possibility distribution, which in turn provides a basis for computing levels of trust and distrust. Moreover, the possibility distribution so obtained may also be summarized under the form of a crisp interval by computing lower and upper expected values. This may be viewed as another way to build summarizing intervals. Besides, partial and complete orders are also proposed for comparing directly histograms of grade values, from a trustworthiness point of view.

The rest of the paper is structured as follows. In Section 2, we discuss different research trends on the problem of evaluating trustworthiness, and we highlight some advantages of our approaches. In Section 3, we present the first one, that is, in Section 3.1, we establish six axioms for summarizing methods, in Section 3.2, we develop a method based on pulling and prove that it satisfies the axioms, and in Section 3.3, we show how summarizing intervals may be used to construct trust intervals. Next, in Section 4, we turn to the second approach. We begin with histograms of grade values, introduce ordering relations between them, build possibility distributions from them, and finally obtain from these distributions levels of trust and distrust, as well as summarizing intervals.

2   Trust Evaluation: Different Research Trends

The problem of evaluating trustworthiness may be considered from many viewpoints. First of all, there are different kinds of representation formats. For example, trustworthiness may be represented by a number, a pair of numbers (usually one for trust and one for distrust), an interval, or even a fuzzy interval. In addition, the same representation format may have different understandings.

For example, in some approaches (e.g. [JK98] and [ZdSM05]), an agent is either trustworthy or not, and the authors manipulate a number which indicates the probability or the belief that it is trustworthy. In other approaches (e.g. [dCdS06]), an agent is trustworthy to a certain degree, and the authors work with a number that indicates to which degree. But, the probability of being trustworthy is certainly not the same thing as a degree of trustworthiness.

Other approaches motivate interval-based representation of trustworthiness by the poorness of the information available, e.g. [Pra07]. This view is compatible with the understanding that trustworthiness is binary and the probability of being trustworthy is imprecise. Similarly, it is compatible with the understanding that trustworthiness is graded and the degree of trustworthiness is ill-known.

Another facet of the problem is that it may refer to quite different types of input data. For example, these data may take the form of opinions of agents about others, e.g. [AMT05], [WJI04], and [MDB06]. This is also the case in [TB04] and [TLU06], where trust evaluation is based on direct opinions, that is, opinions obtained from past interactions. Then, indirect opinions are computed by chaining and combining direct ones, either by means of inference rules [TLU06] or by path semirings [TB04]. Both approaches associate an uncertainty estimate to their trust values. Another option is to view trust assessment as a matter of argumentation, that is, the idea is to balance arguments in favor of deciding to trust an agent with arguments against this choice [Pra07].

In this paper, we evaluate trustworthiness from past performances, which has been rather neglected in the literature. Although purely statistical methods may be considered if enough data are available, we investigate other roads here since data are not necessarily numerous in practice. In e-commerce, there are systems (e.g. Ebay) where agents receive simple rates (e.g. good, bad, or neutral), and their trustworthiness, represented by a number, is evaluated in a rudimentary way from these rates. By our interval-based approaches, we try to exploit the rates in a deeper way. In addition, a number does not give many indications of how the rates are scattered, while an interval does.

3   Trustworthiness as a Summarizing Interval

3.1   Axioms

In this section, we provide desirable properties for summarizing methods.

Definition 1. *A grade structure* $\mathcal{G}$ *is an ordered pair* $\langle G, v \rangle$, *where* G *is a non-empty and finite set of grades and* v *is a function from a superset of* G *to the interval* $[0, 1]$ *(of real numbers). We call* $v(g)$ *the value of* g.

A summarizing method I *is a function which transforms any grade structure into a sub-interval of* $[0, 1]$.

The reader may wonder why we allow the domain of v to be a superset of G, while G would be sufficient. The reason is simply that it helps to increase the readability of certain definitions and proofs. For all $x \in [0, 1]$, we denote by $wei_\mathcal{G}(x)$ the "weight" of x in $\mathcal{G}$, that is, $wei_\mathcal{G}(x) = |\{g \in G : v(g) = x\}|$. When the context is clear we may drop the subscript $\mathcal{G}$. The same goes for all notations.

We turn to a first obvious property. If two structures lead to the same values and to the same weights, then of course they should lead to the same interval.

Definition 2. *Let* $\mathcal{G} = \langle G, v \rangle$ *and* $\mathcal{G}' = \langle G', v' \rangle$ *be two grade structures. We say that* $\mathcal{G}$ *and* $\mathcal{G}'$ *are equivalent (in symbols* $\mathcal{G} \equiv \mathcal{G}'$) *iff* $v(G) = v'(G')$ *and* $\forall x \in v(G)$, $wei_\mathcal{G}(x) = wei_{\mathcal{G}'}(x)$.

A summarizing method I *respects equivalence iff for all grade structures* $\mathcal{G}$ *and* $\mathcal{G}'$, *if* $\mathcal{G} \equiv \mathcal{G}'$, *then* $I(\mathcal{G}) = I(\mathcal{G}')$.

Another obvious property is that the summarizing interval should not exceed the limits of the zone in which the grades are located.

Definition 3. *A summarizing method* I *respects confinement iff for all grade structure* $\mathcal{G}$, $I(\mathcal{G}) \subseteq [min(v(G)), max(v(G))]$.

Next, assume that the grades are regularly scattered over some distance. Then, the summarizing interval should cover exactly this distance.

Definition 4. *A grade structure* $\mathcal{G}$ *is regular iff:*
- $\exists r, s \in \mathbb{R}, \exists n \in \mathbb{N}, v(G) = \{r, r+s, r+2s, \ldots, r+ns\}$
- $\forall x, y \in v(G), wei(x) = wei(y)$

A summarizing method I *respects regularity iff for all regular grade structure* $\mathcal{G}$, $I(\mathcal{G}) = [min(v(G)), max(v(G))]$.

The next property says the following: if the grades are symmetric with respect to some axis, then so should be the summarizing interval. Let $x, a \in \mathbb{R}$. We denote by $mir_a(x)$ is the mirror image of x with respect to a, that is, $mir_a(x) = 2a - x$.

Definition 5. *A grade structure $\mathcal{G}$ is symmetric with respect to $a \in \mathbb{R}$ iff for all $x \in v(G)$, $mir(x) \in v(G)$ and $wei(x) = wei(mir(x))$.*

A summarizing method I respects symmetry iff for all grade structure $\mathcal{G}$ and $\forall a \in \mathbb{R}$, if $\mathcal{G}$ is symmetric with respect to a, then $mir(minI(\mathcal{G})) = maxI(\mathcal{G})$.

Note that we sometimes write $minX$, vX, etc. instead of $min(X)$, $v(X)$, etc. in order to increase readability. We denote by $mean_\mathcal{G}$ the mean of the grades of $\mathcal{G}$ and by $cen_\mathcal{G}$ the center of the zone in which they are located, that is, $cen_\mathcal{G}$ is the middle of $[min(v(G)), max(v(G))]$.

Assume that *mean* is to the right of *cen*. Then, intuitively, $\mathcal{G}$ is leaning to the right. The summarizing interval should reflect this asymmetry, that is, it should "forget" at least a bit the grades on the extreme left. The same goes when $\mathcal{G}$ is leaning to the left.

Definition 6. *A method I respects leaning iff for all grade structure $\mathcal{G}$,*
- *if cen < mean, then $min(v(G)) < minI(\mathcal{G})$*
- *if mean < cen, then $maxI(\mathcal{G}) < max(v(G))$*

Finally, take a grade structure $\mathcal{G}$, add new grades to the right, and call $\mathcal{G}'$ the structure so obtained. Then, the bounds of $I(\mathcal{G}')$ should be at least as to the right as those of $I(\mathcal{G})$. In addition, if some new grades are strictly more to the right than the old ones, then the right bound of $I(\mathcal{G}')$ should be strictly more to the right than that of $I(\mathcal{G})$. The same goes with left.

Definition 7. *Let $\mathcal{G} = \langle G, v \rangle$ and $\mathcal{G}' = \langle G', v' \rangle$ be two grade structures. We denote by $\preceq_r$ the relation such that*

$$\mathcal{G} \preceq_r \mathcal{G}' \quad iff \quad G' = G \cup H, \quad v|_G = v'|_G, \quad and \quad \forall g \in G, \forall h \in H, v'(g) \leq v'(h)$$

We denote by $\prec_r$ the relation such that

$$\mathcal{G} \prec_r \mathcal{G}' \quad iff \quad \mathcal{G} \preceq_r \mathcal{G}' \quad and \quad \exists g' \in G', \forall g \in G, v(g) < v'(g')$$

The definitions of $\preceq_l$ and $\prec_l$ are obtained by replacing $\leq$ by $\geq$, and $<$ by $>$.

Intuitively, $\mathcal{G} \preceq_r \mathcal{G}'$ means that $\mathcal{G}'$ can be obtained from $\mathcal{G}$ by adding new grades to the right, and $\mathcal{G} \prec_r \mathcal{G}'$ means that some new grades are strictly more to the right than the old ones. Note that $v|_G$ denotes the restriction of v to G.

Definition 8. *A method I is coherent iff for all grade structures $\mathcal{G}$ and $\mathcal{G}'$,*
- *if $\mathcal{G} \preceq_r \mathcal{G}'$, then $minI(\mathcal{G}) \leq minI(\mathcal{G}')$ and $maxI(\mathcal{G}) \leq maxI(\mathcal{G}')$*
- *if $\mathcal{G} \prec_r \mathcal{G}'$, then $maxI(\mathcal{G}) < maxI(\mathcal{G}')$*
- *if $\mathcal{G} \preceq_l \mathcal{G}'$, then $minI(\mathcal{G}') \leq minI(\mathcal{G})$ and $maxI(\mathcal{G}') \leq maxI(\mathcal{G})$*
- *if $\mathcal{G} \prec_l \mathcal{G}'$, then $minI(\mathcal{G}') < minI(\mathcal{G})$*

3.2   A Summarizing Method Based on Pulling

Assume a grade structure $\mathcal{G}$ is given. It can be visualized as a set of points above the real interval $[0, 1]$, each point being located above its value. For example, the structure $\mathcal{G}_0$ consisting of 0, 0.4, 0.4, 1, and 1 can be visualized as follows:

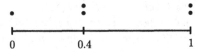

We are now going to construct an interval $I_p(\mathcal{G})$ that summarizes $\mathcal{G}$. Initially, $I_p(\mathcal{G})$ is the smallest interval that contains the values of all points, which seems natural. Next, the idea is to look for "strong" groups of points, that is, groups able to pull the bounds of $I_p(\mathcal{G})$ towards themselves, despite the resistance of certain points. Finally, we move each bound of $I_p(\mathcal{G})$ to the farthest value x such that there exists a group able to pull it to x.

Here is a first simple way to find a group able to pull the left bound of $I_p(\mathcal{G})$ (the case of the right bound is similar). Suppose that the arithmetic mean m of the grades is to the right of the center c of $I_p(\mathcal{G})$. In our opinion, this means that the points above the right half of $I_p(\mathcal{G})$ constitute a group S able to pull the left bound towards the right. The more m is far from c, the more S is able to give it a hard pull. More precisely, S can pull the left bound "until c reaches m", that is, it can pull it to the value x such that if the left bound was equal to x, then c would be equal to m. For example, in $\mathcal{G}_0$, the two 1's are able to pull the left bound of $I_p(\mathcal{G}_0)$ to 0.12.

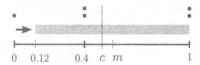

We turn to a more general way to find a group able to pull the left bound of $I_p(\mathcal{G})$. Take some limit l, ignore the points of $\mathcal{G}$ to the right of l, and let $\mathcal{G}'$ be the grade structure so obtained. Next, let $I_p(\mathcal{G}')$ be the smallest interval which contains the values of all grades of $\mathcal{G}'$, and, as before, let us look for a group able to pull the left bound of $I_p(\mathcal{G}')$. If we find such a group, then it is able to pull the left bound of $I_p(\mathcal{G})$ as well.

Indeed, suppose the mean m' of the grades of $\mathcal{G}'$ is to the right of the center c' of $I_p(\mathcal{G}')$. Then, the points above the right half of $I_p(\mathcal{G}')$ constitute a group S' able to pull the left bound of $I_p(\mathcal{G}')$ until c' reaches m'. But, if a group of points can pull the left bound towards the right in a certain context, then of course it can do the same thing in any context obtained by adding new points to the right of this group. This reflects the intuition that he who can do more can do less. Consequently, since, in $\mathcal{G}'$, S' can pull the left bound of $I_p(\mathcal{G}')$ to a certain value x, it follows that, in $\mathcal{G}$, S' can pull the left bound of $I_p(\mathcal{G})$ to x as well.

For example, let $\mathcal{G}_0'$ be the structure obtained from $\mathcal{G}_0$ by removing the two 1's. Then, in $\mathcal{G}_0'$, the two 0.4's can pull the left bound of $I_p(\mathcal{G}_0')$ to 0.133. Therefore, in $\mathcal{G}_0$, the two 0.4's can pull the left bound of $I_p(\mathcal{G}_0)$ to the same value.

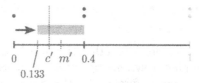

Consequently, in $\mathcal{G}_0$, there are two groups able to pull the left bound of $I_p(\mathcal{G}_0)$, namely the two 1's (to 0.12) and the two 0.4's (to 0.133). It turns out that the second group is able to pull the left bound to a farther value than the first one. This may seem surprising since the first group is farther than the second one, but actually this is normal. Indeed, the two 1's are farther but they face a stronger resistance to pulling, that is, when pulling they are opposed to 0, 0.4, and 0.4, while the two 0.4's are only opposed to 0.

To summarize, we begin with the smallest interval $I_p(\mathcal{G})$ which contains the values of all grades of $\mathcal{G}$, then we identify the groups of grades able to pull the left bound of $I_p(\mathcal{G})$, and finally we move it to the farthest value x such that there exists a group able to pull it to x. The same goes for the right bound.

For example, here is in the final analysis the interval $I_p(\mathcal{G}_0)$ obtained from $\mathcal{G}_0$ by the pulling method (it is represented by the grey bar). Note that, according to our method, no group is able to pull the right bound of $I_p(\mathcal{G}_0)$.

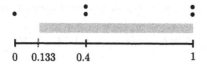

Definition 9. *Let $\mathcal{G} = \langle G, v \rangle$ be a grade structure. We denote by $I_p^s(\mathcal{G})$ the interval that superficially summarizes $\mathcal{G}$ according to the pulling method, that is, the interval obtained by this method when no limit l is considered. More formally,*

$$I_p^s(\mathcal{G}) = \begin{cases} [min(vG), \ max(vG)] & \textit{if } cen = mean \\ [mir_{mean}(max(vG)), \ max(vG)] & \textit{if } cen < mean \\ [min(vG), \ mir_{mean}(min(vG))] & \textit{if } mean < cen \end{cases}$$

A set L is a *left part* of $\mathcal{G}$ iff $\exists\, l \in \mathbb{R}$, $L = \{g \in G : v(g) \leq l\}$. Similarly, a set R is a *right part* of $\mathcal{G}$ iff $\exists\, l \in \mathbb{R}$, $R = \{g \in G : l \leq v(g)\}$. We denote by $L(\mathcal{G})$ (resp. $R(\mathcal{G})$) the set of all non-empty left (resp. right) parts of $\mathcal{G}$.

Definition 10. *Let $\mathcal{G} = \langle G, v \rangle$ be a grade structure. We denote by $I_p(\mathcal{G})$ the interval that summarizes $\mathcal{G}$ according to the pulling method, that is,*

$$I_p(\mathcal{G}) = [max\{minI_p^s\langle L, v\rangle : L \in L(\mathcal{G})\}, \ min\{maxI_p^s\langle R, v\rangle : R \in R(\mathcal{G})\}]$$

Here are some additional examples to give the reader a better idea how I_p behaves. We scattered five grades regularly over some distance. Then, as desired, the interval obtained by the pulling method covers exactly the five grades.

•   •   •   •   •

Next, suppose that we bring closer together the three grades which are closest to the middle, while keeping a symmetric situation. Then, the newly formed concentration of grades makes us forget a bit the two extreme grades.

•   • • •   •

If we do the same thing, but without keeping a symmetric situation, then the concentration of grades makes us forget an extreme grade more than the other.

• $\vdots$ •

More formally, the summarizing method based on pulling satisfies all axioms introduced in Section 3.1.

Proposition 1. *The summarizing method I_p based on pulling satisfies equivalence, confinement, regularity, symmetry, leaning, and coherence.*

Proof. Equivalence, confinement, regularity, and leaning are easy.

Proof for symmetry. Assume $\mathcal{G} = \langle G, v \rangle$ is symmetric with respect to $a \in [0, 1]$. We show later that:
(0) $\forall L \in L(\mathcal{G}),\ \exists R \in R(\mathcal{G}),\ mir(minI_p^s\langle L, v \rangle) = maxI_p^s\langle R, v \rangle$
(1) $\forall R \in R(\mathcal{G}),\ \exists L \in L(\mathcal{G}),\ mir(maxI_p^s\langle R, v \rangle) = minI_p^s\langle L, v \rangle$
By definition, $\exists L \in L(\mathcal{G}),\ minI_p(\mathcal{G}) = minI_p^s\langle L, v \rangle$.
By (0), $\exists R \in R(\mathcal{G}),\ mir(minI_p^s\langle L, v \rangle) = maxI_p^s\langle R, v \rangle$.
Therefore, $maxI_p(\mathcal{G}) \leq maxI_p^s\langle R, v \rangle = mir(minI_p(\mathcal{G}))$.
We show $mir(minI_p(\mathcal{G})) \leq maxI_p(\mathcal{G})$.
  Suppose $maxI_p(\mathcal{G}) < mir(minI_p(\mathcal{G}))$.
  By definition, $\exists R \in R(\mathcal{G}),\ maxI_p(\mathcal{G}) = maxI_p^s\langle R, v \rangle$.
  Thus, by (1), $\exists L \in L(\mathcal{G}),\ mir(maxI_p^s\langle R, v \rangle) = minI_p^s\langle L, v \rangle$.
  Thus, $minI_p(\mathcal{G}) = mir(mir(minI_p(\mathcal{G}))) < mir(maxI_p(\mathcal{G})) = mir(maxI_p^s\langle R, v \rangle)$
  $= minI_p^s\langle L, v \rangle$, which is impossible.

Proof of (0) *((1) is similar).* Let $L \in L(\mathcal{G})$. Then, $\exists l \in \mathbb{R},\ L = \{g \in G : v(g) \leq l\}$.
Let $R = \{g \in G : mir(l) \leq v(g)\}$. We show $mir(v(L)) = v(R)$.
  "$\subseteq$". Let $y \in mir(v(L))$. Then, $\exists x \in v(L),\ y = mir(x)$. But, $x \leq l$.
  Thus, $mir(l) \leq y$. In addition, by symmetry, $\exists g \in G,\ v(g) = y$.
  But, $g \in R$. Therefore, $y \in v(R)$.
  "$\supseteq$". Let $x \in v(R)$. Then, $mir(l) \leq x$. Thus, $mir(x) \leq mir(mir(l)) = l$.
  By symmetry, $\exists g \in G,\ v(g) = mir(x)$. But, $g \in L$. Thus, $mir(x) \in v(L)$.
  Therefore, $x = mir(mir(x)) \in mir(v(L))$.
In addition, $L \neq \emptyset$. Thus, $R \neq \emptyset$. Therefore, $R \in R(\mathcal{G})$.
Let c, m, min, max be shorthands for $cen_{\langle L, v \rangle},\ mean_{\langle L, v \rangle},\ min(v(L)),\ max(v(L))$.

We show $mir(c) = cen_{\langle R,v \rangle}$.

By definition, $\overrightarrow{c\,min} + \overrightarrow{c\,max} = \overrightarrow{0}$. But $\forall\, x,y \in \mathbb{R}$, $\overrightarrow{xy} = \overrightarrow{mir(y)mir(x)}$.

Therefore, $\overrightarrow{mir(min)mir(c)} + \overrightarrow{mir(max)\,mir(c)} = \overrightarrow{0}$.

But, $mir(v(L)) = v(R)$. So, $mir(min) = max(v(R))$ and $mir(max) = min(v(R))$.

Thus, $\overrightarrow{max(v(R))mir(c)} + \overrightarrow{min(v(R))mir(c)} = \overrightarrow{0}$. So, $mir(c) = cen_{\langle R,v \rangle}$.

We show $mir(m) = mean_{\langle R,v \rangle}$.

By definition, $\sum_{x \in v(L)} wei(x)\overrightarrow{m\,x} = \overrightarrow{0}$. Therefore,

$$\sum_{x \in v(L)} wei(x)\overrightarrow{mir(x)mir(m)} = \sum_{x \in v(L)} wei(mir(x))\overrightarrow{mir(x)mir(m)} = \overrightarrow{0}.$$

Consequently, $\sum_{y \in v(R)} wei(y)\overrightarrow{y\,mir(m)} = \overrightarrow{0}$. Thus, $mir(m) = mean_{\langle R,v \rangle}$.

Finally, we show $mir_a(minI_p^s \langle L, v \rangle) = maxI_p^s \langle R, v \rangle$.

Case 1: $c \leq m$. Then, $minI_p^s \langle L, v \rangle = mir_m(max)$ and $mir_a(m) \leq mir_a(c)$.

Therefore, $maxI_p^s \langle R, v \rangle = mir_{mir_a(m)}(min(vR)) = mir_{mir_a(m)}(mir_a(max))$
$= mir_a(mir_m(max))$.

Case 2: $m < c$. Then, $minI_p^s \langle L, v \rangle = min$ and $mir_a(c) < mir_a(m)$.

Thus, $maxI_p^s \langle R, v \rangle = max(v(R)) = mir_a(min)$.

Proof for coherence. Let $\mathcal{G} = \langle G, v \rangle$ and $\mathcal{G}' = \langle G', v' \rangle$ be two grade structure.
Suppose $\mathcal{G} \preceq_r \mathcal{G}'$. We show $minI_p(\mathcal{G}) \leq minI_p(\mathcal{G}')$.

There exists $L \in L(\mathcal{G})$ such that $minI_p(\mathcal{G}) = minI_p^s \langle L, v \rangle$.

Let $L' = \{g \in G' : v'(g) \leq max(vL)\}$. Then, $L' \in L(\mathcal{G}')$.

Let m, m', c, c' be shorthands for $mean_{\langle L,v \rangle}$, $mean_{\langle L',v' \rangle}$, $cen_{\langle L,v \rangle}$, $cen_{\langle L',v' \rangle}$.

Then, $min(vL) = min(v'L')$, $max(vL) = max(v'L')$, $c = c'$ and $m \leq m'$.

Case 1: $c \leq m$ and $c' \leq m'$.

Then, $minI_p^s \langle L, v \rangle = mir_m(max(vL)) \leq mir_{m'}(max(v'L')) = minI_p^s \langle L', v' \rangle$.

Case 2: $c \leq m$ and $m' < c'$. Then, $m' < m$, which is impossible.

Case 3: $m < c$ and $c' \leq m'$.

Then, $minI_p^s \langle L, v \rangle = min(vL) = min(v'L') \leq mir_{m'}(max(v'L')) = minI_p^s \langle L', v' \rangle$.

Case 4: $m < c$ and $m' < c'$.

Then, $minI_p^s \langle L, v \rangle = min(vL) = min(v'L') = minI_p^s \langle L', v' \rangle$.

We show $maxI_p(\mathcal{G}) \leq maxI_p(\mathcal{G}')$.

There exists $R' \in R(\mathcal{G}')$ such that $maxI_p(\mathcal{G}') = maxI_p^s \langle R', v' \rangle$.

Let $R = \{g \in G : min(v'R') \leq v(g)\}$.

Case 1: $R = \emptyset$. Then, $maxI_p(\mathcal{G}) \leq max(vG) < min(v'R') \leq maxI_p(\mathcal{G}')$.

Case 2: $R \neq \emptyset$. Then, $R \in R(\mathcal{G})$. Thus, $maxI_p(\mathcal{G}) \leq maxI_p^s \langle R, v \rangle$.

Let m, m', c, c' be shorthands for $mean_{\langle R,v \rangle}$, $mean_{\langle R',v' \rangle}$, $cen_{\langle R,v \rangle}$, $cen_{\langle R',v' \rangle}$.

Then, $min(vR) = min(v'R')$, $max(vR) \leq max(v'R')$, and $m \leq m'$.

Case 2.1: $c \leq m$ and $c' \leq m'$.

Then, $maxI_p^s \langle R, v \rangle = max(vR) \leq max(v'R') = maxI_p^s \langle R', v' \rangle$.

Case 2.2: $c \leq m$ and $m' < c'$. Then, $maxI_p^s \langle R, v \rangle = max(vR) \leq mir_m(min(vR))$
$\leq mir_{m'}(min(v'R')) = maxI_p^s \langle R', v' \rangle$.

Case 2.3: $m < c$ and $c' \leq m'$.

Then, $maxI_p^s \langle R, v \rangle = mir_m(min(vR)) < max(vR) \leq max(v'R') = maxI_p^s \langle R', v' \rangle$.

Case 2.4: $m < c$ and $m' < c'$.

Then, $maxI_p^s \langle R, v \rangle = mir_m(min(vR)) \leq mir_{m'}(min(v'R')) = maxI_p^s \langle R', v' \rangle$.

Suppose $\mathcal{G} \prec_r \mathcal{G}'$. We show $maxI_p(\mathcal{G}) < maxI_p(\mathcal{G}')$.

The proof is similar to that of $maxI_p(\mathcal{G}) \leq maxI_p(\mathcal{G}')$.

The difference is that this time we have $max(vR) < max(v'R')$ and $m < m'$.

This difference allows us to derive in all cases $maxI_p^s\langle R, v\rangle < maxI_p^s\langle R', v'\rangle$.

The proofs for $\preceq_l$ and $\prec_l$ and similar to those for $\preceq_r$ and $\prec_r$. □

3.3   From Summarizing Intervals to Trust Intervals

In certain contexts, given a grade structure $\mathcal{G} = \langle G, v\rangle$, the user needs a trust interval rather than a summarizing one. Recall that a trust interval is an interval such that it is rational to believe (on the basis of the past grades) that the future grades will essentially fall on it. We think that we get such an interval $T(\mathcal{G})$ if we take a summarizing interval $I(\mathcal{G})$ and add an adequate margin of error.

The question is of course: what is an adequate margin of error? The more the number of past grades is big, the more the margin should be small. A solution is for example to define the left bound of $T(\mathcal{G})$ as the weighted mean of 0 and the left bound of $I(\mathcal{G})$. The weight of the former is 1, while that of the latter is the number of past grades, that is, $|G|$. The same goes for the right bound.

Definition 11. *Let $\mathcal{G} = \langle G, v\rangle$ be a grade structure. We denote by $T_p(\mathcal{G})$ the trust interval obtained from $\mathcal{G}$ according to the pulling method, that is,*

$$T_p(\mathcal{G}) = [\frac{|G|minI_p(\mathcal{G})}{1 + |G|}, \frac{1 + |G|maxI_p(\mathcal{G})}{1 + |G|}]$$

T_p and I_p behave almost in the same way. The essential difference is that two structures may lead to the same summarizing interval, but to different trust intervals. This is possible because there exist structures which contain different numbers of grades, and yet lead to the same summarizing interval. Here is an example. Suppose that there is only one grade of value 0.5. Then, T_p is centered and strictly smaller than $[0, 1]$, which reflects the idea that we are expecting future grades close to 0.5, but we remain cautious.

Next, add two other 0.5's. Then, T_p is still centered and even smaller than before (as desired), while in both cases I_p is the same interval, namely $[0.5, 0.5]$.

Provided that our view of a trust interval is convincing ("trust = summary + margin of error"), T_p provides trustors with an indication of what they can expect from trustees, which may be of a certain help.

4   Trustworthiness as Levels of Trust and Distrust

Recall that the information available about the past behavior of an agent is supposed to take the form of a collection of grades whose values belong to the interval $[0, 1]$. The interval $[0, 1]$ is viewed in this section as a bipolar univariate scale. By convention, 0 is supposed to stand for the worst grade, and 1 for the best one. The value 0.5 will be considered as a neutral value, which means that values in $(0.5, 1]$ will be understood as increasingly good, while values in $[0, 0.5)$ are bad values, which are all the worse as they are closer to 0. Although, it may look natural, the choice of the neutral value in the middle of the interval is not compulsory, and the approach described in the following could be easily adapted to a neutral value differently located in $(0, 1)$.

We also assume that $[0, 0.5)$ (resp. $(0.5, 1]$) is partitioned into a finite number of subintervals of equal length, increasingly ordered $\lambda_{-n}, ..., \lambda_{-j}, ..., \lambda_{-1}$ (resp. $\mu_{+1}, ..., \mu_{+i}, ..., \mu_{+n}$). All grade values belonging to the same interval λ_{-j} (or μ_{+i}) are considered as indistinguishable and equivalent. Thus, a grade structure $\mathcal{G} = \langle G, v \rangle$ will be characterized by the sequence $\langle w_{-n}, ..., w_{-1}, w_{+1}, ..., w_{+n} \rangle$, where $w_{-j} = |\{g \in G : v(g) \in \lambda_{-j}\}|$ and similarly $w_{+i} = |\{g \in G : v(g) \in \mu_{+i}\}|$.

Let us first provide some examples of partial orders for comparing two grade structures. Given two structures $\mathcal{G} = \langle G, v \rangle$ and $\mathcal{G}' = \langle G', v' \rangle$, with respective sequences $\langle w_k \rangle$ and $\langle w'_k \rangle$, a partial order can be defined by comparing the global amounts of grades with good and with bad values. Namely,

$$\mathcal{G} \gg_{card} \mathcal{G}' \text{ iff } \sum_{i=1}^{n} w_{+i} \geq \sum_{i=1}^{n} w'_{+i} \text{ and } \sum_{j=1}^{n} w_{-j} \leq \sum_{j=1}^{n} w'_{-j}$$

Clearly, $\mathcal{G} \gg_{card} \mathcal{G}'$ expresses that the grade structure $\mathcal{G}$ is at least as good (from a trustworthiness viewpoint) as $\mathcal{G}'$ since $\mathcal{G}$ has more grades with good values and less grades with bad values in the wide sense than $\mathcal{G}'$. An even more refined, actually complete, order can then be obtained by taking the difference of the global amounts of grades with good values and bad values.

$$\mathcal{G} \gg_{d\text{-}card} \mathcal{G}' \text{ iff } \sum_{i=1}^{n} w_{+i} - \sum_{j=1}^{n} w_{-j} \geq \sum_{i=1}^{n} w'_{+i} - \sum_{j=1}^{n} w'_{-j}$$

However, it makes no difference between a structure with a few good grade values and no bad ones, and a structure with some bad ones and a few more good ones. Moreover, it is clear that all the grades with good (resp. bad) values have not the same importance. A value is all the better (resp. worse) as it is closer to 1 (resp. 0). So, it would be advisable to use fuzzy cardinality [DP80] in the above definition. Let us first define the fuzzy set *Good* of good value classes and the fuzzy set *Bad* of bad value classes. We take for the membership degrees increasing and decreasing functions respectively:

$$\forall j,\ Good(\lambda_{-j}) = 0, \quad Good(\mu_{+1}) = \frac{1}{n}, ..., Good(\mu_{+i}) = \frac{i}{n}, ..., Good(\mu_{+n}) = 1$$

$$Bad(\lambda_{-n}) = 1, \ldots, Bad(\lambda_{-j}) = \frac{j}{n}, \ldots, Bad(\lambda_{-1}) = \frac{1}{n}, \quad \forall i, Bad(\mu_{+i}) = 0$$

For convenience, let us use the simplified notations $Good(\mu_{+i}) = go_{+i}$ and $Bad(\lambda_{-j}) = ba_{-j}$. Then, a fuzzy cardinality-based partial ordering is defined:

$$\mathcal{G} \gg_{f\text{-}card} \mathcal{G}' \text{ iff } \sum_{i=1}^{n} go_{+i} w_{+i} \geq \sum_{i=1}^{n} go_{+i} w'_{+i} \text{ and } \sum_{j=1}^{n} ba_{-j} w_{-j} \leq \sum_{j=1}^{n} ba_{-j} w'_{-j}$$

Such a comparison between two structures $\mathcal{G}$ and $\mathcal{G}'$ is fair only if they are based on the same number of grades, that is, only if $|G| = |G'|$. Otherwise, if we compare two structures with unequal number of grades, it may be better to use relative cardinality, that is, $\mathcal{G} \gg_{rf\text{-}card} \mathcal{G}'$ iff

$$\frac{1}{|G|} \sum_{i=1}^{n} go_{+i} w_{+i} \geq \frac{1}{|G'|} \sum_{i=1}^{n} go_{+i} w'_{+i} \text{ and } \frac{1}{|G|} \sum_{j=1}^{n} ba_{-j} w_{-j} \leq \frac{1}{|G'|} \sum_{j=1}^{n} ba_{-j} w'_{-j}$$

Le us illustrate on an example the different discriminating powers of the orderings $\gg_{f\text{-}card}$ and $\gg_{rf\text{-}card}$. Let $\mathcal{G}^1$, $\mathcal{G}^2$, and $\mathcal{G}^3$ be three structures defined by:

- $w^1_{-n} = 3$ and $\forall i, \forall j \neq n, w^1_{-j} = w^1_{+i} = 0$
- $w^2_{-n} = 2$ and $\forall i, \forall j \neq n, w^2_{-j} = w^2_{+i} = 0$
- $w^3_{-n} = 2, w^3_{-(n-1)} = 1$ and $\forall i, \forall j < n-1, w^3_{-j} = w^3_{+i} = 0$

Then it can be checked that $\mathcal{G}^2 \gg_{f\text{-}card} \mathcal{G}^1$, while $\mathcal{G}^2 \approx_{rf\text{-}card} \mathcal{G}^1$ (where $a \approx b$ iff $a \gg b$ and $b \gg a$). However $\mathcal{G}^2 \gg_{f\text{-}card} \mathcal{G}^3$ and $\mathcal{G}^3 \gg_{rf\text{-}card} \mathcal{G}^2$. As expected, $\gg_{rf\text{-}card}$ is only sensitive to the percentages of rather good and rather bad cases, but not directly to their actual cardinalities. However, it acknowledges the fact that in average $\mathcal{G}^3$ is not as bad as $\mathcal{G}^2$, although $\mathcal{G}^2$ reports less bad cases.

We now discuss the computation of a level of trust as the certainty (on the basis of the past grades) that a future grade will be good, and a level of distrust as the fear that a future grade may be bad. The idea is that the level of trust should be high if *always* grades with good values are reported, while the level of distrust should be high as soon as *some* grades with bad values are reported.

For computing such levels of trust and distrust, we use a two-step approach: i) transform the grade structure $\mathcal{G}$ into a possibility distribution, then viewed as restricting the possible value of the next outcome; ii) on this basis, compute the level of trust as the necessity measure that a grade with a good value will be obtained, and the level of distrust as the possibility that a bad grade value will be obtained, where "good" and "bad" refer to the fuzzy sets *Good* and *Bad*.

For performing the first step, we first normalize the weighting structure, and then apply a probability-possibility transformation, preserving as much information as possible. For $j = 1, \ldots, n$, let $p_{-j} = \frac{w_{-j}}{|G|}$. For $i = 1, \ldots, n$, let $p_{+i} = \frac{w_{+i}}{|G|}$. Then, in order to apply the probability-possibility transformation [DPS93], we have to re-order the set $\{p_{-n}, \ldots, p_{-1}, p_{+1}, \ldots, p_{+n}\}$ decreasingly, as $p_{\sigma(1)} \geq \cdots \geq p_{\sigma(k)} \geq \cdots \geq p_{\sigma(2n)}$. Next, let $\pi_{\sigma(k)} = \sum_{j=k}^{2n} p_{\sigma(j)}$. Note that

$\pi_{\sigma(1)} \geq \ldots \geq \pi_{\sigma(k)} \geq \ldots \geq \pi_{\sigma(2n)}$, which expresses that the transformation is faithful with respect to the shape of the distribution.

The second step amounts to the computation of the necessity and the possibility of fuzzy events, that is,

$$trust(\mathcal{G}) = \min_x \max(Good(x), 1 - \pi(x)) \quad distrust(\mathcal{G}) = \max_x \min(Bad(x), \pi(x))$$

The level of distrust is high as soon as there exists a really bad grade value that is highly plausible. The level of trust is high as soon as any bad grade value (including the less bad ones) is impossible or almost impossible. Such definitions acknowledge the fact that one should be afraid by bad performances in trust evaluation, which play a more important role than the good ones. It can be checked that the sum of these two levels is always less or equal to 1 (as in most models of trust and distrust, e.g. [dCdS06], however these levels are computed here from past performances, good or bad, in agreement with possibility theory). Thus, from them an interval pertaining to trust (resp. to distrust) can be built as $[trust(\mathcal{G}), 1 - distrust(\mathcal{G})]$ (resp. $[distrust(\mathcal{G}), 1 - trust(\mathcal{G})]$). These levels (and intervals) not only involve the grade structure information $\mathcal{G}$, but also a graded view of goodness and badness.

Besides, the obtained possibility distribution π, or more precisely its convex hull, can be seen as a kind of fuzzy version of summarizing interval in the sense of Section 3.2. This interval may be transformed into a crisp one representing its mean value [DP87]. The bounds of the interval are computed as lower and upper expected values $E_*(\pi)$ and $E^*(\pi)$ (using Choquet integrals)

$$E_*(\pi) = \sum_{k=1}^{n} x_k(\pi_*(x_k) - \pi_*(x_{k-1})) \quad E^*(\pi) = \sum_{k=1}^{n} x_k(\pi^*(x_k) - \pi^*(x_{k+1}))$$

where $\pi_*(x) = \max_{t \leq x} \pi(t)$ and $\pi^*(x) = \max_{t \geq x} \pi(t)$ and the x_k stand for the (increasingly ordered) central values of the $2n$ subintervals partitioning $[0,1]$. It can be shown that the interval $[E_*(\pi), E^*(\pi)]$ satisfies all the axioms of the first approach, presented in Section 3.1, with the exception of the leaning axiom.

Using the possibility distribution π, one may also compute the largest value $\underline{x}$ such that $N(\underline{x} \leq) = 1$ or $\theta \leq N(\underline{x} \leq)$ and the smallest $\overline{x}$ such that $\Pi(\overline{x} \leq) = 0$ or $\Pi(\overline{x} \leq) \leq \rho$, where θ and ρ are thresholds, Π and N are possibility and necessity measures with $\Pi(A) = \max_x \min(A(x), \pi(x))$ and $N(A) = 1 - \Pi(\neg A)$. This is again a summarizing interval $[\underline{x}, \overline{x}]$ (now based on Sugeno integrals).

5   Conclusion

The first contribution of the present paper is that we propose interval-based representations of trustworthiness (i.e. summarizing and trust intervals), which is rather new in the field of trust and reputation. The second contribution is that we provide two approaches for evaluating trustworthiness from a set of past performances, which has also been rather neglected in the literature. Interestingly enough, the first approach is based on a purely horizontal view (based on the idea of pulling values), while the second approach exploits a vertical view (based on histograms, then transformed into possibility distributions).

Besides, general partial orders can be defined for comparing two grade structures, for example, the bipolar ones introduced at the beginning of Section 4, or unipolar ones such as stochastic dominance. This could be the basis of postulates expressing some agreement between partial orderings of grade structures and comparisons of their associated summarizing intervals.

Lines for further research also include a deeper comparison of the two approaches, the validation of the models from a cognitive psychology point of view, and refinements in order to take into account the freshness of the information.

References

[AMT05]   Avesani, P., Massa, P., Tiella, R.: A trust-enhanced recommender system application: Moleskiing. In: Proc. of the 2005 ACM symposium on Applied computing, pp. 1589–1593 (2005)

[dCdS06]   de Cock, M., Pinheiro da Silva, P.: A many valued representation and propagation of trust and distrust. In: Bloch, I., Petrosino, A., Tettamanzi, A.G.B. (eds.) WILF 2005. LNCS (LNAI), vol. 3849, pp. 114–120. Springer, Heidelberg (2006)

[DP80]   Dubois, D., Prade, H.: Fuzzy sets and systems: Theory and applications. Academic Press, London (1980)

[DP87]   Dubois, D., Prade, H.: The mean value of a fuzzy number. Fuzzy Sets and Systems 24, 279–300 (1987)

[DPS93]   Dubois, D., Prade, H., Sandri, S.: On possibility/probability transformations. In: Roubens, M., Lowen, R. (eds.) Fuzzy logic: State of the art, pp. 103–112. Kluwer Academic Publ., Dordrecht (1993)

[JK98]   Jøsang, A., Knapskog, S.J.: A metric for trusted systems. In: Proc. of the 21st NIST-NCSC National Information Systems Security Conference, pp. 16–29 (1998)

[MDB06]   Melaye, D., Demazeau, Y., Bouron, T.: Which adequate trust model for trust networks? In: Proc. of the 3rd IFIP Conference on Artificial Intelligence Applications and Innovations (AIAI), pp. 236–244 (2006)

[Pra07]   Prade, H.: A qualitative bipolar argumentative view of trust. In: Prade, H., Subrahmanian, V.S. (eds.) SUM 2007. LNCS (LNAI), vol. 4772, pp. 268–276. Springer, Heidelberg (2007)

[SS05]   Sabater, J., Sierra, S.: Review on computational trust and reputation models. Artificial Intelligence 24, 33–60 (2005)

[TB04]   Theodorakopoulos, G., Baras, J.S.: Trust evaluation in ad-hoc networks. In: Proc. of the 3rd ACM workshop on Wireless security, pp. 1–10 (2004)

[TLU06]   Toivonen, S., Lenzini, G., Uusitalo, I.: Context-aware trustworthiness evaluation with indirect knowledge. In: Proc. of the 2nd International Semantic Web Policy Workshop (SWPW) (2006)

[WJI04]   Whitby, A., Jøsang, A., Indulska, J.: Filtering out unfair ratings in bayesian reputation systems. In: Proc. of the 7th Int Workshop on Trust in Agent Societies, at AAMAS 2004 (2004)

[ZdSM05]   Zaihrayeu, I., Pinheiro da Silva, P., McGuinness, D.L.: IWTrust: Improving user trust in answers from the web. In: Herrmann, P., Issarny, V., Shiu, S.C.K. (eds.) iTrust 2005. LNCS, vol. 3477, pp. 384–392. Springer, Heidelberg (2005)

A Comparative Study of Six Formal Models of Causal Ascription

Salem Benferhat[1], Jean-François Bonnefon[3], Philippe Chassy[3],
Rui Da Silva Neves[3], Didier Dubois[3], Florence Dupin de Saint-Cyr[3],
Daniel Kayser[2], Farid Nouioua[2], Sara Nouioua-Boutouhami[2], Henri Prade[3],
and Salma Smaoui[1]

[1] Université d'Artois
[2] Université Paris 13
[3] Université de Toulouse

Abstract. Ascribing causality amounts to determining what elements
in a sequence of reported facts can be related in a causal way, on the
basis of some knowledge about the course of the world. The paper offers a comparison of a large span of formal models (based on structural
equations, non-monotonic consequence relations, trajectory preference
relations, identification of violated norms, graphical representations, or
connectionism), using a running example taken from a corpus of car
accident reports. Interestingly enough, the compared approaches focus
on different aspects of the problem by either identifying all the potential
causes, or selecting a smaller subset by taking advantages of contextually
abnormal facts, or by modeling interventions to get rid of simple correlations. The paper concludes by a general discussion based on a battery
of criteria (several of them being proper to AI approaches to causality).

1 Introduction

Causality is a protean and complex notion. Accordingly, multiple models of causation were developed in Artificial Intelligence (AI). Indeed, the idea of causality
pervades several important AI problems, e.g., in the diagnosis of the potential
causes from observed effects; in the induction of causal laws from series of observations; in logics of action; in the qualitative simulation of dynamical systems
(when propagating constraints in influence graphs).

In this article, we focus on the perception of causal relations and causal ascription. Unsurprisingly, models proposed for causal ascription generally agree in
some way with the idea of relating causality to *counterfactuality:* the counterfactual 'Had A not taken place, B would not have occurred' sounds as a necessary
condition for declaring that A causes B. This idea underlies many approaches,
from that initiated in modal logic years ago [1], to the approach more recently
advocated by Pearl [2] in a probabilistic setting. However, as we will see, providing a full account of the way causality is perceived may also benefit from the
identification of facts found 'abnormal' by agents in given contexts, among a
series of reported events.

S. Greco and T. Lukasiewicz (Eds.): SUM 2008, LNAI 5291, pp. 47–62, 2008.
© Springer-Verlag Berlin Heidelberg 2008

It is a daunting task to compare the definitions and properties of models of causal perception and ascription. A preliminary and useful step toward such an achievement, though, consists of illustrating the behavior of the models through a series of well-chosen examples. The examples should be realistic and relevant to the real world—but not so complex that they would no longer be manageable. They should strike the right balance between traditional, simplistic examples (the causal equivalents of the Tweety problem in default reasoning), and intractable scenarios such as the circumstances of Princess Diana's death. Traffic accidents reports offer an excellent source for such examples. They describe genuine events; they naturally lend themselves to causal analysis (in fact, they are often used for that very purpose); and they occur in a relatively self-contained micro-universe. We were able to gain access to a database of traffic accident reports submitted by drivers to insurance companies (the current sample consists of about one hundred reports of accidents that happened in France in recent years). We then submitted these reports to a battery of formal models (based on structural equations, nonmonotonic logics, graphs, or connectionism). Due to space limitations, we will restrict ourselves to one report:

Example 1 (Accident). We were at $* * *$, I was surprised by the person who braked in front of me, not having the option of changing lane and the road being wet, I could not stop completely in time.

All models will use the same common core of variables and pieces of knowledge. Variables are: Acc (occurrence of an accident), Wet (road being wet), $Brak$ (driver B brakes in front of driver A), $Reac$ (driver A brakes in reaction to driver B's braking), with variants $ReacS$ and $ReacL$ (driver A brakes shortly after B brakes, or with a longer delay), Ncl (A does not have the option of changing lane), Sur (A is surprised). Additional variables may be introduced in some models to display interesting variants of the example. Logical constraints exist among the variables: (1) $Reac \equiv ReacS \vee ReacL$, (2) $\neg ReacS \vee \neg ReacL$, (3) $\neg Reac \vee Brak$. The common core of knowledge is: (4) Accidents are abnormal, (5) Being surprised is abnormal, (6) $ReacL$ and Wet promote Acc, (7) $Brak$ and Ncl and Sur promote $ReacL$, (8) $Brak$ and Ncl and $\neg Sur$ promote $ReacS$. Each model will incorporate this common core of knowledge, up to its representational specificities (especially regarding the formalization of what 'abnormal' and 'promote' mean). Again, additional pieces of knowledge may be introduced to highlight interesting aspects of the models. The presentation of each model will follow the same structure: brief motivation, reminder of definitions, summary of characteristic features, treatment of the example, discussion. Although the original purpose of this paper is to compare the models mainly on the basis of formal considerations, their discussion will occasionally point to experimental data, when they exist.

2 Structural Equations Model

Halpern and Pearl [3] propose a model allowing identification of 'actual causes.' The model distinguishes between 'endogenous' and 'exogenous' variables. Assigned values of endogenous variables are governed by structural equations, whereas exogenous variables are assumed to be known and out of control. Only endogenous variables can be causes or be caused. Background knowledge in such model is given by the context and structural equations. A causal model is denoted by $M = (U, V, F)$ where U and V are sets of exogenous and endogenous variables. F is a function that assigns a value to each variable given each value of its parents. Each assignment of the exogenous variables $U = u$ determines a unique value x of each subset X of endogenous variables (i.e. $X \subseteq V$).

Definition 1. *The event $X = x$ is said to be an actual cause of an event ϕ if and only if:*

1. $X(u) = x$ and $\phi(u)$ is true (when U takes the value u).
2. There exists a partition (Z, W) of V with $X \subseteq Z$ and some settings (x', w') of (X, W) such that if $Z(u) = z^*$ (z^* is the value assigned to Z when $U = u$), both of the following conditions hold:
    a) $\phi_{X \leftarrow x', W \leftarrow w'}(u)$ is false, namely, if X is set to x' and W is set to w' then ϕ becomes false.
    b) $\phi_{X \leftarrow x, W' \leftarrow [w'], Z' \leftarrow [z^*]}(u)$ is true for all $W' \subseteq W$ and for all $Z' \subseteq Z$. Namely, if X is set to x, W' is set to $[w']$ ($[w']$ is an instantiation of W' consistent with w'), and Z' is set to $[z^*]$ then ϕ remains true.
3. The subset X is minimal.

Pearl and Halpern also proposed an extended causal model to deal with excluded settings. The extended version of Definition 1 consists of adding to the tuple (U, V, F) a set E that contains allowed settings of endogenous variables. E functions as some kind of integrity constraint. In our example, all settings are considered allowed, and the extended causal model collapses with Definition 1. The causal model described above can be represented using a graph, in which nodes are corresponding to variables in V and an edge from X to Y exists if the value of Y depends from the value of X. This graph is a directed acyclic graph (DAG) representing the relationships between variables which are fully specified by structural equations.

Example. We model the example presented in the introduction using only endogenous variables. Variables *Brak*, *Ncl*, *Sur*, *Wet* and *Acc* have the same meaning as previously given. The variable *Reac* is a ternary variable taking its values in $\{ReacS, ReacL, NoReac\}$ where *NoReac* stands for '*A* does not brake'. For simplicity, we consider that all settings are allowed ($E = \emptyset$). The structural equations are given by:

$$- \; Acc = \begin{cases} 1 \text{ if } wet = 1 \text{ and } Reac = ReacL \\ 0 \text{ otherwise} \end{cases}$$

$$- \; Reac = \begin{cases} NoReac \text{ if } Brak = 0 \text{ or } Ncl = 0 \\ ReacS \quad \text{ if } Sur = 0 \text{ and } Brak = 1 \text{ and } Ncl = 1 \\ ReacL \quad \text{ if } Sur = 1 \text{ and } Brak = 1 \text{ and } Ncl = 1 \end{cases}$$

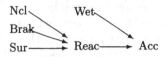

Fig. 1. A causal network

This model can be represented by the DAG given in Figure 1. Assume that the actual context is $Sur = 1$ and $Brak = 1$ and $Ncl = 1$ and $Reac = ReacL$ and $Wet = 1$ and $Acc = 1$. Now let us find causes of the event $Acc = 1$ in this context. We first check if $Ncl = 1$ is a cause of $Acc = 1$. Condition 1 holds since $Ncl = 1$ and $Acc = 1$ is true in the actual world. Given the partition $Z = \{Ncl, Reac, Acc\}$ and $W = \{Sur, Brak, Wet\}$, it is easy to check that maintaining the actual context ($w' = \{Sur = 1, Brak = 1, Wet = 1\}$) and changing the value of Ncl from true to false (i.e. $Ncl = 0$) is enough to change the value of Acc from true to false (i.e. $Acc = 0$). Condition 2a is satisfied for w'. Setting Ncl to true and setting all subsets $\hat{W}$ (e.g. $\{Sur = 1\}$) of W to their values $\hat{w}$ (consistent with w') is not enough to change the value of Acc which remains true (i.e. $Acc = 1$). Thus condition 2b is also satisfied. It is obvious that $Ncl = 1$ is minimal (condition 3). We conclude that $Ncl = 1$ is a cause of $Acc = 1$. Maintaining the same context and setting $W = w'$ we obtain that each event is a cause of $Acc = 1$.

Discussion. Despite the fact that this model allows to handle notorious case studies on causality, it still presents some limitations. Reasoning with structural equations means that all required information must be available (this makes sense in some physics applications where structural equations reflects physical laws among a limited set of variables). Unfortunately, this is not always the case, which may limit the scope of application. For example, rules (4) and (5) in the introduction cannot be easily represented [4], and using non-monotonic rules may be an interesting alternative. Besides, requiring that any assignment of exogenous variables uniquely determines the value of all endogenous variables is not always natural. The apparent lack of selective power of this model may also be considered a weakness, as an event is very easily designated as a cause of another. E.g., in our example, each event is a cause of $Acc = 1$. In order to select preferred causes, it may be interesting to assign 'weights' on the basis of levels of normality assigned to each cause according to its implication in making the event happening.

3   Nonmonotonic Logic Approaches

As discussed by philosophers of law [5], and experimentally checked by psychologists, 'abnormal' facts are privileged when providing causal explanations [6]. Added to the insufficiency of material implication for representing causation, this naturally leads to consider nonmonotonic logic-based approaches for causal ascriptions. Relations between nonmonotonic inference and causality have already been emphasized by authors dealing with reasoning about actions and the frame problem [7,8]. 'Causal rules' are understood there as 'there is a cause for effect B to be true if it is true that A has just been executed,' where 'there is a cause for' is a modal operator. However, we are not interested in the following in the proper modeling of already established causality relations, but rather in the ascription of causality relations in a reported series of facts or events.

3.1 Nonmonotonic Consequence Approach

To reflect the fact that human agents cannot always couch their beliefs in precise probabilistic terms, Bonnefon et al. [9,10] offer a qualitative counterpart to probabilistic conceptions of causality. This approach is based on pieces of default knowledge, and privileges the role of abnormal events in a given context.

Definition 2. *Assume an agent learns of the sequence $\neg B_t$, A_t, B_{t+k}. Call K_t (the context) the conjunction of all other facts known by the agent at time t. Let $\vdash\!\!\!\sim$ denote a nonmonotonic consequence relation. If the agent believes $K \vdash\!\!\!\sim \neg B$ and $K \wedge A \vdash\!\!\!\sim B$, the agent will perceive A to cause B in context K, denoted $A \vartriangleright B$. If the agent believes that $K \vdash\!\!\!\sim \neg B$, and $K \wedge A \not\vdash\!\!\!\sim \neg B$ rather than $K \wedge A \vdash\!\!\!\sim B$, then A is perceived as* facilitating *rather than* causing *B, denoted $A \blacktriangleright B$.[1]*

In the definitions of $\vartriangleright$ and $\blacktriangleright$, $\vdash\!\!\!\sim$ is a preferential entailment in the sense of Kraus et al. [11], and a rational closure entailment, respectively. This definition has noticeable features. E.g., causes and facilitations are abnormal in context: If $A \vartriangleright B$ or $A \blacktriangleright B$ then $K \vdash\!\!\!\sim \neg A$. Furthermore, causality is transitive only in particular cases: If A is the normal way of getting B in context K, i.e., $K \wedge B \vdash\!\!\!\sim A$, and if $A \vartriangleright B$ and $B \vartriangleright C$, then $A \vartriangleright C$. The practical significance of Def. 2 (including the distinction between causation and facilitation), as well as the restricted transitivity property, have been validated by behavioral experiments. Note that a facilitation is abnormal and is not a necessary condition for the effect, in contrast to an enabling condition (see below).

Example. The story that unfolds in the report reads: At any point in time, Wet is true. Initially, Ncl is true, and Acc, $Brak$, $Reac$, and Sur are false. Next, $Brak$ and Sur become true. Next, $ReacL$ becomes true. Finally, Acc becomes true. The formalization of the common core of knowledge is : (4) $\vdash\!\!\!\sim \neg Acc$; (5) $\vdash\!\!\!\sim \neg Sur$; (6) $ReacL \wedge Wet \vdash\!\!\!\sim Acc$; (7) $Brak \wedge Ncl \wedge Sur \vdash\!\!\!\sim ReacL$; (8) $Brak \wedge Ncl \wedge \neg Sur \vdash\!\!\!\sim ReacS$.

From (4) and (6), we derive $ReacL \wedge Wet \vartriangleright Acc$. The cause of the accident is the conjunction of braking late and the road being wet. Now let us consider a few additional plausible nonmonotonic rules. Assume that long-delay braking alone,

---

[1] K may be omitted in practice. Def. 1 corresponds to a basic scenario already considered by von Wright [1]: The falsity of B_t agrees with the piece of general knowledge $K \vdash\!\!\!\sim \neg B$ and after A_t takes place B_{t+k} becomes true, although normally if A_t does not happen, $\neg B$ would have persisted.

although it does not make accidents normal, at least makes them not abnormal ($ReacL \not\hspace{-0.3em}\sim Acc$ together with $ReacL \not\hspace{-0.3em}\sim \neg Acc$). Adding this assumption, we can derive $ReacL \blacktriangleright Acc$; i.e., the long-delay braking alone facilitated the accident (but the cause of the accident is still the conjunction of late braking and the road being wet). Assume now that late braking is abnormal ($\sim \neg ReacL$), and remains so in the context of others braking, and being unable to change lane ($Brak \wedge Ncl \hspace{0.2em}\mid\hspace{-0.3em}\sim \neg ReacL$). Then it follows from (7) that being surprised caused the late braking ($Sur \triangleright ReacL$). For the purpose of further illustration, let us assume that accidents remain abnormal even when roads are wet ($Wet \hspace{0.2em}\mid\hspace{-0.3em}\sim \neg Acc$). Then it is possible to derive than late braking alone caused the accident ($ReacL \triangleright Acc$). Note now that $Sur \triangleright ReacL$ together with $ReacL \triangleright Acc$. Surprise caused the late braking that itself caused the accident. Does it follow by transitivity that $Sur \triangleright Acc$, i.e., that surprise caused the accident? Not necessarily so, for $\triangleright$ is not generally transitive. If, however, we are ready to accept that $ReacL \hspace{0.2em}\mid\hspace{-0.3em}\sim Sur$, i.e., a late braking is usually diagnostic of a surprised driver, then it follows from the restricted transitivity property of $\triangleright$ that the surprise caused the accident. Finally, suppose that that we add to the story that some other car C hit B. Then, the nonmonotonic approach yields a disjunctive causal ascription 'car hitting OR late braking' caused the accident. Only a more detailed report may lead the approach to privilege one of the disjuncts.

Discussion. This approach relies on the beliefs about the 'normal' states and courses of the world. Such beliefs are agent-dependent, which explains that different individuals may have different readings of events. Since the inference engine based on System P is very cautious, many of these normal states must be explicitly coded rather than derived. Causality ascription is localized, thanks to a lack of general transitivity, but also because only events that are explicitly mentioned in the story can be detected as causes. Exceptional events are favored as potential causes, which help discriminating causes; in fact, the approach only exhibits causes that are abnormal events. A notion of 'necessary condition' (or enabling condition) [12] can be defined to deal with normal events without which nothing would have happened. Finally, this approach does not embed the notion of intervention and thus cannot readily distinguish spurious correlation from causation. See nonetheless the *Graphical Models and Interventions* section for an extension of the approach into that direction (both the current approach and graphical models can be encoded in a possibilistic setting).

3.2   Trajectory-Based Preference Relations

This proposal [13][2] starts with the idea that counterfactuality involves the computation of two kinds of evolutions of the world, namely extrapolation [14] and update [15]. If we want to know whether $Sur_{(2)}$ (being surprised at time point 2) is a counterfactual cause of $Acc_{(3)}$, given a scenario Σ ($Brak_{(1)} \wedge Sur_{(2)} \wedge Ncl_{(2)} \wedge Wet_{(2)} \wedge Acc_{(3)}$), we need to (i) compute the most normal evolutions of the world

---

[2] For the sake of brevity, this novel approach is only sketched in this paper.

(called trajectories) that correspond to the scenario $Sur_{(2)}$ and $Acc_{(3)}$. This computation is called extrapolation, it is a process of completing initial beliefs sets stemming from observations by assuming minimal 'abnormalities' in the evolution of the world with respect to generic knowledge. In our example, the preferred trajectories satisfying Σ do satisfy $Sur_{(2)}$ and $Acc_{(3)}$ (since they are mentioned in Σ). (ii) Compute what would have happened to Acc_3 if $Sur_{(2)}$ had not been true. This is done by updating the temporal formula representing the scenario by the formula $\neg Sur_{(2)}$. At this step, update aims at capturing a minimal change w.r.t. the initial scenario. The update operator proposed in [13] is based on a distance between trajectories that take into account the time point of the change and normality. Here, the trajectories that satisfy $\neg Sur_{(2)}$ that are closest to the previous preferred trajectories until the time of the change and that are the most normal satisfy $\neg Acc_{(3)}$. Hence the surprise can be considered as counterfactually causing the accident. One may consider that not all counterfactual causes are important; the lack of selectivity of counterfactuality is tackled here by using normality. Choosing among the 'normal' counterfactual causes, the most abnormal ones in context, would further increase selectivity.

3.3   Norm-Based Approach

This approach [16], too, rests on the idea that norms are crucial for people to find causes of events: if the event is considered normal, its cause is the norm itself; if abnormal, its cause is traced back to the violation of a norm.[3]

Principle. Searching for the cause of an abnormal event E occurring at time t basically amounts to finding an agent who should, according to some norm, adopt behavior b at a time $t' < t$, and actually adopted another behavior b', such that E appears as a normal consequence of b' (in that sense, for example, the lack of liability insurance is a norm violation but cannot usually be considered the cause of an accident, because it arguably does not normally have an accident as a consequence). Another condition must be checked, namely that, at t', the agent had the possibility to have the normal behavior b; otherwise, b' is only a derived anomaly and the search must be pursued to find a primary anomaly, occurring earlier than t' and explaining the impossibility of the agent to have the behavior b at t'. Whenever this search fails, i.e., when the privilege conferred to an 'interventionist' kind of cause gives no result, and only in this case, we look for some non agentive abnormal circumstance that could explain E.

Norm-based reasoning is intrinsically non monotonic, as norms are rules that apply by default. For this reason, in this approach, the knowledge necessary to causal ascription is expressed in a reified first-order logic augmented with default rules (in the sense of R. Reiter); the fact that property P holds for agent A at time t is written $holds(P, A, t)$. A discrete and linear model of time is sufficient, as only what really happened is represented. Two modalities are introduced to

---

[3] The word 'norm' is taken here in the 'normal' rather than 'normative' sense; but as we expect agents to respect their duties, the normative is seen as a special case of the normal.

express norm violations: $should(P, A, t)$ and $able(P, A, t)$ standing for: at time t, A should (resp. has the ability to) achieve P.

Testing this approach in the domain of road accidents requires to gather all the literals of the form $should(P, A, t)$ that are relevant for this domain. To this end, we examined 73 car-crash reports, used as a training sample among the 160 reports in our possession; the remainder being left for validation purposes. For the running example of this paper, we only need a few of these literals: By wet weather, one should reduce one's speed; having had an accident at time t entails that one had at time $t - 1$ the duty of avoiding some obstacle; and having this duty and being unable to change lane amounts to have the duty to stop. This is written ($\rightarrow$ is the material implication):

(1) $Wet \rightarrow should(reduced\_speed, A, t)$

(2) $holds(Acc, A, t) \rightarrow should(avoid\_obs, A, t-1)$

(3) $should(avoid\_obs, A, t) \wedge \neg able(ch\_lane, A, t)$
$\rightarrow should(stop, A, t)$

Expressed in this language, the cause of an abnormal event (the 'primary anomaly' P_ano) obtains as:

(4) $should(F, A, t) \wedge able(F, A, t) \wedge \neg holds(F, A, t+1) \rightarrow P\_ano(F, A, t+1)$

I.e., if at t an agent A should do F and was able to do F, while at $t+1$, F failed to be done, this failure is the cause looked for. Similarly, a 'derived anomaly' D_ano is detected by the rule:

(5) $should(F, A, t) \wedge \neg able(F, A, t) \rightarrow D\_ano(F, A, t)$

Assume as a default that agents having a duty are generally able to comply with it. Exceptions to this default mostly correspond to cases where the situation allows to prove the impossibility of actions known to produce the desired effect.

Example. With the notations adopted in this paper, the example is written: $holds(Brak, B, 0)$, $holds(Sur, A, 1)$, $holds(Ncl, A, 2)$, $holds(Reac, A, 2)$, $holds(Acc, A, 3)$, Wet. Ncl (inability to change lane) translates as:

(6) $holds(Ncl, A, t) \rightarrow \neg able(ch\_lane, A, T)$

Expressing that surprise entails a late brake is written as:

(7) $holds(Sur, A, t-1) \wedge holds(Reac, A, t) \rightarrow holds(ReacL, A, t)$

Whether late braking entails or not an accident depends on the ability of the driver to stop the vehicle, i.e.:

(8) $holds(ReacL, A, t) \rightarrow [holds(Acc, A, t+1) \leftrightarrow \neg able(stop, A, t)]$

Rule (2) and fact $holds(Acc, A, 3)$ yield $should(avoid\_obs, A, 2)$; (6) gives $\neg able(ch\_lane, A, 2)$, hence (3) deduces $should(stop, A, 2)$. From (7) with premises $holds(Reac, A, 2)$ and $holds(Sur, A, 1)$ we get $holds(ReacL, A, 2)$. So (8) shows that something abnormal occurred: agent A should have stopped at time 2 but was unable to. According to (5), this is a derived anomaly, so the search for the cause of the accident must go on. The ability to stop, under the circumstances, is expressed by (9) $able(stop, A, t) \leftrightarrow (\neg Wet \vee holds(reduced\_speed, A, t))$, which gives $\neg holds(reduced\_ speed, A, 2)$. (1) shows that $should(reduced\_speed, A, t)$ for any t. Without proof to the contrary, the default 'agents who should do something are generally able to do it' yields $able(reduced\_speed, A, 1)$, and (4) tells that we have a primary anomaly, i.e., a cause of the accident: 'at time 1, A was able to reduce speed; because of the wetness of the road, A should have done so, but the occurrence of the accident at time 3 shows that he was still driving too fast at time 2.'

Discussion. In traffic accident examples, the norm-based approach views norms as normative duties. To generalize this approach to domains where norms are only what is normal (as opposed to mandatory), it is necessary to organize these norms in a hierarchy, and to conjecture that the most specific violated norm will be perceived as the cause of an abnormal event. Testing this conjecture requires to gather a reasonably complete set of norms for the domain, which is a hard task. This was achieved in the domain of traffic accidents, and the validation process for this domain is underway. We intuitively determined the causes of the 160 accidents in the corpus, translated the gathered norms in Smodels [17], and implemented a system translating natural language sentences into the language of the norm-based approach. This system [16] agrees with the researchers' intuitions in 95% of the training sample and 85% of the validation sample. Behavioral experiments are underway to check whether these intuitions are shared by a majority of subjects.

4   Graphical Models and Interventions

Intervention is a critical route to causation. Ascribing causality becomes easier when experimenting, then observing the effects of the manipulation on the system. Such changes cannot be deduced from a joint probability nor possibility distribution, even fully specified on the variables describing the system. Graphical causal models help make explicit the assumptions needed by allowing inference from interventions as well as observations. A causal Bayesian network is a Bayesian network where directed arcs of the graph are interpreted as elementary causal relations between variables. When there is an influence relation between two variables, intervention allows to determine the causality relation between these variables. In this case, arcs between variables should follow the direction of the causal process. Pearl [2] proposed an approach for handling interventions using causal graphs based on a 'do' operator. Note that causal relations expressed by graphs only concern variables, not complex events. Causal Bayesian networks organize causal knowledge in terms of a few basic mechanisms, each involving a relatively small number of variables. Each intervention entails local change at the level of only one parents-child relation.

This section summarizes manipulation methods for handling interventions in possibilistic causal networks. Indeed graphical models are compatible both with a probabilistic and a possibilistic modeling of uncertainty. The possibilistic setting [18] is adopted here. It is more qualitative, and allows us to more easily relate graphical models to nonmonotonic approaches. In fact, the 'do' operator has been first proposed within Spohn's ordinal conditional functions framework which has strong relationships with possibility theory. The parents-child relation at the level of each variable A_i is governed by a local possibility distribution $\Pi(A_i|U_{A_i})$ where U_{A_i} is the parents set of A_i. The joint possibility distribution is computed using the chain rule: $\pi(A_1, ..., A_n) = \Diamond_{i=1,...,n}\Pi(A_i|U_{A_i})$, where $\Diamond$ is either equal to min or product. An intervention forcing a variable A_i to take the value a_i is denoted $do(A_i = a_i)$ or $do(a_i)$. This intervention consists of making A_i true independently from all its other direct causes (i.e. parents). Graphically, this modification is represented by the deletion of links from U_{A_i} pointing into A_i. The resulting graph is said to be mutilated and we have:

$$\pi(\omega|do(A_i = a_i)) = \pi_{mut}(\omega|A_i = a_i) = \begin{cases} \Diamond_{a_j:A_j \neq A_i}\Pi(a_j|u_{A_j}) & \text{if } \omega[A_i] = a_i \\ 0 & \text{otherwise} \end{cases}$$

where $\omega[A_i] = a_i$ means that ω is consistent with $A_i = a_i$, and π_{mut} is the joint possibility distribution given by the mutilated graph. Another approach [19] consists in adding a new variable denoted DO_{A_i} as a parent node of A_i. DO_{A_i} takes value $do_{A_i-noact}$ when no intervention is observed, and value do_{a_i} when an intervention occurs, forcing A_i to take value a_i (a_i belonging to the domain of A_i). The resulting graph is called augmented. In [20], we showed that the better option to compute the effect of interventions is using augmented graphs, since it allows to reuse existing propagation algorithms without any change.

Example. Let us consider the possibilistic causal network given in Fig. 1. The variables $Brak, Ncl, Sur, Wet$ and Acc are binary variables with a domain $\{0, 1\}$ and have the same meaning as in above examples. However, $Reac$ is a ternary variable taking its values in $\{ReacS, ReacL, NoReac\}$ where $NoReac$ means 'A does not brake', $ReacS$ means 'A brakes as soon as B brakes' and $ReacL$ means 'A brakes later after B braked'. For simplicity's sake, we assume only three levels of normality: 1 (i.e. fully plausible) $> \beta > \alpha > 0$ (i.e. impossible). Prior local possibility distributions are assumed to be: $\Pi(Sur = 0) = 1 > \Pi(Sur = 1) = \alpha$, which encodes rule (5) of the introduction; $\Pi(Brak = 0) = 1 > \Pi(Brak = 1) = \beta > \alpha$, $\Pi(Ncl = 0) = 1 > \Pi(Ncl = 1) = \alpha$, $\Pi(Wet = 0) = 1 > \Pi(Wet = 1) = \alpha$, which respectively express that normally: 'B does not brake', ' there is no possibility to change lane', and 'the road is not wet'. The local possibility distribution for $Reac$ (i.e. $\Lambda_1 = \Pi(Reac|Sur, Brak, Ncl)$) is given by (9):

$$\Lambda_1 = \begin{cases} 1 \text{ if } (Reac = NoReac \text{ and } (Brak = 0 \text{ or } Ncl = 0)) \\ \quad \text{or } (Reac = ReacS \text{ and } Sur = 0 \text{ and } Brak = 1 \text{ and } Ncl = 1) \\ \quad \text{or } (Reac = ReacL \text{ and } Sur = 1 \text{ and } Brak = 1 \text{ and } Ncl = 1) \\ \alpha \text{ otherwise} \end{cases}$$

Rules (7) and (8) of the introduction are encoded. Indeed, for instance regarding rule (8) we have $\Pi(Reac = ReacL \mid Sur = 1, Ncl = 1, Brak = 1) = 1 > \Pi(Reac = ReacS|Sur = 1, Ncl = 1, Brak = 1) = \alpha$ (and $\Pi(Reac = ReacL \mid Sur = 1, Ncl = 1, Brak = 1) = 1 > \Pi(Reac = NoReac|Sur = 1,$

$Ncl = 1, Brak = 1) = \alpha$, which means that if 'when the driver B brakes, A is surprised and there is no a possibility to change lane' then it is more plausible that the driver A brakes with a longer delay than he does not brake or he brakes shortly after B brakes. Lastly, the local possibility distribution at the level of Acc (i.e. $\Lambda_2 = \Pi(Acc|Wet, Reac)$) is given by (10):

$$\Lambda_2 = \begin{cases} 1 \text{ if } (Acc = 1 \text{ and } Wet = 1 \text{ and } Reac = ReacL) \\ \quad \text{or } (Acc = 0 \text{ and } (Wet = 0 \text{ or } Reac = NoReac \text{ or } Reac = ReacS)) \\ \alpha \text{ } otherwise \end{cases}$$

Again, rule (6) is encoded since $\Pi(Acc = 1 \mid Wet = 1 \text{ and } Reac = ReacL) > \Pi(Acc = 1 \mid Wet = 0 \text{ or } Reac \neq ReacL)$. Note that rule (4) is not explicitly represented but is only derived. Indeed, after propagation of weights we obtain $\Pi(Acc = 0) = 1 > \Pi(Acc = 1) = \alpha$ which means that accidents are abnormal.

For binary variables, possibilistic graphical models can encode causality relations as defined by nonmonotonic logic approaches. $E \mathrel{\mid\sim} F$ is interpreted by $\Pi(E \wedge F) > \Pi(E \wedge \neg F)$. This relation satisfies rational monotony in addition to System P, providing more causal relations. Besides, whereas only reported events can be causes as per Definition 1, unreported but strongly plausible events can be causes in the possibilistic frameworks. Lastly, graphical models provide a computational tool for causality ascriptions in presence of interventions. Recall that $\Pi(Acc = 0) = 1 > \Pi(Acc = 1)$, i.e. $Acc = 1$ is rejected in the initial context. Let us consider an external factor (say, an animal crossing the road) forcing the variable $Reac$ to take value $ReacL$. This intervention $do(Reac = ReacL)$ can be represented by mutilating or by augmenting the graph. Assume moreover that the road is wet. After computation, we have $\Pi(Acc = 1|do(Reac = ReacL), Wet = 1) = 1 > \Pi(Acc = 0|do(Reac = ReacL), Wet = 1)$. Namely, after intervention $do(Reac = ReacL)$ and observation $Wet = 1$, event $Acc = 1$ becomes accepted. We conclude that $do(Reac = ReacL)$ and $Wet = 1$ caused $Acc = 1$.

Discussion. Graphical models offer a natural representation of causal relations between elementary events (e.g. variables), thanks to the 'do' operator that models interventions. They can be viewed as complementing or extending nonmonotonic approaches. Indeed, Definition 1 can be naturally extended when reported events include interventions (as illustrated above). A graphical model goes beyond System P without recovering transitivity. It can be used to discriminate between possible causes by considering the most plausible ones, and allows causality ascription in presence of observations and interventions.

5   Theory of Explanatory Coherence (TEC)

Thagard's theory of explanatory coherence [21] and its connectionist implementation (ECHO) view causal ascriptions as attempts to maximize explanatory coherence between propositions. Although this model did not originate from the AI knowledge representation community, it addresses a similar concern to the other models with have reviewed, and it is as much implementable. In the accident example, maximizing coherence would lead to accept the most plausible hypotheses that explain the accident and reject the alternative hypotheses. If one proposition explains another, then there is a positive constraint between them. Negative constraints result from events that prevent or are inconsistent with other events. Maximizing coherence is generally considered to be computationally intractable. Nevertheless, good approximation algorithms are available, in particular connectionist algorithms such as ECHO. ECHO creates a network of units with explanatory and inhibitory non directional links and then makes inference by spreading activation through the network until all activations have reached stable values. Note that links can be excitatory or inhibitory and units can be positively or negatively activated. When units have settled, the acceptation and rejection of hypotheses depend on whether final activation is positive or negative. Some units can be given priority by linking them positively with a special unit whose activation is kept at 1. A coherence problem is defined as follows [22]. Let E be a finite set of elements $\{e_i\}$ and C be a set of constraints on E understood as a set $\{(e_i, e_j)\}$ of pairs of elements of E. C divides into C^+, the positive constraints on E, and C^-, the negative constraints on E. With each constraint is associated a number w, which is the weight (strength) of the constraint. The problem is to partition E into two sets, A and R, in a way that maximizes compliance with the following two coherence conditions:

1. if (e_i, e_j) is in C^+, then e_i is in A iff e_j is in A;
2. if (e_i, e_j) is in C^-, then e_i is in A iff e_j is in R.

Let W be the sum of the weights of the satisfied constraints. The coherence problem is then to partition E into A and R in a way that maximizes W. Let E, C, C^+, and C^- as defined above. ECHO runs as follows:

1. For every e_i of E, construct a unit u_i, a node in a network of units U;
2. For every positive (negative) constraint in C^+ (C^-) on elements e_i and e_j, construct an excitatory (inhibitory) link between the corresponding units u_i and u_j affected with the same positive (negative) weight.
3. Assign each unit u_i an equal initial activation. Update activation of all the units in parallel given current activations and the weights on links [23]
4. When units have settled, hypotheses acceptation and rejection depend on the sign of their final activation. Some units can be given priority by linking them positively with a special unit whose activation is kept at 1.

Example. In Figure 2 each node represents a variable. The three nodes on the left and the Wet node correspond to variables with priority; in this case, initial conditions at the beginning of the accident process. Dotted lines represent

Table 1. Final TEC activation values

	Brak	Wet	Sur	Ncl	ReacL	ReacS	Acc
Brak, *Wet*, *Sur*, *Ncl* initially set to 1	-.22	.72	.68	-.22	.23	-.70	.58
Only *Brak* initially set to 1	.68	-.64	-.65	-.43	.46	.73	-.56

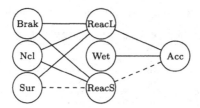

Fig. 2. Accident Example Network in ECHO

inhibitory links. Table 1 shows final activation values of the variables after the units have settled. When initial conditions are $Brak = Wet = Sur = Ncl = 1$ (*All* in Table 1), the hypothesis that the accident occurs is accepted ($Acc = .58$). *Wet*, *Sur*, and *ReacL* are accepted, all other hypotheses are rejected. The most activated causes are *Wet* and *Sur*. When the only initial condition is *Brak*, the accident hypothesis is rejected: *Brak* alone is not a sufficient condition for *Acc*.

Discussion. ECHO establishes an ordering between accepted causes, their final activation representing their causal power. It is of particular interest because previous experimental studies [9] have suggested that human distinction between facilitation and genuine causality is based on the strength of the relation between events. Inference in connectionist models like ECHO is not monotonic, not transitive, and can be forward or backward. Although the only central notion is coherence in TEC, questions of abnormality, temporality and intervention can be introduced in order to compute a more powerful causal inference. ECHO can be translated in Pearl's probabilistic networks [24], and has been used in diverse psychological domains in addition to the computation of causation [25].

6   General Discussion

Causality has always been the matter of hot debates. There exists no consensus about its very nature: is it a means by which the human mind makes sense of the world, or an objective property of the world? Is causation intrinsically deterministic, and only our ignorance makes it admissible to approach it by methods devoted to handle uncertain knowledge; or on the opposite, is its relation to uncertainty fundamental? The models we described are agnostic with respect to such debates—and this should be no surprise to the reader, as this paper is not about causation per se, but about how, under practical circumstances, agents prune among a huge number of potential causal factors.

Although the different models start with the same core of variables and pieces of knowledge (1–8), they rely on representation frameworks of different expressive power, and they may exploit additional pieces of knowledge that are not assumed to be available to other models. For example, the norm-based approach relies on a vast set of norms extracted from driving regulations, while for instance the graphical approach relies on probabilistic or possibilistic information. Although this introduces some heterogeneity in the treatment of the example,

Table 2. Comparison of the models, synthesis

	Structural Eq.	TEC	Norms	Trajectories	Nonmon. Consequences	Graphs
Selectivity	No	Yes	Yes	Yes	Yes	Yes
Abnormality	No	No	Yes	Yes	Yes	Yes
Temporality	No	No	Yes	Yes	Yes	Yes
Cause Present	No	No	No	No	Yes	Yes
Intervention	No	No	No	Yes	No	Yes
Agentivity	No	No	Yes	No	No	No
Backward Cause	Yes	Yes	No	No	No	No

this heterogeneity is irreducible if we want to compare a large span of approaches while respecting their specific modeling strategy.

Table 2 sums up some features of each model.[4] TEC and the structural equation model do not make explicit the temporal relation between the factors they deal with, e.g. braking occurs before stopping (**temporality**). All other models make this temporal link explicit. Accordingly, all models but TEC and the structural equation model assume that effects cannot precede their causes (**backward causation**). The structural equation approach is the least selective of all (but see caveat in section 2), in that sense that it delivers a set of factors that all reasonably have some relevant causal connection to the effect under consideration. All other models strive to select a smaller set of factors, apparently emulating human judgments (**selectivity**). These models privilege different aspects of information to select one event as the main cause. First, all these selective models make explicit the contrast between normal and abnormal states of affairs, to orient the search of causes of an abnormal event towards factors that make a normal course of events become abnormal (**abnormality**). Then, some of them (nonmonotonic consequences, graphical models) consider that the cause is bound to belong to the set of facts given in the description (**cause present**), whereas the other models are allowed to elicit causes among implicit elements derived from these facts, or including as background knowledge in the course of the modelling. Besides, one model (norm-based) privileges as causes events that are under the control of agents (**agentivity**). Finally, some models (trajectories, graphical model) can support explicit intervention-like manipulations, where a variable can be forced to take some value, regardless of what its normal value would be given the values of the other variables (**intervention**).

In addition to the criteria summarized in Table 2, let us note that only the structural equation model is deterministic, in the sense that there is (commonly) no uncertainty in the structural equations relating the variables representing the micro-universe under consideration. This could be seen as a guarantee of accurateness, as far as the description of the micro-universe is reasonably complete.

---

[4] **Transitivity** is not a built-in characteristic in any model we have considered. Depending on the specific setting of some parameters, though, some of them may take causation to be transitive. **Comptutational tractability** is not a truly discriminative criterion here either. All the formalisms underlying the approaches we have reviewed have already been implemented. Moreover, the formal complexity of all these frameworks has already been studied; and in any case, the treatment of traffic accident reports is unlikely to lead to any significant combinatorial explosion.

However, such accurateness would come with a price. Leaving aside the computational cost of ascription itself, a deterministic model is more costly in terms of the acquisition of information that is necessary prior to making any ascription. Furthermore, default, incomplete knowledge is arguably less unrealistic as a model of the kind of knowledge human agents bring to a causal ascription task.

Among the topics that we have not covered, the role of argumentation in causal ascription is worth mentioning. Argumentation is a dynamical process where arguments interact to assess a given claim (here, a causal claim), and processing of causal arguments requires a particular argumentation theory [26]. Agents may argue about where causation takes place in a sequence of events; they may use a weaker notion of causality than, e.g., Def. 2. But agents may also use argumentation in a self-serving way: in the case of a traffic accident, they may attempt to present events in a favorable way; to produce a 'biased description,' that remains respectful of the essential facts, but triggers inferences to conclusions that are in favor of the arguer. For example, one argumentation technique consists in suggesting a causal link between two facts, even if the causation is at best debatable. One typical case is to present the violation of a 'strong' norm as a consequence caused by the adversary's violation of a 'weak' norm, as in the example: 'At the stop sign, the driver on the main road delayed in entering the intersection; I proceeded.' The author wishes to convey that it is normal to overstep a stop sign, in case the vehicle having priority is hesitating. Identifying argumentative strategies may help to get a better understanding of reports, by detecting understatements, and reconstructing what is not explicitly said. In addition, further work will have to compare approaches in terms of their handling of preventative (negative) causation, and of their syntax sensitivity.

Acknowledgments

This research was supported by grant NT05-3-44479 from Agence Nationale de la Recherche. We thank L. Amgoud, D.J. Hilton, and F. Lévy for useful comments.

References

1. von Wright, G.H.: Norm and Action: A Logical Enquiry. Routledge, London (1963)
2. Pearl, J.: Causality: Models, Reasoning, and Inference. Cambridge University Press, Cambridge (2000)
3. Halpern, J., Pearl, J.: Causes and explanations: A structural-model approach — part 1: Causes. British Journal for the Philosophy of Science 56, 843–887 (2005)
4. Hall, N.: Structural equations and causation. Philosophical Studies 132, 109–136 (2007)
5. Hart, H.L.A., Honoré, T.: Causation in the law. Oxford University Press, Oxford (1985)
6. Hilton, D.J., Slugoski, B.R.: Knowledge-based causal attribution: The abnormal conditions focus model. Psychological Review 93, 75–88 (1986)
7. Giunchiglia, E., Lee, J., McCain, N., Lifschitz, V., Turner, H.: Non-monotonic causal theories. Artificial Intelligence 153, 49–104 (2004)

8. McCain, N., Turner, H.: A causal theory of ramifications and qualifications. In: Proc. IJCAI 1995, vol. 95, pp. 1978–1984 (1995)
9. Bonnefon, J.F., Da Silva Neves, R.M., Dubois, D., Prade, H.: Background default knowledge and causality ascriptions. In: Proc. ECAI 2006, pp. 11–15 (2006)
10. Bonnefon, J.F., Da Silva Neves, R.M., Dubois, D., Prade, H.: Predicting causality ascriptions from background knowledge: Model and experimental validation. International Journal of Approximate Reasoning 48, 752–765 (2008)
11. Kraus, S., Lehman, D., Magidor, M.: Nonmonotonic reasoning, preferential models and cumulative logics. Artificial Intelligence 44, 167–207 (1990)
12. Prade, H.: Responsibility judgments: Towards a formalization. In: Proc. IPMU 2008, Malaga, June 22–27 (2008)
13. Dupin de Saint-Cyr, F.: Scenario update applied to causal reasoning. In: Proc. of KR 2008 (2008)
14. Dupin de Saint-Cyr, F., Lang, J.: Belief extrapolation (or how to reason about observations and unpredicted change). In: Proc. KR 2002 (2002)
15. Katsuno, H., Mendelzon, A.: On the difference between updating a knowledge base and revising it. In: Proc. KR 1991, pp. 387–394 (1991)
16. Kayser, D., Nouioua, F.: About norms and causes. International Journal on Artificial Intelligence Tools 1-2, 7–23 (2005)
17. Syrjaänen, T., Niemelä, I.: The Smodels systems. In: Eiter, T., Faber, W., Truszczyński, M. (eds.) LPNMR 2001. LNCS (LNAI), vol. 2173, pp. 434–438. Springer, Heidelberg (2001)
18. Dubois, D., Prade, H.: Possibility theory: Qualitative and quantitative aspects. In: Gabbay, D.M., Smets, P. (eds.) Quantified Representation of Uncertainty and Imprecision, pp. 169–226. Kluwer, Dordrecht (1998)
19. Pearl, J.: Comment: Graphical models, causality and intervention. Statistical Sciences 8 (1993)
20. Benferhat, S., Smaoui, S.: Possibilistic causal networks for handling interventions: A new propagation algorithm. In: Proc. AAAI 2007, pp. 373–378 (2007)
21. Thagard, P.: Explanatory coherence. Behavioral and Brain Sciences 12, 435–467 (1989)
22. Thagard, P., Verbeurgt, K.: Coherence as constraint satisfaction. Cognitive Science 22, 1–24 (1998)
23. McClelland, J., Rumelhart, D.: Explorations in parallel distributed processing. MIT Press, Cambridge (1989)
24. Thagard, P.: Probabilistic networks and explanatory coherence. Cognitive Science Quarterly 1, 91–114 (2000)
25. Read, S., Marcus-Newhall, A.: The role of explanatory coherence in the construction of social explanations. Journal of Personality and Social Psychology 65, 429–447 (1993)
26. Amgoud, L., Prade, H.: Arguing about potential causal relations. In: IAF 2007 (2007)

An Efficient Algorithm for Naive Possibilistic Classifiers with Uncertain Inputs

Salem Benferhat and Karim Tabia

CRIL-CNRS UMR8188, Université d'Artois,
Rue Jean Souvraz SP 18 62307 Lens, Cedex, France
{benferhat,tabia}@cril.univ-artois.fr

Abstract. Possibilistic networks are graphical models particularly suitable for representing and reasoning with uncertain and incomplete information. According to the underlying interpretation of possibilistic scales, possibilistic networks are either quantitative or qualitative. In this paper, we address possibilistic-based classification with uncertain inputs. More precisely, we first analyze Jeffrey's rule for revising possibility distributions by uncertain observations. Then, we propose an efficient algorithm for revising possibility distributions encoded by a naive possibilistic network. This algorithm is particularly suitable for classification with uncertain inputs since it allows classification in polynomial time using different efficient transformations of initial naive possibilistic networks.

Keywords: Possibilistic networks, classification under uncertain inputs.

1 Introduction

Graphical models are powerful tools for representing and reasoning under uncertainty conditions. For instance, probabilistic (Bayesian) networks [9] are suitable for handling uncertain information while possibilistic networks [2][4][5] are more suitable for imprecise and incomplete data. Like probabilistic networks, possibilistic ones are graphical models but use possibility theory to handle imprecise and incomplete knowledge. They factor a global joint possibility distribution into a set of local possibility distributions that can be combined according to the network structure. This factorization allows interesting inference capabilities. Handling imprecise and incomplete (missing) data are main advantages of possibilistic models.

Classification is a special kind of inference: given an observed instance of each observable variable, it is required to determine the class label of the observed instance among a predefined set of class labels. Possibilistic classifiers have not been sufficiently studied in spite of the fact that they are useful for problems where knowledge is imprecise or missing. In fact, only few works used naive possibilistic classifiers [3][1] and few works address possibilistic network classifiers. In this paper, we address possibilistic-based classification with uncertain inputs. More precisely, we propose an efficient algorithm suitable for naive possibilistic

S. Greco and T. Lukasiewicz (Eds.): SUM 2008, LNAI 5291, pp. 63–77, 2008.
© Springer-Verlag Berlin Heidelberg 2008

network classification with uncertain inputs. We first investigate the possibilistic counterpart of Jeffrey's rule [8] for revising possibility distributions given uncertain observations. In fact, Jeffrey's rule cannot be directly applied for revising possibilistic knowledge encoded by a possibilistic network since its computation is exponential in the number of attributes and attribute domains. In order to overcome this limitation, we propose an efficient method for revising naive product-based possibilistic networks suitable for classification with uncertain inputs. Our algorithm is based on a series of equivalent and polynomial transformations of initial possibilistic networks taking into account uncertain inputs.

The rest of this paper is organized as follows: Section 2 briefly presents basics about possibility theory and possibilistic networks. In section 3, we address possibilistic belief revision based on Jeffrey's rule. Section 4 proposes a new efficient algorithm for naive possibilistic network classification with uncertain inputs. Finally, section 5 concludes this paper.

2   Possibilistic Networks

In this section, we present possibilistic networks with emphasis on possibilistic classification. Before going further, let us fix the notations that will be used along with this paper.

$V = \{A_1, A_2, .., A_n\}$ denotes the set of variables. $D_A = \{a_1, a_2, .., a_m\}$ denotes the finite domain of variable A. a_i denotes an instance (value) of variable A_i. A, X,.. denote subsets of variables from V. $D_X = \times_{A_i \in X} D_{A_i}$ represents the cartesian product relative to variables A_i involved in subset X. x denotes any instance of X (namely, $x \in D_X$). $\Omega = \times_{A_i \in V} D_{A_i}$ denotes the universe of discourse (all possible states of the world); it is the cartesian product of all variable domains involved in V. A tuple $w = (a_1, a_2, .., a_n)$ which is an instance of Ω represents a possible state of the world. In $w = (a_1, a_2, .., a_n)$, the value of variable A_i is a_i and it is denoted $w[A_i] = a_i$. ϕ, φ denote subsets of Ω called events while $\overline{\phi}$ denotes the complementary of ϕ in Ω ($\overline{\phi} = \Omega - \phi$).

2.1   Possibility Theory

Possibility theory is an uncertainty theory suitable for handling uncertain and imprecise knowledge. Introduced by Zadeh [11], this theory is based on two dual measures in order to represent knowledge/ignorance relative to event in hand. One of the basic concepts of possibility theory is the one of possibility distribution π which is a mapping from the universe of discourse Ω to the unit scale $[0, 1]$. The possibility degree $\pi(w_i)$ expresses to what extent it is consistent that w_i can be the actual state of the world. Then $\pi(w_i) = 1$ means that w_i is totally possible and $\pi(w_i) = 0$ denotes an impossible event. The relation $\pi(w_i) > \pi(w_j)$ means that w_i is more possible than w_j. A possibility distribution π is said to be normalized if $max_{w_i \in \Omega}(\pi(w_i)) = 1$. It is said to be sub-normalized otherwise. Possibility theory relies on two measures in order to assess knowledge/ignorance:

- **Possibility measure:** The possibility measure, denoted $\Pi(\phi)$, represents the possibility degree relative to any event $\phi \subseteq \Omega$. It evaluates to what extent

ϕ is consistent with the knowledge encoded by possibility distribution π on Ω. This is defined as follows:

$$\Pi(\phi) = max_{w_i \in \phi}(\pi(w_i)) \tag{1}$$

Note that term $\Pi(\phi)$ denotes the possibility degree relative to having one of the events involved in ϕ as the actual state of the world.

- **Necessity measure:** The necessity measure is the dual of possibility measure and evaluates the certainty implied by the current knowledge of the world. Namely, $N(\phi)=1-\Pi(\overline{\phi})$ where $\overline{\phi}$ denotes the complementary of ϕ.

Given a possibility distribution π on Ω, marginal distributions π_X relative to subset of variables X ($X \subseteq V$) are computed using the max operator as follows:

$$\pi_X(x) = max_{w_i \in \Omega}(\pi(w_i) : w_i[X] = x), \tag{2}$$

where term $w_i[X] = x$ denotes the fact that x is the instantiation of X in w_i. According to the interpretation underlying possibilistic scale [0,1], there are two variants of possibility theory:

- **Qualitative possibility theory:** In this case, the possibility measure is a mapping from the universe of discourse Ω to an "ordinal" scale where only the "ordering" of values is important.
- **Quantitative possibility theory:** In this case, the possibilistic scale [0, 1] is numerical. Then possibility degrees are like numeric values that can be manipulated by arithmetic operators. One of possible interpretations of quantitative possibility distributions is viewing $\pi(w_i)$ as degree of surprise as in Spohn's ordinal conditional functions [10].

2.2   Conditioning in Possibilistic Networks

Conditioning is concerned with updating the current knowledge encoded by a possibility distribution π when an evidence (a sure event) is observed.

In the qualitative setting, conditional possibility degree of w_i given an event ϕ is computed as follows (we assume that $\Pi(\phi) \neq 0$):

$$\pi_m(w_i|\phi) \begin{cases} 1 & \text{if } \pi(w_i)=\Pi(\phi) \text{ and } w_i \in \phi; \\ \pi(w_i) & \text{if } \pi(w_i)< \Pi(\phi) \text{ and } w_i \in \phi; \\ 0 & \text{otherwise.} \end{cases} \tag{3}$$

In the quantitative setting, conditioning uses the product operator as follows:

$$\pi_p(w_i|\phi) \begin{cases} \frac{\pi(w_i)}{\Pi(\phi)} & \text{if } w_i \in \phi; \\ 0 & \text{otherwise.} \end{cases} \tag{4}$$

In this paper, we only focus on product-based conditioning.

2.3   Possibilistic Networks

A possibilistic network [4] [6] consists of two components: a **(1) graphical component** consisting in a DAG (Direct Acyclic Graph) which encodes direct influence relations existing between domain variables, and a **(2) numerical component** which is a "quantitative" component composed of a set of local conditional possibility distributions measuring the influence endured by each domain variable A_i in the context of its parents U_{A_i}.

Local possibility distributions relative to nodes without parents ($U_{A_i} = \emptyset$) should satisfy the normalization condition. Namely,

$$max_{a_{i_j} \in D_{A_i}}(\pi(a_{i_j})) = 1 \tag{5}$$

In case where domain variable A_i has parents ($U_{A_i} \neq \emptyset$), the normalization constraint is denoted as follows:

$$max_{a_{i_j} \in D_{A_i}}(\pi(a_{i_j}/U_{A_i})) = 1 \tag{6}$$

The possibility degree associated with an observation is computed using the product-based chain rule. Namely,

$$\Pi(A_1, A_2, .., A_n) = \prod_{i=1}^{n}(\pi(A_i/U_{A_i}) \tag{7}$$

In classification problems, one node represents class variable C while the remaining variables are attributes $A=\{A_1, A_2,..,A_n\}$ that may be observable. Given an observation denoted $A=(a_1,a_2,..,a_n)$ of $\{A1, A_2, .., A_n\}$, the candidate class c is determined as follows:

$$c = argmax_{c_k \in D_C}(\Pi(c_k/A)) \tag{8}$$

Note that term $\Pi(c_k/A)$ denotes possibility degree of having c_k the actual class given the observation $A=(a_1,a_2,..,a_n)$.

2.4   Naive Possibilistic Network Classifier

A naive possibilistic network classifier assumes that attributes are independent[1] in the context of the class node. As it is shown in the following figure, the only dependencies allowed in naive networks are from the class node C to each attribute A_i. The quantitative component of a naive possibilistic network involves

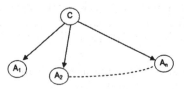

Fig. 1. Naive possibilistic network structure

---

[1] In quantitative possibilistic setting, event $\phi \subseteq \Omega$ is said independent from event $\psi \subseteq \Omega$ given event $\varphi \subseteq \Omega$ if $\Pi(\phi/\psi, \varphi) = \Pi(\phi/\varphi)$.

prior possibility distribution relative to class node and the conditional possibility distributions relative to attributes given the class node. Applying product-based conditioning (see Equation 4) and product-based chain rule (see Equation 7) on term $\Pi(c_k/A)$ leads to the following formula:

$$\Pi(c_k/A) = \frac{\Pi(c_k, A)}{\Pi(A)} = \frac{\pi(c_k) * \pi(A_1/c_k) * \pi(A_2/c_k) * .. * \pi(A_n/c_k)}{\Pi(A_1 A_2 .. A_n)} \qquad (9)$$

Note that term $\Pi(A)$ is a normalization factor and it is the same over all class labels. Then this can be obtained by normalizing numerator of Equation 9. Hence classification in naive product-based possibilistic network is ensured by the following rule:

$$c = argmax_{c_k \in D_C}(\pi(c_k) * \pi(A_1/c_k) * \pi(A_2/c_k) * .. * \pi(A_n/c_k)) \qquad (10)$$

It is important to note that there are only few works which used naive possibilistic network classifiers [1][3] while other networks have not been experimented. To the best of our knowledge, there is no work that addresses the problem of classification under uncertain inputs using naive possibilistic networks.

3   Possibilistic Classification with Uncertain Inputs Using Jeffrey's Rule

In this section, we investigate the application of Jeffrey's rule [8] for revising possibility distributions encoded by a naive possibilistic network given uncertain observations. In our case, uncertainty relative to uncertain/missing attribute A_i is represented by a possibility distribution π'_{A_i} given by the expert (or by observation sensors).

3.1   Possibility Distribution Revision Using Jeffrey's Rule

In [8], Jeffrey proposed a method for revising a probability distribution p into p' given uncertainty bearing on a set of mutually exclusive and exhaustive events λ_i. The uncertainty is of the form (λ_i, α_i) with $\alpha_i = p'(\lambda_i)$. Jeffrey's method relies on the fact that although there is uncertainty about events λ_i, conditional probability of any event $\phi \subseteq \Omega$ given any uncertain event λ_i remains the same in the original and the revised distributions. Namely:

$$P(\phi/\lambda_i) = P'(\phi/\lambda_i) \qquad (11)$$

The underlying interpretation of revision implied by constraint of Equation 11 is that revised probability distribution p' must not change conditional probability degrees of any event ϕ given uncertain events λ_i. In the probabilistic framework, applying Bayes rule then marginalization leads to the following formula:

$$P'(\phi) = \sum_{\lambda_i} P'(\lambda_i) * \frac{P(\phi, \lambda_i)}{P(\lambda_i)} \qquad (12)$$

Note that revised probability distribution p' obtained using Jeffrey's rule is unique. In the following, we consider revising a possibility distribution π in the presence of uncertain observations concerning a set of exhaustive and mutually exclusive events λ_i using Jeffrey's rule. The possibilistic counterpart of this rule has been investigated in [7] from a semantics point of view. Then, in the possibilistic framework, revised possibility distribution π' must comply with the principle stating that uncertainty about events λ_i must not alter the conditional possibility degree of any event $\phi \subseteq \Omega$ given any event λ_i. Namely,

$$\forall \lambda_i \in \Omega, \ \forall \phi \subseteq \Omega, \Pi'(\phi/\lambda_i) = \Pi(\phi/\lambda_i) \tag{13}$$

One can easily check that there is also a unique solution π' that satisfies Equation 13 and that guarantees that $\forall \lambda_i$, $\pi'(\lambda_i)=\alpha_i$. This solution is provided by the following equation:

$$\forall \phi, \Pi'(\phi) = max_{\lambda_i}(\pi'(\lambda_i) * \frac{\Pi(\phi, \lambda_i)}{\pi(\lambda_i)}) \tag{14}$$

Note that there is no algorithm for revising possibility distributions by uncertain observations. In our context (classification with uncertain inputs), uncertainty can bear on any attribute subset or on the whole attribute set. Uncertainty concerning attribute A_i is encoded by a possibility distribution π'_{A_i} given by the expert or by observation sensors. The application of Jeffrey's rule in our context raises two problems:

The first problem is related to the fact that Jeffrey's rule can be applied only if uncertainty concerns a set of exhaustive and mutually exclusive events while in classification with uncertain inputs problems, uncertainty is bearing on a set of events λ_i which are not mutually exclusive. For example, if attributes A_1 and A_2 are uncertain, then this uncertainty is encoded by π'_{A_1} and π'_{A_2} respectively. In order to apply Jeffrey's rule, we must compute another possibility distribution $\pi'_{A_1 A_2}$ relative to $A_1 A_2$. In this way, uncertain events $a_1 a_2$ are exhaustive and mutually exclusive. However, there are several potential possibility distributions for $\pi'_{A_1 A_2}$. The following is an example confirming the multiplicity of $\pi'_{A_1 A_2}$.

Example. Let A_1 and A_2 be two variables whose domains are respectively $D_{A_1}=\{a_{1_1}, a_{1_2}\}$ and $D_{A_2}=\{a_{2_1}, a_{2_2}\}$. Let also π'_{A_1}, π'_{A_2} be the possibility

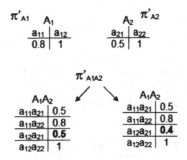

Fig. 2. Example of two possibility distributions

distributions encoding uncertainty relative to A_1 and A_2 respectively. Figure 2 shows that $\pi'_{A_1 A_2}$ is not unique.

When uncertainty is bearing on attributes $A_i,..A_j$, then this uncertainty is encoded by specifying $\pi'_{A_i},..,\pi'_{A_j}$. Given the multiplicity of joint possibility distributions $\pi'_{A_i..A_j}$, we propose to use the distribution preserving attributes' independencies since we are concerned with naive possibilistic classifier which assumes that attributes are independent given the class node. Hence, joint possibility distribution $\pi'_{A_i..A_j}$ is computed as follows:

$$\pi'_{A_i..A_j}(a_i..a_j) = \prod_{k=i}^{j}(\pi'_{A_k}(a_k)) \tag{15}$$

The second problem concerns computational issue. In order to perform classification under uncertain inputs, one cannot directly apply Jeffrey's rule to revise possibility distributions encoded by the naive possibilistic network. Given the initial possibility degrees of class labels c_k (namely, $\pi(c_k)$ involved in the possibilistic network), we want to revise this possibility distribution given uncertain attributes $A_1,..,A_n$ using Jeffrey's rule. Namely, we need to compute $\pi'(c_k) = \pi(c_k|\pi'(A_1,..,A_n))$ defined as follows:

$$\pi(c_k|\pi'(A_1..A_n)) = max_{A_1..A_n}(\Pi(c_k/A_1..A_n) * \pi'(A_1..A_n)) \tag{16}$$

Given that joint possibility distribution $\pi'_{A_1..A_n}$ is the one corresponding to the case where attributes A_i are independent, then

$$\pi'(c_k) = max_{A_1..A_n}(\Pi(c_k/A_1..A_n) * \pi'(A_1) * .. * \pi'(A_n)) \tag{17}$$

Clearly, one cannot use this formula to compute $\pi'(c_k)$ because this computation is exponential in the number of attributes and attribute domains. In the following, we give an example of using Jeffrey's rule to perform classification with uncertain inputs.

3.2 Possibilistic-Based Classification with Uncertain Inputs Based on Jeffrey's Rule

In order to illustrate, on one hand, possibilistic-based classification using Jeffrey's rule and, on the other hand, our algorithm, we will consider for the rest of this paper naive possibilistic network of Figure 3. This figure gives an example of naive product-based possibilistic network encoding the initial knowledge. It includes a class node C and three attribute nodes A_1, A_2 and A_3. Figure 3 also gives initial possibility distributions and the joint distribution obtained using chain rule of Equation 7. Assume now that we have in hand an uncertain observation to classify. Uncertainty bearing on attributes A_1, A_2 and A_3 is encoded by π'_{A_1}, π'_{A_2} and π'_{A_3} are provided by Figure 4.

Note that our objective is to find the most plausible class(es) given the uncertain observations. The following figure gives the results of revising the initial joint possibility distribution (see Figure 3) using Jeffrey's rule:

From revised joint possibility distribution π' of Figure 5, revised local possibility distribution relative to class node C is $\pi'_C(c_1)=1$, $\pi'_C(c_2)=.6667$. Then

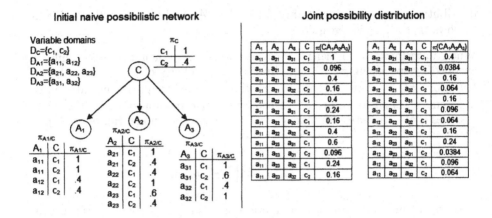

Fig. 3. Naive possibilistic network example

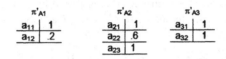

Fig. 4. Uncertain observations example

A_1	A_2	A_3	$\Pi'(A_1A_2A_3)$
a_{11}	a_{21}	a_{31}	1
a_{11}	a_{21}	a_{32}	1
a_{11}	a_{22}	a_{31}	0.6
a_{11}	a_{22}	a_{32}	0.6
a_{11}	a_{23}	a_{31}	1
a_{11}	a_{23}	a_{32}	1
a_{12}	a_{21}	a_{31}	0.2
a_{12}	a_{21}	a_{32}	0.2
a_{12}	a_{22}	a_{31}	0.12
a_{12}	a_{22}	a_{32}	0.12
a_{12}	a_{23}	a_{31}	0.2
a_{12}	a_{23}	a_{32}	0.2

A_1	A_2	A_3	C	$\pi'(CA_1A_2A_3)$
a_{11}	a_{21}	a_{31}	c_1	1
a_{11}	a_{21}	a_{31}	c_2	0.096
a_{11}	a_{21}	a_{32}	c_1	1
a_{11}	a_{21}	a_{32}	c_2	0.4
a_{11}	a_{22}	a_{31}	c_1	0.6
a_{11}	a_{22}	a_{31}	c_2	0.36
a_{11}	a_{22}	a_{32}	c_1	0.24
a_{11}	a_{22}	a_{32}	c_2	0.6
a_{11}	a_{23}	a_{31}	c_1	1
a_{11}	a_{23}	a_{31}	c_2	0.16
a_{11}	a_{23}	a_{32}	c_1	1
a_{11}	a_{23}	a_{32}	c_2	0.6667

A_1	A_2	A_3	C	$\pi'(CA_1A_2A_3)$
a_{12}	a_{21}	a_{31}	c_1	0.1667
a_{12}	a_{21}	a_{31}	c_2	0.016
a_{12}	a_{21}	a_{32}	c_1	0.2
a_{12}	a_{21}	a_{32}	c_2	0.08
a_{12}	a_{22}	a_{31}	c_1	0.12
a_{12}	a_{22}	a_{31}	c_2	0.072
a_{12}	a_{22}	a_{32}	c_1	0.048
a_{12}	a_{22}	a_{32}	c_2	0.12
a_{12}	a_{23}	a_{31}	c_1	0.08
a_{12}	a_{23}	a_{31}	c_2	0.0128
a_{12}	a_{23}	a_{32}	c_1	0.16
a_{12}	a_{23}	a_{32}	c_2	0.1067

$\Pi'(A_1 A_2 A_3)$ obtained by applying Equation 14

Revised joint possibility distribution π' according to Jeffrey's rule:

$$\pi'(C_kA_1A_2A_3) = \pi(C_kA_1A_2A_3) \cdot \frac{\Pi'(A_1A_2A_3)}{\Pi(A_1A_2A_3)}$$

Fig. 5. Revised joint possibility distribution

the only class label totally possible given the instance to classify is c_1. We want to perform same revision without computing global joint possibility distribution since this method is intractable when the number of attributes becomes important. In the following, we propose an efficient algorithm suitable for naive product-based possibilistic network classification with uncertain inputs.

4 A New Algorithm for Naive Possibilistic Network Classification with Uncertain Inputs

The basic idea of our method is to only search for classes that are totally possible (classes having possibility degrees equal to 1) on the basis of uncertain inputs. Since we are concerned with a classification problem (the task is finding the most plausible class label(es) given the uncertain observation to classify), then the method we propose fits classification objectives. Our method goes through a sequence of equivalent transformations on the initial possibilistic network. The following subsections provide and detail the different steps of our algorithms.

4.1 Step 1: Instance Elimination

Recall that revision is performed according to Jeffrey's rule (using Equation 17) and we are only concerned with determining if a given class label c_k is among the most plausible ones (namely, the ones having possibility degrees equal to 1). Given this fact, we can eliminate all instances of $A_1 A_2 .. A_n$ where $\Pi'(A_1 A_2 .. A_n)$ <1 because such instances force the value of $\pi'(c_k)$ to be less than 1. Given that attributes are independent, then this simplification leads to eliminating from each attribute domain $D_{A_i}^{NP}$ (relative to A_i in initial network NP) values whose possibility degrees in π'_{A_i} are less than 1. In this step, attribute domain $D_{A_i}^{NP}$ is changed to $D_{A_i}^{NP_{S_1}}$ which denotes A_i's domain in network NP^{S_1} obtained from NP after Step 1. Namely, $D_{A_i}^{NP_{S_1}} = D_{A_i}^{NP} - \{a_i, if\ \pi'_{A_i}(a_i) < 1\}$. After this step, all the attributes' remaining instances are totally possible. Then we have the following proposition:

Proposition 1. Let NP be the initial naive possibilistic network and π'_{A_1}, π'_{A_2} ,.., π'_{A_n} be the possibility distributions encoding uncertainty relative to attributes A_1, A_2,.., A_n respectively. Let NP^{S_1} be the naive possibilistic network obtained by eliminating not totally possible instances. Then,
$\pi'^{NP}(c_k) = max_{A_1..A_n}(\Pi^{NP}(c_k/a_1..a_n) * \pi'(a_1) * .. * \pi'(a_n)) = 1$
if and only if $\pi^{NP_{S_1}}(c_k) = max_{A_1..A_n}(\Pi^{NP_{S_1}}(c_k/a_1..a_n)) = 1$

Proposition 1 states that if there is a class label which is totally possible in the initial network NP then it is also totally possible in network NP^{S_1} obtained after transformation of Step 1.

Example. The application of instance elimination step on network NP of Figure 3 gives NP^{S_1} as follows:

Network of Figure 6 is obtained by respectively substituting $D_{A_1}^{NP} = \{a_{11}, a_{12}\}$, $D_{A_2}^{NP} = \{a_{21}, a_{22}, a_{23}\}$ and $D_{A_3}^{NP} = \{a_{31}, a_{32}\}$ by $D_{A_1}^{NP_{S_1}} = \{a_{11}\}$, $D_{A_2}^{NP_{S_1}} = \{a_{21}, a_{23}\}$ and $D_{A_3}^{NP_{S_1}} = \{a_{31}, a_{32}\}$. Note that in NP^{S_1}, the possibility distribution relative to node C is exactly the same as in NP.

4.2 Step 2: Unary Variable Elimination

As a consequence of instance elimination step, there might be attributes whose domains only contain one value. This is for instance the case in our example

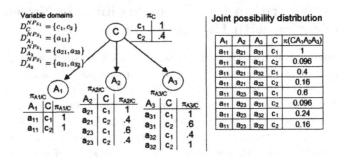

Fig. 6. NP^{S_1}: Possibilistic network after Step 1

where $D_{A_1}^{NP_{S_1}}$ exactly contains one element which is a_{11}. During this step, these singleton variables are eliminated and class node distribution will be adapted so that joint possibility distribution remains unchanged. In the network obtained after Step 1, the possibility degree of any instance $c_k a_1 a_2 .. a_n$ is computed using the chain rule as follows:

$$\Pi^{NP_{S_1}}(c_k a_1 a_2 .. a_n) = \pi^{NP_{S_1}}(c_k) * \pi^{NP_{S_1}}(a_1/c_k) * .. * \pi^{NP_{S_1}}(a_n/c_k) \quad (18)$$

Then we can build a new network NP^{S_2} by eliminating unary attributes but class node distribution has to be changed in order to guarantee that $\pi^{NP_{S_1}}(c_k a_1 a_2 .. a_n)$ remains the same. For a singleton attribute A_i whose domain $D_{A_i}^{NP_{S_1}}$ contains only one value a_i, it is possible to achieve this transformation by substituting each $\pi^{NP_{S_1}}(c_k)$ with $\pi^{NP_{S_2}}(c_k) = \pi^{NP_{S_1}}(c_k) * \pi^{NP_{S_1}}(a_i/c_k)$.

Proposition 2. Let NP^{S_1} be the naive possibilistic network whose nodes involve class node C and attribute nodes A_1, $A_2, .., A_n$. Assume that A_1 is a unary attribute whose domain only contains the instance a_1 and let NP^{S_2} be the naive possibilistic network involving C, $A_2, .., A_n$ such that: $\pi^{NP_{S_2}}(a_i) = \pi^{NP_{S_1}}(a_i)$ for $i = 2, .., n$ and $\pi^{NP_{S_2}}(c_k) = \pi^{NP_{S_1}}(a_1/c_k) * \pi^{NP_{S_1}}(c_k)$. Then, $\forall c_k \in D_C, \forall a_i \in D_{A_i}^{NP_{S_1}}$ for $i = 1, .., n$, $\pi^{NP_{S_1}}(c_k a_1 a_2 .. a_n) = \pi^{NP_{S_2}}(c_k a_2 .. a_n)$

Example (continued): This transformation on network of Figure 6 leads to the following:

Note that node A_1 which is a unary attribute has been removed and possibility distribution relative to class node C has been altered such that joint possibility distributions of Figure 6 and Figure 7 remain equal.

4.3   Step 3: Renormalizing Local Possibility Distributions

After Steps 1 and 2, local possibility distributions of some attributes might not be normalized (even if global joint possibility distribution is normalized). Namely, it may exist a variable A_i and a class label c_k such that $max_{A_i}(\pi^{NP_{S_2}}(a_i/c_k)) = \alpha$ ($\alpha < 1$). Step 3 deals with this problem considering two cases:

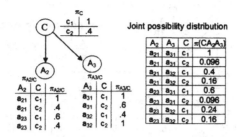

Fig. 7. NP^{S_2}: Possibilistic network after Step 2

- If $\alpha = 0$, then $\forall c_k$, $\pi^{NP_{S_2}}(c_k a_1 a_2 .. a_n) = 0$. This means that whatever is the value of A_i, this forces $\pi^{NP_{S_2}}(c_k a_1 a_2 .. a_n) = 0$. In this case, the class c_k cannot be among plausible ones, and can be removed from $D_C^{NP_{S_2}}$.

- If $0 < \alpha < 1$, normalization of A_i can be done by building a new network NP^{S_3} by substituting $\pi^{NP_{S_2}}(a_i/c_k)$ with $\pi^{NP_{S_3}}(a_i/c_k) = \frac{\pi^{NP_{S_2}}(a_i/c_k)}{\alpha}$ and substituting $\pi^{NP_{S_2}}(c_k)$ with $\pi^{NP_{S_3}}(c_k) = \pi^{NP_{S_2}}(c_k) * \alpha$. In this way, $\pi^{NP_{S_3}}(c_k a_1 a_2 .. a_n)$ remains unchanged and local possibility distribution becomes normalized.

Proposition 3. Let NP^{S_2} be the naive possibilistic network involving nodes $C, A_1, A_2, .., A_n$ obtained from Step 2. Assume that conditional possibility distribution relative to node A_1 is not normalized ($\exists c_k$ such that $max_{A_1}(\pi^{NP_{S_2}}(a_1/c_k)) = \alpha$ and $0 < \alpha < 1$). Let NP^{S_3} be the naive possibilistic network having same structure as NP^{S_2} where $\pi^{NP_{S_3}}(a_1/c_k) = \frac{\pi^{NP_{S_2}}(a_1/c_k)}{\alpha}$ and $\pi^{NP_{S_3}}(a_i/c_k) = \pi^{NP_{S_2}}(a_i/c_k)$ for i=2,..,n and $\pi^{NP_{S_3}}(c_k) = \pi^{NP_{S_2}}(c_k) * \alpha$. Then, $\forall c_k \in D_C^{NP_{S_3}}$, $\forall a_i \in D_{A_i}^{NP_{S_3}}$, $\pi^{NP_{S_3}}(c_k a_1 a_2 .. a_n) = \pi^{NP_{S_2}}(c_k a_1 a_2 .. a_n)$

Example (continued): On network NP^{S_2} of Figure 7, local possibility distribution relative to attribute A_2 is sub-normalized (because $max_{a_i \in D_{A_2}^{NP_{S_2}}}$ $(\pi^{NP_{S_2}}(a_i/c_2)) = .4$). Transformation of Step 3 on NP^{S_2} gives the following network:

Note that possibility distribution relative to A_2 has been renormalized and possibility distribution relative to class node C has been adjusted accordingly. Consequently, joint possibility distributions of Figure 7 and Figure 8 are equal.

4.4　Step 4: Prior Totally Possible Class Lookup

Steps 1, 2 and 3 allow to simplify the initial network by eliminating not totally possible instances, eliminating unary variables and impossible classes and renormalizing the obtained network. In this step, we search for class labels which are totally possible in network NP^{S_3} obtained after Steps 1, 2 and 3. Then every class c_k having its prior possibility degree $\pi^{NP_{S_3}}(c_k) = 1$ is totally possible given the uncertain instance to classify. Hence, we have the following proposition:

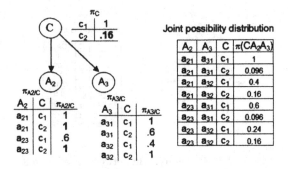

Fig. 8. NP^{S_3}: Possibilistic network after Step 3

Proposition 4. $\forall c_k \in D_C^{NP_{S_3}}$ such that $\pi^{NP_{S_3}}(c_k)=1$ then
$$max_{A_1..A_n}(\pi^{NP_{S_3}}(c_k/a_1..a_n)) = 1$$

Proposition 4 states that there exists an attribute configuration $a_1 a_2..a_n$ making it possible for a class c_k having $\pi^{NP_{S_3}}(c_k)=1$ to be totally possible (namely $\pi^{NP_{S_3}}(c_k/a_1 a_2..a_n)=1$).

Example (continued): On network NP^{S_3} of Figure 8, class c_1 is totally possible since $\pi^{NP_{S_3}}(c_1) = 1$ and $\exists a_{21}$ such that $\pi^{NP_{S_3}}(a_{21}/c_1) = 1$ and $\exists a_{31}$ such that $\pi^{NP_{S_3}}(a_{31}/c_1) = 1$. Then, $\Pi^{NP_{S_3}}(c_1/a_{21}a_{31})=1$.

4.5   Step 5: Conditionally Totally Possible Class Lookup

Unfortunately, Proposition 4 only provides a subset of plausible classes. Indeed, it may happen that an other class c_k having $\pi^{NP_{S_3}}(c_k) = \alpha$ $(0<\alpha<1)$ is totally possible given uncertain instance to classify. Namely, it may exists an attribute configuration $a_1 a_2..a_n$ such that $\Pi^{NP_{S_3}}(c_k/a_1 a_2..a_n)=1$ even if $\pi^{NP_{S_3}}(c_k)<1$. Ofcourse, we would like to avoid exploring all configurations of $\Pi^{NP_{S_3}}(c_k/a_1 a_2..a_n)$. For sake of simplicity, we assume in this step that C is a binary variable (namely, $D_C^{NP_{S_3}}=\{c_1,c_2\}$ but this can be easily extended to non-binary variables) and class label c_1 is totally possible $(\pi^{NP_{S_3}}(c_1)=1)$ while $\pi^{NP_{S_3}}(c_2)<1$. Hence, we would like to determine whether there is an attribute configuration $a_1 a_2..a_n$ such that $\Pi^{NP_{S_3}}(c_2/a_1 a_2..a_n)=1$ without exploring all configurations of $\Pi^{NP_{S_3}}(c_2/a_1 a_2..a_n)$. Therefore, we propose to proceed by comparing these configurations with those which were previously found totally possible. The basic idea is to compare every configuration $\Pi^{NP_{S_3}}(c_2/a_1 a_2..a_n)$ with $\Pi^{NP_{S_3}}(c_1/a_1 a_2..a_n)$ (c_1 is such that $\pi^{NP_{S_3}}(c_1) = 1$). In case where $\Pi^{NP_{S_3}}(c_2/a_1 a_2..a_n)>\Pi^{NP_{S_3}}(c_1/a_1 a_2..a_n)$, then this means that c_2 is more possible that c_1 conditionally to $a_1 a_2..a_n$, consequently, $\Pi^{NP_{S_3}}(c_2/a_1 a_2..a_n)=1$. In order to find such a configuration, we can use the following decomposition:

Recall that we search for a configuration $a_1..a_n$ ensuring
$$\Pi^{NP_{S_3}}(c_2/a_1..a_n)=\frac{\pi^{NP_{S_3}}(c_2 a_1..a_n)}{\Pi^{NP_{S_3}}(a_1..a_n)} = 1$$

Given that $\Pi^{NP_{S_3}}(a_1..a_n)=max_{c_i \in D_C^{NP_{S_3}}}(\pi(c_i a_1 a_2..a_n))$, then $\forall c_i \in D_C^{NP_{S_3}}$, $\Pi^{NP_{S_3}}(a_1 a_2..a_n) \geq \pi^{NP_{S_3}}(c_i a_1 a_2..a_n)$. Consequently if $\Pi^{NP_{S_3}}(c_2/a_1..a_n)=1$ then, $\dfrac{\pi^{NP_{S_3}}(c_2 a_1 a_2..a_n)}{\pi^{NP_{S_3}}(c_1 a_1 a_2..a_n)} = \dfrac{\pi^{NP_{S_3}}(c_2)}{\pi^{NP_{S_3}}(c_1)} * \dfrac{\pi^{NP_{S_3}}(a_1/c_2)}{\pi^{NP_{S_3}}(a_1/c_1)} * .. * \dfrac{\pi^{NP_{S_3}}(a_n/c_2)}{\pi^{NP_{S_3}}(a_n/c_2)} \geq 1$.

Since c_1 denotes a class whose prior possibility degree $\pi^{NP_{S_3}}(c_1)=1$, then,

$$\frac{\pi^{NP_{S_3}}(c_2 a_1 a_2..a_n)}{\pi^{NP_{S_3}}(c_1 a_1 a_2..a_n)} = \pi^{NP_{S_3}}(c_2) * \frac{\pi^{NP_{S_3}}(a_1/c_2)}{\pi^{NP_{S_3}}(a_1/c_1)} * .. * \frac{\pi^{NP_{S_3}}(a_n/c_2)}{\pi^{NP_{S_3}}(a_n/c_1)} \geq 1 \qquad (19)$$

Decomposition of Equation 19 can be used to build a new network NP^{S_4} by transforming conditional possibility distributions relative to each attribute A_i in NP^{S_3} by substituting every term $\pi^{NP_{S_3}}(a_i/c_2)$ by $\pi^{NP_{S_4}}(a_i/c_2)=\dfrac{\pi^{NP_{S_3}}(a_i/c_2)}{\pi^{NP_{S_3}}(a_i/c_1)}$ and discarding c_1 since it is known to be totally possible. Substituting $\pi^{NP_{S_3}}(a_i/c_2)$ by $\pi^{NP_{S_4}}(a_i/c_2)$ aims at upgrading/downgrading each term $\pi^{NP_{S_3}}(a_i/c_2)$ according to the corresponding term $\pi^{NP_{S_3}}(a_i/c_1)$ in order to determine whether a_i is more/less possible in class c_2 than in c_1. Note that terms $\pi^{NP_{S_4}}(a_i/c_2)$ may be greater than 1 (in case when $\pi^{NP_{S_3}}(a_i/c_2)<\pi^{NP_{S_3}}(a_i/c_1)$). Hence, they will no longer represent possibility degrees. In order to avoid such a problem, let us define an unbound possibility distribution, denoted $\gamma\pi$, as a function from $\Omega \longrightarrow \Re$. Unbound possibility degrees are induced in the same way as in standard possibility setting (for event $\phi \subseteq \Omega$, $\gamma\Pi(\phi) = max_{w_i \in \phi}(\gamma\pi(w_i))$. Note that unbound possibility distributions are similar to the so-called potentials in junction tree algorithms [9]; they are only needed for computational issues. An unbound naive possibilistic network is exactly a naive possibilistic network, except that γ-possibility distributions have no upper bound (they may involve possibility degrees greater than 1). In particular, each unbound possibilistic network induces a unique joint γ-possibility distribution $\gamma\pi$ using chain rule of Equation 7.

Then, using decomposition of Equation 19, we can transform network NP^{S_3} (obtained after Steps 1, 2 and 3) into an unbound possibilistic network UNP. As a consequence of this transformation, some local conditional γ-possibility distributions in network UNP may not be normalized. Repeating Step 2 (Re-normalization) on $\gamma\pi_{A_i}$ (local γ-distributions relative to attributes in network UNP) allows to normalize them. Hence, once re-normalization accomplished, the new possibility distribution $\gamma\pi_C^{UNP}$ relative to class node shows whether class label c_2 is totally possible. Then we have the following proposition:

Proposition 5. Let NP^{S_3} be the naive possibilistic network obtained after Steps 1, 2 and 3, and let $D_C^{NP_{S_3}} = \{c_1, c_2\}$, $\pi^{NP_{S_3}}(c_1)=1$ and $\pi^{NP_{S_3}}(c_2)<1$. Let UNP be the unbound naive possibilistic network having same structure as NP^{S_3} where $D_C^{UNP}=\{c_2\}$. Let $\gamma\pi^{UNP}(a_i/c_2)=\dfrac{\pi^{NP_{S_3}}(a_i/c_2)}{\pi^{NP_{S_3}}(a_i/c_1)}$ for $i=1,..,n$. Then, $\gamma\pi^{UNP}(c_2) \geq 1$ if and only if it exists an attribute configuration $a_1..a_n$ such that $\Pi^{NP_{S_3}}(c_2/a_1..a_n)=1$.

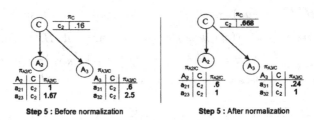

Fig. 9. UNP: Possibilistic network after Step 5

Proof of Proposition 8

In network UNP (where conditional possibility distribution relative to attributes are normalized), $\gamma\pi^{UNP}(c_k)\geq1$ means that $max_{A_1..A_n}(\gamma\pi^{UNP}(c_k a_1..a_n))\geq1$. This implies that $max_{A_1..A_n}(\gamma\pi^{UNP}(c_k)*\gamma\pi^{UNP}(a_1/c_k)*..*\gamma\pi^{UNP}(a_n/c_k))\geq1$. Given that for i=1..n, $\gamma\pi^{UNP}(a_i/c_k)=\frac{\pi^{NP_{S_3}}(a_i/c_k)}{\pi^{NP_{S_3}}(a_i/c_j)}$ and $\gamma\pi^{UNP}(c_k)= \frac{\pi^{NP_{S_3}}(c_k)}{\pi^{NP_{S_3}}(c_j)}$, then $\gamma\pi^{UNP}(c_k)\geq1$ implies that $max_{A_1..A_n}(\frac{\pi^{NP_{S_3}}(c_k a_1..a_n)}{\pi^{NP_{S_3}}(c_j a_1..a_n)})\geq1$.

Example (continued): Transformation of Step 5 on network NP^{S_3} and its re-normalization gives network UNP of Figure 9.

On the left side, we provide network UNP before normalization while network of right side represents UNP after re-normalization. This latter shows that class c_2 is not totally possible ($\pi^{UNP}(c_2) < 1$). At the end, clearly only c_1 is totally possible given the uncertain instance to classify (see Figure 4). This result is exactly the same as the one achieved by directly applying Jeffrey's rule (see Figure 5).

5   Conclusion

This paper deals with possibilistic-based classification with uncertain inputs. More precisely, we first addressed revising possibilistic knowledge encoded by a naive product-based possibilistic network classifier using Jeffrey's rule which cannot be directly applied (since it is exponential in the number of attributes and attribute domains). Then we proposed a new and efficient algorithm for revising a naive product-based possibilistic network given uncertain inputs. This algorithm ensures same classification results as Jeffrey's rule while computations are accomplished in polynomial time in the number of attributes. Future work will address classification with uncertain inputs using non naive possibilistic classifiers as well as min-based possibilistic networks.

References

1. Haouari, Z.E.B., Amor, N.B., Mellouli, K.: Naive possibilistic network classifier. In: Proceedings of The Thirteenth Congress of International Association for Fuzzy-Set Management and Economy, SIGEF 2006 (2006)

2. Benferhat, S., Dubois, D., Garcia, L., Prade, H.: Possibilistic logic bases and possibilistic graphs. In: Proceedings of the 15th Conference on Uncertainty in Artificial Intelligence UAI 1999, Stockholm, pp. 57–64 (1999)
3. Borgelt, C., Gebhardt, J.: A naive bayes style possibilistic classifier. In: Proceedings of the 7th European Congress on Intelligent Techniques and Soft Computing EUFIT 1999, Aachen, Germany (1999)
4. Borgelt, C., Kruse, R.: Graphical Models: Methods for Data Analysis and Mining. John Wiley & Sons, Inc., New York (2002)
5. Borgelt, C., Kruse, R.: Learning from imprecise data: possibilistic graphical models. Computational Statistics & Data Analysis 38(4), 449–463 (2002)
6. Kruse, R., Borgelt, C., Gebhardt, J.: Possibilistic graphical models. In: Proceedings of International School for the Synthesis of Expert Knowledge (ISSEK 1998), Udine, Italy, pp. 51–68 (1998)
7. Dubois, D., Prade, H.: A synthetic view of belief revision with uncertain inputs in the framework of possibility theory. Int. J. of Approximate Reasoning 17(2–3), 295–324 (1997)
8. Jeffrey, R.C.: The Logic of Decision. McGraw Hill, New York (1965)
9. Pearl, J.: Probabilistic reasoning in intelligent systems: networks of plausible inference. Morgan Kaufmann Publishers Inc., San Francisco (1988)
10. Spohn, W.: Ordinal conditional functions: A dynamic theory of epistemic states. In: Harper, W.L., Skyrms, B. (eds.) Causation in decision, belief change, and statistics, vol. II, pp. 105–134. Kluwer Academic Publishers, Dordrecht (1988)
11. Zadeh, L.A.: Fuzzy sets as a basis for a theory of possibility. Fuzzy Sets and Systems 1(3) (1978)

Transitive Observation-Based Causation, Saliency, and the Markov Condition

Jean-François Bonnefon[1], Didier Dubois[2], and Henri Prade[2]

[1] CLLE-CNRS, Toulouse
bonnefon@univ-tlse2.fr
[2] IRIT-CNRS, Toulouse
{dubois,prade@irit}.fr

Abstract. If A caused B and B caused C, did A caused C? Although causality is generally regarded as transitive, some philosophers have questioned this assumption, and models of causality in artificial intelligence are often agnostic with respect to transitivity: They define causation, then check whether the definition makes all, or only some, causal arguments transitive. We consider two formal models of observation-based causation, which differ in the way they represent uncertainty. The quantitative model uses a standard probabilistic definition; the qualitative model uses a definition based on nonmonotonic consequence. The two models identify different sufficient conditions for the transitivity of causation: The Markov condition on events for the quantitative model, and a Saliency condition (if B is true then generally A is true) for the qualitative model. We explore the formal relations between these sufficient conditions, and between the underlying definitions of observation-based causation. These connections shed light on the range of applicability of both models.

1 Causal Transitivity

Making yourself some tea, you put your kettle on the fire. Moments later, the kettle whistles because the water is boiling. The water is boiling because it has been heated to 100 degrees. Is the kettle whistling because the water has been heated to 100 degrees?

Most of us agree that it is the case. The kettle example is one where it seems natural to accept that 'A causes C' results from 'A causes B' and 'B causes C.' That is, it makes causal transitivity appear unproblematic. Although it has always been a strong temptation to consider that causality on events is necessarily a transitive relation, philosophers have cogently argued that transitivity is not a natural property of causation [1,2,3] (and, more recently, [4,5,6]). Accordingly, models of causality in artificial intelligence such as [7] often take an agnostic stance with respect to transitivity, by defining causation first and then checking whether the definition makes all, or only some, causal arguments transitive. For example, Pearl [8] explains (p. 237) that the transitivity of causality becomes natural if it is understood in terms of indirect influence under a Markovian condition: if A causes B, B causes C *regardless of* A, then A is understood

S. Greco and T. Lukasiewicz (Eds.): SUM 2008, LNAI 5291, pp. 78–91, 2008.
© Springer-Verlag Berlin Heidelberg 2008

as causing (indirectly) C. We will indeed have more to say on the connection between transitivity and the Markov condition.

In this article, we consider two models of uncertain causation, which differ in the way they represent uncertainty. The first model uses the standard quantitative, probabilistic definition of 'A causes B' as $\Pr(B|A) > \Pr(B)$, or equivalently $\Pr(B \mid A) > \Pr(B \mid \bar{A})$, originally discussed by Goodman [9,10]. Note that this definition is appropriate for *observation-based causation*, rather than for intervention-based causation [8]. Accordingly, this article addresses with causality relations that are perceived (correctly or incorrectly) from merely observing the world, rather than from intervening on the world like an experimenter. Because information about the effects of intervention is not always available, intuitions of causation must sometimes do with observation and time only.[1]

The second model, recently proposed by the authors, uses a qualitative representation of uncertainty, based on nonmonotonic consequence relations. As we will see, sufficient conditions for the transitivity of causation laid bare by these two models are different. The quantitative model predicts that causation is transitive as soon as the causal chain is Markovian; and the qualitative model predicts that causation is transitive as soon as the first event in the chain is a salient, normal cause of the middle event. The question then arises of whether the two transitivity conditions are formally related at all; and if so, whether their formal relations reflect formal relations between the two underlying definitions of causation. To answer these questions, we need to:

1. Adapt the Markov condition to a qualitative setting;
   (a) check whether it is a sufficient condition for causal transitivity, in the qualitative sense;
   (b) check whether it is distinct from, stronger than, or weaker than the Saliency condition;
2. Adapt the Saliency condition to a quantitative setting;
   (a) check whether it is a sufficient condition for causal transitivity, in the quantitative sense;
   (b) check whether it is distinct from, stronger than, or weaker than the Markov condition;
3. Compare the notions of causality captured by the qualitative and quantitative conditions; in particular, we will:
   (a) Translate the qualitative definition in a probabilistic setting, and check whether it is stronger or weaker than the standard definition;
   (b) investigate the transitivity conditions of this translated definition.

We eventually point out a gap between the concepts of causation captured by each framework, which may explain the disagreement between them despite the fact that the qualitative framework can be viewed as a mathematical limit of the quantitative one, in terms of extreme, non-standard probabilities. Let us note that these quantitative and qualitative frameworks are both eligible for predicting judgments of causality from reported sequences of events [11]. In particular,

---

[1] See [11] in this volume for a more general review of causality formalisms.

their implementation does not raise significant problems from a computational point of view, and is not discussed any further in this article.

2   The Quantitative Markov Condition

The standard definition of causation, from a probabilistic perspective, is that the presence of the cause increases the probability of the effect. That is, 'A causes B' (where A, B, are events, not variables) if and only if $\Pr(B|A) > \Pr(B|\bar{A})$. Note that this expression precludes the cases where either $\Pr(A)$ or $\Pr(B)$ is equal to 0 or 1,[2] and that it can also be written $\Pr(B|A) > \Pr(B)$. Note also that, although it can be written in a symmetrical way expressing positive correlation, $\Pr(AB) > \Pr(A)\Pr(B)$, we will maintain the tradition of abusively assigning A and B the asymmetric roles of 'cause' and 'effect,' respectively (provided that the cause temporally precedes the effect). Still, the correlation might be spurious, but in the absence of appropriate interventions, a cause-effect relation may be indeed perceived by humans.

Causation in the probabilistic sense is not necessarily transitive. The fact that $\Pr(B|A) > \Pr(B|\bar{A})$, i.e., 'A causes B', together with the fact that $\Pr(C|B) > \Pr(C|\bar{B})$, i.e., 'B causes C', does not always imply that $\Pr(C|A) > \Pr(C|\bar{A})$, i.e., 'A causes C.' A detailed counterexample is presented later on (see Table 1; all tables display integer numbers, corresponding to the number of observations in each cell).

Table 1. A Counterexample to the transitivity of probabilistic causation when $\Pr(C|AB) = \Pr(C|B)$

	$\bar{A}$	A	
	$\bar{B}$ B	$\bar{B}$ B	
$\bar{C}$	2 4	3 4	
C	3 4	0 4	

Probabilistic causation, however, is transitive as soon as the two following conditions are jointly satisfied:

$$\Pr(C|AB) = \Pr(C|B) \qquad (1)$$
$$\Pr(C|A\bar{B}) = \Pr(C|\bar{B}) \qquad (2)$$

Conditions (1) and (2) are the two sides of the Markov condition on events. They express that C is independent of A in the context of B, and in the context of $\bar{B}$, respectively. In the following, we will speak of the 'positive' and 'negative' sides of the Markov condition on events, respectively.

---

[2] In this paper, all probabilities are positive for the sake of simplicity. Using zero conditional probabilities would require a full conditional probabilities framework[12], which is outside the scope of this paper.

Remark 1. Both sides are covered by the symmetric expression of the Markov condition $\Pr(abc)\Pr(b) = \Pr(ab)\Pr(bc)$, for Boolean variables a, b, c having values A, $\bar{A}$, etc. This symmetric expression allows for $\Pr(b) = 0$, which is not the case for the conditional, asymmetric formulation, using Kolmogorov conditional probabilities.

Proposition 1. *If the two sides of the Markov condition on events are satisfied, then it follows from* $\Pr(B|A) > \Pr(B|\bar{A})$ *and* $\Pr(C|B) > \Pr(C|\bar{B})$ *that* $\Pr(C|A) > \Pr(C|\bar{A})$.

Proof. $\Pr(C|A) = \Pr(C|AB)\Pr(B|A) + \Pr(C|A\bar{B})(1 - \Pr(B|A))$. Likewise, $\Pr(C|\bar{A}) = \Pr(C|\bar{A}B)\Pr(B|\bar{A})+\Pr(C|\bar{A}\bar{B})(1-\Pr(B|\bar{A}))$. From (1), $\Pr(C|AB) = \Pr(C|\bar{A}B) = \Pr(C|B)$; From (2), $\Pr(C|A\bar{B}) = \Pr(C|\bar{A}\bar{B}) = \Pr(C|\bar{B})$. Hence, $\Pr(C|A) - \Pr(C|\bar{A}) = (\Pr(C|AB) - \Pr(C|A\bar{B}))(\Pr(B|A) - \Pr(B|\bar{A})) = (\Pr(C|B)-\Pr(C|\bar{B}))(\Pr(B|A)-\Pr(B|\bar{A}))$. This quantity is strictly positive from the definitions of 'A causes B' and 'B causes C.'   □

Remark 2. This proof is inspired from Eells and Sober [13], who studied the transitivity of their own version of probabilistic causation.

It will be relevant later on to note that (1) alone is not sufficient to ensure transitivity. Table 1 presents an example where A causes B and B causes C, in the probabilistic sense: $\Pr(B|A) = 8/11$ is greater than $\Pr(B) = 16/24$, and $\Pr(C|B) = 8/16$ is greater than $\Pr(C) = 11/24$. Furthermore, the positive aspect (1) of the Markov condition on events is satisfied since $\Pr(C|BA) = 4/8 = \Pr(C|B\bar{A})$. However, A cannot be said to cause C, since $\Pr(C|A) = 4/11$ is *less* than $\Pr(C) = 11/24$. As it can be expected, the negative aspect (2) of the Markov condition on events is not satisfied, since $\Pr(C|\bar{B}A) = 0$ is different from $\Pr(C|\bar{B}\bar{A}) = 3/5$.

Table 2. Postulates and characteristic properties of System P

	PREMISE 1	PREMISE 2	CONCLUSION
LEFT EQUIVALENCE	$E \equiv F$	$E \mathrel{\vert\!\sim} G$	$F \mathrel{\vert\!\sim} G$
RIGHT WEAKENING	$E \mathrel{\vert\!\sim} F$	$F \models G$	$E \mathrel{\vert\!\sim} G$
AND	$E \mathrel{\vert\!\sim} F$	$E \mathrel{\vert\!\sim} G$	$E \mathrel{\vert\!\sim} F \wedge G$
OR	$E \mathrel{\vert\!\sim} G$	$F \mathrel{\vert\!\sim} G$	$E \vee F \mathrel{\vert\!\sim} G$
CAUTIOUS MONOTONY	$E \mathrel{\vert\!\sim} F$	$E \mathrel{\vert\!\sim} G$	$E \wedge F \mathrel{\vert\!\sim} G$
CUT	$E \mathrel{\vert\!\sim} F$	$E \wedge F \mathrel{\vert\!\sim} G$	$E \mathrel{\vert\!\sim} G$

3   A Qualitative Saliency Condition

Because probabilistic information is not always available for causal inference, Bonnefon and colleagues [14,15] offered a qualitative counterpart to probabilistic conceptions of causality. This framework takes advantage of so-called *non-monotonic consequence relations,* which make it possible to express that the occurrence of B is generally, normally a consequence of the occurrence of A, but that exceptional situations may arise—without the need for specifying how frequent these exceptions are.

Formally, the relation 'If A is true then normally B is true' is written $A \mathrel{|\!\sim} B$, read A 'snake' B. The snake operator follows the requirements of System P [16]. That is, $\mathrel{|\!\sim}$ is reflexive and satisfies the postulates and properties summarized in Table 2. Empirical studies repeatedly demonstrated that the postulates of System P provide an adequate description of the way human reasoners handle exception-laden rules [17,18].

Based on this representation of background knowledge, perceived causation is defined in the following terms: an event A is perceived to cause another event B in a context K if B was false before A took place (which was normal in context K), and became true afterwards (B is normal as well in context $A \wedge K$). Formally:

Definition 1. *Assume that an agent learns of the sequence* $\neg B_{t1}$, A_{t1}, B_{t2} *where* $t_2 > t_1$. *Call* K_{t1} *(the* context*) the conjunction of all other facts known by the agent at time* t_1. *If the agent possesses the pieces of default knowledge that* $K \mathrel{|\!\sim} \neg B$ *and* $A \wedge K \mathrel{|\!\sim} B$, *the agent will perceive* A_{t1} *to cause* B_{t2} *in context* K_{t1}, *denoted* $K_{t1} : A_{t1} \rhd B_{t2}$, *and abridged* $A \rhd B$ *when there is no risk of ambiguity.*

This definition has a number of formal properties that are explored in [15]. Especially relevant to our current purpose is the fact that perceived causality defined in this way is not generally transitive: it is not always possible to infer $A_{t1} \rhd C_{t3}$ from $A_{t1} \rhd B_{t2}$ and $B_{t2} \rhd C_{t3}$ (where $t_3 > t_2 > t_1$; for the sake of simplicity, we shall drop the time indices from now on). Transitivity holds, however, as soon as the following requirement is satisfied:

$$K \wedge B \mathrel{|\!\sim} A \tag{3}$$

The proof is given in [15], and uses CAUTIOUS MONOTONY and CUT. The condition $K \wedge B \mathrel{|\!\sim} A$ means that observing B in context K normally leads one to expect that A has occurred. In other terms, it means that A is a very common and salient cause of B, so common and so salient that it is normally the first explanation that one will imagine, by default, to explain the occurrence of B.

4   A Qualitative Markov Condition

In this section, we focus on the qualitative case by (a) exploring the links between the qualitative Saliency condition and a qualitative rendition of the Markov condition; and (b) exploring the links between this qualitative rendition and the transitivity of qualitative causation. One qualitative rendition of (1) and (2) is:

$$K \wedge A \wedge B \mathrel{|\!\sim} C \text{ if and only if } K \wedge B \mathrel{|\!\sim} C \tag{4}$$

$$K \wedge A \wedge \bar{B} \mathrel{|\!\sim} C \text{ if and only if } K \wedge \bar{B} \mathrel{|\!\sim} C \tag{5}$$

The qualitative Saliency condition implies half of the qualitative Markov condition. More precisely, the Saliency condition (3) implies the positive side (4) but not the negative side (5).

Proposition 2. *If $K \wedge B \hspace{0.5mm}\vdash\hspace{-2mm}\sim A$, then $K \wedge A \wedge B \hspace{0.5mm}\vdash\hspace{-2mm}\sim C$ if and only if $K \wedge B \hspace{0.5mm}\vdash\hspace{-2mm}\sim C$.*

Proof. The proof simply uses CUT on $K \wedge B \hspace{0.5mm}\vdash\hspace{-2mm}\sim A$ and $K \wedge A \wedge B \hspace{0.5mm}\vdash\hspace{-2mm}\sim C$ for $\Rightarrow$, and CAUTIOUS MONOTONY on $K \wedge B \hspace{0.5mm}\vdash\hspace{-2mm}\sim A$ and $K \wedge B \hspace{0.5mm}\vdash\hspace{-2mm}\sim C$ for $\Leftarrow$. □

However, $K \wedge B \hspace{0.5mm}\vdash\hspace{-2mm}\sim A$ does not imply the negative aspect of the Markov condition. It is possible to have $K \wedge B \hspace{0.5mm}\vdash\hspace{-2mm}\sim A$ but not $K \wedge A \wedge \bar{B} \hspace{0.5mm}\vdash\hspace{-2mm}\sim C \equiv K \wedge \bar{B} \hspace{0.5mm}\vdash\hspace{-2mm}\sim C$. For example, it is possible to have both $K \wedge B \hspace{0.5mm}\vdash\hspace{-2mm}\sim A$ and $K \wedge \bar{B} \hspace{0.5mm}\vdash\hspace{-2mm}\sim \bar{A}$; and this last relation prohibits to derive $K \wedge A \wedge \bar{B} \hspace{0.5mm}\vdash\hspace{-2mm}\sim C$ from $K \wedge \bar{B} \hspace{0.5mm}\vdash\hspace{-2mm}\sim C$. In a qualitative setting, the Saliency condition does not necessarily imply the negative side of the Markov condition on events.

Remark 3. Note that (5) could easily be derived from $K \wedge \bar{B} \hspace{0.5mm}\vdash\hspace{-2mm}\sim A$. However, if both $K \wedge B \hspace{0.5mm}\vdash\hspace{-2mm}\sim A$ and $K \wedge \bar{B} \hspace{0.5mm}\vdash\hspace{-2mm}\sim A$ hold, then (by OR) $(K \wedge B) \vee (K \wedge \bar{B}) \hspace{0.5mm}\vdash\hspace{-2mm}\sim A$, and ultimately $K \hspace{0.5mm}\vdash\hspace{-2mm}\sim A$. As shown in [15], the fact that $K \hspace{0.5mm}\vdash\hspace{-2mm}\sim A$ precludes that $A \triangleright B$ for any B: In the qualitative model, normal events cannot be perceived as causes of abnormal events. Thus, adding the condition $K \wedge \bar{B} \hspace{0.5mm}\vdash\hspace{-2mm}\sim A$ to $K \wedge B \hspace{0.5mm}\vdash\hspace{-2mm}\sim A$ would allow to derive (4) and (5) instead of just (4), but would defeat the whole point of reasoning about causes.

Remarkably, and contrary to the quantitative case, the positive side of the qualitative Markov condition is sufficient to give transitivity.

Proposition 3. *If $K \wedge A \hspace{0.5mm}\vdash\hspace{-2mm}\sim B$, $K \wedge B \hspace{0.5mm}\vdash\hspace{-2mm}\sim C$, and $(K \wedge A \wedge B \hspace{0.5mm}\vdash\hspace{-2mm}\sim C$ if and only if $K \wedge B \hspace{0.5mm}\vdash\hspace{-2mm}\sim C)$, then $K \wedge A \hspace{0.5mm}\vdash\hspace{-2mm}\sim C$.*

Proof. From $K \wedge B \hspace{0.5mm}\vdash\hspace{-2mm}\sim C$ and $(K \wedge A \wedge B \hspace{0.5mm}\vdash\hspace{-2mm}\sim C$ if and only if $K \wedge B \hspace{0.5mm}\vdash\hspace{-2mm}\sim C)$, we get $K \wedge A \wedge B \hspace{0.5mm}\vdash\hspace{-2mm}\sim C$. From this relation and $K \wedge A \hspace{0.5mm}\vdash\hspace{-2mm}\sim B$ we arrive at $K \wedge A \hspace{0.5mm}\vdash\hspace{-2mm}\sim C$ by applying CUT. □

Corollary 1. *If an agent is in position to believe $A \triangleright B$ and $B \triangleright C$ as per Definition 1, and if the agent believes that $(K \wedge A \wedge B \hspace{0.5mm}\vdash\hspace{-2mm}\sim C$ if and only if $K \wedge B \hspace{0.5mm}\vdash\hspace{-2mm}\sim C)$, then the agent is in a position to believe $A \triangleright C$.*

Proof. To be in a position to believe $A \triangleright C$, as per Definition 1, it is enough that the agent (i) believes $K \hspace{0.5mm}\vdash\hspace{-2mm}\sim \neg C$. This condition is satisfied because the agent is in a position to believe $B \triangleright C$; (ii) the agent believes $K \wedge A \hspace{0.5mm}\vdash\hspace{-2mm}\sim C$. This condition is satisfied as shown by Proposition 3; and (iii) the agent knows of a sequence $\neg C_t, A_t, C_{t'}$ where $t' > t$. Condition (iii) is satisfied as shown in [15]. □

Nevertheless, it can be checked that the positive side of the qualitative Markov condition does not imply the Saliency condition. To show this, we use a model of System P where the former holds but not the latter. Consider a qualitative possibility distribution induced by the well-ordered partition [19]: $(\bar{A} \wedge \bar{B} \wedge \bar{C}, C), (A \cup B) \setminus C)$. Namely $\forall s \notin A \cup B \cup C, \pi(s) = 1$; $\forall s \in C, \pi(s) = \alpha$; $\forall s \in (A \cup B) \setminus C, \pi(s) = \beta$, with $1 > \alpha > \beta$. Translating $A \hspace{0.5mm}\vdash\hspace{-2mm}\sim B$ as $\Pi(A \cap B) > \Pi(A \cap \bar{B})$, where $\Pi(A) = \max_{s \in A} \pi(s)$ it is easy to check that:

- $\not\hspace{-0.3em}\sim \bar{B}$ and $\not\hspace{-0.3em}\sim \bar{C}$ since $\Pi(B) < 1$ and $\Pi(C) < 1$
- $A \hspace{-0.3em}\sim B, B \hspace{-0.3em}\sim C$ since $\Pi(A \wedge B) = \Pi(B \wedge C) = \alpha$, assuming $A \cap B \cap C \neq \emptyset$; assuming $A \cap \bar{B} \cap C = \emptyset$, $\Pi(A \wedge \bar{B}) = \Pi(B \wedge \bar{C}) = \beta$
- Assuming that $\bar{A} \cap B \cap C \neq \emptyset$, $B \hspace{-0.3em}\sim A$ does not hold since $\Pi(\bar{A} \wedge B) = \alpha$.

It may seem surprising that, in the qualitative setting, the positive side of the Markov condition is sufficient for transitivity, although it is weaker than the Saliency condition. We can explain this by exploiting the natural connection between conditional assertions of the form $A \hspace{-0.3em}\sim B$ and conditional probabilities $\Pr(B \mid A)$. Indeed, $A \hspace{-0.3em}\sim B$ can be formally interpreted as a pair of events of the form $(AB, A\bar{B})$, and the logic of conditional assertions has a three-valued semantics based on this representation [20]. $\Pr(B \mid A)$ is entirely determined by $\Pr(AB)$ and $\Pr(A\bar{B})$, and there is a closely related semantics of conditional assertions, whereby the statement of $A \hspace{-0.3em}\sim B$ comes down to an infinitesimal probability statement:

$$A \hspace{-0.3em}\sim B \iff \Pr(B \mid A) > 1 - \epsilon,$$

where ϵ is a positive number arbitrarily close to 0. The properties of reasoning with such extreme probability statements were studied in [21,22] and turned out to be the properties of nonmonotonic reasoning laid bare in System P. In fact, the calculus of infinitesimal conditional probabilities of this form is equivalent to System P [23].

Now, it is clear that $B \rhd C$ reads $\Pr(C \mid B) > 1 - \epsilon$ and $\Pr(C) < \epsilon$. Hence:

- From $A \rhd B$ and $B \rhd C$ we get $\Pr(AB) > (1 - \epsilon)\Pr(A)$ and $\Pr(BC) > (1 - \epsilon)\Pr(B)$; it yields:
- $\Pr(AB)\Pr(BC) > (1 - O(\epsilon))\Pr(A)\Pr(B)$.
- Which, with the positive Markov condition, yields: $\Pr(ABC)\Pr(B) > (1 - O(\epsilon))\Pr(A)\Pr(B)$.
- Simplifying by $\Pr(B)$: $\Pr(AC) \geq \Pr(ABC) > (1 - O(\epsilon))\Pr(A)$. Hence $A \rhd C$.

5   A Quantitative Saliency Condition

In this section, we focus on the quantitative case by (a) exploring the links between the quantitative Markov condition and a quantitative rendition of the Saliency condition; and (b) exploring the links between this quantitative rendition and the transitivity of quantitative causation. In agreement with the broadest probabilistic understanding of $\hspace{-0.3em}\sim$, we use the following quantitative rendition of the Saliency condition (3):

$$\Pr(A \mid B) \geq k > 0.5. \tag{6}$$

for some appropriate value of the threshold k. We first consider the limit case where $k = 1$. As we will see, this limit case is already informative enough; we will only briefly consider the general case where $0.5 < k < 1$.

The fact that $k = 1$ in (6), i.e., that $\Pr(A \mid B) = 1$, implies the positive side of the quantitative Markov condition. More precisely, $\Pr(A \mid B) = 1$ implies (1) but not (2).

Table 3. A Counterexample to $\Pr(C \mid A\bar{B}) = \Pr(C \mid \bar{B})$ where $\Pr(A \mid B) = 1$

	$\bar{A}$	A		
	$\bar{B}$	B	$\bar{B}$	B
$\bar{C}$	4	0	1	1
C	2	0	1	1

Proposition 4. *If* $\Pr(A \mid B) = 1$ *then* $\Pr(C|AB) = \Pr(C|B)$.

Proof. $\Pr(A \mid B) = 1$ implies $\Pr(\bar{A}B) = 0$, and therefore both $\Pr(AB) = \Pr(B)$ and $\Pr(ABC) = \Pr(BC)$. Therefore, $\Pr(ABC)\Pr(B) = \Pr(AB)\Pr(BC)$, which gives (1). □

Just like qualitative, the positive aspect of the Markov condition does not imply the qualitative Saliency condition, (1) does not imply $\Pr(A \mid B) = 1$. See again Table 1 for a counterexample. $\Pr(A \mid B) = 1$ is thus a stronger condition than the positive aspect (1) of the Markov condition on events. However, no such relation exists between $\Pr(A \mid B) = 1$ and the negative aspect of the Markov condition on events: $\Pr(A \mid B) = 1$ does not imply (2). Table 3 displays a simple counterexample where $\Pr(A \mid B) = 1$ but $\Pr(C \mid A\bar{B}) = 1/2$ is different from $\Pr(C \mid \bar{B}) = 3/8$.

Neither does $\Pr(A \mid B) = 1$ imply transitivity. Table 4 displays an example where A causes B and B causes C, in the probabilistic sense: $\Pr(B \mid A) = 1/6$ is greater than $\Pr(B) = 1/20$, and $\Pr(C \mid B) = 1$ is greater than $\Pr(C) = 8/20$. Furthermore, $\Pr(A \mid B) = 1$. But A cannot be said to cause C, as $\Pr(C \mid A) = 2/6$ is *lower* than $\Pr(C) = 8/20$. Unsurprisingly, the negative Markov condition is not satisfied, since $\Pr(C \mid \bar{B}A) = 1/5$ is different from $\Pr(C \mid \bar{B}\bar{A}) = 6/14$.

We have considered so far the limit case where $K \wedge B \mathbin{\mid\!\sim} A$ is translated as $\Pr(A \mid B) = 1$. Even in this limit case, causation is not necessarily transitive, since $\Pr(C \mid A)$ is not necessarily greater than $\Pr(C)$ when $\Pr(C \mid B) > \Pr(C)$ and $\Pr(B \mid A) > \Pr(B)$. Now, it can be shown that the optimal lower bound of $\Pr(C \mid A)$ is an *increasing function* of the threshold k with $\Pr(A \mid B) = k$.

Indeed, as shown in [24], the optimal lower bound of $\Pr(C \mid A)$ expresses as:

$$\Pr(C \mid A) \geq \Pr(B \mid A) \cdot \max\left(0, 1 - \frac{1 - \Pr(C \mid B)}{\Pr(A \mid B)}\right) \qquad (7)$$

Table 4. A Counterexample to transitivity where $\Pr(A \mid B) = 1$

	$\bar{A}$	A		
	$\bar{B}$	B	$\bar{B}$	B
$\bar{C}$	8	0	4	0
C	6	0	1	1

It is easily checked from (7) that the optimal lower bound of $\Pr(C \mid A)$ increases with $\Pr(A \mid B)$, and is thus an increasing function of k. Therefore, all other probabilities being equal, if it is not guaranteed that $\Pr(C \mid A) > \Pr(C)$ when $k = 1$, then it cannot be guaranteed that $\Pr(C \mid A) > \Pr(C)$ for any value of $k > 0.5$.

6   Discussion

In summary, the following results have been obtained. In the qualitative setting, using the nonmonotonic Definition 1 of causation, the positive Markov condition on events is sufficient for transitivity to hold: there is no need for the negative Markov condition to hold. Because the Saliency condition implies the positive aspect of the Markov condition (albeit not its negative aspect), it is itself a sufficient condition for transitivity.

In the quantitative setting, using the probabilistic definition of causation as $\Pr(B \mid A) > \Pr(B)$, the positive Markov condition on events alone (without the negative side) is not a sufficient condition for transitivity. In this setting, the Saliency condition implies the positive aspect of the Markov condition, but not its negative aspect; and it is not itself a sufficient condition for transitivity. In this section, we consider whether the pattern of results obtained for the transitivity conditions is a consequence of formal relations between the underlying definitions of causation in the two models.

6.1   Two Views of Causation

The connection between nonmonotonic inference and conditional probability, as recalled above, clarifies the difference between probabilistic causality developed after [9], and nonmonotonic causality. The nonmonotonic definition, couched in probabilistic terms, comes down to the following requirements: A causes B if and only if B is little probable per se and very probable in the context where A is true. The weakest quantitative rendition of this definition is:

$$\Pr(B) < \Pr(\bar{B}) \text{ and } \Pr(B \mid A) > \Pr(\bar{B} \mid A). \tag{8}$$

Remark 4. Note that this definition of causation is genuinely asymmetric, contrary to the standard probabilistic definition, which expresses a positive correlation between events.

This weakest rendition already implies $\Pr(B \mid A) > \Pr(B)$ since (8) implies $\Pr(B \mid A) > 0.5 > \Pr(B)$. Hence, the qualitative approach leads to a definition of causality that, even in its weakest quantitative counterpart, is clearly stronger than Good's standard probabilistic definition. Causes in the qualitative sense are always causes in the quantitative sense, but there are probabilistic causes that the qualitative setting does not recognize as causes.

There are two classes of such situations. First, situations where, although the presence of the cause does increase the probability of the effect, this latter probability stays lower than .5:

$$\Pr(B) < P(B \mid A) < \frac{1}{2}. \tag{9}$$

In these situations, 'A causes B' in the probabilistic but not in the qualitative sense, since the normal course of things is to observe $\bar{B}$ in the context of A.

Remark 5. From the perspective of scientific discovery, it certainly makes sense to talk about the causal role of A in situation (9). And indeed, the probabilistic definition of causality was proposed with a view to capture the nature of scientific explanation in experimental fields (see [25] for a retrospective collection of essays). It may be more debatable whether (9) corresponds to what lay persons would declare as expressing causality. The close inspection of available experimental data [26,27] shows that perceptions of causality in this situation are at best moderate. Note, however, that $\Pr(B)$ and $P(B \mid A)$ always have the same order of magnitude in these experiments.

Although (9) is not a situation recognized as causation by the qualitative model, it may qualify as a situation of 'facilitation.' In [14,15] the facilitation relation is defined as one where B is abnormal, but becomes neither abnormal nor normal when A occurs. There is another class of situations of probabilistic causation that does not match the requirements for qualitative causation. This class of situations corresponds to cases when the cause increases the probability of an effect that was already highly probable:

$$\Pr(B \mid A) > \Pr(B) > \frac{1}{2}. \tag{10}$$

There is no way to express this reinforcement effect in the qualitative setting, due to a lack of expressive power. For A to cause B in the qualitative sense, it is necessary that the perception of B changes from that of an abnormal event, to that of a normal event when A occurs. A cannot be said to be a qualitative cause of B when B belongs to the normal course of the world even in the absence of A.

Remark 6. A limit situation occurs when B is neither intrinsically normal nor abnormal, but becomes normal in the presence of A. In other terms, one is totally ignorant about whether B is true or not, but starts believing that B is the case when learning that A has occurred. In a qualitative setting, this expresses as:

$$K \not\hspace{-2pt}\sim B \text{ and } K \not\hspace{-2pt}\sim \bar{B} \text{ and } K \wedge A \hspace{-1pt}\sim B$$

The probabilistic counterpart to this limit situation may be considered to be that wherein $\Pr(B) = \Pr(\bar{B})$. This is debatable, though, as it presupposes that ignorance about B is confused with knowledge about the randomness of B. This situation is not considered one of causation in [15]. Rather, following [28], it is considered one of 'justification.' That is, one where, rather than seeing A as the cause of the occurrence of B, agents may consider A the justification in their belief that B was going to happen.

Table 5. Counterexample to transitivity under saliency and strengthened causation

	$\bar{A}$	A		
	$\bar{B}$	B	$\bar{B}$	B
$\bar{C}$	55	0	13	8
C	10	0	4	10

6.2   Consequences for Transitivity

There is a difference of nature between the standard probabilistic definition of causation and the definition inspired by the qualitative model (notwithstanding the fact that the first is based on a symmetric property, whilst the second is asymmetric). Quantitatively, causality is understood in terms of a positive influence of one event on another one, regardless of the prior probability or this last event. Qualitatively, causality is restricted to situations of tendency reversal, where an abnormal state of affairs becomes normal upon the occurrence of some event.

Because the quantitative rendition (8) of the qualitative definition is stronger than the standard probabilistic model, the question arises of whether Saliency would ensure the transitivity of this stronger notion of causation. The following counterexample shows that this is not the case. Suppose A causes B and B causes C in the sense of (8), and that Saliency strictly holds, i.e., $\Pr(A \mid B) = 1$. Suppose observations as in Table 5. Note that $\Pr(B) < \frac{1}{2}$; $\Pr(C) < \frac{1}{2}$. Moreover $\Pr(B \mid A) = \frac{18}{35} > \frac{1}{2}$; $\Pr(C \mid B) = \frac{10}{18} > \frac{1}{2}$; However, $\Pr(C \mid A) = \frac{14}{35} < \frac{1}{2}$. One may think of strengthening again the definition of causation by increasing the threshold k and change (8) into what could be called k-causation:

$$\Pr(B) \leq 1 - k < 0.5 \text{ and } \Pr(B \mid A) \geq k. \tag{11}$$

However we can show by means of the generic counterexample in Table 6 that the Saliency condition is not sufficient to ensure transitivity of k-causation, however close is k to 1. Indeed, the conditions $\Pr(B) \leq 1 - k$; $\Pr(C) \leq 1 - k$ can be achieved by choosing a sufficiently high value of x, tuning w accordingly for a fixed value of k. Furthermore, when $0.5 < k < 1$, it is clear that $\Pr(B \mid A) = \frac{4+k}{6-k} > k$; $\Pr(C \mid B) = \frac{5k}{4+k} > k$; but $\Pr(C \mid A) = \frac{5k}{6-k} < k$. What it means is that when k increases and the notion of k-causation becomes more demanding, there always exists a small range of situations that do not sanction transitivity. This range shrinks when k increases—and it vanishes when $k = 1$.

Table 6. Counterexample to the transitivity of k-causation under saliency

	$\bar{A}$		A	
	$\bar{B}$	B	$\bar{B}$	B
$\bar{C}$	x	0	w	$2w$
C	y	0	0	$\frac{5wk}{2(1-k)}$

Note that replacing Saliency by the two Markov conditions will not do any better at ensuring the transitivity of k-causation. Indeed, suppose $\Pr(C|B) = \Pr(B|A) = k > 0.5$. Using both Markov conditions, $\Pr(C|A) = \Pr(C|B)\Pr(B|A) + \Pr(C|\bar{B})(1 - \Pr(B|A))$. Therefore: $\Pr(C|A) = k^2 + \Pr(C|\bar{B})(1 - k)$. Letting $\Pr(C|\bar{B}) < k$, we arrive at $\Pr(C|A) < k$.

Although, in the strictest sense, the transitivity of k-causation can fail under Markov conditions and Saliency, the condition $\Pr(C|A) \geq \Pr(C \mid B)\Pr(B \mid A) > k^2$ is always derivable from $\Pr(B|A) > k$ and $\Pr(C|B) > k$, under the saliency condition $\Pr(A|B) = 1$, from equation (7), with no other assumption. If $\Pr(B|A)$ and $\Pr(C|B)$ are largely greater than k, then it is possible that $\Pr(C|A) \geq \Pr(C \mid B)\Pr(B \mid A) > k$. Furthermore, from a psychological perspective, it is conceivable that, for some high values of k^2, some individuals may perceive the causal chain as transitive in situations where $k^2 < \Pr(C|A) < k$.

7   Final Words

A case can be made for the idea that the two models we have compared in this article do not address the same phenomenon. The probabilistic definition of causation introduced after Good, and popularized by epistemologists, aims at detecting a positive influence in data observed from natural phenomena. Such causal relations can be read from a careful scrutiny of contingency tables. In contrast, the qualitative model captures a more mundane, commonsense, everyday variant of causation— whereby the change of a state of affairs is understood as caused by the prior occurrence of some abnormal event. This form of causal thinking often comes down to explaining an abnormal fact by some unexpected circumstances. These two kinds of causal thinking are quite distinct, as shown in this article, and perhaps it is no surprise that their transitivity conditions observe a complex pattern of relations.

This observation raises the (largely unaddressed) empirical question of the transitivity of everyday causal thinking. Are everyday inferences on causal chains sensitive to Saliency, or to Markovian considerations? In parallel to the present formal research, we collected data on the perceived transitivity of causal chains. These chains were always *quantitatively* Markovian, but did or did not meet the *qualitative* Saliency condition [29]. E.g., of the two following quantitatively Markovian chains, the first meets the qualitative Saliency condition, but the second does not:

1. Émilie had put her kettle on the fire. The kettle whistled because the water was boiling. The water was boiling because it had been heated to 100 degrees.
2. Alice was asleep under an apple tree. She woke up because an apple fell on her. The apple fell on her because it was ripe.

All results so far show that chains like the first are perceived as transitive (the kettle whistled because the water had been heated to 100 degrees), whereas chains like the second are not (Alice did not wake up because the apple was ripe). These results suggest that lay reasoners may be prone to bypass Markovian considerations in favor of qualitative Saliency considerations. If we accept that qualitative Saliency is more easily noticed and processed that Markovian considerations, then it can be expected that individuals will tend to reject transitivity when Saliency is not satisfied, even though the causal chain is Markovian.

Acknowledgements. This research was supported by a grant from the Agence Nationale de la Recherche, project number NT05-3-44479.

References

1. Hesslow, G.: The transitivity of causation. Analysis 41, 130–133 (1981)
2. Lowe, E.J.: For want of a nail. Analysis 40, 50–52 (1980)
3. Mackie, J.L.: The transitivity of counterfactuals and causation. Analysis 40, 53–54 (1980)
4. Bjornsson, G.: How effects depend on their causes,why causal transitivity fails, and why we care about causation. Philosophical Studies 133, 349–390 (2007)
5. Hall, N.: Causation and the price of transitivity. Journal of Philosophy 97, 198–222 (2000)
6. Hitchcock, C.: The intransitivity of causation revealed in equations and graphs. Journal of Philosophy 98, 273–299 (2001)
7. Halpern, J., Pearl, J.: Causes and explanations: A structural-model approach — part 1: Causes. British Journal for the Philosophy of Science 56, 843–887 (2005)
8. Pearl, J.: Causality: Models, Reasoning, and Inference. Cambridge University Press, Cambridge (2000)
9. Good, I.J.: A causal calculus I. British Journal for the Philosophy of Science 11, 305–318 (1961)
10. Good, I.J.: A causal calculus II. British Journal for the Philosophy of Science 12, 43–51 (1962)
11. Benferhat, S., Bonnefon, J.F., Chassy, P., Da Silva Neves, R.M., Dubois, D., Dupin de Saint-Cyr, F., Kayser, D., Nouioua, F., Nouioua-Boutouhami, S., Prade, H., Smaoui, S.: A comparative study of six formal models of causal ascription. In: SUM 2008 (2008)
12. Coletti, G., Scozzafava, R.: Probabilistic Logic in a Coherent Setting. Kluwer Academic Publishers, Dordrecht (2002)
13. Eells, E., Sober, E.: Probabilistic causality and the question of transitivity. Philosophy of Science 50, 35–57 (1983)
14. Bonnefon, J.F., Da Silva Neves, R.M., Dubois, D., Prade, H.: Background default knowledge and causality ascriptions. In: Brewka, G., Coradeschi, S., Perini, A., Traverso, P. (eds.) Proceedings of the 17th European Conference on Artificial Intelligence (ECAI 2006), Zurich, pp. 11–15. IOS Press, Amsterdam (2006)
15. Bonnefon, J.F., Da Silva Neves, R.M., Dubois, D., Prade, H.: Predicting causality ascriptions from background knowledge: Model and experimental validation. International Journal of Approximate Reasoning 48, 752–765 (2008)
16. Kraus, S., Lehmann, D., Magidor, M.: Nonmonotonic reasoning, preferential models and cumulative logics. Artificial Intelligence 44, 167–207 (1990)
17. Benferhat, S., Bonnefon, J.F., Da Silva Neves, R.M.: An overview of possibilistic handling of default reasoning, with experimental studies. Synthese 146, 53–70 (2005)
18. Pfeifer, N., Kleiter, G.D.: Coherence and nonmonotonicity in human nonmonotonic reasoning. Synthese 146, 93–109 (2005)

19. Benferhat, S., Dubois, D., Prade, H.: Possibilistic and standard probabilistic semantics of conditional knowledge bases. Journal of Logic and Computation 9, 873–895 (1999)

20. Dubois, D., Prade, H.: Conditional objects as nonmonotonic consequence relations: Main results. In: Doyle, J., Sandewall, E., Torasso, P. (eds.) KR 1994: Principles of Knowledge Representation and Reasoning, pp. 170–177. Morgan Kaufmann, San Francisco (1994)

21. Adams, E.: The logic of conditionals: An application of probability to deductive logic. Reidel, Dordrecht (1975)

22. Pearl, J.: Probabilistic Reasoning in Intelligent Systems. Morgan Kaufmann, San Mateo (1988)

23. Benferhat, S., Dubois, D., Prade, H.: Nonmonotonic reasoning, conditional objects and possibility theory. Artificial Intelligence 92, 259–276 (1997)

24. Dubois, D., Godo, L., Lopez de Mantaras, R., Prade, H.: Qualitative reasoning with imprecise probabilities. Journal of Intelligent Information Systems 2, 319–363 (1993)

25. Salmon, W.C.: Causality and Explanation. Oxford University Press, New York (1998)

26. Buehner, M., Cheng, P., Clifford, D.: From covariation to causation: A test of the assumption of causal power. Journal of Experimental Psychology: Learning, Memory, and Cognition 29, 1119–1140 (2003)

27. Lober, K., Shanks, D.: Is causal induction based on causal power? Critique of Cheng. Psychological Review 107(2000), 195–212 (1997)

28. Dubois, D., Fariñas Del Cerro, L., Herzig, A., Prade, H.: A roadmap of qualitative independence. In: Dubois, D., Prade, H., Klement, E.P. (eds.) Fuzzy Sets, Logics and Reasoning about Knowledge. Applied Logic series, vol. 15, pp. 325–350. Kluwer, Dordrecht (1999)

29. Bonnefon, J.F., Da Silva Neves, R.M., Dubois, D., Prade, H.: Is causality transitive? It depends on the alternatives. In: The European Cognitive Science Conference, Delphi, Greece (May 2007)

A Family of Tolerant Antidivision Operators for Database Fuzzy Querying

Patrick Bosc and Olivier Pivert

Irisa – Enssat, University of Rennes 1
Technopole Anticipa 22305 Lannion Cedex France
bosc@enssat.fr, pivert@enssat.fr

Abstract. In this paper, we present an algebraic relational operator called antidivision and we describe a range of interpretations that can be attached to this operator in the context of databases with fuzzy relations (i.e., relations that contain weighted tuples). We also study the way(s) this operator can be made tolerant to exceptions in order to limit the risk of obtaining empty answers.

1 Introduction

The idea of extending usual Boolean queries with preferences has become a hot topic in the database community. One of the advantages of this approach is to deliver discriminated answers rather than flat sets of elements. Fuzzy sets are a natural means to represent preferences and many works have been undertaken to define queries where fuzzy predicates can be introduced inside user queries. The objective of this article is to illustrate the expressiveness of fuzzy sets with a certain type of queries, that we call antidivision queries, in the context of regular databases. Like other operators, the regular antidivision is not flexible at all and small variations in the data may lead to totally different results. To counter this behavior, two types of tolerant antidivision operators founded on fuzzy sets are suggested. First, let us make clear what we mean by antidivision. Let r be a relation of schema $R(X, A)$ and s a relation of schema $S(B, Y)$, with A and B compatible (sets of) attributes. We call antidivision the operator $\ddagger$ defined the following way:

$$r[A \ddagger B]s = \{x \mid \forall b \in s[B], (x, b) \notin r\}.$$

In other words, an antidivision query $r[A \ddagger B]s$ retrieves the X-values present in relation r which are associated in r with none of the B-values present in s. In the following, in order to simplify the formulas and with no loss of generality, we will assume that the schema of s is $S(B)$. Some examples of (non-fuzzy) antidivision queries are given hereafter:

– A consumers' association aims at assessing some chemical products (e.g. cosmetics) in order to give them quality labels so as to express their level of safety. In this context, an antidivision query could be: retrieve the products which do not contain any noxious component in a proportion higher than 5%.

S. Greco and T. Lukasiewicz (Eds.): SUM 2008, LNAI 5291, pp. 92–105, 2008.
© Springer-Verlag Berlin Heidelberg 2008

– The Atomic Energy Research Center aims at finding a site for implanting a nuclear waste processing plant. In this context, an antidivision query could be: retrieve the sites which are at least hundred miles away from any geographic point where the seismic risk is higher than 2 (on a given scale).

It can be noticed that an antidivision is nothing but an antijoin followed by a projection over X: $r[A \ddagger B]s = (r \rhd s)[X]$. We call this operator antidivision by analogy with the relation between a semijoin and an antijoin: a division query $r[A \div B]s$ (resp. a semi-join query $r \ltimes s$) retrieves the X-values which are associated in r with *all* of the B-values present in s (resp. the tuples from r which join with at least one tuple from s) while an antividision query $r[A \ddagger B]s$ (resp. an antijoin query $r \rhd s$) retrieves those X-values which are associated with none of the B-values from s (resp. the tuples from r which join with none of the tuples from s).

Our purpose is not to introduce a superfluous algebraic operator but to show that the concept of antidivision seen as an atomic operator allows to reach a wide range of useful semantics when one moves from regular relations to fuzzy ones. An additional outcome is that it becomes much easier to make that operator tolerant to exceptions, in order to overcome (as much as possible) the empty answer problem. The tolerance aspect is central to the present contribution which constitutes a follow-up to [6] where a non-tolerant antidivision operator was introduced.

The remainder of the paper is organized as follows. In section 2, we deal with the possible formulations of the antidivision operator in a regular database context (in both relational algebra and SQL) and with its tolerant version. Section 3 is devoted to the antidivision in the context of databases involving fuzzy relations (i.e., relations which contain weighted tuples). We first give some basic notions concerning fuzzy relations and fuzzy queries, then we point out the different semantics that can be attached to the antidivision operator in such a context. The way this operator can be made tolerant to exceptions is also dealt with. The conclusion recalls the main contributions and mentions some perspectives for future work.

2   Antidivision of Regular Relations

2.1   Principle and Possible Formulations

In the framework of relational algebra, an antidivision can be expressed as:

$$r[X] - (r \bowtie s)[X] \tag{1}$$

where $\bowtie$ denotes the join operator. In SQL, a possible formulation is:

select X **from** r **where** X **not in** (**select** X **from** r, s **where** $r.A = s.B$)

or equivalently:

select X **from** r $r1$ **where not exists**
    (**select** * **from** s **where** A **in** (**select** A **from** r $r2$ **where** $r2.X = r1.X$)).

Table 1. Extension of relation *prod*

p	c	*prop*
p_1	c_1	3
p_1	c_2	4
p_1	c_3	93
p_2	c_1	9
p_2	c_4	91
p_3	c_2	8
p_3	c_6	92

Example 1. Let us consider the relations *prod* which describes the composition of some chemical products and *nox* which gathers the identifications of noxious components. Let us consider the query "retrieve the products which do not contain any noxious component in a proportion higher than 5%." Let us suppose that $nox = \{c_1, c_2, c_5\}$ and *prod* is represented in Table 1.

This query can be expressed as:

$$((Prod : prop > 5)[p, c]) \, [c \ddagger c] \, Nox$$

and its result is $\{p_1\}$. ⋄

Another vision of the antidivision in an SQL-like language can be based on an inclusion:

select X **from** r **group by** X
        having set(A) includes_none (**select** A **from** s)

where the Boolean predicate includes_none is defined as:

includes_none $(E, F) \equiv (E \cap F) = \emptyset \equiv (E \subseteq cp(F)) \equiv (F \subseteq cp(E))$.

where $cp(E)$ denotes the complement of set E. This vision corresponds to the following definition of the antidivision:

$$r[A \ddagger B]s = \{x \in r[X] \mid s \cap \Omega(x) = \emptyset\} = \{x \in r[X] \mid s \subseteq cp(\Omega(x))\} \quad (2)$$
$$= \{x \in r[X] \mid \Omega(x) \subseteq cp(s)\}$$

where $\Omega(x) = (r : X = x)[A]$ i.e., is the set of A-values associated with x in r.

2.2   Tolerant Antidivision of Regular Relations

Among other reasons (see section 3), it is interesting to define the antidivision in terms of an inclusion because it then becomes easy to make this operator tolerant (and then to limit the risk of obtaining empty answers). In the case of regular relations, tolerance consists in relaxing the quantifier "none" and thus to authorize a certain number (or proportion) of exceptions: one looks for the X-values from r which are connected in r with at most k of the B-values from relation s. So as to capture that type of semantics with an algebraic expression, it is necessary to use two copies of relation r and to replace in expression (1) the part $(r \bowtie s)[X]$ with:

$$((r_1 \bowtie s)[X_1, A_1])[X_1 = X_2](r_2 \bowtie s)[X_2, A_2]) : (A_1 \neq A_2))[X_1]$$

if one wants to authorize one exception, and so on (two self-joins are necessary if two exceptions are allowed, etc). In SQL, one would have to use an expression such as:

select X **from** r **where** X **not in**
  (**select** X **from** r **where** A **in** (**select** B **from** s) **group by** X
    having count(**distinct** A) > k).

If the goal is to authorize a proportion of exceptions (for instance, one wants to retrieve the X-values which are connected in r with at most k % of the values present in s), the problem becomes more tricky. It is not expressible in relational algebra (due to the lack of a counting operator), and in SQL one would have to use:

select X **from** r **where** X **not in**
  (**select** X **from** r **where** A **in** (**select** B **from** s) **group by** X
    having count(**distinct** A) > (**select** $k/100$ * **count**(*) **from** s)).

On the other hand, the tolerant antidivision can be expressed simply by relaxing the set-oriented operator "includes_none(E, F)" into "includes_almost_none (E, F, k)" meaning that E does not include more than k % of the elements of F. Let x be an element of $r[X]$ and n the cardinality of s. The number of authorized exceptions equals $e = k \times n/100$ i.e., the greatest integer smaller or equal to $k \times n/100$. Let e' be the number of elements b in s such that b is not associated with x in r. If $e \leq e'$ then includes_almost_none $(\Omega(x), s, k)$ is true, otherwise it is false.

3 Antidivision of Fuzzy Relations

In this section, we first recall some basic notions related to fuzzy relations and fuzzy queries, before defining the antidivision operator in a context of databases with fuzzy relations and proposing some tolerant versions of it.

3.1 About Fuzzy Relations and Fuzzy Queries

Let us recall that fuzzy set theory [16] aims at representing sets whose boundaries are not sharp. A fuzzy set F defined on a domain X is associated with a membership function F from X into the unit interval [0, 1]. The closer to 1 the membership degree $\mu_F(x)$, the more x belongs to F. The support $S(F)$ and the core $C(F)$ of a fuzzy set F are defined respectively as the following two crisp sets:

$$S(F) = \{x \in X \mid F(x) > 0\}$$
$$C(F) = \{x \in X \mid F(x) = 1\}$$

Table 2. Extension of relation fy-emp

num	name	salary	age	living-city	degree
76	Martin	12,500	40	New York	0.3
26	Tanaka	12,000	37	Chiba	0.4
12	Smith	12,000	39	London	0.4
55	Lucas	13,000	35	Miami	0.8

In the database domain, fuzzy set theory can serve as a basis for defining a flexible querying approach [9]. The key concept is that of a fuzzy relation, i.e., a relation designed as a fuzzy subset of Cartesian products of domains. Thus, any such fuzzy relation r can be seen as made of weighted tuples, denoted by μ/t, where μ expresses the extent to which tuple t belongs to the relation, i.e., is compatible with the concept conveyed by r. Of course, since regular databases are assumed to be queried, initial relations (i.e., those stored in the database) are special cases of fuzzy relations where all the tuple weights are equal to 1.

Example 2. Let us consider a database with the relation *employee(num, name, salary, age, living-city)*. From a given initial extension of this regular relation, it is possible to get the intermediate fuzzy relation *fy-emp* shown in Table 2 containing those employees who are "fairly young." It is assumed that the membership function associated with the flexible predicate "fairly young" is defined as follows: $\mu_{fy}(x) = 0$ if $age \geq 45$, $\mu_{fy}(x) = 1$ if $age \leq 30$, linear in between.

It can be noticed that no element is a full member of the fuzzy relation *fy-emp* since no employee reaches the maximal degree 1. In the fuzzy relation obtained, only the tuples t such that $\mu_{fy}(t) > 0$ appear.   ◇

The regular relational operations can be straightforwardly extended to fuzzy relations by considering fuzzy relations as fuzzy sets on the one hand and by introducing gradual predicates in the appropriate operations (selections and joins especially) on the other hand. If r and s are two fuzzy relations defined over the same domains $D_1, ..., D_k$, the following three set-oriented operations can be defined:

- Union: $\mu_{union(r, s)}(t) = \bot(\mu_r(t), \mu_s(t))$, where $\bot$ is a triangular co-norm,
- Intersection: $\mu_{inter(r, s)}(t) = \top(\mu_r(t), \mu_s(t))$, where $\top$ is a triangular norm,
- Difference: $\mu_{differ(r, s)}(t) = \top(\mu_r(t), 1 - \mu_s(t))$, which stems from the fact that in the Boolean framework $r - s = r \cap cp(s)$. Some other definitions are possible, but this is the most commonly used.

The Cartesian product of any two fuzzy relations r and s defined respectively on the sets of domains X and Y is given by: $\mu_{prod(r, s)}(tu) = \top(\mu_r(t), \mu_s(u))$.

Selection, projection and join operations are defined as follows:

- Selection: $\mu_{select(r, cond)}(t) = \top(\mu_r(t), \mu_{cond}(t))$ where cond is a fuzzy predicate,
- Projection: $\mu_{project(r, Y)}(u) = max_{v \in r}(uv)$ where Y is a subset of X and u one of its values, while v takes its value in $(X - Y)$,

- Join: $\mu_{join(r,\ s,\ A,\ B,\ \theta)}(tu) = \top(\mu_r(t), \mu_s(u), \mu_\theta(t.A, u.B))$ where A (resp. B) is a subset of X (resp. Y), A and B are defined over the same domains, θ is a binary relational operator (possibly fuzzy), $t.A$ (resp. $u.B$) stands for the value of t over A (resp. u over B).

As to the division of fuzzy relation, it is studied in [8] and a tolerant version of this operator is defined in [3]. For more details about query language aspects, the reader may refer to [4] where a fuzzy SQL-like language is described.

3.2 Principle and Formulation of the Antidivision of Fuzzy Relations

Starting from expression (1), and denoting by *res* the relation resulting from the antidivision query, one gets, for an element x *present in relation* r, the degree:

$$\mu_{res}(x) = min(\mu_{support(r[X])}(x), 1 - \mu_{proj(r\bowtie s,\ X)}(x)) \quad (3)$$
$$= min(1, 1 - max_{a\in s}\top(\mu_s(a), \mu_r(x, a)))$$
$$= min_{a\in s}(1 - \top(\mu_s(a), \mu_r(x, a)))$$

As to the expression based on an inclusion, it becomes:

$$r[A \ddagger B]s = \{\mu/x \mid x \in support(r[X])\text{ and }\mu = Inc(s, cp(\Omega(x)) > 0\} \quad (4)$$

where $Inc(s, cp(\Omega(x))$ denotes the degree of inclusion ($\in [0, 1]$) of s in $cp(\Omega(x))$. The graded inclusion indicator Inc can be defined the following way [1]:

$$Inc(E, F) = min_{x\in X}(\mu_E(x) \to \mu_F(x)) \quad (5)$$

where $\to$ denotes a fuzzy implication operator, i.e., a mapping from $[0, 1]^2$ into $[0, 1]$. There are several families of fuzzy implications, notably R-implications [11]:

$$p \to_R q = sup_{u\in[0,1]}\{u \mid \top(u, p) \le q\}$$

It is possible to rewrite these implications as:

$$p \to_R q = 1 \text{ if } p \le q, f(p, q) \text{ otherwise}$$

where $f(p, q)$ expresses a degree of satisfaction of the implication when the antecedent (p) exceeds the conclusion (q). The implications of Gödel ($p \to_{Gd} q = 1$ if $p \le q$, q otherwise), Goguen ($p \to_{Gg} q = 1$ if $p \le q$, q/p otherwise) and Lukasiewicz ($p \to_{Lu} q = 1$ if $p \le q$, $1 - p + q$ otherwise) are the three most used R-implications and they are obtained resp. with the norms $\top(x, y) = min(x, y)$, $\top(x, y) = x \times y$ and $\top(x, y) = max(x + y - 1, 0)$.

As to S-implications [11], they generalize the (usual) material implication $p \Rightarrow q = ((not\ p)\text{ or }q)$ by: $p \to_S q = \bot(1 - p, q)$. The minimal element of this class, namely Kleene-Dienes' implication obtained with $\bot = max$ expresses the inclusion of the support of E in the core of F (1 is reached then). This is also the case for Reichenbach's implication (obtained with the norm product).

Let us discuss the impact of the type of implication (R- or S-) on the semantics of the antidivision. The degrees in the divisor (relation s) act as:

- Importance levels if Kleene-Dienes' implication is used; in this case, the higher the degree attached to an element a of s, the more the degree attached to $<a, x>$ in r impacts the final degree attached to x in the result; the complement of the degree attached to a (i.e., $1 - s(a)$) corresponds to a guaranteed satisfaction level;
- Thresholds with any R-implication; here, the higher the degree attached to an element a of s, the smaller the degree attached $<a, x>$ in r must be so as to get a final degree attached to x equal to 1; when the degree attached to $<a, x>$ in r is higher than 1 minus the degree attached to a in s, a penalty is applied, which varies with the R-implication considered.

Example 3. Let us come back to the context of example 1 and consider relations *prod* and *nox* again. This time, these relations are supposed to be fuzzy in order to express that a component can be more or less noxious and that the proportion of a component in a chemical product can be more or less important. Let us consider the query "retrieve the products which do not contain any highly noxious component in a significant proportion". The fuzzy term "significant" can

prod	p	c	μ
	p_1	c_1	0.3
	p_1	c_2	0.85
	p_1	c_3	1
	p_2	c_1	1
	p_2	c_4	0.7
	p_3	c_2	1
	p_3	c_6	0.9

nox	c	μ
	c_1	0.8
	c_2	0.3
	c_4	0.1
	c_5	0.6
	c_6	0.4

be defined for instance as $\mu_{sig}(x) = 0$ if $x \leq 3$, $\mu_{sig}(x) = 1$ if $x \geq 7$, linear in-between. This fuzzy term is used to obtain the relation *prod* above by means of a selection applied on a relation of schema $(p, c, proportion)$ such as that from Example 1. The degrees in relation *nox* are supposed to be specified explicitly (the divisor relation can be given in extension in the query). Let us consider the extensions of *prod* and *nox* above. The antidivision query can be expressed as: $(prod[p, c])\,[c \ddagger c]\,nox$.

With Gödel's implication, one gets the result: $\{0.15/p_1\}$, with Goguen's implication: $\{0.5/p_1\}$, with Lukasiewicz' implication: $\{0.85/p_1, 0.2/p_2, 0.7/p_3\}$, and with Kleene-Dienes' implication: $\{0.7/p_1, 0.2/p_2, 0.6/p_3\}$. ◇

Now, let us give a semantic justification of expression (4). It is important to notice that if an R-implication is used in (5), one loses the equivalence valid in the Boolean case between $Inc(s, cp(\Omega(x)))$ and $Inc(\Omega(x), cp(s))$. Indeed, with an R-implication, the truth value of $(p \to_R q)$ is not equal to $[(not\ q) \to_R (not\ p)]$ in general. On the other hand, the equivalence between $Inc(s, \Omega(x))$ and $Inc(\Omega(x), cp(s))$ is preserved by S-implications. In the case of an R-implication, the "correct" choice for defining the antidivision is thus to use $Inc(s, cp(\Omega(x)))$

— as in expression (4) — and not $Inc(\Omega(x),\,cp(s))$. Indeed, the expected behavior is that the degrees attached to the elements of the divisor act as thresholds, and not the opposite. Finally, we have:

$$\mu_{r[A\ddagger B]s}(x) = Inc(s,\,\Omega(x)) = min_{a\in s}(\mu_s(a) \to 1 - \mu_r(x,\,a)) \qquad (6)$$

Dubois and Prade [10] have shown that R-implications and S-implications can be expressed using a common format, i.e., $p \to q = 1 - cnj(p,\,1-q)$ where cnj denotes a triangular norm $\top$ when the implication is an R-implication, and a non-commutative conjunction ncc when it is an R-implication. For example, the operators ncc associated with G''odel's and Goguen's implications are respectively:

$ncc_{Gd}(x,y) = 0$ if $x + y \leq 1$, y otherwise

$ncc_{Gg}(x,y) = 0$ if $x + y \leq 1$, $(x + y - 1)/x$ otherwise.

Hence, we get the generic expression for the antidivision of fuzzy relations:

$$\mu_{r[A\ddagger B]s}(x) = min_{a\in s}(1 - cnj(\mu_s(a),\,\mu_r(x,\,a))) \qquad (7)$$

which generalizes (3) by also taking into account non-commutative conjunctions.

Remark. Expression (4) — whose interpretation rests on formula (7) — also generalizes the definition of the antidivision based on an intersection, i.e.:

$$R[A \ddagger B]S = \{x \mid s \cap \Omega(x) = \emptyset\} \qquad (8)$$

Indeed, from this expression, it comes:

$$\mu_{r[A\ddagger B]s}(x) = 1 - \mu_\cap(s,\,\Omega(x))$$
$$= 1 - max_{a\in s}\top(\mu_s(a),\,\mu_r(x,\,a))$$
$$= min_{a\in s}(1 - \top(\mu_s(a),\,\mu_r(x,\,a)))$$

which is nothing but formula (3).

In order to obtain the generic semantics that we propose for the antidivision in relational algebra, it would be necessary to parameterize the Cartesian product by the conjunction operator. On the one hand, this would not be very easy to do for an end-user (it is not obvious how to choose the right conjunction operator to get the desired threshold-based or importance-based behavior) and, on the other hand, this raises a semantic difficulty since the Cartesian product is by nature a symmetrical operator (but it would not stay so if it were based on a non-commutative conjunction).

In an SQL-like language, the most simple solution is to parameterize the operator *includes_none* introduced above by the fuzzy implication desired. We get an expression of the form:

select x **from** r
group by x
having set(A) includes_none$_{fuzzy\ implication}$ (**select** B **from** s)

where includes_none$_{fuzzy\ implication}$ $(E,\,F) = Inc_{fuzzy\ implication}\,(F,\,cp(E))$.

Besides the better "readability" of this formulation, another advantage is that it provides a simple way to make the antidivision tolerant to exceptions, as will be described in the following subsection.

3.3 Tolerant Antidivisions of Fuzzy Relations

In [5], we defined a tolerant inclusion based on the relaxation of the universal quantifier underlying the definition of the non-tolerant inclusion according to formulas 5 (where the universal quantifier is interpreted as a minimum). The principle was to weaken the universal quantifier into "almost all" [15,17] so as to obtain a tolerant inclusion, denoted by $\subseteq_{almost\ all}$ (as the non-tolerant graded inclusion, this operator is parameterized by a fuzzy implication as it will be made clear in the following). An informal definition of this quantitative tolerant inclusion can be given in reference to the quantifier "almost all" as follows:

$$(E \subseteq_{almost\ all} F) \Leftrightarrow \text{"almost all" of the elements of } E \text{ are included in } F \quad (9)$$
$$\text{in the sense of the fuzzy implication considered.}$$

The key for interpreting formula (9) resides in the use of the degrees (denoted later by w_i) induced by the fuzzy quantifier "almost all". The mechanism suggested in [5] has a natural semantics in the following sense: any degree w_i issued from the quantifier "almost all" defines a level of "ignoration" (or a guaranteed level of satisfaction). This means that the implication value $(\mu_E(x) \rightarrow \mu_F(x))$ is somewhat ignored. This behavior is modeled by:

$$max(w_i, (\mu_E(x) \rightarrow \mu_F(x))) \quad (10)$$

where the weight w_i is defined as $\mu_{almost\ all}(1 - i/n)$, and n is the cardinality of the support of E. The method suggested in [5] consists in using the largest ignoration degree for the compensation of the smallest degree of implication, the second largest ignoration degree for the compensation of the second smallest degree of implication, and so on.

Here, we want to relax a statement of the form "find the x's which are connected in r with none of the B-values from s" into "find the x's which are connected in r with almost none of the B-values from s", where *almost none* is a fuzzy quantifier. This can be translated into: "find the x's such that *almost all* of the B-values from s are included in $cp(\Omega(x))$" where *almost all* is the antonym of *almost none*, i.e., $\mu_{almost\ all}(x) = \mu_{almost\ none}(1 - x)$ where $x \in [0, 1]$ denotes a proportion. The corresponding SQL-like expression is:

select x **from** r **group by** x
having set(A) incl_alm_none$_{(fuzzy\ impl.,\ alm\ none)}$ (**select** B **from** s)

where:

incl_alm_none$_{(fuzzy\ impl.,\ alm\ none)}(E,\ F) = F \subseteq_{(fuzzy\ impl.,\ alm\ all)} (cp(E))$.

Example 4. Let us consider the quantifier "almost none" defined as:

$\mu_{almost\ none}(p) = 1$ for any $p \in [0, 0.1]$, $\mu_{almost\ none}(p) = 0$ for any $p \in [0.25, 1]$, $\mu_{almost\ none}$ is linearly increasing between 0.1 and 0.25.

From this definition, we can derive the interpretation of "almost all":

$\mu_{almost\ all}(p) = 0$ for any $p \in [0, 0.75]$, $\mu_{almost\ none}(p) = 1$ for any $p \in [0.9, 1]$, $\mu_{almost\ all}$ is linearly increasing between 0.75 and 0.9.

Let us consider the following extensions of relations r and s:

$$r = \{0.9/<x_1, a_1>, 0.8/<x_1, a_2>, 0.6/<x_1, a_3>, 0.4/<x_1, a_4>,$$
$$0.2/<x_1, a_5>, 0.1/<x_1, a_6>, 0.9/<x_1, a_9>, 0.5/<x_1, a_{10}>, 1/<x_2, a_1>\}$$

$$s = \{0.5/<a_1>, 0.8/<a_2>, 0.7/<a_3>, 1/<a_4>, 0.9/<a_5>, 0.8/<a_6>,$$
$$1/<a_7>, 0.2/<a_8>, 0.1/<a_9>, 0.4/<a_{10}>\}.$$

The regular antidivision of these two relations using Gödel's implication yields $\{0.1/<x_1>\}$. Let us now compute the tolerant antidivision of r by s with the quantifier "almost none" above. From the definition of its antonym "almost all", we get the set of weights $W = \{w_1 = 1, w_2 = 0.33, w_3 = ... = w_{10} = 0\}$. Using formula 10, the degree obtained for x_1 and x_2 are respectively given by:

$$min(max(1, 0.1), max(0.33, 0.2), max(0, 0.4), max(0, 0.6), max(0, 0.8),$$
$$max(0, 1), max(0, 1), max(0, 1), max(0, 1), max(0, 1)) = 0.33,$$

$$min(max(1, 0), max(0.33, 1), max(0, 1), max(0, 1), max(0, 1), max(0, 1),$$
$$max(0, 1), max(0, 1), max(0, 1), max(0, 1)) = 1.$$

One observes that, according to what is expected, this new result $\{0.33/<x_1>, 1/<x_2>\}$ is a superset of the previous one, i.e., $\{0.1/<x_1>\}$.

Using Kleene-Dienes' implication, the result of the regular antidivision of r by s is: $\{0.2/<x_1>, 0.5/<x_2>\}$. The tolerant antidivision of r by s with the same quantifier "almost none" as before leads to the result $\{0.4/<x_1>, 1/<x_2>\}$.

With Lukasiewicz' implication, the regular antidivision yields $\{0.4/<x_1>, 0.5/<x_2>\}$, and the tolerant antidivision: $\{0.6/<x_1>, 1/<x_2>\}$. ◇

In the case of an antidivision of fuzzy relations, there is another way of introducing tolerance: one can choose to ignore (to some extent) the low-intensity exceptions (this corresponds to a qualitative vision of the exceptions). Because of space limitation, we only deal with the case of R-implications here (see [7] for the way to handle S-implications). When the graded inclusion $E \subseteq F$ is based on an R-implication, the idea is to take into account the gap between the membership degrees to E and to F respectively. More precisely, one considers that the situation where $\mu_E(x)$ exceeds $\mu_F(x)$ is totally acceptable if the difference $(\mu_E(x) - \mu_F(x))$ is in a given interval $[0, \alpha]$, and is more or less acceptable when it is in the interval $[\alpha, \beta]$. With respect to the informal definition of the quantitative tolerant inclusion (formula 9), the change consists in stating that:

$$(E \subseteq_{[\alpha,\ \beta]} F) \Leftrightarrow \text{all the elements of } E \text{ are "almost included" in } F$$
$$\text{in the sense of the R-implication considered.}$$

The principle proposed in [7] consists in in splitting the compensation mechanism both in the antecedent and in the consequent part of the R-implication used.

$$deg(E \subseteq_{[\alpha, \beta]} F) = min_{x \in X} (\mu_E(x) - \delta_1) \rightarrow_R (\mu_F(x) + \delta_2) \qquad (11)$$

where $\delta = \delta_1 + \delta_2 = 0$ if $\mu_E(x) - \mu_F(x) \geq \beta$ or $\mu_E(x) - \mu_F(x) \leq 0$
$$= \mu_E(x) - \mu_F(x) \text{ if } 0 \leq \mu_E(x) - \mu_F(x) \leq \alpha,$$
$$= \frac{\alpha}{\beta - \alpha}(\beta - (\mu_E(x) - \mu_F(x))) \text{ otherwise.} \qquad (12)$$

Special cases are obtained letting $\delta = \delta_1$, $\delta_2 = 0$ or $\delta = \delta_2$, $\delta_1 = 0$. In the following, we consider that $\delta_1 = \delta \times k$ and $\delta_2 = (1 - k) \times \delta$ where k is a user-specified constant belonging to the unit interval.

Remark. In the case of Gödel's implication, it appears logical to choose $k = 0$, i.e., $\delta = \delta_2$, $\delta_1 = 0$ since the implication degree $p - \delta_1 \rightarrow q + \delta_2$ does not depend on the premise when $(p - \delta_1) > (q + \delta_2)$. With Lukasiewicz' implication, the result does not depend on k since $p - \delta_1 \rightarrow q + \delta_2 = 1 - (p - \delta_1) + (q + \delta_2) = 1 - p + k\delta + q + (1 - k)\delta = 1 - p + q + \delta$ when $p > q$. On the other hand, with Goguen's implication, the choice of k has an impact on the compensation degree.

The generic form of an SQL-like qualitative tolerant antidivision query is:

select x **from** r **group by** x
having set(A) includes_none$_{(fuzzy\ impl.,\ \alpha,\ \beta)}$ (**select** B **from** s)

where includes_none$_{(fuzzy\ impl.,\ \alpha,\ \beta)}$ $(E, F) \equiv F \subseteq_{(fuzzy\ impl.,\ [\alpha,\ \beta])} cp(E)$.

Example 5. Let us consider the following extensions of relations r and s:

$r = \{< 0.2/ <x_1, a_1>, 0.1/ <x_1, a_2>, 0.6/ <x_1, a_4>, 0.2/ <x_1, a_5>,$
$\quad 0.2/ <x_2, a_2>, 0.8/ <x_2, a_3>, 0.3/ <x_3, a_1>, 0.8/ <x_3, a_5>\}$

$s = \{1/ <a_1>, 0.7/ <a_2>, 0.3/ <a_3>\}$

and let us use the thresholds $\alpha = 0.2$, $\beta = 0.4$. The non-tolerant antidivision of r by s based on Gödel's implication yields: $\{0.8/ <x_1>, 0.2/ <x_2>, 0.7/ <x_3>\}$ while the tolerant antidivision based on Gödel's implication (and $k = 0$) yields: $\{1/ <x_1>, 1/ <x_2>, 0.75/ <x_3>\}$. $\diamond$

3.4   Implementation Aspects

The question arises of defining efficient processing algorithms suited to these new types of queries. As a starting point, we will consider the work presented in [3] which dealt with processing methods for the division of fuzzy relations. In that work, three processing techniques were outlined and compared:

1. Translation into an SQL query involving a comparison of cardinalities and a user-defined function in order to calculate the satisfaction degrees,
2. Translation into an SQL query involving an inclusion and a user-defined function in order to calculate the satisfaction degrees,

3. Compilation of the original division query into a processing algorithm encoded in a procedural language such as Pro*C or PL/SQL.

It appears that the third strategy is by far the most efficient. The experimental measures reported in [3] show that, using the Oracle DBMS, for a dividend relation made of 60,000 tuples and a divisor made of 1000 tuples, the processing time is 1 min. 2 sec. for the cardinality-based approach, 36 sec. for the inclusion-based one, and only 18 sec. for the one based on a compiled algorithm. Another interesting result is that a similar division query addressed to crisp (instead of fuzzy) relations takes 15 sec. instead of 18 sec. to be processed. The additional cost induced by the fuzziness of the relations is thus around 20% only. In the following, the latter method is used. Hereafter, we give the principle of the algorithm based on that presented in [3]. One considers the problem of antidividing relation r of schema $R(A, X, mu)$ by relation s of schema $S(B, mu)$ where mu denotes in both cases the membership degree associated with each tuple. Let us recall that the evaluation of the antidivision is based on formula (6). The idea is to use two nested loops. The first one scans the different X-values present in relation r. For a given x, the inner loop scans the B-values b in the divisor, checks by means of a *select* query whether $< b, x >$ is in the dividend (and if so, with which degree) and updates the satisfaction degree associated with x in the result. In the algorithm, $impl$ ($\rightarrow$ above) denotes the fuzzy implication underlying the division. Let λ be the user-specified threshold (if the user does not specify any, $\geq \lambda$ can be replaced by > 0).

```
define cursX = select distinct X from r;
define cursB = select mu, B from s;
div ← ∅;
for all x in cursX do
   val_imp ← 1;
   for all <mu1, b> in cursB and val_imp > 0 do
      select mu into mu2 from r where X = x and A = b;
         -- we assume that if <b, x> ∉ r, then mu equals zero
      val_imp ← min(val_imp, impl(mu1, 1 - mu2));
   enddo;
   if val_imp ≥ λ then div ← div ∪ {<val_imp/x>} endif
enddo;
rank-order(div) according to the satisfaction degrees val_imp.
```

So as to tolerate quantitative exceptions, the preceding algorithm has to go through a few modifications. First, it is not possible anymore to calculate *val_imp* incrementally since the implication degrees attached to a given X-value x must be ranked in order to apply the weights w_i's appropriately. Consequently, it is necessary to store the different implication degrees attached to a given x. As to the weights, they depend on the cardinality of the divisor and on the fuzzy quantifier Q. Therefore, they can be computed before entering the outer loop of the previous algorithm.

Since *val_imp* cannot be computed incrementally anymore, it is not possible to stop the inner loop as soon as one gets a zero implication degree (for a certain value b from s). However, it is still possible in some cases to stop that loop before scanning s entirely. Let us denote by k the number of w_i's greater than zero. As soon as than k implication values equal to zero have been found (for a given x), one can conclude that x does not belong to the result. In the case where the user specifies a threshold λ (> 0), this pruning criterion can be refined in the following way. Let k' denote the number of w_i's greater than or equal to λ. As soon as more than k' implication degrees lower than λ are found (for a given x) one can conclude that x is not an answer.

Compared to the reference algorithm suited to the classical division of fuzzy relations, the additional cost is related to: i) the necessity of scanning relation s once in order to compute its cardinality and then the weights w_i's, ii) the fact that the inner loop cannot be stopped as often. The pruning condition is not as favorable in the tolerant case, but this does not change the nature of the worst case that can be encountered (and thus the maximal complexity).

In the qualitative exception case, the impact on the algorithm is even more limited. One just has to replace the calls $impl(mu_1, mu_2)$ with $relaxed\_impl(mu_1, mu_2)$ which takes the thresholds α and β into account. The extra cost is thus practically neglectable (since the number of accesses remains the same).

4   Conclusion

In this paper, we have introduced the concept of an antidivision operator, which, in the classical relational framework, corresponds to a non-primitive operator since it can be expressed by means of a antijoin, a projection and a difference. Seeing this operator as an atomic operator becomes particularly interesting when i) one wants to make it tolerant to exceptions, and ii) one moves to the framework of fuzzy relations. We have provided a generic definition for the antidivision operator, based on a graded inclusion, which captures a wide range of semantics when it comes to the interaction between the degrees in the divisor and those in the dividend. A second step was to introduce some more flexibility into the antidivision operator, by making the inclusion indicator tolerant to exceptions, and two visions of exceptions have been considered: a quantitative one and a qualitative one.

Among the perspectives for future work, it would be worthy dealing with the optimization of antidivision queries both in the regular relational database model and the fuzzy extension of this model. In particular, it would be interesting to study whether some optimization mechanisms proposed for antijoin queries, such as those described in [14], could be adapted to process antidivisions.

Another extension of this work concerns the application of the antidivision operator proposed here to the context of information retrieval. In different information retrieval models, it is indeed possible to specify inside a user query a set of (possibly weighted) unwanted keywords [12,13]. We thus believe that the flexible antidivision operator would be a well suited tool for interpreting the "negative part" of a query, in the same way that a fuzzy division operator can be used to interpret its "positive part" (i.e., the set of required keywords), as described in [2].

References

1. Bandler, W., Kohout, L.: Fuzzy power sets and fuzzy implication operators. Fuzzy Sets and Systems 4, 13–30 (1980)
2. Bordogna, G., Bosc, P., Pasi, G.: Fuzzy inclusion in database and information retrieval query interpretation. In: ACM SAC 1996, pp. 547–551 (1996)
3. Bosc, P., Hadjali, A., Pivert, O.: Preference-based divisions to overcome empty answers. In: 3rd Multidisciplinary Workshop on Advances on Preference Handling (M-PREF 2007), in conjunction with VLDB 2007, Vienna, Austria (2007)
4. Bosc, P., Pivert, O.: SQLf: a relational database language for fuzzy querying. IEEE Transactions on Fuzzy Systems 3, 1–17 (1995)
5. Bosc, P., Pivert, O.: About approximate inclusion and its axiomatization. Fuzzy Sets and Systems 157, 1438–1454 (2006)
6. Bosc, P., Pivert, O.: On a parameterized antidivision operator for database flexible querying. In: 19th Int. Conference on Database and expert Systems Applications (DEXA 2008), Torino, Italy (2008)
7. Bosc, P., Pivert, O.: On two qualitative approaches to tolerant inclusion operators. Fuzzy Sets and Systems (to appear, 2008)
8. Bosc, P., Pivert, O., Rocacher, D.: About quotient and division of crisp and fuzzy relations. Journal of Intelligent Information Systems 29, 185–210 (2007)
9. Bosc, P., Prade, H.: An Introduction to the Treatment of Flexible Queries and Uncertain or Imprecise Databases. In: Motro, A., Smets, P. (eds.) Uncertainty Management in Information Systems, pp. 285–324. Kluwer Academic Publishers, Dordrecht (1997)
10. Dubois, D., Prade, H.: A theorem on implication functions defined from triangular norms. Stochastica 8, 267–279 (1984)
11. Fodor, J.: On fuzzy implication operators. Fuzzy Sets and Systems 42, 293–300 (1991)
12. Lee, J.H., Kim, W.Y., Kim, M.H., Lee, Y.J.: On the evaluation of Boolean operators in the extended Boolean retrieval framework. In: SIGIR 1993, pp. 291–297 (1993)
13. Pasi, G.: A logical formulation of the Boolean model and of weighted Boolean models. In: Workshop on Logical and Uncertainty Models for Information Systems (LUMIS 1999), pp. 1–11 (1999)
14. Rao, J., Lindsay, B.G., Lohman, G.M., Pirahesh, H., Simmen, D.E.: Using EELs, a practical approach to outerjoin and antijoin reordering. In: ICDE 2001, pp. 585–594 (2001)
15. Yager, R.R.: Interpreting linguistically quantified propositions. International Journal of Intelligent Systems 9, 541–569 (1994)
16. Zadeh, L.A.: Fuzzy sets. Inf. Control. 8, 338–353 (1965)
17. Zadeh, L.A.: A computational approach to fuzzy quantifiers in natural languages. Computer Mathematics with Applications 9, 149–183 (1983)

Uncertainty Management for the Retrieval of Economic Information from Distributed Markets

René Brunner, Felix Freitag, and Leandro Navarro

Computer Architecture Department, Polytechnic University of Catalonia
08034, Barcelona, Spain
{rbrunner,felix,leandro}@ac.upc.edu

Abstract. The provision of real-time and highly accurate information in large-scale distributed systems is technically difficult and approximations imply uncertainty. In economic science, however, reliable information about markets, its specifications, and the behavior of its participants is essential for sophisticated and efficient negotiation strategies. There is the need for a system that provides and allows consulting an overall knowledge of economic information in distributed markets, while managing the accuracy of information for the user. This paper evaluates the influences of uncertainties for information retrieval within distributed Grid markets. It proposes an uncertainty management component for a Decentralized Market Information System (DMIS), which regulates the accuracy of information and the number of messages for the retrieval of economic data from a scalable market. First, we analyze the properties and the completeness of information in Grid markets. Therefore, we simulate Grid market specific scenarios under complete and incomplete information provision by varying the information accessibility. The results confirm the influence of the accuracy on the stability of the market. Based on these results, an optimization mechanism, which uses approximations is introduced for the retrieval of information. The approximations are controlled by the uncertainty management to find a trade-off between the amount of messages and the accuracy of information.

1 Introduction

In the last few years the emergence of Grid markets have put the focus on market mechanisms. The distributed nature of Grid applications has inspired to use distributed markets for resource allocation. Examples of such approaches are the market-based Grid platforms developed in several projects such as Grid4All [9], GridEcon [10], Tycoon [15] or SORMA [20]. These markets use auction mechanisms like the Continuous Double Auction (CDA) or the English auction. Other market mechanisms apply bargaining like the Catallaxy-based Grid Market [8].

A problem arising from scalable distributed markets is the gathering of information about the market, its prices, its products and the participating traders. The knowledge about the market is essential for sophisticated and efficient negotiation strategies. Examples are computational approaches like the game theory,

S. Greco and T. Lukasiewicz (Eds.): SUM 2008, LNAI 5291, pp. 106–119, 2008.
© Springer-Verlag Berlin Heidelberg 2008

predicting the future through forecasting and using learning rules on former and current trading information. Currently, no completely researched system provides and allows consulting an overall knowledge of economic information in a distributed manner.

Bergemann's survey [3] shows that the economic aspect of information acquisition in market mechanisms such as auctions has attracted a significant attention by the economic research community. Moreover, the study demonstrates the importance of the economic information disclosure for market participants. The need for this information lies in both, being able to apply sophisticated economic strategies and to feed the business models. In scalable distributed environments, however, the retrieval of real-time and accurate information is very cost intensive or even impossible due to the snapshot problem in distributed systems [16], the number of messages and the limited capacities of the individual peers.

The objective of this paper is first to analyze the influence of uncertainties, in terms of inaccuracy and obsolete data, for markets. Second is, based on the obtained results, to propose an uncertainty management for distributed and scalable market environments. This uncertainty management has to reduce the network load in number of sent messages and the duration of an information retrieval process with the help of approximations. Finally, a self-management approach will control the uncertainty automatically.

This paper is organized as follows: we present first the motivation for the need of economic information retrieval in Section 2 and the incompleteness caused by the distributed occurrence of information in Section 3. Afterwards, we analyze the uncertainties in distributed markets and evaluate their influences in Section 4. Experimental evaluations show the proof-of-concept and the advantages of our uncertainty management in Section 5. Section 6 compares our work to the existing related work of uncertainties in distributed systems and to other market evaluations.

2   Motivation

Auction-based and bargaining-based distributed marketplaces require economic information provision to enable a fair and equilibrium prices. Examples for such markets are non-centralized trading places for Grid services like envisioned in the projects Grid4All [9] and SORMA [20]. These trading places enable resource providers and service providers to sell their products such as resources or computing services on a Grid market. However, the buyers and sellers need to obtain information about the market in order to optimize their trading strategy, which mostly results to higher benefits.

Figure 1 (a) shows a scenario, which motivates the use of on economic information system like the Distributed Market Information System (DMIS). Coordinated by auctioneers, the sellers and buyers trade on different marketplaces. An auctioneer uses for example an English Auction or a Continuous Double Auction (CDA). From this separation of marketplaces follows that no information will be exchanged amongst them without any interaction. More reasons for such a separation of markets arise from different currencies, geographical locations, privacy, and trust constraints or political aspects.

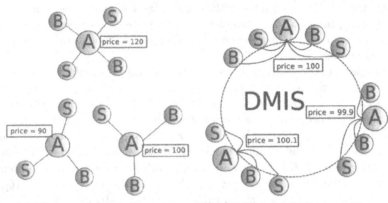

(a) Without global information.   (b) DMIS information provision.

Fig. 1. Possible trading places containing auctioneers A, buyers B and sellers S

Introducing the DMIS to that scenario of an electronic market (see Fig. 1 (b)) enables explicitly an information exchange among all participants. Traders can now obtain information from other traders or directly from every auctioneer. Alternatively, an auctioneer can be distributed on several nodes, depending on its type and implementation. Interested participants could execute queries for certain values or could subscribe to new events such as the arriving of new products or concluded trades.

3   Incomplete Information Retrieval in Markets

The information retrieval in distributed markets is an important feature to guarantee trading at fair and equilibrated prices. In markets, equilibrium prices (P_0) are finally reached by human traders, but works in research show that bidding strategies are more successful than human traders. Even simple negotiation strategies like Zero Intelligence Plus (ZIP) agents [17] outperform human trading in finding the market equilibrium price. Both, sophisticated and simple negotiation strategies need prior price information from the past. For example, the ZIP strategy bases on the maximum bid (B_{max}) or minimum offer (O_{min}) of the previous trading round.

In distributed markets, these strategies need information which occurs in a distributed manner, meaning a geographical or logical separation. Therefore, it is impossible to provide a global summary of the economic data for each individual bidding agent within the regular trading or bargaining process. Figure 2, derivated from Minkowski's space-time model, shows the occurrence of information at a set of n bidders, indexed by $i \in 1,2, ..., n$. Each bidder B_i possess Information $I_{P_1}^{T_1}(B_i)...I_{P_p}^{T_t}(B_i)$, where the location of the occurring is defined by time T indexed by $t \in 1,2, ..., n$ and place P indexed by $p \in 1,2, ..., n$.

The economic information about the market occurs at different places within the Space S $i \otimes B_i$ at a certain time T and a certain place P. Figure 2 depicts

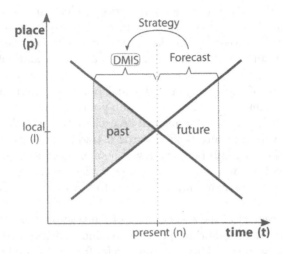

Fig. 2. Distributed information occurrence in markets

the differentiation of *past*, *present* and *future* information. To gain the optimal benefit while trading, a bidder agent need to know future offers and behavior of the market. Therefore, forecasting mechanisms are trying to predict future events and prices. This allows the bidding strategy to select an optimal price. However, the forecasting is based on information from the past. Therefore, the DMIS provides the information from the distributed system for an individual bidding agent by aggregating the local information I_L from each bidding agent A_i. The local information is defined by the following:

$$I_L^{B_n}(B_x) = I_{P_j}^{T_s}(B_x) \cup I_{P_j}^{T_s}(B_n)0 \leq j \leq p, 0 \leq s \leq t \tag{1}$$

Normally, two bidding agents meet each other at the same time at the same place, when an offer matches a bid from both and a trade is concluded. This allows them to know about the price of the agent participating in the same matchmaking process. Otherwise, an agent has to consult an information service provided by the auction mechanism. As this is limited to the auctions view, an external market information service provides the ability to retrieve a global view of the scalable market system.

4   Analysis of Uncertainties in Markets

Grid Markets consist of a number of traders, sellers that have an item that they wish to sell, and buyers that have a certain amount of money, limited by the budget to buy resources. In this work, we consider a simplified market with only one type of resource being traded. A controlled amount of information supports the traders as a base of the bidding strategy to simulate the uncertainty in the market.

The Reservation Price (R_0) is the price that traders are willing to pay and accumulating R_0 of all traders within the market create the supply and the demand. For a seller R_0 is the minimum price, which can be derived by the own costs and the least desired profit. A buyer defines R_0 with its maximum budget it is willing to invest. If a market is setting up or when the agent has non information, then an agent has no information about P_0 and enters a market with its R_0.

The intersection of the supply and demand builds the equilibrium price P_0 and equilibrium quantity Q_0. This equilibrium point is the price and quantity at which the maximum number of items will be exchanged. According to economic theory, markets will naturally tend towards a trading at this price P_0. If the market price is above equilibrium, there will be more sellers competing to trade with fewer buyers thus bringing the price down. Vice versa, if the price is below equilibrium, there will be more buyers wanting to buy items for sale, that pushes the price up.

Thus, a measurement of the effectiveness of a market mechanism is how close the traders are to this equilibrium price. Also, since markets with no prior history will most likely start making negotiations far from the equilibrium, a second important measure is how quickly the equilibrium is reached. In this work we consider agents trading in a CDA. In auctions, market prices are determined through bidding rounds in which buyers and sellers shout the current price that they are willing to pay for an exchange of one item (identical commodity good). If these prices match, the involved traders make a deal, otherwise the traders need to update the price willing to pay for the next round. In a CDA, both, buyers and sellers announce their current prices, which stays valid until an update in a later round.

Table 1 summarizes the symbols used for the following description of simulation experiments, in order to assess the influence of incomplete market information:

Before comparing the market behavior with the different information types, we establish a baseline simulation. In our market experiments, we assign to each seller agent a reservation price of 50 money units and to each buyer agents 100 money units. Agents have initial shouts to enter the market with a random price, for sellers from the interval $[R_0, R_0 + 2]$, and for buyers from the interval $[R_0 - 2, R_0]$, where R_0 is the reservation price for that particular agent. After a successful trade, the bidding agents (sellers and buyers) return into the market with a re-entering rate E_r initialized with the probability of $\frac{1}{3}$.

Table 1. Table of symbols

Symbol	Meaning
R_0	reservation price
P_0	equilibriums price
β	learning beta
γ	learning gamma
B_i	bidding agent
α	deviation to P_0
O_{min}	seller's minimum offer
B_{max}	buyer's maximum bid

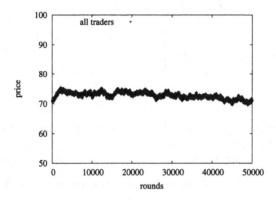

Fig. 3. Price evolution during 50.000 rounds

Figure 3 shows the prices traded at P_t with 2000 bidding agents (each for seller agents and buyer agents) over 50000 rounds. As the prices are slightly falling after 20000 rounds, we had to adjust the learning beta (β) of the buyer agents. We assigned $\beta = 0.05145$ and $\gamma = 0.005145$ for buyer agents and $\beta = 0.05$ and $\gamma = 0.005$ for seller agents.

Smith introduced in [19] a way of appraising how close a set of n trading prices p_i are to equilibrium P_0,

$$\alpha = 100 * \left(\sqrt{\frac{\sum_{i=1}^{n}(p_i - P_0)^2}{n}} \right) / P_0 \qquad (2)$$

which measures the standard deviation of trading prices from the equilibrium trading price. Graphing α over time gives us a quantification of how quickly an auction converges to equilibrium, and how closely it matches that equilibrium after convergence. For the baseline experiment, we obtained an α of 1.5 for 50,000 rounds and about 200,000 successful trades, if the traders have global price information. The calculated α is close to that shown in Priest et al. experiments in [17]. In Smith's experiments with humans, α reached a value between 0.6 and 13.2. Thus we consider an alpha between 1 and 2, obtained in the baseline simulator as reasonably low.

We modify the baseline simulation to vary the accessibility of information, to simulate an artificial uncertainty. Therefore, we create imperfect information by modifying O_{min} and B_{max}. Randomly, the simulator adds or subtracts a value v between 0 and the imperfection rate r_I ($v \in 0 \leq v \leq r_I$). Figure 4(a) shows α under varying the accuracy of the bids. A small variation until a maximum imperfection of $r_I = 2$ produces an α of better than 2, which is still reasonable for a well operating market. However, α increases rapidly under a higher inaccuracy. The market strives to a P_0 with a r_I of over 3.

We simulate the influence of uncertainties in form of obsolete information to a market using a CDA where agents trade with a ZIP strategy. The CDA is controlled by rounds where each bidder can propose its bid. The highest bid is

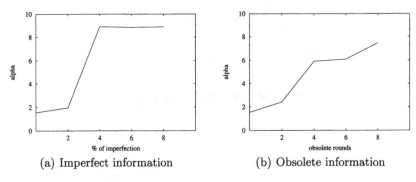

(a) Imperfect information   (b) Obsolete information

Fig. 4. Influence of uncertainty on the stability of market α

matched to the lowest offer, the next highest bid to the next lowest offer until no matches are made. Figure 4(b) depicts α for a controlled obsolete information. The agents obtain information (O_{min} and B_{max}), which occurred 2, 4, 6 or 8 rounds before the current bidding. A low delay of information of 2 rounds leads to a reasonable α of 2. A longer delay follows a strong increase of α.

Our preliminary measurements illustrate how the information acquisition in distributed Grid markets influences the performance of the market. The results show the importance of a market information system. By revealing the disequilibrium of the market without complete information, the simulations indicate important requirements for the design of a distributed market information system. The results show that the market information system has a small margin for the provision of real-time and accurate information.

A margin for the delay of the information provision is important in distributed, scalable systems. The delay in such systems can increase exponentially as the provision requires the aggregation of routing structures. Even a multiplicity of these structures are required to retrieve more complex data. Moreover, retrieving a 100% accurate value needs a request to all participants that probably results in a higher delay, when the slowest or most restricted participant, in terms of uncertainty, builds a bottleneck.

The awareness of the margin for inaccurate information retrieval, shown by the experimental results, opens new aspects for the design and the uncertainty management of the DMIS architecture. Handling of failures in the technical level results in cost intensive algorithm like replication to avoid the failure of the system or loss of data. However, if the system will work in a satisfactory way in terms of α then that tolerance allows the technical layer to have a more efficient design regarding the number of messages.

However, the results also indicate the finding of a trade-off between real-time and accurate information provision. A possibility is to obtain faster response in new information, while decreasing the level of accuracy. For example, even relatively simple statistical approximations calculate nearly exact values while they need only the information from a small and randomly selected subset of participants to manage the uncertainty.

5 Evaluation

The evaluation is based on the results of uncertainty margins for a stable market, which have been obtained by the simulations explained in the previous section. In the following, we analyze the self-management component, which maintains the uncertainty within user specified limits based on approximations (using a trade-off between fast and accurate information retrieval). This component is deployed by the DMIS prototype [4].

The DMIS has to handle the economic requirements, while it also addresses the technical challenges arising from the decentralization. Primarily, the technical challenges result from the support for a large scalability in number of users and information and by the provision of a high robustness against failures and churn in a P2P-based system. The chosen solution uses Scribe [18] to apply the advantages from its key-based routing (KBR), distributed hash table (DHT) and its subscription mechanism. A widely deployed concept to allow aggregation and scalability in information systems are tree structures, which build the basis structure for the information retrieval of the DMIS.

Based on the previous results and taking into account the performance of routing mechanisms in large-scale systems such as DHTs, a number of determined parameters influence on the accuracy of information. An increase on performance can be reached by finding a trade-off between accurate data and faster results, obtained by fewer messages. For example, querying all nodes in a large-scale system needs more messages and has a longer duration but obtains an optimal accuracy. On the other side, an approximation made from a random subset of nodes reduces the delay for the information retrieval and the number of messages while the uncertainty increases as well.

5.1 Uncertainty Results

Distributed large-scale systems involve uncertainties, which result from the delay of the information transmission, possible malicious peers, failures or churn. Mattern [16] described the problem of a snapshot in distributed systems to obtain a "true" state of the system. In practice, the retrieval of 100% accurate information at one time is not feasible in large-scale and high-dynamic distributed systems. An approach, however, are approximations to obtain a nearly global view of the system, which have the advantage of reducing the duration of the retrieval process and the number of messages. In certain cases, an approximation can even lead to more accurate results, regarding the fact that it returns faster results, than retrieving accurate information, which is already obsolete.

We define the uncertainty management parameter *hops* which defines the height in a balanced binary tree (balanced through random 128-bit key IDs), used by the DMIS as an example for n-ary trees. Consequently, the *hops* define the maximal number of messages, needed for one retrieval process (2^{hops}). The DMIS uses the *hops* to manage the uncertainty level by increasing and decreasing the number of queried nodes to reach a predefined level of uncertainty μ. In our experiments, μ is set to an uncertainty level of maximal 2%. This value is deduced by the previous simulation results in Section 4, but it can be modified by the user or be flexibly applied to other environments. The calculation of μ is described in Equation 3, where σ is the standard deviation of the retrieved sample $\in 1, 2, ..., n$. $M = \dfrac{1}{n} \sum\limits_{i=0}^{n} P_i$. The mean of the samples of the prices $P_0...P_n$ and t is the value obtained from the $t - distribution$ with n and the Confidence Interval (CI).

$$\mu = \frac{t_{(n,CI)} * \sigma * 100}{\sqrt{n} * M} \tag{3}$$

We measure the number of *hops*, since it is a significant value. On one side, this describes the duration of a request: many connectivity scenarios for a DMIS vary from 1 GB Intranet connections to low bandwidth connections like analog modems. The real time can be calculated by the average connection time between peers, within the focused network and the number of hops. On the other side, the number of hops represents a part of the consumed bandwidth for the whole system, because this shows the total number of send messages within a balanced binary tree 2^{hops}.

In our experiments, we show the functioning of the self-management component for uncertainties in an information system for distributed markets. Smith's experiments with humans [19] resulted in an α between 0.6 and 13.2. Therefore, increasing α after each retrieval process until it reaches 15, emulates an extreme value of real markets. For each node, the price is randomly assigned after each query process. Figure 5 shows an increase of α until 15, while in the meantime, the uncertainty μ stays below 2. This means that a user can obtain the average price with an accuracy (at a CI of 95%) of at least 98%.

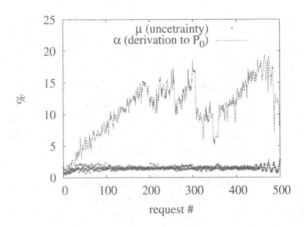

Fig. 5. Uncertainty self-management in experiments with 10000 nodes and a CI of 95%, while the variation of α simulates trends and finer variations of real markets

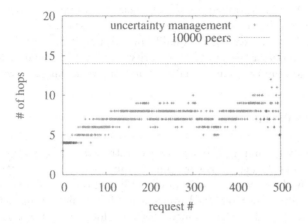

Fig. 6. Number of hops as indicator for the duration and number of messages. The uncertainty management reduces the *hops* to below 10, without the uncertainty management, querying for 10000 nodes would result in more than 14 *hops*.

An advantage of the applied approximation for the average price based on the CI results in a shorter response time for the request and fewer messages for the query process. Figure 6 shows the number of hops for each query request. The duration for one request can be calculated by the number of hops multiplied by the average duration for the connection, depending on the network type. Although α increases linear in Figure 5, the number of hops increases only logarithmically. This is an import property for the scalability in distributed environments and to ensure a fast information provision (measured in number of hops).

The number of totally send messages for a request is reduced through the approximations. Instead of sending messages to all 10000 peers, the uncertainty management system sends only 2^{hops} messages, depending on the level of uncertainty. Figure 6 shows that an α of about 16 leads to an $h = 9$, which has a maximum of 512 messages in contrary to *hops* $>= 14$ for querying all 10000 peers.

5.2   Outlook

In future work, we will evaluate the obtained results to apply them in more efficient routing structures, which will increase the optimization of the information provision. This is the evaluation of faster mechanisms for the information retrieval in scalable systems, which builds a bottleneck according to our measurements of the delay for distributed information retrieval. However, a trade-off will be necessary as a faster retrieval of messages results in higher maintaining costs, in number of messages and network overhead. An alternative approach to decrease the delay of messages is an approximation, which has the disadvantage of inaccurate information.

The uncertainties caused by failures and churn in distributed environments can be optimized in another aspect; we plan to reduce these uncertainties with the help of replication. Although, this approach increases the number of messages, but it could also improve the accuracy and the delay of the process for the information retrieval. Especially, increasing the quality of the sample data of the approximations in form of a better reliability on security and fault tolerance is supposed to decrease the uncertainty of the global information in the entire system.

6   Related Work

A survey from Bergemann [3] discusses the retrieval and aggregation of information in markets. Other literature puts emphasis on the theoretical analysis of the influence of information to markets [13] and on the acquisition of information [2]. Results about required information for economic markets are given in [11]. However, the above mentioned literature focuses on theoretical analysis indicating principally the need for information availability. In our work, we aim to make empirical analysis from simulations and from a deployed prototype.

Uncertainties in distributed environments can be caused by incoherence or inconsistence. Our idea of the DMIS is similar to the failure detectors of [5], that studies the solution for uncertainty management in asynchronous systems through the terms of completeness and accuracy. Large-scale systems over partially unreliable networks induce uncertainties through failures and churn. Surveys and discussions on fault-tolerant and scalable solutions to the problem of accuracy and scalability are made and measured by the correctness of query results [1] [12].

The quality of markets and bidding strategies is often measured by the level of reaching the market's equilibrium price [19]. At this theoretical price the most products are traded, which can be considered as an optimum. Preist et. al [17] introduced zero intelligence plus (ZIP) agents that use a simple learning algorithm to make use of past information, that results in a better performance than human traders. In distributed environments such as peer-to-peer (P2P) systems, however, the past information is uncertain. Therefore, [7] handles this inaccuracy with approximations based on historical data. In our work, an uncertainty metric μ characterizes the efficiency, fairness and stability for distributed markets based on current market data. With this metric we define the influence of uncertainty to markets executed on a distributed environment, which is compared to [19] (measured by *alpha*).

It is known and reported by [6], [16] and [14], that the "true" value of a current state in a distributed environment can only be consulted with a perfect view over the whole system, while simulations vary as a result of imperfection. Jain et. al [14] introduces a *network imprecision* metric to characterize the uncertainty through the accuracy in distributed network systems. Our proposed market information system needs therefore to manage the uncertainty and imprecision of information in distributed markets to allow agents to take appropriate economic decisions.

We conclude from the related work the need for information retrieval in distributed markets. In distributed system, however, obtaining information for a "true" global view as a snapshot remains a challenge. Many projects present algorithms to handle the network imprecision and uncertainty and to provide or to retrieve accurate information from a distributed system. Our approach simulates the margin for economic uncertainty for the provision of economic information. Afterwards, we described an approximation approach within the DMIS to handle the uncertainty and the need for fast information provision.

7   Conclusions

This paper analyzed the economic information provision in scalable markets, which is affected by the uncertainties caused from the distributed system. These uncertainties result from the snapshot problem in distributed systems and from failures and churn in distributed large-scale applications. Therefore, we analyzed the market to identify the behavior of information accuracy and to propose a solution for the uncertainty of information, a problem arising from the distributed environments.

Simulations showed the influence of different kind of incomplete information to the stability within the market. Our results showed that a small information inaccuracy of less than 2% keeps a reasonable market stability. Similarly, a small margin of obsolete information still ensures a stable market. This result is important, since the identified margin allows design decisions within the DMIS regarding the implemented mechanisms for the implemented methods, while maintaining the scalability and the robustness.

We proposed an approach for the uncertainty management which bases on the result of simulations. They showed that the cost in number of messages and in form of time delay is very important for information provision in real market scenarios. Defining guarantees for the accuracy in form of a confidence interval allows the reducing of the time for the information provision and the number of messages. In an environment with 10000 participants, the approximation reduces the time by about a half and the total number of messages by $\frac{1}{20}$. Both reached a fixed value, even within a large and scalable environment. Moreover, when increasing the deviation α from the equilibrium price of the market, the number of messages and the time of provision increases only logarithmically.

Furthermore, we introduced an uncertainty self-management component for the DMIS. This component follows an algorithm to keep the uncertainty within a predefined limit. Therefore, we applied the constraints obtained by the simulations to show that the self-management component helps to keep automatically the stability of the market. While this uncertainty management is proposed for a scalable economic market, it could principally also be suitably for being applied to other scalable distributed information management systems such as Grid monitoring systems, where the accuracy of a parameter also needs maintenance during the application execution.

Acknowledgments. This work was supported in part by the European Union under Contract Grid4All EU IST-FP6-034567, under Contract SORMA EU

IST-FP6-034286, and the Ministry of Education and Science of Spain under Contract TIN2007-68050-C03-01.

References

1. Bawa, M., Gionis, A., Garcia-Molina, H., Motwani, R.: The price of validity in dynamic networks. In: SIGMOD 2004: Proceedings of the 2004 ACM SIGMOD international conference on Management of data, pp. 515–526. ACM Press, New York (2004)
2. Bergemann, D., Valimaki, J.: Information acquisition and efficient mechanism design. Econometrica 70(3), 1007–1033 (2002), http://ideas.repec.org/a/ecm/emetrp/v70y2002i3p1007-1033.html
3. Bergemann, D., Valimaki, J.: Information in mechanism design. In: Richard Blundell, W.N., Persson, T. (eds.) Proceedings of the 9th World Congress of the Econometric Society, ch. 5, pp. 186–221. Cambridge University Press, Cambridge (2007)
4. Brunner, R., Freitag, F., Navarro, L.: Towards the development of a decentralized market information system: Requirements and architecture. In: Parallel and Distributed Computing in Finance (PDCoF 2008). Proceedings of the 22nd IPDPS, Miami, FL, USA (2008)
5. Chandra, T.D., Toueg, S.: Unreliable failure detectors for reliable distributed systems. Journal of the ACM 43(2), 225–267 (1996)
6. Considine, J., Li, F., Kollios, G., Byers, J.: Approximate aggregation techniques for sensor databases. In: Proceedings of 20th International Conference on Data Engineering, 2004, pp. 449–460 (2004)
7. Despotovic, Z., Usunier, J.-C., Aberer, K.: Towards peer-to-peer double auctioning. In: HICSS 2004: Proceedings of the Proceedings of the 37th Annual Hawaii International Conference on System Sciences (HICSS 2004) - Track 9, p. 90289.1. IEEE Computer Society Press, Washington (2004)
8. Eymann, T., Reinicke, M., Streitberger, W., Rana, O., Joita, L., Neumann, D., Schnizler, B., Veit, D., Ardaiz, O., Chacin, P., Chao, I., Freitag, F., Navarro, L., Catalano, M., Gallegati, M., Giulioni, G., Schiaffino, R.C., Zini, F.: Catallaxy-based grid markets. Multiagent Grid Syst. 1(4), 297–307 (2005)
9. Grid4All (2008), http://grid4all.elibel.tm.fr/
10. GridEcon (2008), http://www.gridecon.eu/
11. Grossklags, J., Schmidt, C.: Interaction of human and artificial agents on double auction markets - simulations and laboratory experiments. In: IAT 2003: Proceedings of the IEEE/WIC International Conference on Intelligent Agent Technology, p. 400. IEEE Computer Society Press, Washington (2003)
12. Gupta, I., van Renesse, R., Birman, K.: Scalable fault-tolerant aggregation in large process groups (2001)
13. Jackson, M.O.: Efficiency and information aggregation in auctions with costly information. Review of Economic Design 8(2), 121–141 (2003)
14. Jain, N., Kit, D., Mahajan, D., Yalagandula, P., Dahlin, M., Zhang, Y.: Known unknowns in large-scale system monitoring. In: Review (October 2007)
15. Lai, K., Huberman, B.A., Fine, L.: Tycoon: A distributed market-based resource allocation system. Technical report (2004) HP:arXiv:cs.DC/0404013
16. Mattern, F.: Efficient algorithms for distributed snapshots and global virtual time approximation. J. Parallel Distrib. Comput. 18(4), 423–434 (1993)

17. Preist, C., van Tol, M.: Adaptive agents in a persistent shout double auction. In: ICE 1998: Proceedings of the first international conference on Information and computation economies, pp. 11–18. ACM Press, New York (1998)
18. Rowstron, A.I.T., Kermarrec, A.-M., Castro, M., Druschel, P.: Scribe: The design of a large-scale event notification infrastructure. In: NGC 2001: Proceedings of the Third International COST264 Workshop on Networked Group Communication, London, UK, pp. 30–43. Springer, Heidelberg (2001)
19. Smith, V.L.: An experimental study of competitive market behavior. Journal of Political Economy 70(3), 322 (1962)
20. SORMA. Sorma project (2008), http://www.iw.uni-karlsruhe.de/sormang/

Loopy Propagation in a Probabilistic Description Logic

Fabio Gagliardi Cozman and Rodrigo Bellizia Polastro

Escola Politécnica, Universidade de São Paulo - São Paulo, SP - Brazil
fgcozman@usp.br, rodrigopolastro@gmail.com

Abstract. This paper introduces a probabilistic description logic that adds probabilistic inclusions to the popular logic $\mathcal{ALC}$, and derives inference algorithms for inference in the logic. The probabilistic logic, referred to as CR$\mathcal{ALC}$ ("credal" $\mathcal{ALC}$), combines the usual acyclicity condition with a Markov condition; in this context, inference is equated with calculation of (bounds on) posterior probability in relational credal/Bayesian networks. As exact inference does not seem scalable due to the presence of quantifiers, we present first-order loopy propagation methods that seem to behave appropriately for non-trivial domain sizes.

1 Introduction

A description logic offers a formal language where one can describe concepts such as "A mother is a woman who has a child" [2]. To do so, a description logic typically uses a decidable fragment of first-order logic, and tries to reach a practical balance between expressivity and complexity. The last decade has seen a significant increase in interest in description logics as a vehicle for large-scale knowledge representation, for instance in the *semantic web* [4]. Indeed, the language OWL, proposed by the W3 consortium as the "data layer" of their architecture for the semantic web, is an XML encoding for quite expressive description logics [21].

Description logics are not geared towards the representation of uncertainty about individuals and concepts: one cannot express that "with high probability, a bird is a flying animal". The literature contains a number of proposals that add probabilistic uncertainty to description logics, as this is central to the management of semantic data in large repositories. The goal of this paper is to contribute in such a direction.

In this paper we consider a probabilistic extension of the popular logic $\mathcal{ALC}$, where we allow *probabilistic inclusions* such as $P(\mathsf{FlyingBird}|\mathsf{Bird}) = 0.99$. Section 2 offers a brief appraisal of related work in the literature. The syntax and semantics of our proposed probabilistic logic are introduced in Section 3. A notable feature of our proposal is that we adopt an interpretation-based semantics that avoids the challenges of direct inference and lets us deal smoothly with probabilities over assertions. We then adopt a Markov condition, attached to the usual acyclicity condition of description logics, that connects the logic with the theory of relational credal/Bayesian networks. In Section 4 we discuss the inference problem for the logic, and note that exact inference does not seem to be scalable when quantified concepts are employed. Thus we derive a first-order version of loopy propagation, and show evidence of the scalability of the method even when probabilities are not uniquely specified. We briefly discuss infinite domains in Section 5.

S. Greco and T. Lukasiewicz (Eds.): SUM 2008, LNAI 5291, pp. 120–133, 2008.
© Springer-Verlag Berlin Heidelberg 2008

2 Probabilistic Description Logics

This section reviews the literature on probabilistic description logics; some basic concepts are defined in this paragraph. Assume a vocabulary containing *individuals*, *concepts*, and *roles* [2]. Concepts and roles are combined to form new concepts using a set of *constructors*; constructors in the $\mathcal{ALC}$ logic [45] are *conjunction* ($C \sqcap D$), *disjunction* ($C \sqcup D$), *negation* ($\neg C$), *existential* restriction ($\exists r.C$), and *value* restriction ($\forall r.C$). *Concept inclusions/definitions* are denoted respectively by $C \sqsubseteq D$ and $C \equiv D$, where C and D are concepts. A set of concept inclusions and definitions is a *terminology*. Concept ($C \sqcup \neg C$) is denoted by $\top$, and concept ($C \sqcap \neg C$) is denoted by $\bot$ (when we use $\top$ or $\bot$, we assume them to be defined through some C that does not appear anywhere else in the terminology). If an inclusion/definition contains a concept C in its right hand side and a concept D in its left hand side, say that C *directly uses* D. Indicate the transitive closure of "directly uses" by *uses*. A terminology is *acyclic* if it is a set of concept inclusions/definitions such that no concept in the terminology uses itself [2]. Typically terminologies only allow the left hand side of a concept inclusion/definition to contain a concept name (and no constructors). Usually one is interest in *concept subsumption*: whether $C \sqsubseteq D$ for concepts C and D. A terminology may be associated to a set of *assertions* about individuals, such as Fruit(appleFromJohn) and buyFrom(houseBob, John). A set of assertions $\mathcal{A}$ is called an *Abox*. An assertion $C(a)$ directly uses assertions of concepts (resp. roles) directly used by C instantiated by a (resp. by (a, b) for $b \in \mathcal{D}$), and likewise for the "uses" relation in a recursive fashion. The semantics of a description logic is almost always given by a *domain* $\mathcal{D}$ and an *interpretation* $\mathcal{I}$. The domain $\mathcal{D}$ is a nonempty set; we often assume its cardinality to be given as input. The interpretation function $\mathcal{I}$ maps each individual to an element of the domain, each concept name to a subset of the domain, each role name to a binary relation on $\mathcal{D} \times \mathcal{D}$. The interpretation function is extended to other concepts as follows: $\mathcal{I}(C \sqcap D) = \mathcal{I}(C) \cap \mathcal{I}(D)$, $\mathcal{I}(C \sqcup D) = \mathcal{I}(C) \cup \mathcal{I}(D)$, $\mathcal{I}(\neg C) = \mathcal{D} \backslash \mathcal{I}(C)$, $\mathcal{I}(\exists r.C) = \{x \in \mathcal{D} | \exists y : (x, y) \in \mathcal{I}(r) \wedge y \in \mathcal{I}(C)\}$, $\mathcal{I}(\forall r.C) = \{x \in \mathcal{D} | \forall y : (x, y) \in \mathcal{I}(r) \rightarrow y \in \mathcal{I}(C)\}$. An inclusion $C \sqsubseteq D$ is entailed iff $\mathcal{I}(C) \subseteq \mathcal{I}(D)$, and $C \equiv D$ is entailed iff $\mathcal{I}(C) = \mathcal{I}(D)$. An assertion $C(a)$ is *consistent* iff $\mathcal{I}(a) \in \mathcal{I}(C)$ for some interpretation, and likewise for $r(a, b)$; an Abox is consistent iff all its assertions are consistent at once. Logics in the literature offer significantly larger sets of features, such as numerical restrictions, role hierarchies, inverse and transitive roles (the OWL language contains several such features [21]). Most description logics have direct translations into multi-modal logics [44] and fragments of first-order logic [5] (the translation to first-order logic is particularly important here: each concept C is interpreted as a unary predicate $C(x)$; each role r is interpreted as a binary predicate $r(x, y)$; other constructs have direct translations into first-order logic, such as $\exists r.C$ to $\exists y : r(x, y) \wedge C(y)$ and $\forall r.C$ to $\forall y : r(x, y) \rightarrow C(y)$).

Several probabilistic descriptions logics have appeared in the literature. Heinsohn [20], Jaeger [24] and Sebastiani [46] consider probabilistic inclusion axioms such as $P_{\mathcal{D}}(\text{Plant}) = \alpha$, meaning that a randomly selected individual is a Plant with probability α. That is, probabilities are assigned to subsets of the domain $\mathcal{D}$; this characterizes a *domain-based* semantics. Sebastiani allows assessments such as $P(\text{Plant}(\text{Tweety})) = \alpha$ as well, specifying probabilities over the interpretations themselves. For example one interprets $P(\text{FlyingBird}(\text{Tweety})) = 0.001$ as assigning 0.001 to the probability of all interpretations where Tweety is a flying bird. This characterizes an *interpretation-based* semantics. Overall, most proposals for probabilistic description logics have adopted a domain-based semantics [13,14,18,20,24,30,33,46,52], while relatively few have adopted an interpretation-based semantics [6,46]. The difficulty with domain-based semantics is the problem of *direct inference* [31]: statistical information about the domain does not translate into information about individuals. For example, suppose we learn that $P(\text{FlyingBird}) = 0.3$; a domain-based semantics takes a fixed domain and fixed interpretation and assigns 0.3 to the probability that an element of the domain is a flying bird. However, we learn nothing about $P(\text{FlyingBird}(\text{Tweety}))$, as the interpretation is fixed and Tweety either is a flying bird, or not. For this reason, most proposals for probabilistic description logics with a domain-based semantics simply do not handle assertions. We note that Dürig and Studer do avoid direct inference by only allowing probabilisties over assertions [14]. Lukasiewicz has proposed another strategy, where probabilities over terminologies and assertions blend through an entailment relation with nonmonotonic properties, *lexicographic entailment* [18,33]. Lukasiewicz considers probabilistic versions of very expressive description logics; his logic P-$\mathcal{SHOIN}$(D) is currently the most expressive probabilistic description logic in the literature. In this paper we prefer not to employ nonmonotonic reasoning.

The probabilistic description logics discussed so far share the property that a set of formulas may be satisfied by one *or more* probability measures (in fact, semantics based on *sets of probability measures* are often adopted by probabilistic logics [19]). Another characteristic shared by the probabilistic description logics mentioned so far is that they do not express judgements of independence. However, there has been significant effort in combining logical constructs with Bayesian and Markov networks in the last fifteen years, so as to benefit from independence judgements rather than to suffer from their complexities [17,36]. Indeed, several recent probabilistic description logics have adopted semantics based on Bayesian networks. The first logic to do so, P-CLASSIC, enlarges the logic CLASSIC with a set of Bayesian networks ("p-classes") so as to specify a single probability measure over the domain [30]. A limitation is that P-CLASSIC does not handle assertions. Some characteristics of P-CLASSIC are present in the logics proposed in this paper (acyclicity and Markov conditions); however our interest in obtaining meaningful probabilities over assertions, by resorting to interpretation-based semantics, is a major difference.

Other logics that combine terminologies with Bayesian networks are Yelland's Tiny Description Logic [52], Ding and Peng's BayesOWL language [13], and Staker's logic [49] (none can handle assertions). Costa and Laskey's PR-OWL language [6] adopts an interpretation-based semantics inherited from Multi-entity Bayesian networks (MEBNs) [7], and quite similar to the semantics used in this paper. The PR-OWL language is more expressive than ours, with less guarantees concerning inference and infinite domains; their inference algorithms are based on incremental propositionalization. Finally, most constructs in this paper can be also emulated in Nottelmann and Fuhr's probabilistic version of the OWL language, however our inference methods are completely different from theirs [40]. Besides the literature just reviewed, there is a large body of relevant work on knowledge databases [22] and on fuzzy description logics [34].

3 A Probabilistic Description Logic: CR$\mathcal{ALC}$

Probabilistic inclusions and inferences. Start with a fragment of $\mathcal{ALC}$ by discarding roles for a moment. That is, if C and D are concepts, then $\neg C$, $C \sqcap D$ and $C \sqcup D$ are concepts as well. Concept inclusions and definitions are allowed, denoted by $C \sqsubseteq D$ and $C \equiv D$ where D is a concept and C is a concept name (that is, we do not allow *general concept axioms* [2]). Now introduce *probabilistic inclusions* $P(C|D) = \alpha$, where D is a concept and C is a concept name. If D is $\top$, then we simply write $P(C) = \alpha$. We are interested in computing a *query* $P(A_0(a_0)|\mathcal{A})$ for an Abox $\mathcal{A} = \{A_j(a_j)\}_{j=1}^M$ (this is an *inference*).

Acyclicity. Given a probabilistic inclusion $P(C|D) = \alpha$, say that C "directly uses" B if B appears in the expression of D; again, "uses" is the transitive closure of "directly uses", and a terminology is acyclic if no concept uses itself (Section 2). We assume that every terminology is acyclic; this is in fact a common assumption for description logics [2]. The acyclicity assumption allows one to draw any terminology $\mathcal{T}$ as a directed acyclic graph $\mathcal{G}(\mathcal{T})$: each concept name is a node, and if a concept C directly uses concept D, then D is a *parent* of C in $\mathcal{G}(\mathcal{T})$.

Domain/interpretation semantics. As noted in Section 2, in a domain-based semantics we consider measures over the domain $\mathcal{D}$, and the natural interpretation for a probabilistic inclusion is $P(\text{set of } Cs \mid \text{set of } Ds) = \alpha$. An interpretation-based semantics instead postulates probability measures over interpretations (that is, over complete assignments of individuals to concepts: for m concepts and $|\mathcal{D}| = n$, there are 2^{mn} interpretations). The most natural interpretation-based semantics for $P(C|D) = \alpha$ seems to be (as discussed for instance by Lukasiewicz [32]):

$$\forall x : P(C(x)|D(x)) = \alpha. \tag{1}$$

We favor this interpretation-based semantics because it can smoothly interpret a query $P(A(a)|B(b))$ for concepts A and B and individuals a and b. A domain-based semantics would assign 0 or 1 to the probability $P(A(a)|B(b))$, depending on the particular fixed interpretation. That is, the semantics (1) lets us bypass direct inference (the problem of moving from probabilities over domains to probabilities for individuals).[1] Note that asserted facts must be conditioned upon: there is no contradiction between assessment $\forall x : P(C(x)) = \alpha$ and assertion $C(a)$, as we can have $P(C(a)|C(a)) = 1$ while $P(C(a)) = \alpha$.

  Following Bacchus [3], we harmonize the semantics (1) and assertions such as $C(a)$ by assuming that all individuals are rigid designators (that is, an individual corresponds to the same element of the domain in all interpretations).

Adding roles: relational networks. We now introduce restrictions $\exists r.C$ and $\forall r.C$ into the logic. To simplify the presentation, without loss of generality we assume that C in

---

[1] As a digression, we note that the most elaborate attempt to address, rather than bypass, direct inference in probabilistic description logics are Lukasiewicz's. He uses lexicographic entailment to produce direct inference [18,33], and also tries to avoid a drawback of semantics (1): the fact that it forbids exceptions such as $P(C(a)|D(a)) < \alpha$ for some individual a.

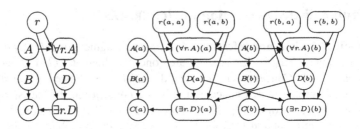

Fig. 1. Graph $\mathcal{G}(\mathcal{T}_1)$ for terminology $\mathcal{T}_1$ in Example 1, and its grounding for domain $\mathcal{D} = \{a, b\}$

these restrictions is a concept name (an auxiliary definition may specify a concept C of arbitrary complexity). As probabilistic inclusions must only have concept names in their conditioned concept, assessments such as $P(\forall r.C|D) = \alpha$ are not allowed.

Now, each restriction $\exists r.C$ and $\forall r.C$ is added as a node to the graph $\mathcal{G}(\mathcal{T})$. As each one of these restrictions directly uses r and C, the graph $\mathcal{G}(\mathcal{T})$ must contain a node for each role r, and an edge from r to each restriction directly using it. Each node $\exists r.C$ or $\forall r.C$ is a *deterministic* node in that its value is completely determined by its parents; again, we emphasize that a direct assessment such as $P(\exists r.C|D) = \alpha$ is not allowed.

Example 1. Consider a terminology $\mathcal{T}_1$ with concepts A, B, C, D. Suppose $P(A) = \alpha_1$, $B \sqsubseteq A$, $C \sqsubseteq B \sqcup \exists r.D$, $P(B|A) = \alpha_2$, $P(C|B \sqcup \exists r.D) = \alpha_3$, and $P(D|\forall r.A) = \alpha_4$. The last three assessments specify beliefs about partial overlap among concepts. Suppose also $P(D|\neg\forall r.A) = \epsilon \approx 0$ (conveying the existence of exceptions to the inclusion of D in $\forall r.A$). Figure 1 depicts $\mathcal{G}(\mathcal{T})$. □

Independence and Markov condition. Probabilistic description logics such as P-CLASSIC, BayesOWL and PR-OWL employ judgements of independence, encoded by a Markov condition, to constrain probability values (down to uniqueness) and to decompose models into small pieces. Other probabilistic logics adopt similar Markov conditions for graph-based assessments [16,36], and a few logics adopt graphs with Markov conditions and allow assessments "outside" of the graphs [1,9].

We take the position that the structure of the "directly uses" relation encodes stochastic independence through a Markov condition. First, for every concept $C \in \mathcal{T}$ and for every $x \in \mathcal{D}$, $C(x)$ is independent of every assertion that does not use $C(x)$, given assertions that directly use C. Second, for every $(x, y) \in \mathcal{D} \times \mathcal{D}$, $r(x, y)$ is independent of all other assertions, except ones that use $r(x, y)$.

The interaction between logical constructs and this Markov condition has its subtleties. For instance, if $\mathcal{G}(\mathcal{T})$ is $A \rightarrow C \leftarrow B$ because $A \sqsubseteq \neg C$ and $B \sqsubseteq C$, then the Markov condition imposes independence of A and B, but this is possible only if $P(A) = 0$ or $P(B) = 0$, as $A \sqcap B$ must be empty [10]. Thus CR$\mathcal{ALC}$ does not exactly match the behavior of standard $\mathcal{ALC}$ when probabilities are unspecified, as logical constraints may interact with the Markov condition; we leave for the future a detailed study of the relationship between CR$\mathcal{ALC}$ and standard $\mathcal{ALC}$.

Homogeneity. Note that a terminology in CR$\mathcal{ALC}$ may not specify a single measure over interpretations (in Example 1, the assessment $P(C|B \sqcup \exists r.D) = \alpha_3$ does not guarantee that $P(C|B \sqcap \exists r.D)$ is constrained down to a single value). We assume the following *homogeneity condition* always holds. We assume that, given a concept C with parents $D_1, \ldots, D_m$, then for any conjunction of the m concepts $\pm D_i$, where $\pm D_i$ is either D_i or $\neg D_i$, $P(C(x)| \pm D_1(x) \sqcap \pm D_2(x) \sqcap \cdots \sqcap \pm D_m(x))$ is a constant across individuals x. Without this condition, a probability left unspecified in a terminology may take a distict value for each individual in the domain, a situation we wish to preclude. With the homogeneity condition, any terminology can be viewed as a non-recursive relational Bayesian network [25], except for the fact that some probabilities may not be precisely specified. Indeed, for a fixed finite domain $\mathcal{D}$, the propositionalization of a terminology $\mathcal{T}$ produces a *credal network*; that is, a Bayesian network where probabilities are not precisely specified [8]. Figure 1 shows a propositionalized version of $\mathcal{T}_1$ (Example 1).

Thus we have a logic with the constructs of $\mathcal{ALC}$, including assertions (with rigidity for individuals), plus probabilistic inclusions with semantics (1), acyclicity and the extended Markov condition, and homogeneity. We refer to the resulting logic as CR$\mathcal{ALC}$ (for "credal" $\mathcal{ALC}$).

Uniqueness. There is a way to guarantee uniqueness of probabilities that may be useful in practice. First, adopt the *unique names assumption*; that is, distinct names for individuals correspond to distinct elements of the domain. Second, assume the following *uniqueness condition*: (i) for each concept C: if C has no parents, then $P(C) = \alpha$ is given; and if C has parents, then either C is specified by a definition, or C has a single parent D and probabilistic inclusions with respect to D and $\neg D$ (that is, either C is determined by its parents or C is a "fully probabilistic" node); and (ii) for each role r, an assessment $P(r) = \alpha$ is made, whose semantics is $\forall x, y : P(r(x, y)) = \alpha$.

The unique names assumption and the uniqueness condition guarantee that, when we ground a terminology, we obtain a Bayesian network (different assumptions guarantee uniqueness in P-CLASSIC and PR-OWL).

Example 2. Consider a terminology $\mathcal{T}_2$ with concepts A, B, C, D, where: $P(A) = \alpha_1$, $B \sqsubseteq A$, $P(B|A) = \alpha_2$, $D \equiv \forall r.A$, $C \equiv B \sqcup \exists r.D$, and $P(r) = \alpha_3$. Figure 1 also applies, but now all probabilities are precisely specified.

4 Inference: First-Order Elimination and Loopy Propagation

Consider an inference in a CR$\mathcal{ALC}$ terminology, defined as the calculation of query $Q = P(A_0(a_0)|\mathcal{A})$ for $\mathcal{A} = \{A_j(a_j)\}_{j=1}^{M}$ (where $|\mathcal{D}| > M$). We start with both the uniqueness condition and *domain closure* (domain with finite cardinality n that is known and given as part of the input). Later we discuss removal of these assumptions.

We first derive the joint probability distribution over the set $V_{\mathcal{T}}^n$ containing all assertions generated from $\mathcal{T}$ and a domain $\mathcal{D}$ with cardinality n. To do so, introduce random variables that are indicator functions of grounded relations. We use the same notation for an assertion and its associated random variable. For instance, $C(a)$ and $r(a, b)$ refer both to assertions and to random variables that yield 1 if the assertion holds and 0 otherwise. Denote by $\mathcal{C}$ the set of concept names in $\mathcal{T}$, plus restrictions such as $\exists r.C$

and $\forall r.C$ (where C is always a concept name); by $\mathcal{R}$ the set of role names in $\mathcal{T}$; and by $\text{pa}(C_i(x))$ the parents of concept C_i. Then our assumptions imply:

$$P(V_{\mathcal{T}}^n) = \prod_{C_i \in \mathcal{C};\, x \in \mathcal{D}} P(C_i(x)|\text{pa}(C_i(x))) \times \prod_{r \in \mathcal{R};\, x,y \in \mathcal{D}} P(r(x,y)).$$

One can propositionalize any terminology and do inference in the resulting network; such a strategy is clearly not scalable. Our strategy is instead to employ techniques from *first-order variable elimination* [11,12,42]. The first step then is to write Q and $P(V_{\mathcal{T}}^n)$ in a *shattered* form [11]; that is, so that every pair of atoms can be grounded either into identical or disjoint sets of grounded atoms, taking into account constraints on the possible assertions.

A key insight is that in CR$\mathcal{ALC}$ we can syntactically shatter the query and the distribution at once. Define $\mathcal{D}' \doteq \{a_0, \ldots, a_M\}$ and $\mathcal{D}'' \doteq \mathcal{D} \backslash \mathcal{D}'$. The following theorem can be proved by inspecting Expression (2) and noting that it satisfies all conditions required for shattering [12]:

Theorem 1. *Query Q and $P(V_{\mathcal{T}}^n)$ are shattered when $P(V_{\mathcal{T}}^n)$ is written as:*

$$\prod_{C_i \in \mathcal{C};\, a' \in \mathcal{D}'} P(C_i(a')|\text{pa}(C_i(a'))) \quad \times \prod_{r \in \mathcal{R};\, a',a'' \in \mathcal{D}'} P(r(a',a''))$$

$$\times \prod_{r \in \mathcal{R};\, a' \in \mathcal{D}';\, x_0 \in \mathcal{D}''} P(r(a',x_0))\, P(r(x_0,a')) \tag{2}$$

$$\times \prod_{C_i \in \mathcal{C};\, x_0 \in \mathcal{D}''} P(C_i(x_0)|\text{pa}(C_i(x_0))) \quad \times \prod_{r \in \mathcal{R};\, x_0,x_1 \in \mathcal{D}''} P(r(x_0,x_1)),$$

where $\text{pa}(C_i(x))$ denotes the parents of C_i if C_i is a concept name; and if C_i is a restriction $\exists r.C$ or $\forall r.C$, then $\text{pa}(C_i(a'))$ denotes $\{r(a',a''), C(a'') : a'' \in \mathcal{D}'\} \cup \{r(a',x_0), C(x_0) : x_0 \in \mathcal{D}''\}$, and $\text{pa}(C_i(x_0))$ denotes $\{r(x_0,a'), C(a') : a' \in \mathcal{D}'\} \cup \{r(x_0,x_1), C(x_1) : x_1 \in \mathcal{D}''\}$. □

The first line of Expression (2) encodes a propositional Bayesian network over individuals in Q. These individuals are connected to other individuals through roles $P(r(a',x_0))$ and $P(r(x_0,a'))$ (in $\text{pa}(C_i(a'))$, $\text{pa}(C_i(x_0))$ and in the second line of Expression (2)). The third line builds a relational Bayesian network with "generic" individuals x_0 and x_1, with connections $P(r(x_0,x_0))$ and $P(r(x_0,x_1))$. Figure 2 offers a visual translation of shattering on terminology $\mathcal{T}_2$ and query $P(C(a_0))$. A benefit from explicit shattering of the Q and $P(V_{\mathcal{T}}^n)$ is that we can apply "first-order" d-separation on the shattered network, thus eliminating unnecessary parts of the terminology. For instance, node $(\exists r.D)(x_0)$ can be removed from Figure 2 when we compute $P(C(a_0))$.

First-order variable elimination is, in essence, variable elimination in the shattered network. Some gains are apparent. For instance, node $B(x_0)$ in Figure 2 can be eliminated for all x_0 at once, as $\sum_{B(x_0)} P(V_{\mathcal{T}_2}^n) \propto \sum_{B(x_0)} \prod_{x_0 \in \mathcal{D}''} P(B(x_0)|A(x_0)) \times P(C(x_0)|B(x_0),(\exists r.A)(x_0))$, and we can invert summation and product in the last expression (this is an *inversion elimination* [11]). The elimination of nodes containing restrictions requires new techniques. Note that, while Braz et al do not have quantification in their language [11,12], Poole discusses the network where $\exists x : A(x)$ has single

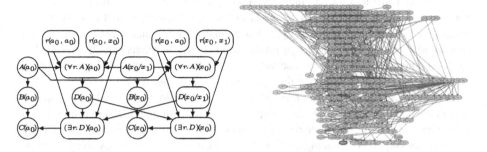

Fig. 2. A shattered version of T_2 and query $P(C(a_0))$; grounded network for T_2 and $|\mathcal{D}| = 10$

parent $A(x)$. Poole shows that $P(\exists x : A(x)) = 1 - (1 - P(A(x)))^n$ when the groundings of $A(x)$ are independent [42]. Such a nice result does not apply when restrictions are themselves parameterized, as is the case here (but approximations proposed later do use this insight).

We first note the algebraic structure of distributions $P(C_i|\text{pa}(C_i))$ when C_i is a restriction, using indicator functions. Remember that such distributions only yield 0 or 1 probabilities, as a restriction is completely determined by its parents. In the next two expressions, $\forall$ stands for the indicator function of $\forall r.C(x)$, $\exists$ stands for the indicator function of $\exists r.C(x)$, and likewise C stands for $C(x)$ and r stands for $r(x, y)$. Then:

$$P(\forall|\text{pa}(\forall)) = (\forall)\left(\prod_{y \in \mathcal{D}} 1 - r + rC\right) + (1 - \forall)\left(1 - \prod_{y \in \mathcal{D}} 1 - r + rC\right); \quad (3)$$

$$P(\exists|\text{pa}(\exists)) = (\exists)\left(1 - \prod_{y \in \mathcal{D}} 1 - rC\right)(1 - \exists)\left(\prod_{y \in \mathcal{D}} 1 - rC\right). \quad (4)$$

In theory, one could apply these expressions to the shattered network produced by Theorem 1, and then run first-order variable elimination. Our experience in trying the algorithm on small examples (such as the examples discussed previously) suggests that exact inference in the shattered network is rarely viable. The difficulty is that, *in exactly those cases where propositionalization does not work due to the presence of quantifiers, first-order inference seems to fail as well, at least in practice.* Note that first-order variable elimination does not guarantee elimination of "first-order" nodes beforehand; in the worst case the network (or vast parts of it) must be propositionalized. The difficulty is that restrictions typically lead to many connections between grounded nodes due to their quantifiers. To illustrate this fact, Figure 1 (right) shows a propositionalization of terminology T_2 with a $n = 10$, produced using the Primula system for relational Bayesian networks (www.cs.aau.dk/~jaeger/Primula/). The network is dense due to auxiliary nodes that must be inserted to encode deterministic relations (mostly quantifiers); without these auxiliary nodes the probability tables cannot even be stored. Exact inference in this network does not seem possible even with the best available algorithms (calculation of $P(C(a_0))$ was possible up to $n = 9$ and failed for $n > 9$ due to memory exhaustion).

Instead of insisting on exact methods, a wiser and more scalable strategy is to look for approximations. Here the challenge is to find approximations that can exploit the structure of quantifiers. We investigate variational methods that "break" connections in networks; among those, the *loopy propagation* algorithm seems particularly suitable [39]. Another idea would be to use variational approximations of Noisy-OR [29] in Expressions (3) and (4); we leave this possibility for the future.

A natural strategy then is to propositionalize a terminology and run loopy propagation in the resulting network. Loopy propagation deals with quantifiers in a straightforward manner: a restriction node receives messages from its neighbors, and then locally produces messages by replacing the "local" distribution $P(C|\mathrm{pa}(C))$ by an appropriate Expression (3) or (4). Note that Poole's analysis of quantifiers, mentioned previously, applies locally during loopy propagation.

However, we can do *much better*, and this is one of the main insights of this paper. We can use the shattered network produced by Theorem 1 directly, and concoct a *first-order* version of loopy propagation: simply run loopy propagation in the shattered network, and combine the local messages using Expressions (3) or (4) as appropriate; if a message flows from a parameterized node to a restriction node, then it must be raised to a power (equal to the number of individuals that can be substituted for the parameter) before combination in Expressions (4) or (3). Note that it is not just the case that we are running loopy propagation in a conveniently modified version of $\mathcal{G}(\mathcal{T})$; we are indeed running a first-order version of loopy propagation, because all the messages that are sent in the parameterized portion of the shattered network would be replicated were the terminology propositionalized. Thus, the same excellent empirical performance that has been observed for loopy propagation (in propositional networks) is necessarily transferred to this first-order loopy propagation scheme.

Example 3. Consider node $(\forall r.A)(x_0)$ in Figure 2. A possible schedule of messages has nodes $A(a_0)$, $A(x_0/x_1)$, $r(x_0, a_0)$ and $r(x_0, x_1)$ sending messages to $(\forall r.A)(x_0)$. A message to be sent to node $D(x_0/x_1)$ is easily produced as, locally to the approximation scheme, $P((\forall r.A)(x_0) = 1) = \prod_{y \in \mathcal{D}} 1 - P(r(x_0, y)) (1 - P(A(y)))$.

The idea that a first-order loopy propagation scheme can be built in probabilistic relational models was advanced by Jaimovich et al [28] for Markov networks without observed variables, and more recently by Sigla and Domingos [48] for Markov logic. What the shattered network allows us to do is to apply first-order loopy propagation on a structure that is fixed beforehand even when observations are made.

To illustrate the performance of this first-order loopy propagation scheme, consider again Example 2. The next table shows $P(C(a_0))$ for a domain containing individuals $a_0, \ldots, a_{n-1}$, for several n. Whenever possible we show the result of exact inference with a state-of-art algorithm (in the SamIam package at reasoning.cs.ucla.edu/samiam, using the recursive decomposition algorithm). Note that inferences converge to a stable value for n large; the analysis of Section 5 sheds light on this issue.

n	1	2	3	5	9	10	20	50
Loopy: $P(C(a_0))$	0.5175	0.5383	0.5291	0.4885	0.4296	0.4223	0.4049	0.4050
Exact: $P(C(a_0))$	0.4350	0.4061	0.4050	0.4050	0.4050	—	—	—

As another example, we have built a larger terminology containing 15 nodes, with 3 restrictions and a considerable amount of arcs amongst nodes (details are omitted due to lack of space). Exact inference became unfeasible even for small domains; loopy propagation produced inferences in seconds for $n = 10, 20$.

We have worked so far under the uniqueness assumption. In practice it may be useful to drop such a demanding assumption, as one may for instance choose not to specify $P(r)$ for all roles. In theory, lack of uniqueness (in the presence of homogeneity) is easy to handle: instead of a single probability measure, we must now deal with a set of probability measures; instead of computing a single value for an inference, we must compute a minimum and a maximum value for the probabilities of interest [8]. In practice, the calculation of exact probability bounds without uniqueness appears quite challenging computationally. However, the picture is different for approximate algorithms. Indeed, the *L2U algorithm* [23] is a version of loopy propagation for credal networks with binary variables that has been observed empirically to have excellent performance. One can extend L2U to first-order just as we did for loopy propagation, now letting messages carry probability intervals. Again, messages are locally combined and quantifiers can be dealt with in a local fashion. And again, the first-order algorithm has the property that its performance is identical to what would be obtained were the terminology grounded and L2U performed in the grounded network.

To illustrate the performance of this first-order L2U scheme, we return again to Example 2. But now we take $P(r)$ to be *entirely unspecified*; that is, it can be any value in the interval $[0, 1]$. This is in accord with the usual description logics where no information is provided for roles except through their use in restrictions. In the next table we show inferences for $P(C(a_0))$ for a domain for several n (an inference now produces an interval containing lower/upper probabilities). Note the convergence of probabilities as n increases. Perhaps more surprisingly, note the little influence $P(r)$ has in the value of $P(C(a_0))$; this suggests that one may leave various probabilities free in a knowledge base and still get meaningful answers.

n	1	3	5	10	20	50
L2U: $P(C(a_0))$	[0.405000 0.464500]	[0.405000 0.406783]	[0.405000 0.405030]	[0.405000 0.405000]	[0.405000 0.405000]	[0.405000 0.405000]

5 Infinite Domains

Infinite domains are useful, when a domain is finite but very large, and necessary, when the available information does not constrain the cardinality of the domain. However, infinite domains are challenging: there are issues concerning existence and uniqueness of a joint measure, and then there are obvious difficulties with inference based on propositionalization. Indeed, first-order variable elimination may fail for infinite domains when probabilities are expressed in Braz et al's language [12].

We use results by Jaeger [26,27] to prove existence and uniqueness for CR$\mathcal{ALC}$:

Theorem 2. *Every terminology $\mathcal{T}$ in* CR$\mathcal{ALC}$ *defines a unique joint distribution under the uniqueness condition, and* $P(V_{\mathcal{T}}^{\infty}) = \lim_{n \to \infty} P(V_{\mathcal{T}}^{n})$.

Proof. As every terminology in CR$\mathcal{ALC}$ under the given assumptions defines a non-recursive relational Bayesian network, it defines a unique joint distribution over an appropriate algebra [27, Th. 4.7]. Now note that all restrictions can be rewritten as *max-based combination functions* [25], and consequently they are *exponentially convergent* [26, Def. 3.4]. The limit of the joint distribution as n grows is then the joint distribution for an infinite domain [26, Th. 3.9].   □

Similar results have been proved for the BLOG language [35]. Existence has also been proved for other probabilistic description logics where infinite domains may lead to violation of uniqueness [7,41,47]; existence also obtains for logics that assign probabilities over domains (even without uniqueness) [18,33].

We now turn to inference with infinite domains, restricting ourselves to queries conditioned on ⊤. Here again Theorem 1 comes handy. We simply analyze the shattered graph top down, taking limits at each Expression (3) or (4) that we meet. (Gaifman's theorem [15] is necessary here to prove correctness, as it shows that probabilities for restrictions are obtained by taking limits over disjunctions/conjunctions.)

For example, if $P(r) > 0$ and $P(A) > 0$, then for any x, we have both limits $\lim_{n \to \infty} P((\exists r.A)(x)|\mathrm{pa}((\exists r.A)(x))) = 1$, $\lim_{n \to \infty} P((\forall r.A)(x)|\mathrm{pa}((\forall r.A)(x))) = 0$ whenever the conditioning events have nonzero probability. There are several other possibilities, by taking combinations of $P(r) = 0$, $P(r) = 1$, $P(A) = 0$, $P(A) = 1$; all of these cases lead to probability 0 or 1 for restrictions. This rationale constructs a *zero-one law* for CR$\mathcal{ALC}$. A similar zero-one law for description logics has been proved by Ycart and Rousset [51] for a uniform distribution over possible assertions; Jaeger's analysis of infinite domains [27] also implies several related zero-one laws. An interesting side effect is that we can make a linear number of queries in $\mathcal{G}(\mathcal{T})$ (one for each restriction, from top to bottom) to build a relational Bayesian network *without roles* on which inferences can be made. The next example should be sufficient to illustrate how these ideas can be used when computing queries for infinite domains.

Example 4. Consider terminology $\mathcal{T}_2$, with $\alpha_1 = 2\alpha_2 = 3\alpha_3 = 0.9$, query $P(C(a_0))$ and an infinite domain. From top down: as $P(r) > 0$ and $P(A) > 0$, $P(\forall r.A) = 0$; thus $P(D) = 0$ and $P(C) = P(B) = P(B|A)P(A) + P(B|\neg A)P(\neg A) = \alpha_2 \alpha_1$ and $P(C(a_0)) = 0.405$. Compare this value with the values obtained in the previous section for n large.

6 Conclusion

This paper started from the desire to represent terminologies with probabilities over concepts, in such a way that queries involving assertions can be handled. A probabilistic version of the $\mathcal{ALC}$ description logic has been introduced, with an interpretation-based semantics that allows probabilistic inclusions and queries on the probability of assertions (thus bypassing the problem of direct inference). The paper contributed with techniques for first-order inference algorithms in finite domains (and to a limited extent, in infinite domains) and in particular with a first-order loopy propagation scheme that is based on the "shattered" version of a terminology. Such techniques may be useful to other languages such as Costa and Laskey's PR-OWL [6]. The use of shattering and loopy propagation may be useful in other logics as well, a point that we leave for future investigation.

The paper clearly left a few topics for the near future: investigation of inference in infinite domains *with observations*, and more empirical testing with improved variational approximations. In the future we plan to investigate extensions of the language, such as at-least and at-most restrictions (these can be handled through loopy propagation) or role inclusions, leading gradually to a full-blown version of the OWL language.

A few closing words on the assumptions we have adopted seem appropriate. Some of them could easily be relaxed; for instance, we could allow probabilistic inclusions with a set of conditioned concepts, provided no such concept is a restriction. Other assumptions seem difficult to remove, such as the rigidity and unique names assumptions on individuals, and the homogeneity condition on probabilities. Also, it seems difficult to remove the acyclicity condition (and the associated Markov condition). Undirected graphs would seem more amenable to a mix of logical and probabilistic constructs as cycles are not a concern [43,50]; however, undirected graphs interact awkwardly with probabilistic logic, as the usual Markov condition for undirected graphs fails to imply factorization of measures in the presence of logical constraints [38]. A possibility is to postulate a factorization from the outset [43,47]; we have preferred to stay with the Markov condition of directed acyclic graphs, even though probabilistic description logics based on undirected graphs certainly deserve more study.

As a final comment, we note that it would also be desirable to drop the domain closure assumption, as description logics never assume anything about cardinality of the domain [37]. Interest must then be in computing minima/maxima of probabilities as n varies. Given the rigidity assumption, a query fixes observations with respect to elements of the domain, and leaves other elements unobserved. Even though no general technique for such optimization problems seems to be developed at this point, in some simple cases one can find bounds and optimal n:

Example 5. Consider terminology T_1 with $\alpha_1 = 2\alpha_2 = 3\alpha_3 = 4\alpha_4 = 1000\epsilon = 0.9$, and query $P(C(a_0))$, with no information about domain cardinality. This terminology is simple enough that we can write down the expressions for the query and optimize over them. We obtain $P(C(a_0)) \in [0.1215, 0.3]$; the lower bound is obtained for $P(r) = 0$ (any n) and the upper bound for $P(r) = 1$ and $n = \infty$.

Acknowledgements

This work was partially funded by FAPESP (04/09568-0); the first author is partially supported by CNPq, and the second author is supported by HP Brazil R&D. We thank all these organizations.

References

1. Andersen, K.A., Hooker, J.N.: Bayesian logic. Decision Support Systems 11, 191–210 (1994)
2. Baader, F., Calvanese, D., McGuinness, D.L., Nardi, D., Patel-Schneider, P.F.: Description Logic Handbook. Cambridge University Press, Cambridge (2002)
3. Bacchus, F.: Representing and Reasoning with Probabilistic Knowledge: A Logical Approach. MIT Press, Cambridge (1990)

4. Berners-Lee, T., Hendlers, J., Lassila, O.: The semantic web. In: Scientific American, pp. 34–43 (2001)
5. Borgida, A.: On the relative expressiveness of description logics and predicate logics. Artificial Intelligence 82(1-2), 353–367 (1996)
6. Costa, P.C.G., Laskey, K.B.: PR-OWL: A framework for probabilistic ontologies. In: Conf. on Formal Ontology in Information Systems (2006)
7. da Costa, P.C.G., Laskey, K.B.: Of Klingons and starships: Bayesian logic for the 23rd century. In: Conf. on Uncertainty in Artificial Intelligence (2005)
8. Cozman, F.G.: Credal networks. Artificial Intelligence 120, 199–233 (2000)
9. Cozman, F.G., de Campos, C.P., Ferreira da Rocha, J.C.: Probabilistic logic with independence. Int. Journal of Approximate Reasoning (in press, September 7, 2007) doi: 10.1016/j.ijar.2007.08.002
10. Polpo de Campos, C., Cozman, F.G., Luna, J.E.O.: Assessing a consistent set of sentences in relational probabilistic logic with stochastic independence. Journal of Applied Logic (to appear)
11. de Salvo Braz, R., Amir, E., Roth, D.: Lifted first-order probabilistic inference. In: Int. Joint Conf. in Artificial Intelligence (IJCAI) (2005)
12. de Salvo Braz, R., Amir, E., Roth, D.: MPE and partial inversion in lifted probabilistic variable elimination. AAAI (2006)
13. Ding, Z., Peng, Y., Pan, R.: BayesOWL: Uncertainty modeling in semantic web ontologies. In: Soft Computing in Ontologies and Semantic Web. Studies in Fuzziness and Soft Computing, vol. 204. Springer, Berlin (2006)
14. Dürig, M., Studer, T.: Probabilistic ABox reasoning: preliminary results. In: Description Logics, pp. 104–111 (2005)
15. Gaifman, H.: Concerning measures on first-order calculi. Israel Journal of Mathematics 2, 1–18 (1964)
16. Getoor, L., Friedman, N., Koller, D., Taskar, B.: Learning probabilistic models of relational structure. In: Int. Conf. on Machine Learning, pp. 170–177 (2001)
17. Getoor, L., Taskar, B.: Introduction to Statistical Relational Learning. MIT Press, Cambridge (2007)
18. Lukasiewicz, T., Giugno, R.: P-SHOQ(D): A probabilistic extension of SHOQ(D) for probabilistic ontologies in the semantic web. In: Flesca, S., Greco, S., Leone, N., Ianni, G. (eds.) JELIA 2002. LNCS (LNAI), vol. 2424, pp. 86–97. Springer, Heidelberg (2002)
19. Halpern, J.Y.: Reasoning about Uncertainty. MIT Press, Cambridge (2003)
20. Heinsohn, J.: Probabilistic description logics. In: Conf. on Uncertainty in Artificial Intelligence, pp. 311–318 (1994)
21. Horrocks, I., Patel-Schneider, P.F., van Harmelen, F.: From SHIQ and RDF to OWL: The making of a web ontology language. Journal of Web Semantics 1(1), 7–26 (2003)
22. Hung, E., Getoor, L., Subrahmanian, V.S.: Probabilistic interval XML. ACM Transactions on Computational Logic 8(4) (2007)
23. Ide, J.S., Cozman, F.G.: Approximate algorithms for credal networks with binary variables. Int. Journal of Approximate Reasoning 48(1), 275–296 (2008)
24. Jaeger, M.: Probabilistic reasoning in terminological logics. Principles of Knowledge Representation (KR), pp. 461–472 (1994)
25. Jaeger, M.: Relational Bayesian networks. In: Uncertainty in Artificial Intelligence, pp. 266–273. Morgan Kaufmann, San Francisco (1997)
26. Jaeger, M.: Convergence results for relational Bayesian networks. LICS (1998)
27. Jaeger, M.: Reasoning about infinite random structures with relational Bayesian networks. In: Knowledge Representation. Morgan Kaufmann, San Francisco (1998)
28. Jaimovich, A., Meshi, O., Friedman, N.: Template based inference in symmetric relational Markov random fields. Uncertainty in Artificial Intelligence, Canada. AUAI Press (2007)

29. Jordan, M.I., Ghahramani, Z., Jaakkola, T.S.: An introduction to variational methods for graphical models. Machine Learning 37, 183–233 (1999)
30. Koller, D., Pfeffer, A.: Object-oriented Bayesian networks. In: Conf. on Uncertainty in Artificial Intelligence, pp. 302–313 (1997)
31. Kyburg Jr., H.E., Teng, C.M.: Uncertain Inference. Cambridge University Press, Cambridge (2001)
32. Lukasiewicz, T.: Probabilistic logic programming. In: European Conf. on Artificial Intelligence, pp. 388–392 (1998)
33. Lukasiewicz, T.: Expressive probabilistic description logics. Artificial Intelligence (to appear)
34. Lukasiewicz, T., Straccia, U.: Managing uncertainty and vagueness in description logics for the semantic web (submitted, 2008)
35. Milch, B., Marthi, B., Sontag, D., Russell, S., Ong, D.L., Kolobov, A.: BLOG: Probabilistic models with unknown objects. In: IJCAI (2005)
36. Milch, B., Russell, S.: First-order probabilistic languages: into the unknown. In: Int. Conf. on Inductive Logic Programming (2007)
37. Motik, B., Horrocks, I., Rosati, R., Sattler, U.: Can OWL and logic programming live together happily ever after? In: Cruz, I., Decker, S., Allemang, D., Preist, C., Schwabe, D., Mika, P., Uschold, M., Aroyo, L.M. (eds.) ISWC 2006. LNCS, vol. 4273, pp. 501–514. Springer, Heidelberg (2006)
38. Moussouris, J.: Gibbs and Markov random systems with constraints. Journal of Statistical Physics 10(1), 11–33 (1974)
39. Murphy, K.P., Weiss, Y., Jordan, M.I.: Loopy belief propagation for approximate inference: An empirical study. In: Uncertainty in Artificial Intelligence, pp. 467–475 (1999)
40. Nottelmann, H., Fuhr, N.: Adding probabilities and rules to OWL lite subsets based on probabilistic datalog. Int. Journal of Uncertainty, Fuzziness and Knowledge-based Systems 14(1), 17–42 (2006)
41. Pfeffer, A., Koller, D.: Semantics and inference for recursive probability models. In: AAAI, pp. 538–544 (2000)
42. Poole, D.: First-order probabilistic inference. In: Int. Joint Conf. on Artificial Intelligence (IJCAI), pp. 985–991 (2003)
43. Richardson, M., Domingos, P.: Markov logic networks. Machine Learning 62(1-2), 107–136 (2006)
44. Schild, K.: A correspondence theory for terminological logics: Preliminary report. In: Int. Joint Conf. on Artificial Intelligence, pp. 466–471 (1991)
45. Schmidt-Schauss, M., Smolka, G.: Attributive concept descriptions with complements. Artificial Intelligence 48, 1–26 (1991)
46. Sebastiani, F.: A probabilistic terminological logic for modelling information retrieval. In: Int. ACM Conf. on Research and Development in Information Retrieval (SIGIR), Dublin, Ireland, pp. 122–130. Springer, Heidelberg (1994)
47. Sigla, P., Domingos, P.: Markov logic in infinite domains. In: Uncertainty in Artificial Intelligence, pp. 368–375. AUAI Press (2007)
48. Sigla, P., Domingos, P.: Lifted first-order belief propagation. AAAI (2008)
49. Staker, R.: Reasoning in expressive description logics using belief networks. In: Int. Conf. on Information and Knowledge Engineering, Las Vegas, USA, pp. 489–495 (2002)
50. Taskar, B., Abbeel, P., Koller, D.: Discriminative probabilistic models for relational data. In: Conf. on Uncertainty in Artificial Intelligence, Edmonton, Canada (2002)
51. Ycart, B., Rousset, M.-C.: A zero-one law for random sentences in description logics. Colloquium on Mathematics and Computer Science (2000)
52. Yelland, P.M.: Market analysis using a combination of Bayesian networks and description logics. Technical Report SMLI TR-99-78, Sun Microsystems Laboratories (1999)

On the Performance of Fuzzy Data Querying*

Mariela Curiel[1], Claudia González[1], Leonid Tineo[1], and Angélica Urrutia[2]

[1] Universidad Simón Bolívar, Departamento de Computación y T.I,
Caracas, Venezuela
{mcuriel,claudia,leonid}@ldc.usb.ve
[2] Universidad Católica del Maule, Departamento de Computación e Informática,
Talca, Chile
aurrutia@ucm.cl

Abstract. We are interested in providing databases with fuzzy data representation and flexible querying capabilities. This work concerns with a performance analysis based on statistical techniques to evaluate methods for fuzzy queries over fuzzy data. We introduce the application of Derivation Principle for this kind of queries and show its practical benefit using a prototype that we have built on top of Oracle's DBMS.

Keywords: Fuzzy Database, Query Processing, Querying Performance.

1 Introduction

Semantics of fuzzy sets application to databases for data representation and querying have received special attention of many database researchers ([1] [2] [3] [4]). Nevertheless the problem of fuzzy databases is not only a semantic matter but also a practical performance problem. In conventional DBMS, the problem of query evaluation remains somewhat open since given a query in general the optimal evaluation way cannot be reached. For fuzzy queries the process becomes more complex for two reasons: i) the available access paths cannot be directly used, and ii) the number of selected rows with fuzzy conditions number is larger than those selected by boolean conditions based result sets cardinality. In this sense few works have been done at present time ([5] [6] [3]). Main efforts try to take advantage of connections between fuzzy conditions and boolean ones, so that fuzzy query processing can come down to boolean query processing (at least partly). It has been proposed first by Bosc and Pivert [5] for the evaluation of SQLf and is widely known as the Derivation Principle. This principle has been applied to different kinds of vague queries over crisp data ([7], [8], [9], [10], [11], [12], [6], [13], [14],[15]).

---

* This work was supported in part by the Venezuelan Foundation for Science, Innovation and Technology FONACIT Grant G-2005000278. Main reason of doing this scientific work is to glorify our lovely God: "Whatever you do, work at it with all your heart, as working for the Lord, not for men, since you know that you will receive an inheritance from the Lord as a reward. It is the Lord Christ you are serving." (Colossians 3:23-24).

S. Greco and T. Lukasiewicz (Eds.): SUM 2008, LNAI 5291, pp. 134–145, 2008.
© Springer-Verlag Berlin Heidelberg 2008

Derivation Principle states that: *Given a fuzzy query, in most cases we may derive a crisp query that retrieves the same set of rows that the fuzzy query (it is known as Strong Derivation), furthermore, in worst case we may derive a crisp query that retrieves a set with rows that fuzzy one retrieves and some (low number of) undesired rows (it is known as Weak Derivation).* This worst case occurs when some *mean operator* (such as the *arithmetic mean* or the *harmonic mean* and so on) is used as connector for combining fuzzy conditions, nevertheless it has been demonstrated that the number of undesired rows is rather low [5]. Applying this principle, the fuzzy query is evaluated over the derived query answer set, keeping low the number of accessed rows and the extra cost of truth degree calculation.

At present time we are specially interested in the integration of SQLf and FSQL in a standard for fuzzy databases and it upgrade to SQL:2003 [16][4]. In this way it is necessary the extension of the Derivation Principle to vague queries over fuzzy data [17]. It suggests to offer an improvement because is not necessary to process the degree of membership to all rows. However, is possible that the condition to evaluate according to filter the registers adds some additional costs and affects the performance. Furthermore, no-atomic representation needed for fuzzy data storage could affect the performance because his storage requirements are bigger, this can bring more blocks to be recovered to the databases and more CPU use because requires more processing. These reasons make necessary a performance study by means of statistical models and descriptive analysis [18]. It would confirm or refuse the use of this principle for the evaluation of vague queries in presence of fuzzy data.

Rest of this paper is organized as follows: Section 2 concerns with of vague queries over fuzzy data and the Derivation Principle; Section 3 presents the for the statistics based performance study; Section 4 shows in detail the and parameters configuration for the study; Section 5 is devoted to the Descriptive Analysis of experimental results; and, finally Section 6 Points out the Conclusions and Future Work.

2   Semantics Aspects

In its original definition SQLf [1] does not allow fuzzy data values for attributes while FSQL does [2]. For the integration of these languages in a sole standard [16], four kinds of fuzzy attributes have been proposed. These are, lightly different form those of FSQL. Proposed types are: Type 1: attributes with precise data and an ordered domain. Fuzzy predicates could be defined over it. Example: the age has an ordered domain between [0,1000] years old, and defined labels like young, old, etc. Type 2: attributes with precise data, but with a non ordered domain. Similitude relations and fuzzy predicates could be defined over it. Example: colors are not ordered, but green is more similar to blue than red. Type 3: fuzzy data with an ordered domain. We could define an age as young when it is between 0 and 30 years old and adult for 31 to 60 years old, and clearly young<adult. Type 4: fuzzy data with a not ordered domain. Also we

could define a new color as 0.5/orange, 0.5/pink and similarity relation. The syntax to specify the data type of an attribute in the in the CREATE/ALTER TABLE statement will be: NAME FUZZYTYPEn CLASSICTYPE, where NAME is the name of the attribute, n is the fuzzy attribute type number, and CLASSICTYPE is the underlying basic domain. Possibilistic reasoning provides two truth measures for logic propositions: possibility (II) and necessity (N). In fuzzy conditions over classic (crisp) data, case of SQLf, necessity is unsuccessful [1][4], because it gets the same result as possibility measure. Thus, SQLf uses only the possibility measure. On the other hand, FSQL involves fuzzy data and fuzzy conditions. Then, FSQL allows using either possibility or necessity according to user desires. Nevertheless, we would like queries returning fuzzy relations defined by user preferences. Therefore, in the integration of FSQL and SQLf [16] the use of possibility measure as default has been proposed, also, when user desires, there is a way to specify that one wishes to use the necessity. Despite diverse querying structures in fuzzy set based extensions of SQL, we focus our attention here to basic block query:

```
SELECT <attribute expressions> FROM <relations>
WHERE <fuzzy_condition> THRESOLD < α >
```

The answer of this query is the fuzzy bag of rows in the Cartesian product of the relations in the FROM clause that satisfy the fuzzy condition with possibility measure greater or equal to the threshold α, membership degree to the result for each row is given by the possibility measure.

We also restrict the scope of our study in this paper to fuzzy conditions of form $T_1 = T_2$, being T_1 a fuzzy attribute of type 3 whose value is a trapezium shape fuzzy set with $\text{core}(T_1) = [b, c]$ and $\text{support}(T_1) = [a, d]$ and $T2$ a predicate defined by a fuzzy set also with a trapezium shape membership function having $\text{core}(T_2) = [f, g]$ and $\text{support}(T_2) = [e, h]$. In this case the truth degree is that of (1).

$$\mu(T_1 = T_2) = \begin{cases} 1 & \text{when } (b \leq f \leq c \vee f \leq g \leq c) \\ \frac{(d-e)}{(f-e)-(c-d)} & \text{when } (e < d \wedge c < f) \\ \frac{(a-h)}{(g-h)-(b-a)} & \text{when } (a < h \wedge g < b) \\ 0 & Otherwise \end{cases} \tag{1}$$

The answer of this query is the fuzzy bag of rows in the Cartesian product of the relations in the FROM clause that satisfy the fuzzy condition with possibility measure greater or equal to the threshold α, membership degree to the result for each row is given by the possibility measure.

In order to apply the Derivation Principle, it might be shown that [17], we can derive the Boolean condition $DNC(T_1 = T_2, \leq, \alpha)$ in (2) obtaining the derived query:

```
SELECT <attribute expressions> FROM <relations>
WHERE DNC(T₁ = T₂, ≤, α)
```

$$DCN(T_1 = T_2, \geq, \alpha) = (b \leq f \wedge f \leq c) \vee (b \leq g \wedge g \leq c) \vee$$
$$(f \leq b \wedge b \leq g)$$
$$\vee (e < d \wedge c < f \wedge \tfrac{d-e}{(f+d)-(e+c)} \geq \alpha) \qquad (2)$$
$$\vee (a < h \wedge g < b \wedge \tfrac{a-h}{(g+a)-(h+b)} \geq \alpha)$$

3 Methodology and Hypotheses

The performance evaluation methodology consists of the definition of working hypothesis and the study of their feasibility through controlled experiments and statistical methods. The set of experiments allow us to obtain data to fit a lineal model that describes the total consumed time in the prototype as a function of different factors. With the support of ANOVA, F-Tests and plots we study the importance of different factors and their interactions. The importance of a factor is measured by the proportion of the total variation in the response that is explained by it. The model and the descriptive analyses allow us to discern the right hypotheses. Hypotheses are posed to study the performance of queries over imperfect (fuzzy) and perfect (crisps) data with vague (fuzzy) criteria, also the performance of derivation mechanism over fuzzy data. We deal with the following working hypotheses:

- (H1) The use of fuzzy data will increment the total expend time in database engine.
- (H2) The total expend time in database engine using the Derivation Principle will be lower than that the generated using the Naïve Strategy.
- (H3) The use of the Derivation Principle would make total expend time in database less sensible to difference between fuzzy and crisp data.
- (H4) The use of Naïve Strategy would make total expend time in database less sensible to different user desired satisfaction levels.
- (H5) The Derivation Principle improves its performance when the query is more selective.

4 Experimental Design

For the experiments we have extended the fuzzy querying system SQLf-pl [19] that is based on SQLf and implemented on top of Oracle 9i. Fuzzy querying logic in SQLf-pl is implemented in PL/SQL. Translator for Derivation Principle and Naïve Strategy was developed in SWI-Prolog. SQLf-pl originally supports only precise (crisp) data, our extension supports also imprecise (fuzzy) data with trapezium shape representation.

We adopt a 2^k factorial design [18]. The observed or response variable in our study is the TCT: Total Consumed Time (TCT) that is measured by the Oracle RDBMS and obtained by trace feature and *tkprof* utility. Despite there is an

Table 1. Experimental factors and corresponding chosen levels for our 2^k factorial design

D:Data	S:Strategy	P:Predicate	V:Volume	H:Threshold
D1=CRISP	S1=NAIVE	P1=UNIMODAL	V1=SMALL	T1= LOW
D2=FUZZY	S2=DERIVATION	P1=MONOTONIC	V2=LARGE	T2= HIGH

external layer for fuzzy query recognition and translation in the corresponding PL/SQL evaluation procedure, it is reasonable to assume that the spent time for this layer is constant. On the other hand, Oracle TCT measures the effective time used by the query engine isolating waiting times due to other processes in the server and networking.

Several relevant factors were considered important to explain the response variable. For each factor we choose two representative levels. Table 1 summarizes factors and their levels. The first considered factor is named DATA (D), it concerns with the nature of data, whose levels are D1 = CRISP (traditional precise data) and D2 = FUZZY (imprecise data represented with a trapezium shape possibility distribution). Second factor is the STRATEGY (S) with levels S1 = NAïVE Strategy and S2 = DERIVATION Principle. Third factor is the PREDICATE (P) behaviour, with levels P1 = UNIMODAL and P2 = MONO-TONIC. The fourth considered factor is the VOLUME (V) of data set, whose levels are V1 = SMALL (8912 registers) and V2 = LARGE (101250 registers). These sizes have been fixed due to generation procedure and platform restrictions. Fifth factor is the THRESHOLD (H) of user desired minimum satisfaction level, with factors T1 = LOW (1/3) and T2 = HIGH (2/3). With this setting, the number of runs in the experiment is 32 ($2^k, k = 5$).

This experimental design corresponds to the additive model (3) that supposes the response variable to be a linear combination of the factors and theirs interactions in combination of two, three, four and five.

$$
\begin{aligned}
T = \hat{T} &+ \beta_1 V + \beta_2 D + \beta_3 S + \beta_4 H + \beta_5 P + \\
&\beta_6 VD + \beta_7 VS + \beta_8 VH + \beta_9 VP + \beta_{10} DS + \beta_{11} DH \\
&\beta_{12} DP + \beta_{13} SH + \beta_{14} SP + \beta_{15} HP \\
&\beta_{16} VSD + \beta_{17} VDH + \beta_{18} VDP + \beta_{19} VSH + \beta_{20} VSP + \\
&\beta_{21} VHP + \beta_{22} DSH + \beta_{23} DSP + \beta_{24} DHP + \beta_{25} SHP \\
&\beta_{26} VDSH + \beta_{27} VDSP + \beta_{28} VDHP + \beta_{29} VSHP + \\
&\beta_{30} DSHP + \beta_{31} VDSHP + \epsilon
\end{aligned}
\tag{3}
$$

Experimental fuzzy queries are addressed to a table with the schema:
SURVEY(name, arrival_hour, time_between_stations, service_quality)

According to factors DATA, PREDICATE and THRESHOLD, the query may present eight variations. It is expressed in the querying structure variables: $< t >$ either the table with precise data of the table with fuzzy data; $< fp >$ either the decreasing shape fuzzy predicate or the unimodal one; and $< \alpha >$ either the threshold 1/3 or 2/6. Two vague predicates were used describing the

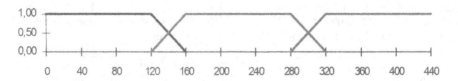

Fig. 1. Membership function of fuzzy predicates over *time_between_stations* (in seconds): *brief* (monotonic decreasing), *regular* (unimodal) and *long* (monotonic increasing)

Table 2. Observed value for Total Consumed Time (in milliseconds), per level of factor

| | | | PREDICATE → UNIMODAL | | MONOTONIC | |
| | | | THRESHOLD → LOW | HIGH | LOW | HIGH |
VOLUME ↓	DATA ↓	STRATEGY ↓				
SMALL	CRISP	NAIVE	1060	1180	980	940
		DERIVATION	760	630	640	630
	FUZZY	NAIVE	3120	2490	2460	2000
		DERIVATION	2400	1070	800	310
LARGE	CRISP	NAIVE	14949	13880	13710	13160
		DERIVATION	11490	9450	9030	8300
	FUZZY	NAIVE	41810	31800	27210	24180
		DERIVATION	35580	13120	9230	3070

time_between_stations: the monotonic decreasing *brief* and non monotonic unimodal regular, defined in Fig. 1. Predicates with increasing membership function were not considered due to design 2^k.

We have performed our experiment in a SUN-Fire-V440 Server with two 1281 MHz 1024 KB Sparc Processors and 16 GB of RAM running SOLARIS 10. The Oracle 9i DBMS was set with 305 MB for the SGA and 236 MB for the PGA. Measured values are shown in Table 2.

5   Descriptive Analysis

This section is devoted to present the results of performed experiments and make the descriptive analysis of such results. Table 2 presents the measured times. Due to the great difference between the lowest and the highest value of observed variable it is necessary to perform a logarithmic transformation. This variation is not amazing at all due to variation between low and high volume of rows populating the database table. A logarithmic transformation is often used in this kind of studies [20] [18]. With transformed data we have fitted the initial model by means of ANOVA and F-Test. Table 3 shows the ANOVA for

Table 3. Analysis Of Variance for the fitted model. Significance codes at rightmost column are: 0 '***' 0.001 '**' 0.01 '*' 0.05 '.' 0.1 ' ' 1. Observe that most significant factors are VOLUME, DATA and STRATEGY with its interactions.

	Df	Sum sq	Mean Sq	F value	Pr(>F)	
VOLUME	1	52.574	52.574	7542.610	< 2.2e-16	***
STRATEGY	1	4.204	4.204	603.096	7.404e-16	***
DATA	1	2.170	2.170	311.316	3.068e-13	***
THRESHOLD	1	0.848	0.848	121.725	1.056e-09	***
PREDICATE	1	1.659	1.659	238.073	3.346e-12	***
STRATEGY:DATA	1	0.773	0.773	110.933	2.267e-09	***
STRATEGY:THRESHOLD	1	0.375	0.375	53.801	5.934e-07	***
STRATEGY:PREDICATE	1	0.519	0.519	74.501	5.327e-08	***
DATA:THRESHOLD	1	0.537	0.537	77.084	4.099e-08	***
DATA:PREDICATE	1	0.882	0.882	126.505	7.673e-10	***
STRATEGY:DATA:THRESHOLD	1	0.211	0.211	30.210	2.656e-05	***
STRATEGY:DATA:PREDICATE	1	0.471	0.471	67.544	1.121e-07	***
Residuals	19	0.132	0.007			

the final fitted model (4) . We can observe the fit of considered factors and their interactions. Next we will make a performance analysis by observing the corresponding pairs of factors in interaction plots.

$$
\begin{aligned}
log(T) = \overline{log(T)} + \beta_1 V + \beta_2 D + \beta_3 S + \beta_4 H + \beta_5 P + \\
\beta_6 SD + \beta_7 SH + \beta_8 SP + \beta_9 DH + \beta_{10} DP + \\
\beta_{11} SDH + \beta_{12} SDP + \epsilon
\end{aligned} \quad (4)
$$

It is obvious in the ANOVA of Table 3 that VOLUME is the most influent factor in the TCT $Pr(> F) < 2.2e - 16$. Despite this factor has no shown significant interaction with none other factor, it is convenient to see its interaction plot with the STRATEGY factor due to its great influence in the response variable behavior. We must remark that STRATEGY is the second most influent factor $(Pr(> F)7.404e - 16$ in Table 3). Remember also that the purpose of this study is to show the behavior of the Derivation Principle strategy. So, it would be convenient to see the interaction of the Strategy·with the most influent factor. Figure 2 shows this interaction. We can see that Naïve Strategy increasing rate is higher. It obeys to the fact that this strategy does not takes advantage form the fuzzy condition in order to keep low the number of accessed rows as Derivation Principle does. It is more evident while the data set is larger. This result confirms the hypothesis (H2): *The total expend time in database engine using the Derivation Principle will be lower than that the generated using the Naïve Strategy.*

Third factor in significance according to ANOVA Table 3 is just the DATA factor $(Pr(> F)3.068e - 13)$. Its interaction with STRATEGY factor is very meaningful: $Pr(> F)2.267e - 09$ (Table 3). The first observation of these factors interaction plot (Fig. 3) is the fulfillment of the hypothesis (H1): *The use of fuzzy data will increment the total expend time in database engine.* Moreover, this

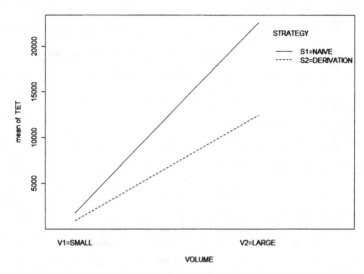

Fig. 2. VOLUME-STRATEGY Factors Interaction Plot: Derivation Principle Strategy shows the lowest Total Expend Times and the best tendency to scale with volume increase

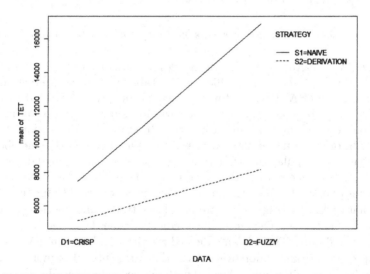

Fig. 3. DATA-STRATEGY Factors Interaction Plot: Derivation Principle Strategy shows the lowest Total Expend Times and the lowest added cost for processing fuzzy data

increment is higher for the Naïve Strategy than that observed for the Derivation Principle. In fact this improved evaluation mechanism has shown its benefit despite complexity of derived condition and representation of fuzzy data values. If confirms our hypothesis (H3): *The use of the Derivation Principle would make*

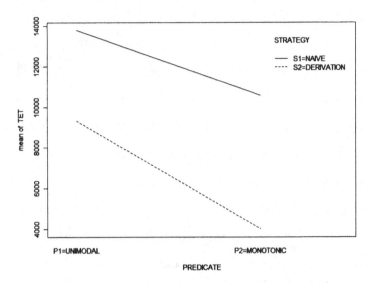

Fig. 4. PREDICATE-STRATEGY Factors Interaction Plot: Derivation Principle Strategy shows the lowest Total Expend Times and the best tendency of response to query selectivity. Data was generated with normal distribution and the used unimodal predicate was centered in the universe domain.

total expend time in database less sensible to difference between fuzzy and crisp data.

PREDICATE factor is the fourth in relevance according to its contribution to explain the TCT: $Pr(> F)3.346e - 12$ in Table 3. Also its interactions with the DATA and STRATEGY factors are very meaningful: $Pr(> F)7.673e - 10$ and $Pr(> F)5.327e - 08$, respectively. We will focus our attention to the second interaction because our main interest here is to study the Derivation Principle behavior. In order to understand the results in Fig. 4, we must remember that the database was populated with data being generated with normal distribution. This distribution concentrates the highest frequencies for values in the centre of the universe domain. On the other hand, our chosen unimodal shape fuzzy predicate regular (defined in Fig. 4) is represented as a trapezium function centered in the domain of abscissas. Therefore, this predicate defines less selective queries for these generated data. There is an expected relationship between query selectivity and processing times, moreover, Derivation Principle takes more advantage of selectivity due to filtering performed with derived condition. We confirm thus the hypothesis (H5): *The Derivation Principle improves its performance when the query is more selective.*

Finally, let's study the interaction between the THRESHOLD and STRATEGY factors (Fig. 5) that is related to the hypothesis (H4): *The use of Naïve Strategy would make total expend time in database less sensible to different user desired satisfaction levels.* It is clear that Derivation Principle has the best behaviour. It shows the lowest times and the highest rate of decreasing of times, whiles user specified desired threshold increases. As ever, the filtering of desired

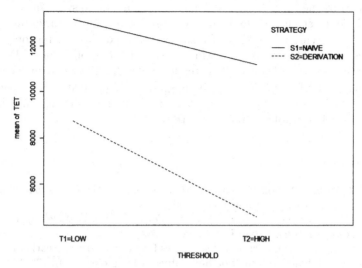

Fig. 5. THRESHOLD-STRATEGY Factors Interaction Plot: Derivation Principle Strategy shows the lowest Total Expend Times and the best tendency of response to threshold increasing that is an indicator of selectivity in fuzzy querying

rows before the calculation of satisfaction degrees makes the difference between both mechanisms. It confirms the related hypothesis.

6   Conclusions and Future Work

We have shown in this article how to apply the Derivation Principle for processing vague queries over fuzzy data. This principle takes advantage of existing connections between fuzzy sets and regular ones in order to keep low the extra computational effort supposed for fuzzy query processing. We have restricted our work to conditions where the imprecise data value is expressed with a trapezium shape fuzzy set as well as the vague predicate. However it is easy to extend it to other fuzzy sets representations. We have made an experimental performance study supported by statistical techniques: a 2^k factorial experimental design, analysis of variance and F Tests. Considered factors and levels were: volume (small or large), strategy (naïve or derivation), data (crisp or fuzzy), predicate (unimodal or monotonic) and threshold (low or high). This study ensures that, for this kind of queries, the processing time using the Naïve Strategy is higher than that of the Derivation Principle. As we might suppose, the use of fuzzy data adds extra cost to query evaluation, nevertheless, the Derivation Principle keeps it low. Finally, it was found that for high volumes of data, selectivity filters applied to queries with influence over time of evaluation of the queries, which should highlight that *while predicates are more selective will be felt more the performance benefits incurred by the principle of derivation*. This happens because the evaluation of the condition avoids calculating the degree of membership of the records that will not appear in the answer. In future work we would like to study the implementation and behaviour of fuzzy queries over fuzzy data involving other kind of fuzzy terms in conditions, not only atomic predicates. It would be also interesting to exploit the application of Derivation Principle in the core of a DBMS extended for fuzzy data and querying. The integration of SQLf and FSQL and its upgrade to SQL:2003 involves some new complex data and querying structures that would be necessary to study in order to provide efficient implementation strategies.

References

1. Bosc, P., Pivert, O.: Sqlf: A relational database language for fuzzy querying. IEEE Transactions on Fuzzy Systems 3(1) (1995)
2. Galindo, J., Urrutia, A., Piattini, A.: M. Fuzzy Database Modeling, Design and Implementation. Idea Group Publishing (2006)
3. Ma, Z., Yan, L.: Generalization of strategies for fuzzy query translation in classical relational databases. Information and Software Technology 4(9), 172–180 (2007)
4. Urrutia, A., Tineo, L., González, C.: FSQL and SQLf: Towards a Standard in Fuzzy Databases. In: Galindo, J. (ed.) Handbook of Research on Fuzzy Information Processing in Databases, IGI Global, pp. XI–1 – XI–30 (2008)
5. Bosc, P., Pivert, O.: Sqlf query functionality on top of a regular relational database management system. Knowledge Management in Fuzzy Databases, 171–190 (2000)
6. López, Y., Tineo, L.: About the performance of sqlf evaluation mechanisms. CLEI Electronic Journal 9(2), 8-1–8-9 (2006)
7. Goncalves, M., Tineo, L.: An evaluation mechanism for procedural sqlf. In: Actas de la XXXI Conferencia Latinoamericana de Informática CLEI 2005, pp. 425–434 (2005)
8. Goncalves, M., Tineo, L.: Derivation principle in advanced fuzzy queries. In: Proceedings of the 14th Anual IEEE International Conference on FUZZY Systems FUZZ-IEEE, pp. 579–584 (2005) ISBN 0-7803-9158-6
9. Goncalves, M., Tineo, L.: Derivation principle in sqlf2 algebra operators. In: Proceedings of International Conference on Fuzzy Information Processing Theories and Applications FIP 2003, pp. 453–459 (2003) ISBN 7-302-06299-4
10. Goncalves, M., Tineo, L.: Sqlf vs. skyline - expressivity and performance. In: Proceedings of the 15th Anual IEEE International Conference on FUZZY Systems FUZZ-IEEE (2006)
11. Goncalves, M., Tineo, L.: Towards flexible skyline queries. In: Actas de la XXXII Conferencia Latinoamericana de Informática CLEI 2006 (2006)
12. Goncalves, M., Tineo, L.: Fuzzy dominance skyline queries. In: Wagner, R., Revell, N., Pernul, G. (eds.) DEXA 2007. LNCS, vol. 4653, pp. 469–478. Springer, Heidelberg (2007)
13. Tineo, L.: Extending rdbms for allowing fuzzy quantified queries. In: Ibrahim, M., Küng, J., Revell, N. (eds.) DEXA 2000. LNCS, vol. 1873, pp. 407–416. Springer, Heidelberg (2000)
14. Tineo, L.: Sqlf horizontal fuzzy quantified query processing. In: Actas de la XXXI Conferencia Latinoamericana de Informática CLEI 2005 (2005)
15. Tineo, L.: Una Contribución a la Interrogación Flexible de Bases de Datos Relacionales: Evaluación de Consultas Cuantificadas. PhD thesis, Simón Bolívar University, Caracas, Venezuela (2006)

16. Galindo, J., González, C., Tineo, L.: Falta titulo. In: Proceedings of FSKD 2008 (to appear, 2008)
17. González, C., Tineo, L.: Procesamiento de consultas vagas sobre datos difusos: Principio de derivación (under revision for CLEI 2008 conference)
18. Jain, R.: The Art of Computer Systems Performance. John Wiley & Sons, Inc., Chichester (1991)
19. González, E., Tineo, L.: Experimental prototype for flexible database querying: Sqlf-pl (under revision for ODBASE 2008 conference)
20. Burnham, K., Anderson, D.: Multimodel inference: understanding aic and bic in model selection. In: Amsterdam Workshop on Model Selection (2004)

Tractable Reasoning with Bayesian Description Logics

Claudia d'Amato[1], Nicola Fanizzi[1], and Thomas Lukasiewicz[2,3]

[1] Dipartimento di Informatica, Università degli Studi di Bari
Campus Universitario, Via Orabona 4, 70125 Bari, Italy
{claudia.damato,fanizzi}@di.uniba.it
[2] Computing Laboratory, University of Oxford
Wolfson Building, Parks Road, Oxford OX1 3QD, UK
thomas.lukasiewicz@comlab.ox.ac.uk
[3] Institut für Informationssysteme, Technische Universität Wien,
Favoritenstraße 9-11, 1040 Wien, Austria
lukasiewicz@kr.tuwien.ac.at

Abstract. The *DL-Lite* family of tractable description logics lies between the semantic web languages RDFS and OWL Lite. In this paper, we present a probabilistic generalization of the *DL-Lite* description logics, which is based on Bayesian networks. As an important feature, the new probabilistic description logics allow for flexibly combining terminological and assertional pieces of probabilistic knowledge. We show that the new probabilistic description logics are rich enough to properly extend both the *DL-Lite* description logics as well as Bayesian networks. We also show that satisfiability checking and query processing in the new probabilistic description logics is reducible to satisfiability checking and query processing in the *DL-Lite* family. Furthermore, we show that satisfiability checking and answering unions of conjunctive queries in the new logics can be done in LogSpace in the data complexity. For this reason, the new probabilistic description logics are very promising formalisms for data-intensive applications in the Semantic Web involving probabilistic uncertainty.

Keywords: Bayesian description logics, tractable reasoning, description logics, ontologies, *DL-Lite*, Bayesian networks, Semantic Web.

1 Introduction

The *Semantic Web (SW)* is a web of data to be shared by machines in order to help them to understand the information in the Web and to perform various complex tasks autonomously, such as data integration, discovery, etc. Ontology languages such as OWL have been proposed to express concepts and relations in this context. These are ultimately based on *description logics (DLs)* [1].

Intuitively, description logics model a domain of interest in terms of concepts and roles, which represent classes of individuals resp. binary relations on classes of individuals. A description logic knowledge base (or ontology) encodes in particular (i) subsumption relationships between concepts, (ii) subsumption relationships between roles, (iii) instance relationships between individuals and concepts, and (iv) instance relationships between pairs of individuals and roles.

S. Greco and T. Lukasiewicz (Eds.): SUM 2008, LNAI 5291, pp. 146–159, 2008.
© Springer-Verlag Berlin Heidelberg 2008

The heterogeneity of the data sources clearly introduces degrees of uncertainty in the data manipulation process, which causes purely logical methods to fall short. Hence, extended forms of ontology languages have been proposed in order to deal with uncertainty through probabilistic reasoning [20].

There is a plethora of applications with an urgent need for handling uncertain knowledge in ontologies, especially in areas like medicine, biology, defense, and astronomy. Furthermore, there are strong arguments for the critical need of dealing with probabilistic uncertainty in ontologies in the Semantic Web (in order to encode ambiguous information, such as "John is a student with the probability 0.7 and a teacher with the probability 0.3", which is very different from vague/fuzzy information, such as "John is tall with the degree of truth 0.7"):

- Concepts of a probabilistic ontology are probabilistically related. For example, two concepts either may be logically related via a subsumption or disjointness relationship, or they may show a certain degree of overlap. Probabilistic ontologies allow for quantifying these degrees of overlap, for reasoning about them, and for using them in semantic web applications, e.g., information retrieval. The degrees of concept overlap may also be exploited in personalization and recommender systems.
- The Semantic Web will consist of a huge collection of different ontologies. So, in semantic web applications of reasoning and retrieval, one may have to align the concepts of different ontologies, which is called ontology matching/mapping. In general, the concepts of different ontologies do not match exactly, and we have to deal with degrees of concept overlap as above, which are determined by automatic or semi-automatic tools or experts. These degrees of concept overlap are then represented in probabilistic ontologies, which thus allows for inference about the degrees of overlap between other concepts and about uncertain instance relationships.
- The Semantic Web will likely contain controversial information in different web sources. This can be handled via probabilistic data integration by associating with every web source a probability describing its degree of reliability. As resulting pieces of data, such a probabilistic data integration process necessarily produces probabilistic facts, i.e., probabilistic knowledge at the instance level. Such probabilistic instance relationships can be encoded in probabilistic ontologies and there be enhanced by further classical and/or terminological probabilistic knowledge, which then allows for inference about other probabilistic instance relationships.

Although there are many previous approaches to probabilistic description logics and probabilistic ontology languages in the literature, including some that are specifically designed for the Semantic Web, there is only little work on tractable probabilistic description logics (see Section 7), and to date no work on tractable probabilistic description logics for the Semantic Web. In this paper, we try to fill this gap. We present a novel combination of description logics with probabilistic uncertainty, which is especially directed towards tractable formalisms for reasoning under probabilistic uncertainty with ontologies in the Semantic Web. More concretely, we present an extension of the *DL-Lite* family of description logics [2] by probabilistic uncertainty as in Bayesian networks. The main contributions of this paper can be summarized as follows:

- We present a probabilistic generalization of the *DL-Lite* family of description logics, which is based on Bayesian networks.

- We show that the new probabilistic description logics are rich enough to properly extend both the *DL-Lite* description logics as well as Bayesian networks.
- We also show that satisfiability checking and query processing in the new logics can be reduced to satisfiability checking and query processing in the *DL-Lite* family.
- Finally, we show that satisfiability checking and answering unions of conjunctive queries in the new logics can be done in LogSpace in the data complexity.

Compared to previous tractable probabilistic description logics, our new approach to tractable probabilistic description logics is especially well-suited for data-intensive applications in the Semantic Web, such as the ones listed above (see also Section 7).

The rest of this paper is organized as follows. In the next section, the preliminaries of the *DL-Lite* family of description logics and of Bayesian networks are presented. In Section 3, we introduce our new probabilistic description logics. Sections 4 to 6 provide semantic, computational, and data tractability results, respectively, around the new logics. In Section 7, we survey related work in neighboring research areas. Finally, Section 8 concludes the paper and outlines possible future directions of research. Note that detailed proofs of all results in this paper are given in the extended report.

2   Preliminaries

In this section, we first recall the main concepts of the *DL-Lite* family of tractable description logics, and we then recall the basics of Bayesian networks.

2.1   The *DL-Lite* Family

We now recall the *DL-Lite* family of tractable description logics [2], which include the core language $DL\text{-}Lite_{core}$ and its extensions *DL-Lite* (also called $DL\text{-}Lite_{\mathcal{F}}$) and $DL\text{-}Lite_{\mathcal{R}}$. They are a restricted class of classical description logics for which the main reasoning tasks in description logics can be done in deterministic polynomial time in the size of the knowledge base and some of these tasks even in LogSpace in the size of the ABox in the data complexity. The *DL-Lite* description logics are the most common tractable description logics in the semantic web context. They are especially directed towards data-intensive applications. We now first preliminarily recall the language and its semantics, and we then recall tractability results.

Syntax. We first define *DL-Lite* (also called $DL\text{-}Lite_{\mathcal{F}}$). Let $\mathbf{A}$, $\mathbf{R}_A$, and $\mathbf{I}$ be pairwise disjoint sets of atomic concepts, abstract roles, and individuals, respectively.

A *basic role (in DL-Lite)* is either an atomic role $P \in \mathbf{R}_A$ or its inverse P^-. *Roles (in DL-Lite)* are defined as follows. Every basic role P and negation of a basic role $\neg P$ is a role. A *basic concept (in DL-Lite)* is either an atomic concept from $\mathbf{A}$ or an existential restriction on a basic role R, denoted $\exists R.\top$ (abbreviated as $\exists R$). *Concepts (in DL-Lite)* are defined as follows. Every basic concept B and negation of a basic concept $\neg B$ is a concept.

An *axiom (in DL-Lite)* is either (1) a *concept inclusion axiom* $B \sqsubseteq \phi$, where B is a basic concept, and ϕ is a concept, or (2) a *functionality axiom* (funct R), where R is a basic role, or (3) a *concept membership axiom* $A(a)$, where A is an atomic concept and $a \in \mathbf{I}$, or (4) a *role membership axiom* $R(a, c)$, where $R \in \mathbf{R}_A$ and $a, c \in \mathbf{I}$. A *TBox (in DL-Lite)* is a finite set of concept inclusion and functionality axioms. An *ABox (in DL-Lite)* is a finite set of concept and role membership axioms. A *knowledge base (in DL-Lite)* $KB = (\mathcal{T}, \mathcal{A})$ consists of a TBox $\mathcal{T}$ and an ABox $\mathcal{A}$. A *query* ϕ is an open formula of first-order logic with equalities. A *conjunctive query* is of the form $\exists \mathbf{y} \, \phi(\mathbf{x}, \mathbf{y})$, where ϕ is a conjunction of atoms and equalities with free variables $\mathbf{x}$ and $\mathbf{y}$. A *union of conjunctive queries* is of the form $\bigvee_{i=1}^{n} \exists \mathbf{y}_i \, \phi_i(\mathbf{x}, \mathbf{y}_i)$, where each ϕ_i is a conjunction of atoms and equalities with free variables $\mathbf{x}$ and $\mathbf{y}_i$.

The description logic *DL-Lite*$_{core}$ does not allow for functionality axioms in knowledge bases, while *DL-Lite*$_{\mathcal{R}}$ allows for (5) *role inclusion axioms* $R \sqsubseteq E$, rather than functionality axioms, where R is a basic role, and E is a role.

The following example from semantic web services illustrates the above notions.

Example 1 (Flight Services). Given an ontology as a shared knowledge base, we use description logic concepts to describe semantic web services, and their instances to represent the real procedures implementing the services (see [11] for more details).

More specifically, we consider flight services. The following knowledge base $KB = (\mathcal{T}, \mathcal{A})$ in *DL-Lite*$_{\mathcal{R}}$ encodes an ontology with airports and air connections between them (where conjunctions are used to compactly represent several concept inclusion axioms with the same body by one concept inclusion axiom):

$\mathcal{T} = \{ Service \sqsubseteq Top;\ Airport \sqsubseteq Top;\ Country \sqsubseteq Top;$
$\qquad Service \sqsubseteq \neg Airport \sqcap \neg Country;\ Airport \sqsubseteq \neg Country;$
$\qquad Italy \sqsubseteq Country;\ Germany \sqsubseteq Country;\ UK \sqsubseteq Country;$
$\qquad Italy \sqsubseteq \neg Germany \sqcap \neg UK;\ Germany \sqsubseteq \neg UK;$
$\qquad Rome \sqsubseteq Airport;\ Cologne \sqsubseteq Airport;\ Frankfurt \sqsubseteq Airport;\ London \sqsubseteq Airport;$
$\qquad Rome \sqsubseteq \neg Cologne \sqcap \neg Frankfurt \sqcap \neg London;\ \ldots;\ Frankfurt \sqsubseteq \neg London;$
$\qquad RomLon \sqsubseteq Service;\ CgnLon \sqsubseteq Service;\ FraLon \sqsubseteq Service;$
$\qquad RomLon \sqsubseteq \neg CgnLon \sqcap \neg FraLon;\ CgnLon \sqsubseteq \neg FraLon;$
$\qquad FraLgw \sqsubseteq FraLon;\ FraLhr \sqsubseteq FraLon;\ FraLgw \sqsubseteq \neg FraLhr;$
$\qquad Service \sqsubseteq \exists From;\ Airport \sqsubseteq \exists From^-;$
$\qquad Service \sqsubseteq \exists To;\ Airport \sqsubseteq \exists To^- \},$

$\mathcal{A} = \{ Rome(FCO);\ Rome(CIA);\ Cologne(CGN);\ Frankfurt(FRA);\ London(LHR);$
$\qquad FraLon(LH456);\ CgnLon(GermanWings123);\ RomLon(BA789);$
$\qquad From(LH456, FRA);\ From(GermanWings123, CGN);\ From(BA789, FCO);$
$\qquad To(LH456, LHR);\ To(GermanWings123, LHR);\ To(BA789, LHR) \}.$

In particular, the concepts *FraLon*, *CgnLon*, and *RomeLon* describe flight services from Frankfurt, Cologne, and Rome, respectively, to London. For each such concept, also an instance is specified. The above TBox $\mathcal{T}$ is partially illustrated in Fig. 1.

The union of conjunctive queries $Q(x) = \exists y(To(x, y) \wedge Rome(y)) \vee \exists y(From(x, y) \wedge Rome(y))$ then asks for all flight services that are ending or starting in Rome.

Semantics. An *interpretation* $\mathcal{I} = (\Delta^{\mathcal{I}}, \cdot^{\mathcal{I}})$ consists of a nonempty *(abstract) domain* $\Delta^{\mathcal{I}}$ and a mapping $\cdot^{\mathcal{I}}$ that assigns to each atomic concept $C \in \mathbf{A}$ a subset of $\Delta^{\mathcal{I}}$, to each abstract role $R \in \mathbf{R}_A$ a subset of $\Delta^{\mathcal{I}} \times \Delta^{\mathcal{I}}$, and to each individual $a \in \mathbf{I}$ an element

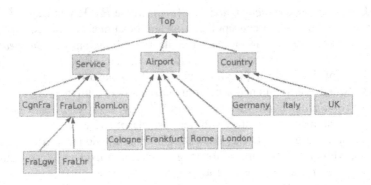

Fig. 1. TBox (partially) for the Flight Services Example

of $\Delta^{\mathcal{I}}$. Here, different individuals are associated with different elements of $\Delta^{\mathcal{I}}$ (*unique name assumption*). The mapping $\cdot^{\mathcal{I}}$ is extended to all concepts and roles as follows:

- $(R^-)^{\mathcal{I}} = \{(a, b) \mid (b, a) \in R^{\mathcal{I}}\}$;
- $(\neg R)^{\mathcal{I}} = \Delta^{\mathcal{I}} \times \Delta^{\mathcal{I}} \setminus R^{\mathcal{I}}$;
- $(\exists R)^{\mathcal{I}} = \{x \in \Delta^{\mathcal{I}} \mid \exists y \colon (x, y) \in R^{\mathcal{I}}\}$;
- $(\neg B)^{\mathcal{I}} = \Delta^{\mathcal{I}} \setminus B^{\mathcal{I}}$.

The *satisfaction* of an axiom F in the interpretation $\mathcal{I} = (\Delta^{\mathcal{I}}, \cdot^{\mathcal{I}})$, denoted $\mathcal{I} \models F$, is defined as follows: (1) $\mathcal{I} \models B \sqsubseteq \phi$ iff $B^{\mathcal{I}} \subseteq \phi^{\mathcal{I}}$; (2) $\mathcal{I} \models (\text{funct } R)$ iff $(o, o') \in R^{\mathcal{I}}$ and $(o, o'') \in R^{\mathcal{I}}$ implies $o' = o''$; (3) $\mathcal{I} \models A(a)$ iff $a^{\mathcal{I}} \in A^{\mathcal{I}}$; (4) $\mathcal{I} \models R(a, b)$ iff $(a^{\mathcal{I}}, b^{\mathcal{I}}) \in R^{\mathcal{I}}$; and (5) $\mathcal{I} \models R \sqsubseteq E$ iff $R^{\mathcal{I}} \subseteq E^{\mathcal{I}}$. The interpretation $\mathcal{I}$ *satisfies* the axiom F, or $\mathcal{I}$ is a *model* of F, iff $\mathcal{I} \models F$. The interpretation $\mathcal{I}$ *satisfies* a knowledge base $KB = (\mathcal{T}, \mathcal{A})$, or $\mathcal{I}$ is a *model* of KB, denoted $\mathcal{I} \models KB$, iff $\mathcal{I} \models F$ for all $F \in \mathcal{T} \cup \mathcal{A}$. We say that KB is *satisfiable* (resp., *unsatisfiable*) iff KB has a (resp., no) model. An axiom F is a *logical consequence* of KB, denoted $KB \models F$, iff every model of KB satisfies F. An *answer* for a query ϕ to KB is a ground substitution θ for all free variables in ϕ such that $\phi\theta$ is a logical consequence of KB.

Example 2 (Flight Services (cont'd)). Consider again the knowledge base $KB = (\mathcal{T}, \mathcal{A})$ in *DL-Lite*$_{\mathcal{R}}$ from Example 1. It is not difficult to verify that KB is satisfiable, and that some logical consequences of KB are given by *FraLhr* $\sqsubseteq$ *Service* and *Service(LH456)*. The only answer for the query $Q(x)$ of Example 1 to KB is $\theta = \{x/BA789\}$.

Tractability. We briefly recall the tractability results for reasoning with *DL-Lite* (resp., *DL-Lite*$_{\mathcal{R}}$) that we will use in the probabilistic generalization. The following result from [2] shows that deciding the satisfiability of *DL-Lite* (resp., *DL-Lite*$_{\mathcal{R}}$) knowledge bases can be done in LogSpace in the size of the ABox in the data complexity.

Theorem 1 (see [2]). *Given a DL-Lite (resp., DL-Lite*$_{\mathcal{R}}$*) knowledge base $KB = (\mathcal{T}, \mathcal{A})$, deciding whether KB is satisfiable can be done in LogSpace in the size of the ABox $\mathcal{A}$ in the data complexity.*

The next result from [2] shows that computing the answers for unions of conjunctive queries to *DL-Lite* (resp., *DL-Lite$_\mathcal{R}$*) knowledge bases can also be done in LogSpace in the size of the ABox in the data complexity.

Theorem 2 (see [2]). *Given a DL-Lite (resp., DL-Lite$_\mathcal{R}$) knowledge base $KB = (\mathcal{T}, \mathcal{A})$ and a union of conjunctive queries $Q = \bigvee_{i=1}^{n} \exists \mathbf{y}_i \, \phi_i(\mathbf{x}, \mathbf{y}_i)$, computing all answers for Q to KB can be done in LogSpace in the size of the ABox $\mathcal{A}$ in the data complexity.*

2.2 Bayesian Networks

We now briefly recall *Bayesian networks* (see especially [25, 15]). Let V be a finite set of *random variables*. Each variable $X \in V$ may take on *values* from a finite *domain* $D(X)$. A *value* for a set of variables $X = \{X_1, \ldots, X_n\} \subseteq V$ is a mapping $x \colon X \to \bigcup_{i=1}^{n} D(X_i)$ such that $x(X_i) \in D(X_i)$ (where the empty mapping $\emptyset$ is the unique value for $X = \emptyset$). The *domain* of X, denoted $D(X)$, is the set of all values for X. For $Y \subseteq X$ and $x \in D(X)$, we use $x|Y$ to denote the restriction of x to Y. We often identify singletons $\{X_i\} \subseteq V$ with X_i, and their values x with $x(X_i)$.

A *Bayesian network* $BN = (G, Pr)$ over V is defined by a directed acyclic graph $G = (V, E)$ over the random variables in V as nodes and by a conditional probability distribution $Pr(X = \cdot \mid Y = y) \colon D(X) \to [0, 1]$ for each variable $X \in V$ and each value $y \in D(Y)$ of the parents $Y \subseteq V$ of X in G, denoted $\mathrm{Pa}(X)$. It specifies a unique joint probability distribution Pr_{BN} over all values for V by:

$$Pr_{BN}(V = v) = \prod_{X \in V} Pr(X = v|X \mid \mathrm{Pa}(X) = v|\mathrm{Pa}(X)) \quad \text{(for every } v \in D(V)\text{)}.$$

That is, the joint probability distribution Pr_{BN} is uniquely determined by the conditional probability distributions $Pr(X = \cdot \mid Y = y)$. This implicitly assumes conditional probabilistic independencies encoded in the directed acyclic graph G. One then specifies a probability Pr_{BN} for every $X \subseteq V$ and $x \in D(X)$ as follows:

$$Pr_{BN}(X = x) = \sum_{v \in D(V),\, v|X = x} Pr_{BN}(V = v).$$

3 Bayesian *DL-Lite$_\mathcal{R}$* (*BDL-Lite$_\mathcal{R}$*)

In this section, we introduce the novel probabilistic description logic *Bayesian DL-Lite$_\mathcal{R}$* (or *BDL-Lite$_\mathcal{R}$*), which combines classical knowledge bases in *DL-Lite$_\mathcal{R}$* with Bayesian networks. Informally, every description logic axiom is annotated with an event, which is in turn associated with a probability value via a Bayesian network. Like *DL-Lite$_\mathcal{R}$*, *BDL-Lite$_\mathcal{R}$* is especially directed towards data-intensive applications. Note that a very similar probabilistic generalization can be defined for *DL-Lite$_\mathcal{F}$*.

3.1 Syntax

We first define the syntax of *BDL-Lite$_\mathcal{R}$*. As for the elementary ingredients, as in Section 2.1, let $\mathbf{A}$, $\mathbf{R}_A$, and $\mathbf{I}$ be pairwise disjoint sets of atomic concepts, abstract roles, and individuals, respectively. As in Section 2.2, we assume a finite set of random variables V, where each $X \in V$ may take on values from a finite domain $D(X)$.

We next define the concept of a probabilistic knowledge base, which consists of a set of probabilistic axioms and a Bayesian network. Every probabilistic axiom in turn consists of a classical axiom in *DL-Lite$_\mathcal{R}$* and a probabilistic annotation, which connects it to a set of value assignments $V = v$ with $v \in D(V)$ of a Bayesian network over V along with their probability values. Formally, a *probabilistic annotation* is an expression of the form $X = x$, where $X \subseteq V$ and $x \in D(X)$. We also use $\top$ to denote the probabilistic annotation for $X = \emptyset$. Informally, every probabilistic annotation represents a scenario (or an event) which is associated with the set of all value assignments $V = v$ with $v \in D(V)$ that are compatible with $X = x$ (that is, $v | X = x$) and their probability value $Pr_{BN}(V = v)$ in a Bayesian network BN over V. We next formally define *probabilistic axioms* as follows. A *probabilistic concept membership* (resp., *role membership, concept inclusion, functionality, role inclusion) axiom in BDL-Lite$_\mathcal{R}$* is an expression of the form $\phi \colon X = x$, where ϕ is a concept membership (resp., role membership, concept inclusion, functionality, role inclusion) axiom in *DL-Lite$_\mathcal{R}$*, and $X = x$ is a probabilistic annotation. Informally, such a probabilistic axiom $\phi \colon X = x$ encodes that in the scenario $X = x$, the description logic axiom ϕ holds. We often abbreviate probabilistic axioms of the form $\top \colon X = x$ (resp., $\phi \colon \top$) by $X = x$ (resp., ϕ). A *probabilistic TBox in BDL-Lite$_\mathcal{R}$* is a finite set of probabilistic concept inclusion and probabilistic role inclusion axioms in *BDL-Lite$_\mathcal{R}$*. A *probabilistic ABox in BDL-Lite$_\mathcal{R}$* is a finite set of probabilistic concept and probabilistic role membership axioms in *BDL-Lite$_\mathcal{R}$*. A *probabilistic knowledge base $KB = (\mathcal{T}, \mathcal{A}, BN)$ in BDL-Lite$_\mathcal{R}$* consists of (i) a probabilistic TBox $\mathcal{T}$ in *BDL-Lite$_\mathcal{R}$*, (ii) a probabilistic ABox $\mathcal{A}$ in *BDL-Lite$_\mathcal{R}$*, and (iii) a Bayesian network $BN = ((V, E), Pr)$.

We finally define probabilistic queries to probabilistic knowledge bases in *BDL-Lite$_\mathcal{R}$*. A *probabilistic query* is of the form $\psi \colon X = x$, where ψ is a first-order formula, and $X = x$ is a probabilistic annotation. We often abbreviate probabilistic queries of the form $\top \colon X = x$ (resp., $\psi \colon \top$) by $X = x$ (resp., ψ). A *probabilistic union of conjunctive queries* is a probabilistic query $\psi \colon X = x$ such that ψ is a union of conjunctive queries.

Example 3 (Flight Services (cont'd)). Consider again the knowledge base $KB = (\mathcal{T}, \mathcal{A})$ in *DL-Lite$_\mathcal{R}$* given in Example 1. We may now know that, given that a service belongs to a concept, then it also belongs to another concept with a certain probability. For example, we may know that a service in *FraLon* is also a service in *FraLhr* with the probability 0.8. This probabilistic information may be useful, for example, when searching for services in *FraLon*, to speed up the service discovery process [6]. It can be encoded by the following probabilistic concept inclusion axiom:

$$FraLon \sqsubseteq FraLhr \colon LonLhr = \mathbf{true},$$

where *LonLhr* is a random variable, which is true with the probability 0.8. Similarly, functionality axioms and role inclusion axioms can be annotated with probabilities.

In the same way, we may know that the individual *GermanWings456* is an instance of the service description *FraLon* with the probability 0.9, which can be expressed by the following probabilistic concept membership axiom:

$$FraLon(GermanWings456) \colon FraLonGW = \mathbf{true},$$

where *FraLonGW* is a random variable, which is true with the probability 0.9.

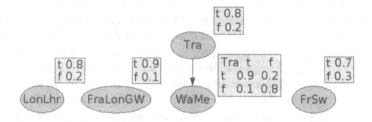

Fig. 2. Bayesian network (with CPTs) for the Flight Services Example

Similarly, we can express that (1) the individual *Swiss123* belongs to the concept *Transatlantic* with the probability 0.8, (2) the individual *Swiss123* belongs to the concept *WarmMeal*, given that it belongs (resp., does not belong) to the concept *Transatlantic* with the probability 0.9 (resp., 0.2), and (3) the pair of individuals (*Swiss123*, *CIA*) belongs to the role *From* with the probability 0.7 by the following probabilistic concept membership axioms and probabilistic role membership axiom:

$$Transatlantic(Swiss123):\ Tra = \textbf{true}\,,$$
$$WarmMeal(Swiss123):\ WaMe = \textbf{true}\,,$$
$$From(Swiss123,CIA):\ FrSw = \textbf{true}\,,$$

where (1) *Tra* is a random variable, which is true with the probability 0.8, (2) *WaMe* is a random variable, which is true with the probability 0.9 (resp., 0.2), given *Tra* is true (resp., false), and (3) *FrSw* is a random variable, which is true with the probability 0.7.

The above random variables along with their probabilities and conditional probabilities form a Bayesian network, which is shown in Fig. 2, where the probabilities and conditional probabilities are represented in conditional probability tables (CPTs).

The probabilistic union of conjunctive queries $Q(x) = \exists y(To(x,y) \land Rome(y)) \lor \exists y(From(x,y) \land Rome(y))$ then asks for all flight services that are ending or starting in Rome, along with their probabilities. Whereas the probabilistic conjunctive query $Q'(x) = \exists y(From(x,y) \land Rome(y) \land WarmMeal(x))$ asks for all flight services that are starting in Rome and are offering a warm meal, along with their probabilities.

From the engineering viewpoint, there are two different ways of designing probabilistic knowledge bases $KB = (\mathcal{T}, \mathcal{A}, BN)$ in *BDL-Lite$_\mathcal{R}$*. One is to start to model the Bayesian network $BN = ((V, E), Pr)$, and to collect for every probabilistic annotation $V = v$ with $v \in D(V)$ a set of probabilistic axioms $\phi: V = v$, which is then simplified to a set of probabilistic axioms of the type $\phi: X = x$ with $X \subseteq V$ and $x \in D(X)$. Another way is to start to model a set of probabilistic axioms $\phi: X = x$ with single binary random variables X, which are then used to form the nodes of the Bayesian network $BN = ((V, E), Pr)$. In this paper, we adopt especially the first viewpoint.

3.2   Semantics

We now define a formal semantics of probabilistic knowledge bases in *BDL-Lite$_\mathcal{R}$*, in terms of probability distributions over classical interpretations.

We first define annotated interpretations, which extend standard first-order interpretations (under the unique name assumption) by value assignments $V = v$ in a Bayesian network over V. Formally, an *annotated interpretation* $\mathcal{I} = (\Delta^{\mathcal{I}}, \cdot^{\mathcal{I}})$ is defined in the same way as a classical first-order interpretation under the unique name assumption (see Section 2.1) except that $\cdot^{\mathcal{I}}$ maps additionally the set of random variables V to a value $v \in D(V)$. The annotated interpretation $\mathcal{I}$ *satisfies* (or is a *model* of) a probabilistic axiom $\phi\colon X = x$, denoted $\mathcal{I} \models \phi\colon X = x$, iff $V^{\mathcal{I}}|X = x$ is equivalent to $\mathcal{I} \models \phi$.

We next define probabilistic interpretations, which are finite probability distributions over annotated interpretations. Formally, a *probabilistic interpretation* Pr is a probability function over the set of all annotated interpretations that associates only a finite number of annotated interpretations with a positive probability. The *probability* of a probabilistic axiom $\phi\colon X = x$ in Pr, denoted $Pr(\phi\colon X = x)$, is the sum of all $Pr(\mathcal{I})$ such that $\mathcal{I}$ is an annotated interpretation that satisfies $\phi\colon X = x$. A probabilistic interpretation Pr *satisfies* (or is a *model* of) a probabilistic axiom $\phi\colon X = x$ iff $Pr(\phi\colon X = x) = 1$. We say Pr *satisfies* (or is a *model* of) a set of probabilistic axioms $\mathcal{F}$ iff Pr satisfies all $F \in \mathcal{F}$. The probabilistic interpretation Pr *satisfies* (or is a *model* of) a probabilistic knowledge base $KB = (\mathcal{T}, \mathcal{A}, BN)$ in *BDL-Lite$_{\mathcal{R}}$* iff (i) Pr is a model of $\mathcal{T} \cup \mathcal{A}$ and (ii) $Pr(V = v) = Pr_{BN}(V = v)$ for all $v \in D(V)$. We say KB is *satisfiable* iff it has a model Pr.

We finally define answers for probabilistic queries as follows. An annotated interpretation $\mathcal{I}$ *satisfies* (or is a *model* of) a ground query $\psi\colon X = x$, denoted $\mathcal{I} \models \psi\colon X = x$, iff $V^{\mathcal{I}}|X = x$ and $\mathcal{I} \models \psi$. The *probability* of a ground query $\psi\colon X = x$ in Pr, denoted $Pr(\psi\colon X = x)$, is the sum of all $Pr(\mathcal{I})$ such that $\mathcal{I}$ is an annotated interpretation that satisfies $\psi\colon X = x$. An *answer* for a probabilistic query $Q = \psi\colon X = x$ to a probabilistic knowledge base $KB = (\mathcal{T}, \mathcal{A}, BN)$ is a pair (θ, pr) consisting of a ground substitution θ for the variables in Q and some $pr \in [0, 1]$ such that $Pr(\psi\theta\colon X = x) = pr$ for all models Pr of KB. An answer (θ, pr) for Q to KB is *positive* iff $pr > 0$.

Example 4 (Flight Services (cont'd)). Consider again the probabilistic knowledge base KB in *BDL-Lite$_{\mathcal{R}}$* and the two probabilistic queries $Q(x)$ and $Q'(x)$ described in Example 3. It is not difficult to verify that KB is satisfiable. The only positive answers (θ, pr) for $Q(x)$ to KB are $(\{x/BA789\}, 1)$ and $(\{x/Swiss123\}, 0.7)$, while the only positive answer (θ, pr) for $Q'(x)$ to KB is $(\{x/Swiss123\}, 0.76)$. If KB would additionally contain the probabilistic concept membership axiom *Transatlantic(Swiss123)*, then the only positive answer (θ, pr) for $Q'(x)$ to KB would be $(\{x/Swiss123\}, 0.9)$.

4   Semantic Properties

An important property of hybrid knowledge representation and reasoning formalisms is that they faithfully extend their integrated formalisms. In this section, we show that *BDL-Lite$_{\mathcal{R}}$* faithfully extends both *DL-Lite$_{\mathcal{R}}$* and Bayesian networks.

The following theorem shows that probabilistic knowledge bases in *BDL-Lite$_{\mathcal{R}}$* faithfully extend Bayesian networks. That is, querying any Bayesian network is equivalent to querying any of its extensions to a satisfiable probabilistic knowledge base in *BDL-Lite$_{\mathcal{R}}$*.

Theorem 3. *Let $BN = ((V, E), Pr)$ be a Bayesian network, and let $KB = (T, A, BN')$ be any probabilistic knowledge base in BDL-Lite$_R$ such that $BN' = BN$. Let $X \subseteq V$ and $x \in D(X)$. Then, the probabilistic query $Q = X = x$ to KB has the pair $(\theta, pr) = (\emptyset, Pr_{BN}(X = x))$ as an answer. If KB is satisfiable, then this pair (θ, pr) is also the only answer for Q to KB.*

We next show that probabilistic knowledge bases in *BDL-Lite$_R$* also faithfully extend classical knowledge bases in *DL-Lite$_R$*. In detail, querying any satisfiable knowledge base in *DL-Lite$_R$* is equivalent to querying any of its extensions in *BDL-Lite$_R$*.

Theorem 4. *Let $KB = (T, A)$ be a satisfiable knowledge base in DL-Lite$_R$, let ψ be a query to KB, and let $BN = ((V, E), Pr)$ be any Bayesian network. Then, the probabilistic query $Q = \psi$ to $KB' = (T, A, BN)$ has as positive answers (θ, pr) exactly all pairs $(\theta, 1)$ such that θ is an answer for ψ to KB.*

5 Computation

In this section, we show that satisfiability checking and query processing in *BDL-Lite$_R$* can be reduced to satisfiability checking and query processing in *DL-Lite$_R$*.

The following theorem shows that the satisfiability of probabilistic knowledge bases in *BDL-Lite$_R$* can be reduced to the satisfiability of knowledge bases in *DL-Lite$_R$*. Note that all negated axioms in the theorem can be simulated by positive ones.

Theorem 5. *Let $KB = (T, A, BN)$ be a probabilistic knowledge base in BDL-Lite$_R$. For every $v \in D(V)$, let T_v (resp., A_v) be the set of all axioms ϕ and $\neg\phi$ for which there exists a probabilistic axiom $\phi: X = x$ in T (resp., A), such that $v|X = x$ and $v|X \neq x$, respectively. Then, KB is satisfiable iff the knowledge base $KB_v = (T_v, A_v)$ in DL-Lite$_R$ is satisfiable for every $v \in D(V)$ with $Pr_{BN}(V = v) > 0$.*

The next theorem shows that query processing in probabilistic knowledge bases in *BDL-Lite$_R$* can be reduced to query processing in knowledge bases in *DL-Lite$_R$*. Note that all negated axioms in the theorem can be simulated by positive ones.

Theorem 6. *Let $KB = (T, A, BN)$ be a satisfiable probabilistic knowledge base in BDL-Lite$_R$, and let $Q = \psi: X = x$ be a probabilistic query to KB. For every $v \in D(V)$, let T_v (resp., A_v) be the set of all ϕ and $\neg\phi$ for which there exists some $\phi: X = x$ in T (resp., A) such that $v|X = x$ and $v|X \neq x$, respectively. Let θ be a ground substitution for the variables in Q and let $pr \in (0, 1]$. Then, (θ, pr) is an answer for Q to KB iff pr is the sum of all $Pr_{BN}(V = v)$ such that (i) $v \in D(V)$ with $Pr_{BN}(V = v) > 0$, (ii) θ is an answer for ψ to $KB_v = (T_v, A_v)$, and (iii) $v|X = x$.*

6 Tractability Results

As an important result of this paper, we now show that both satisfiability checking and query processing in *BDL-Lite$_R$* can be done in LogSpace in the data complexity. Note that we adopt the notion of data complexity from logic programming [5].

The following theorem shows that deciding whether a probabilistic knowledge base in *BDL-Lite$_R$* is satisfiable can be done in LogSpace in the data complexity.

Theorem 7. *Given a probabilistic knowledge base* $KB = (\mathcal{T}, \mathcal{A}, BN)$ *in BDL-Lite$_\mathcal{R}$, deciding whether KB is satisfiable can be done in LogSpace in the size of $\mathcal{A}$ in the data complexity.*

The next theorem shows that computing all positive answers for probabilistic unions of conjunctive queries can also be done in LogSpace in the data complexity.

Theorem 8. *Given a satisfiable probabilistic knowledge base* $KB = (\mathcal{T}, \mathcal{A}, BN)$ *in BDL-Lite$_\mathcal{R}$ and a probabilistic union of conjunctive queries $Q = \psi \colon X = x$, computing the set of all positive answers (θ, pr) for Q to KB can be done in LogSpace in the size of the ABox $\mathcal{A}$ in the data complexity.*

7   Related Work

There are several related approaches to probabilistic description logics in the literature, which can be classified according to the generalized description logics, the supported forms of probabilistic knowledge, and the underlying probabilistic reasoning.

Closest in spirit to this paper is perhaps the work by Koller et al. [17], which presents P-CLASSIC, which is a probabilistic generalization of the CLASSIC description logic, rather than the *DL-Lite* family. Like our approach, theirs allows for terminological probabilistic knowledge about concepts and roles, but unlike ours, theirs does not support assertional knowledge about instances of concepts and roles. Like ours, their approach is based on inference in Bayesian networks as underlying probabilistic reasoning formalism. Closely related work by Yelland [29] combines a restricted description logic close to $\mathcal{FL}$ with Bayesian networks, rather than the *DL-Lite* family. It also allows for terminological probabilistic knowledge about concepts and roles, but does not support assertional knowledge about instances of concepts and roles. The main differences to our work are summarized as follows. First, we allow for both terminological probabilistic knowledge about concepts and roles, and assertional knowledge about instances of concepts and roles. Second, as a closely related aspect, unlike the above two works, we provide LogSpace data complexity results, and we consider the problem of answering probabilistic unions of conjunctive queries. Third, the above two probabilistic description logics essentially lie in the intersection of tractable description logics and Bayesian networks, and are thus limited in their expressive power, while ours orthogonally and faithfully combine the two components, and thus keep their expressive power. For this reason, our approach allows for much richer terminological knowledge. Hence, compared to previous tractable probabilistic description logics, our new approach to tractable probabilistic description logics is especially well-suited for data-intensive applications in the Semantic Web, such as the ones listed in the introduction.

Also closely related are the probabilistic description logics in [20], which are probabilistic extensions of the expressive description logics $\mathcal{SHIF}(\mathbf{D})$ and $\mathcal{SHOIN}(\mathbf{D})$ behind OWL Lite and OWL DL, respectively, towards sophisticated formalisms for reasoning under probabilistic uncertainty in the Semantic Web.[1] They allow for expressing

---

[1] See [16] for an implementation of the probabilistic description logics in [20].

both terminological probabilistic knowledge about concepts and roles, and also assertional probabilistic knowledge about instances of concepts and roles. Our present work is more flexible in the sense that terminological and assertional pieces of probabilistic knowledge can be freely combined, while [20] partitions the probabilistic knowledge into terminological pieces of probabilistic knowledge and object-centered assertional pieces of probabilistic knowledge. Rather than on Bayesian networks, they are based on probabilistic lexicographic entailment from probabilistic default reasoning [19] as underlying probabilistic reasoning formalism, which treats terminological and assertional probabilistic knowledge in a semantically way as probabilistic knowledge about random resp. concrete instances. Differently from [20], we here provide LogSpace data complexity results, and we consider probabilistic unions of conjunctive queries.

Heinsohn [12] presents a probabilistic extension of $\mathcal{ALC}$, which allows to represent terminological probabilistic knowledge about concepts and roles, and which is essentially based on probabilistic reasoning in probabilistic logics, similar to [23, 18]. Heinsohn, however, does not allow for assertional knowledge about concept and role instances. Jaeger's work [13] proposes another probabilistic extension of $\mathcal{ALC}$, which allows for terminological and assertional probabilistic knowledge about concepts / roles and about concept instances, respectively, but does not support assertional probabilistic knowledge about role instances (although a possible extension in this direction is mentioned). The uncertain reasoning formalism in [13] is essentially based on probabilistic reasoning in probabilistic logics, as the one in [12], but coupled with cross-entropy minimization to combine terminological probabilistic knowledge with assertional probabilistic knowledge. Jaeger's recent work [14] is less closely related, as it focuses on interpreting probabilistic concept subsumption and probabilistic role quantification through statistical sampling distributions, and develops a probabilistic version of the guarded fragment of first-order logic.

Related works on probabilistic web ontology languages focus especially on combining the web ontology language OWL with probabilistic formalisms based on Bayesian networks. In particular, da Costa et al. [4, 3] propose a probabilistic generalization of OWL, called PR-OWL, which is based on multi-entity Bayesian networks.

Ding et al. [8] propose a probabilistic generalization of OWL, called BayesOWL, which is based on standard Bayesian networks. BayesOWL provides a set of rules and procedures for the direct translation of an OWL ontology into a Bayesian network that supports ontology reasoning, both within and across ontologies, as Bayesian inferences. The authors also describe an application of this approach in ontology mapping. In closely related work, Mitra et al. [22] introduce a technique to enhancing existing ontology mappings by using a Bayesian network to represent the influences between potential concept mappings across ontologies.

Yang and Calmet [28] present an integration of the web ontology language OWL with Bayesian networks. The approach makes use of probability and dependency-annotated OWL to represent uncertain information in Bayesian networks. Pool and Aikin [26] also provide a method for representing uncertainty in OWL ontologies, while Fukushige [9] proposes a basic framework for representing probabilistic relationships in RDF. Finally, Nottelmann and Fuhr [24] present two probabilistic extensions of variants of OWL Lite, along with a mapping to locally stratified probabilistic Datalog.

8   Summary and Outlook

We have presented probabilistic generalizations of the *DL-Lite* description logics, which are based on Bayesian networks. We have shown that the new probabilistic description logics properly extend both the *DL-Lite* description logics as well as Bayesian networks. We have also shown that satisfiability checking and query processing in the new probabilistic description logics can be reduced to satisfiability checking and query processing in the *DL-Lite* family. Furthermore, satisfiability checking and answering probabilistic unions of conjunctive queries can be done in LogSpace in the data complexity.

Other classical description logics can be extended similarly by probabilistic uncertainty in Bayesian networks. All results of this paper carry over to such extensions, except for the tractability results, which generally will not hold for extensions of classical description logics that are more expressive than those of the *DL-Lite* family.

We leave for future work the implementation of the new probabilistic description logics and the investigation of efficient algorithms for the general case beyond the data complexity (where tractable cases and efficient techniques from Bayesian networks may come into play). Another interesting topic for future research is to investigate the use of the new tractable probabilistic description logics in important tasks such as web search and database querying. Furthermore, it would be very interesting to develop techniques for learning the new tractable probabilistic description logics (e.g., from web data).

Acknowledgments. Thomas Lukasiewicz is supported by the German Research Foundation (DFG) under the Heisenberg Programme. We thank the reviewers for their constructive and useful comments, which helped to improve this work.

References

[1] Baader, F., Calvanese, D., McGuinness, D., Nardi, D., Patel-Schneider, P.F. (eds.): The Description Logic Handbook: Theory, Implementation, and Applications. Cambridge University Press, Cambridge (2003)

[2] Calvanese, D., De Giacomo, G., Lembo, D., Lenzerini, M., Rosati, R.: DL-Lite: Tractable description logics for ontologies. In: Proceedings AAAI 2005, pp. 602–607. AAAI Press/MIT Press (2005)

[3] da Costa, P.C.G., Laskey, K.B.: PR-OWL: A framework for probabilistic ontologies. In: Proceedings FOIS 2006, pp. 237–249. IOS Press, Amsterdam (2006)

[4] da Costa, P.C.G., Laskey, K.B., Laskey, K.J.: PR-OWL: A Bayesian ontology language for the Semantic Web. In: Proceedings URSW 2005, pp. 23–33 (2005)

[5] Dantsin, E., Eiter, T., Gottlob, G., Voronkov, A.: Complexity and expressive power of logic programming. ACM Comput. Surv. 33(3), 374–425 (2001)

[6] d'Amato, C., Staab, S., Fanizzi, N., Esposito, F.: Efficient discovery of services specified in description logics languages. In: Proceedings of the ISWC-2007 Workshop on Service Matchmaking and Resource Retrieval in the Semantic Web (SMR^2 2007) (2007)

[7] Ding, Z., Peng, Y.: A probabilistic extension to ontology language OWL. In: Proceedings HICSS 2004 (2004)

[8] Ding, Z., Peng, Y., Pan, R.: BayesOWL: Uncertainty modeling in Semantic Web ontologies. In: Ma, Z. (ed.) Soft Computing in Ontologies and Semantic Web. Studies in Fuzziness and Soft Computing, vol. 204, Springer, Heidelberg (2006)

[9] Fukushige, Y.: Representing probabilistic knowledge in the Semantic Web. In: Proceedings of the W3C Workshop on Semantic Web for Life Sciences, Cambridge, MA, USA (2004)

[10] Lukasiewicz, T., Giugno, R.: P-$\mathcal{SHOQ}(D)$: A Probabilistic Extension of $\mathcal{SHOQ}(D)$ for probabilistic ontologies in the Semantic Web. In: Flesca, S., Greco, S., Leone, N., Ianni, G. (eds.) JELIA 2002. LNCS (LNAI), vol. 2424, pp. 86–97. Springer, Heidelberg (2002)

[11] Grimm, S., Motik, B., Preist, C.: Variance in e-business service discovery. In: Proceedings of the ISWC 2004 Workshop on Semantic Web Services (2004)

[12] Heinsohn, J.: Probabilistic description logics. In: Proceedings UAI 1994, pp. 311–318. Morgan Kaufmann, San Francisco (1994)

[13] Jaeger, M.: Probabilistic reasoning in terminological logics. In: Proceedings KR 1994, pp. 305–316. Morgan Kaufmann, San Francisco (1994)

[14] Jaeger, M.: Probabilistic role models and the guarded fragment. In: Proc. IPMU 2004, pp. 235–242 (2004); Extended version in Int. J. Uncertain. Fuzz., 14(1), 43–60 (2006)

[15] Jensen, F.V.: Bayesian Networks and Decision Graphs. Springer, Heidelberg (2001)

[16] Klinov, P.: Pronto: A non-monotonic probabilistic description logic reasoner. In: System demo at ESWC 2008 (2008)

[17] Koller, D., Levy, A., Pfeffer, A.: P-CLASSIC: A tractable probabilistic description logic. In: Proceedings AAAI 1997, pp. 390–397. AAAI Press/MIT Press (1997)

[18] Lukasiewicz, T.: Probabilistic deduction with conditional constraints over basic events. J. Artif. Intell. Res. 10, 199–241 (1999)

[19] Lukasiewicz, T.: Probabilistic default reasoning with conditional constraints. Ann. Math. Artif. Intell. 34(1–3), 35–88 (2002)

[20] Lukasiewicz, T.: Expressive probabilistic description logics. Artif. Intell. 172(6/7), 852–883 (2008)

[21] Lukasiewicz, T., Straccia, U.: Managing uncertainty and vagueness in description logics for the Semantic Web. J. Web Sem. (in press)

[22] Mitra, P., Noy, N.F., Jaiswal, A.: OMEN: A probabilistic ontology mapping tool. In: Gil, Y., Motta, E., Benjamins, V.R., Musen, M.A. (eds.) ISWC 2005. LNCS, vol. 3729, pp. 537–547. Springer, Heidelberg (2005)

[23] Nilsson, N.J.: Probabilistic logic. Artif. Intell. 28(1), 71–88 (1986)

[24] Nottelmann, H., Fuhr, N.: Adding probabilities and rules to OWL Lite subsets based on probabilistic Datalog. Int. J. Uncertain. Fuzz. 14(1), 17–42 (2006)

[25] Pearl, J.: Probabilistic Reasoning in Intelligent Systems: Networks of Plausible Inference. Morgan Kaufmann, San Francisco (1988)

[26] Pool, M., Aikin, J.: KEEPER and Protégé: An elicitation environment for Bayesian inference tools. In: Proceedings of the Workshop on Protégé and Reasoning held at the 7th International Protégé Conference (2004)

[27] Smyth, C., Poole, D.: Qualitative probabilistic matching with hierarchical descriptions. In: Proceedings KR 2004, pp. 479–487. AAAI Press, Menlo Park (2004)

[28] Yang, Y., Calmet, J.: OntoBayes: An ontology-driven uncertainty model. In: Proceedings IAWTIC 2005, pp. 457–463. IEEE Computer Society Press, Los Alamitos (2005)

[29] Yelland, P.M.: An alternative combination of Bayesian networks and description logics. In: Proceedings KR 2000, pp. 225–234. Morgan Kaufmann, San Francisco (2000)

Approximate Reasoning for Efficient Anytime Induction from Relational Knowledge Bases

Nicola Di Mauro, Teresa M.A. Basile, Stefano Ferilli, and Floriana Esposito

Università degli Studi di Bari, Dipartimento di Informatica, 70125 Bari, Italy
{ndm,basile,ferilli,esposito}@di.uniba.it

Abstract. In most real-world applications the choice of the right representation language represents a fundamental issue, since it may give opportunities for generalization and make inductive reasoning computationally easier or harder. While the setting of First Order Logic (FOL) is the most suitable one to model the multi-relational data of real and complex domains, on the other hand it puts the question of the computational complexity of the knowledge induction that represents a challenge for multi-relational data mining algorithms. Indeed, the complexity of most real domains, in which a lot of relationships are required to model the objects involved, calls for both an efficient and effective search method for exploring the space of candidate solutions and a deduction procedure assessing the validity of the discovered knowledge. A way of tackling the complexity of such domains is to use a method that reformulates a multi-relational learning task into an attribute-value one. In this paper we propose an *approximate reasoning* technique that decreases the complexity of a relational problem changing both the language and the inference operation used for the deduction. The complexity of the FOL language is decreased by means of a stochastic propositionalization method, while the NP-completeness of the deduction is tackled using an *approximate query evaluation*. The induction is performed with an *anytime algorithm*, implemented by a population based method, able to efficiently extract knowledge from structured data in form of complete FOL definitions. The validity of the proposed technique has been proved making an empirical evaluation on a real-world dataset.

1 Motivations

Over the last decades large volumes of data in digital form have been acquired. Most of these data are stored using relational databases consisting of multiple tables and associations. Moreover, the data used in the fields of weather prediction, financial risk analysis and drug design are relational in nature. The induction of conceptual definitions to model the knowledge of such complex real-world domains is a hard and crucial task. The challenges posed by such domains are due to various elements such as the noise in the descriptions, the lack of data, but also the choice of the right representation language exploited to describe them.

Representation is a fundamental as well as a critical aspect in the process of knowledge discovery. Indeed, the choice of the right representation has a significant impact on the performance of the learning algorithms but also on the possibility to interpret and

S. Greco and T. Lukasiewicz (Eds.): SUM 2008, LNAI 5291, pp. 160–173, 2008.
© Springer-Verlag Berlin Heidelberg 2008

reuse the discovered knowledge. The most suitable representation language to describe the objects and their relationships of complex real-world domains is a logic-based representation such as the first-order logic language (FOL) and the research area implementing algorithms working on this kind of representation is popularly known as Inductive Logic Programming (ILP). ILP systems represent examples, background knowledge, hypotheses and target concepts in Horn clause logic. The core of ILP is the use of logic for representation and the search for syntactically legal hypotheses constructed from predicates provided by the background knowledge.

However, this representation language allows a potentially large number of mappings between descriptions. The obvious consequence of such a representation is that both the space of candidate solutions to search and the test to assess the validity of the induced model result more costly. A possible solution is represented by *approximate reasoning* techniques [1], that try to decrease the complexity of a problem changing either the adopted language or the inference operation used for the deduction. In this way, the results may be unsound or incomplete but with a consequent speed-up and a reduced reasoning complexity.

A possible approximate reasoning technique consists in reformulating the original multi-relational learning task in a propositional one (i.e., *propositionalization*). This reformulation can be partial (heuristic), in which information is lost and the representation change is incomplete, or complete, in which no information is lost. In general, however, it is not possible to efficiently transform multi-relational data into an equivalent propositional form without an exponentially increasing complexity [2]. Alternative approaches concern the possibility to apply propositionalization directly on the original FOL context by a sort of flattening of the multi-relational data substituting them with all (or a subset of) their matchings with a pattern that can be provided by the users or previously built by the system.

This work proposes a method to decrease the dimensionality of the space of candidate solutions of multi-relational data to search by means of a propositionalization technique in which the transposition of the relational data is performed by an *online* flattening of the examples. The proposed method is a population based (genetic) algorithm that stochastically propositionalizes the training examples in which the learning phase may be viewed as a bottom-up search in the hypotheses space. The objective of this paper is twofold:

O1: Providing an efficient and scalable method for inductive reasoning on relational databases, combining a genetic approach to navigate the search space of candidate solutions with a partial transposition of the relational knowledge base in a propositional one;

O2: Incorporating an approximate reasoning strategy in a relational inductive learner, making incomplete a) the validation test (*query answering*) of the acquired knowledge, and b) the inductive generalization task.

The resulting learning algorithm, of the objective O1, belongs to the class of *anytime* algorithms [3] whose quality of results improves gradually as computation time increases, hence trading this quality against the cost of computation. They are resource constrained algorithms that return the best solution within a specified computational budget.

The validation test of the acquired knowledge, in objective O2, corresponds to the classical query answering task, that in relational learning is obtained by solving a subsumption problem known to be NP-complete. In many cases it is less important to obtain an exact query result than keeping query response time short. For instance, the following conjunctive FOL query

$$author(A1, P1), journal(P1, J), impact(J, IF), author(A2, P2), journal(P2, J)$$

may be used to test if there exist two authors $A1$ and $A2$ that have published a paper (resp. $P1$ and $P2$) in a journal J with an impact factor IF. Sometimes, instead of a correct answer, it may be suitable knowing the response for a subset of the authors in the domain, sacrificing the accuracy to improve running time. The approximate query answering used in this work is a *sampling* based technique, in which a random sample of the individuals involved in the domain is selected and used to solve the query.

2   Related Work

Various strategies have been proposed in order to overcome the limitation imposed by the inborn complexity of most real-word applications whose descriptions involve many relationships. One of the classical approaches consists in the reformulation of the relational learning in a propositional one followed by the application of well known propositional learners and by the mapping back in relational form of the resulting hypotheses. During the reformulation, a fixed set of structural features is built from relational background knowledge and the structural properties of the individuals occurring in the examples. In such a process, each feature is defined in terms of a corresponding program clause whose body is made up of a set of literals derived from the relational background knowledge. When the clause defining the feature is called for a particular individual (i.e., if its argument is bound to some example identifier) and this call succeeds at least once, the corresponding boolean feature is defined to be true for the given example; otherwise, it is defined to be false. Examples of systems that implement such kind of propositionalization process are LINUS [4], and its extensions DINUS [5] and SINUS [6], and RSD [7].

Alternative approaches avoid the reformulation process and apply propositionalization directly on the original FOL context: the relational examples are *flattened* by substituting them with all (or a subset of) their matchings with a pattern. To this concern, it was noted [8,9,10] that a most suitable setting for supervised relational learning is that of multiple instance problems (MIP), first introduced by Dietterich [11], where each example consists of a set of literals (instances) built on a same predicate symbol. The multiple instances representation is an extension that offers a good trade-off between the expressive power of relational learning and the low complexity of propositional learning. Unfortunately, most of the existing inductive learning systems are not able to face efficiently with this problem. In some cases the learning system has an incomplete knowledge about each training example: It does not know the features vector but it only knows that each example can be represented by means of one (or more) potential feature vectors (a bag of instances).

Following this idea, [12,9,10] proposed a multi-instance propositionalization. In such a framework each relational example is reformulated in its multiple matchings with a pattern (a formula of the initial hypotheses space that can be built from the training data or provided by the user). After the reformulation, each initial observation corresponds to many feature vectors and the search for hypotheses may be recasted in this propositional representation as the search for rules that cover at least one instance per observation. Consequently, the learning task is no longer to induce an hypothesis that is consistent with all the feature vectors reformulated but an hypothesis that covers at least one reformulated example of each positive initial training example and no reformulated example of any negative initial training example.

Specifically, the approach proposed in [9] consists in limiting the number of possible mappings by means of a selective mapping and then searching inductive generalizations in the hypotheses space defined by the selected mapping type. The type of mapping, i.e. the relevant propositionalization pattern, is provided by the user/expert and represents a (strong) bias which allows to dramatically reduce the matching space. On the contrary, in [12] the propositionalization process is done through a stochastic selection on each example of a user-defined number of example matchings with the pattern, which allows to reduce the dimensionality of the reformulated problem. In other words, for each example it is constructed the set of a user-defined number of hypotheses covering the example and not covering any example belonging to other classes. Then a representative of such a set for each example is learned that classifies unseen examples via a nearest-neighbour-like process. Finally, [10] proposed a method that selectively propositionalizes the relational data by interleaving attribute-value reformulation and algebraic resolution avoiding, as much as possible, the generation of reformulated data which are not relevant with respect to the discrimination task and obtaining a reformulated learning problem of tractable size. The obtained set of attribute-value instances is then used to solve the initial relational problem by applying a data-driven strategy.

Based on this kind of more suitable propositionalization and on the existing effective and efficient techniques for feature selection, [13] proposed an extension of classical feature selection methods for coping with the problem of relational data by firstly transforming the original relational data in propositional ones by means of a multi-instance propositionalization and successively applying methods for feature selection on such a new transformation.

3   The Anytime Induction Method

In this paper we propose a technique that, reformulating the training positive and negative examples, solves the multi-relational learning problem by applying a data-driven bottom-up strategy.

3.1   Logic Background

We used Datalog [14] as representation language for the domain and induced knowledge, that here is briefly reviewed. For a more comprehensive introduction to logic programming and ILP we refer the reader to [15,16,5].

A first-order *alphabet* consists of a set of *constants*, a set of *variables*, a set of *function symbols*, and a non-empty set of *predicate symbols*. Each function symbol and each predicate symbol has a natural number (its *arity*) assigned to it. The arity assigned to a function symbol represents the number of arguments the function has. Constants may be viewed as function symbols of arity 0. A *term* is a constant symbol, a variable symbols, or an n-ary function symbol f applied to n terms $t_1, t_2, \ldots, t_n$.

An atom $p(t_1, \ldots, t_n)$ (or atomic formula) is a predicate symbol p of arity n applied to n terms t_i. Both l and its negation $\bar{l}$ are said to be *literals* (resp. positive and negative literal) whenever l is an atomic formula. A *clause* is a formula of the form $\forall X_1 \forall X_2 \ldots \forall X_n (L_1 \vee L_2 \vee \ldots \vee \bar{L}_i \vee \bar{L}_{i+1} \vee \ldots \vee \bar{L}_m)$ where each L_i is a literal and $X_1, X_2, \ldots X_n$ are all the variables occurring in $L_1 \vee L_2 \vee \ldots \bar{L}_i \vee \ldots \bar{L}_m$. Most commonly the same clause is written as an implication $L_1, L_2, \ldots L_{i-1} \leftarrow L_i, L_{i+1}, \ldots L_m$, where $L_1, L_2, \ldots L_{i-1}$ is the *head* of the clause and $L_i, L_{i+1}, \ldots L_m$ is the *body* of the clause. Clauses, literals and terms are said to be *ground* whenever they do not contain variables. A *Horn clause* is a clause which contains at most one positive literal. A *Datalog clause* is a clause with no function symbols of non-zero arity; only variables and constants can be used as predicate arguments.

A *substitution* θ is defined as a set of bindings $\{X_1 \leftarrow a_1, \ldots, X_n \leftarrow a_n\}$ where $X_i, 1 \leq i \leq n$ is a variable and $a_i, 1 \leq i \leq n$ is a term. A substitution θ is applicable to an expression e, obtaining the expression $e\theta$, by replacing all variables X_i with their corresponding terms a_i.

The learning problem for ILP can be formally defined:

Given: A finite set of clauses $\mathcal{B}$ (*background knowledge*) and sets of clauses E^+ and E^- (positive and negative *examples*).

Find: A theory Σ (a finite set of clauses), such that $\Sigma \cup \mathcal{B}$ is *correct* with respect to E^+ and E^-, i.e.: a) $\Sigma \cup \mathcal{B}$ is *complete* with respect to E^+: $\Sigma \cup \mathcal{B} \models E^+$; and, b) $\Sigma \cup \mathcal{B}$ is *consistent* with respect to E^-: $\Sigma \cup \mathcal{B} \not\models E^-$.

Given the formula $\Sigma \cup \mathcal{B} \models E^+$, deriving E^+ from $\Sigma \cup \mathcal{B}$ is *deduction*, and deriving Σ from $\mathcal{B}$ and E^+ is *induction*. In the simplest model, $\mathcal{B}$ is supposed to be empty and the deductive inference rule $\models$ corresponds to θ-*subsumption* between clauses.

Definition 1 (θ-**subsumption**). *A clause c_1 θ-subsumes a clause c_2 if and only if there exists a substitution σ such that $c_1\sigma \subseteq c_2$. c_1 is a generalization of c_2 (and c_2 a specialization of c_1) under θ-subsumption. If c_1 θ-subsumes c_2 then $c_1 \models c_2$.*

θ-subsumption is the test used in relational learning for query answering. It corresponds to the most time consuming task of the induction process being it a problem NP-complete. In Section 3.4 we will present an approximate θ-subsumption test based on a sampling method described in the following section.

3.2 Data Reformulation

The method we propose is based on a stochastic reformulation of examples that, differently from other proposed propositionalization techniques, does not use the classical subsumption relation. For instance, in PROPAL [10], each example E, described in FOL, is reformulated into a set of matchings of a propositional pattern P with E by using the classical θ-subsumption procedure, being in this way still bound to the FOL context. On the contrary, in our approach the reformulation is based on a *syntactic rewriting* of the training examples based on a fixed set of domain constants.

Let E be an example, represented as a Datalog ground clause, and let $consts(E)$ be the set of the constants appearing in E. One can write a new example E' from E by changing one or more constants in E, i.e. by renaming. In particular, E' may be obtained by applying an antisubstitution (i.e., a mapping from terms onto variables) and a substitution under Object Identity (OI) to E, $E' = E\sigma^{-1}\theta_{OI}$, where σ^{-1} is an antisubstitution that maps terms to variables, and θ_{OI} is a substitution under OI. In the Object Identity framework, within a clause, terms that are denoted with different symbols must be distinct, i.e. they must represent different objects of the domain. In the following we will omit the OI notation, and we will consider substitutions under the Object Identity framework.

Definition 2 (Renaming of an example). *A ground renaming of an example E, $R(E)$, is obtained by applying a substitution $\theta = \{V_1/t_1, V_2/t_2, \ldots V_n/t_n\}$ to $E\sigma^{-1}$, i.e. $R(E) = E\sigma^{-1}\theta$, such that σ^{-1} is an antisubstitution, $\{V_1, V_2, \ldots V_n\} \subseteq vars(E\sigma^{-1})$, and $\{t_1, t_2, \ldots t_n\}$ are distinct constants of $consts(E)$, $n = consts(E)$.*

Example 1. Let $E : h(a) \leftarrow q(a,b), c(b), t(b,c)$ an example, $C = consts(E) = \{a, b, c\}$, and $\sigma^{-1} = \{a/X, b/Y, c/Z\}$ an antisubstitution. All the possible ground renamings of E, $\mathcal{R}(E)$ in the following, are

$$E_1 : h(a) \leftarrow q(a,b), c(b), t(b,c),$$
$$E_2 : h(a) \leftarrow q(a,c), c(c), t(c,b),$$
$$E_3 : h(b) \leftarrow q(b,a), c(a), t(a,c),$$
$$E_4 : h(b) \leftarrow q(b,c), c(c), t(c,a),$$
$$E_5 : h(c) \leftarrow q(c,a), c(a), t(a,b),$$
$$E_6 : h(c) \leftarrow q(c,b), c(b), t(b,a)$$

obtained by applying to $E\sigma^{-1} : h(X) \leftarrow q(X,Y), c(Y), t(Y,Z)$ all the possible injective substitutions from $vars(E\sigma^{-1}) = \{X, Y, Z\}$ to $consts(E)$.

In this way, we do not need to use the θ-subsumption test to compute the renamings of an example E, we just have to rewrite it considering the permutations of the constants in $consts(E)$.

Lemma 1. *Given an example E, let $m = |\ consts(E)\ |$. The number of all possible renamings of E, $|\mathcal{R}(E)|$, is equal to the number of permutations on a set of m constants, i.e. $|\mathcal{R}(E)| = P_m^m = m!$.*

Proof. Let $consts(E) = \{c_1, c_2, \ldots, c_m\}$, and $\sigma^{-1} = \{c_1/V_1, c_2/V_2, \ldots, c_m/V_m\}$ be an antisubstitution. By Definition 2, a renaming $R(E) \in \mathcal{R}(E)$ is obtained by choosing a substitution $\theta_i = \{V_1/t_{1i}, V_2/t_{2i}, \ldots, V_m/t_{mi}\}$, where $\{t_{1i}, t_{2i} \ldots, t_{mi}\}$ are elements of $consts(E)$, s.t. $R(E) = E\sigma^{-1}\theta_i$. Letting fixed variables $V_j, j = 1 \ldots m$, all the possible substitutions θ_i can be obtained by selecting permutations $(t_{1i}t_{2i} \cdots t_{mi})_i$ of the elements in the set $\{c_1, c_2, \ldots, c_m\}$. Being $P_m^m = m!$, it follows that $|\mathcal{R}(E)| = |\{R(E) \mid R(E) = E\sigma^{-1}\theta_i\}| = P_m^m = m!$. ◁

Table 1. Renamings of the clause $h(a) \leftarrow q(a,b), c(b), t(b,c)$

	h(a)	h(b)	h(c)	q(a,b)	q(a,c)	q(b,a)	q(b,c)	q(c,a)	q(c,b)	c(a)	c(b)	c(c)	t(a,b)	t(a,c)	t(b,a)	t(b,c)	t(c,a)	t(c,b)
E_1	•			•							•					•		
E_2	•				•							•						•
E_3		•				•				•				•				
E_4		•					•					•					•	
E_5			•					•		•			•					
E_6			•						•		•				•			

Lemma 2. *All the renamings of an example E belong to the same equivalence class,
$[E] = \mathcal{R}(E) = \{R(E) \in \mathcal{E} \mid R(E) \sim_s E\}$, based on the equivalence relation $\sim_s$
defined by $a \sim_s b$ iff a is syntactically equivalent to b, where $\mathcal{E}$ is the set of all the
possible ground clauses. In particular, given an example E, $\forall E' \in [E], \exists \theta, \sigma^{-1}$ s.t.
$E'\sigma^{-1}\theta = E$.*

Proof. Let $consts(E) = \{c_1, c_2, \ldots, c_m\}$. If $R, Q \in \mathcal{R}(E)$ then, by Definition 2,
$\exists \sigma^{-1} = \{c_1/V_1, c_2/V_2, \ldots, c_m/V_m\}$, and $\theta_R = \{V_1/t_{1R}, \ldots, V_m/t_{mR}\}$ and $\theta_Q =
\{V_1/t_{1Q}, \ldots, V_m/t_{mQ}\}$, where $(t_{1R} \cdots t_{mR})$ and $(t_{1Q} \cdots t_{mQ})$ are permutations of
the elements in the set $consts(E)$, s.t. $R = E\sigma^{-1}\theta_R$ and $Q = E\sigma^{-1}\theta_Q$. Now, $R\theta_R^{-1}\sigma =
Q\theta_Q^{-1}\sigma$, where $\theta_R^{-1} = \{t_{1R}/V_1, \ldots, t_{mR}/V_m\}$, $\theta_Q^{-1} = \{t_{1Q}/V_1, \ldots, t_{mQ}/V_m\}$ and
$\sigma = \{V_1/c_1, \ldots, V_m/c_m\}$, and hence R and Q are syntactically equivalent, $R \sim_s Q$. ◁

Table 1 reports the propositional representation of the renamings belonging to the equivalence class of the clause reported in the Example 1.

3.3   Approximate Model Construction

In the general framework of ILP, the generalization of clauses, and hence the model construction, is based on the concept of *least general generalization* originally introduced by Plotkin. Given two clauses C_1 and C_2, C_1 generalizes C_2 (denoted by $C_1 \leq C_2$) if
C_1 subsumes C_2, i.e. there exists a substitution θ such that $C_1\theta \subseteq C_2$.

In our propositionalization framework, a generalization C (a non-ground clause) of
two positive examples E_1 and E_2 may be calculated by turning constants into variables
in the intersection between a renaming of E_1 and a renaming of E_2.

Definition 3. *Let E_1 and E_2 be two positive examples, n and m the number of constants in E_1 and E_2 respectively. Let C be a set of p constants such that $p \geq n$ and
$p \geq m$. $R(E_1)_{\{C\}}$ and $R(E_2)_{\{C\}}$ indicate two generic renamings of the examples E_1
and E_2, respectively, onto the set of constants C.*

Proposition 1 (Generalization). *Given E_1, E_2 examples, a generalization G such that
subsumes both E_1 and E_2, $G \leq E_1, E_2$ is*

$$G = (R(E_1)_{\{C\}} \cap R(E_2)_{\{C\}})\sigma^{-1}.$$

Proof. We must show, by generalization definition, that there exist θ_1, θ_2 substitutions,
such that $G\theta_1 \subseteq E_1$ and $G\theta_2 \subseteq E_2$. $\forall l_j \in G\theta_i : l_j \in (R(E_1)_{\{C\}} \cap R(E_2)_{\{C\}})\sigma^{-1}\theta_i$,
and hence $l_j \in R(E_i)_{\{C\}}\sigma^{-1}\theta_i$. θ_i are substitutions that map variables in G onto terms
in E_i. Since $R(E_i)_{\{C\}}\sigma^{-1}\theta_i \in [E_i]$ then $R(E_i)_{\{C\}}\sigma^{-1}\theta_i \sim_s E_i$ by Lemma 2. Thus,
$\forall l_j \in G\theta_i : l_j \in E_i$, hence $G\theta_i \subseteq E_i$.   ◁

In order to obtain consistent intersections, it is important to note that all the renamings, for both E_1 and E_2, must be calculated on the same fixed set of constants. Hence, given $E_1, E_2, \ldots, E_n$ examples, the set C of the constants useful to build the renamings may be chosen equal to

$$C = \operatorname*{argmax}_{E_i}(|consts(E_i)|).$$

Furthermore, to avoid empty generalizations, the constants appearing in the head literal of the renamings must be take fixed.

Example 2. Given two positive examples
  $E_1 : h(a) \leftarrow q(a, b), c(b), t(b, c), p(c, d)$ and
  $E_2 : h(d) \leftarrow q(d, e), c(d), t(e, f)$.
We calculate C as:

$$C = \operatorname*{argmax}_{E_i}(|consts(E_i)|) = consts(E_1) = \{a, b, c, d\}.$$

Now,
  $R(E_1)_{\{C\}} = \{h(a), \neg q(a, b), \neg c(b), \neg t(b, c), \neg p(c, d)\}$,
  $R(E_2)_{\{C\}} = \{h(a), \neg q(a, b), \neg c(a), \neg t(b, c)\}$
A generalization G of E_1 and E_2 is
  $G = (R(E_1)_{\{C\}} \cap R(E_2)_{\{C\}})\sigma^{-1} = \{h(a), \neg q(a, b), \neg t(b, c)\}\sigma^{-1} =$
  $= (h(a) \leftarrow q(a, b), t(b, c))\sigma^{-1} = h(X) \leftarrow q(X, Y), t(Y, Z)$
with $\sigma^{-1} = \{a/X, b/Y, c/Z\}$.

3.4   Approximate Model Validation

The model validation we adopt in the proposed framework to assess and exploit the generated model on the seen and unseen data is based on a syntactic lazy matching.

Corollary 1 (Subsumption). *Given a generalization G and an example E, G subsumes E iff $R(G\theta)_{\{C\}} \cap R(E)_{\{C\}} \sim_s G\theta$.*

Proof. $\rightarrow$) If G subsumes E then, by definition, there exists a substitution θ s.t. $G\theta \subseteq E$. This means that $\forall l \in G\theta : l \in E$ and hence $G\theta \cap E = G\theta \sim_s R(G\theta)_{\{C\}} = R(G\theta \cap E)_{\{C\}} = R(G\theta)_{\{C\}} \cap R(E)_{\{C\}}$.
  $\leftarrow$) If $R(G\theta)_{\{C\}} \cap R(E)_{\{C\}} \sim_s G\theta$, then by Proposition 1,
    $(R(G\theta)_{\{C\}} \cap R(E)_{\{C\}})\sigma^{-1} \leq E$
  $\Rightarrow R(G\theta)_{\{C\}}\sigma^{-1} \leq E$
  $\Rightarrow \exists \delta : R(G\theta)_{\{C\}}\sigma^{-1}\delta \subseteq E$
  $\Rightarrow (G\theta\sigma'^{-1}\delta')\sigma^{-1}\delta \subseteq E$
  $\Rightarrow G\theta' \subseteq E$

$\triangleleft$

To be complete, the procedure must prove the test $G\theta \cap E = G\theta$ for all $P_r^n = \frac{n!}{(n-r)!}$ renamings of $G\theta$ and E, where $n = \max\{|consts(G\theta)|, |consts(E)|\}$ and $r = \min\{|consts(G\theta)|, |consts(E)|\}$ and by taking fixed the renaming for the clause $G\theta$ or E containing less constants. However, we can make the test approximate by randomly choosing a number α of all the possible permutations.

Algorithm 1. Sprol

Input: E^+: positive examples; E^-: negative examples; α: the parameter for negative coverage; β: the parameter for positive coverage; k: the dimension of the population; r: number of restarts;

Output: the hypotheses h

1: $C = \text{argmax}_{E_i \in E = E^+ \cup E^-} (|consts(E_i)|)$;
2: **while** $E^+ \neq \emptyset$ **do**
3:      select a seed e from E^+
4:      /* select k renamings of e */
5:      Population $\leftarrow ren(k, e, C)$;
6:      PopPrec $\leftarrow$ Population; $i \leftarrow 0$;
7:      **while** $i < r$ **do**
8:          P $\leftarrow \emptyset$;
9:          **for** each element $v \in$ Population **do**
10:             **for** each positive example $e^+ \in E^+$ **do**
11:                 /* select t renamings of e^+ */
12:                 $V_{e^+} \leftarrow ren(t, e^+, C)$;
13:                 /* generalization */
14:                 P $\leftarrow$ P $\cup \{u | u = v \cap w_i, w_i \in V_{e^+}\}$;
15:         Population $\leftarrow$ P;
16:         /* Consistency check */
17:         **for** each negative example $e^- \in E^-$ **do**
18:             /* select α renamings of e^- */
19:             $V_{e^-} \leftarrow ren(\alpha, e^-, C)$;
20:             **for** each element $v \in$ Population **do**
21:                 **if** v covers an element of V_{e^-} **then**
22:                     remove v from Population
23:         /* Completeness check */
24:         **for** each element $v \in$ Population **do**
25:             completeness$_v \leftarrow 0$;
26:         **for** each positive example $e^+ \in E^+$ **do**
27:             /* select β renamings of e^+ */
28:             $V_{e^+} \leftarrow ren(\beta, e^+, C)$;
29:             **for** each element $v \in$ Population **do**
30:                 **if** $\exists u \in V_{e^+}$ s.t. $u \cap v = v$ **then**
31:                     completeness$_v \leftarrow$ completeness$_v + 1$;
32:         $i \leftarrow i + 1$;
33:         **if** $|$Population$| = 0$ **then**
34:             /* restart with the previous population */
35:             Population $\leftarrow$ PopPrec;
36:         **else**
37:             leave in Population the best k generalizations only;
38:             PopPrec $\leftarrow$ Population;
39:     add the best element $b \in$ Population to h;
40:     remove from E^+ the positive exs covered by b

Definition 4 (Subsumption degree). *Let be n the number of all possible renamings of $G\theta$ and E, and α, $\alpha \leq n$, the renamings to test the subsumption between G and E. The subsumption degree between G and E is defined as*

$$sd(G, E) = \begin{cases} 1 & \text{if } R(G\theta)_{\{C\}} \cap R(E)_{\{C\}} \sim_s G\theta; \\ \text{argmax}_\alpha \frac{|R(G\theta)_{\{C\}} \cap R(E)_{\{C\}}|}{|R(G\theta)_{\{C\}}|} & \text{otherwise.} \end{cases}$$

In this paper we do not use the subsumption degree to access the validity of generalizations. Each generalization G is considered complete with respect to a positive example E if $R(G\theta)_{\{C\}} \cap R(E)_{\{C\}} \sim_s G\theta$ (*exact completeness*) for a given renaming, and it is considered consistent with respect to a negative example E' if $R(G\theta)_{\{C\}} \cap R(E')_{\{C\}} \sim_s G\theta$ does not hold for all the chosen α renamings (*approximate consistency*). The induction with subsumption degree represents a future work.

To reduce the set of possible permutations we can fix the associations for the variables in the head of the generalization G. In particular if $G : h(V_1, V_2, \ldots, V_d) \leftarrow \ldots$ and $E : h(c_1, c_2, \ldots, c_d) \leftarrow \ldots$ then we can fix in all the generated permutations the associations $\{V_1/c_1, V_2/c_2, \ldots, V_d/c_d\}, d \leq r, n$.

Finally, we can further reduce the set of permutations by taking into account the positions of the costants in the literals. Suppose $p(V_1, V_2, \ldots, V_k)$ be a literal of the generalization G. Then, all the constants that may be associated to V_i, $1 \leq i \leq k$, are all those appearing in position i in the literals p/k of the example E.

3.5 Sprol System

Algorithm 1 reports the sketch of the Sprol system, implemented in Yap Prolog 5.1.1, that incorporates ideas of the propositional framework we proposed. Sprol is a population based algorithm where several individual candidate solutions are simultaneously maintained using a constant size population implementing the anytime nature of the algorithm. The population of candidate solutions provides a straightforward means for achieving search diversification and hence for increasing the exploration capabilities of the search process. In our case, the population is made up of candidate generalizations over the training positive examples. In many cases, local minima are quite common in search algorithms and the corresponding candidate solutions are typically not of sufficiently high quality. The strategy we used to escape from local minima is a *restart strategy* that simply reinitializes the search process whenever a local minimum is encountered.

Sprol takes as input the set of positive and negative examples of the training set and some user-defined parameters characterizing its approximate and anytime behaviour. In particular, α and β represent the number of renamings of a negative, respectively positive, example to use for the covering test; k is the size of the population; and r is the number of restarts.

As reported in Algorithm 1, Sprol tries to find a set of clauses that cover all the positive examples and no negative one, by using an iterative population based covering mechanism. It sets the initial population made up of k randomly chosen renamings of a positive example (lines 3-5). Then, the elements of the population are iteratively generalized on the positive examples of the training set (lines 9-15). All the generalizations that cover at least one negative example are taken out (lines 16-22), and the quality of each generalization, based on the number of covered positive examples, is calculated (lines 23-31). Finally, best k generalizations are taken into account for the next iteration (line 37). In case of an empty population a restart is generated with the previous population (line 35).

Renamings of an example are generated according to the procedure reported in Algorithm 2, that randomly chooses k renamings of the example E onto the set of constants C. This procedure implements the approximate and anytime nature of the method. Indeed, the parameter k represents at the same time both the approximation degree and the time allocated for the algorithm. The more renamings the algorithm select, the more accurate generalizations and subsumptions will be, but the more time to compute them will be needed.

It is important to note that our approach constructs hypotheses that are only approximately consistent. Indeed, in the consistency check it is possible that there exists a matching between an hypothesis and a negative example. The number α of allowed permutations is responsible of the induction cost as well as of the consistency of the produced hypotheses. An obvious consequence is that the more permutations allowed, the more consistent the hypotheses found and, perhaps, the more learning time.

Algorithm 2. $ren(k, E, C)$

Input: $\underline{k}$: the number of renamings; $\underline{E}$: the example; $\underline{C}$: a set of constants;
Output: a set S of renamings of E
1: $S \leftarrow \emptyset$
2: **for** $i = 1$ to k **do**
3:     $S \leftarrow S \cup \{R(E)_{\{C\}}\}$

---

4 Experiments

In order to evaluate the system Sprol, we performed experiments on the classical ILP mutagenesis dataset [17] consisting of structural descriptions of molecules. The Mutagenesis dataset has been collected to identify mutagenic activity in a compound based on its molecular structure and is considered to be a benchmark dataset for multi-relational learning. The Mutagenesis dataset consists of the molecular structure of 230 compounds, of which 138 are labelled as mutagenic and 92 as non-mutagenic. The mutagenicity of the compounds has been determined by the Ames Test. The task is to distinguish mutagenic compounds from non-mutagenic ones based on their molecular structure. The Mutagenesis dataset basically consists of atoms, bonds, atom types, bond types and partial charges on atoms. The dataset also consists of the hydrophobicity of the compound (logP), the energy level of the compound's lowest unoccupied molecular orbital (LUMO), a boolean attribute identifying compounds with 3 or more benzyl rings (I1), and a boolean attribute identifying compounds which are acenthryles (Ia). Ia, I1, logP and LUMO are relevant properties in determining mutagencity.

The size of the population has been set to 50, the parameter α to 50, the parameter β to 50, and making 5 restarts. As measures of performance, we use predictive accuracy and execution time. Results have been compared to those obtained by running, on both the same machine and dataset, the system Progol [18]. A 10-fold cross-validation produced the results reported in Table 2, averaged over the 10-folds, where we can note that there is an evident improvement of the execution time with respect to Progol obtaining a comparable predictive accuracy of the learned theory.

A second experiment, whose result are reported in Table 3, has been made in order to evaluate how the behaviour of the algorithm change by altering parameters k, α and β.

As we can see in Table 3, the first row reports the case in which we fixed α and β and letting k to change. Obviously, taking more elements in the population make grow the execution time. Furthermore, the second and the third row show that changing β does not change the accuracy of the theory. On the contrary α seems to be more important than β in improving the system performances. A further investigation of this behaviour deserve a more accurate experiment on an ad-hoc artificial dataset.

Table 2. Execution time (in seconds) and accuracy of Progol and Sprol on the mutagenesis dataset

	Progol		SPROL	
	Time	Accuracy	Time	Accuracy
M1	330.76	84.21	56.73	57.89
M2	479.03	78.95	41.15	89.47
M3	535.95	84.21	48.51	73.68
M4	738.54	68.42	63.67	84.21
M5	699.90	89.47	55.56	84.21
M6	497.08	78.95	53.55	78.49
M7	498.22	84.21	71.97	84.21
M8	584.00	78.95	56.29	89.47
M9	511.88	68.42	50.44	83.33
M10	587.18	82.35	65.63	70.59
Mean	546.25	79.81	56.35	79.60

Table 3. Results on parameter settings

		Time	Accuracy
	$k = 50$	75.49	71.14
$\alpha = 50 \; \beta = 50$	$k = 75$	96.80	75,35
	$k = 100$	117.29	71.67
	$\beta = 40$	78.84	78.67
$\alpha = 50 \; k = 50$	$\beta = 50$	75.49	71.14
	$\beta = 60$	74.39	76.85
	$\beta = 100$	114	78.02
	$\alpha = 40$	75.49	70.19
$\beta = 50 \; k = 50$	$\alpha = 50$	75.49	71.14
	$\alpha = 60$	56.35	79.6

5 Conclusion

Efficient multi-relational data mining algorithms have to tackle the problem of selecting the best search method for exploring the hypotheses space and the problem of reducing the complexity of the coverage procedure that assessis the validity of the learned theory against the training examples. A way of tackling the complexity of this kind of learning systems is to use a propositional method, that reformulates a multi-relational learning problem into an attribute-value one.

In this paper we proposed a population based algorithm able to efficiently solve multi-relational problems by using an approximate propositional method. The result of an empirical evaluation on the mutagenesis dataset of the proposed technique is very promising and proves the validity of the method.

As a future work, we plan to perform more in-depth experiments, on a purposely defined artificial dataset, in order to evaluate the method dependence from the parameters k, α and β. A solution should be to automatically discover, in an online manner, the correct input parameters of Sprol for a given learning task.

Furthermore, we want to investigate the behaviour of the algorithm in the case of approximate completeness. In particular, we want to use the subsumption degree between clauses in order to induce theories when noisy or uncertain data are available.

Acknowledgements

This work is partially founded by the Italian MIUR FAR project "Laboratorio di Biologia Computazionale per la Biodiversità Molecolare" (Computational Biology Laboratory for Molecular Biodiversity).

References

1. Zilberstein, S., Russell, S.: Approximate reasoning using anytime algorithms. Imprecise and Approximate Computation 318, 43–62 (1995)
2. Raedt, L.D.: Attribute value learning versus inductive logic programming: The missing links (extended abstract). In: Page, D. (ed.) ILP 1998. LNCS, vol. 1446, pp. 1–8. Springer, Heidelberg (1998)
3. Boddy, M., Dean, T.L.: Deliberation scheduling for problem solving in time-constrained environments. Artificial Intelligence 67(2), 245–285 (1994)
4. Lavrac, N., Dzeroski, S., Grobelnik, M.: Learning nonrecursive definitions of relations with linus. In: Proceedings of the European Working Session on Machine Learning, pp. 265–281. Springer, Heidelberg (1991)
5. Lavrac, N., Dzeroski, S.: Inductive Logic Programming: Techniques and Applications. Ellis Horwood, New York (1994)
6. Krogel, M.-A., Rawles, S., Zelezny, F., Flach, P., Lavrac, N., Wrobel, S.: Comparative evaluation of approaches to propositionalization. In: Horváth, T., Yamamoto, A. (eds.) ILP 2003. LNCS (LNAI), vol. 2835, pp. 194–217. Springer, Heidelberg (2003)
7. Lavrač, N., Železný, F., Flach, P.A.: RSD: Relational subgroup discovery through first-order feature construction. In: Matwin, S., Sammut, C. (eds.) ILP 2002. LNCS (LNAI), vol. 2583, pp. 149–165. Springer, Heidelberg (2003)
8. Sebag, M., Rouveirol, C.: Induction of maximally general clauses consistent with integrity constraints. In: Wrobel, S. (ed.) Proceedings of the 4th International Workshop on Inductive Logic Programming. GMD-Studien, vol. 237, pp. 195–216. Gesellschaft für Mathematik und Datenverarbeitung MBH (1994)
9. Zucker, J.-D., Ganascia, J.-G.: Representation changes for efficient learning in structural domains. In: Proceedings of 13th International Conference on Machine Learning, pp. 543–551. Morgan Kaufmann, San Francisco (1996)
10. Alphonse, E., Rouveirol, C.: Lazy propositionalization for relational learning. In: Horn, W. (ed.) Proc. of the 14th European Conference on Artificial Intelligence, pp. 256–260. IOS Press, Amsterdam (2000)
11. Dietterich, T., Lathrop, R., Lozano-Perez, T.: Solving the multiple instance problem with axis-parallel rectangles. Artificial Intelligence 89(1-2), 31–71 (1997)
12. Sebag, M., Rouveirol, C.: Tractable induction and classification in first order logic via stochastic matching. In: 15th International Join Conference on Artificial Intelligence, pp. 888–893. Morgan Kaufmann, San Francisco (1997)
13. Alphonse, E., Matwin, S.: A dynamic approach to dimensionality reduction in relational learning. In: Hacid, M.-S., Raś, Z.W., Zighed, D.A., Kodratoff, Y. (eds.) ISMIS 2002. LNCS (LNAI), vol. 2366, pp. 255–264. Springer, Heidelberg (2002)

14. Ullman, J.D.: Principles of Database and Knowledge-Base Systems, vol. I. Computer Science Press (1988)
15. Bratko, I.: Prolog programming for artificial intelligence, 3rd edn. Addison-Wesley Longman Publishing Co., Amsterdam (2001)
16. Muggleton, S., De Raedt, L.: Inductive logic programming: Theory and methods. Journal of Logic Programming 19/20, 629–679 (1994)
17. Srinivasan, A., Muggleton, S., King, R.D.: Comparing the use of background knowledge by inductive logic programming systems. In: Raedt, L.D. (ed.) Proceedings of the 5th International Workshop on Inductive Logic Programming, pp. 199–230. Springer, Heidelberg (1995)
18. Muggleton, S.: Inverse Entailment and Progol. New Generation Computing, Special issue on Inductive Logic Programming 13(3-4), 245–286 (1995)

Fusing Uncertain Structured Spatial Information*

Florence Dupin de Saint-Cyr[1], Robert Jeansoulin[2], and Henri Prade[1]

[1] IRIT, CNRS, Univ. Toulouse III, 31062 Toulouse Cedex 09, France
[2] Institut Gaspard Monge, CNRS, Univ. Paris Est, 77453 Marne-la-Vallée, France

Abstract. Spatial information associates properties to labeled areas. Space is partitioned into (elementary) parcels, and union of parcels constitute areas. Properties may have various level of generality, giving birth to a *taxonomy* of properties for a given universe of discourse. Thus, the set of properties pertaining to a conceptual taxonomy, as the set of areas and parcels, are structured by a natural partial order. We refer to such structures as ontologies. In fusion problems, information coming from distinct sources may be expressed in terms of different conceptual and/or spatial ontologies, and may be pervaded with uncertainty. Dealing with several conceptual (or spatial) ontologies in a fusion perspective presupposes that these ontologies be aligned. This paper introduces a basic representation format called *attributive formula*, which is a pair made of a property and a set of parcels (to which the property applies), possibly associated with a certainty level. Uncertain attributive formulas are processed in a possibilistic logic manner, augmented with a two-sorted characterization: the property may be true *everywhere* in an area, or at least true *somewhere* in the area. The fusion process combines the factual information encoded by the attributive formulas provided by the different sources together with the logical encoding of the conceptual and spatial ontologies (obtained after alignment). Then, inconsistency encountered in the fusion process may be handled by taking advantage of the existence of different fusion modes, or by relaxing when necessary a closed world-like assumption stating by default that what is true somewhere in an area may be also true everywhere in it (if nothing else is known). A landscape analysis toy example illustrates the approach.

Keywords: spatial information, ontology, uncertainty, possibilistic logic, fusion.

1 Introduction

The management of multiple sources raises many fusion problems due to the uncertainty and the heterogeneity of the information. Geographical information has

---

* This work was funded by the Midi-Pyrénées and Provence-Alpes-Côte d'Azur Regional Councils (Inter-Regional Project n° 05013992 "GEOFUSE"). A preliminary version is electronically available [6].

S. Greco and T. Lukasiewicz (Eds.): SUM 2008, LNAI 5291, pp. 174–188, 2008.
© Springer-Verlag Berlin Heidelberg 2008

all these problems [4,2,12,18], its specific aspect being to deal with geographical-space areas, called *parcels*, on which we need to operate union and intersection.

A popular representation is the so called "field model", $f{:}(x,y) \to f(x,y)$, with a Cartesian coordinate domain as space, and real numbers as target domain. Though widely used in geophysics, meteorology, etc. and in most applications that involve imagery, terrain or any "gridded data", it is much too limited in many situations that deal with non quantitative data. Landscape analysis is one such situation. Spatial information may involve a mix of numeric and symbolic attributes, using different vocabularies more or less structured, but rarely unstructured. The sources may use different space partitions. Moreover, there may exist several kinds of dependencies, and spatial fusion must keep consistent with all of them. A previous paper [7] started an informal discussion of these problems. The present paper provides a logical framework for handling spatial information and ontological information. Another step is made by handling the merging of spatial information in the general setting of logical information fusion. Lastly, both numeric and symbolic information may be pervaded by several forms of uncertainty and imprecision [14]. This is why we allow for "uncertain attributive formulas" linking parcels to a property associated with a certainty degree: it expresses that for *any* parcel of a given set, we are sure at least at this degree that a property is true.

Hence, dealing with spatial data requires relatively powerful representation languages, as discussed in [15]. Ontology is often used for representing a structured vocabulary [12], and the fusion of ontology-based geospatial information must face the problem of heterogeneous vocabularies [10]. This paper deals with terminology integration and discusses the merging of information provided by different sources using multiple space partitions, and expressed with more or less precise labels from the same ontology resulting from a preliminary alignment.

Following Papini *et al.* [23], we use a logical framework for processing ontological information, and "attributive formulas" to link sets of parcels to property or attribute statements. We need a simple type of ontology that can be logically expressed by three and only three conditions: 1) a label may be a sub-label of another label, 2) a label is the reunion of its sub-labels, 3) labels referring to the most specific classes are mutually exclusive two by two. This representation allows us to express both ontological information and attributive formulas. Besides, the spatial extent on which an attributive formula applies may vary within a parcel: it means that we must distinguish between statements true everywhere, or only somewhere in a parcel.

The paper is organized as follows. Section 2 discusses representation needs, proposes a logical formalism for representing geographic information in ontologies, and introduces the notion of an *attributive formula* as a reified formula that links space and labels. Section 3 details the fusion process that helps to merge heterogeneous descriptions of the same space. In Section 4, "uncertain attributive formulas" are defined, and we introduce the explicit precision of the "somewhere" or "everywhere" reading associated to an attributive formula.

Section 5 shows how to integrate possibilistic principles in the context of "attributive formulas". It is illustrated on a landscape information fusion example.

2   Geographic Ontologies and Attributive Formulas

In *geographic information* we can distinguish the *geo* part, the *info* part, and the association that links them (the *what*, the *there* and the *is*, of Quine[20]). Hence, three aspects should be considered for representing geographic information:

1) The *(attributed) space*: one single space for all applications, but many different ways to split it into parts. *Parcels* have a spatial extent, and it is assumed that after intersecting all parcels from the different splittings, the most elementary parcels form a finite partition of the space. This is called a *partonomy structure*.
2) The *(attribute) properties*: many *property domains*, more or less independent, can serve different purposes. A *taxonomy structure* can represent a hierarchy of properties, reflecting some partial order. A consistent fusion of partial orders may help to detect, and to remove errors when mixing such structures.
3) The *attribution*: it results from an observation process, where the associations are often multiple, and largely pervaded by uncertainty for space and properties.

A similar, but not formalized, approach was proposed in [17]: *an ontology is built on three main concepts: (1) a partonomy of physical objects of which the attributes represent most of the relevant information, (2) a simple taxonomy of informational objects, (3) a relation between the informational objects and those physical objects they inform about.* In order to have a representation model more appropriate than the "field model", we use a logical "attributive formalism" to represent "property-parcel" information. Beside the attributive link, there are two other basic links: *property-property* (from the knowledge encoded in a property taxonomy), and *parcel-parcel* (from a partonomy). The logical representation is satisfactory for encoding such qualitative links too. The ontology representation we use is simpler than the ones offered by description logics since we remain propositional. The ontological relations are not uncertain here.

2.1   A Logical Encoding of an Ontology of Information

In fusion problems, it is advantageous to encode taxonomies in a logical manner, which makes the information merging easier. Let $\{\langle set\ of\ nodes \rangle, \subseteq\}$ be a *poset* structure that we name *ontology* [22], where nodes are concepts, and $\subseteq$ encodes specialization/subsumption relations: these relations are represented graphically by edges where arrow direction refers to generalization. Let $\mathscr{L}$ be a propositional logical language built on a vocabulary $\mathscr{V}$ with connectives $\wedge$, $\vee$, $\rightarrow$ ("and", "or", material implication).

Definition 1 (poset definition of an ontology). *An ontology is a directed acyclic graph (dag) $G = (X, U)$. $X \subseteq \mathscr{L}$ is a set of formulas (one per concept, or node); U is a set of directed arcs (φ, ψ) denoting that φ is a subclass of ψ. An ontology admits one single source, $\bot$, and one single sink $\top$.*

Definition 2 (levels in an ontology). Levels *are defined inductively: L_0 is the set of formulas that have no predecessor (it contains only the contradiction $\perp$) L_i is the set of formulas that have no predecessor in $G \setminus (L_0 \cup \ldots L_{i-1})$, etc. $\Gamma^+(x)$ and $\Gamma^-(x)$ are the sets of successors and predecessors of x.*

Level L_1 nodes are called leaves (i.e., formulas φ s.t. the edge $(\perp, \varphi) \in U$). Moreover, we impose: (a) G: to be a lattice, (b) all the sub-classes of a class: to appear in the ontology, (c) all the leaves: to be mutually exclusive two by two.

Proposition 1. *Providing that*
(1) we add the appropriate formulas and arcs that turn a dag into a lattice;
(2) we add to each not-leave formula φ, a sub-formula "other elements of φ";
(3) we split leaves, wherever necessary, to make them mutually exclusive;
then, we can insure properties (a), (b) and (c) because the operations (1), (2) and (3) can always be done in the finite case.

Hence, an ontology will be encoded in the following way.

Definition 3 (logical encoding of an ontology). *Any dag $G = (X, U)$ representing an ontology can be associated to a set L_G of formulas that hold:*

1. $\forall (\varphi, \psi) \in U$,   *it holds that $\varphi \to \psi$.*
2. $\forall \varphi \in X \setminus \{L_1 \cup L_0\}$,   *it holds that $\varphi \to \bigvee_{\varphi_i \in \Gamma^-(\varphi)} \varphi_i$.*
3. $\forall \varphi, \psi \in L_1$,   *it holds that $\varphi \wedge \psi \to \perp$.*
4. $\forall (\varphi, \psi) \in X \times X$, s.t. $\varphi \vdash \psi$, *it exists a directed path from φ to ψ in G.*

Rule 1 expresses that an inclusion relation holds between two classes, 2 is a kind of closed world assumption version of property (b), 3 expresses property (c), 4 expresses completeness, as follows: if all the inclusion relations are known in the ontology, hence all corresponding paths must exist in G. From this, it follows that: $\forall \varphi \in X$, $\varphi \to \bigwedge_{\varphi_i \in \Gamma^+(\varphi)} \varphi_i$. and $\forall \varphi \in X$, $\varphi \to \top$. Given any pair of formulas $(\varphi, \psi) \in X \times X$, the logical encoding of the ontology $G = (X, U)$ allows us to decide if $\{\varphi \wedge \psi\} \cup L_G$ is consistent or not; and if $\varphi \cup L_G \vdash \psi$ or not. Taxonomy 1 of Figure 2 provides a toy example of such an ontology, where e.g. $L_0 = \{\perp\}$, $L_1 = \{conifer, wetland, agriculture\}$.

2.2 Attributive Formulas

Since we need to express binary links, our representational language is built on ordered pairs of formulas of $\mathscr{L}_i \times \mathscr{L}_s$, here denoted (φ, p). Such formulas should be understood as formulas of $\mathscr{L}_i$ reified by association with a set of parcels described by a formula of $\mathscr{L}_s$. In other words, to each formula is attached a set of parcels, where this formula applies. More precisely, (φ, p) expresses that φ is true for *each* elementary parcels satisfying p. Another understanding would view (φ, p) as the material implication $\neg p \vee \varphi$ in the language based on the union of the two vocabularies $\mathscr{V}_i$ and $\mathscr{V}_s$. Alternatively, in a first order logic language view, this may be also understood as $\forall x, p(x) \to \varphi(x)$, here $p(x)$ means that the parcel x satisfies p, equating formula p with the union of elementary parcels x_0 satisfying p. A pair (φ, p) will be called an *attributive formula*.

Definition 4 (attributive formula). *An attributive formula f, denoted by a pair (φ, p), is a propositional language formula based on the vocabulary $\mathcal{V}_i \cup \mathcal{V}_s$ where the logical equivalence $f \equiv \neg p \vee \varphi$ holds and p contains only variables of the vocabulary $\mathcal{V}_s$ $(p \in \mathcal{L}_s)$ and φ contains only variables of $\mathcal{V}_i$ $(\varphi \in \mathcal{L}_i)$.*

The intuitive meaning of $f = (\varphi, p)$ is that *for the set of elementary parcels that satisfy p, the formula φ is true*. Observe that there exist formulas built on the vocabulary $\mathcal{V}_i \cup \mathcal{V}_s$ which cannot be put under the attributive form, e.g., $a \wedge p_1$ where a is a literal of $\mathcal{V}_i$ and p_1 a literal of $\mathcal{V}_s$. The introduction of connectives $\wedge$, $\vee$ and $\neg$ does make sense, since any pair (φ, p) is a classical formula. From the above definition of (φ, p) as being equivalent to $\neg p \vee \varphi$, several inference rules straightforwardly follow from classical logic:

Proposition 2 (inference rules on attributive formulas)
1. $(\neg \varphi \vee \varphi', p), (\varphi \vee \varphi'', p') \vdash (\varphi' \vee \varphi'', p \wedge p')$
2. $(\varphi, p), (\varphi', p) \vdash (\varphi \wedge \varphi', p);$ 3. $(\varphi, p), (\varphi, p') \vdash (\varphi, p \vee p')$
4. *if $p' \vdash p$ then $(\varphi, p) \vdash (\varphi, p');$* 5. *if $\varphi \vdash \varphi'$ then $(\varphi, p) \vdash (\varphi', p)$*

From these rules, we can deduce the converse of 2: $(\varphi \wedge \varphi', p) \vdash (\varphi, p), (\varphi', p)$ and that $(\varphi, p), (\psi, p') \vdash (\varphi \vee \psi, p \vee p')$ and $(\varphi, p), (\psi, p') \vdash (\varphi \wedge \psi, p \wedge p')$. Thus, reification allows us to keep potential inconsistency *local*, namely restricted to a subset of parcels rather than pervading the whole knowledge base.

2.3 Taxonomy of Properties and Partonomy of Parcels

The previous formalization of an ontology can be applied both to parcels, which gives birth to partonomies, and to properties for describing conceptual taxonomies. The properties associated to parcels can be labels taken from a *vocabulary*. It might seem more suitable to develop first on parcels, before developing on properties that we will attribute to parcels. But, in fact we agree with [13] who says that *"the taxonomic basis of single-resource classifications precludes their direct placement in a spatially based ecological hierarchy (partonomy)."*
    Taxonomies divide and organize items into hierarchies of *kind-of* relations [21]. *"They work well for arranging entities possessing distinct, identifiable characteristics [...] (soils, vegetation, etc.). But, this strict and rigid identification is also a limitation, as announced in [13]: Applying taxonomic classifications to characterize ecological patterns over space proves difficult."* A *taxonomy* is an ontology, hence a lattice where the nodes are labeled on a given *vocabulary*, and where the partial order entails a relation, named *sort-of* or *is-a*, with the following peculiarities in practice: (i) Any level can exist without antecedent; (ii) If *a sort-of b*, then *a* may be unique. Let's name *taxon* a node of this graph.
    Partonomies reflect *part-of* relations based on space or proximity [21]. [13] says: *"Recognition of patterns at different spatial resolutions is fundamental to partonomies. Fortunately, there is a natural tendency for humans to perceive and subdivide the environment on the basis of part-whole relationships [5]. [...] most patterns or structures originate from ecological processes that are inherently spatial and thus partonomic in nature."* In a partition of a territory, particular

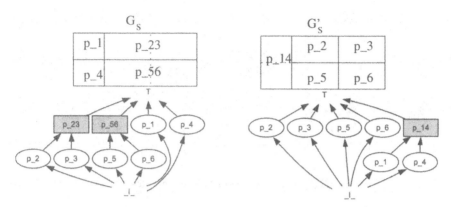

Fig. 1. Two partonomies (space ontologies) for the same set of parcels

subsets of parcels may have names, hence any partition equipped with the set inclusion relation, can be represented by partonomy. We further assume that all these partonomies share the same set of elementary parcels. Fig.1 exhibits two partonomies Gs and Gs' and their common elementary parcels $p_1, \ldots, p_6$.

A *partonomy* [1] is an ontology, hence a lattice, where the nodes are labeled by the elementary parcels, and the partial order entails a part-of relation which, in practice, has the following properties: (i) A class exists if and only if all its sub-classes exist; (ii) Only leaves can exist without antecedent; (iii) If *a part-of b*, then *b made-of a*, and it exists *c* (in the parcel vocabulary), complement of *a* in *b*. The union of two taxons can always exist, but it is not the case for two elements of a partonomy (partons), because taxons are classes, but partons are individuals that must exist when used by an operator. Figure 1 represents two partitions G_s and G_s' of the same space, leading to two partonomies where elementary parcels are identified by ovals.

3 Fusion of Properties as an Ontology Alignment Problem

Because the vocabulary is often insufficient for describing any subset of objects in a non-ambiguous way; or conversely because there may be no proper set of objects that satisfy a given set of properties and only them, only many-to-many relationships are really useful for representing geographic information. For a many-to-many relationship between the parcels of a given subset P_i of the partonomy, and the properties of a given list L_j of excerpts from the taxonomy, we need classically to build three database relations:

- R_s that distributes the subset P_i over its parcels;
- R_p that distributes the subset L_j over its properties;
- R_a made of the attributive formulas: pairs from $R_s \times R_p$ (learning samples).

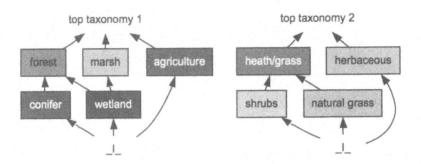

Fig. 2. An example of two taxonomies

What interests us is to discover if some additional knowledge emerges from the fusion of two information sources (R_{s1}, R_{p1}, R_{a1}) and (R_{s2}, R_{p2}, R_{a2}). The fusion of partonomies is not a problem, if we accept to ignore data matching issues, and that the geometric intersection between parcels of R_{s1} and R_{s2}, become leaves of the fusion R_s. The fusion of taxonomies is more difficult (many papers in FCA, semantic web, database integration), and it converges now to the notion of *ontology alignment* (see: Euzenat and Shvaiko [11]). We can distinguish several aspects: (a) the construction of $R_a = R_{a1} + R_{a2}$ (concatenation), (b) the structural alignment that will identify th number of nodes for candidate attributive formulas, and their partial order (classical FCA); (c) the labeling of this nodes that may unify them possibly on either R_{p1} or R_{p2}, or may need to form a new label by coupling (sign &) concepts from both R_{p1} and R_{p2}; (d) the decision to keep or discard these candidates nodes, according to one or several criteria (this aspect is skipped here, but similar to the discussion of section 5).

Let's now illustrate the problem with a landscape analysis example. Fig. 2 exhibits two concurrent taxonomies about land cover, as often, when experts from different disciplines try to build a domain ontology that reflects their own knowledge. Here, taxonomy 1, seems broader than taxonomy 2, which focuses on moor lands (shrubs, heath, and grass that can be natural or cultivated). We also notice that taxonomy 1 accepts multi-heritage, while the second does not.

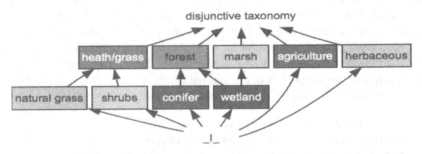

Fig. 3. Mutual exclusion taxonomy (solution 1)

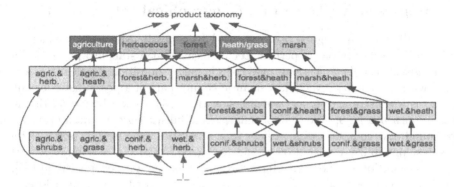

Fig. 4. Corresponding cross product taxonomy (solution 2)

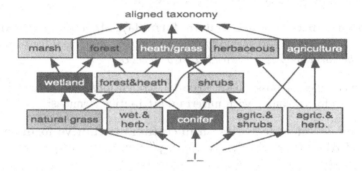

Fig. 5. Corresponding aligned taxonomy (solution 3)

One solution is to combine the two taxonomies with the assumption that they are totally disjoint, and that only one type of information is possible at one parcel (full mutual exclusion: Fig.3). This first solution means that for each parcel, we must choose only one label, from either taxonomy. This is a much too strong constraint, e.g.: *Agriculture* and *Herbaceous* are not necessarily incompatible.

A second approach is to consider every association as equally possible, under the only constraint to preserve both original partial orders (Fig.4). It doesn't impose anything: consequently, it doesn't provide any additional knowledge.

The third solution is to use the relation R_a, built for each p with all the attributive formulas (φ^1_i, p) expressed in taxonomy 1, together with all the (φ^2_j, p) expressed in taxonomy 2. Using a FCA algorithm [16], we can compute the taxonomy of Fig. 5: this is the most informative solution, which filters only the concepts that fit with the actual observations. The principle of the algorithm is to 'learn', among several partial orders compatible with both taxonomies, the minimal which complies with the given set of observations. Of course, this data-mining technique, if used with different observations, may lead to different "learned taxonomies", but a stability can be obtained with reliable enough samples.

4   Representing Uncertain Geographical Information

Our attributive language is now extended in a possibilistic logic manner, by allowing uncertainty on properties. Let us recall that a standard propositional possibilistic formula [8] is a pair made of a logical proposition (Boolean), associated with a certainty level. The semantic counterpart of a possibilistic formula (φ, α) is a constraint $N(\varphi) \geq \alpha$ expressing that α is a lower bound on the necessity measure N [9] of logical formula φ. Possibilistic logic has been proved to be sound and complete with respect to a semantics expressed in terms of the greatest possibility distribution π underlying N $(N(\varphi) = 1 - \sup_{\omega \models \neg \varphi} \pi(\omega))$. This distribution rank-orders interpretations according to their plausibility [8].

Note that a possibilistic formula (φ, α) can be viewed at the meta level as being only true or false, since either $N(\varphi) \geq \alpha$ or $N(\varphi) < \alpha$. This allows us to introduce possibilistic formula instead of propositional formula inside our attributive pair, and leads to the following definition.

Definition 5 (uncertain attributive formula). *An* uncertain attributive formula *is a pair* $((\varphi, \alpha), p)$ *meaning that for the set of elementary parcels that satisfy* p, *the formula* φ *is certain at least at level* α.

The inference rules of possibilistic logic [8] straightforwardly extend into the following rules for reasoning with uncertain attributive formulas:

Proposition 3 (inference rules on uncertain attributive formulas)
1. $((\neg\varphi \vee \varphi', \alpha), p), ((\varphi \vee \varphi'', \beta), p') \vdash ((\varphi' \vee \varphi'', \min(\alpha, \beta)), p \wedge p')$
2. $((\varphi, \alpha), p), ((\varphi', \beta), p) \vdash ((\varphi \wedge \varphi', \min(\alpha, \beta)), p)$
3.A. $((\varphi, \alpha), p), ((\varphi, \beta), p') \vdash ((\varphi, \min(\alpha, \beta)), p \vee p')$
3.B. $((\varphi, \alpha), p), ((\varphi, \beta), p') \vdash ((\varphi, \max(\alpha, \beta)), p \wedge p')$
4. *if* $p \vdash p'$ *then* $((\varphi, \alpha), p') \vdash ((\varphi, \alpha), p)$; 5. *if* $\varphi \vdash \varphi'$ *then* $((\varphi, \alpha), p) \vdash ((\varphi', \alpha), p)$

Rules 3.B. and 3.A. correspond respectively to the fact that either i) we locate ourselves in the parcels that satisfy both p and p', and then the certainty level of the formula φ can reach the maximal upper bound of the certainty levels known in p or in p', or ii) we consider any parcel in the union of the models of p and p' and then the certainty level is only guaranteed to be greater than the minimum of α and β. Note that this formalism allows us to express a greater uncertainty about a rather specific label than about a more general label, as in:

Example 1. In order to express that parcel p_1 has either "Conifer" or "Wetland" and more plausibly "Conifer", we use the two uncertain attributive formulas: $((Conifer, \alpha_1), p_1)$ and $((Wetland \vee Conifer, \alpha_2), p_1)$ where $\alpha_1 \leq \alpha_2$. At the semantic level, this is represented by the possibility distribution π_1 for p_1:

$$\pi_1(\omega) = \begin{cases} 1 & \text{if } \omega \models Conifer, \\ 1 - \alpha_1 < 1 & \text{if } \omega \models Wetland \wedge \neg Conifer, \\ 1 - \alpha_2 & \text{otherwise.} \end{cases}$$

Suppose that parcel p_2 has almost certainly Forest and more plausibly Conifer, knowing that Conifer are Forest $((\neg Conifer \vee Forest, 1), \top)$. Then for p_2:

$$\pi_2(\omega) = \begin{cases} 0 & \text{if } \omega \models Conifer \wedge \neg Forest, \\ 1 - \alpha_2 & \text{if } \omega \models \neg Conifer \wedge \neg Forest, \\ 1 - \alpha_1 & \text{if } \omega \models \neg Conifer \wedge Forest, \\ 1 & \text{if } \omega \models Conifer \wedge Forest, \end{cases}$$

This distribution can be syntactically encoded by the three formulas $((\neg Conifer \vee Forest, 1), p_2)$, $((Forest, \alpha_2), p_2)$ and $((Conifer, \alpha_1), p_2)$, with $\alpha_2 \geq \alpha_1$.

Fusion operations. The syntactic counterpart of the pointwise combination of two possibility distributions π_1 and π_2 into a distribution $\pi_1 \oplus \pi_2$ by any monotonic combination operator $\oplus$ such that $1 \oplus 1 = 1$, can be easily computed. Namely, if Σ_1 is associated with π_1 and Σ_2 with π_2, a possibilistic base that is semantically equivalent to $\pi_1 \oplus \pi_2$ can be computed as [3]:

$$\Sigma_{1 \oplus 2} = \begin{vmatrix} \{(\varphi_i, 1 - (1 - \alpha_i) \oplus 1) & \text{s.t. } (\varphi_i, \alpha_i) \in \Sigma_1\}, \\ \cup \{(\psi_j, 1 - 1 \oplus (1 - \beta_j)) & \text{s.t. } (\psi_j, \beta_j) \in \Sigma_2\}, \\ \cup \{(\varphi_i \vee \psi_j, 1 - (1 - \alpha_i) \oplus (1 - \beta_j)) & \text{s.t. } (\varphi_i, \alpha_i) \in \Sigma_1, (\psi_j, \beta_j) \in \Sigma_2\}. \end{vmatrix}$$

For $\oplus = \min$, we get $\pi_{\Sigma_1 \cup \Sigma_2} = \min(\pi_1, \pi_2)$ as expected. For $\oplus = \max$, we get $\Sigma_{\max(\pi_1, \pi_2)} = \{(\varphi_i \vee \psi_j, \min(\alpha_i, \beta_j)) \text{ s.t. } (\varphi_i, \alpha_i) \in \Sigma_1, \text{ and } (\psi_j, \beta_j) \in \Sigma_2\}$.

Localization of attributive knowledge. Still, attributive information itself may have two different intended meanings, namely when stating (φ, p) one may want to express that:

- *Everywhere* in each parcel satisfying p, φ holds as true, denoted by (φ, p, e). Then, for instance, $(Agriculture, p, e)$ cannot be consistent with $(Forest, p, e)$ since "Agriculture" and "Forest" are mutually exclusive in taxonomy 1.
- *Somewhere* in each parcel satisfying p, φ holds as true, denoted by (φ, p, s). Then, replacing e by s in this example is no longer inconsistent, since in each parcel there may exist "Agricultural" parts and "Forest" parts.

Note that these two meanings differ from the case where two exclusive labels such as "Water" and "Grass" might be attributed to the same parcel because they are intimately mixed, as in a "Swamp". This latter case should be handled by adding a new appropriate label in the ontology. More formally, for a given parcel p in the partonomy, if p is:

-not a leaf, (φ, p, s) means: $\forall p', p' \vdash p, (\varphi, p', s)$ holds;
-a leaf, but made of parts o, (φ, p, s) means that $\exists o \in p, \varphi(o)$.

Thus, it is clear that inference rules that hold for "everywhere", not necessarily hold for "somewhere". Indeed, the rule 2.2 $(\varphi, p), (\psi, p) \vdash (\varphi \wedge \psi, p)$ is no longer valid since $\exists o \in p, \varphi(o)$ and $\exists o' \in p, \psi(o')$ doesn't entail $\exists o'' \in p, \varphi(o'') \wedge \psi(o'')$. More generally, here are the rules that hold for the "somewhere" reading:

Proposition 4 (inference rules on attributive formulas)

1'. $(\neg\varphi \vee \varphi', p \wedge p', e)$, $(\varphi \vee \varphi'', p', s) \vdash (\varphi' \vee \varphi'', p \wedge p', s)$

2'. $(\varphi, p, s), (\varphi', p, e) \vdash (\varphi \wedge \varphi', p, s)$; *3'.* $(\varphi, p, s), (\varphi, p', s) \vdash (\varphi, p \vee p', s)$

4'. if $p' \vdash p$ *then* $(\varphi, p, s) \vdash (\varphi, p', s)$; *5'. if* $\varphi \vdash \varphi'$ *then* $(\varphi, p, s) \vdash (\varphi', p, s)$

where (φ, p, s) *stands* $\forall p', p' \vdash p \ \exists o \in p', \varphi(o)$, *and* (φ, p, e) *for* $\forall o \in p, \varphi(o)$.

Moreover, between "somewhere" and "everywhere" formulas, we have:

6'. $\neg(\varphi, p, s) \equiv (\neg\varphi, p, e)$

Taxonomy information and attributive information *should be handled separately,* because they refer to different types of information, *and, more importantly,* because taxonomy distinctions expressed by mutual exclusiveness of taxons do not mean that they cannot be simultaneously true in a given area: the taxonomy-formula $(a \leftrightarrow \neg b)$, with $a, b \in \mathcal{V}_i$ coming from the same taxonomy, differs from the attributive-formula $(a \leftrightarrow \neg b, \top)$, applied to every parcel (with the *everywhere* reading), since it may happen that for a parcel p, we have $(a, p) \wedge (b, p)$ (with a *somewhere* reading). The latter may mean that p contains at least two distinct parts, and that $\exists o \in p, \varphi(o) \wedge \exists o' \in p, \psi(o')$.

However, subsumption properties can be added to attributive formulas without any problem. Indeed $\varphi \vdash \psi$ means $\forall o, \varphi(o) \to \psi(o)$, and if we have (φ, p), implicitly meaning that $\exists o \in p, \varphi(o)$, then we obtain $\exists o \in p, \psi(o)$, i.e., (ψ, p). Thus we can write the subsumption property as $(\varphi \to \psi, \top)$.

5   Information Fusion: General Discussion on an Example

Generally speaking, fusing *consistent* knowledge bases merely amounts to apply logical inference to the union of the knowledge bases. In presence of inconsistency, another combination process should be defined and used. In this section, we develop an example, represented in the language of section 4, on two sources using the same taxonomy (possibly aligned: section 3), but different partonomies.

Possibilistic information fusion easily extends to attributive formulas: each given (φ, p) is equivalent to the conjunction of the (φ, p_i), where the p_i's are the leaves of the partonomy, such that $p_i \models p$. Using finite partonomies, it is always possible to refine them by taking the non-empty intersection of pairs of leaves, and possibilistic information fusion takes place for each p_i.

Let us detail the example of Fig.6: two sources report observations about an area which is partitioned in four elementary parcels, after refinement: $p_1, p_2, p_3, p_4,$

Source 1			Source 2	
Heath	*Conifer* p_2		*Forest*	p_{12}
Natural grass	*Forest*			
p_{13}	*Marsh* p_4		*Herbaceous* p_3	*Wetland*
			Natural grass	p_4

Fig. 6. The information given by the sources (inspired from [19])

using the aligned taxonomy from Fig.5. Clearly, we have four possible logical readings of two labels a and b associated with an area covered by two elementary parcels p_1 and p_2:

i. $(a \wedge b, p_1 \vee p_2)$: means that both a and b apply to each of p_1 and p_2.

ii. $(a \wedge b, p_1) \vee (a \wedge b, p_2)$: both a and b apply to p_1 or both apply to p_2.

iii. $(a \vee b, p_1 \vee p_2)$: a applies to each of p_1, p_2 or b applies to each of p_1, p_2.

iii. $(a \vee b, p_1) \vee (a \vee b, p_2)$: we don't know what of a or b applies to what of p_1 or p_2. This may be particularized by adding the mutual exclusiveness constraint $\neg(a, p_1 \vee p_2) \wedge \neg(b, p_1 \vee p_2)$: that a label cannot apply to both parcels.

When a and b are mutually exclusive the everywhere meaning is impossible (if we admit that sources provide consistent information).

Another ambiguity is about if the "closed world assumption" (CWA) holds or not, e.g.: if a source says that p_i contains *Conifer* and *Agriculture*, does it exclude that p_i would also contain *Marsh* ? It would be indeed excluded by applying CWA. Also, CWA may help to induce "everywhere" information from "somewhere" information. Indeed, if we know that all formulas attached to p are $\varphi_1, \ldots \varphi_n$ with a somewhere meaning: $(\varphi_1, p, \text{s}) \wedge \ldots \wedge (\varphi_n, p, \text{s}))$, then CWA entails that if there were another ψ that holds somewhere in p, it would have been already said, hence we can jump to the conclusion that $(\bigvee_{i=1,n} \varphi_i, p, \text{e})$.

Let's consider the non ambiguous reading i. of the example with the formulas:

Spatial formulas	*Property formulas*	
1. $p_1 \to p_{12}$,	14. Natgrass $\to$ Wetland,	22. AgriHerb $\to$ Herbac,
2. $p_1 \to p_{13}$,	15. Natgrass $\to$ ForHeath,	23. AgriHerb $\to$ Agric,
3. $p_2 \to p_{12}$,	16. WetHerb $\to$ Wetland,	24. Wetland $\to$ Marsh,
4. $p_3 \to p_{13}$,	17. WetHerb $\to$ Herbac,	25. Wetland $\to$ Forest,
5. $p_{12} \vee p_{13} \vee p_4$,	18. Conifer $\to$ ForHeath,	26. ForHeath $\to$ Forest,
6. $p_{12} \to p_1 \vee p_2$,	19. Conifer $\to$ Shrubs,	27. ForHeath $\to$ Heath,
7. $p_{13} \to p_1 \vee p_3$,	20. AgriShrub $\to$ Shrubs,	28. Shrubs $\to$ Heath,
8. $p_1 \wedge p_2 \to \bot$,	21. AgriShrub $\to$ Agric,	29. + 20 mutual excl.
9. + 5 mut. excl.		

Under the CWA:

Source 1	Source 2
49. (Heath, p_{13}, s)	
50. (Natural grass, p_{13}, s)	54. (Forest, p_{12}, s)
51. (Conifer, p_2, s)	55. (Herbaceous, p_3, s)
52. (Forest, p_2, s)	56. (Natural grass, p_3, s)
53. (Marsh, p_4, s)	57. (Wetland, p_4, s)

Let's project on: $p_1 \equiv p_{12} \wedge p_{13}$, using formula 7: $p_{13} \to p_1 \vee p_3$, and inference rule 4' (with $p_1 \vdash p_{13}$ and $p_3 \vdash p_{13}$). Idem with p_{12}. We obtain:

Source 1	Source 2
58. (Heath, p_1, s)	
59. (Heath, p_3, s)	62. (Forest, p_1, s)
60. (Natural grass, p_1, s)	63. (Forest, p_2, s)
61. (Natural grass, p_3, s)	

With the closed world assumption, we deduce:

Source 1	Source 2
64. (Heath $\vee$ Natural grass, p_1, e)	68. (Forest, p_1, e)
65. (Heath $\vee$ Natural grass, p_3, e)	69. (Forest, p_2, e)
66. (Conifer $\vee$ Forest, p_2, e)	70. (Herbaceous $\vee$ Natural grass, p_3, e)
67. (Marsh, p_4, e)	71. (Wetland, p_4, e)

Now we can proceed with the fusion step, in the conjunctive mode. We obtain:

parcel p_1: (64) and (68) yields (Conifer, p_1, e), which contradicts (60).

parcel p_2: the conjunction of (51), (52), (66), (63) is consistent, and yields (Woods, p_2, e) $\wedge$ (Conifer, p_2, s).

parcel p_3: the conjunction of (59), (61), (65), (55), (56),(70) consistently yields (Herbaceous $\vee$ Naturalgrass, p_3, e) $\wedge$ (Herbaceous, p_3, s) $\wedge$ (Naturalgrass, p_3, s)

parcel p_4: (67) and (71) yields (Rivers, p_4, e).

Conclusion:

$\bot$	$(Conifer, s)$
	$(Forest, e)$
$(Herbaceous, s)$	$(Wetland, e)$
$(Naturalgrass, s)$	

Sources 1 and 2 are conflicting on p_1: we can perform a disjunction of their formulas on this parcel. This conflict may come from the application of CWA to each source prior the fusion: the induction from (Forest, p_1, s) to (Forest, p_1, e) is perhaps too adventurous. We can check that (Forest, p_1, s) would yield (Conifer $\vee$ Natural grass, p_1, e) $\wedge$ (Conifer, p_1, s) $\wedge$ (Natural grass, p_1, s).

The treatment of this kind of fusion problem in [19] and [16] distinguishes between pessimistic and optimistic fusion modes. Our approach uses i) a pure logical representation setting (with an explicit distinction between conjunction and disjunction of labels), ii) distinguishes between somewhere and everywhere statements, iii) allows to express CWA (or not), iv) applies the general setting of logic-based information fusion. Our fusion result may also be more precise, thanks to a greater expressivity power of the representation framework.

Our logical framework also allows us to have a possibilistic handling of uncertainty, and then a variety of combination operations, which may depend on the level of conflict between the sources, or on their relative priority [3], can be encoded. The uncertainty setting enables us to enrich the reading of the example. Consider the information given by source 1 on p_2, namely "Conifer, Forest". As discussed in section 4.2, such an information may express that p_2 is covered by Forest, and plausibly by Conifer. With the "everywhere" reading, this can be syntactically encoded by the possibilistic formulas $((Forest, 1), p_2, e)$ and $((Conifer, \alpha), p_2, e)$, with $\alpha < 1$, together with the ontology information $((\neg Conifer \vee Forest, 1), \top)$. Similarly, the information given by source 2 on p_2 can be encoded as $((Forest, 1), p_2, e)$. Here, there is no inconsistency, hence $((Forest, 1), p_2, e) \wedge ((Conifer, \alpha), p_2, e)$.

Imagine that, now, source 2 says $((Forest, 1), p_2, e)$ and $((Wetland, \beta), p_2, e)$. The two sources are now partially inconsistent on p_2, and it can be checked that the level of possibilistic inconsistency of the information provided by the two sources, about p_2, is $Inc = \min(\alpha, \beta)$.

Different fusion modes can be used. One may use a renormalized conjunction [3]: the syntactic counterpart of this operator yields, if we assume $\alpha > \beta$, $((Woods, 1), p_2, e) \wedge ((Conifer, \alpha), p_2, e)$. Or one may choose a disjunctive attitude ($\oplus = \max$), one gets $((Forest, 1), p_2, e) \wedge ((Conifer \vee Wetland, \beta), p_2, e)$.

In case we again combine the two previous results obtained with the above fusion modes, by a product-based conjunction ($\oplus$ =product), one would obtain $((Woods, 1), p_2, e) \wedge ((Orchards \vee Wetland, 1 - (1 - \alpha)(1 - \beta)), p_2, e) \wedge ((Conifer, \alpha), p_2, e)$. This is a more refined result, since it keeps track of the conflict, and of a preference for the more certain information $((Conifer, \alpha), p_2, e)$ since $\alpha > \beta$. Observe however that $1 - (1 - \alpha)(1 - \beta)) > \alpha$, which makes the statement $Conifer \vee Wetland$ more certain.

6   Conclusion

After having identified representational needs (use of two vocabularies referring respectively to parcels and to properties, references to ontologies, uncertainty) when dealing with spatial information and restating ontology alignment procedures, a general logical setting has been proposed. It offers a non-ambiguous representation, propagates uncertainty in a possibilistic manner, and provides also the basis for handling multiple source information fusion. Moreover, we have seen that it is often important to explicitly distinguish between the cases where a property holds everywhere or somewhere into a parcel. An issue of interest for further research would be to allow for uncertain or default inheritance in ontologies. Note that, since subsumption relations can be easily added to the pieces of attributive spatial information, it would be possible to make some of these relations uncertain in our framework.

References

1. Rosse, C., Smith, B.: The role of foundational relations in the alignment of biomedical ontologies. In: Fieschi, M., et al. (eds.) MedInfo, Amsterdam. IOS Pres, IMIA (2004)
2. Balley, S., Parent, C., Spaccapietra, S.: Modelling geographic data with multiple representations. Int. J. of Geographical Information Science 18(4), 327–352 (2004)
3. Benferhat, S., Dubois, D., Prade, H.: A computational model for belief change and fusing ordered belief bases. In: Williams, M.-A., Rott, H. (eds.) Frontiers in Belief Revision, pp. 109–134. Kluwer Academic Publishers, Dordrecht (2001)
4. Bloch, I., Hunter, A. (eds.): Fusion: General Concepts and Characteristics. International Journal of Intelligent Systems 16(10), 1107–1134 (2001)
5. Tversky, B., Mark, D., Smith, B.: Ontology and geographic objects: An empirical study of cognitive categorization. In: Freksa, C., Mark, D.M. (eds.) COSIT 1999. LNCS, vol. 1661, pp. 283–298. Springer, Heidelberg (1999)
6. Dupin de Saint-Cyr, F., Jeansoulin, R., Prade, H.: Spatial information fusion: Coping with uncertainty in conceptual structures. In: ICCS Supplement, pp. 66–74 (2008), http://ceur-ws.org/Vol-354/p36.pdf

7. Dupin de Saint, F., Prade, H.: Multiple-source data fusion problems in spatial information systems. In: 11th Int. Conf. on Inf. Processing and Management of Uncertainty in Knowledge-Based Systems (IPMU 2006), pp. 2189–2196 (2006)
8. Dubois, D., Lang, J., Prade, H.: Possibilistic logic. In: Gabbay, D.M., Hogger, C.J., Robinson, J.A. (eds.) Handbook of logic in Artificial Intelligence and logic programming, vol. 3, pp. 439–513. Clarendon Press, Oxford (1994)
9. Dubois, D., Prade, H.: Possibility Theory. Plenum Press (1988)
10. Duckham, M., Worboys, M.: An algebraic approach to automated information fusion. Intl. Journal of Geographic Information Systems 19(5), 537–557 (2005)
11. Euzenat, J., Shvaiko, P.: Ontology matching. Springer, Heidelberg (2007)
12. Fonseca, F., Egenhofer, M., Agouris, P., Cmara, G.: Using ontologies for integrated geographic information systems. Transactions in GIS 6(3), 231–257 (2002)
13. Sorokine, A., Nowacki, G.: The limitations of applying single-resource taxonomies to ecological partonomies. In: Ecological Interpretations and Principles: Soil info. for a changing world. NCSS conf., Plymouth MA, August 2003, pp. 17–20 (2003)
14. Goodchild, M., Jeansoulin, R.: Data Quality in Geographic Information: from Error to Uncertainty, p. 192. Hermés, Paris (1998)
15. Goodchild, M.F., Yuan, M., Cova, T.J.: Towards a general theory of geographic representation in gis. Int. J. of Geogr. Information Science 21(3), 239–260 (2007)
16. Jeansoulin, R., Pham, T.T., Phan-Luong, V.: A quality-aware theme fusion for spatial information. In: Int. Conf. on Formal Concept Analysis (FCA 2007) (2007)
17. Klischewski, R.: How to 'rightsize' an ontology: a case of ontology-based web information management to improve the service for handicapped persons. In: 15th Int. Workshop on Database and Expert Systems Applications, pp. 158–162 (2004)
18. Petry, F., Cobb, M., Wen, L., Yang, H.: Design of system for managing fuzzy relationships for integration of spatial data in querying. Fuzzy Sets and Systems 140(1), 51–73 (2003)
19. Trung Pham, T.: Fusion de l'information géographique hiérarchisée. PhD thesis, Université de Provence, septembre (2005)
20. Quine, W.V.O.: On What There Is. In: From a Logical Point of View, pp. 1–19. Harper and Row, New York (1953)
21. Smith, B.: Mereotopology: A theory of parts and boundaries. Data and Knowledge Engineering 20, 287–303 (1996)
22. Staab, S., Studer, R. (eds.): Handbook on Ontologies. Springer, Heidelberg (2004)
23. Wurbel, E., Papini, O., Jeansoulin, R.: Revision: an application in the framework of GIS. In: 7th Int. Conf. on Principles of Knowledge Representation and Reasoning (KR 2000), pp. 505–516 (2000)

A Neuro Fuzzy Approach for Handling Structured Data

Alessio Ferone and Alfredo Petrosino

Department of Applied Science
University of Naples "Parthenope"
Centro Direzionale Isola C4
80143 Naples, Italy
{alessio.ferone,alfredo.petrosino}@uniparthenope.it

Abstract. Dealing with structured data has always represented a huge problem for classical neural methods. Although many efforts have been performed, they usually pre-process data and then use classic machine learning algorithm. Another problem that machine learning algorithm have to face is the intrinsic uncertainty of data, where in such situations classic algorithm do not have the means to handle them. In this work a novel neuro-fuzzy model for structured data is presented that exploits both neural and fuzzy methods. The proposed model called Fuzzy Graph Neural Network (F-GNN) is based on GNN, a model able to handle structure data. A proof of F-GNN approximation properties is provided together with a training algorithm.

Keywords: Structured pattern recognition, fuzzy systems, neural networks.

1 Introduction

Although neural methods have proved their powerful in dealing with various machine learning problems, sometimes they have failed because of the intrinsic data uncertainty. For this reason a growing interest has been addressed towards the integration of neural nets and approximated logics with a particular interested for the most famous, i.e. fuzzy logic[18,19]. Synergy between these two computational methods leads to the definition of new models called neuro-fuzzy systems. The basic idea behind neuro-fuzzy system is transforming fuzzy control system so to get neural net learning feature and hence exploiting advantages from both models. In neuro-fuzzy models, neural nets supply to fuzzy systems the connectionist structure and the learning ability, while fuzzy systems allow the use of a framework for approximated reasoning by means of rules in the IF-THEN form.

Fuzzy logic and neural nets are complementary technologies. Neural nets get information from systems that have to learn and control, while fuzzy logic based techniques use linguistic information from experts. It is natural that the synergy between these two techniques brings benefits to the final model. For example, it

S. Greco and T. Lukasiewicz (Eds.): SUM 2008, LNAI 5291, pp. 189–200, 2008.
© Springer-Verlag Berlin Heidelberg 2008

is possible to use a fuzzy system to represent experience from an expert and to use neural nets to calibrate their operation. In general, neuro-fuzzy model can be classified in three categories[6]:

1. *Neural fuzzy systems*: neural nets are used into fuzzy model
2. *Fuzzy neural networks*: fuzzification of neural nets
3. *Fuzzy-neural hybrid systems*: hybrid systems that incorporate fuzzy techniques and neural techniques.

In the first approach the goal is to provide fuzzy systems with tuning techniques used for neural nets without modifying their functionalities. In these models neural nets are used for numeric processing of fuzzy systems.

A fuzzy system of the first type are the *fuzzy basis function network* (FBFN), a type of neuro-fuzzy controller originally proposed by Wang and Mendel in [14]. In a FBFN, a fuzzy system is presented like an expansion series of fuzzy basis function (FBF), that is algebraic superimposition of membership functions. For this reason each FBF codes a fuzzy rule.

In the second approach, some typical elements of neural nets are fuzzified. In particular in fuzzy neural nets fuzzy neuron with activation signal obtained from a fuzzy relation are used[9].

In the third approach, both techniques play a fundamental role: each one operates in distinct part of the system so to incorporate complete functionalities of the other one[2].

A major drawback of the existing neural fuzzy systems is that their application domain is limited to static problems due to their inherent feedforward network structure. However, these kinds of studies are very interesting in all the application domains where the patterns are strongly correlated through structure, the processing is both numerical and symbolic and the nature of the data is imprecise and incomplete. Hence neural fuzzy systems capable for solving structure dependent problems are needeed.

The use of more complex data structures can lead to a better representation of data, so to simplify the solution of a given problem that deals with such data. Many efforts have been performed to handle structured data by pre-processing them and then apply classical machine learning algorithms. This approach not only add complexity to the final algorithm, but also introduce approximation errors and implementation difficulties. Moreover these kind of techniques tend to be specific for a problem and hence can be hardly reused for other problems. Neural methods are an example of techniques that evolved to handle with structured data[8][16][17][10]: original connectionist models have been modified to process sequences, trees and graphs. Some models[3][1] been proposed to deal directly with structured data, also able to approximate showing in probability every function defined on graph till an arbitrary precision degree.

Recently, much work has been focused on the representational capabilities of recursive networks. The idea which motivates these studies is that if a network model cannot *represent* a certain structure, then it certainly cannot *learn* it either. The main question is then whether or not a given recursive network architecture can represent a specific structure [4]. Recursive neural networks can be initialized with prior knowledge provided by training structured data; this ability makes recursive neural networks useful tools for modeling tree automata, where prior knowledge is available.

The purpose of the present paper is to report how to construct neural fuzzy models for dealing with structured data in recursive manner. The work extends the model Graph neural network [11,12], letting to handle fuzziness. The learning algorithm of the reported model and its approximation capabilities are reported and demonstrated.

2 The Proposed F-GNN Model

The model is based on the idea that computing "concepts" is more efficient if performed by means of linguistic elements coded as fuzzy rules. A node can represent an object with some physical attributes, but it can also represent a concept; in this case a crisp computation is not adequate. A model able to elaborate such nodes should deal with an intrisic uncertainty, hence fuzzy logic can support this kind of computation with poweful tools. In the same way, edges represent relationships between nodes that can be better expressed in terms of linguistic concepts. Once again, fuzzy computation allows the use of powerful tools to deal with the uncertainty of these linguisitc elements. Based on these considerations, the information processing at each node and each edge is made by means of fuzzy systems in the form of *multi-input-single-output* (MISO). The idea is that each node computes input information using fuzzy rules.

Let us assume the fuzzy rules for each node have the following form:

$$R^j: \text{IF } x_1 \text{ is } A_1^j \text{ AND } x_2 \text{ is } A_2^j \text{ AND } ... \text{ AND } x_n \text{ is } A_n^j \text{ THEN } y \text{ is } B^j$$

where $x_i, i = 1, 2, ..., n$ are the input variables, y is the output variable and A_i^j and B^j are linguistic terms characterized by membership functions $\mu_{A_i^j}(x_i)$ and $\mu_{B^j}(y)$ with $j = 1, 2, ..., M$.

Each node in the graph is encoded by a fuzzy control multi-input-single-output system $(X \subset \mathbb{R}^n \rightarrow Y \subset \mathbb{R})$ and in case of multiple output system, it can be decomposed in more multi-input-single-output systems.

Given an input graph, an encoding map is built using a MISO for each node of the graph. Each connection between nodes of the graph corresponds to connection between MISOs. Moreover for each output node another MISO is used. Figure 1 shows the structure of an encoding map where f_w and g_w are MISOs.

Connections between nodes are necessary to collect the states from adjacent nodes to a given node. In this way a node output will depend not only on the state and labels of the node itself but also on states and labels of adjacent nodes. Once the encoding map has been built, it is unfolded following the input graph connections (fig.2) and, once the fixed state has been reached, g-unit are added (encoding network). g-unit is unique in case of focused map; in general, we can say that they equal the number of output nodes.

From the definition of MISO and from the structure of encoding network, it is possible to note how in the proposed model f-unit input data are fuzzified and

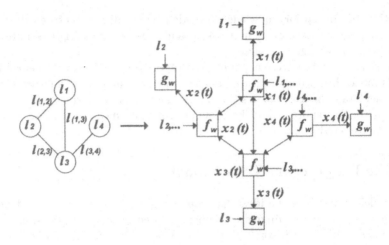

Fig. 1. Structure of an encoding map

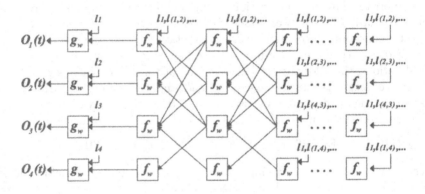

Fig. 2. Unfolding

defuzzified before they become input of the next f-unit. It is well known [5] that when more fuzzy rules are linked, problems can arise if the output of the first rule is not defuzzified before it is given in input to the next rule: this problem, called *fuzzy modus ponens*[13], has been faced by a large number of fuzzy logic researchers.

The above described procedure can be formalized by the following equation:

$$\begin{cases} x_n = f_w(l_n, l_{cp[n]}, x_{ne[n]}, l_{ne[n]}) \\ o_n = g_w(x_n, l_n) \end{cases} \tag{1}$$

where l_n is the label of node n, $l_{cp[n]}$ are the labels of its edges, $x_{ne[n]}$ are the states of the nodes in the neighborhood of n, $l_{ne[n]}$ are the labels of the nodes in the neighborhood of n, and x_n is the state of node n, i.e. it represents the concept denoted by node n. This value, along with the label l_n, is used to produce an output, i.e. a decision about the concept.

However, for non-positional graphs it is useful to replace function f_w of Eq.1 with the following equation

$$x_n = \sum_{u \in ne[n]} h_w(l_n, l_{(n,u)}, x_u, l_u) \tag{2}$$

where h_w is a parametric function. This transition function, already used in recursive neural networks, is not affected by the positions and the number of the children.

Assuming that the fuzzy system implemented on each node is composed by the following elements:

- Singleton fuzzifier
- Product inference
- Centroid defuzzifier
- Gaussian membership function.

Each MISO could be modeled as follows:

$$y = f(x) = \frac{\sum_{j=1}^{M} \bar{y}^j (\prod_{i=1}^{n} \mu_{A_i^j}(x_i))}{\sum_{j=1}^{M} (\prod_{i=1}^{n} \mu_{A_i^j}(x_i))} \tag{3}$$

where $f : X \subset \mathbb{R}^n \to \mathbb{R}$, $\bar{y}^j$ is the point in the output space Y where $\mu_{B^j}(\bar{y}^j)$ reaches its maximum value and $\mu_{A_i^j}(x_i)$ is a Gaussian membership function defined as:

$$\mu_{A_i^j}(x_i) = a_i^j exp[-\frac{1}{2}(\frac{x_i - m_i^j}{\sigma_i^j})^2] \tag{4}$$

where a_i^j, m_i^j and σ_i^j are real parameters and $0 < a_i^j \leq 1$.

From Eq. 4, it is possible to define *fuzzy basis functions* (FBFs) as:

$$p_j(\mathbf{x}) = \frac{\prod_{i=1}^{n} \mu_{A_i^j}(x_i)}{\sum_{j=1}^{m} (\prod_{i=1}^{n} \mu_{A_i^j}(x_i))}, j = 1, 2, ..., M. \tag{5}$$

and a *FBF network* (FBFN) like a FBF expansion:

$$f(\mathbf{x}) = \sum_{j=1}^{M} p_j(\mathbf{x})\theta^j \tag{6}$$

where $\theta^j = \bar{y}^j \in \mathbb{R}$, i.e. a FBFN can be thought as a linear combination of FBFs.

This asserts also the computational equivalence between a MISO fuzzy system and a FBFN.

Figure 3 shows the structure of a FBFN where Gaussian membership functions composed with product are present in layer 1. The output of layer 1 is composed using the sums in layer 2, while in layer 3 the output is defuzzified. It has to be noted that, although FBFN structure for f-unit and g-unit is the same, rules implemented by the two nets are not necessarily the same.

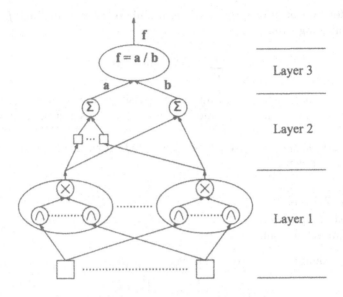

Fig. 3. FBFN structure

3 F-GNN: Universal Approximator

In the following, theorems that demonstrate approximation properties of the F-GNN model will be reported.

Firstly we introduce the concept of *unfolding equivalence*. Let us assume that $\tau : D \rightarrow R^m$ is a generic map constrained to produce the same output on nodes that are equivalent, i.e. given two nodes n and u of a grah G, $n \sim u$ implies $\tau(G, n) = \tau(G, u)$. The equivalence $\sim$ is called *unfolding equivalence* and is defined using the concept of *unfolding tree* T_n^d, that is the graph obtained by unfolding G up to the depth d using n as root.

Definition 1 Unfolding Equivalence. *Let $G = (N, E)$ be an undirected graph[1]. The nodes $n, u \in N$ are said to be unfolding equivalent, i.e. $n \sim u$, if $T_n = T_u$.*

Theorem 1 Approximation by non positional GNN[11]. *Let D be the non-positional graph domain. For each measurable function $\tau \in \mathcal{F}(D)$ that preserves the unfolding equivalence, each norm $\| \cdot \|$ over R^m, each probability measure P over D and every real ϵ, μ, λ with $\epsilon > 0, 0 < \lambda < 1, 0 < \mu < 1$, exist two continuous derivable function h and g*

$$x_n = \sum_{u \in ne[n]} h_w(l_n, l_{(n,u)}, x_u, l_u)$$
$$o_n = g_w(x_n, l_n), n \in N \tag{7}$$

---

[1] The definition can be extended also to directed graph.

such that the global transition function F is a contraction with constant μ, state dimension is $s = 1$ and the function defined by $\phi(G, n) = o_n$ satisfy the condition

$$P(\|\tau(G, n) - \phi(G, n)\| \geq \epsilon) \leq 1 - \lambda \tag{8}$$

where the global transition function F is a stacked version of $|N|$ instances of f_w.

Theorem 2 Approximation by non-positional non-linear F-GNN. *Let assume true the hypothesis of the previous theorem, then exists a set of parameters w and two FBFNs h_w and g_w with continuous derivative such that the thesis of the previous theorem is verified.*

Previous theorem relies on the following Lemma, which demonstrates that FBFNs are universal approximators.

Lemma 1 Stone-Weierstrass theorem. *Let Z be a set of continuous real functions on a compact set U. If*

1. *Z is an algebra, that is the set Z is closed with respect to sum, product and scalar product operations*
2. *Z separates points in U, that is for each $x, y \in U$, $x \neq y$*

then Z uniform closure consists of all the continuous real functions on U, that is (Z, d_∞) is dense in $(G[U], d_\infty)$.

<u>Proof</u>: *Firstly, we show the proof that (Y, d_∞) is an algebra. Let $f_1, f_2 \in Y$ such that:*

$$f_1(x) = \frac{\sum_{j=1}^{K1}(\overline{z}1^j \prod_{i=1}^{n} \mu_{A1_i^j}(x_i))}{\sum_{j=1}^{K1}(\prod_{i=1}^{n} \mu_{A1_i^j}} \tag{9}$$

$$f_2(x) = \frac{\sum_{j=1}^{K2}(\overline{z}2^j \prod_{i=1}^{n} \mu_{A2_i^j}(x_i))}{\sum_{j=1}^{K2}(\prod_{i=1}^{n} \mu_{A2_i^j}} \tag{10}$$

from which we have:

$$f_1(x) + f_2(x) = \frac{\sum_{j1=1}^{K1} \sum_{j2=1}^{K2}(\overline{z}1^{j1} + \overline{z}2^{j2})(\prod_{i=1}^{n} \mu_{A1_i^{j1}}(x_i)\mu_{A2_i^{j2}}(x_i))}{\sum_{j1=1}^{K1} \sum_{j2=1}^{K2}(\prod_{i=1}^{n} \mu_{A1_i^{j1}}(x_i)\mu_{A2_i^{j2}}(x_i))} \tag{11}$$

Given that $\mu_{A1_i^{j1}}$ and $\mu_{A2_i^{j2}}$ are Gaussian membership functions, their product $\mu_{A1_i^{j1}}\mu_{A2_i^{j2}}$ is still a Gaussian function, hence $f_1 + f_2$ is in the form a FBFN ($f_1 + f_2 \in Y$). Similarly we have that:

$$f_1(x)f_2(x) = \frac{\sum_{j1=1}^{K1} \sum_{j2=1}^{K2}(\overline{z}1^{j1}\overline{z}2^{j2})(\prod_{i=1}^{n} \mu_{A1_i^{j1}}(x_i)\mu_{A2_i^{j2}}(x_i))}{\sum_{j1=1}^{K1} \sum_{j2=1}^{K2}(\prod_{i=1}^{n} \mu_{A1_i^{j1}}(x_i)\mu_{A2_i^{j2}}(x_i))} \tag{12}$$

is also in the form of a FBFN, hence $f_1 f_2 \in Y$. Finally, for an arbitrary $c \in \mathbb{R}$,

$$cf_1(x) = \frac{\sum_{j=1}^{K1}(c\overline{z}1^j \prod_{i=1}^{n} \mu_{A1_i^j}(x_i))}{\sum_{j=1}^{K1}(\prod_{i=1}^{n} \mu_{A1_i^j})} \tag{13}$$

we still have a FBFN, hence $f_1 f_2 \in Y$.

Next step consist in demonstrating that (Y, d_∞) separates points U.

Build a function $f \in Y$, such that $f(x_0) \neq f(y_0)$ with arbitrary $x_0, y_0 \in U$ and $x_0 \neq y_0$. Then two fuzzy rules are chosen in the form:

$$R_j: \text{ IF } x_1 \text{ is } A_1^j \text{ AND } x_2 \text{ is } A_2^j \text{ ... AND } x_n \text{ is } A_n^j \text{ THEN}$$
$$z \text{ is } B^j$$

as base fuzzy rule ($M = 2$).

Let $x^0 = (x_1^0, x_2^0, ..., x_n^0)$ and $y^0 = (y_1^0, y_2^0, ..., y_n^0)$. Se $x_i^0 \neq y_i^0$, two fuzzy sets are defined $(A_i^1, \mu_{A_i^1})$ and $(A_i^2, \mu_{A_i^2})$ where

$$\mu_{A_i^1}(x_i) = exp[-\frac{(x_i - x_i^0)^2}{2}] \tag{14}$$

$$\mu_{A_i^2}(x_i) = exp[-\frac{(x_i - y_i^0)^2}{2}] \tag{15}$$

If $x_i^0 = y_i^0$, then $A_i^1 = A_i^2$ and $\mu_{A_i^1} = \mu_{A_i^2}$, hence only a fuzzy set is defined. Two fuzzy sets are defined $(B_i^1, \mu_{B_i^1})$ and $(B_i^2, \mu_{B_i^2})$ where

$$\mu_{B_i^j}(z) = exp[-\frac{(z - \bar{z}^j)^2}{2}] \tag{16}$$

with $j = 1, 2$ and $\bar{z}^j$ specified in the following. Hence all parameters have been defined except $\bar{z}^j$ ($j = 1, 2$), then a function f, in the FBFN form, has been defined, with $M = 2$ and $\mu_{A_i^j}$ specified before. With such f we have:

$$f(x^0) = \frac{\bar{z}^1 + \bar{z}^2 \prod_{i=1}^n exp[-(x_i^0 - y_i^0)^2/2]}{1 + \prod_{i=1}^n exp[-(x_i^0 - y_i^0)^2/2]} = \alpha \bar{z}^1 + (1 - \alpha)\bar{z}^2 \tag{17}$$

$$f(y^0) = \frac{\bar{z}^2 + \bar{z}^1 \prod_{i=1}^n exp[-(x_i^0 - y_i^0)^2/2]}{1 + \prod_{i=1}^n exp[-(x_i^0 - y_i^0)^2/2]} = \alpha \bar{z}^2 + (1 - \alpha)\bar{z}^1 \tag{18}$$

where

$$\alpha = \frac{1}{1 + \prod_{i=1}^n exp[-(x_i^0 - y_i^0)^2/2]} \tag{19}$$

Given that $x^0 \neq y^0$, it must exist some i such that $x_i^0 \neq y_i^0$, so that $\prod_{i=1}^n exp[-(x_i^0 - y_i^0)^2/2] \neq 1$, or $\alpha \neq 1 - \alpha$. If $z^1 = 0$ and $z^2 = 1$, then $f(x^0) = 1 - \alpha \neq \alpha = f(y^0)$. Hence (Y, d_∞) separates all points in U.

(Y, d_∞) in not null for any point in U, just choosing all the $\bar{z}^j > 0$ with $j = 1, 2, .., M$, i.e. every $f \in Y$ with $\bar{z}^j > 0$ can be used as the requested f.

4   F-GNN: Training Algorithm

Before introducing F-GNN training algorithm, we have to show how a neuro-fuzzy system and a FBFN in particular can be trained:

1. If a_i^j, m_i^j and σ_i^j are free parameters, then the FBFN is non-linear and an optimization technique like backpropagation has to be used.
2. If all the parameters in $p_j(\mathbf{x})$ are given and the only free parameter is θ^j, then $f(\mathbf{x})$ is linear and the *orthogonal least-squares* (OLS)[14] algorithm can be used.

In particular in the second case, *Gram-Schmidt OLS* algorithm is employed, which can be determine automatically the number of significant FBFs. This algorithm is a hybrid learning method because other than the number of the most significant FBFs, it can compute the relative parameters.

4.1   FBFN Backpropagation Algorithm

In the most general case, where optimization has to be performed with respect to all the parameters, backpropagation algorithm is adopted for FBFN[15]. In particular FBFN has to be continuous differentiable with respect to parameters m, σ, θ, where m and σ represent mean and variance of the Gaussian membership function and θ represents the weight associated with each fuzzy basis function. Differentiability conditions are ensured by use of Gaussian membership function, because it is continuous differentiable with respect to both m and σ, hence FBFN is differentiable too with respect to the same parameters and also with respect to states x. For parameter θ, FBFN compact form

$$f(\mathbf{x}) = \sum_{j=1}^{M} p_j(\mathbf{x})\theta^j \tag{20}$$

shows that f is differentiable with respect to θ.

Given a pair $(\underline{x}^P, d^P)$, $\underline{x}^P \in U \subset \mathbb{R}^n$ and $d^P \in \mathbb{R}$, we want to minimize

$$e^P = \frac{1}{2}[f(\underline{x}^P) - d^P]^2 \tag{21}$$

where f is a FBFN. If we consider e, f, d as $e^P, f(\underline{x}^P), d^P$, respectively, we have:

1. To modify $\bar{z}^j$ it is used:

$$\bar{z}^j(k+1) = \bar{z}^j(k) - \alpha \frac{\partial e}{\partial \bar{z}^j}\Big|\bar{z}^j = \bar{z}^j(k) \tag{22}$$

where $j = 1, ..., M$ and $k = 0, 1, 2, ...$ and α is the learning rate. Because f and hence e depend on $\bar{z}^j$ only through a, where $f = a/b$ with $a = \sum_{j=1}^{M}(\bar{z}^j y^j)$ and $b = \sum_{j=1}^{M} y^j$ and $y^j = \prod_{i=1}^{n} \mu_{A_i^j}(x_i^P)$, using the chain rule we have:

$$\frac{\partial e}{\partial \bar{z}^j} = (f-d)\frac{\partial f}{\partial a}\frac{\partial a}{\partial \bar{z}^j} = (f-d)\frac{1}{b}y^j \tag{23}$$

from which:

$$\bar{z}^j(k+1) = \bar{z}^j(k) - \alpha\frac{f-d}{b}y^j \tag{24}$$

where $j = 1, ..., M$ e $k = 0, 1, 2, ...$

2. To modify $\bar{x}_i^j$ it is used:

$$\bar{x}_i^j(k+1) = \bar{x}_i^j(k) - \alpha \frac{\partial e}{\partial \bar{x}_i^j} |\bar{x}_i^j = \bar{x}_i^j(k) \tag{25}$$

where $i = 1, 2, ..., n$, $j = 1, 2, ..., M$ and $k = 0, 1, 2, ...$ Because f and hence e depend on $\bar{x}_i^j$ only through y^j, using the chain rule we have:

$$\frac{\partial e}{\partial \bar{x}_i^j} = (f - d)\frac{\partial f}{\partial y^j}\frac{\partial y^j}{\partial \bar{x}_i^j} = (f - d)\frac{\bar{z}^j - f}{b}y^j\frac{\bar{x}_i^P - \bar{x}_i^j}{\sigma_i^{j2}} \tag{26}$$

from which:

$$\bar{x}_i^j(k+1) = \bar{x}_i^j(k) - \alpha\frac{f - d}{b}(\bar{z}^j - f)y^j\frac{\bar{x}_i^P - \bar{x}_i^j(k)}{\sigma_i^{j2}(k)} \tag{27}$$

where $j = 1, ..., M$ e $k = 0, 1, 2, ...$
3. Using the same method, we have the following update of parameter σ_i^j:

$$\sigma_i^j(k+1) = \sigma_i^j(k) - \alpha\frac{\partial e}{\partial \sigma_i^j}|\sigma_i^j = \sigma_i^j(k)$$

$$= \sigma_i^j(k) - \alpha\frac{f - d}{b}(\bar{z}^j - f)y^j\frac{(x_i^P - \bar{x}_i^j(k))^2}{\sigma_i^{j3}(k)} \tag{28}$$

where $j = 1, ..., M$ and $k = 0, 1, 2, ...$

Based on such considerations, F-GNN learning algorithm see F as a stacked version of the FBFNs which implement f-units, G is the stacked version of the FBFNs which implement g-units and vector w contains free parameters to be modified (mean and variance of the membership functions and weights associated with each FBF).

To obtain a fast convergence of the algorithm, it is important to initialize parameters with values consistent with input data, rather than random. Mean and variance of the nodes label membership functions and of the edges labels membership functions can be computed as sampled mean and variance (or by using a clustering algorithm) because these data are part of the input data. On the contrary, parameters of the states membership functions cannot be computed

---

Algorithm 1. F-GNN Training algorithm

1: x = FORWARD-1ST(w)
2: **repeat**
3:     $\frac{\partial e_w}{\partial w}$=BACKWARD(x,w)
4:     w = w - $\lambda \cdot \frac{\partial e_w}{\partial w}$
5:     x = FORWARD(w);
6: **until** stop criterion is reached
7: return w

previously and hence it is necessary, during operation of FORWARD-1st function, to apply a clustering algorithm or to compute sampled mean and variance of the produced states.

Next, the output node states are first computed (by FORWARD step) and then computes the gradient (by BACKWARD step).

Once all parameters have been updated, a new FORWARD step is performed, until the desired accuracy is reached.

5 Conclusion

The aim of the proposed research is the theoretic definition of a neuro-fuzzy model for structured data. The model employs neural nets to capture information contained in each node of a graph as well as the information contained at each adjacent node. This allows to produce a new state, that is a concept defined by a node and its adjacent nodes. Motivations behind the study of the proposed model relies on the consideration that a concept can be expressed more effectively in terms of natural language rather than with numeric values. This aspect imposes the use of a logic that could handle linguistic terms in the framework of a numeric model. The chosen logic is the one that more then the others has contributed to bring "human experience" into expert systems: fuzzy logic.

Although fuzzy logic is often used in static system, the challenge for many researchers has been that of introducing it into dynamic systems, like neural nets, which has lead to a new field of computer science: neural fuzzy systems. This is particularly demanded when the data are too complex, incomplete and, as the topic of the present paper, are characterized by an inner structure. Synergy of systems based on fuzzy logic and neural nets to deal structured data aims to put together two complementary techniques, so to get the best from both of them. This synergy is mainly required in many application fields where structured data play a fundamental role, like bioinformatics and computer vision.

The reported model is in this direction and extends in the fuzzy framework recent works on this subject. In the reported model, named by us F-GNN, nodes and edges labels (which represents an event) are fuzzy data as well as fuzzy results the state computation. A remarkable result is presented for the proposed model in that it is a universal approximator. A learning algorithm based on the FBFN backpropagation is also sketched to handle structured data.

References

1. Bianchini, M., Maggini, M., Sarti, L., Scarselli, F.: Recursive neural networks for processing graphs with labelled edges: Theory and applications. Neural Networks - Special Issue on Neural Network and Kernel Methods for Structured Domains 18, 1040–1050 (2005)
2. Challoo, R., Clark, D.A., McLauchlan, R.A., Omar, S.I.: A fuzzy neural hybrid system. IEEE World Congress on Computational Intelligence 3, 1654–1657 (1994)

3. Gori, M., Maggini, M., Sarti, L.: A Recursive neural network model for processing directed acyclic graph with labeled edges. In: Procedings of the International Joint Conference on Neural Networks, vol. 2, pp. 1351–1355 (2003)

4. Gori, M., Petrosino, A.: Encoding nondeterministic fuzzy tree automata into recursive neural networks. IEEE Transactions on Neural Networks 15(6), 1435–1449 (2004)

5. Gorrini, V., Bersini, H.: Recurrent fuzzy systems. FUZZ-IEEE World Congress on Computional Intelligence, pp. 193–198 (1994)

6. Lin, C.T., Lee, C.S.G.: Neural Fuzzy Systems: A Neuro-Fuzzy Synergism to Intelligent Systems, p. 482. Prentice-Hall, Englewood Cliffs (1996)

7. Lin, C.T., Lee, C.S.G.: Real-time supervised structure/parameter learning for fuzzy neural networks. In: Proc. IEEE International Conference of Fuzzy Systems, vol. 2(1), pp. 1283–1291 (1992)

8. Nowlan, S.J.: Gain variation in recurrent error propagation networks. Complex Systems 2, 305–320 (1988)

9. Pal, S.K., Mitra, S.: Multilayer perceptron, fuzzy sets, and classification. IEEE Trans. Neural Networks 3(5), 683–697 (1992)

10. Pineda, F.: Generalization of back-propagation to recurrent neural networks. Physical Review Letters 59, 2229–2232 (1987)

11. Scarselli, F., Gori, M., Tsoi, A.-C., Hagenbuchner, M., Monfardini, G.: The Graph Neural Network Model. IEEE Transactions on Neural Networks (to appear, 2008)

12. Scarselli, F., Gori, M., Tsoi, A.-C., Hagenbuchner, M., Monfardini, G.: Computational Capabilities of Graph Neural Networks. IEEE Transactions on Neural Networks (to appear, 2008)

13. Smets, P.: Implications and Modus Ponens in Fuzzy Logic. In: Conditional Logic in Expert Systems, pp. 235–268. Elsevier Science Publisher, Amsterdam (1991)

14. Wang, L.X., Mendel, J.M.: Fuzzy basis functions, universal approximation, and orthogonal least-squres learning. IEEE Transaction on Neural Networks 3(5), 807–814 (1992)

15. Wang, L.X., Mendel, J.M.: Back-Propagation fuzzy system as nonlinear dynamic system identifier. IEEE Transaction on Neural Networks 3(5), 1409–1418 (1992)

16. Werbos, P.J.: Backpropagation through time: what it does and how to do it. Proceedings of the IEEE 78(10), 1550–1560 (1990)

17. Williams, R., Zipser, D.: A learning algorithm for continually running fully recurrent neural networks. Neural Computation (1), 270–280 (1989)

18. Zadeh, L.: Fuzzy sets. Information and Control 8(3), 338–353 (1965)

19. Zadeh, L.: Fuzzy sets as a basis for a theory of possibility. Fuzzy Sets and Systems 1, 3–28 (1978)

A Framework for the Partial Evaluation
of SPARQL Queries

Sergio Flesca, Filippo Furfaro, and Andrea Pugliese

DEIS - Università della Calabria
Via Bucci - 87036 Rende (CS) Italy
{flesca,furfaro,apugliese}@deis.unical.it

Abstract. A framework for the partial evaluation of SPARQL queries on multiple RDF data sources, both at a local and global level, is proposed. According to the proposed approach, global evaluation of queries is accomplished by first performing local evaluation on each data source, then merging the obtained results. When merging the results, term equivalence across different sources is evaluated by looking at the context of each term. Moreover, the framework allows scoring partial answers by evaluating how much a partial answer is able to capture each concept expressed in the query. Finally, a distributed index structure is proposed that supports early pruning of useless intermediate results.

1 Introduction

With the increasing adoption of the *Resource Description Framework* (RDF) [1] for describing resources in a semantically-rich and machine-readable way, the integration and querying of data coming from distributed autonomous sources has gained more and more importance. Moreover, it is often mandatory to provide a single querying interface to different data sources, viewing all the available RDF databases as a single *federated* database [2]. The standard query language for RDF, SPARQL [3], allows targeting RDF graphs coming from different sources, and supports the specification of a different pattern to be matched to each different graph.

In this paper we focus on SPARQL queries consisting of graph patterns, that must be matched against a set of RDF data sources seen as a whole. In this setting, we propose a framework for supporting *partial* answers, in the sense that some of the conditions in the query can be left unsatisfied.

In the proposed framework, queries are evaluated by first performing local (partial) evaluation on each data source, then merging the results. This is done with the aim of retrieving information which can be extended (and possibly completed) with the information provided by other sources. The final answer is obtained by combining local partial answers. Observe that our approach differs from the most common approach currently adopted in the RDF scenario, that is moving all data into a single repository then merging and querying them locally. Indeed, the latter is unfeasible in the presence of, e.g., data access limitations, frequently-changing data, large volumes of data, or on-the-fly creation of RDF views of relational or object-oriented databases.

Moreover, the framework supports the recognition of "implicit" equivalence among RDF terms: we aim at identifying terms that, across different sources, represent the

S. Greco and T. Lukasiewicz (Eds.): SUM 2008, LNAI 5291, pp. 201–214, 2008.
© Springer-Verlag Berlin Heidelberg 2008

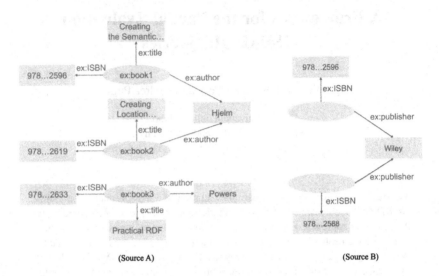

Fig. 1. Two example RDF graphs

same real-world objects. This way, an object description provided by a source can be completed by looking at the information about the same object extracted from other sources. In our framework, term equivalence is recognized by exploiting information about functional and inverse functional properties (such properties can be specified using OWL [4]). This process also involves blank RDF nodes, that are unidentified nodes providing connectivity between different parts of an RDF graph[1].

Example 1. Consider two RDF data sources exporting information about books (Fig. 1). A user that looks for the title of the books wrote by "Hijelm" and published by "Wiley" would write a SPARQL query containing the clauses

```
SELECT   ?title
WHERE { ?book ex:title ?title .
            ?book ex:author "Hjelm" .
            ?book ex:publisher "Wiley"
}
```

Evaluating this query against each of the RDF graphs by itself would yield no answer. However, we can recognize that "Creating the Semantic..." is an answer to the query if we take into account all the available information about ex:book1. In fact, the first blank node in the RDF graph can be recognized to represent ex:book1, because it has the same value for an inverse functional property (ISBN). Moreover, source A provides information about the book's author and source B about its publisher. If we extract this partial information and combine them, we can provide a complete answer to the query.   □

Our framework also supports partial final answers. As a consequence, we aim at distinguishing among partial answers by trying to quantify how close they are to a complete

---

[1] SPARQL manages blank nodes coming from different sources by replacing them with "fresh" ones, each with a different local identifier [5], and applying the query to the merged graph.

answer. Our proposed scoring technique looks at the "independent" concepts specified in the query, corresponding to connected subgraphs of the query graph. In particular, for each concept, the score quantifies to which extent the concept is captured, by considering the "largest" (in terms of triple patterns) of its captured sub-concepts. The framework is also capable of taking into account the importance given by the user, in the form of weights, to the triple patterns in the query.

Finally, we propose a distributed index structure supporting the independent evaluation of graph pattern queries at each data source. The main idea is that each source maintains information about the possibility of finding, in other sources, RDF terms that are equivalent to local ones. This way, early pruning of useless intermediate results can be performed.

1.1 Related Work

Past works on partial distributed SPARQL querying tackled different aspects of the scenario described above. [6] proposes a system for the support of SPARQL querying of multiple relational databases. In [7], a mediator-based engine is proposed for SPARQL queries over federated RDF databases. The idea is to decompose the original query into subqueries to be routed to the different sources. To this aim, *service descriptions* are employed to declaratively describe the data available at each source. Subqueries are then identified in such a way that local evaluation always yields a (possibly partial) answer; final answers are always complete. The main focus of the proposal is distributed query planning and optimization, mainly based on existing techniques from the relational realm such as query rewriting and cost based optimization; the authors also propose specific techniques for result size estimation.

A similar approach is proposed in [8,9], where an extension of the *Sesame* RDF repository is proposed to support distributed queries over multiple repositories. An index structure is used to determine the relevant sources for different parts of a query, then query optimization is performed by viewing the paths in RDF graphs as relation instances. The approach is thus restricted to path queries. A technique is also proposed for the recognition of implicit term equivalence that is based on a predefined set of keys. In [10], a technical infrastructure based on this framework is presented.

Other proposals aim at the support of "relaxed" RDF query answers in the centralized scenario. A formal framework is proposed in [11] that supports a complex set of *query transformations*: besides dropping entire triple patterns, they allow replacing a constant with a variable, breaking join dependencies, and predicate-to-domain and predicate-to-range relaxations. The focus of the proposal is an efficient algorithm for computing relaxed answers. The framework also attacks the problem of ranking results by providing a formal characterization of rank functions, but no proposal is made for a suitable rank function.

The proposal in [12] allows similarity joins by allowing sets of variables to be declared as imprecise. To rank the results, they look at the imprecise variables and compare them based on a specified similarity measure, such as edit distance. In [13] conjunctive queries over a terminological knowledge base are considered. Query containment is viewed as a form of query approximation, and query evaluation proceeds from less complex queries to more complex ones (the original one is evaluated last). A "query graph" is exploited to establish which parts of the original query are successively added to the approximate query.

1.2 Main Contributions and Plan of the Paper

To the best of our knowledge, the framework presented in this paper is the first attempt at supporting, in an integrated way:

- Partial evaluation of SPARQL queries both at a local and global level, in a distributed scenario;
- Scoring of partial query results;
- Recognition of term equivalence based on the context of each term;
- Early pruning of useless intermediate results through the use of a distributed index.

The remainder of the paper is organized as follows. In Section 2 we briefly formalize some basic RDF-related notions. In Section 3 we propose our framework for partial querying of RDF data. Section 4 describes the distributed index and its usage. Finally, Section 5 outlines conclusions.

2 Preliminaries

We assume the reader is familiar with ordinary RDF. In this section we briefly describe how we formalize RDF graphs, queries, and query answers.

Let $\mathcal{U}$ denote a set of *Internationalized Resource Identifiers* (IRIs), $\mathcal{B}$ a set of blank nodes, $\mathcal{L}$ a set of literals (with $\mathcal{U}$, $\mathcal{B}$, and $\mathcal{L}$ being pairwise disjoint), $\mathcal{P} \subseteq \mathcal{U}$ a set of IRIs denoting properties, and $\mathcal{P}_f, \mathcal{P}_{if} \subseteq \mathcal{P}$ two sets of *functional* and *inverse functional* RDF properties [4], respectively. An RDF triple is a triple of the form $\langle s, p, o \rangle$ where $s \in \mathcal{U} \cup \mathcal{B}$ is the subject, $p \in \mathcal{P}$ is the property, and $o \in \mathcal{U} \cup \mathcal{B} \cup \mathcal{L}$ is the object (s, p, and o are called *terms*). An RDF database is a finite set of RDF triples[2]. We say that a term t belongs to an RDF database D (and write $t \in D$) if t appears in at least one triple of D. The graph induced by an RDF database contains, for each triple $\langle s, p, o \rangle$, two nodes corresponding to s and o, respectively, and a p-labeled edge between them. From now on we will refer to a set of RDF triples as to an *RDF graph*.

The kind of queries we are interested in are graph patterns, that essentially correspond to conjunctive SPARQL queries.

Definition 1 (Graph pattern query). *A graph pattern query is a 5-tuple* (V, N, E, ω, C) *where:*

- *V is the set of variables;*
- *$N \subseteq \mathcal{U} \cup \mathcal{B} \cup \mathcal{L} \cup V$ is the set of nodes;*
- *$E \subseteq N \times (V \cup \mathcal{P}) \times N$ is the set of edges;*
- *$\omega : E \rightarrow \mathbb{R}$ is the edge weight function;*
- *C is a set of constraints of the form $\sigma_1 \psi \sigma_2$, where $\sigma_1 \in V$, $\sigma_2 \in V \cup \mathcal{L}$, and $\psi \in \{=, <, \leq, >, \geq, \neq\}$.*

---

[2] We assume we are dealing with RDF databases where all subclass/subproperty inferences have been drawn.

Fig. 2. The query graph of Example 1

A graph pattern query (V, N, E, ω, C) is said to be *safe* if every variable in V appears in at least one triple in E. In the remainder of the paper we assume that our queries are always safe.

We view a graph pattern query (V, N, E, ω, C) as a graph containing, for each triple $\langle s, p, o \rangle \in E$, two nodes corresponding to s and o, respectively, and a p-labeled edge between them. For instance, Fig. 2 shows the graph associated with the query of Example 1. By a little abuse of notation, given a graph pattern query $q = (V, N, E, \omega, C)$ and a node $v \in V$ (resp., edge $e \in E$), we will equivalently write $v \in q$ (resp., $e \in q$).

The answer to a graph pattern query $q = (V, N, E, \omega, C)$ with respect to a graph D is the set of substitutions for the variables in V that map each variable to a term in D such that structural relationships are preserved and constraints are satisfied.

Definition 2 (Query answer). *Let D be an RDF graph and $q = (V, N, E, \omega, C)$ be a graph pattern query. The answer to q over D, denoted as $q(D)$, is the set of substitutions $\{\theta_1, \ldots, \theta_k\}$ with $\forall i \in [1, k], \theta_i : V \cup \mathcal{U} \cup \mathcal{B} \cup \mathcal{L} \rightarrow \mathcal{U} \cup \mathcal{B} \cup \mathcal{L}$, such that:*

1. *$\forall t \in \mathcal{U} \cup \mathcal{B} \cup \mathcal{L}$ it holds that $t\theta_i = t$;*
2. *$\forall i \in [1, k], \forall e \in E$, it holds that $e\theta_i \in D$;*
3. *$\forall i \in [1, k], \forall \sigma_1 \psi \sigma_2 \in C$, it holds that $\sigma_1 \theta_i \psi \sigma_2 \theta_i$.*

Example 2. The following query, when applied over the RDF graph of source A in Example 1, retrieves ISBNs and titles of all the books:

```
SELECT  *
WHERE {  ?book ex:title ?title .
              ?book ex:ISBN ?ISBN
}
```

The answer to this query is the set of substitutions $\{\langle$?ISBN/"978...2596", ?book /ex:book1, ?title/"Creating the Semantic..."$\rangle$, $\langle$?ISBN/"978...2619", ?book/ex:book2, ?title/"Creating Location..."$\rangle$, $\langle$?ISBN/"9782633", ?book/ex:book3, ?title/"Practical RDF"$\rangle\}$. □

3   Partial Answers to Graph Pattern Queries

In this section we present a framework for supporting partial answers to graph pattern queries. A partial answer can be viewed as the result of evaluating a new query where some of the conditions in the original one have been removed. The aim of our framework is that of providing answers to queries that result from removing conditions from the original query up to a certain extent.

We first introduce the notion of *partial* substitution, then we discuss the notion of *score* of a partial substitution, which is a measure of the extent to which a partial substitution satisfies query conditions, and finally we define partial answers.

Definition 3 (Partial substitution). *Let* $q = (V, N, E, \omega, C)$ *be a graph pattern query and D an RDF graph. A partial substitution for q on D is a (partial) function θ : $V \cup \mathcal{U} \cup \mathcal{B} \cup \mathcal{L} \to \mathcal{U} \cup \mathcal{B} \cup \mathcal{L}$ such that the following conditions hold:*

1. *$\forall t \in \mathcal{L}$ it holds that $t\theta = t$ and $\forall t \in \mathcal{U} \cup \mathcal{B}$ either t is not mapped by θ or $t\theta = t$;*
2. *$\forall \langle s, p, o \rangle \in E$, if s, p, and o are mapped then $\langle s\theta, p\theta, o\theta \rangle \in D$;*
3. *$\forall \sigma_1 \psi \sigma_2$ in C, if σ_1 and σ_2 are mapped then $\sigma_1 \theta \psi \sigma_2 \theta$ holds;*
4. *$\forall \langle s, p, o \rangle \in E$ such that $p\theta = $ rdf:type, if s is mapped, then o is mapped;*
5. *$\forall \langle s, p, o \rangle \in E$ such that $p\theta$ is a functional property, if s is mapped and there is a triple $\langle s\theta, p\theta, x \rangle$ in D, then $o\theta = x$;*
6. *$\forall \langle s, p, o \rangle \in E$ such that $p\theta$ is an inverse functional property, if o is mapped and there is a triple $\langle y, p\theta, o\theta \rangle$ in D, then $s\theta = y$.*
7. *$\forall v \in V$ if v is mapped then there is a triple $e \in E$ such that v appears in e and e does not contain unmapped variables.*

Condition 1 of Definition 3 ensures that θ does not scramble constant terms. Conditions 2 and 3 impose that θ preserves the structural relationships and the constraints specified in q. Condition 4 states that, if θ maps a term having an rdf:type specified in q, then its image must be a node of the correct type. Conditions 5 and 6 entail that, if a term n is mapped, then the triples in q that express (inverse) functional properties of n must be mapped and thus correctly preserve the (inverse) functionality. Condition 7 means that mapped variables are indeed used to satisfy at least one triple in q.

Obviously, given a query q and a data graph D, several partial substitutions for q on D may exist. As it will be clearer in the following, it is important to distinguish among these partial substitutions, by trying to quantify how close they are to a total substitution. We now discuss our proposal for the ranking of partial substitutions that is based on this criterion, and define a measure for estimating the closeness of a partial substitution to a (total) substitution. From now on, we say that a triple, constraint, or graph is mapped iff it does not contain unmapped variables.

In the light of Definition 3, a partial substitution can be viewed as an incomplete substitution, in the sense that it may leave some of the query variables unmapped. Some of the constraints in the query may also be disregarded; however, due to Condition 3 in Definition 3, this happens only if at least one of the two terms in the constraint is not mapped. Thus, since all the variables occurring in a query appear in at least one triple, a constraint is disregarded when at least one triple of the query is not mapped. This reasoning suggests that the degree of completeness of a partial substitution θ can be measured by counting the number of triples of the query which are mapped by θ (as explained above, this takes into account the constraints which are disregarded by the partial substitution as well).

The measure explained above is based on the assumption that each triple in the query represents a concept independently from the concepts represented by the other triples. A more reasonable completeness measure must distinguish among the independent concepts specified in the query, and evaluate, for each of them, with which degree of completeness this concept is mapped onto the data graph by the partial substitution. Intuitively enough, it is reasonable to assume that each concept expressed in the query corresponds to a connected subgraph of the query graph. Consequently, we measure the completeness of a partial substitution by taking the average of the degrees of completeness with which each connected subgraph of the query graph is mapped. Specifically, we measure the completeness of a partial substitution w.r.t. each connected subgraph c as the ratio between the size of the largest mapped connected subgraph of c and the size of c itself.

More formally, given a graph pattern query q, we denote the set of maximal connected subgraphs of q as $C(q)$. Moreover, given a subgraph q' of q and a partial substitution θ, we denote the set of maximal connected subgraphs of q' which are mapped by θ as $CG(q', \theta)$. Finally, we define the *score* of θ, denoted as $\mathrm{score}(\theta, q, D)$, as

$$\mathrm{score}(\theta, q, D) = \mathrm{avg}_{q' \in C(q)} \left(\frac{max_{g \in CG(q', \theta)} \left(\sum_{e \in g} w(e) \right)}{\sum_{e \in q'} w(e)} \right).$$

Observe that, since query triples are associated with a weight, graph sizes are evaluated by considering the weights of their triples.

Example 3. Consider a query q corresponding to the following SPARQL query (we consider an extended syntax, where the weights associated with triple patterns are written in square brackets):

```
SELECT  ?a1 ?b1
WHERE { ?a1 p ?a2 [1]. ?a2 p ?a3 [1]. ?a3 p A [1].
        ?b1 q ?b2 [2]. ?b2 q ?b3 [2]. ?b3 q B [2]
}
```

When evaluated over an RDF graph D, the query retrieves all the pairs of nodes $n_1, n_2 \in D$, such that A is reachable from node n_1 through 3 p-labeled edges, and B is reachable from node n_2 through 3 q-labeled edges. Now consider two partial substitutions θ and θ', where θ maps triples $\langle ?a1\ p\ ?a2 \rangle$, $\langle ?a3\ p\ A \rangle$, and $\langle ?b1\ q\ ?b2 \rangle$, and θ' maps triples $\langle ?a1\ p\ ?a2 \rangle$, $\langle ?a2\ p\ ?a3 \rangle$, and $\langle ?a3\ p\ A \rangle$. Both substitutions map 3 of the triples in the query, but θ' is able to completely map the path between the image of ?a1 and A. If we measure the completeness of the substitutions as the overall weight of the mapped triples, substitutions θ and θ' have scores 4 and 3, respectively; with our characterization, we obtain: $\mathrm{score}(\theta, q, D) = \mathrm{avg}(\frac{1}{3}, \frac{2}{6}) = \frac{1}{3}$, and $\mathrm{score}(\theta', q, D) = \mathrm{avg}(\frac{3}{3}, \frac{0}{6}) = \frac{1}{2}$, thus capturing the fact that θ' can be considered more complete than θ. □

The notion of query answer introduced in Definition 2 as a set of (total) substitutions can be naturally extended to the notion of partial query answer. In our framework, a partial answer is a set of partial substitutions whose score is greater than a given threshold.

Definition 4 (Partial answer). *Let q be a graph pattern query, D an RDF graph, and $\kappa \in [0, 1]$. The partial answer of q on D w.r.t the threshold κ (denoted as $q^\kappa(D)$) is the set of all the partial substitutions θ for q on D such that*

1. $Score(\theta, q, D) \geq \kappa$;
2. *There is no partial substitution θ' for q on D such that (i) for each variable v mapped by θ it holds that $\theta'(v) = \theta(v)$, and (ii) there exists a variable in V that is mapped by θ' and not by θ.*

Basically, Condition 2 ensures maximality of the partial substitutions. Obviously, $q^1(D) = q(D)$, and $q^0(D)$ consists of all the maximal partial substitutions for q on D.

3.1   Partial Answers over Multiple RDF Graphs

In the previous section we introduced the notion of partial answer for queries posed against a single RDF graph. We now extend this notion to the case of distributed data. In this scenario, a partial description of a concept can be provided by a single source, but the description can still be extended (and possibly completed) by looking at the information about the same concept given by other sources (as explained in Example 1). In defining the notion of partial answer in the distributed scenario, we take advantage of this possibility. To this aim, we introduce the notion of *term equivalence*, which will be exploited to detect whether the same concept is described by different sources.

Definition 5 (Term equivalence). *Let $D_1, \ldots, D_k$ be RDF graphs and $D = \bigcup_{i=1}^k D_i$. Let t_1, t_2 be two terms in D. Terms t_1 and t_2 are said to be* equivalent *w.r.t. D (denoted as $t_1 \equiv t_2$) iff one of the following conditions holds:*

1. *t_1 and t_2 are the same term (same IRI or same literal);*
2. *there is a property $p \in \mathcal{P}_f$ and there are triples $\langle t_1', p, t_1 \rangle$, $\langle t_2', p, t_2 \rangle$ in D such that $t_1' \equiv t_2'$;*
3. *there is a property $p \in \mathcal{P}_{if}$ and there are triples $\langle t_1, p, t_1' \rangle$, $\langle t_2, p, t_2' \rangle$ in D such that $t_1' \equiv t_2'$;*
4. *there is a term t_3 in D such that $t_1 \equiv t_3$ and $t_2 \equiv t_3$.*

Basically, Definition 5 means that two terms are equivalent if they refer to the same "real-world" object. Specifically, Conditions 2 and 3 exploit functional and inverse functional properties to detect term equivalence. For instance, Condition 3 captures the fact that, if two distinct terms are related through an inverse functional property to the same term (or, more generally, to a pair of equivalent terms), then they represent the same concept, as inverse functional property values uniquely identify concepts (see Example 1).

The term equivalence relation defines equivalence classes of terms; we denote the equivalence class containing a term t as $c(t)$. Let $\mathcal{C}_{(\equiv)}$ be the set of equivalence classes of the terms of D implied by relation $\equiv$ and let $\gamma : \mathcal{C}_{(\equiv)} \rightarrow \mathcal{U} \cup \mathcal{B} \cup \mathcal{L}$ be the function defined as follows:

- If $c \in \mathcal{C}_{(\equiv)}$ contains a term in $\mathcal{U}$, then $\gamma(c)$ is the first IRI in c according to any given total order on $\mathcal{U}$;
- If c contains a literal $l \in \mathcal{L}$, then $\gamma(c) = l$;[3]

---

[3] Two literals are equivalent only if they represent the same value, thus all the literals in the same equivalence class represent the same value.

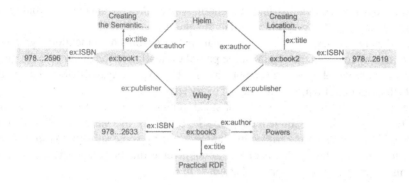

Fig. 3. Global RDF graph for Example 1

- Otherwise, $\gamma(c)$ is a blank node not appearing in D and such that $\forall c' \in \mathcal{C}_{(\equiv)}$ s.t. $c' \neq c, \gamma(c') \neq \gamma(c')$.

Function γ associates a single representative term with each equivalence class in $\mathcal{C}_{(\equiv)}$. We define the *global* graph over a set of RDF graphs $D_1, \ldots, D_k$ as the graph obtained by merging graph $D_1, \ldots, D_k$ after substituting every term with the representative of its equivalence class.

Definition 6 (Global graph). *Let $D_1, \ldots, D_k$ be RDF graphs and $D = \bigcup_{i=1}^{k} D_i$. The* global *graph over $D_1, \ldots, D_k$ is*

$$global(D_1, \ldots, D_k) = \{\langle \gamma(c(s)), \gamma(c(p)), \gamma(c(o)) \rangle \mid \langle s, p, o \rangle \in D\}.$$

Fig. 3 shows the global graph obtained from the RDF graphs of Example 1.

The partial answer of a query over multiple RDF graphs is defined as the partial answer over the corresponding global graph.

Definition 7 (Partial answer over multiple RDF graphs). *Let $D_1, \ldots, D_k$ be RDF graphs, q be a graph pattern query and $\kappa \in [0, 1]$. The partial answer of q over $D_1, \ldots, D_k$ w.r.t κ is $q^{\kappa}(global(D_1, \ldots, D_k))$.*

Thus, with our proposed query semantics for multiple graphs, partial evaluation is performed on the global graph. For instance, the evaluation of the query of Example 1 is performed on the global RDF graph of Fig. 3. It should be noted that, if we set $\kappa = 1$, our semantics is able to correctly provide the complete answer $\{\langle ?book/ex:book1, ?title/"Creating the Semantic..." \rangle\}$.

4   Evaluation of Graph Pattern Queries

Following Definition 7, the answer to a graph pattern query q over a set of RDF graphs can be evaluated by first computing the corresponding global graph D and then evaluating q over D. However, this may require large amounts of data to be exchanged, and thus be unfeasible in practice. In this section, we propose an approach for evaluating a graph pattern query in a distributed scenario which takes advantage of partial results computed on each RDF graph involved in the query.

Specifically, we first show that the partial answer evaluated on the global graph can be obtained by merging the results of the partial evaluation of the query on each graph. Then, we show that this strategy can be enhanced by exploiting a distributed index that counts the number of equivalent terms of every term.

We start by introducing the notion of subgraph induced by a set of partial substitutions Θ of a query q on a single RDF graph D. Basically, this subgraph consists of the triples of D onto which the triples in q are mapped by some substitution in Θ, along with triples of D defining chains of functional/inverse-functional properties connected to terms mapped onto D by some substitution in Θ.

Definition 8 (Induced subgraph). *Let $q = (V, N, E, \omega, C)$ be a graph pattern query and D an RDF graph. The subgraph of D induced by a set of (partial) substitutions Θ for q on D (denoted as $sub(\Theta, D)$) is the RDF graph satisfying the following conditions:*

1. *$\forall e \in E$ and $\forall \theta \in \Theta$, if $e\theta \in D$, then $e\theta \in sub(\Theta, D)$;*
2. *$\forall x \in \mathcal{U} \cup \mathcal{B}$ such that there is a triple of the form $\langle x, p, o \rangle$ or of the form $\langle s, p, x \rangle$ in $sub(\Theta, D)$,*
   (a) if there is a triple $\langle s', p, x \rangle$ in D where $p \in \mathcal{P}_f$, then $\langle s', p, x \rangle \in sub(\Theta, D)$;
   (b) if there is a triple $\langle x, p, o' \rangle$ in D where $p \in \mathcal{P}_{if}$, then $\langle x, p, o' \rangle \in sub(\Theta, D)$.

Proposition 1 below ensures that the partial answer to a query q over a set of RDF graphs $D_1, \cdots, D_k$ w.r.t. a threshold κ can be evaluated by performing the following steps:

1. Evaluate $q^0(D_1), \ldots, q^0(D_k)$, i.e., the partial answers of q on $D_1, \cdots, D_k$ w.r.t. the threshold 0;
2. For each D_i, compute its subgraph induced by $q^0(D_i)$;
3. Build the global graph from the k induced subgraphs;
4. Evaluate q on the graph obtained at the previous step w.r.t. the threshold κ.

Proposition 1. *Let $D_1, \ldots, D_k$ be RDF graphs, q be a graph pattern query, $\kappa \in [0, 1]$ and $\forall i \in [0..k]$, $S_i = sub(q^0(D_i), D_i)$. It holds that $q^\kappa(global(D_1, \ldots, D_k)) = q^\kappa(global(S_1, \ldots, S_k))$.*

We now show how the above-described strategy for computing partial answers on multiple RDF graphs can be further enhanced by exploiting a suitable distributed index on the equivalent terms. Specifically, the information represented in this index will allow us to prune, from each $q^0(D_i)$, the substitutions which cannot contribute to the final answer, i.e., the substitutions which cannot be extended up to a substitution satisfying the specified threshold.

Definition 9 (Equivalent-term index). *Let $D_1, \ldots, D_k$ be RDF graphs. The local equivalent-term index I_i of D_i is a set containing, for each term $t \in D_i$, the pair $\langle t, n \rangle$, where n is the number of terms in $D_1 \cup \cdots \cup D_{i-1} \cup D_{i+1} \cup \cdots \cup D_k$ that are equivalent to t. The equivalent-term index on $D_1, \ldots, D_k$ is the set $I = \{I_1, \ldots, I_k\}$.*

On the basis of the information represented in the equivalent-term index, we introduce the notion of *forbidden term*. Basically, given a query q and a partial substitution θ, a term t of q is forbidden if it is not mapped by θ and cannot be mapped by any substitution extending θ, as t is connected (through an edge in q) to a term t' which is mapped by θ onto a node of the local RDF graph that has no equivalent terms in any other data source.

Definition 10 (Forbidden term and extension-candidate subgraph). *Given a graph pattern query $q = (V, N, E, \omega, C)$, an RDF graph D_i, a partial substitution θ for q on D_i, and the local equivalent-term index I_i, we say that a term t is* forbidden *if it appears in a triple $e \in E$ and the following conditions hold:*

1. *θ does not map t;*
2. *There is a term t' in e such that t' is mapped by θ and there is no pair $\langle t'\theta, n \rangle \in I_i$ with $n > 0$;*
3. *If t appears as the subject or object of e, then the property p specified in e is mapped by θ.*

The extension-candidate subgraph *of q w.r.t. θ and I_i (denoted as $\mathcal{EC}(q, \theta, I_i)$) is a graph consisting of the triples in E containing no forbidden terms.*

Given a graph pattern query $q = (V, N, E, \omega, C)$, an RDF graph D_i, a local equivalent term index I_i, and a partial substitution θ for q on D_i, we say that θ is an *extension-candidate substitution* for q w.r.t. I_i up to a threshold κ iff

$$\kappa \leq \mathrm{avg}_{q' \in \mathcal{C}(q)} \left(\frac{max_{g \in A(q')} \left(\sum_{e \in g} \omega(e) \right)}{\sum_{e \in q'} \omega(e)} \right)$$

where $A(q') = \mathcal{C}(\mathcal{EC}(q, \theta, I_i) \cap q')$, i.e., $A(q')$ is the set of maximally connected subgraphs of $\mathcal{EC}(q, \theta, I_i)$ which are subgraphs of q' as well.

Proposition 2. *Let $D_1, \ldots, D_k$ be RDF graphs, q a graph pattern query, and, for each $i \in [1..k]$, let Θ_i be the set of the extension-candidate substitutions for q on D_i w.r.t. I_i up to a threshold κ. It holds that $q^\kappa(global(D_1, \ldots, D_k)) = q^\kappa(global(sub(\Theta_1, D_1), \ldots, sub(\Theta_k, D_k)))$.*

Maintaining the equivalent-term index. We now discuss how the equivalent-term index is maintained up-to-date w.r.t. bulk updates performed at each data source. A bulk update is a pair of the form $\langle U^+, U^- \rangle$, where U^+ and U^- are disjoint sets consisting of the triples to be inserted and deleted, respectively.

Triple insertions and deletions may cause insertions and deletions of terms, and may change the subgraphs induced by already existing terms. These three forms of changes may modify the number of terms equivalent to a term stored in the equivalent-term index. It is straightforward to see that both the insertion and the deletion of a term t changes the entries of the equivalent-term index I corresponding to terms equivalent to t. Moreover, the insertion/deletion of a triple may also change the number of detectable equivalents of terms not occurring in the triple. In fact, the equivalence between two terms t_i, t_j occurring in two distinct RDF graphs D_i, D_j is decided on the basis of the subgraphs of D_i, D_j induced by t_i and t_j, which, as explained above, may be changed by a triple insertion/deletion.

When a bulk update is applied on the local RDF graph D_i, D_i is changed accordingly, and several messages are exchanged between D_i and the other data sources, to update the equivalent-term index. The algorithm in Fig. 4 is executed at each data source D_i where a bulk update U is performed. It first computes the set T_U of the terms in the local RDF graph whose induced subgraphs are affected by U. Then, for each term t in T_U, a message is sent to all the other data sources, depending on which of the following cases occurs:

- If t has been inserted into D_i, a message insert is sent, with the specification of t and the subgraph induced by t on the updated local RDF graph;
- If t has been deleted from D_i, a message delete is sent, with the specification of t and the subgraph induced by t on the old local RDF graph;
- If t is a term which has been neither inserted nor deleted from D_i and the induced subgraph of t has been changed by U, a message update is sent, with the specification of t and both the subgraphs induced by t on the updated and the old local RDF graph.

The algorithm in Fig. 5 is executed at each data source D_r which receives a message from another data source D_s. The following cases may occur:

- If an insert(t, G) message is received (where G is the subgraph induced by t in D_s), the algorithm looks for a term t' equivalent to t in the local RDF graph D_r. In order to check the equivalence, both D_r and G are exploited, i.e., $t \equiv t'$ is tested on $D' = D_r \cup G$, as this enables terms related to t and t' through (inverse) functional properties to be taken into account. Then, if an equivalent term is found, the local equivalent-term index is updated accordingly, and a reply is sent back to D_s, so that D_s will be aware of the presence of term equivalent to t and will increase the counter associated with t in its local index.
- If a delete(t, G) message is received, the algorithm looks for a term t' equivalent to t among those referred in the local equivalent-term index. Again, the equivalence

---

Algorithm Update
Input: $U = \langle U^+, U^- \rangle$: update to the local RDF graph D
Output: Updated D and transmission of the appropriate messages

1	$D' \leftarrow D \cup U^+ \setminus U^-$
2	$T_U = \{t \mid \exists t' \text{ s.t. } t' \text{ appears in } U \text{ and } t' \text{ appears in } \mathsf{sub}(D,t) \text{ or in } \mathsf{sub}(D',t)\}$
3	**for each** term $t \in T_U$
4	**if** $t \in D' \setminus D$ **then** send insert$(t, \mathsf{sub}(D',t))$
5	**if** $t \in D \setminus D'$ **then** send delete$(t, \mathsf{sub}(D,t))$
6	**if** $t \in D \cap D'$ and $\mathsf{sub}(D,t) \neq \mathsf{sub}(D',t)$ **then** send update$(t, \mathsf{sub}(D,t), \mathsf{sub}(D',t))$
7	**end for**
8	$D \leftarrow D'$

Fig. 4. Performing bulk updates

	Algorithm Apply update messages **Input:** Update message m, local RDF graph D, equivalent-term index I **Output:** Updated equivalent-term index I
1	**if** $m =$insert(t, G)
2	**for all** terms $t' \in D$
3	**if** $t \equiv t'$ w.r.t. $D \cup G$ **then**
4	replace $\langle t', n \rangle$ with $\langle t', n + 1 \rangle$ in I
5	reply increase(t)
6	**if** $m =$delete(t, G)
7	**for all** pairs $\langle t', n \rangle \in I$ with $n > 0$
8	**if** $t \equiv t'$ w.r.t. $D \cup G$ **then**
9	replace $\langle t', n \rangle$ with $\langle t', n - 1 \rangle$ in I
10	**if** $m =$update(t, G_{new}, G_{old})
11	**for all** terms $t' \in D$
12	**if** $t \equiv t'$ w.r.t. $D \cup G_{old}$ **and** $t \not\equiv t'$ w.r.t. $D \cup G_{new}$ **then**
13	replace $\langle t', n \rangle$ with $\langle t', n - 1 \rangle$ in I
14	reply decrease(t)
15	**if** $t \equiv t'$ w.r.t. $D \cup G_{new}$ **and** $t \not\equiv t'$ w.r.t. $D \cup G_{old}$ **then**
16	replace $\langle t', n \rangle$ with $\langle t', n + 1 \rangle$ in I
17	reply increase(t)

Fig. 5. Updating an equivalent-term index after receiving an update message

test $t \equiv t'$ is accomplished w.r.t. $D_r \cup G$. Then, if an equivalent term is found, the local equivalent-term index is updated accordingly. Observe that in this case no message is sent back to D_s, since D_s deletes the entry corresponding to t from its local-term index independently on whether t has equivalents or not.

- If an update(t, G_{new}, G_{old}) message is received (where G_{new} and G_{old} are the subgraphs induced by t in the version of D_s after and before the update, respectively), the algorithm looks for a term t' in the local RDF graph D_r satisfying one of the following conditions:

1. t' *is equivalent to t w.r.t. $D_r \cup G_{old}$, but not w.r.t. $D_r \cup G_{new}$*: this means that the update resulted in removing some triple from the induced subgraph of t. In this case, the number of terms equivalent to t' in the local equivalent-term index is decreased by 1, and a message is sent to D_s calling for the decrease of the counter associated to t in the local equivalent-term index of D_s.

2. t' *is equivalent to t w.r.t. $D_r \cup G_{new}$, but not w.r.t. $D_r \cup G_{old}$*: this means that the update resulted in inserting some triple into the induced subgraph of t. In this case, the number of terms equivalent to t' in the local equivalent-term index is increased by 1, and a message is sent to D_s calling for the increase of the counter associated to t in the local equivalent-term index of D_s.

Observe that, if a term t' is found in D_r which is equivalent to t w.r.t. both $D_r \cup G_{new}$ and $D_r \cup G_{old}$, no change must be performed on the equivalent-term index.

5   Conclusions

In this work, a framework for the partial evaluation of SPARQL queries in a distributed scenario has been proposed. The framework supports, in an integrated way, the partial evaluation of SPARQL queries both at local and global level, by exploiting implicit equivalence among terms. Moreover, a scoring function for partial answers has been defined that looks at the independent concepts expressed in the query. Finally, a distributed index for the early pruning of useless intermediate results has been proposed.

References

1. Klyne, G., Carroll, J.J.: Resource description framework (rdf): Concepts and abstract syntax. W3C recommendation (February 2004)
2. Sheth, A.P., Larson, J.A.: Federated database systems for managing distributed, heterogeneous, and autonomous databases. ACM Comput. Surv. 22(3), 183–236 (1990)
3. Seaborne, A., Prud'hommeaux, E.: Sparql query language for rdf. W3C recommendation (January 2008)
4. Dean, M., Schreiber, G.: Owl web ontology language reference. W3C recommendation (February 2004)
5. Hayes, P.: Rdf semantics. W3C recommendation (February 2004)
6. Chen, H., Wang, Y., Wang, H., Mao, Y., Tang, J., Zhou, C., Yin, A., Wu, Z.: Towards a semantic web of relational databases: A practical semantic toolkit and an in-use case from traditional chinese medicine. In: Cruz, I., Decker, S., Allemang, D., Preist, C., Schwabe, D., Mika, P., Uschold, M., Aroyo, L.M. (eds.) ISWC 2006. LNCS, vol. 4273, pp. 750–763. Springer, Heidelberg (2006)
7. Quilitz, B., Leser, U.: Querying distributed rdf data sources with sparql. In: Bechhofer, S., Hauswirth, M., Hoffmann, J., Koubarakis, M. (eds.) ESWC 2008. LNCS, vol. 5021, pp. 524–538. Springer, Heidelberg (2008)
8. Stuckenschmidt, H., Vdovjak, R., Houben, G.-J., Broekstra, J.: Index structures and algorithms for querying distributed rdf repositories. In: WWW, pp. 631–639 (2004)
9. Stuckenschmidt, H., Vdovjak, R., Broekstra, J., Houben, G.-J.: Towards distributed processing of rdf path queries. Int. J. Web Eng. Technol. 2(2/3), 207–230 (2005)
10. Adamku, G., Stuckenschmidt, H.: Implementation and evaluation of a distributed rdf storage and retrieval system. In: Web Intelligence, pp. 393–396 (2005)
11. Hurtado, C.A., Poulovassilis, A., Wood, P.T.: A relaxed approach to rdf querying. In: Cruz, I., Decker, S., Allemang, D., Preist, C., Schwabe, D., Mika, P., Uschold, M., Aroyo, L.M. (eds.) ISWC 2006. LNCS, vol. 4273, pp. 314–328. Springer, Heidelberg (2006)
12. Bernstein, A., Kiefer, C.: Imprecise rdql: towards generic retrieval in ontologies using similarity joins. In: SAC, pp. 1684–1689 (2006)
13. Stuckenschmidt, H., van Harmelen, F.: Approximating terminological queries. In: Andreasen, T., Motro, A., Christiansen, H., Larsen, H.L. (eds.) FQAS 2002. LNCS (LNAI), vol. 2522, pp. 329–343. Springer, Heidelberg (2002)

An Evolutionary Perspective on Approximate RDF Query Answering

Christophe Guéret, Eyal Oren, Stefan Schlobach, and Martijn Schut

Vrije Universiteit Amsterdam, de Boelelaan 1081a, Amsterdam, The Netherlands

Abstract. RDF is increasingly being used to represent large amounts of data on the Web. Current query evaluation strategies for RDF are inspired by databases, assuming perfect answers on finite repositories. In this paper, we focus on a query method based on evolutionary computing, which allows us to handle uncertainty, incompleteness and unsatisfiability, and deal with large datasets, all within a single conceptual framework. Our technique supports approximate answers with "anytime" behaviour. We present scalability results and next steps for improvement.

1 Introduction

The Resource Description Framework (RDF) standard [22] is increasingly being used to represent large amounts of data on the Web [10], such as the openly available datasets for the billion triple challenge[1]. Such Semantic Web data is intrinsically incomplete, is too large to represent entirely, and contains errors, omissions and ambiguity. However, most query languages and evaluation strategies for Semantic Web data are inspired by databases: the SPARQL [27] query language assumes perfect answers on finite repositories and most RDF stores rely on database back-ends or database-style implementations [6, 17].

We introduced *evolutionary RDF query answering* [25] as an alternative to these approaches, a new querying paradigm which, we claim, has the potential to efficiently produce approximate answers for large RDF datasets. In short, our algorithm finds variable assignments such that the data graph entails the query graph after variable substitution. Instead of using database-style indices, we randomly generate various "individuals" with complete variable assignments and evolve these individuals using an evolutionary algorithm. A fitness function rewards approximate answers and yields maximum value for perfect solutions. At the current state, our implementation shows some good convergence properties, even though the quality of the answers is not yet fully satisfying.

In this paper, we investigate evolutionary RDF query answering from the perspectives of approximation and scalability; first, studying how our evolutionary approach behaves in the light of uncertainty, incompleteness and unsatisfiability, and secondly, how it scales when applied to realistic datasets. The outcome of our analysis is encouraging, as it indicates nice computational properties of our method, and that it effectively deals with different kinds of uncertainty.

---

[1] http://challenge.semanticweb.org

S. Greco and T. Lukasiewicz (Eds.): SUM 2008, LNAI 5291, pp. 215–228, 2008.
© Springer-Verlag Berlin Heidelberg 2008

After giving some background in section 2 we describe our evolutionary algorithm for RDF query answering in section 3. In section 4, we study the space and run-time requirements of our algorithm. In section 5, we discuss the application of our technique to approximate queries on imperfect data.

2   Background

We first introduce an example which will be used throughout the paper to illustrate our approach. A short snippet of RDF, taken from the SwetoDblp publications dataset [1], is shown in Listing 1.1. It states that the "Principles of Database Systems" book was written by some unnamed blank node, whose first element is Jeff Ullman, with a homepage at Stanford. All authors in the SwetoDblp dataset are RDF sequences (ordered lists). A simple SPARQL query over the SwetoDblp dataset, selecting the titles of all books, is shown in Listing 1.2. In the rest of the paper, we use a subset of this SwetoDblp[2] dataset containing 3m triples and a collection[3] of FOAF profiles containing 15k triples for evaluation.

Listing 1.1. RDF snippet from SwetoDBLP dataset

```
<Ullman88> rdf:type opus:Book .
<Ullman88> rdfs:label "Principles of Database and Knowledge-Base Systems" .
<Ullman88> opus:author _:b1 .
_:b1 rdf:_1 dblp:ullman .
dblp:ullman foaf:homepage <http://www-db.stanford.edu/~ullman/> .
```

Listing 1.2. SPARQL query for book title

```
SELECT ?title WHERE {
  ?publication rdf:type opus:Book .
  ?publication rdfs:label ?title .
}
```

2.1   Formal Problem Description

The formal definitions for the problem we address are standard and closely follow the formalism presented in [23, 26]. RDF [22], the data model of the Semantic Web, is a language for asserting statements about arbitrary identifiable resources. Formally, given three infinite sets I, B and L called respectively URI references, blank nodes and literals, an *RDF triple* (s, p, o) is an element of $(I \cup B) \times I \times (I \cup B \cup L)$. Here, s is called the subject, p the predicate, and o the object of the triple. An *RDF graph* (or dataset) is then a set of RDF triples.

For querying RDF, we restrict ourselves to a subset of SPARQL [27]: SELECT and CONSTRUCT queries with one or more WHERE clauses of simple graph patterns. *Graph patterns* are subsets of $(I \cup L \cup V) \times (I \cup V) \times (I \cup L \cup V)$, where V is a set of variables (disjoint from $U \cup I \cup B$). The rest of SPARQL can be supported

---

[2] http://eardf.few.vu.nl/dblp3m.nt.gz

[3] http://eardf.few.vu.nl/foaf.nt.gz

within the same conceptual framework. In the remainder of the paper we refer to this sub-language. We define the semantics of a query through a mapping μ which is a partial function $\mu : V \rightharpoonup U \cup I \cup B$. For a triple pattern t, $\mu(t)$ is the triple obtained when the variables in t are replaced according to μ.

The set of solutions to a query Q over a data-set D is now defined as follows: let D be an RDF data-set over $U \cup I \cup B$, and Q a graph pattern. Then we say that a mapping μ is *a solution* for Q in D if, and only if, $\mu \in \bigcap_{t \in Q} \{\mu \mid dom(\mu) = var(t)$ and $\mu(t) \in D\}$, where $var(t)$ is the set of variables occurring in t. In the following we will often call the graph pattern Q a *query*, a solution for Q in D an *assignment*, and will refer to a triple pattern within a query as a *clause*.

2.2 Evolutionary Algorithms

Evolutionary algorithms [14] are based on a population of individuals that evolve based on natural selection and inheritance. Each individual represents a candidate solution which competes with its siblings based on "survival of the fittest". Evolutionary algorithms have proven to be efficient on a wide range of optimisation, modeling, and simulation problems; using them for satisfiability problems (as we do here) leads to good results when some knowledge about the problem is incorporated in the evolution process [8, 13].

In general, convergence of an evolutionary algorithm depends on the algorithm, the type of problem, and the fitness landscape (how the fitness is distributed over the solutions). For an evolutionary algorithm with elitist selection as we use here, lower and upper bounds on convergence can be determined [19]. Recently, Teytaud and Gelly [29] have shown that evolutionary algorithms that only *compare* fitness values can converge linearly at best, and suggest *ranking* solutions instead; we do so, by weighting parts of the solutions. Later in the paper, we empirically demonstrate convergence for some RDF queries.

2.3 Evolutionary RDF Querying

Existing RDF stores such as Sesame [6] or YARS [17] mostly employ standard database techniques for query answering. Generally speaking, all systems construct partial indices for simple triple patterns such as (*po*) and (*sp*) during loading time. During query execution, single patterns can be answered with direct index lookups, while joins require nested loops with backtracking.

We propose a different approach which consists of, iteratively, guessing a set of complete assignments for the query variables (a "candidate solution"), verifying those assignments, and if no solutions are found, loop and trying again [25]. The main difference with traditional database querying approaches is that we verify candidate solutions instead of generating them.

In order to minimize query answering time, our evolutionary algorithm should improve its assignments with each loop, arrive at some solution relatively fast, and verify each candidate solution rapidly. To achieve those goals, we combine an evolutionary algorithm with Bloom filters [3], to respectively generate candidate solutions and to test them. Additionally, we use a dictionary encoding to reduce memory usage during evolution.

Verification of solutions. Bloom filters [3] are compact data representations that support only set insertion and membership evaluation. On insertion, a bitmask is computed by applying k hash functions to the inserted key. Bits indicated by the mask are set to 1 in the filter (default value is 0). For membership evaluation, the element's bitmask is computed and evaluated against the stored mask of the set. Since computed hash functions may collide, a lookup may result to false positives (if all k hash functions collide). This collision rate p depends on the ratio m/n between filter bitsize and number of stored elements, and on the k number of hash functions used: $p = (1 - e^{-\frac{kn}{m}})^k$.

In our application, the size of our filters can be adjusted during data loading time to achieve a given collision rate; alternatively, with a given filter and domain size, we can estimate the confidence of false positives in the answers using the same equation. Typically, the number of hash functions is set to $k = 4$, to achieve good collision rates with varying data sizes.

Dictionary. During graph parsing a term dictionary is constructed, which maps terms to integer keys and vice versa. The domain of each variable (candidate assignments) and all generated individuals (selected assignments) are expressed as integer vectors, holding dictionary keys. For readibility, those integers are substitued by their corresponding terms throughout the examples in this paper.

3   An Evolutionary Algorithm for RDF Querying

We now describe the details of our evolutionary encoding: the representation of variable assignments as individuals, the fitness evaluation, the evolutionary operators that modify the population, and some convergence results.

3.1   Encoding of Individuals and Constraints

To setup our evolutionary algorithm, we need to choose a representation for the individuals (candidate solutions) and for the query (constraints). Each individual is a fully instantiated solution to our problem, ie. an assignment for all variables. Therefore, the encoding template for the individuals is the set of terms defined by the query, as shown in Table 1(a). In order to increase the genetic material, and in contrast to our earlier encoding [25], each variable is considered separately, resulting in two different genes for the same variable ?publication.

The domain of a variable depends on its usage in the graph. In total, we have seven possible domains: s, p, o, sp, so, po, spo. During graph parsing we populate the three domains s, p and o with nodes occurring at subject, predicate and object position. Then a variable's domain is the intersection of its position in the query clauses. Table 1(b) shows the domains for our standard example.

A candidate solution is optimal if it satisfies all of the Bloom filter tests and equality constraints. Each constraint is associated to a reward. We use four filters (spo, sp, so, po) to check both complete and partial triple assignments to increase fitness granularity. Table 2 shows the constraints for the query in Listing 1.2. Constraints 1–4 are generated from the first WHERE clause (?publication rdf:type

Table 1. Encoding of individuals (candidate solutions)

(a) Encoding template for individuals

?publication$_1$	?publication$_2$	?title

(b) Domain snippets for the variables

Variable	Domain
?publication$_1$	s: <Ullman88>, _:b1, dblp:ullman
?publication$_2$	s: <Ullman88>, _:b1, dblp:ullman
?title	o: <http:/...>, _:b1, dblp:ullman, "Principles...", opus:Book

Table 2. Translation of SPARQL query into constraints

	Constraint to satisfy	Expected reward
❶	bloom(spo|?publication$_1$ rdf:type opus:Book)	$3 \times w_1$
❷	bloom(sp|?publication$_1$ rdf:type)	w_1
❸	~~bloom(po|rdf:type opus:Book)~~	w_1
❹	bloom(so|?publication$_1$ opus:Book)	w_1
❺	bloom(spo|?publication$_2$ rdfs:label ?title)	$3 \times w_2$
❻	bloom(sp|?publication$_2$ rdfs:label)	w_2
❼	bloom(po|rdfs:label ?title)	w_2
❽	bloom(so|?publication$_2$?title)	w_2
❾	equal(?publication$_1$, ?publication$_2$)	$w_3 \times \frac{w_1+w_2}{2}$

opus:Book), 5–8 correspond to (?publication rdfs:label ?title), the last one is created by the double usage of ?publication. Constraint 3 is removed from the list as it is satisfied by definition.

3.2 Fitness Evaluation

A fitness function should be designed in such a way that individuals closer to the optimal solution can be identified by the system. For our application, an optimal solution consist of a valid variable assignment.

A candidate solution is optimal if it satisfies all constraints. The quality of individuals is therefore related to the number of satisfied constraints. To illustrate the fitness consider Table 3(a). The query instantiated with the assignment corresponding to the individual is checked against all relevant corresponding Bloom filters and Equality constraints. For each constraint that is validated this candidate solution is rewarded, as shown in Table 3(b). Table 3(c) shows the complete fitness evaluation for this individual; half of the constraints are validated, leading to a total reward of $6 \times w_2$.

In addition to this overall evaluation, each variable involved in a satisfied contraint receives a reward This information is used later to determine how to control mutation.

Table 3. Evaluation of a candidate solution

(a) Candidate solution to evaluate

dblp:ullman	<Ullman88>	"Principles..."

(b) Evaluation of the total reward for that candidate assignment

	Constraint to satisfy	Result	Reward
❶	bloom(spo | dblp:ullman rdf:type opus:Book)	*false*	0
❷	bloom(sp | dblp:ullman rdf:type)	*false*	0
❹	bloom(so | dblp:ullman opus:Book)	*false*	0
❺	bloom(spo | <Ullman88> rdfs:label "Principles...")	*true*	$3 \times w_2$
❻	bloom(sp | <Ullman88> rdfs:label)	*true*	w_2
❼	bloom(po | rdfs:label "Principles...")	*true*	w_2
❽	bloom(so | <Ullman88> "Principles...")	*true*	w_2
❾	equal(dblp:ullman <Ullman88>)	*false*	0

(c) For satisfied constraints, reward is equally distributed to each variable involved

	?publication$_1$	?publication$_2$	?title
❺	0	$\frac{3 \times w_2}{2}$	$\frac{3 \times w_2}{2}$
❻	0	w_2	0
❼	0	0	w_2
❽	0	$\frac{w_2}{2}$	$\frac{w_2}{2}$

3.3 Evolution Process

In the basic form, starting with an initial population, individuals recombine and mutate to produce offspring. In each iteration, individuals are evaluated using the fitness function: the unfittest are removed and replaced by new individuals. When a stop criterion, such as minimal fitness or maximum number of generations, is satisfied the best individuals are presented as final solutions.

During a loop, the evolution consists of the consecutive execution of four "operators": parent selection, recombination (crossover), mutation and survivor selection. We now describe our implemented choice for each of these operators.

Parent selection. Evolution loops create new individuals and destroy previous ones. Parent selection is aimed at selecting from the current population the individuals that will be allowed to mate and create offspring, and is commonly aimed at the best individuals. Several parent selection schemes can be used. We employ a tournament-based selection, in which two individuals are randomly picked from the population, the best one is kept as the first parent. This process is repeated to get more parents.

Recombination. Recombination acts as exploration during the search process. This operator is aimed at creating new individuals in unexplored regions of the search space. Its operation takes two parents and combines them into two children. After various experiments, we opted for a classical one-point crossover

Table 4. One-point crossover operator process

(a) Selection of a random pivot gene

dblp:ullman	<Ullman88>	"Principles..."
<Ullman88>	dblp:ullman	_:b1

(b) Creation of two children

dblp:ullman	<Ullman88>	_:b1
<Ullman88>	dblp:ullman	"Principles..."

Table 5. Mutation operator process

(a) Select the gene with lowest reward

dblp:ullman	<Ullman88>	"Principles..."
0	$3 \times w_2$	$3 \times w_2$

(b) Assign a random new value

<Ullman88>	<Ullman88>	"Principles..."

operator, in which one pivot gene is randomly selected and the parts around it are swapped between the parents, demonstrated in Table 4.

Mutation. As compared with the crossover operator whose objective is to do "big jumps" in the search space, the mutation operator is meant to explore the neighbourhood of an individual. A slight modification is applied to one or more genes. This perturbation is commonly referred to as an exploitation scheme. In a standard genetic algorithm mutation is blind, ie., the gene to modify is randomly selected. After some experimentation, we instead designed a mutation operator which is biased towards mutating badly performing genes, based on the score per variables computed during fitness evaluation. The process of this operator is depicted in Table 5.

Such a mutation operator improves convergence of a population by identifying the less efficient assignments. However, such a greedy strategy may lead to local optima without reaching global optima. To reduce the risk of premature convergence we therefore also apply blind mutation after our optimised local search. This mutation is applied randomly, with low probability, to one gene.

Survivor selection. At this point of the evolution we have both a parent population and an offspring population (created by the parents). During survivor selection we select the individuals to keep for the next evolution round. We chose a generational selection: after each evolutionary cycle the parent population is discarded and replaced by its offspring.

3.4 Convergence Results

Figure 1(a) shows the fitness of the best individual when trying to answer an example query on the FOAF dataset (using 200 individuals, for 500 generations). Three phases can be observed: first a rapid improvement during initialisation,

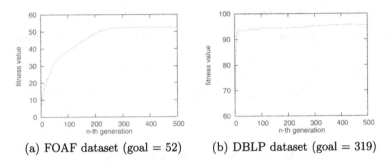

(a) FOAF dataset (goal = 52)   (b) DBLP dataset (goal = 319)

Fig. 1. Best fitness on FOAF and DBLP queries, avg. over 100 runs

when constraints are easy to satisfy, then a slower improvement when individuals solve the more difficult (join) constraints, and finally near-constant fitness when an optimum is found. The curve is typical for evolutionary algorithms and confirms the expected convergence behaviour.

Figure 1(b) shows the result on the DBLP dataset, with same evolution parameters. Now only the first phase is visible and the evolution stops during the second one. Although a partial solution during the initialisation phase is reached quickly, the individuals have difficulty finding further improvements; more work is needed to prevent a local optimum.

4   Discussion on Scalability

Using an evolutionary approach combined with Bloom filters has several scalability benefits. First, during query evaluations users can decide to trade soundness for speed, by stopping the evolution before perfect solutions are found, and to trade soundness for memory size, by using smaller bloomfilters with higher collision rate. In this section, we explore such scalability advantages in more detail.

4.1   Fast Dictionary Construction

Dictionaries often improve performance when handling large amounts of data. All terms are rewritten into dictionary keys (in our case, integer indices).Using these keys during computation improves performance because keys require on average less memory space than the full terms and because integer comparison is faster than a string comparison of the terms.

Constructing dictionaries is however not trivial, as during construction a list of all seen terms and their assigned keys must be kept [20]. For building the dictionary, we employ move-to-front hashtables [30], which are a particular type of chained hashtables using linked lists for overflow entries. When accessed, elements are moved to the front of their list. This simple heuristic relies on the Zipfian distribution of terms in texts, so that often used terms are on average available in the front of the list. Since terms in RDF data follow a similar distribution [24], we use the same data structure and heuristic.

Table 6. Average memory usage using 200 individuals

(a) parsing		(b) querying	
dataset	memory	dataset	memory
FOAF	65 MB	FOAF	15 MB
DBLP	230 MB	DBLP	140 MB

To insert a term in these hashtables, its hash value is computed using some hash function, and used as index into an array of lists. The term is compared to the other terms in the list at that position. If found, the corresponding key is returned, and the list element is moved to the front of the list. If not found, this term is added to the end of the list along with a new key, incremented using some counter, is assigned to him.

An expensive computation in the move-to-front hashtable is the string term comparison, performed at each list element to see whether the existing list term is the same as the one being inserted. To improve performance, we store and compare only the Adler-32 fingerprint [9] of each term. Comparing these fingerprints is a fast bitwise operation, while collision rate is extremely low since both hash value and fingerprint value need to collide.

4.2   Small Memory Footprint

Since the bloom filters, the domain, and all individuals are compactly represented, all runtime data fits in memory, avoiding the disk I/O bottleneck [4, 18]. Actual memory usage during prototype experiments is shown in Table 6, for the smaller FOAF dataset and the larger DBLP dataset. During parsing, most memory is used during dictionary and bloom filters construction; during evolution the memory is used to hold the bloom filters, the assignments of all individuals and the hash table of the dictionary, used for printing final solutions. Both parse and query actions indeed require a reasonable amount of memory; more compact bloomfilter variations are possible, eg. for network distribution [5].

4.3   Short and Fast Evolution Cycles

During evolution, we verify whether solutions are present in each of the bloomfilters. Membership testing in the bloomfilter consists of computing the k hashvalues, which are used as a bitmask for the filter. All computation stays in memory, and all bitwise operations are very fast.

Secondly, we perform the evolutionary operations (cross-over, mutation, etc.) and sometimes assign new values to individuals. Again, since individuals are encoded as integer vectors, these operations are very efficient.

4.4   Suitable for Parallel Computation

Since evolution of individuals is in principal independent the computation can be easily parallelised. Our evolutionary algorithm could use an island model with independent demes [7], to evolve sub-populations in parallel.

Since our Bloom filters are relatively compact, they can be transported over the network, allowing local evolution on distributed clients in a "thinking at home" manner [15]. In a P2P setting, the dictionary itself may also be stored in the network using distributed hashtables [28].

5   Discussion on Approximations and Applicability

In our technique, we have several points in which some approximation of data or query can be performed. Generally speaking, when querying a dataset KB with query Q, we can distinguish three kinds of approximations: one can approximate the query Q by Q', one can approximate KB by KB', and one can approximate the reasoning strategy, by for example returning unsound, partial, matches.

Our method can be seen as an approximation of all three kinds simultaneously. We approximate the dataset, somewhat similar to random sampling, since the evolution can be stopped at any point without all constraints necessarily satisfied, and without having explored the complete search space. At the same time, we also approximate the query, using a simple form of query relaxation, and approximate the reasoning strategy by returning unsound answers.

5.1   Approximate Anwers through Query Relaxation

Query rewriting approximates the original, possibly unsatisfiable, query Q by Q'. Relaxation through query rewriting can be done eg. by making clauses optional, by breaking join dependencies, by replacing constants by variables, by replacing constants using the class and property hierarchy in an associated ontology, or by deleting (ignoring) problematic clauses [11, 21]

Hurtado et al. [21] add an explicit RELAX clause to SPARQL queries, which are automatically and successively relaxed based on schema information such as subClassOf and subPropertyOf. Similarly, Dolog et al. [11] explicitly model user preferences and domain preferences, and use these preferences to automatically relax query clauses by replacing values and predicates in the query with preferred alternatives (eg. synonym values or related predicates).

We employ a similar but less fine-grained form of query relaxation, by returning answers from individuals with sub-optimal fitness. The solutions encoded by these individuals have found partial matches, and thus ignored some of the clauses or clause parts in the query.

5.2   Approximate Answers through Unsoundness

On top of the notion of approximation by ignoring some triple patterns in the query graph, we also introduce approximation by using an unsound method for checking whether a mapping μ is indeed a solution to a query Q for a graph D. The reason for this is that Bloom filters are fast but unsound lookup mechanisms.

Because we generate several constraints for each query clause, and because we have a population-based algorithm which returns only the best solution for each problem, the error rate of answers returned to the user is several factors lower.

For the basic approach which uses four constraints for each clause (for each pair and triple in the clause) the confidence level is:

$$1 - p(query) = 1 - \prod_C (p_{sp} \cdot p_{so} \cdot p_{po} \cdot p_{spo}) = 1 - \prod_{4C} p \qquad (1)$$

For instance, using a collision probability of 10%, the confidence level for query with c clauses is: $1 - (0.10)^{4c} \simeq 1$, indicating the absence of false positives in the solution.

5.3 Dealing with Imperfect Queries

When users lack sufficient knowledge about the dataset that they are querying, they are unable to formulate queries that return the intended result. In the context of the Semantic Web, users frequently lack such knowledge, since data come from multiple sources, with different schemas and often lacking any schema information. Research on cooperative query answering [16] focuses on interactive query formulation, helping users to refine their query until suitable results can be returned.

In our case, when users investigate some dataset, eg. "what can I learn about Tim from this FOAF file?", a potential query would be "SELECT ?prop WHERE ?sub foaf:name "Tim". ?sub ?prop ?obj". Though thousands of properties may exist, the user is likely not to be interested in seeing all of them. And here is where the approximation is made: instead of fetching all the results, the evolutionary process is executed until some reasonable number of answers becomes available.

Evolutionary algorithms are designed to have a population of candidate solution evolving towards a given optimum (according to a fitness function). The initial population may be created randomly or using any other initialisation scheme. Thus, a first set of answers can be such a starting point for a new evolution. Besides, the optimum to reach could be adapted to take into account some new constraints. By taking advantage of those restart and robustness capabilities, an incremental query answering system can be designed.

5.4 Dealing with Imperfect Data

Our initial approach for translating SPARQL queries into a constraint satisfaction problem [25], gave equal importance to all the WHERE clauses; in practical queries, such equal importance might not be the case. In this paper, the introduction of specific weights for different constraints caters for such differences, allowing more "useful" approximate answers. The constraint weights can be tuned using three different strategies: a "static" strategy based on statistical information, a "dynamic" one based on adjustment during evolution, and an "adaptative" scheme based on interactive user feedback.

Static. Relative importance of the clauses could be deduced from their probability, depending on their occurrence frequency. We can simply count each triple occurrence into six wildcard patterns: (?s,p,o), (s,?p,o), (s,p,?o), (?s,?p,o), (s,?p,?o) and (?s,p,?o). The first one, for instance, will count all combinations of p and o. During query time, the value of the counter associated to a pattern gives a hint on the difficulty of finding a variable binding for it.

Dynamic. The importance of a clause can also be discovered dynamically, based on the difficulty of solving them during evolution: a constraint that appears to be hard to satisfy should be solved first. We can assume that a WHERE clause is hard to satisfy if no valid assignment is found for that particular constraint within a finite time [12]. Initially, the weights associated to each clauses are set to a default value. After each n iterations, the weight of a clause is incremented if the best individual could not find a valid assignment for it. Once a valid assignment has been found, those weights are set back to the default, neutral, value. Using this scheme, hard constraints will gain importance until they are satisfied. Once solved, more attention will be paid to the remaining unsatisfied constraints.

Interactive. The third weighting schema allows users to explicitly indicate their preferences. In terms of evolutionary algorithms, the user is then involved in the variation-selection loop, which is called *interactive evolutionary computation* [2]. In terms of the weighting scheme mentioned above, involving the user in the search process means that he is able to change the weights according to fitness values he sees. Then, the weights are used to correct the direction of the search process towards "good" enough answers. Technically, the weights are incorporated in the EA to determine either the fitness of candidate answers and/or the operators to generate new candidates. For the former, one has to take into account that users can only evaluate a small number of candidates, meaning that these candidates have to represented to the user in an intelligible way. Even when using a static fitness function, considerable speed-up can be achieved by user involvement during the generation of new candidates.

6   Conclusion

We have introduced a novel method for querying RDF datasets based on an evolutionary algorithm. Our method is not focused on finding perfect solutions but on providing approximate solutions efficiently. We study this approach from two perspectives: scalability and uncertainty. Regarding scalability, three aspects show the positive behaviour of our method: the potential for parallelisation, small memory usage, and minimal execution time of evolutionary cycles. Furthermore, we show that our approach allows to deal very naturally with different types of uncertainty: approximate queries, approximate answers, and uncertain data. Although the evolutionary operators still need improvement, we believe that our analysis justifies further development of evolutionary methods for RDF querying.

Future work. In this paper, we have focused on finding the best, possibly approximate, solution to a given query. How to efficiently return many results instead is an open issue. One direction for research is evolutionary taboo-search, using individuals as scouts that explore the solution space; once a local optimum is found, the area is tabooed and individuals focus on another part.

We currently do not support aggregation functions, since these are currently not part of the SPARQL standard. Still, we can employ the evolutionary search as a method to compute approximate aggregations "along the way", without requiring complete solutions before aggregating.

References

[1] Aleman-Meza, B., Hakimpour, F., Arpinar, I., Sheth, A.: SwetoDblp ontology of computer science publications. Journal of Web Semantics 5(3), 151–155 (2007)

[2] Banzhaf, W.: Interactive evolution. In: Handbook of Evolutionary Computation, ch. 2.10. IOP Press (1997)

[3] Bloom, B.H.: Space/time trade-offs in hash coding with allowable errors. Communications of the ACM 13(7), 422–426 (1970)

[4] Boncz, P., Manegold, S., Kersten, M.L.: Database architecture optimized for the new bottleneck: Memory access. In: Proceedings of the International Conference on Very Large Data Bases (VLDB), pp. 54–65 (1999)

[5] Broder, A., Mitzenmacher, M.: Network applications of Bloom filters: A survey. Internet Mathematics 1, 485–509 (2005)

[6] Broekstra, J., Kampman, A., van Harmelen, F.: Sesame: A generic architecture for storing and querying RDF and RDF Schema. In: Horrocks, I., Hendler, J. (eds.) ISWC 2002. LNCS, vol. 2342, pp. 54–68. Springer, Heidelberg (2002)

[7] Cantú-Paz, E.: A survey of parallel genetic algorithms. Calculateurs Paralleles, Reseaux et Systemes Repartis 10(2), 141–171 (1998)

[8] Craenen, B., Eiben, A., Marchiori, E.: Solving constraint satisfaction problems with heuristic-based evolutionary algorithms. In: Proceedings of the Congress on Evolutionary Computation, pp. 1571–1577 (2000)

[9] Deutsch, P., Gailly, J.-L.: ZLIB compressed data format specification v3.3. RFC 1950 (1996)

[10] Ding, L., Finin, T.: Characterizing the Semantic Web on the web. In: Cruz, I., Decker, S., Allemang, D., Preist, C., Schwabe, D., Mika, P., Uschold, M., Aroyo, L.M. (eds.) ISWC 2006. LNCS, vol. 4273. Springer, Heidelberg (2006)

[11] Dolog, P., Stuckenschmidt, H., Wache, H., Diederich, J.: Relaxing RDF queries based on user and domain preferences. Journal on Intelligent Information Systems (2008)

[12] Eiben, A.E., van der Hauw, J.K.: Adaptive penalties for evolutionary graph coloring. In: Proceedings of the European Conference on Artificial Evolution, pp. 95–108 (1997)

[13] Eiben, A.E., van Hemert, J.I., Marchiori, E., Steenbeek, A.G.: Solving binary constraint satisfaction problems using evolutionary algorithms with an adaptive fitness function. In: Eiben, A.E., Bäck, T., Schoenauer, M., Schwefel, H.-P. (eds.) PPSN 1998. LNCS, vol. 1498, pp. 201–210. Springer, Heidelberg (1998)

[14] Eiben, A.E., Smith, J.E.: Introduction to Evolutionary Computing. Springer, Berlin (2003)

[15] Fensel, D., van Harmelen, F., Andersson, B., et al.: Towards LarKC: a platform for web-scale reasoning. In: Proceedings of the International Conference on Semantic Computing (2008)

[16] Gaasterland, T., Godfrey, P., Minker, J.: An overview of cooperative answering. Journal on Intelligent Information Systems 1(2), 123–157 (1992)

[17] Harth, A., Decker, S.: Optimized index structures for querying RDF from the web. In: Proceedings of the Latin-American Web Congress (LA-Web), pp. 71–80 (2005)

[18] Harth, A., Umbrich, J., Hogan, A., Decker, S.: YARS2: A federated repository for querying graph structured data from the web. In: Aberer, K., Choi, K.-S., Noy, N., Allemang, D., Lee, K.-I., Nixon, L., Golbeck, J., Mika, P., Maynard, D., Mizoguchi, R., Schreiber, G., Cudré-Mauroux, P. (eds.) ASWC 2007 and ISWC 2007. LNCS, vol. 4825, Springer, Heidelberg (2007)

[19] He, J., Yu, X.: Conditions for the convergence of evolutionary algorithms. Journal of Systems Architecture 47(7), 601–612 (2001)

[20] Heinz, S., Zobel, J., Williams, H.E.: Burst tries: A fast, efficient data structure for string keys. ACM Transactions on Information Systems 20(2), 192–223 (2002)

[21] Hurtado, C.A., Poulovassilis, A., Wood, P.T.: Query relaxation in RDF. Journal on Data Semantics 10, 31–61 (2008)

[22] Klyne, G., Carroll, J.J. (eds.): Resource Description Framework: Concepts and Abstract Syntax. W3C Recommendation (2004)

[23] Muñoz, S., Pérez, J., Gutierrez, C.: Minimal deductive systems for RDF. In: Franconi, E., Kifer, M., May, W. (eds.) ESWC 2007. LNCS, vol. 4519. Springer, Heidelberg (2007)

[24] Oren, E., Delbru, R., Catasta, M., Cyganiak, R., et al.: Sindice.com: A document-oriented lookup index for open linked data. International Journal of Metadata, Semantics and Ontologies 3(1) (to appear, 2008a)

[25] Oren, E., Guéret, C., Schlobach, S.: Anytime query answering in RDF through evolutionary algorithms. In: Proceedings of the International Semantic Web Conference (ISWC) (to appear, 2008b)

[26] Pérez, J., Arenas, M., Gutierrez, C.: Semantics and complexity of SPARQL. In: Cruz, I., Decker, S., Allemang, D., Preist, C., Schwabe, D., Mika, P., Uschold, M., Aroyo, L.M. (eds.) ISWC 2006. LNCS, vol. 4273. Springer, Heidelberg (2006)

[27] Prud'hommeaux, E., Seaborne, A. (eds.): SPARQL Query Language for RDF. W3C Recommendation (2007)

[28] Stoica, I., Morris, R., Karger, D., Kaashoek, M.F., et al.: Chord: A scalable peer-to-peer lookup service for internet applications. SIGCOMM Comput. Commun. Rev. 31(4), 149–160 (2001)

[29] Teytaud, O., Gelly, S.: General lower bounds for evolutionary algorithms. In: Parallel Problem Solving from Nature, pp. 21–32. Springer, Heidelberg (2006)

[30] Zobel, J., Heinz, S., Williams, H.E.: In-memory hash tables for accumulating text vocabularies. Information Processing Letters 80(6), 271–277 (2001)

Clustering Uncertain Data Via K-Medoids

Francesco Gullo, Giovanni Ponti, and Andrea Tagarelli

DEIS, University of Calabria, Via P.Bucci 41c, Rende (CS) I87036, Italy
{fgullo,gponti,tagarelli}@deis.unical.it

Abstract. Uncertain data are usually represented in terms of an uncertainty region over which a probability density function (pdf) is defined. In the context of uncertain data management, there has been a growing interest in clustering uncertain data. In particular, the classic K-means clustering algorithm has been recently adapted to handle uncertain data. However, the centroid-based partitional clustering approach used in the adapted K-means presents two major weaknesses that are related to: *(i)* an accuracy issue, since cluster centroids are computed as deterministic objects using the expected values of the pdfs of the clustered objects; and, *(ii)* an efficiency issue, since the expected distance between uncertain objects and cluster centroids is computationally expensive.

In this paper, we address the problem of clustering uncertain data by proposing a K-medoids-based algorithm, called *UK-medoids*, which is designed to overcome the above issues. In particular, our UK-medoids algorithm employs distance functions properly defined for uncertain objects, and exploits a K-medoids scheme. Experiments have shown that UK-medoids outperforms existing algorithms from an accuracy viewpoint while achieving reasonably good efficiency.

1 Introduction

Handling uncertainty in data management has been requiring more and more importance in a wide range of application contexts. Indeed, data uncertainty naturally arises from, e.g., implicit randomness in a process of data generation/acquisition, imprecision in physical measurements, and data staling. Various notions of uncertainty have been defined depending on the application domain (e.g., [2,3,4,5,6,7,8]). In general, uncertainty can be considered at table, tuple or attribute level [9], and is usually specified by fuzzy models [10], evidence-oriented models [11,12], or probabilistic models [13].

In this paper, we focus on data containing attribute-level uncertainty, which is modeled according to a probabilistic model. We hereinafter refer to this data as *uncertain objects*. An uncertain object is usually represented by means of *probability density functions* (pdfs), which describe the likelihood that the object appears at each position in a multidimensional space [14,15,1], rather than by a traditional vectorial form of deterministic values.

Attribute-level uncertainty expressed by means of probabilistic models is present in several application domains. For instance, sensor measurements may be imprecise at a certain degree due to the presence of various noisy factors

S. Greco and T. Lukasiewicz (Eds.): SUM 2008, LNAI 5291, pp. 229–242, 2008.
© Springer-Verlag Berlin Heidelberg 2008

(e.g., signal noise, instrumental errors, wireless transmission) [16,14]. To address this issue, it is advisable to model sensor data as continuous pdfs [17,18]. Another example is given by data representing moving objects, which continuously change their location so that exact positional information at a given time instant may be unavailable [19]. Further examples come from distributed applications, privacy preserving data mining, and forecasting or other statistical techniques used to generate data attributes [20].

Dealing with uncertain objects has raised several issues in data management and knowledge discovery. In particular, organizing uncertain objects is challenging since the intrinsic difficulty underlying the various notions of uncertainty. As a major exploratory task of data mining, *clustering* is organizing a collection of objects (whose classification is unknown) into meaningful groups (clusters), based on interesting relationships discovered in the data. Objects within a cluster will be each other highly similar, but will be very dissimilar from objects in other clusters. One of the most popular clustering approaches is represented by partitional (or partitioning) clustering [21], which iteratively assigns objects to the clusters according to a certain distance/similarity function. A major cruciality in partitional clustering is how to devise a notion of cluster prototype. In particular, a cluster prototype can be defined as a *centroid*, which is the "mean" object in the cluster, or as a *medoid*, which is an actual object that is nearest to all the other objects in the cluster. The K-means [22] and K-medoids [23] algorithms are the exemplary methods of centroid-based and medoid-based partitional clustering, respectively.

In a recent work [1], the K-means algorithm has been adapted to the uncertain data domain. However, the resulting algorithm, named UK-means, has two major weak points. First, cluster centroids are defined as deterministic objects and computed as the mean of the expected values over the pdfs of the uncertain objects in the cluster; defining centroids in this way may result in loss of accuracy, since only the expected values of the pdfs of the uncertain objects are taken into account. Second, the computation of the Expected Distance (ED) between cluster centroids and uncertain objects is computationally expensive, as it requires non-trivial numerical integral estimations; this represents an efficiency bottleneck at each iteration of the algorithm.

In this paper, we present *UK-medoids*, an algorithm for clustering uncertain objects based on the K-medoids clustering scheme. The proposed algorithm exploits a distance function for uncertain objects, which is not limited to consider only scalar values derived from the pdfs associated to the objects (e.g., pdf expected values). This allows for better estimating the real distance between two uncertain objects, leading to significant improvement of the clustering quality. Also, our algorithm does not require any expensive operation to be repeated at each iteration; indeed, the computation of the distances between uncertain objects in the dataset is performed only once, thus guaranteeing a significant improvement of the efficiency w.r.t. UK-means. Experiments have shown that our method outperforms existing algorithms from an accuracy viewpoint while achieving reasonably good efficiency.

The rest of the paper is organized as follows. The next section discusses some related work. Section 3 describes the uncertain data models used in the paper. Section 4 describes the notion of uncertain distance and the UK-medoids algorithm. Section 5 provides experimental evaluation of our algorithm and the competing methods. Finally, Section 6 concludes the paper.

2   Related Work

In the context of uncertain data management, a lot of research has been mainly focused on data representation and modeling, indexing, query processing, and data mining (e.g., [20]). In particular, data mining applications have involved various tasks, such as classification [24], outlier detection [25], association analysis [26], and clustering [27,15,1,28,29].

As above mentioned, one of the earliest attempts to solve the problem of clustering uncertain objects is UK-means [1]. In order to improve the UK-means efficiency, [28] proposes some pruning techniques to avoid the computation of redundant EDs. Such techniques make use of lower- and upper-bounds that are ad-hoc defined for each ED to be calculated; these bounds allow for eliminating some candidate assignments of objects to cluster centroids, avoiding the corresponding ED computation. However, a major problem of this approach is that it cannot guarantee high pruning (and, hence, high efficiency), as it depends on the features of the objects in the specific dataset. In [29], the *CK-means* is proposed as a variant of UK-means that resorts to the moment of inertia of rigid bodies in order to reduce the execution time needed for computing EDs. Unfortunately, the soundness of the CK-means criterion for the ED computation is guaranteed only if the mean squared error for the definition of the EDs is used and the distance function is based on the Euclidean norm.

It should be noted that all the UK-means variants have to face the issue of computing cluster centroids, whose effectiveness depends on how well the aggregated values (e.g., the expected values) extracted from the object pdfs represent the real location of the uncertain objects. Also, computing the distance between uncertain objects is usually accomplished by calculating the Euclidean distance between the vectors of the (deterministic) expected values.

A more refined approach to the distance computation consists in defining a univariate pdf, or *fuzzy distance function*, for each pair of objects. This univariate pdf computes a probability for each distance value for two objects, and the distance between the objects is finally computed by extracting an aggregated, representative value (e.g., expected value) from the pdf of those objects. This method has been originally presented in [27] and has been proved to be more effective than the standard Euclidean distance applied to vectors of deterministic values.

Devising a fuzzy distance function is a key aspect in density-based approaches that have been proposed for clustering uncertain objects [15,27]. In [15], a fuzzy version of the popular DBSCAN [30] algorithm, $\mathcal{F}$DBSCAN, is proposed. Fuzzy distance functions are used to compute core object and reachability probabilities, which are at the basis of the density-based clustering strategy of the algorithm. A similar approach is presented in [27], where $\mathcal{F}$OPTICS is proposed as a fuzzy version of the popular hierarchical density-based clustering algorithm OPTICS [31].

It is important to note that [15,27] focus on how to efficiently compute reachability probabilities; however, they do not provide a formal definition of fuzzy distance function that can be applied to any clustering algorithm. By contrast, we provide a definition of fuzzy distance function that does not depend on a particular clustering scheme and is well-suited to continuous as well as discrete pdfs.

3   Modeling Uncertain Data

Representing attribute-level uncertain objects is traditionally accomplished by using two models, namely *multivariate uncertainty* and *univariate uncertainty* models.

Using a multivariate uncertainty model, an m-dimensional uncertain object is defined in terms of an m-dimensional region and a multivariate probability density function, which stores the probability according to which the exact representation of the object coincides with any point in the region. In a univariate uncertainty model, an m-dimensional uncertain object has, for each attribute, an interval and a univariate probability density function that assigns a probability value to any point within the interval. Formally:

Definition 1 (multivariate uncertain object). *A* multivariate uncertain object *o is a pair* (R, f)*, where* $R \subseteq \Re^m$ *is the region in which o is defined and* $f : \Re^m \rightarrow \Re_0^+$ *is the probability density function of o at each point* $z \in R$.

Definition 2 (univariate uncertain object). *A* univariate uncertain object *o is a tuple* $(a^{(1)}, \ldots, a^{(m)})$*. Each attribute* $a^{(h)}$ *is a pair* $(I^{(h)}, f^{(h)})$*, for each* $h \in [1..m]$*, where* $I^{(h)} = [l^{(h)}, u^{(h)}]$ *is the interval of definition of* $a^{(h)}$*, and* $f^{(h)} : \Re \rightarrow \Re_0^+$ *is the probability density function that assigns a probability value to each* $z \in I^{(h)}$.

For each multivariate uncertain object, the probability density function involved in its representation can be either *continuous* or *discrete*. A continuous multivariate m-dimensional probability density function defined over a region $R \subseteq \Re^m$ is a function $f : \Re^m \rightarrow \Re_0^+$ such that:

$$\int_{z \in R} f(z) \, \mathrm{d}z = 1 \qquad \text{and} \qquad \int_{z \in \Re^m \setminus R} f(z) \, \mathrm{d}z = 0$$

A discrete multivariate m-dimensional probability density function defined over a set of points $S = \{z_1, \ldots, z_v\}$ ($z_u \in \Re^m$, for each $u \in [1..v]$) is a function $f : \Re^m \rightarrow \Re_0^+$ such that:

$$\sum_{z \in S} f(z) = 1 \qquad \text{and} \qquad \int_{z \in \Re^m \setminus S} f(z) \mathrm{d}\,z = 0$$

For the univariate model, a continuous (resp. discrete) univariate probability density function can be trivially defined in terms of a continuous (resp. discrete) multivariate probability density function, in which the region (resp. set) of definition is a subset of $\Re$ (i.e., $m = 1$).

We hereinafter refer to uncertainty models involving continuous probability functions. Note that this assumption does not result in loss of generality, since the corresponding "discrete" version can be obtained by simply replacing integrals with sums in the equations.

4   Clustering Uncertain Data

4.1   Computing Uncertain Distance

To measure the distance between uncertain objects, we need to devise a suitable notion of *uncertain distance*, which is involved in the proposed clustering algorithm. Uncertain distance is defined in terms of an *uncertain distance function*. In order to make the uncertain distance independent from the chosen uncertainty model, we provide definitions of uncertain distance function for both multivariate and univariate uncertainty models.

Definition 3 (uncertain distance function). *Given a set of uncertain objects $D = \{o_1, \ldots, o_n\}$, the uncertain distance function defined over D is a function $\Delta : D \times D \times \Re \rightarrow \Re_0^+$, for which the following conditions hold:*

$$\int\limits_{z \in \Re} \Delta(o_i, o_j, z) \, \mathrm{d}z = 1, \quad \forall o_i, o_j \in D,$$

$$\Delta(o_i, o_j, z) = \begin{cases} 1, & if \ i = j, z = 0 \\ 0, & if \ i = j, z \neq 0 \end{cases}$$

For any pair of uncertain objects $o_i, o_j, i \neq j$, Δ can be derived from the pdfs associated to the uncertain objects. The definition of Δ depends on the uncertainty model used for representing o_i and o_j (Sect. 3).

Uncertain distance function for multivariate objects. If $o_i = (R_i, f_i)$, $o_j = (R_j, f_j)$ are multivariate uncertain objects, Δ is defined as:

$$\Delta(o_i, o_j, z) = \int\limits_{\boldsymbol{x} \in R_i} \int\limits_{\boldsymbol{y} \in R_j} I[dist(\boldsymbol{x}, \boldsymbol{y}) = z] \, f_i(\boldsymbol{x}) \, f_j(\boldsymbol{y}) \, \mathrm{d}\boldsymbol{x} \, \mathrm{d}\boldsymbol{y} \tag{1}$$

where $dist(\boldsymbol{x}, \boldsymbol{y})$ is a distance measure between any pair $\boldsymbol{x}, \boldsymbol{y} \in \Re^m$ (e.g., Euclidean distance), and $I[A]$ is the *indicator function*, which is equal to 1 when the event A occurs, 0 otherwise.

Uncertain distance function for univariate objects. If $o_i = ((I_i^{(1)}, f_i^{(1)}), \ldots, (I_i^{(m)}, f_i^{(m)}))$, $o_j = ((I_j^{(1)}, f_j^{(1)}), \ldots, (I_j^{(m)}, f_j^{(m)}))$ are univariate uncertain objects, Δ is defined as:

$$\Delta(o_i, o_j, z) = \int_{x_1 \in \Re} \cdots \int_{x_m \in \Re} I[f_{dist}(x_1, \ldots, x_m) = z] \prod_{h=1}^{m} \Psi^{(h)}(o_i, o_j, x_h) \, dx_1 \cdots dx_m$$

$$(2)$$

where

- $\Psi^{(h)} : D \times D \times \Re \to \Re,$
- $\Psi^{(h)}(o_i, o_j, x_h) = \int_{u \in I_i^{(h)}} \int_{v \in I_j^{(h)}} I[|u - v| = x_h] \, f_i^{(h)}(u) \, f_j^{(h)}(v) \, du \, dv, \quad h \in [1..m],$
- $f_{dist} : \Re^m \to \Re$ is a function that computes a scalar value from the components of a vector $(x_1, \ldots, x_m)$. In this work, this function is defined as $f_{dist} = \sqrt{(1/m) \sum_{h=1}^{m} x_h^2}$.

It can be proved that the condition $\int_{z \in \Re} \Delta(o_i, o_j, z) \, dz = 1$ holds for both the definitions of Δ, for all o_i, o_j in the dataset.

Given an uncertain distance function Δ, we now provide a definition of uncertain distance by extracting a single, well-representative numerical value from Δ.

Definition 4 (uncertain distance). *Given a set of uncertain objects $D = \{o_1, \ldots, o_n\}$, let Δ be the uncertain distance function defined over D. The uncertain distance is a function $\delta : D \times D \to \Re_0^+$, which is defined as:*

$$\delta(o_i, o_j) = \int_{z \in \Re} z \Delta(o_i, o_j, z) \, dz \qquad (3)$$

According to Eq. (3), $\delta(o_i, o_j)$ is the expected value of the uncertain distance function Δ between o_i and o_j. Note that, if o_i, o_j are multivariate uncertain objects, $\delta(o_i, o_j)$ can be directly computed as:

$$\delta(o_i, o_j) = \int_{x \in R_i} \int_{y \in R_j} dist(x, y) \, f_i(x) \, f_j(y) \, dx \, dy \qquad (4)$$

whereas, if o_i, o_j are univariate uncertain objects, $\delta(o_i, o_j)$ can be calculated as:

$$\delta(o_i, o_j) = f_{dist}(\psi^{(1)}(o_i, o_j), \ldots, \psi^{(m)}(o_i, o_j)) \qquad (5)$$

where

$$\psi^{(h)}(o_i, o_j) = \int_{x \in I_i^{(h)}} \int_{y \in I_j^{(h)}} |x - y| \, f_i^{(h)}(x) \, f_j^{(h)}(y) \, dx \, dy, \quad h \in [1..m].$$

4.2   The UK-Medoids Algorithm

In this section we present our K-medoids-based algorithm for clustering uncertain objects, named *UK-medoids*. The outline of UK-medoids is given in Algorithm 1.

Algorithm 1. UK-medoids

Input: a set of uncertain objects $D = \{o_1, \ldots, o_n\}$; the number of output clusters k
Output: a set of clusters $\mathcal{C}$

1. compute distances $\delta(o_i, o_j), \forall o_i, o_j \in D$
2. compute the set $S = \{m_1, \ldots, m_k\}$ of initial medoids
3. **repeat**
4. $S' \leftarrow S$
5. $S \leftarrow \emptyset$
6. $\mathcal{C} = \{C_1, \ldots, C_k\} \leftarrow \{\emptyset, \ldots, \emptyset\}$
7.   **for all** $o \in D$ **do**
8.   {*assign each object to the closest cluster, based on its uncertain distance to cluster medoids*}
9. $m_j \leftarrow \arg\min_{o' \in S'} \delta(o, o')$
10. $C_j \leftarrow C_j \cup \{o\}$
11.   **end for**
12.   **for all** $C \in \mathcal{C}$ **do**
13.   {*recompute the medoid of each cluster*}
14. $m \leftarrow \arg\min_{o \in C} \sum_{o' \in C} \delta(o, o')$
15. $S \leftarrow S \cup \{m\}$
16.   **end for**
17. **until** $S \neq S'$
18. **return** $\mathcal{C}$

The input for the UK-medoids algorithm is a dataset D of n uncertain objects and the number k of clusters to be discovered, and the output is a set $\mathcal{C}$ of k clusters. Initially, all the uncertain distances between any pair of objects $o_i, o_j \in D$ are computed (Line 1). The distances are calculated only once and are used at each iteration of the algorithm. Then, the set of k initial medoids is computed (Line 2). The initial medoids can be selected by means of either random chance or a suitable procedure aimed to choose well-separated medoids (e.g., that proposed for the *Partitioning Around Medoids* (PAM) algorithm [32]).

After the initialization steps, the algorithm performs the main loop (starting from Line 3) which is comprised of two phases. In the first phase (Lines $7 - 11$), each object o in D is assigned to the cluster represented by the medoid m closest to o. In the second phase, the medoids in the set S are recomputed according to the objects assigned to each cluster (Lines $12 - 16$). Such phases are iteratively repeated until a local optimum has not been reached, i.e., there has been some change in the current S w.r.t. the previous iteration (Line 17).

Proposition 1. *Given a dataset D of n uncertain objects, Algorithm 1 works in $\mathcal{O}(n^2 \, I)$, where I is the maximum number of iterations.*

5 Experimental Evaluation

We devised an experimental evaluation aimed to assess the ability of our algorithm in clustering uncertain objects, both in terms of accuracy and efficiency.

Table 1. Datasets used in the experiments

dataset	objects	attributes	classes
Iris	150	4	3
Wine	178	13	3
Glass	214	10	6
Ecoli	327	7	5

We also compared our UK-medoids to K-means-based uncertain data clustering algorithms, i.e., UK-means and its variant CK-means.

5.1 Evaluation Methodology

Datasets. Experimental analysis was performed on benchmark datasets from the UCI Machine Learning Repository.[1] We chose four datasets with numerical real-value attributes, namely Iris, Wine, Glass, and Ecoli.

Table 1 shows the main characteristics of the datasets. Iris contains measurements on different iris plants. Wine reports results of a chemical analysis of Italian wines derived from three different cultivars. In Glass, each glass instance is described by the values of its chemical components. Ecoli contains data on the Escherichia Coli bacterium, which are identified with values coming from different analysis techniques.

All the selected datasets originally contain deterministic values, hence the uncertainty was synthetically generated for each object of any dataset. In case of univariate uncertain objects, we generated the uncertain interval $I^{(h)}$ and the pdf $f^{(h)}$ defined over $I^{(h)}$, for each attribute $a^{(h)}$, with $h \in [1..m]$ of the object o. The interval $I^{(h)}$ was randomly chosen as a subinterval within $[min_{o_h}, max_{o_h}]$, where min_{o_h} (resp. max_{o_h}) is the minimum (resp. maximum) deterministic value of the attribute h, over all the objects belonging to the same ideal class of o. As concerns $f^{(h)}$, we considered two continuous density functions, namely *Uniform* and *Normal* pdfs, and *Binomial* as a discrete mass function. We set the parameters of Normal and Binomial pdfs in such a way that their mode corresponded to the deterministic value of the h-th attribute of the object o.

We performed experiments for multivariate uncertain objects as well. In this case, we generated uncertainty starting from the univariate model, assuming statistical independence for the pdfs of the attributes of any object. Since univariate and multivariate models gave similar results, here we report only results on the univariate models for the sake of brevity.

Clustering validity criteria. To assess the quality of clustering solutions we exploited the availability of reference classifications for the datasets. The objective was to evaluate how well a clustering fits a predefined scheme of known classes (natural clusters). To this purpose, we resorted to the *F-measure* [33], which is one of the most commonly used external validity criteria, and is defined in terms of the Information Retrieval notions' *Precision* and *Recall*.

---

[1] http://archive.ics.uci.edu/ml/

Given a collection D of uncertain objects, let $\Gamma = \{\Gamma_1, \ldots, \Gamma_H\}$ be the reference classification of the objects in D, and $\mathcal{C} = \{C_1, \ldots, C_K\}$ be the output partition yielded by a clustering algorithm. Precision of cluster C_j with respect to class Γ_i is the fraction of the objects in C_j that has been correctly classified:

$$P_{ij} = \frac{|C_j \cap \Gamma_i|}{|C_j|}$$

Recall of cluster C_j with respect to class Γ_i is the fraction of the objects in Γ_i that has been correctly classified:

$$R_{ij} = \frac{|C_j \cap \Gamma_i|}{|\Gamma_i|}$$

Using a macro-averaging strategy on the local values of precision and recall, the overall precision (P) and recall (R) are computed as:

$$P = \frac{1}{H} \sum_{i=1}^{H} \max_{j \in [1..K]} P_{ij}, \qquad R = \frac{1}{H} \sum_{i=1}^{H} \max_{j \in [1..K]} R_{ij},$$

Finally, in order to score the quality of $\mathcal{C}$ w.r.t. Γ by means of a single value, the overall F-measure ($F \in [0,1]$) is computed as the harmonic mean of the overall precision and recall:

$$F = \frac{2PR}{P + R} \tag{6}$$

Settings. In K-means-based approaches, the set of initial centroids is randomly selected. Therefore, to avoid that clustering results were biased by random chance, we averaged accuracy and efficiency measurements over 100 different runs. We made a similar choice also for UK-medoids, since we noted that the use of a refined strategy for selecting initial medoids (e.g., the procedure proposed in [32]) gave no significant improvement w.r.t. random selection.

We computed the integrals involved into the distances calculation by taking into account lists of samples derived from the pdfs. To accomplish this, we employed the classic *Monte Carlo* sampling method.[2] We also performed a preliminary tuning phase to properly set the number of samples S; in particular, for each method and dataset, we chose S in such a way that there was no significant improvement in accuracy for any $S' > S$. In general, the optimal S depended on the width of the uncertainty interval/region; however, according to our experiments, 50 and 400÷500 samples represented a reasonably good choice, for univariate and multivariate uncertainty model, respectively.

5.2 Results

Accuracy. Table 2 summarizes the F-measure results obtained by UK-medoids and the other methods. We can observe that UK-medoids drastically outperformed UK-means and CK-means on all the datasets, with Uniform and Binomial

---

[2] We used the SSJ library, available at http://www.iro.umontreal.ca/~simardr/ssj/

Table 2. Clustering quality results (F-measure)

dataset	pdf	UK-means	CK-means	UK-medoids
Iris	Uniform	0.45	*0.50*	**0.84**
	Normal	0.84	*0.85*	**0.88**
	Binomial	*0.62*	0.58	**0.87**
Wine	Uniform	0.46	*0.50*	**0.80**
	Normal	0.69	*0.70*	**0.70**
	Binomial	*0.63*	0.58	**0.73**
Glass	Uniform	0.26	*0.29*	**0.71**
	Normal	*0.63*	0.59	**0.68**
	Binomial	0.27	*0.29*	**0.67**
Ecoli	Uniform	0.30	*0.33*	**0.73**
	Normal	0.73	*0.74*	**0.77**
	Binomial	*0.50*	0.44	**0.72**

pdfs. In particular, compared to best competing method, the accuracy improvement obtained by our UK-medoids was from 34% to 42% with Uniform pdfs and from 10% to 38% with Binomial pdfs. In case of Normal pdfs, UK-medoids performed 3÷5% better than the other methods on three datasets, whereas all the methods behaved similarly in Wine. The reduction of gap between UK-medoids

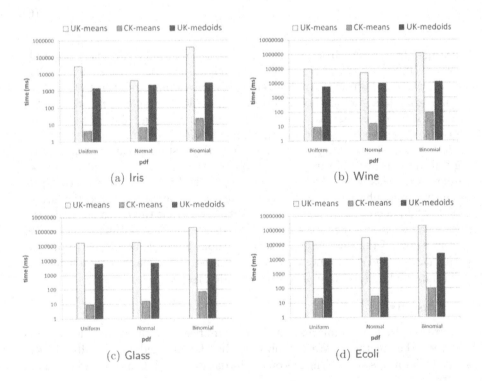

Fig. 1. Clustering time performances

and K-means-based approaches on Normal pdfs can be explained in that, according to our uncertainty generation scheme, the expected value of a Normal pdf associated to any attribute of each uncertain object was set equal to the deterministic value of the attribute for that object. This allowed the centroid generation strategy of UK-means and CK-means to perform well in that case.

It should be also noted that UK-means and CK-means performed similarly for all the pdfs and datasets, as expected, since they employ a similar clustering scheme; the only differences between the two methods are due to random choices, such as selection of initial centroids and pdf sampling for the computation of the integrals.

Efficiency. To evaluate the efficiency of UK-medoids and the competing methods, we measured their time performances in clustering uncertain objects.[3] Figure 1 shows the total execution times (in milliseconds) obtained by the methods on the various datasets. For UK-medoids and CK-means, we calculated the sum of the times obtained for the pre-computing phase (i.e., uncertain distances computation for UK-medoids and cluster centroids computation for CK-means), together with the algorithm runtimes.

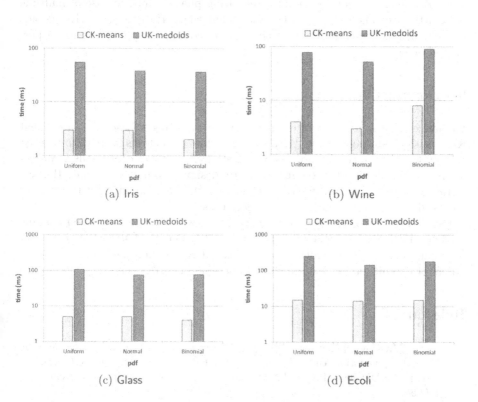

Fig. 2. Performance of the algorithm runtimes (pre-computing phases are ignored)

---

[3] Experiments were conducted on a platform Intel Pentium IV 3GHz with 2GB memory and running Microsoft WinXP Pro.

In the figure, it can be noted that our UK-medoids was $1 \div 2$ orders of magnitude faster than UK-means, which was the slowest method on all datasets. The slowness of UK-means is mainly due to the EDs computation needed for each object in the dataset, at each iteration of the algorithm.

As expected, CK-means outperformed UK-medoids on all datasets, which is explained by a difference between the computational complexities of the two algorithms. Indeed, both the phases of pre-computing and algorithm execution are quadratic (resp. linear) with the number of objects in the dataset for UK-medoids (resp. CK-means). However, it should be emphasized that the CK-means algorithm is less general than the other methods, as it works only if the mean squared error for the definition of the EDs is used and the distance function is based on the Euclidean norm.

We also measured separately the times of the pre-computing phases, which involve the calculation of uncertain distances (in UK-medoids) and cluster centroids (in CK-means). Figure 2 shows that the gap between UK-medoids and CK-means was reduced w.r.t. that measured by including the total runtimes (Figure 1). This result confirms that the major difference between UK-medoids and CK-means is given by the pre-computing phase. Thus, in case of multiple runs of the two algorithms, we can state that the performance of UK-medoids and CK-means are comparable, since the pre-computing phase has to be performed once.

6   Conclusion

We addressed the problem of clustering uncertain objects based on an efficient K-medoids clustering scheme. We provided distance functions for both univariate and multivariate uncertain objects, which are well-suited to continuous as well as discrete pdfs. Moreover, these functions are designed to better estimate the real distance between two uncertain objects since they are not limited to consider only scalar values derived from the object pdfs.

Our UK-medoids has been experimentally shown to outperform other existing methods in terms of accuracy, regardless of the choice of uncertainty density function. Also, from an efficiency viewpoint, UK-medoids performs up to two orders of magnitude faster than the baseline method UK-means.

References

1. Chau, M., Cheng, R., Kao, B., Ng, J.: Uncertain Data Mining: An Example in Clustering Location Data. In: Ng, W.-K., Kitsuregawa, M., Li, J., Chang, K. (eds.) PAKDD 2006. LNCS (LNAI), vol. 3918, pp. 199–204. Springer, Heidelberg (2006)
2. Imielinski, T., Lipski Jr., W.: Incomplete Information in Relational Databases. Journal of the ACM 31(4), 761–791 (1984)
3. Abiteboul, S., Kanellakis, P., Grahne, G.: On the Representation and Querying of Sets of Possible Worlds. In: Proc. SIGMOD Conf., pp. 34–48 (1987)

4. Sadri, F.: Modeling Uncertainty in Databases. In: Proc. ICDE Conf., pp. 122–131 (1991)

5. Lakshmanan, L.V.S., Leone, N., Ross, R.B., Subrahmanian, V.S.: ProbView: A Flexible Probabilistic Database System. ACM TODS 22(3), 419–469 (1997)

6. Dalvi, N.N., Suciu, D.: Efficient Query Evaluation on Probabilistic Databases. In: Proc. VLDB Conf., pp. 864–875 (2004)

7. Green, T., Tannen, V.: Models for Incomplete and Probabilistic Information. IEEE Data Engineering Bulletin 29(1), 17–24 (2006)

8. Aggarwal, C.C.: On Density Based Transforms for Uncertain Data Mining. In: Proc. ICDE Conf., pp. 866–875 (2007)

9. Tao, Y., Xiao, X., Cheng, R.: Range Search on Multidimensional Uncertain Data. TODS 32(3), 15–62 (2007)

10. Galindo, J., Urrutia, A., Piattini, M.: Fuzzy Databases: Modeling, Design, and Implementation. Idea Group Publishing (2006)

11. Lee, S.K.: An Extended Relational Database Model for Uncertain and Imprecise Information. In: Proc. VLDB Conf., pp. 211–220 (1992)

12. Lim, E.-P., Srivastava, J., Shekhar, S.: An Evidential Reasoning Approach to Attribute Value Conflict Resolution in Database Integration. TKDE 8(5), 707–723 (1996)

13. Sarma, A.D., Benjelloun, O., Halevy, A., Widom, J.: Working Models for Uncertain Data. In: Proc. ICDE Conf., pp. 7–18 (2006)

14. Cheng, R., Kalashnikov, D.V., Prabhakar, S.: Evaluating probabilistic queries over imprecise data. In: Proc. SIGMOD Conf., pp. 551–562 (2003)

15. Kriegel, H.-P., Pfeifle, M.: Density-Based Clustering of Uncertain Data. In: Proc. ACM SIGKDD Conf., pp. 672–677 (2005)

16. Cantoni, V., Lombardi, L., Lombardi, P.: Challenges for Data Mining in Distributed Sensor Networks. In: Proc. ICPR Conf., pp. 1000–1007 (2006)

17. Faradjian, A., Gehrke, J., Bonnet, P.: GADT: A Probability Space ADT for Representing and Querying the Physical World. In: Proc. ICDE Conf., pp. 201–211 (2002)

18. Deshpande, A., Guestrin, C., Madden, S., Hellerstein, J.M., Hong, W.: Model-based approximate querying in sensor networks. VLDB Journal 14(4), 417–443 (2005)

19. Li, Y., Han, J., Yang, J.: Clustering Moving Objects. In: Proc. ACM SIGKDD Conf., pp. 617–622 (2004)

20. Aggarwal, C.C., Yu, P.S.: A Survey of Uncertain Data Algorithms and Applications. Technical Report RC24394, IBM Research Division, Thomas J. Watson Research Center (October 2007)

21. Jain, A.K., Dubes, R.C.: Algorithms for Clustering Data. Prentice-Hall, Englewood Cliffs (1988)

22. MacQueen, J.B.: Some methods for classification and analysis of multivariate observations. In: Proc. Berkeley Symposium on Mathematical Statistics and Probability, pp. 281–297 (1967)

23. Kaufman, L., Rousseeuw, P.J.: Finding Groups in Data: An Introduction to Cluster Analysis. Wiley, Chichester (1990)

24. Bi, J., Zhang, T.: Support Vector Classification with Input Data Uncertainty. In: Proc. NIPS Conf., pp. 483–493 (2004)

25. Aggarwal, C.C., Yu, P.S.: Outlier Detection with Uncertain Data. In: Proc. SDM Conf., pp. 483–493 (2008)

26. Chui, C.K., Kao, B., Hung, E.: Mining Frequent Itemsets from Uncertain Data. In: Zhou, Z.-H., Li, H., Yang, Q. (eds.) PAKDD 2007. LNCS (LNAI), vol. 4426, pp. 47–58. Springer, Heidelberg (2007)
27. Kriegel, H.-P., Pfeifle, M.: Hierarchical Density-Based Clustering of Uncertain Data. In: Proc. ICDM Conf., pp. 689–692 (2005)
28. Ngai, W.K., Kao, B., Chui, C.K., Cheng, R., Chau, M., Yip, K.Y.: Efficient Clustering of Uncertain Data. In: Proc. ICDM Conf., pp. 436–445 (2006)
29. Lee, S.D., Kao, B., Cheng, R.: Reducing UK-means to K-means. In: Proc. ICDM Workshops, pp. 483–488 (2007)
30. Ester, M., Kriegel, H.-P., Sander, J., Xu, X.: A Density-Based Algorithm for Discovering Clusters in Large Spatial Databases with Noise. In: Proc. ACM SIGKDD Conf., pp. 226–231 (1996)
31. Ankerst, M., Breunig, M.M., Kriegel, H.-P., Sander, J.: OPTICS: Ordering Points To Identify the Clustering Structure. In: Proc. SIGMOD Conf., pp. 49–60 (1999)
32. Kaufmann, L., Rousseeuw, P.J.: Clustering by means of medoids. In: Proc. Statistical Data Analysis based on the L_1 Norm Conf., pp. 405–416 (1987)
33. van Rijsbergen, C.J.: Information Retrieval. Butterworths (1979)

Speeding Up the NRA Algorithm

Peter Gurský[1] and Peter Vojtáš[2]

[1] University of P.J. Šafárik, Košice, Slovakia
[2] Charles University, Prague, Czech Republic
peter.gursky@upjs.sk, peter.vojtas@mff.cuni.cz

Abstract. Methods of top-k search with no random access can be used to find k best objects using sorted access to the sources of attribute values. In this paper we present new heuristics over the *NRA* algorithm that can be used for fast search of top-k objects using wide range of user preferences. *NRA* algorithm usually needs a periodical scan of a large number of candidates during the computation. In this paper we propose methods of no random access top-k search that optimize the candidate list maintenance during the computation to speed up the search. The proposed methods are compared to a table scan method typically used in databases. We present results of experiments showing speed improvement depending on number of object attributes expressed in a user preferences or selectivity of user preferences.

Keywords: top-k search, no random access, *TA*-sorted variants, user preferences.

1 Introduction

Top-k search became popular with growing use of the web services and increasing datasets sizes. Users are usually interested in few best objects rather than a big list of objects as a result. Top-k algorithms usually follow two main goals. Firstly, they minimize the number of source data to be processed i.e. they find the correct top-k objects using only a part of data. Secondly, the algorithms tend to minimize the number of accesses to the sources and the computation time as well.

1.1 Motivation

In the family of Threshold algorithms (*TA*) the basic assumption is a monotone combination function over ordered sources. The expressivity of a monotone combination function over domain ordering is low. Many authors [22,23] face the problem of more expressive queries by complicate analysis of ranking functions and they offer a kind of multidimensional search.

Example 1. Imagine a user u_1 looking for a low price flat with size about $60m^2$. His overall ranking function F can be expressed as follows:

$$F_{u_1}(price, size) = (1 - \frac{price}{max_{price}}) \cdot max\{0, (1 - |1 - \frac{size}{60}|)\} \qquad (1)$$

S. Greco and T. Lukasiewicz (Eds.): SUM 2008, LNAI 5291, pp. 243–255, 2008.
© Springer-Verlag Berlin Heidelberg 2008

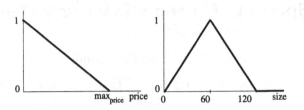

Fig. 1. Local preferences of user u_1

We can see that F_{u_1} is not a monotone function and *TA* cannot to be used ad-hoc.

Instead of a difficult function analysis we prefer a different form of query compound of local preferences and a monotone combination function. Local preference represents user's notion about the suitability of values from the attribute domain. Local preference can be expressed e.g. by fuzzy predicate that maps attribute domain into the interval $[0, 1]$, where 1 means the most preferred domain value and 0 means the least preferable value.

The monotone combination function is used to compare objects incomparable in particular local preferences (one flat can be better in price, another one in size). Typical monotone combination functions are weighted average, minimum, maximum or a set of ranking rules [10].

The ranking function F_{u_1} of user u_1 can be written as a monotone combination (product) of partially linear scoring functions f_p and f_s as depicted on Figure 1.

Formally the preferences of user u for a set of objects with m attributes $a_1, \ldots, a_m$ are described by m arbitrary scoring functions of one variable $f_{a_1}, \ldots, f_{a_m}$ (local preferences) and one monotone combination function F (global preferences). For every object X with attribute values $x_1, \ldots, x_m$ the preference of user u for object X is equal to $F(f_{a_1}(x_1), \ldots, f_{a_m}(x_m))$.

In the naïve approach, we could sort both attributes according to local preferences and use any effective *TA*-like algorithm to find top-k flats. Unfortunately, the meaning of good values of attributes (specified by local preferences), as well as the combination function, can be different for each user.

Example 2. Consider a user u_2 with preferences for rather large flats but mainly the flats with the price about $50k:

$$F_{u_2}(price, size) = 3 \cdot f_{p_2}(price) + f_{s_2}(size), \text{where}$$
$$f_{p_2}(price) = \begin{cases} \frac{price}{10k} - 4 & , price \in \langle 40k, 50k \rangle \\ 6 - \frac{price}{10k} & , price \in (50k, 60k) \\ 0 & , \text{otherwise} \end{cases} \tag{2}$$
$$f_{s_2}(size) = \frac{size}{max_{size}}$$

We can see that the local preferences induce different ordering of the attributes than functions on figure 1. Now the naïve approach fails - reordering in the time of the query is unacceptable.

In this paper we present the heuristics for *3P-NRA* algorithm, which is similar to *NRA* algorithm - a member of the Threshold algorithms. We use the *NRA*-like algorithms because they work with data obtained by sorted access from the sources ordered from the best to the worst in particular attributes and as presented in [10] sorted access can be simulated using an index structure depending on an attribute type. For an ordinal attribute a B+ tree traversed according to user local preference can be used. In example 2 the price tree is traversed from maximal value in descending order using leaf pointers. In the size tree we have to create two pointers, both starting at $60m^2$. First pointer traverses the tree in descending direction and the second one in ascending direction. For a simulation we need to identify local maxima, then the scoring function is used as a black box. Having simple functions (partially linear) we can easily find points of extremes to identify the pointers and directions. Arbitrary functions expressing local preferences would need function analysis. This analysis is much more simple than in case of multidimensional analysis used in [22]. Besides ordinal and nominal attributes presented in [10] we can simulate sorted access over metric and hierarchical attributes, too (not published yet).All simulation algorithms have their speed close to a simple scan of tables sorted in.

In order to enable different users to express top-k queries we designed an intuitive user friendly interface. As an alternative to complicated input users can also use an inductive procedure. Our system was integrated in the *UPRE* system [9]. In *UPRE*, user can define his/her preference by ordering or evaluating a sample of objects. The system creates input for top-k search based on user's evaluation in a two step learning process. First, local fuzzy preference functions have to be induced for each attribute. Second, using these functions, the monotone combination function in the form of fuzzy rules is learned by an inductive logic programming method *IGAP* described in [12]. Alternatively we can use the SVM based system [21].

1.2 Contribution

Having simulations of sorted access it is natural to find top-k objects using the *NRA* algorithm requiring sorted access and monotone combination function only. The original *NRA* algorithm is rather slow because of inefficient management of candidates during the computation. In this paper we present several variants of *NRA* algorithm that speed up the computation of top-k objects.

• Our first contribution includes new heuristics in *3P-NRA* algorithm (an extension of *NRA* algorithm) named 3P-NRAz and 3P-NRA2z that make the computation fast and more stable than the previous approaches.

• The second contribution is the execution of experiments in different directions. We compared time efficiency of a table scan over joined data to several variants of our *3P-NRA* algorithm with data in one index per attribute architecture. We describe common situations in which our approach is better than simple table scan. In section 3 we also show that the *3P-NRA* algorithm with heuristics outperforms the previous *NRA* algorithm significantly.

2   3P-NRA Algorithm

In this section we present the modification of *NRA* algorithm [6] named *3P-NRA*
(3-phased no random access) proved to be better than *NRA* in several aspects.
The presentation of *3P-NRA* algorithm without the support of local preferences
is accepted for ADBIS conference [8].

In the rest of this paper we use the following notation. Value m represents the
number of attributes of objects or the number of sources. An arbitrary object is
denoted as $X = (x_1, \ldots, x_m)$, where $x_1, \ldots, x_m$ are real attribute values of X.
$f_1, \ldots, f_m$ are arbitrary scoring functions of one variable that represent local preferences to attribute values. For each $i \in \{1, \ldots, m\}$, $f_i(x_i)$ represents a user preference to the real value of the i-th attribute of X. Let $V(X) = \{i_1, \ldots, i_n\} \in
\{1, \ldots, m\}$ be a subset of known attributes $x_{i_1}, \ldots, x_{i_n}$ of X, we define $W_V(X)$ (or
shortly $W(X)$ if V is known from context) to be minimal (worst) possible value
of the combination function F for the object X. We assume that F is a monotone
combination function. We compute $W_V(X)$ so that we substitute each missing attribute by the minimum of appropriate scoring function. For example if $V(X) =
\{1, \ldots, g\}$ then $W_V(X) = F(f_1(x_1), \ldots, f_g(x_g), min(f_{g+1}), \ldots, min(f_m))$.

Analogously we define maximal (best) possible value of the combination function F for object X as $B_V(X)$ (or shortly $B(X)$ if V is known from context). Since
we know that sorted access returns values in descending order, we can substitute
each missing value by the corresponding value from the vector $u = (u_1, \ldots, u_m)$,
where $u_1, \ldots, u_m$ are the last scoring values seen from each source. For example
if $V(X) = 1, \ldots, g$ then $B_V(X) = F(f_1(x_1), \ldots, f_g(x_g), u_{g+1}, \ldots, u_m)$.

The real value of the object X is $W(X) \leq F(f_1(x_1), \ldots, f_m(x_m)) \leq B(X)$.
Note that during the computation unseen objects (no values are known) have
$B(X) = F(u_1, \ldots, u_m)$. The value $\tau = F(u_1, \ldots, u_m)$ is known as the threshold
value.

In the algorithm we use the top-k list T ordered by the worst value. The
object in T with the smallest worst value is labeled T_k. In the (unordered) set
C we store the candidates with the worst value smaller or equal to $W(T_k)$ but
with the best value larger than $W(T_k)$. These are the objects with a chance to
get into T later. We call the objects in C candidates.

In *3P-NRA* we implemented C as a hash table with object identifiers as a key.
To recognize the sources with all known values among the objects in $T \cup C$ we
maintain the number of missing values for each source.

3P-NRA algorithm works as follows:

```
Input: k, F, m sources
Output: k ranked objects if exist
T = ∅ , C = ∅
```

Phase 1:
```
Do the sorted access in parallel to all sources.
For every object X seen under sorted access compute W(X) and do
    If |T| < k then put X to T
```

```
Else If W(X) > W(T_k) then
        If X ∉ T move T_k to C, put X to T
     Else put X to C
If W(T_k) ≥ threshold τ goto Phase 2
repeat Phase 1
```

Phase 2:
Do the sorted access in parallel to the sources for which there
are unknown values for objects in C and T.
For every object X seen under sorted access do
```
     If X ∉ T ∪ C ignore it
     Else If B(X) ≤ W(T_k) remove X from C
        If |C| = 0 return T and exit
        If W(X) > W(T_k) and X ∉ T move T_k to C, put X to T
If (W(T_k) increased) OR (threshold τ decreased) then
     heuristic H can choose to go to Phase 3
repeat Phase 2
```

Phase 3:
For every object $X \in C$ compute $B(X)$;
If X is no more relevant (i.e. $B(X) \leq W(T_k)$) remove X from C
If $|C| = 0$ return T and exit; otherwise goto Phase 2.

Phase 1 works similarly to the standard *NRA* algorithm with the exception of
the threshold test and the absence of candidate set search. The heuristic H in
3P-NRA algorithm can be used to skip an expensive computation of phase 3. On
the other hand, if H always chooses to do the phase 3 the *3P-NRA* algorithm is
proved to be instance optimal. The instance optimality of *NRA* means, that if
NRA finds top k objects using y sorted accesses, then there are no algorithms
reading the sources only by sorted access, that can find top k objects using less
than $\frac{y}{m}$ sorted accesses (see [6]).

Theorem 1. *Let F to be a monotone combination function, then algorithm* 3P-
NRA *correctly finds top-k objects.*

Theorem 2. *Let F be a monotone combination function. If heuristic H always chooses to go to phase 3, then algorithm* 3P-NRA *makes at most the same
number of sorted accesses as* NRA *algorithm i.e.* 3P-NRA *algorithm is instance
optimal.*

Proofs excluding the local preferences of can be found in [8]. The improvements
of the *3P-NRA* algorithm in contrast to *NRA* [6] are the following:

- New objects are considered in phase 1 only. Other objects are ignored. This
  is the most significant difference between *3P-NRA* and *NRA*.
- Many computations of the best values are omitted. This feature allows the
  speedup of the computation especially for large number of candidates.
- After acquisition of all unknown values of any attribute among objects in
  $T \cup C$ the algorithm stops working with the corresponding source (no more

sorted accesses to the source will be done). This feature decreases the number of disk accesses significantly.

– A good choice of heuristic H can yield a massive speedup of the algorithm, however it can slightly increase the number of disk accesses according to H.

In [8] we discussed also the modification of 3P-NRA algorithm for the cases when the candidate set C do not fit into the available memory. The proposed modification allows efficient computation of top-k objects with less than $1/100$ of candidates in memory.

2.1 Heuristics

Two the most expensive points of instance optimal *3P-NRA* algorithm are partial join of data form the sources and the computation of the best values in the candidate set C. All heuristics presented in this section follow the idea of decreasing the number of expensive best values computation in phase 3. Nevertheless, we need to do this computation occasionally to prevent the processing of all input data.

The first approach to decrease the number of computations of the best values in phase 3 is to use the heuristic H mentioned in phase 2. In our tests in section 3 we use the heuristic that goes to phase 3 only each 1000th loop of phase 2. A number 1000 is an approximated number of sorted accesses to the sources that is done by reading one disk page per attribute when user preferences cover 5 attributes of the objects. Thus we can be near the optimal number of disk accesses. In the tests we show orders of magnitude speedup against algorithms without the heuristic. This heuristic was used in [8] too. We will call the algorithm having this heuristic *3P-NRA2*.

Our new heuristic of decreasing the number of computations of the best values modifies the phase 3 as follows:

Phase 3:
```
Iterate over objects X ∈ C and compute B(X)
  If X is relevant (i.e. B(X) > W(Tₖ))
    break the cycle and goto Phase 2
  Else Remove X from C
      numberOfRemoved++
  If |C| = 0 return T and exit;
  If numberOfRemoved ≥ 100
    Create new set CNew
    For every object X ∈ C compute B(X)
      If X is relevant, copy X to CNew
    If |CNew| = 0 return T and exit;
    Free memory used by C, set C = CNew
    Set numberOfRemoved = 0 and goto Phase 2;
```

The main idea behind this heuristic is to skip the computation of the best values when there are still many relevant candidates. By iteration through random elements of set C there is a high probability that after erasing of 100 not relevant

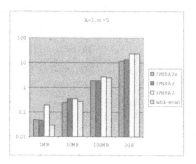
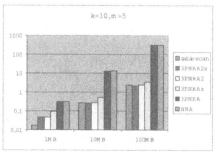

Fig. 2. Computation time in seconds over different size of datasets

objects the candidate set C will have less than 1% of relevant objects. It is more effective to create a new small set rather than deletion of 99% objects from C. We will call this algorithm *3P-NRAz*. Note that the algorithm having this modification of phase 3 is correct and instance optimal. Both the correctness and the instance optimality come from the fact that every time the previous version of phase 3 returns list T, so does the new version.

We have also the possibility of combination of proposed heuristics. The result of the combination is the algorithm called *3P-NRA2z*. This new algorithm is the best in our tests especially for bigger data sizes and restrictive local preferences.

3   Experiments

This section reports the experiments with algorithms using only sorted access over artificial data. The experiments were conducted on a PC having Intel Core 2 1,86 GHz CPU and 2 GB RAM running on Windows XP. We minimized the number of other processes during the tests to keep a stable test environment. Algorithms are implemented in Java. The size of the disk pages was set to 4 kB. All table scan computations were tested using InnoDB table organized as a heap file with no index support in MySQL 6 database.

In the first experiment we compare the mentioned algorithms over different size of datasets: 1 MB (10k objects), 10 MB (100k objects), 100 MB (1M objects) and 1GB (10M objects). Each dataset consists of 5 attributes $x_1, \ldots, x_5$. Each attribute has values in range $[0, 1]$ and Gaussian distribution (the most difficult distribution for *TA*-like algorithms). Tests were computed with 5 different combination functions $F(X) = \sum_{i=1}^{5} a_i \cdot x_i$ where a_i were randomly generated from interval $\langle 1, 5 \rangle$. Results presented on figure 2 are average times of all the tests. *NRA* and *3P-NRA* algorithms without any heuristic are significantly worse than the algorithms with heuristics. For example the computation of top-10 objects over 100MB dataset with *NRA* algorithm took 308 seconds. The same result was computed in 2 seconds using the fastest *3P-NRA2z* algorithm. Table scan took 2,5 seconds. Because of the low performance of the original *NRA* algorithm and instance optimal *3P-NRA* algorithm we do not compare them in all our tests. The

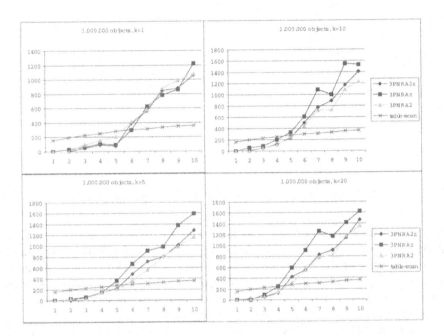

Fig. 3. Computation time in ms over different number of attributes in user preferences

graph on the left shows the computation time needed to search the best object from the datasets. The proposed methods become more effective in comparison to table scan with the growing data size. For example the table scan over 1GB dataset takes more than 23 seconds while the *3P-NRA2z* algorithm needs 11,5 seconds. We have to admit that with the growing k the computation times become longer than table scan times e.g. when $k = 20$ the *3P-NRA2z* algorithm needs 42 seconds to present the results, whilst the table scan time remains 23 seconds.

Our second experiment was motivated by our experiences in project NAZOU (see http://nazou.fiit.stuba.sk). In NAZOU, our target domain are job offers. We identified more than 15 attributes of job offers. Users usually express their preferences by a small subset of attributes (2 to 5). In this experiment we used 10 randomly generated attributes with uniform distribution of values having 1 million tuples (100MB). The base combination function used in this experiment was $F(X) = 3x_1 + 2x_2 + x_3 + 2x_4 + 2x_5 + 3x_6 + 2x_7 + x_8 + 2x_9 + 2x_{10}$. In each run of the test we have a different number of the attributes. The test with m attributes uses the first m elements of the combination function. From the results presented on Figure 3 we can conclude that our methods of top-k search become efficient when user preferences covers up to 5 attributes. These advantages of top-k search grow with the number of stored attributes. For example cars, notebooks or mobile phones are domains with more than 25 attributes.

In NAZOU we also face the problem of one object having more than one value of an attribute e.g. required education level of a job offer can be expressed as "bachelor or master degree". When computing the overall value of an object

Table 1. Computation time in ms over data with 2 attribute values per object over 100.000 objects

k	1	5	10	20
3PNRA2z	157	203	218	250
3PNRAz	234	297	422	484
3PNRA2	141	188	203	235
3PNRA	3782	4484	9031	10890
NRA	3766	4500	9078	10875
table-scan	5890	5890	5890	5890

we use the fuzzy value of more preferred attribute value. For example in this attribute the mentioned job offer would suit a young man who has just ended the bachelor studies. In this experiment each source has 2 values of attribute per object. By joining the data from 5 sources holding 50k objects (100k values per source), we got 1.6M tuples. Results in table 1 show the significant difference between table scan of joined data and our methods. Even low effective algorithms *NRA* and *3P-NRA* are faster than table scan when searching the best object only.

Another significant property that influences the computation time of top-*k* search is the selectivity of user local preferences i.e. the number of values having minimal fuzzy value equal to zero. The situation with many zeros is typical also when the attribute values are unknown. In this case they can be marked as not preferred values (we need some value to compute the overall value of the objects). Unknown values are typical for web extracted data.

Domain values having minimal fuzzy value do not need to be processed from the sources. After reaching the first object with the minimal fuzzy value, the unknown values of this attribute can be substituted by the minimal fuzzy value in all objects not seen in the given attribute. In Figure 4 there are the results of

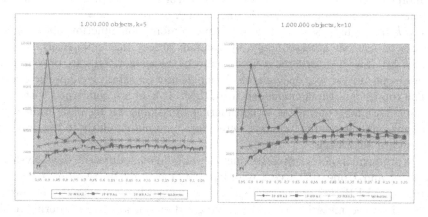

Fig. 4. Computation time in ms over different selectivity of local preferences. X-axis represents the number of objects that have fuzzy value zero (in %).

tests with 5 attributes over sources with uniform distribution. The combination function in this experiment was $F(X) = 3f_1(x_1) + 2f_2(x_2) + f_3(x_3) + 2f_4(x_4) + 2f_5(x_5)$ where $f_i = max\{0, \frac{100 \cdot x_i - d}{100 - d}\}$, and d have values $0.05, \ldots, 0.95$. It is not surprising that for high selective local preferences the top-k search is better than table scan. Results show an interesting behavior of *3P-NRA2* algorithm for high selective queries. We have analyzed it and found out that after a short phase 1 there was a long and expensive computation of phases 2 and 3 with the candidate set of high cardinality. Even if the number of computations of phase 3 has decreased 1000 times compared to *NRA* algorithm, the number of best value evaluations is still high. The new heuristic with restrictive phase 3 is very stable and resistant against long-term large candidate set.

All tests indicate the situations in which the *3P-NRA* style of computation is suitable. All the mentioned situations are typical for the advanced web based search applications that allow complicate user preferences. Users are usually interested in a few best objects only and express their preferences with a small part of attributes. Local preferences are often restrictive (they prefer specific job positions or they want to find houses in a small region). Data sets of objects grow every day. Objects can have more values of one attribute and many attribute values are unknown.

The original *TA*-like algorithms were developed to aggregate the data from the distributed sources having the form of web services. If we combine all the features of data and queries, the use of *3P-NRA* algorithm with heuristics becomes profitable even for local repositories.

4   Related Work

In our approach we face the problem of complex queries by simulation of sorted access over various attribute types. The simulation is directed by an arbitrary local preference function. The combination of arbitrary local preference functions and monotone combination function has a high expressive power.

Top-k query processing using monotone combination function and ordered sources or sources accessed only by random access was extensively studied [1,2,3,6,11]. If we have ordered sources, many of these algorithms are proven to be instance optimal for the top-k search of a single user (constant local preferences).

The top-k algorithms embedded in RDBMS [14,15] are concerned with augmenting the query optimizer to considering rank-joins during plan evaluation. The rank-join algorithms require ordered data on input similarly to the previous middleware algorithms.

The problem of more expressive queries was studied in different ways. Systems MPro [5] and Upper [4] access unordered sources only by random access. In system PREFER [13] the sorted access is provided by choosing one of several prepared ranked materialized views having ordering near to the ordering made by ranked query.

Zhang et al in [23] present the OPT* algorithm combining discrete selection condition and continuous optimization over arbitrary ranking function to find the first best object. Xin et al [22] analyze the ranking function of many variables similarly to [23] to navigate through the huge set of states over m B+ trees. If we can analyze the ranking function over any domain subregion (to find the minimum and possibly recognize monotonicity) this approach should be able to find top-k objects in an effective way. Authors in [22] made many tests and compared their approaches to the table scan as we did. Nevertheless it is difficult to compare our results with theirs because of questionable results of their tests. For example the table scan over 1M tuples having 3 attributes took over 30 seconds in their tests. Our results of the table scan over 1M tuples with 5 attributes shows times from 2 to 3 seconds on a common workstation machine.

Another possible view of recent research distinguishes two branches. One branch of research generalizes types of data to uncertain (see e.g. [19,18]) or to XML data (see e.g. [20]). The other branch focuses on top-k query optimization.

5 Discussion

In this paper we have studied methods of top-k search with no random access which can be used to find k best objects using sources that can be read only by sorted access. Such methods usually need to work with a huge set of candidates during the computation and management of candidates is an important issue.

We have introduced new methods for top-k search with sorted access and implementation of own experimental environment. New versions of *3P-NRA* algorithm were tested with different heuristics that improve the computational time.

We can say that it is suitable to use our methods of top-k search for systems allowing various user preferences. Our motivation comes from querying a big repository with data extracted and/or retrieved from the web relevant to job search. Such data typically contain several dozens of different attributes and single user query typically uses a constant fraction of them, nevertheless all of them are used by some user. System shows better performance if objects have more values of the same attribute. Top-k search with the proposed algorithms should be preferred when the specified local preferences are restrictive.

Moreover the combination of the methods presented in this paper together with the sorted access simulation algorithms over ordinal, nominal, hierarchical and metric attributes becomes a powerful tool for top-k search with a high expressive power [10].

Our system uses a light weight proprietary disk data structures used to simulate the sorted access. This serves only to top-k search, we do not need the full functionality of a transactional multiuser RDBMS.

In the project NAZOU (see http://nazou.fiit.stuba.sk), we use the sorted access to process the output from different methods, which produce data with respect to user preferences to attribute values. There are different methods over various index structures for different types of attributes: ordinal, nominal, hierarchical and metric attributes. To obtain the combination function for different users, our system uses learning user preferences from a sample of objects (see

[12]) or a recommendation for a similar user based on it. The learned preferences have a form of monotone fuzzy rules (instead of the analytical form).

Considering that users are interested only in a part of the attributes and that attribute domains can be complex structures, the new methods of top-k search become very useful.

References

1. Akbarinia, R., Pacitti, E., Valduriez, P.: Best Position Algorithms for Top-k Queries. In: VLDB (2007)
2. Bast, H., Majumdar, D., Schenkel, R., Theobald, M., Weikum, G.: IO-Top-k: Index-Access Optimized Top-k Query Processing. In: VLDB (2006)
3. Balke, W., Güntzer, U.: Multi-objective Query Processing for Database Systems. In: VLDB (2004)
4. Bruno, N., Gravano, L., Marian, A.: Evaluating top-k queries over web-accessible databases. In: ICDE (2002)
5. Chang, K.C.C., Hwang, S.W.: Minimal probing: Supporting expensive predicates for top-k queries. In: SIGMOD (2002)
6. Fagin, R., Lotem, A., Naor, M.: Optimal Aggregation Algorithms for Middleware. In: ACM PODS (2001)
7. Gurský, P., Lencses, R., Vojtáš, P.: Algorithms for user dependent integration of ranked distributed information. In: Böhlen, M.H., Gamper, J., Polasek, W., Wimmer, M.A. (eds.) TCGOV 2005. LNCS (LNAI), vol. 3416. Springer, Heidelberg (2005)
8. Gurský, V., Vojtáš, P.: On top-k search with no random access using small memory. In: ADBIS (accepted, 2008), http://klud.ics.upjs.sk/~gursky/papers/2008adbis.pdf
9. Gurský, P., Horváth, T., Novotný, R., Vaneková, V., Vojtáš, P.: UPRE: User preference based search system. In: IEEE/WIC/ACM Web Inteligence (2006)
10. Gurský, P., Vaneková, V., Pribolová, J.: Fuzzy User Preference Model for Top-k Search. In: Zurada, J.M., Yen, G.G., Wang, J. (eds.) Computational Intelligence: Research Frontiers. LNCS, vol. 5050. Springer, Heidelberg (2008)
11. Güntzer, U., Balke, W., Kiessling, W.: Towards efficient multi-feature queries in heterogeneous enviroments. In: ITCC (2001)
12. Horváth, T., Vojtáš, P.: Ordinal Classification with Monotonicity Constraints. In: Perner, P. (ed.) ICDM 2006. LNCS (LNAI), vol. 4065. Springer, Heidelberg (2006)
13. Hristidis, V., Papakonstantinou, Y.: Algorithms and Applications for answering Ranked Queries using Ranked Views. VLDB Journal 13(1) (2004)
14. Ilyas, I., Aref, W., Elmagarmid, A.: Supporting top-k join queries in relational database. In: VLDB (2003)
15. Ilyas, I., Shah, R., Aref, W.G., Vitter, J.S., Elmagarmid, A.K.: Rank-aware query optimization. In: SIGMOD (2004)
16. Li, C., Chang, K., Ilyas, I., Song, S.: RankSQL: Query algebra and optimization for relational top-k queries. In: SIGMOD (2005)
17. Ramakrishnan, R., Gherke, J.: Database management systems, 3rd edn. McGraw-Hill, New York (2003)
18. Soliman, M.A., Ilyas, I.F., Chang, K.C.C.: Top-k Query Processing in Uncertain Databases. In: Proc. ICDE (2007)

19. Re, Ch., Dalvi, N.N., Suciu, D.: Efficient Top-k Query Evaluation on Probabilistic Data. In: Proc. ICDE (2007)
20. Theobald, M., Schenkel, R., Weikum, G.: An Efficient and Versatile Query Engine for TopX Search. In: VLDB (2005)
21. Yu, H., Hwang, S., Chang, K.: Enabling Soft Queries for Data Retrieval. Information Systems. Elsevier, Amsterdam (2007)
22. Xin, D., Han, J., Chang, K.: Progressive and Selective Merge: Computing Top-K with Ad-Hoc Ranking Functions. In: SIGMOD (2007)
23. Zhang, Z., Hwang, S., Chang, K., Wang, M., Lang, C., Chang, Y.: Boolean + Ranking: Querying a Database by K-Constrained Optimization. In: SIGMOD (2006)

Uncertain Context Modeling of Dimensional Ontology Using Fuzzy Subset Theory

Ying Jiang and Hui Dong

School of Information Management, Wuhan University,
Wuhan 430072, P.R. China
jpz6311whu@gmail.com, lhjdh@126.com

Abstract. Context-sensitive knowledge is widespread in Semantic Web, but traditional RDF triples lack references to situations, points in time, or generally contexts. In order to resolve this problem, Dimensional Ontology (DO) theory is put forward, which features dimensional relations, dimensional operators as well as reasoning mechanism for context-sensitive knowledge. The notion of context in DO is actuarially a vector of dimensions, which are crisp sets representing certain contextual aspects. We propose an approach of modeling uncertain contexts of DO through fuzzy subsets instead of crisp ones. In this way, DO provides the ability of representing fuzzy triples in uncertain contexts. Apart from describing uncertain context model of DO, we discuss how dimensional operators and reasoning mechanism can be applied to uncertain contexts to allow more complex manipulations.

Keywords: Uncertain Context, Dimensional Ontology, Fuzzy Subset Theory.

1 Introduction

Context-sensitive knowledge is widespread in Semantic Web, such as temporary evolution, spatial situation, trust and provenance. Dimensional Ontology (DO) theory [1] provides the abilities of representing contexts and applying them to traditional RDF tripes [2]. For example, the RDF triple ⟨eg:Jim, eg:hasHeight, 1.80⟩ needs a specified time point denoting the context, because the height of a person usually upgrades with the evolution of time. What's more, 1.80 is only for measurement in meters, while 180 is for centimeters. Suppose the time point granular is year, we can construct a dimensional statement (see Definition 12) $\rho_1 = (\langle eg{:}Jim, eg{:}hasHeight, 1.80\rangle, \{d_{Y2004}, d_{meter}\})$ to represent "Jim was 1.80 meters tall in the year of 2004". In DO, the notion of context is represented by mathematical sets. d_{Y2004} is a temporal set, which can further perform set operations like $d_{Y2004} \cup d_{Y2005}$. Suppose $\rho_2 = (\langle eg{:}Jim, eg{:}hasHeight, 1.80\rangle, \{d_{Y2004} \cup d_{Y2005}, d_{meter}\})$, which means "Jim was 1.80 meters tall both in the year of 2004 and 2005", it's obvious that ρ_1 can be inferred by ρ_2 because of the subset relation of temporal context.

Besides crisp ones, there're fuzzy triples in Semantic Web as well. For example, the RDF triple ⟨eg:Jim, eg:hasHeight, eg:TALL⟩ is a vague qualitative

S. Greco and T. Lukasiewicz (Eds.): SUM 2008, LNAI 5291, pp. 256–269, 2008.
© Springer-Verlag Berlin Heidelberg 2008

statement of a person's tallness. It also requires the context of time, which is not a precise time point but a fuzzy time period. Because we can not tell exactly the time period when Jim is tall or not. For a specified time point, the degree of tallness should be modeled to represent to what extent Jim is tall. In a word, context-sensitive fuzzy triples in Semantic Web request uncertain context modeling mechanism, which is the main motivation of this paper.

We propose to extend DO theory with fuzzy logic for uncertain context modeling. The approach is to substitute fuzzy subsets for crisp ones when the context is uncertain. For example, if Jim grew up rapidly and linearly in the year of 2004, we can replace crisp set of d_{Y2004} with, e.g. trapezoidal fuzzy subset. This kind of extension of DO is smooth because fuzzy logic does not dramatically overthrow traditional crisp set theory. Another reason why this approach is applicable is that DO accommodates different types of contexts, which are semantically decoupled (see Definition 1). It means crisp contexts and fuzzy ones can cooperate well without interfering with each other in the extended version of DO.

The remainder of this paper is organized as follows. Sect. 2 discusses the related work. Sect. 3 presents a brief description of partial the DO theory; Sect. 4 illustrates how to model uncertain context of DO, followed by the description of corresponding fuzzy operations and reasoning mechanism; and finally the conclusion is drawn in Sect. 5.

2   Related Work

Uncertain context has been drawing much attention from researchers in the ubiquitous and pervasive computing domain, real time systems or mobile computing. In the novel scenario of the Semantic Web, context representation has been a hot topic as well [6]. As for uncertain context modeling related to Semantic Web or ontology, some researchers have proposed a few approaches, among which the following 4 are typical representatives.

In the paper [7] and [8] , an approach is proposed to support fuzzy, similarity-based matchmaking between real-world situation parameters and predefined semantic situation descriptions by incorporating semantic context information on a conceptual level into common symbolic Semantic Web descriptions utilizing a novel metamodel of Conceptual Situation Spaces (CSS). Based on Conceptual Spaces [9], CSS adopts quality dimensions to describe entities at the conceptual level in terms of their natural characteristics. Note that dimensions and dimension types in DO are towards representing (fuzzy) contexts of assertions/statements of RDF triples, while quality dimensions are entity-oriented or concept-oriented. Another difference is that CSS is for fuzzy context matchmaking, but the goal of DO is (uncertain) context modeling and reasoning.

The project of VICODI [10] develops an ontology of European history used for semantical indexing of historical documents. It presents a fuzzy interval-based temporal model capable of representing imprecise historical temporal knowledge. The ontology model is constructed by KOAN [11] based on HiLog semantics [12], while there's another fuzzy temporal model independent of the ontology model.

These two heterogeneous semantics are orthogonal and need to be integrated at the syntactical and at the semantic level. Although the approach for integrating temporal and ontology models is general and not tied to any particular model, it still separates uncertain context knowledge with domain ontology. On the contrary, DO enhanced with fuzzy subset theory is a unified solution for modeling uncertain context. What's more, the fuzzy temporal model is only for temporal knowledge , but other types of uncertain context are not supported. DO provides the ability of modeling any types of uncertain context through different fuzzy dimension types.

Paper [13] introduces an OWL context model to provide a shared semantic understanding for context-driven adaptation of mobile services. Continuing, the authors propose a simple and lightweight yet generic approach to extend context ontologies with quality of context properties and discuss the use of these quality properties for context ontology matching under uncertainty using fuzzy set theory [14]. This is also a domain-specific approach, in which merely such contexts as User, Platform, Service, Environment for adaptation of mobile services are supported. The fuzzy parameters representing the quality of context only include Precision, Correctness, Trust and Resolution. It's similar to uncertain context with discrete membership mapping function described in Sect. 4.1. But the context modeling mechanisms are quite different: it follows the design patterns in the guideline for defining OWL N-ary relations introduced in [15], while DO theory provides a brand new approach beyond triple-based ontology framework of W3C standards.

Paper [16] presents algorithms of computationally efficient handling of large but sparse fuzzy relations, and theory of knowledge representation, thematic categorization and user modeling. The following work is put forward in paper [17], which introduces how these diverse algorithms and methodologies can be combined in order to approach a greater goal, that of semantic multimedia personalization. The fuzzy semantic relations discussed is merely related to MPEG-7. It proposes to use RDF Reification [18] in order to achieve the desired expressiveness and obtain the enhanced functionality introduced by fuzziness. It's known that RDF Reification is redundant and clumsy, which arises performance doubt of this approach. On the contrary, DO does not adopts RDF Reification at all. Instead, DO utilizes "statement-id" as a OWL DatatypeProperty pointing at a DStatement reference [1].

Besides the four approaches related to Semantic Web and ontology, some efforts have been taken to model different types of contexts of possibility through extending modal logic [19], which attempts to deal with modalities, namely, possibility, probability, and necessity. For example, temporal logic [20] and further linear temporal logic [21] discuss representing, and reasoning about, propositions qualified only in the context of time. But DO supports multiple context types including but not limited to time. As another example, dynamic logic [22] extends modal logic by associating to every action a the modal operators, in which the context refers to the dynamic action performed. On the contrary, DO is toward modeling the contexts of static contextual statues of RDF triples/statements.

3 Brief Description of DO Theory

This section presents a brief introduction of DO Theory. It presents only partial the theory. The full one can be found in paper [1].

3.1 Dimension Type, Dimension and Dimension Container

Definition 1 (Dimension Type). *We define τ to be a dimension type standing for a context aspect, and T to be the set of all context aspects. T is also called the context environment. All the elements in T are disjoint in semantics.*

Definition 2 (Dimension). *We define d to be a concrete dimension for a dimension type τ restricting one certain context aspect, which it's a mathematical set containing a context scope of τ. Let D to be the set of all such dimensions, then $\Psi_d : D \rightarrow T$ maps a specific dimension to its dimension type.*

Definition 3 (Universal Dimension). *We define μ^τ to be the universal dimension for the dimension type τ, which is the universal superset of τ imposing no context restriction on τ. There is one and only one universal dimension for each dimension type .Any dimension is a sub set of a universal dimension of the same type: $\mu^\tau \supseteq d$, if $\Psi_d(d) = \tau$, $d \in D$. We define $\mathcal{M}$ to be the set of all the universal dimensions in the context environment of T, therefore $|\mathcal{M}| = |T|$.*

Example 1 (Dimension). Suppose τ_{time} to be the temporal dimension type, then $\mu^{\tau_{time}}$ is the universal dimension of all the time. Let $d_{Y2008} \in D$ to be a temporal dimension restricting the context of time within year of 2008, then $\Psi_d(d_{Y2008}) = \Psi_d(\mu^{\tau_{time}}) = \tau_{time}$ and $\mu^{\tau_{time}} \supseteq d_{Y2008}$. Note that all the dimensions here are crisp sets without vagueness.

Definition 4 (Dimension Container). *A dimension container o is a set of dimensions restricting certain contexts. A dimension container is an intersection combination of the context restrictions of different dimension types. which satisfies :*

$$\forall d_i \forall d_j (\Psi_d(d_i) \neq \Psi_d(d_j)), \quad d_i, d_j \in o \text{ and } i \neq j.$$

Let DC to be the set of all the dimension containers, then $DC \subseteq P(D)$. The function $\Psi_o : DC \rightarrow P(T)$ is defined as: $\Psi_o(o) = \{\Psi_d(d_1), \ldots, \Psi_d(d_n)\}$, $o = \{d_1, \ldots, d_n\}$ and $o \in DC$.

Example 2 (Dimension container). Let $T = \{\tau_{time}, \tau_{loc}\}$; let τ_{loc} to be the dimension type of location; suppose there is a dimension d_{USA} denoting the location within USA; then $\{d_{Y2007}\}$, $\{d_{Y2008}\}$, $\{d_{USA}\}$, and $\{d_{Y2008}, d_{USA}\}$ are all dimension containers, while $\{d_{Y2007}, d_{Y2008}\}$ and $\{d_{Y2007}, d_{Y2008}, d_{USA}\}$ are not. $\{d_{Y2007}, d_{USA}\}$ restricts the context to be "time within the year of 2007" and "location in USA". The temporal dimension that denotes "time between the year 2007 and 2008" can be constructed through set union operator $d_{Y2007} \cup d_{Y2008}$ (note that it's not $\{d_{Y2007}\} \cup \{d_{Y2008}\}$), but these two dimensions can not exist in the same dimension container at the same time.

3.2   Dimensional Relations

Each dimensional relation is a binary relation between two dimension containers. We introduce only two dimensional relations here: dimensional equivalency and dimensional superset.

Definition 5 (Dimensional equivalency). *We define $\overset{T}{=}$ to be the relation denoting dimensional equivalency in the context environment of T as follows: Let $\mathcal{M}' \subseteq \mathcal{M}$ and $\Psi_o(o) \cap \Psi_o(\mathcal{M}') = \emptyset$, $o, \mathcal{M}' \in \mathcal{DC}$; then $o \overset{T}{=} o \cup \mathcal{M}'$, $o \cup \mathcal{M}' \in \mathcal{DC}$.*

Definition 6 (Overline Normalized Dimension Container). *Let $o \in \mathcal{DC}$. We define $\overline{o}$ to be the overline normalized dimension container of o in the context environment of T, which satisfies: $\overline{o} \overset{T}{=} o$ and $\Psi_o(\overline{o}) = T$. We define $\overline{\mathcal{DC}}$ to be the set of all the overline normalized dimension containers. We define $\Omega : (T, \overline{\mathcal{DC}}) \to \mathcal{D}$ mapping a overline normalized dimension container and a dimension type to the dimension in the dimension container that belongs to the specified dimension type.*

Example 3 (Normalized Dimension Container). Suppose $T = \{\tau_{time}, \tau_{loc}\}$; let $\Psi_d(d_1) = \tau_{time}, o = \{d_1\}, o \in \mathcal{DC}$; then $\overline{o} = \{d_1, \mu^{\tau_{loc}}\}$, and $o \overset{T}{=} \overline{o}$. Both of them restrict the context to be "time within d_1 and in any location ". In this case, $\Omega(\tau_{time}, \overline{o}) = d_1$ and $\Omega(\tau_{loc}, \overline{o}) = \mu^{\tau_{loc}}$.

Definition 7 (Dimensional superset). *We define $\overset{T}{\supseteq}$ to be the relation denoting dimensional superset in the context environment of T as follows: Suppose $o, o' \in \mathcal{DC}$; $o \overset{T}{\supseteq} o'$, iff $\forall \tau(\Omega(\tau, \overline{o}) \supseteq \Omega(\tau, \overline{o'}))$, $\tau \in T$.*

3.3   Dimensional Operators

We introduce three dimensional operators here: dimensional intersection, dimensional partial union and dimensional partial complement.

Definition 8 (Dimensional intersection). *We define $\overset{T}{\cap}$ to be the operator denoting dimensional intersection in the context environment of T: $o \overset{T}{\cap} o' \overset{T}{=} \{\Omega(\tau_1, \overline{o}) \cap \Omega(\tau_1, \overline{o'}), \ldots, \Omega(\tau_n, \overline{o}) \cap \Omega(\tau_n, \overline{o'})\}, o \overset{T}{\cap} o' \in \mathcal{DC}$, if $o, o' \in \mathcal{DC}$ and $T = \{\tau_1, \ldots, \tau_n\}$.*

Definition 9 (Dimensional union). *We define $\overset{T}{\cup}$ to be the operator denoting dimensional union in the context environment of T.*

Note that dimension union is not what performs union operations on each dimension type of a dimension container. As is illustrated in Fig. 1, the dimensional union of o and o' ($o \overset{T}{\cup} o'$) is the bold area, which is not a dimension container at all ($o \overset{T}{\cup} o' \notin \mathcal{DC}$). However dimensional partial union (see Definition 10) makes the operation results dimension containers in any case.

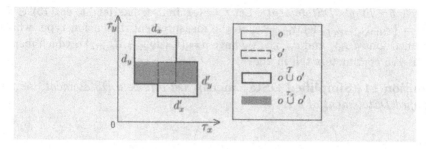

Fig. 1. Dimensional partial union

Definition 10 (Dimensional partial union). *We define $\overset{\tau}{\cup}$ to be the operator denoting dimensional union of two dimension containers on the specified dimension type τ:* $o \overset{\tau}{\cup} o' \overset{\mathcal{T}}{=} \{\Omega(\tau_1,\bar{o}) \cap \Omega(\tau_1,\bar{o}), \ldots, \Omega(\tau,\bar{o}) \cup \Omega(\tau,\bar{o}), \ldots, \Omega(\tau_n,\bar{o}) \cap \Omega(\tau_n,\bar{o})\}$, $\mathcal{T} = \{\tau_1, \ldots, \tau, \ldots, \tau_n\}, o \overset{\tau}{\cup} o' \in \mathcal{DC}$.

Example 4 (Dimensional partial union). Fig. 1 demonstrates dimensional partial union of o and o' on τ_x in the grey area. It performs union operation on τ_x, while performs intersection operations on the other dimension types (τ_y). It can be inferred [1] that $(o \overset{\mathcal{T}}{\cup} o') \overset{\mathcal{T}}{\supseteq} (o \overset{\tau_x}{\cup} o')$.

Definition 11 (Dimensional partial complement). *We define $\overset{\tau}{\neg}$ to be the operator denoting dimensional complement of a dimension container on a specified dimension type:* $\overset{\tau}{\neg} o = \{\mu^{\tau_1}, \ldots, \neg\Omega(\tau,\bar{o}), \ldots, \mu^{\tau_n}\}$, $\mathcal{T} = \{\tau_1, \ldots, \tau, \ldots, \tau_n\}$.

3.4 DStatement

Dimensional containers are devoted to represent context. We can further apply dimension containers to RDF triples to construct contextual assertions.

Definition 12 (DStatement). *A dimensional statement (i.e. DStatement) is an ordered, strongly binary tree [3] ρ that is defined recursively in terms of left and right subtrees of the root as follows:*

$$\rho = \left(\left\{ \begin{matrix} t \\ \rho' \end{matrix} \right., o \right), \quad \rho, \rho' \in \mathcal{DS}, \ t \in T, \ o \in \mathcal{DC}$$

DStatement is an assertion which means the left subtree exists in the context of the right dimension container, or the left one is truth for the right one. We define $\mathcal{DS}$ to be the set of all DStatements . The function $\Upsilon_\rho : (\mathcal{DS}, \mathbb{N}) \to \mathcal{DS} \cup T$ maps a DStatement to its left child in the specified depth. The function $\Phi_\rho : (\mathcal{DS}, \mathbb{N}) \to \mathcal{DC}$ maps a DStatement to its right child in the specified depth. We define H_ρ to be the height of ρ.

Definition 13 (Simple DStatement). *A DStatement ρ is a simple DStatement, iff $\Upsilon_\rho(\rho, 1) \in T$. And $\mathcal{SDS}$ is the set of all the simple DStatements.*

Example 5 (Simple DStatement). Let $t = \langle$eg:Jim, eg:hasHeight, eg:175$\rangle \in T$; let $\mathcal{T} = \{\tau_{time}, \tau_{mea}\}$; let τ_{mea} to be the measurement dimension type, which has dimensions d_{centi} and d_{meter}, we have $\rho = (t, \{d_{Y2007}, d_{centi}\})$, which means "Jim is 175 centimeters tall in 2007".

Definition 14 (Simplified DStatement). *Let ρ to be a DStatement, the the simplified DStatement of ρ is :*

$$\hat{\rho} = \left(\Upsilon_\rho(\rho, H_\rho), \bigcap_{d=1}^{H_\rho \atop \mathcal{T}} \Phi_\rho(\rho, d) \right), \quad d \in \mathbb{N}, \ \rho \in \mathcal{DS}.$$

Proposition 1. $\hat{\rho} \in \mathcal{SDS}$, *if* $\rho \in \mathcal{DS}$.

Example 6 (Simplified DStatement). Let $t_1 = \langle$eg:Jim, eg:hasHeight, eg:185$\rangle$; let $\mathcal{T} = \{\tau_{time}, \tau_{prov}\}$; let τ_{prov} to be the provenance dimension type, which has dimension d_{Lucy} (i.e. Lucy says/said) ; let $\rho_1 = ((t_1, d_{Y2008}), \{d_{Lucy}\})$,$\rho_2 = ((t_1, d_{Lucy}), \{d_{Y2008}\})$ and $\rho_3 = (t_1, \{d_{Lucy}, d_{Y2008}\})$; then ρ_1 means "Lucy says 'Jim was 185 tall in 2008'", while ρ_2 means "In 2008 Lucy said 'Jim is 185 tall'" and ρ_2 means " 'Jim is 185 tall' is truth, if time is in 2008 and it's from Lucy's words ". Note that the semantic meanings of the three are not equivalent. We have $\hat{\rho}_1 = \hat{\rho}_2 = \rho_3$.

4   Uncertain Context Extension of DO

This section discusses how to model uncertain context of DO using fuzzy subset theory. The basic idea is to create new dimension types for different uncertain contexts and construct corresponding dimensions and dimension containers with fuzzy subsets instead of crisp ones. In this way, the universe of discourse of all the fuzzy subsets is the set of DStatements including RDF triples (RDF triples are special cases of DStatements in Definition 12). And dimension containers with dimensions of fuzzy subsets can be applied to DStatements in order to denote ambiguous contextual assertions. Note that it's not required for a dimension container to encapsulate only fuzzy subsets or merely crisp ones. They can be mixed within a dimension container for different contextual aspects.

The membership function of a fuzzy subset can be either discrete or continuous.

4.1   Discrete Membership Function

Fuzzy subset F of a set S can be defined as a set of ordered pairs, each with a first element that is an element of the set S, and a second element that is a value in the interval [0,1], with exactly one ordered pair present for each element of S. If $S = \{x_1, \ldots, x_n\}$ is a finite set and F is a fuzzy subset in S then we can use the notation: $F = \mu_1/x_1 + \cdots + \mu_n/x_n$, where term $\mu_i, i = 1, \ldots, n$ signifies that μ_i is the degree of membership of x_i in F and the plus sign represents the union. Suppose F contains finite n mappings from DStatements to [0,1]. We can introduce a new dimension type τ_f denoting the extent of uncertainty with a property value between 0 and 1.

For example, in order to modeling tallness of Jim at discrete time points, we can define $\mathcal{T} = \{\tau_{time}, \tau_f\}$. Let $t = \langle$eg:Jim, eg:hasHeight, eg:TALL$\rangle, t \in T$, we have such DStatements as $\rho_1 = (t, \{d_{Y2002}, d_{f0.25}\})$, $\rho_2 = (t, \{d_{Y2004}, d_{f0.50}\})$ and $\rho_3 = (t, \{d_{Y2008}, d_{f1.00}\}), \rho_1, \rho_2, \rho_3 \in \mathcal{DC}$. ρ_1 represents "In the year of 2002, degree of truth of the statement 'Jim is TALL' is 0.25", while ρ_3 interprets "Jim is 100% TALL in 2008". Note that both τ_{time} and τ_f are ordinary crisp sets. We don't use fuzzy subsets in this approach. Instead, we utilize crisp dimensions for modeling discrete fuzzy subsets.

In fact, dimension types of DO can be so diverse that we can establish a new dimension type denoting the extent of uncertainty to modeling uncertain context for each DStatement. But the limitation of this approach is that it is merely suitable for fuzzy subsets with finite and discrete mappings instead of infinite continuous ones.

4.2   Continuous Membership Function

Sometimes, a more general definition is used, where membership functions take values in an arbitrary fixed algebra or structure $F = \{(x, \mu_F(x))|x \in S\}$. And $\mu_F : S \rightarrow [0, 1]$ is defined as a mapping between elements of the set S and values in the interval [0,1]. $\mu_F(x)$ is the degree is interpreted as the degree of membership of element x in fuzzy set F. The value zero is used to represent complete non-membership, the value one is used to represent complete membership, and values in between are used to represent intermediate degrees of membership. The set S is referred to as the universe of discourse for the fuzzy subset F.

Taking tallness as an example, we can define a fuzzy subset F which answers the question "to what degree is person x tall?". To each person in the universe of discourse, we have to assign a degree of membership to $\mu_F(x)$. The easiest way to do this is with a membership function based on the person's height.

$$\mu_F(x) = \begin{cases} 0 & \text{if } height(x) \leq 1.6 \\ 2.5 \cdot height(x) - 4 & \text{if } 1.6 < height(x) \leq 2.0 \\ 1 & \text{if } height(x) > 2.0 \end{cases} \quad (1)$$

Furthermore, we can also make it based on time with certain assumption. Suppose Jim's height has a linear relation with time, we can define:

$$height(t) = 0.05 \cdot t - 98.4, \quad 1968 \leq t \leq 2020 \quad (2)$$

Therefore we can construct a fuzzy subset F of Jim's tallness in time set through combining Equation 1 and Equation 2:

$$\mu_F(t) = \begin{cases} 0 & \text{if } 1968 < t \leq 2000 \\ 0.125 \cdot t - 250 & \text{if } 2000 < t \leq 2008 \\ 1 & \text{if } 2008 < t \leq 2020 \end{cases} \quad (3)$$

In this example, it is actually a normal trapezoidal fuzzy subset [5] on the real line. Due to its linear nature, a normal trapezoidal fuzzy subset can be specified

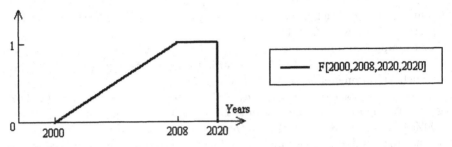

Fig. 2. Trapezoidal fuzzy subset of F[2000,2008,2020,2020]

by four parameters, a, b, c and d, which is represented as F[a,b,c,d]. The fuzzy subset of Jim's tallness in time set is F[2000,2008,2020,2020], which is illustrated in Fig. 2.

As is showed in the example of Jim's tallness in Equation 3, Jim was born in 1968 and died in 2020. During the 52 years of his life, Jim's tallness can be judged at any time point. It's not possible to enumerate all the mappings and construct infinite DStatements of Jim's tallness for any time points. On the other hand, τ_{time} and τ_f are strongly related, which is in conflict with the principle in Definition 1: dimension types are desired to be decoupled with each other. The design of the dimension environment in the example of Sect. 4.1 may lead to unexpected consequence of dimensional union operation. Paper [1] discusses the harmfulness of this situation. It's better to combine the two strongly related dimension types into an intergraded one.

We denote the combined dimension type to be τ_{ftime}. All the dimensions of τ_{ftime} are fuzzy subsets of time set. For modeling Jim's tallness, the dimension of τ_{ftime} has 4 property values representing the 4 parameters of trapezoidal fuzzy subset. Let $t = \langle$eg:Jim, eg:hasHeight, eg:TALL$\rangle, t \in T$; let $d_{F[2000,2008,2020,2020]}$ $\in \mathcal{D}$ and $\Psi_d(d_{F[2000,2008,2020,2020]}) = \tau_{ftime}$; then $\rho = \{t, \{d_{F[2000,2008,2020,2020]}\}\}$ $\in \mathcal{DC}$ represents Jim's tallness perfectly.

4.3   Operation and Entailment on Uncertain Context

Uncertain context can be modeled through the methods introduced in Sect. 4.1 or Sect. 4.2. This section discusses how to further manipulate uncertain contexts for fuzzy dimensional operations and corresponding reasoning.

The definition of entailment in DO are presented here with useful theorems and corollaries. They apply well to both crisp and fuzzy context reasoning.

Definition 15 (Dimensional Interpretation). *A dimensional interpretation I of a vocabulary $\mathcal{V}$ consists of:*

1. *A non-empty set of RDF triples T_I.*
2. *A set of dimension containers $\mathcal{DC}_I$.*
3. *A set of DStatements $\mathcal{DS}_I$.*
4. *A dimensional context mapping $P_I : T_I \cup \mathcal{DS}_I \to \mathcal{DC}_I$.*
5. *A vocabulary interpretation mapping $I_{\mathcal{V}} : \mathcal{V} \to T_I \cup \mathcal{DC}_I \cup \mathcal{DS}_I$.*

We define the mapping: $I : V \rightarrow T_I \cup DC_I \cup \{True, False\}$ such that:

1. $I(x) = I_V(x), \forall x \in V \cap (T \cup DC)$.
2. Let $x \in V \cap DS$, then $I(x) = True$, if $I_V(\Phi_\rho(x,1)) \in P_I(I_V(\Upsilon_\rho(x,1)))$, otherwise $I(x) = False$.

Definition 16 (Dimensional Entailment). Let $\rho, \rho' \in DS$ and T is the dimensional environment. We say that ρ dimensional-entails ρ' ($\rho \models^T \rho'$) iff for every dimensional interpretation I, if $I \models \rho$ then $I \models \rho'$.

Theorem 1. Let $\rho, \rho' \in DS, H_\rho = H_{\rho'} = h \in \mathbb{N}$ and $\Upsilon_\rho(\rho, H_\rho) = \Upsilon_\rho(\rho', H_{\rho'}) = t \in T$; let $\forall i(\Phi_\rho(\rho, i) \overset{T}{\supseteq} \Phi_\rho(\rho, i)), i \leq h \in \mathbb{N}$; then $\rho \models^T \rho'$.

Theorem 2. Let $\rho, \rho' \in DS, H_\rho = H_{\rho'} = h \in \mathbb{N}$ and $\Upsilon_\rho(\rho, H_\rho) = \Upsilon_\rho(\rho', H_{\rho'})$

$$= t \in T; \; let \; \rho'' = \left(\begin{cases} t & if \; i = h \\ \Upsilon_\rho(\rho'', i) & if \; i < h \end{cases} , \; \begin{cases} \Phi_\rho(\rho, j) \overset{T}{\cup} \Phi_\rho(\rho', j) & if \; j = k \\ \Phi_\rho(\rho, j) \overset{T}{\cap} \Phi_\rho(\rho', j) & otherwise \end{cases} \right),$$

$$\rho''' = \left(\begin{cases} t & if \; i = h \\ \Upsilon_\rho(\rho''', i) & if \; i < h \end{cases} , \; \begin{cases} \Phi_\rho(\rho, j) \overset{T}{\cup} \Phi_\rho(\rho', j) & if \; j = k \\ \Phi_\rho(\rho, j) \overset{T}{\cap} \Phi_\rho(\rho', j) & otherwise \end{cases} \right), \tau \in T,$$

$i, j, k \leq h \in \mathbb{N}$. i, j are variables denoting tree node depth, while k is a predefined constant; then $\{\rho, \rho'\} \models^T \rho'' \models^T \rho'''$.

Corollary 1. Let $\rho = (\rho_1, o_1), \rho' = (\rho_1', o_1'), \rho, \rho_1, \rho', \rho_1' \in DS$ and $\Upsilon_\rho(\rho, H_\rho) = \Upsilon_\rho(\rho', H_{\rho'}) = t \in T$; let $\rho_1'' = \left(t, \Phi_\rho(\widehat{\rho_1}, 1) \overset{T}{\cap} \overset{\tau}{\neg} \Phi_\rho(\widehat{\rho_1'}, 1) \right), \rho'' = \left(\rho_1'', o_1 \overset{T}{\cap} \overset{\tau}{\neg} o_1' \right);$ then $\{\rho, \rho'\} \models^T \rho''$.

Example 7. Let $t_1 = \langle eg\text{:}Jim, eg\text{:}hasName, \text{"Jackson"} \rangle$; let $T = \{\tau_{time}, \tau_{prov}\}$; let τ_{prov} to be the dimension type denoting provenance, which has dimensions d_{dairy} and $d_{archive}$ (i.e. recorded in the private diary and personal identify archive) ; let $\rho_1 = ((t_1, \{d_{BY2006}\}), \{d_{dairy}\})$, which means "It's recorded in the diary that Jim's name was 'Jackson' before 2006 " (informal provenance); let $\rho_2 = ((t_1, \{d_{BY2007}\}), \{d_{archive}\})$, which means "It's recorded in the personal identity archive that Jim's name was 'Jackson' before 2007 " (official provenance); let $\rho_3 = ((t_1, \{d_{BY2006}\}), \{d_{dairy} \cup d_{archive}\})$, which means "It's recorded both in the diary and in the personal identity archive that Jim's name was 'Jackson' *at least* before 2006 "; if we want to merge the two statements and find what is true from both the two provenances, we can perform entailment of Theorem 2 and get $\{\rho_1, \rho_2\} \models^T \rho_3$. Note that "in both of provenances" implies that the union operation is performed on τ_{prov}, but intersection should be performed on the other dimension types (τ_{time}) at the same time, according to Theorem 2. Let $\rho_4 = \left(\left(t_1, \Phi_\rho(\widehat{\rho_2}, 1) \overset{T\tau_{time}}{\cap \neg} \Phi_\rho(\widehat{\rho_1}, 1) \right), \Phi_\rho(\rho_2, 1) \overset{T\tau_{prov}}{\cap \neg} \Phi_\rho(\rho_1, 1) \right) = ((t_1, \{d_{Y0607}\}), \{d_{archive}\}) \in DS$, which means "It's recorded in the personal identity archive but not in the diary that Jim's name was 'Jackson' between 2006 and 2007". We have $\{\rho_1, \rho_2\} \models^T \rho_4$ according to Corollary 1.

The entailment of Example 7 shows the crisp dimensional operation results of DO. We can further introduce fuzzy operations on fuzzy subsets and perform uncertain context reasoning.

Here are the definitions of fuzzy operations. Let A and B are fuzzy subsets of a nonempty (crisp) set S, we have:

Definition 17 (Fuzzy Intersection). *The intersection of A and B is defined as:* $\mu_{(A \cap B)}(x) = \min(\mu_A(x), \mu_B(x))$, *for all* $x \in S$.

Definition 18 (Fuzzy Union). *The union of A and B is defined as:* $\mu_{(A \cup B)}(x) = \max(\mu_A(x), \mu_B(x))$, *for all* $x \in S$.

Definition 19 (Fuzzy Complement). *The complement of a fuzzy subset A is defined as:* $\mu_{(\neg A)}(x) = 1 - \mu_A(x)$, *for all* $x \in S$.

Some dimension types for uncertain context modeling, such as τ_{ftime}, are fuzzy subsets by nature. Therefore the dimensional operations (see Sect 3.3) on them are also fuzzy ones, which should be performed according to Definition 17, 18 and 19.

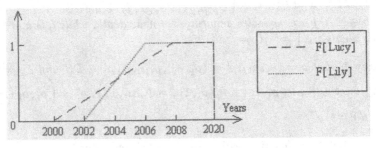

Fig. 3. Fuzzy subsets of F[Lucy] and F[Lily]

Let's introduce a new dimension type of provenance τ_{prov} to illustrate fuzzy dimensional operations. We suppose τ_{prov} has two dimensions d_{Lucy} and d_{Lily} (i.e. Lucy says and Lily says). Since everybody's view of tallness is subjective, Lucy and Lily may have different options of Jim's tallness. For example, Lucy says the fuzzy subset of F[2000,2008,2020,2020] (i.e. F[Lucy] for short) represents Jim's tallness, but Lily says it should be F[2002,2006,2020,2020] (i.e. F[Lily] for short). Suppose $t = \langle eg{:}Jim, eg{:}hasHeight, eg{:}TALL\rangle, t \in T$ and $T = \{\tau_{ftime}, \tau_{prov}\}$, we have two DStatements: $\rho_{Lucy} = ((t, \{d_{F[Lucy]}\}), \{d_{Lucy}\})$ and $\rho_{Lily} = ((t, \{d_{F[Lily]}\}), \{d_{Lily}\})$. Their fuzzy subsets are showed in Fig. 3 .

If we want to find out what both Lucy and Lily say, we can perform fuzzy intersection on the two fuzzy time dimensions. Let $\rho_{LucyLily} = ((t, \{d_{F[Lucy]}\} \overset{\tau}{\cap} \{d_{F[Lily]}\}), \{d_{Lucy}\} \overset{\tau_{prov}}{\cup} \{d_{Lily}\}) = ((t, d_{F[Lucy] \cap F[Lily]}), \{d_{Lucy} \cup d_{Lily}\}) \in \mathcal{DS}$, we have $\{\rho_{Lucy}, \rho_{Lily}\} \models^T \rho_{LucyLily}$ according to Theorem 2. Let's take the year of 2003 as an example. In this year, Lucy believes the extent of Jim's tallness is 0.33, while Lily regards it as 0.25. Therefore we can infer that both Lucy and

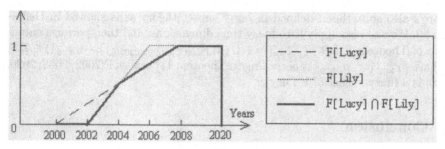

Fig. 4. Fuzzy subset of F[Lucy] ∩ F[Lily]

Lily think Jim's tallness attains the extent of 0.25 in 2003. Note that in this entailment, the dimensional intersection of $\{d_{F[Lucy]}\}$ and $\{d_{F[Lily]}\}$ are fuzzy intersection merging two fuzzy subsets of Jim's tallness in time set. But the union on d_{Lucy} and d_{Lily} are ordinary crisp union operation for denoting the combination two persons' views. The reasoning result of Jim's tallness in this case is showed in Fig. 4.

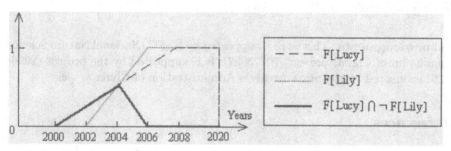

Fig. 5. Fuzzy subset of F[Lucy] ∩¬ F[Lily]

In a similar way, if we want to find out what Lucy says but Lily disagrees, we can first perform fuzzy complement on Lily's fuzzy time dimension and then perform fuzzy intersection with Lucy's. Let $\rho_{LucyNotLily} = ((t, \{d_{F[Lucy]}\} \overset{T}{\cap}$ $\{d_{\neg F[Lily]}\}), \{d_{Lucy}\} \overset{T}{\cap} \overset{T_{prov}}{\neg} \{d_{Lily}\}) = ((t, \{d_{F[Lucy]\cap\neg F[Lily]}\}), \{d_{Lucy}\cap\neg d_{Lily}\})$ $\in \mathcal{DS}$. Since Lucy and Lily are different persons, we have $d_{Lucy}\cap\neg d_{Lily} = d_{Lucy}$. Therefore $\rho_{LucyNotLily} = ((t, \{d_{F[Lucy]\cap\neg F[Lily]}\}), \{d_{Lucy}\}) \in \mathcal{DS}$. Finally we have $\{\rho_{Lucy}, \rho_{Lily}\} \models^T \rho_{LucyNotLily}$ according to Corollary 1. Taking the year of 2005 as an example, we have Lucy's view on Jim's tallness is 0.66. But Lily thinks it should be 0.75, therefore the extent that Lily disagrees with Jim's tallness is 0.25. We can further infer that Lucy says but Lily disagrees on the extent of Jim's tallness in 2005 is 0.25 (i.e. MIN of 0.66 and 0.25). The reasoning result of Jim's tallness in this case is showed in Fig. 5.

Definition 20 (Subsethood of Fuzzy Subset). *Let A and B are fuzzy subsets of a classical set X. We say that A is a subset of B if $\mu_A(x) \leq \mu_B(x)$, for all $x \in S$.*

268   Y. Jiang and H. Dong

There's also subsethood defined in fuzzy subset theory as is showed in Definition 20. We can also apply it to fuzzy time dimensions, and then perform entailment of Theorem 1. Let $\rho_{LucySub} = ((t, \{d_{F[2002,2008,2020,2020]}\}), \{d_{Lucy}\}) \in \mathcal{DS}$, we have $\rho_{Lucy} \models^T \rho_{LucySub}$ according to Theorem 1, because F[2002, 2008, 2020, 2020] is a fuzzy subset of F[Lucy].

5 Conclusion

In this paper we propose to extend DO's crisp dimensions with fuzzy ones based on fuzzy subset theory in order to model uncertain contexts. Crisp dimension types and fuzzy ones can cooperate with each other well within DO theory. Uncertain contexts modeled in this way can be applied to RDF triples or generally DStatements to construct ambiguous contextual assertions. Fuzzy dimensional operations and related reasoning mechanism are also discussed, which still work well in DO based on fuzzy subset theory. One of the advantages of our proposal is that it's a domain-independent solution. Other strong points are mainly the great features of DO compared with other approaches, such as theory uniformity and implementation flexibility/efficiency.

Acknowledgments. This work is supported by NSFC (National Nature Science Foundation of China) project (70773087). It is supported by the project (2006-x-29) sponsored by the State Archives Administration of China as well.

References

1. Jiang, Y., Dong, H.: Beyond Triples, Dimensional Ontology Theory for Context-Sensitive Knowledge. In: The 3rd Asian Semantic Web Conference, ASWC 2008 (2008)
2. Lassila, O., Swick, R.: Resource Description Framework (RDF) Model and Syntax Specification. W3C Recommendation (1999)
3. Strongly Binary Tree – from Wolfram MathWorld, http://mathworld.wolfram.com/StronglyBinaryTree.html
4. Zadeh, L.A.: Fuzzy Sets. Information and Control. J. Mol. Biol. 8, 338–353 (1965)
5. Dubois, D., Prade, H.: Fuzzy Numbers. An Overview. In: Bezdek (ed.) The Analysis of Fuzzy Information. CRS Press, Boca Raton (1985)
6. Bontas, E.P.: Context Representation and Usage for the Semantic Web: A State of the Art. Technical report, B-04-30 (2004)
7. Dietze, S., Gugliotta, A., Domingue, J.: Conceptual Situation Spaces for Situation-Driven Processes. In: Bechhofer, S., Hauswirth, M., Hoffmann, J., Koubarakis, M. (eds.) ESWC 2008. LNCS, vol. 5021. Springer, Heidelberg (2008)
8. Dietze, S., Gugliotta, A., Domingue, J.: Fuzzy Context Adaptation through Conceptual Situation Spaces. In: Proceedings of 2008 IEEE International Conference on Fuzzy Systems (FUZZ-IEEE 2008). IEEE Press, New York (2008)
9. Gärdenfors, P.: How to make the semantic web more semantic. In: Proccedings of Formal Ontology in Information Systems, pp. 19–36. IOS Press, Amsterdam (2004)

10. Nagypál, G., Motik, B.: A Fuzzy Model for Representing Uncertain, Subjective, and Vague Temporal Knowledge in Ontologies. In: Goos, G., Hartmanis, J., van Leeuwen, J. (eds.) CoopIS 2003, DOA 2003, and ODBASE 2003. LNCS, vol. 2888, pp. 906–923. Springer, Heidelberg (2003)
11. KAON framework, http://kaon.semanticweb.org/
12. Chen, W., Kifer, M., Warren, D.S.: Hilog: A foundation for higher-order logic programming. Journal of Logic Programming 15, 183–230 (1993)
13. Preuveneers, D., Van den Bergh, J., Wagelaar, D., Georges, A., Rigole, P., Clerckx, T., Berbers, Y., Coninx, K., Jonckers, V., De Bosschere, K.: Towards an extensible context ontology for ambient intelligence. In: Hutchison, D., Kanade, T., Kittler, J., et al. (eds.) EUSAI 2004. LNCS, vol. 3295, pp. 148–159. Springer, Heidelberg (2004)
14. Preuveneers, D., Berbers, Y.: Quality Extensions and Uncertainty Handling for Context Ontologies. In: Proceedings of Context and Ontologies: Theory Practice and Applications, pp. 62–64. CEUR-WS.org (2006)
15. Defining N-ary Relations on the Semantic Web, http://www.w3.org/TR/swbp-n-aryRelations/
16. Akrivas, G., Stamou, G., Kollias, S.: Semantic Association of Multimedia Document Descriptions through Fuzzy Relational Algebra and Fuzzy Reasoning. Systems, Man, and Cybernetics, part A 34(2), 1397–1402 (2004)
17. Mylonas, P., Wallace, M.: Using ontologies and fuzzy relations in multimedia personalization. In: Proceedings of the First International Workshop on Semantic Media Adaptation and Personalization, pp. 146–150. IEEE Press, New York (2006)
18. W3C RDF Reification, http://www.w3.org/TR/rdf-concepts/
19. Blackburn, Patrick, de Rijke, M., Venema, Y.: Modal Logic. Cambridge University Press, Cambridge (2001)
20. Venema, Y.: Temporal Logic. In: Goble, L. (ed.) The Blackwell Guide to Philosophical Logic. Blackwell, Malden (2001)
21. Gerth, R., Peled, D., Vardi, M.Y., Wolper, P.: Simple on-the-fly automatic verification of linear temporal logic. In: Proceedings of the Fifteenth IFIP WG6.1 International Symposium on Protocol Specification, Testing and Verification XV. Chapman and Hall, Ltd, London (1995)
22. Pratt, V.R.: Semantical Considerations on Floyd-Hoare Logic. In: Proccedings of 17th Annual IEEE Symposium on Foundations of Computer Science, pp. 109–121. Massachusetts Institute of Technology Cambridge, MA (1976)

A Personalized Approach to Experience-Aware Service Ranking and Selection

Friederike Klan and Birgitta König-Ries

Institute of Computer Science, Friedrich-Schiller-University Jena, Ernst-Abbe-Platz
1-4, 07743 Jena, Germany
{friederike.klan,koenig}@informatik.uni-jena.de

Abstract. Existing approaches to service ranking and selection evaluate the suitability of available services for a given request based on the advertisement created by the service provider. They will compare how well the advertisement matches the service request and will choose the service with the best matching advertisement. Unfortunately, at this point in time, it is uncertain whether the service that will actually be performed will match the request as well as the advertisement promised. In this paper, we present an approach that reduces the degree of this uncertainty by taking previous experiences with the service provider (which reflect the performance of the actual service *not* the advertisement) into account. Contrary to many other approaches our solution accounts for the subjective nature of rating-based experiences by considering the preferences of the experience creators. Moreover it exploits the number of available experiences more effectively by considering not only experiences for a given service, but also experiences for similar services of the same provider. Our solution utilizes indirect user information and avoids explicit sharing of personal consumer information.

1 Introduction

Over the last decade the Web evolved from a collection of static web sites offered by a relatively small number of providers to a platform for sharing and collaboration where everyone can provide content and offer functionality. This shift of web usage behavior and the consequent rise of available information and resources as well as their growing heterogeneity poses new challenges to application integration. A paradigm that has proved to be appropriate to enable this is service-oriented computing. It allows to provide functionality or information as stand-alone services, that can be described by a service offer, then published, automatically discovered, and ranked by comparing (matching) a given service request with available offers, selected, composed and executed. Facing the overwhelming flood of information effective mechanisms for matching and ranking available resources according to their relevance become crucial to support consumers when selecting a service. In this context much work has been done on improving the expressiveness of service descriptions, particularly by applying semantic techniques, as well as on effective matchmaking algorithms to select

S. Greco and T. Lukasiewicz (Eds.): SUM 2008, LNAI 5291, pp. 270–283, 2008.
© Springer-Verlag Berlin Heidelberg 2008

suitable service offers based on a given request. However, there is a critical point here that has not been paid much attention to so far. Existing matchmaking approaches implicitly assume that the service advertised in the offer corresponds to the actually provided service. However, it is unrealistic to assume to have a 1:1 correspondence here. In fact one cannot be sure about the degree of correspondence between offer and actual service. This is due to several reasons. On the one hand service providers may advertise more than they are able to provide to be preferred over competing providers. On the other hand discrepancies between the promised and the actually provided service naturally arise from the dynamics of services as well as from the finiteness of service descriptions. In general, there is a tradeoff between the accuracy and the size of a service description and thus the cost of matchmaking. Thus service descriptions tend to be inaccurate to some degree [1]. Though this problem can be mitigated by introducing a negotiation step it cannot be solved completely. It is obvious that the bigger the difference between the advertised and the actually provided service the less meaningful are the results of the service matchmaker and the more arbitrary is the offer ranking and thus the selection decision based on those results, since available services are solely compared on the basis of their offer descriptions. Service ranking and selection algorithms should take this point into consideration by 1) quantifying the difference between the offer and the actual service (*offer conformance*) and thus the preciseness of the matching results and 2) considering this information when ranking available services.

In this context collaborative feedback mechanisms seem to be promising to reduce the uncertainty in service selection [2]. However existing mechanisms for experience-aware service selection exhibit a number of disadvantages. In most of the approaches offer conformance is a rather abstract concept [2], neither related to the attributes of a service nor to the service promised in the offer. A specific class of approaches in that context are those that recommend suitable services based on selections of other users [3,4]. In our opinion these approaches suffer from a major drawback: they do not consider whether the decision of the user was a good one or not, i.e., they record user satisfaction with the offer *not* with the actual service delivered. Often solutions that measure the performance of a service in terms of its attributes captured in the offer description assume consumer feedback to be objective and measurable [5,6,7,8,9]. Thus, they mainly focus on QoS attributes [10,8,9]. Though some service properties' values can be measured automatically, most of them, particularly in the field of information services, cannot. Imagine for instance a service that provides digital contents like a mp3-file containing a song. In that case one can automatically verify that the downloaded file is an mp3-file, but automatically checking that it contains the song you wanted by the interpreter you wanted is not possible. Moreover, measuring a service's performance with respect to several aspects can be very costly and has to be based on commonly agreed upon measuring methods. Due to these facts we advocate personalized experiences in terms of consumer ratings. Ratings are personalized, i.e they depend on a consumer's expectations expressed in his preferences. These preferences capture how important certain aspects of a service are to a consumer. Consequently experiences of specific consumers are only transferable to situations where the involved service consumer has similar preferences. Most of the existing rating based approaches [10,11,12] do not account for that fact. Some solutions, e.g. [7], that consider the subjective nature of ratings rely on the explicit exchange of consumer requests and preferences. In our opinion this would divulge valuable personal information. Moreover comparing user requests and preferences directly would be very costly. Consumer ratings for a specific service are scarce. For that reason feedback should be exploited effectively. Only a few approaches consider this [5,10].

In this paper we propose an approach for experience-aware service ranking and selection that solves the described problems. It is designed as an extension for existing matchmakers and utilizes consumer experiences in former service interactions to allow for proper service ranking and selection. The remainder of the paper is organized as follows. First we provide definitions for basic notions and specify our assumptions about the underlying service description language as well as on the underlying matchmaker (Sect. 2). Afterwards we present our solution for experience-aware service selection in Sect. 3. We discuss and present experimental results in Sect. 4 and conclude the paper in Sect. 5.

2   Prerequisites

Before describing the entire approach in the following sections we define basic notions and make some general assumptions about the underlying service description language as well as on the underlying *basic matchmaker*. We consider a *service* as a set of instances that can be executed. It is characterized by a set of attributes. Each *service instance* is characterized by a particular combination of values for those attributes. Service descriptions are set-based, i.e. they describe a service by means of its instances.[1] A *service offer or advertisement* specifies which instances a given service provides. For instance a service offer for a bookseller might describe that this offer contains the set of service instances where the effect is that ownership of a book changes. These books have a title, prices and so on. An example of a service instance would be the service selling the book with the title "Pope Joan" for 14.90 Euro, to be delivered by 01.04.08 to a certain address. A *service request* characterizes a *service consumer's* goal by describing the service instances that are suitable for solving that goal. Additionally, a service request contains an implicit mapping that assigns a *match value* to each service instance in the request. This value indicates how well a given instance fits to the service consumer's goal. W.l.o.g. we assume that the match value is a real number from the interval $[0, 1]$. The mapping can be interpreted as the *consumer's preferences* with respect to the given request. A service request could be the set of instances where the effect is that ownership

---

[1] We assume this set to be finite. Though this is not necessarily true for real service descriptions, we argue that an infinite instance set can be sufficiently approximated by a finite instance set.

of a book with the title "Pope Joan" changes to me, where the delivery address is my address, the price is less than 20 Euro and delivery happens within the next 2 days. We do not set any further restrictions on the underlying service description language. We assume that the basic matcher implements a pessimistic set-based matchmaking approach. Specifically that means that an offer matches to a given request, if it is a subset of the request. The *match value* of an offer and a request is the smallest match value of the service instances described in the offer according to the request. It indicates how well the considered offer fits to the request. The pessimistic approach ensures that the executed service instance has a match value that is at least as high as the match result for the whole service. This is reasonable, since we will not know in advance which of the service instances described in the offer is executed by the service provider. Once available offers are discovered the matcher determines a sorted vector containing the match values for the offers according to a given request (*match result vector*) in a completely automatic fashion. The best fitting offer, i.e. the offer yielding the highest match value, is chosen and the corresponding service is invoked, i.e. one of its instances is executed, without requiring additional human intervention. Among other approaches the semantic service description language DSD [13,14] and the DIANE service matcher meet these assumptions.

3   Experience-Aware Service Selection

Our solution is designed as an extension for existing matchmakers, i.e. we assume to have the matching results provided by a basic matcher based on a given request and available offer descriptions. To allow for proper service ranking we evaluate how reliable those results are. More precisely we have to quantify the degree of conformance between the offer, the matching result is based on, and the service that will be actually provided (*offer conformance*). For that reason each service consumer provides the offer conformance of a provider perceived during service interaction as experience to others. Obviously, experiences of users that had similar requirements are more valuable in this context. If, for instance, two users requested a mp3-file but with different encoding and bit rates, and one of them is dissatisfied with the service, that does not imply that the other will be, too. The offer conformance of a specific service provider with respect to a given request and thus the reliability of the matching results for his services can then be predicted based on *relevant experiences* provided by other consumers. Finally, available offers are ranked based on their match value provided by the underlying matcher, the offer conformance prediction and the confidence of that prediction. In this section, we will describe how offer conformance can be formalized (Subsect. 3.1), how it can be used to predict the future offer conformance of a provider (Subsect. 3.3), how relevance of experiences can be determined (Subsect. 3.2) and how services can be ranked based on this information (Subsect. 3.3). Algorithm 1 is the resulting overall algorithm.

Algorithm 1. ExperienceAwareServiceSelection(request r, offer set O)

---
1. get the matching results mr for the request r and the offers in O from the basic matcher;
2. drop all offers with a match value of 0;
3. **if** (mr contains more than one offer of the same provider) **then**
4.   keep the offer with the highest match value among them and drop all the others;
5. **end if**
6. **for** (each provider with an offer in mr) **do**
7.   get all available experiences that are relevant for predicting the offer conformance of that provider with respect to r;
8.   calculate the overall offer conformance value and its confidence;
9. **end for**
10. rank the available offers based on mr, their predicted offer conformance and its confidence;
11. **return** t he offer with the highest rank;

3.1 Offer Conformance

Inspired by the concept of quality conformance proposed by Vu et al. [8], we measure the conformance between the service promised and that actually provided by comparing the match value calculated by the basic matcher and the rating the consumer provides after service execution. More specifically consider a consumer c posing a request r. Once the best fitting offer o among the set of available offers is determined, the corresponding service s is invoked. After service execution the consumer rates the service in terms of its suitability for reaching the goals captured in the request. Given the consumer c and the request r we measure the conformance $oc \in [0,1]$ of the offer o and the service s actually provided by

$$oc(c,s,r,o) = \begin{cases} \frac{ra(c,s,r)}{mv(r,o)} & \text{if } mv(r,o) \geq ra(c,s,r) \\ 1 & \text{otherwise} \end{cases} \tag{1}$$

where $mv(r,o)$ is the match value for r and o provided by the basic matcher. The value $ra(c,s,r) \in [0,1]$ is the personalized rating for the service s provided by the consumer c (with respect to the request r). It is the higher the more the service outcome suited to the consumer's needs. Note that we consider only negative deviations from the match value.

3.2 Relevance of Experiences

Once suitable offers and their providers are determined by the basic matcher, we have to identify consumer experiences that are *relevant* for predicting the offer conformance of every single provider with respect to the specified request. We define the set of experiences that are relevant for the offer conformance prediction of a given provider p with respect to the request r as those experiences that refer to a service stemming from p. An experience is the more relevant the more similar r and the request the experience is based on are. The first postulation is due to the fact that experiences with one provider cannot be transferred to another, the second accounts for the fact that ratings and thus offer conformance experiences are personalized and request-specific, i.e. experiences based on similar service demands and similar preferences are more valuable in this context. More specifically this means that observing the same service instance, the considered consumer and the experience provider should produce similar offer conformance values. This is true, if the given requests are similar. Moreover it is required that given similar requests the matcher provides similar match values. Presuming that the similarity of requests implies similarity of all their instances, this assumption holds if we choose 1− the mean deviation of corresponding service instances' match values (instances not contained in one of the requests were assumed to have a match value of 0) as a measure for request similarity. The relevance of a given experience may then be determined by directly comparing the two requests involved. However this is not a satisfying solution. The reasons are twofold. On the one hand the computation would be very costly, on the other hand consumers had to divulge much of their personal information including their preferences to allow for that comparison. Due to these facts we propose to approximate the similarity of the requests by indirectly comparing their match result vectors containing the match values for several offers. Note that this will not raise additional effort, since the match result vectors are created by the basic matchmaker anyway.

Approximating the request similarity. Without loss of generality we assume that both requests r_1 and r_2 are matched against the same set of offers,[2] i.e. all offers, and both resulting match result vectors mr_1 and mr_2 are in the same order with respect to the offers. The algorithm is based on two assumptions:

1. The result of the comparison between two corresponding match values $mr_1[i]$ and $mr_2[i]$, $0 \leq i \leq n$, where $n + 1$ is the length of mr_1 resp. mr_2, provides an indication for request similarity/dissimilarity, if at least one of the corresponding match values is high. It is the more significant, the higher $\max(mr_1[i], mr_2[i])$ is.
2. If the result of a comparison is significant, the following holds: The smaller the differences between the corresponding match values, the higher the similarity of the corresponding requests.

Figure 1 illustrates the motivation for those assumptions. It shows three diagrams each indicating the service instances of a sample offer with 10 instances and their match values with respect to two different requests (black and gray points). The lines correspond to the match value of the overall offer with respect to the requests. Diagram 1(a) presents the case where the offer has a low match value with respect to both requests, 0.1 and 0.2 respectively. In that case the difference between the match values of a single service instance with respect to the two requests is between 0 and $1 - 0.1 = 0.9$, so we cannot draw any conclusions about the similarity of the requests. Diagram 1(b) shows the case where the offer has a high match value with respect to one request and a low match value with

---

[2] Note that this is a simplified assumption, since existing matchmakers often do not match a given offer but a request-specific configuration of an offer (specialization of the offer). Consequently we do not necessarily compare the match values for the same offers. However our algorithm will provide meaningful results, if the available offers are not too generic. In this case the configured offers do not differ that much.

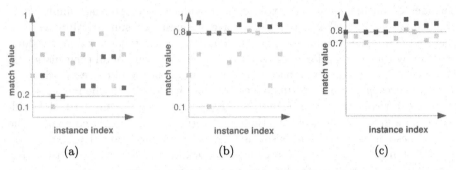

Fig. 1. Motivation for the assumptions

Algorithm 2. ApproximateSimilarity(minimalMV,threshold,mr_1,mr_2)

---

1. sumOfDeviations = 0;
2. sumOfWeights = 0;
3. **for** (i < mr_1.length) **do**
4. $maximum = max(mr_1[i], mr_2[i])$;
5.   **if** ($maximum \geq minimalMV$) **then**
6. $maximum = maximum^2$;
7.   sumOfDeviations+=| $mr_1[i] - mr_2[i]$ | · $maximum$;
8.   sumOfWeights+=$maximum$;
9.   **end if**
10. **end for**
11. **if** (sumOfWeights $\geq$ threshold) and (sumOfWeights > 0) **then**
12.   **return** 1-(sumOfDeviations/sumOfWeights);
13. **else**
14.   **return** 0;
15. **end if**

---

respect to the other. In that case the difference between the match values of a single service instance with respect to the two requests is also between 0 and 0.9, but we presume that it is most often high, since we believe that in real requests the match values of the described service instances are similar to some degree. Thus case 1(b) is an indication for the dissimilarity of the two requests. Diagram 1(c) depicts the case where the offer has a high match value with respect to both requests. In that case the difference between the match values of a single service instance with respect to the two requests is between 0 and $1 - 0.7 = 0.3$. Thus we have a strong indication for the similarity of the two requests. Based on the above assumptions we calculate the approximate similarity sim_{approx} of two requests r_1 and r_2 according to Alg. 2 by comparing their corresponding match values for a set of comparison offers given by the match result vectors mr_1 and mr_2. The algorithm calculates the weighted mean of the match value deviations. Following Assumption 1 the weights $max^2(mv_1, mv_2)$ correspond to the significance of each comparison result. Moreover for calculating the approximate similarity only those pairs are considered where at least one of the match values exceeds the value `minimalMV`. The output of the algorithm is only meaningful, if it is based on a sufficient number of significant comparisons. This is true, if the sum of the weights exceeds a given `threshold`, otherwise the algorithm returns 0, which means that the requests are not similar. Consequently the corresponding experiences are not considered for the offer conformance prediction. Appropriate values for $minimalMV$ and $threshold$ are application-specific and thus parameters of the algorithm. They can be determined based on test data (see Sect. 4).

Quality of the measure. The quality of our approximate similarity measure depends on the diversity and the number of available offers. This is due to the fact that we need a sufficient number of offers that lead to a high match value for at least one of the two requests to be compared to have enough match results that provide an indication for request similarity/dissimilarity. Since each single match value comparison allows to draw conclusions only about the request similarity referring to the service instances contained in the offer, a sufficient number of diverse offers is needed. On the other hand if a subset of the service instances covered by a request is not contained in any of the available offers, the quality of the similarity approximation with respect to those instances would be bad, but it does not matter, because those instances are never executed and thus never rated. However we argue that the algorithm provides meaningful results in real world scenarios, since in those settings we have a variety of offers. The quality of the approximate similarity measure will be evaluated in Sect. 4.

3.3 Service Ranking

Having determined the set of relevant experiences $E_{rel}(p,r)$ for each provider p with respect to the specified request r, we predict its future offer conformance $oc_p(r)$ based on those experiences. Moreover we calculate a confidence value $conf(oc_p(r))$ indicating the reliability of the offer conformance prediction $oc_p(r)$. Afterwards we rank the offers in the match result vector based on those values and the initial match values provided by the basic matcher.

Predicting the offer conformance. The future offer conformance $oc_p(r) \in [0,1]$ for p's offers with respect to the specified request r is calculated as the weighted mean of the observed oc-values (see Equ. 1) provided by the experiences in $E_{rel}(p,r)$.

$$oc_p(r) = \begin{cases} \frac{\sum_{i \in E_{rel}(p,r)} w(i) \cdot oc(i)}{\sum_{i \in E_{rel}(p,r)} w(i)} & \text{if } E_{rel}(p,r) \neq \emptyset \\ 0 & \text{otherwise} \end{cases} \quad (2)$$

with

$$w(i) = w_a(age(i)) \cdot sim_{approx}(r_i, r), \quad (3)$$

where $w(i)$ is a weight indicating the relevance of an experience i for the given request r. An experience is the more relevant the smaller its age $age(i)$ and the higher the similarity $sim_{approx}(r_i, r)$ of r_i and the considered service request r. The weight w_a with $w_a(a_{max}) = 0$ and $w_a(0) = 1$ is a monotonically decreasing function taking into account the age of an experience. Experiences older than a_{max} are not considered.

Confidence calculation. The confidence $conf(oc_p(r))$ of the predicted offer conformance value $oc_p(r)$ is determined by the number, age, and relevance of the experiences its calculation is based on. It is the higher the higher the number of experiences and the newer and the more relevant the experiences are. The confidence $conf(oc_p(r))$ of the offer conformance prediction $oc_p(r)$ is

$$conf(oc_p(r)) = \begin{cases} f(|E_{rel}(p,r)|, \min_{i \in E_{rel}(p,r)} w(i)) & \text{if } E_{rel}(p,r) \neq \emptyset \\ 0 & \text{otherwise,} \end{cases} \quad (4)$$

where f is an application-specific function to the interval $[0,1]$. It increases with the number of experiences and the minimal weight $w(i)$ of the experiences $i \in E_{rel}(p,r)$. It can be determined based on test data in the given field of application. We may also consider weights that account for the trustworthiness of the experience providers. However assessing the trustworthiness of experiences is a challenging topic in itself. It is not considered in this paper.

Service ranking. Once the $oc_p(r)$ and $conf(oc_p(r))$ values are calculated for the providers, we rank the offers based on those values and the initial match value of each offer. The rank $rank(o_p) \in [0,1]$ of an offer o_p from the provider p with the match value $mv(r, o_p)$ is calculated by

$$rank(o_p) = mv(r, o_p) \cdot conf(oc_p(r)) \cdot (oc_p(r)^2 - 1) + mv(r, o_p). \quad (5)$$

The rank of an offer o_p is equal to $mv(r, o_p)$ as long as no experiences are available and decreases linear to $mv(r, o_p) \cdot oc_p(r)^2$ with increasing confidence. Intuitively spoken this means that unknown services are preferred to give newcomers a chance. On the other hand inaccurate description providers are punished, where the penalty is the higher the lower the offer conformance is. Algorithm 1 summarizes the overall service ranking and selection procedure. Given a request r it ranks the available offers O based on the match result vector provided by the basic matcher and available experiences.

4   Evaluation and Discussion

We implemented the service model and a basic matcher as described in Sect. 2 as well as our approach to experience-aware service selection introduced in this paper. We performed several simulative experiments to evaluate the effectiveness of our solution.[3]

In a first series of tests we evaluated the quality of our approximate similarity measure, in a second series we investigated the quality of the offer conformance prediction. In both cases we studied the dependency of the quality from several parameters.

---

[3] The simulation environment as well as the implementation of the tests described in this section are available under
http://fusion.cs.uni-jena.de/professur/?content=fklan.

Algorithm 3. TestApproxSim($|I|,|C|,minMV$)

---

1. create two random requests of randomly chosen similarity containing maximal $|I|$ instances
2. create $|C|$ random comparison offers having at least a match value of $minMV$ with the first request
3. calculate approximate and actual similarity for the requests as described in Sect. 3.2
4. **return** t he percental deviation of the approximate similarity from the actual similarity

---

Quality of the approximate similarity measure. We evaluated the quality of our approximate similarity measure (Alg. 2) depending on the maximum number of instances per request $|I|$, the cardinality of the comparison set of offers $|C|$, i.e. the number of offers considered in the match result vectors which are input to the approximate similarity algorithm, and the match values of the offers in that set. For the latter we introduced a parameter $minMV$ indicating the smallest match value of all offers in the comparison set with respect to a given requests. The quality was measured in terms of the percental deviation of the approximate measure's results from the actual similarity calculated by comparing requests directly as described in Sect. 3.2.

The test was performed according to Alg. 3. It was run with several parameter settings. The average quality was calculated over 10000 runs (50000 for the quality-$|I|$-dependency plot). We tested our approximate similarity measure with several parameter configurations. We identified *threshold* = 10 and *minimalMV* = 0.5 as a good combination. Decreasing one or both of the values leads to lower quality results. Increasing the parameter values does not result in a significant improvement of the result's quality. All test series are based on this parameter setting. Figure 2(a) shows the quality of the approximate similarity measure depending on the maximum number of instances per request.[4] After an initial phase the average deviation of the approximated similarity is about 17% for $|I| \approx 100$ and slightly increases with higher $|I|$-values. Another series of experiments showed that the absolute deviation for $|I| \approx 100$ is 0.1. Further increasing of $|I|$ up to 5000 instances results in a deviation of about 20%. The bad quality for small request lengths originates from the small number of possible offers in the comparison set. We evaluated the quality of the approximate similarity measure depending on the minimal match value of the offers in the comparison set with respect to the given request. Resulting from the higher match values of the comparison offers and thus a higher significance of the single comparison results, the quality increases with higher values for $minMV$ and reaches its optimum around $minMV = 0.5$. Further increasing of $minMV$ leads to results of worse quality. This is due to the decreasing number of possible comparison offers. The dependency between the quality of the approximate similarity measure and the cardinality of the set of comparison offers is illustrated in Fig.2(b). The quality is plotted for 3 different values of $|I|$. After an initial phase the quality remains stable at a level of about 17% for $|C| = 20$. Further increasing of $|C|$ does not result in a better quality. Summarizing the results for this test series we point out that a number of 20 comparison offers with a match value of at least 0.5

---

[4] The brackets indicate the standard error of the sample mean assuming that the discrepancy values follow a Gaussian distribution.

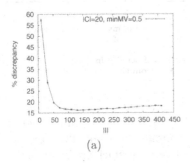
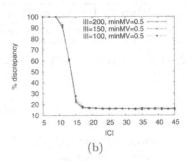

(a)   (b)

Fig. 2. Quality of the approximate similarity measure depending from the maximal number of instances per request (a) and the cardinality of the comparison set (b)

with respect to at least one of the two requests to be compared is sufficient to assure a measure quality of about 17%. The quality just slightly decreases with the maximal number of instances per request.

Quality of the offer conformance prediction. The quality of the offer conformance prediction was evaluated depending on the number of relevant experiences $|E_{rel}|$ and the minimal similarity $minExpSim$ between the given request and those the experiences are based on. We simplified our experiments in that we considered only service providers offering a single service. We did not consider providers with changing behavior over time, i.e. the actually provided service of a provider remained stable over time. Finally we did not account for the age of experiences, i.e. we assumed $age(i) = 0$ for all experiences i. Studying of those aspects is subject to our future research. The quality of the offer conformance prediction was measured in terms of its percental deviation from the actual offer conformance. Given a request r and an offer o the actual offer conformance was calculated as the mean offer conformance of all instances in o with respect to r. This is reasonable, since this is the expected offer conformance when executing the service belonging to o, presuming that all service instances are executed with equal probability. As already mentioned a provider offers a single service. He is characterized by the offer for that service and by the actually provided service. The latter is represented as an offer that differs from the advertised offer. The differences between the offer and the actually provided service are generated by replacing instances, uniformly chosen from the instances contained in the advertised offer, by others uniformly chosen from the basic instance set. We introduced a provider parameter indicating the maximum number of differing instances per offer. The plots are based on a provider where maximal 50% of the instances differ from the advertised offer. If executed, a service uniformly chooses one of its instances and provides it to the consumer. The consumer may rate this service by determining the match value of this instance with respect to the posed request. Afterwards the offer conformance can be calculated based on this rating and the match value for the whole service offer.

Algorithm 4. TestOfferConf($|E_{rel}|$, $minExpSim$)

1. create a request r and a set R of $|E_{rel}|$ requests having at least a similarity of $minExpSim$ to r
2. create a provider p based on a random offer o
3. create a set of $|C|$ comparison offers each having at least a match value of $minMV$ with the request r
4. **for** (each of the requests in R) **do**
5.   generate an experience with p as well as the matching result vector based on the set of comparison offers
6. **end for**
7. get the offer conformance of the provider p with respect to r based on the generated experiences according to formula (2)
8. get the actual offer conformance of the provider p with respect to r as described in this section
9. **return** t he percental deviation of the predicted from the actual offer conformance value

The test was performed according to Alg. 4. It was run with several parameter settings and the average quality over 10000 runs was calculated. Figure 3(a) shows the quality of the offer conformance prediction depending on the minimal similarity between the given request and those the experiences are based on. The test was performed with the parameter values $|C| = 20$, $|I| = 100$ and $minMV = 0.5$. The quality is plotted for 20, 30 and 50 experiences. As expected the quality of the prediction increases with $minMV$, since the relevance of the considered experiences is higher. The optimal quality of about 10% deviation is reached for $minMV \approx 0.9$. When calculating the offer conformance by assigning the same weight to all experiences, the quality of the prediction is much worse. The dependency between the quality of the offer conformance prediction and

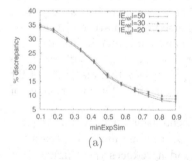

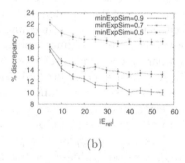

(a)   (b)

Fig. 3. Quality of the offer conformance prediction depending on the minimal experience similarity (a) and the number of experiences (b)

the number of experiences is illustrated in Fig. 3(b). The test was performed with the parameter values $|C| = 50$, $|I| = 100$ and $minMV = 0.5$. The quality is plotted for similarity thresholds of 0.5, 0.7 and 0.9. As expected the quality of the prediction increases with the number of experiences and remains stable after a threshold specific number of experiences. This number is the smaller the smaller the minimal similarity of the experiences is. Considering an experience similarity of 0.9 we need about 50 experiences to have a prediction deviation of 10%. A number of 20 experiences is sufficient to have a prediction deviation of 12%. The described test series is based on the assumption that we know about the actual similarity of the requests, but in fact we have to rely on the approximate similarity when selecting the experiences to be considered for the offer conformance prediction. We can simply infer results for this case. Assuming a similarity deviation of 20% the average deviation of the offer conformance prediction is between 7% and 14% when having a minimal similarity of 0.8 and a number of 20 experiences (see Fig. 3(a)).

Based on a test series like this one may derive an appropriate function f defining the confidence of the prediction (see Def. 4). In our experiments requests and offers are created randomly. The distribution of their instances differs from that of real world service descriptions in that the match value distribution for the latter is smoother, i.e. the match values of the single instances within a request are more similar. Due to this observation we expect that the approximation of the request similarity and thus the offer conformance prediction will be even more accurate when working with real world service descriptions.

5   Conclusion

We introduced our approach for experience aware service ranking and selection. Designed as an extension it augments the functionality of existing matchmakers by allowing them to predict a service's future performance more accurately based on offer conformance experiences in former service interactions and thereby reducing the uncertainty encountered in this step. The services discovered by those matchers are then ranked based on their match values, the predicted offer conformance and the confidence of this prediction. The approach relies on subjective feedback in terms of ratings and considers the personalized nature of those experiences while avoiding explicit sharing of personal consumer information by comparing consumer preferences indirectly. It exploits available feedback effectively by considering not only ratings for a single service but also ratings for similar services of the same provider when evaluating the offer conformance of a specific service.

In our future work we plan to elaborate on mechanisms for providing request and preference templates as proposed in [3,15]. On the one hand this eases the creation of service descriptions, on the other hand it reduces the ambiguity of descriptions. Moreover it allows for more efficient storage and gathering of experiences. The presented approach considers experiences where service consumers rated a service as a whole. We plan to extend our solution by also allowing for refined experience, where consumers may rate partial aspects of a service. Another interesting point that is important when dealing with experiences of other consumers is that of dishonest experience providers. We have to question how to recognize those experiences, how to deal with them and how to prevent them. It is planned to adopt the reputation system solution of Obreiter et al. [16] for this purpose. Beside those extending features we will expand our evaluation by testing our solution with service descriptions based on existing description languages.

References

1. Küster, U., König-Ries, B.: Supporting Dynamics in Service Descriptions - The Key to Automatic Service Usage. In: 5th International Conference on Service Oriented Computing, Vienna (2007)
2. Josang, A., Ismail, R., Boyd, C.: A Survey of Trust and Reputation Systems for Online Service Provision. Decis. Support Syst. 43(2), 618–644 (2007)
3. Kerrigan, M.: Web Service Selection Mechanisms in the Web Service Execution Environment (WSMX). In: 21st ACM Symposium on Applied Computing, Dijon, pp. 1664–1668 (2006)
4. Kokash, N., Birukou, A., D'Andrea, V.: Web Service Discovery Based on Past User Experience. In: Abramowicz, W. (ed.) BIS 2007. LNCS, vol. 4439, pp. 95–107. Springer, Heidelberg (2007)
5. Billhardt, H., Hermoso, R., Ossowski, S., Centeno, R.: Trust-based Service Provider Selection in Open Environments. In: 22nd ACM Symposium on Applied Computing, Seoul, pp. 1375–1380 (2007)
6. Maximilien, E.M., Singh, M.P.: Conceptual Model of Web Service Reputation. SIGMOD Rec. 31(4), 36–41 (2002)
7. Sensoy, M., Pembe, F.C. (eds.): Experience-Based Service Provider Selection in Agent-Mediated E-Commerce. Eng. Appl. Artif. Intell. 20(3), 325–335 (2007)
8. Vu, L.-H., Hauswirth, M., Aberer, K.: QoS-based Service Selection and Ranking with Trust and Reputation Management. In: Meersman, R., Tari, Z. (eds.) OTM 2005. LNCS, vol. 3760, pp. 446–483. Springer, Heidelberg (2005)
9. Vu, L.-H., Porto, F., Hauswirth, M., Aberer, K.: An Extensible and Personalized Approach to QoS-enabled Service Discovery. In: 11th Intl. Database Engineering & Applications Symposium, Banff (2007)
10. Caballero, A., Bota, J.A., Gmez-Skarmeta, A.F.: On the Behaviour of the TRSIM Model for Trust and Reputation. In: 5th German Conf. on Multiagent System Technologies, Leipzig, pp. 182–193 (2007)
11. Manikrao, U.S., Prabhakar, T.V.: Dynamic Selection of Web Services with Recommendation System. In: Intl. Conf. on Next Generation Web Services Practices, p. 117. IEEE Computer Society, Washington (2005)
12. Wang, H.-C., Lee, C.-S., Ho, T.-H.: Combining Subjective and Objective QoS Factors for Personalized Web Service Selection. Expert Syst. Appl. 32(2), 571–584 (2007)
13. Küster, U., König-Ries, B.: Semantic Service Discovery with DIANE Service Descriptions. In: Intl. Workshop on Service Composition & SWS Challenge at the WI 2007, Silicon Valley (2007)
14. Klein, M., König-Ries, B., Müssig, M.: What is Needed for Semantic Service Descriptions? A Proposal for Suitable Language Constructs. Int. J. of Web and Grid Services 1(3/4), 328–364 (2005)
15. Stollberg, M., Hepp, M., Hoffmann, J.: A Caching Mechanism for Semantic Web Service Discovery. In: ISWC/ASWC, pp. 480–493 (2007)
16. Obreiter, P., König-Ries, B.: A New View on Normativeness in Distributed Reputation Systems - Beyond Behavioral Beliefs. In: 4th Intl. Workshop on Agents and Peer-to-Peer Computing, Utrecht (2005)

Performance Evaluation of Algorithms for Soft Evidential Update in Bayesian Networks: First Results

Scott Langevin and Marco Valtorta*

Department of Computer Science and Engineering
University of South Carolina
Columbia, SC 29208, USA
{langevin,mgv}@cse.sc.edu

Abstract. In this paper we analyze the performance of three algorithms for soft evidential update, in which a probability distribution represented by a Bayesian network is modified to a new distribution constrained by given marginals, and closest to the original distribution according to cross entropy. The first algorithm is a new and improved version of the big clique algorithm [1] that utilizes lazy propagation [2]. The second and third algorithm [3] are wrapper methods that convert soft evidence to virtual evidence, in which the evidence for a variable consists of a like-lihood ratio. Virtual evidential update is supported in existing Bayesian inference engines, such as Hugin. To evaluate the three algorithms, we implemented BRUSE (Bayesian Reasoning Using Soft Evidence), a new Bayesian inference engine, and instrumented it. The resulting statistics are presented and discussed.

Keywords: Bayesian networks, Iterative Proportional Fitting Procedure, Soft Evidence, Virtual Evidence, Cross Entropy.

1 Introduction and Motivation

The issue of how to deal with uncertain evidence in Bayesian networks appears in Pearl's foundational text [4, sections 2.2.2, 2.3.3] and has recently been the subject of methological inquiry and algorithm development (e.g., [1,5,6,7,8,9,3,10]). A result of these studies has been to clarify the distinction between soft and virtual evidence. Briefly, representing uncertain probabilistic evidence as virtual evidence is appropriate when we model the reliability of an information source, while the soft evidence representation is appropriate when we want to incorporate the distribution of a variable of interest into a probabilistic model. Update based on virtual evidence (sometimes called likelihood evidence) is supported

---

* This work was funded in part by the Intelligence Advanced Research Projects Activity (IARPA) Collaboration and Analyst System Effectiveness (CASE) Program, contract FA8750-06-C-0194 issued by the Air Force Research Laboratory (AFRL). The views and conclusions are those of the authors, not of the US Government or its agencies. We thank three anonymous reviewers for their comments.

S. Greco and T. Lukasiewicz (Eds.): SUM 2008, LNAI 5291, pp. 284–297, 2008.
© Springer-Verlag Berlin Heidelberg 2008

in several existing Bayesian inference engines, such as Hugin[1]. This paper is concerned with soft evidence only.

For the purpose of this paper, we define evidence in a Bayesian network as a collection of findings on variables of the Bayesian network. A hard finding specifies which value (state) the variable is in. A soft finding specifies the probability distribution of a variable. Hard evidence is a collection of hard findings. Soft evidence is a collection of soft findings. See [1] for more general definitions of evidence. Some authors describe the problem of update in the presence of soft evidence as a model revision or parameter tuning problem. In the case of soft evidential update, all evidence (hard and soft) is presented simultaneously; in the case of model revision, the soft evidence is better considered as a constraint on the probability distribution encoded by the model, which is modified before evidence is applied. Despite the clear difference in the problems that are solved, similar algorithms can be used to solve both problems, as can be seen by contrasting [9], which takes the model revision approach, with [3], which takes the evidential update approach.

Belief update in the presence of hard evidence is carried out by conditioning. As observed by many authors, conditioning cannot be used to update beliefs in the presence of soft evidence. The general soft evidential update method of [1] will be used in this paper; this general method admits several detailed algorithmic variants, which have different efficiency characteristics with respect to network topologies and evidence presentations. The input to the method consists of a Bayesian network and a set of soft and hard findings. The method computes implicitly a joint probability that has two properties: (1) the evidence is respected, i.e. the findings are marginals for the joint probability distribution; (2) the joint probability is as close as possible to the initial distribution represented in the input Bayesian network, where distance is measured by cross-entropy (I-divergence). The joint probability is computed implicitly in that only its single-variable marginals are output. The focus of this paper is the experimental comparison of three such variants: the big clique algorithm of [1,6], and the two wrapper-based methods of [3]. The authors of [3] prove that the three variants compute the same distribution. The three variants are described in the following section. We aim (in future work) to provide further insight into the appropriateness of the three variants for different network topologies and evidence presentations.

2 Algorithms

In this section we first describe lazy propagation, an efficient probabilistic update algorithm that is used as the core update mechanism for the three algorithms analyzed in this paper. We then describe the big clique algorithm and the two variations of wrapper algorithms that can utilize any inference engine without modification. In this paper we only consider wrappers for lazy propagation. Finally, we list various other methods that have been proposed for soft evidential update.

---

[1] Virtual evidence is, confusingly, called soft evidence in [11].

2.1   Lazy Propagation

Lazy propagation [2] is an efficient junction tree algorithm that utilizes d-separation properties of the original Bayesian network by maintaining a multiplicative decomposition of clique and separator potentials. It merges the ideas of belief update algorithms that compute all marginals and direct query-based algorithms that compute a marginal for a query and better exploit evidence-induced d-separation.

Lazy propagation can be used with any computational tree structure that maintains the d-separation properties of the original Bayesian network. Our implementation uses the junction tree structure as does Hugin propagation, rather than the original Lauritzen-Spiegelhalter or the Shafer-Shenoy structures. In particular, two mailboxes per separator are used, one for messages sent during the collect evidence phase and the other for the distribute evidence phase [12]. Cliques and separators in the junction tree maintain sets of potentials and combination of potentials is delayed as long as possible to take advantage of d-separation and unity potential properties of the Bayesian network.

Lazy propagation consists of two phases: collecting evidence to the designated root clique, and distributing evidence from the designated root clique to the rest of the junction tree. Evidence is collected and distributed by message passing, where each message is a collection of potentials.

Following is a description of the lazy propagation algorithm:

1. Build a junction tree for the Bayesian network (see [13] and [2] for details).
2. Apply hard evidence (see procedure on page 287 for details).
3. Invoke *Collect Evidence* on designated root of junction tree.
4. Invoke *Distribute Evidence* on designated root of junction tree.
5. Invoke *Calculate Posterior Marginals*.

Collect Evidence. Let C_i and C_j be adjacent cliques in the junction tree and let S be the separator between C_i and C_j. Let Φ_{C_i} and Φ_{C_j} be the set of potentials associated with C_i and C_j. Let $\Phi^\uparrow$ and $\Phi^\downarrow$ be the set of potentials stored in the collect and distribute mailboxes of S respectively. If *Collect Evidence* is invoked on C_j from C_i, then:

1. C_j invokes *Collect Evidence* on all adjacent cliques except C_i.
2. The message $\Phi^\uparrow$ from C_j to C_i is calculated (using the algorithm on page 287) and stored in the collect mailbox of S.
3. Update $\Phi_{C_i} = \Phi_{C_i} \cup \Phi^\uparrow$.

Distribute Evidence. Let C_i and C_j be adjacent cliques in the junction tree and let S be the separator between C_i and C_j. Let Φ_{C_i} and Φ_{C_j} be the set of potentials associated with C_i and C_j. Let $\Phi^\uparrow$ and $\Phi^\downarrow$ be the set of potentials stored in the collect and distribute mailboxes of S respectively. If *Distribute Evidence* is invoked on C_j from C_i, then:

1. The message $\Phi^\downarrow$ from C_i to C_j is calculated (using the algorithm on page 287) and stored in the distribute mailbox of S.
2. Update $\Phi_{C_j} = \Phi_{C_j} \cup \Phi^\downarrow \backslash \Phi^\uparrow$.
3. C_j invokes *Distribute Evidence* on all adjacent cliques except C_i.

Calculate Message. Let C_i and C_j be adjacent cliques in the junction tree and let S be the separator between C_i and C_j. Let Φ_{C_i} be the set of potentials associated with C_i. Let $dom(A)$ be the set of variables associated with A (where A is either a potential or a separator). The message passed from C_i to C_j is calculated as follows:

1. Set $\mathcal{R}_S =$ Invoke *Find Relevant Potentials* on Φ_{C_i} for $dom(S)$.
2. For each variable $\mathcal{X}$ in $\{\mathcal{X} \in dom(\phi)|\phi \in \mathcal{R}_S, \mathcal{X} \notin dom(S)\}$
   (a) Marginalize $\mathcal{X}$ out of $\mathcal{R}_S$:
      i. Set $\Phi_{\mathcal{X}} = \{\phi \in \mathcal{R}_S | \mathcal{X} \in dom(\phi)\}$.
      ii. Let $\phi_{\mathcal{X}}^* = \sum_{\mathcal{X}} \prod_{\phi \in \Phi_{\mathcal{X}}} \phi$.
      iii. Update $\mathcal{R}_S = \{\phi_{\mathcal{X}}^*\} \cup \mathcal{R}_S \backslash \Phi_{\mathcal{X}}$
3. Return $\mathcal{R}_S$.

A detailed presentation on alternative ways to perform the second step can be found in [14].

Find Relevant Potentials. Let Φ be a set of potentials and let S be a set of variables. The relevant potentials of Φ for calculating the joint probablity of S are calculated as follows:

1. Let $\mathcal{R}_S = \{\exists \mathcal{X} \in dom(\phi) | \mathcal{X}$ is d-connected to $\mathcal{Y} \in S\}$.
2. Use the unity-potential axiom to remove from $\mathcal{R}_S$ all potentials containing only barren head variables (defined in, e.g., [13]) to obtain $\mathcal{R}_S'$.
3. Return $\mathcal{R}_S'$.

Apply Hard Evidence. In the lazy propagation algorithm, hard evidence is incorporated by applying hard evidence on a variable $\mathcal{X}$ with all cliques C_i where $\mathcal{X} \in dom(C_i)$. This is done to fully exploit d-separation properties of the Bayesian network induced by the evidence. Hard evidence on a variable $\mathcal{X} = x$ is incorporated by the reduction of the domain of all potentials ϕ_i where $\mathcal{X} \in dom(\phi_i)$ to only include configurations of the potential where $\mathcal{X} = x$. All configurations where $\mathcal{X} \neq x$ are simply removed. This process is called an instantiation of ϕ_i.

Calculate Posterior Marginals. In the lazy propagation algorithm, marginals of all variables in the Bayesian network can be calculated by first applying any hard evidence entered, then performing the collect evidence and distribute evidence phases, known collectively as a full propagation of evidence. Let $\mathcal{P}(\mathcal{X}|\epsilon)$ be the posterior marginal of $\mathcal{X}$. Calculation of marginals is then performed on each variable $\mathcal{X}$ by the following:

1. For each variable $\mathcal{X}$
   (a) Let $\Phi_{\mathcal{X}} = \{argmin_{\Phi_{C_i}}\, dom(C_i)|\mathcal{X} \in dom(C_i)\}$.
   (b) Set $\mathcal{R}_{\mathcal{X}} =$ Invoke *Find Relevant Potentials* on $\Phi_{\mathcal{X}}$ for $dom(\{\mathcal{X}\})$.
   (c) For each variable $\mathcal{Y}$ in $\{\mathcal{Y} \in dom(\phi)|\phi \in \mathcal{R}_{\mathcal{X}}, \mathcal{Y} \neq \mathcal{X}\}$

i. Marginalize $\mathcal{Y}$ out of $\mathcal{R}_{\mathcal{X}}$:
   A. Set $\Phi_{\mathcal{Y}} = \{\phi \in \mathcal{R}_{\mathcal{X}} | \mathcal{X} \in dom(\phi)\}$.
   B. Let $\phi_{\mathcal{Y}}^* = \sum_{\mathcal{Y}} \prod_{\phi \in \Phi_{\mathcal{Y}}} \phi$.
   C. Update $\mathcal{R}_{\mathcal{X}} = \{\phi_{\mathcal{Y}}^*\} \cup \mathcal{R}_{\mathcal{X}} \backslash \Phi_{\mathcal{Y}}$

(d) Calculate

$$P(\mathcal{X}|\epsilon) = \frac{\prod_{\phi \in \mathcal{R}_{\mathcal{X}}} \phi}{\sum_{\mathcal{X}} \prod_{\phi \in \mathcal{R}_{\mathcal{X}}} \phi}$$

The above algorithm can be modified to also calculate posterior marginals using the separators as well as the cliques.

2.2   Lazy Big Clique Algorithm

The big clique algorithm [1] incorporates soft evidence by combining two methods: junction tree propagation and Iterative Proportional Fitting Procedure (IPFP; [15,16,1]). The original big clique algorithm modified the Hugin propagation algorithm and therefore did not exploit d-separation properties of the underlying Bayesian network. A new version of the big clique algorithm was developed (the lazy big clique algorithm), that is more efficient by taking advantage of d-separation using the lazy propagation algorithm described in the previous section.

The lazy big clique algorithm modifies the lazy propagation algorithm as follows:

1. Construct a junction tree that includes all variables that have soft evidence in one clique - the big clique C_1.
2. Apply hard evidence and invoke the lazy propagation routine *Collect Evidence* on C_1.
3. Combine all potentials associated with C_1 to produce the joint probability distribution $P(C_1)$.
4. Absorb all soft evidence in C_1 (with the algorithm described on page 289).
5. Invoke the *Big Clique Distribute Evidence* routine. A special method is needed to distribute evidence from the big clique since during absorption of soft evidence the decomposition of potentials in C_1 is lost, and therefore a division by the evidence received from a neighboring clique is necessary when calculating messages to avoid passing back redundant information.

Big Clique Distribute Evidence

1. For each clique C_i adjacent to C_1, combine potentials of message in collect mailbox of separator S between C_i and C_1, call this result Φ_i^* - the evidence C_1 received from C_i.
2. Calculate message passed from C_1 to C_i as follows:

$$\Phi_i^\downarrow = \frac{\Phi_{C_1}}{\Phi_i^*}$$

3. For each variable $\mathcal{X}$ in $\{\mathcal{X} \in dom(\Phi_i^{\downarrow}) | \mathcal{X} \notin \mathcal{S}\}$
   (a) Marginalize out $\mathcal{X}$.
4. Let $\Phi_i^{\downarrow*}$ be the potential obtained.
5. Store $\Phi_i^{\downarrow*}$ in the distribute mailbox of $\mathcal{S}$.
6. Update $\Phi_{C_i} = \Phi_{C_i} \cup \Phi_i^{\downarrow*}$.
7. C_i invokes the lazy propagation routine *Distribute Evidence* on all adjacent cliques except C_1.

Absorption of Soft Evidence. We define absorption in the special big clique C_1 as the process by which the joint probability $\mathcal{P}(C_1)$ is updated to satisfy the constraints imposed by soft evidence on variables $\mathcal{S} \subseteq C_1$, where $\mathcal{S} = \{S_1, S_2, .., S_k\}$. Let $\mathcal{Q}(C_1)$ be the joint probability after absorption.

Then $\forall i \sum_{C_1 \backslash S_i} \mathcal{Q}(C_1) = \mathcal{P}(S_i)$, where $\mathcal{P}(S_i)$ is the soft evidence on S_i, $i = 1, ..., k$. Absorption of soft evidence in clique C_1 is done using IPFP and consists of cycles of k steps, one per finding. Each step corresponds to one soft finding. The procedure is as follows:

$$\mathcal{Q}_0(C_1) = \mathcal{P}(C_1)$$
$$\mathcal{Q}_i(C_1) = \frac{\mathcal{Q}_{i-1}(C_1) \cdot \mathcal{P}(S_j)}{\mathcal{Q}_{i-1}(S_j)}$$

where $j = (i - 1) \bmod k + 1$.

2.3   Wrapper Method 1: Iterate over Network

Both wrapper methods [3] utilize any existing Bayesian inferencing engine that supports virtual evidence by converting soft evidence findings into virtual evidence that are applied to the Bayesian network using standard inference. Convergence is achieved using an iterative method. For wrapper method 1, at each iteration one soft evidence finding is converted to virtual evidence and applied. The process is performed repeated until convergence as follows:

Let $\mathcal{P}(\mathcal{X})$ be the joint probability of the Bayesian network $\mathcal{N}$ obtained using standard BN inference. Let $\mathcal{S}$ be the variables with soft evidence, where $\mathcal{S} = \{S_1, S_2, .., S_k\}$, and $\mathcal{P}(S_i)$ is the soft evidence on $S_i, i = 1, .., k$. This algorithm applies soft evidence by iterating over the whole network as follows:

1. $\mathcal{Q}_0 = \mathcal{P}(\mathcal{X})$; $k = 1$;
2. Repeat the following until convergence:
   (a) $i = 1 + (k - 1) \bmod m$; $j = 1 + \lfloor (k - 1)/m \rfloor$;
   (b) (Convert the soft evidence to virtual evidence) Construct virtual evidence $\mathcal{V}_{i,j}$ with likelihood ratio:

$$\mathcal{L}(S_i) = \frac{\mathcal{P}(S_i)}{\mathcal{Q}_{k-1}(S_i)}$$

   (c) Obtain $\mathcal{Q}_k(\mathcal{X})$ by updating $\mathcal{Q}_{k-1}(\mathcal{X})$ with $\mathcal{V}_{i,j}$ using standard BN inference.
   (d) $k = k + 1$

2.4   Wrapper Method 2: Iterate over Soft Evidence

Wrapper method 2 is similar to the big clique algorithm in that both methods calculate the joint probability of the soft evidence variables and use IPFP to absorb soft evidence. The big clique performs IPFP on all variables in the big clique, while the wrapper 2 method only performs IPFP on the soft evidence variables. The wrapper 2 method converts the soft evidence to virtual evidence that is applied to the Bayesian network using standard inference. As a result, the wrapper 2 method requires two full propagations: one to calculate the joint probability of the soft evidence variables, and another to calculate the posterior marginals. The process is as follows:

Let $\mathcal{P}(\mathcal{X})$ be the joint probability of the Bayesian network $\mathcal{N}$ obtained using standard BN inference. Let $\mathcal{S}$ be the variables with soft evidence, where $\mathcal{S} = \{\mathcal{S}_1, \mathcal{S}_2, .., \mathcal{S}_k\}$ and $\mathcal{P}(\mathcal{S}_i)$ is the soft evidence on $\mathcal{S}_i, i = 1, .., k$. Let $\mathcal{P}(\mathcal{S})$ be the joint probability of $\mathcal{S}$. This algorithm applies soft evidence as follows:

1. Use any BN inference method on $\mathcal{N}$ to obtain $\mathcal{P}(\mathcal{S})$.
2. Absorb all soft evidence in $\mathcal{P}(\mathcal{S})$ (with the algorithm described below) to obtain $\mathcal{Q}(\mathcal{S})$.
3. (Convert the soft evidence to virtual evidence) Construct virtual evidence $\mathcal{V}$ with likelihood ratio:
$$\mathcal{L}(\mathcal{S}) = \frac{\mathcal{Q}(\mathcal{S})}{\mathcal{P}(\mathcal{S})}$$
4. Update the beliefs in $\mathcal{N}$ with $\mathcal{V}$ using standard BN inference.

Bayesian network engines of the "all-marginal" variety (junction tree based) do not compute joint probabilities, but rather calculate single-variable marginals for all variables. Junction tree algorithms can be modified to calculate joint probabilities for a set of variables by adding pairwise edges between all variables of interest to the moral graph before performing triangulation. This ensures the resulting junction tree will contain a clique that contains all variables of interest. After propagation, the joint probability of the variables can be constructed by combining all potentials associated with this clique. Our implementation of the wrapper 2 method uses this technique to calculate the joint probability of the soft evidence variables. See [17] and [13, Section 5.2] for a discussion of other methods to calculate joint probabilities in "all-marginal" algorithms.

Absorption of Soft Evidence. We define absorption of soft evidence as the process by which the joint probability $\mathcal{P}(\mathcal{S})$ is updated to satisfy the constraints imposed by soft evidence on variables $\mathcal{S}$, where $\mathcal{S} = \{\mathcal{S}_1, \mathcal{S}_2, .., \mathcal{S}_k\}$. Let $\mathcal{Q}(\mathcal{S})$ be the joint probability after absorption. Then $\forall i \sum_{\mathcal{S}\backslash \mathcal{S}_i} \mathcal{Q}(\mathcal{S}) = \mathcal{P}(\mathcal{S}_i)$, where $\mathcal{P}(\mathcal{S}_i)$ is the soft evidence on $\mathcal{S}_i$, $i = 1, ..., k$. Absorption of soft evidence is done using the Iterative Proportional Fitting Procedure (IPFP) and consists of cycles of k steps, one per finding. Each step corresponds to one soft finding. The procedure is as follows:

$$\mathcal{Q}_0(\mathcal{S}) = \mathcal{P}(\mathcal{S})$$

$$Q_i(\mathcal{S}) = \frac{Q_{i-1}(\mathcal{S}) \cdot \mathcal{P}(\mathcal{S}_j)}{Q_{i-1}(\mathcal{S}_j)}$$

where $j = (i - 1) \bmod k + 1$.

2.5   Other Methods

Here, we only list several other methods for soft evidence update: the space-saving implementation of IPFP [18,19,20]; the soft updating algorithm of [10]; and the approximate update algorithms by Peng and Ding [9].

3   Experimental Setup

To evaluate the lazy big clique (referred to as big clique from here on) and wrapper algorithms, a new Bayesian reasoning engine was constructed that utilizes lazy propagation, the Bayesian Reasoning Using Soft Evidence (BRUSE) engine. BRUSE was developed using the Java framework and implements the three discussed algorithms for soft evidential update. In order to evaluate algorithm performance, an instrumentation framework was implemented into BRUSE to gather statistics during inferencing. Statistics collected are: number of table multiplication operations performed, number of table addition operations performed, number of table division operations performed, IPFP iterations required for convergence, domain size of the IPFP table, and time to perform inference. Our testing was done on a Dell Optiplex Intel Core 2 Duo, 2.4 GHz machine with 2GB of RAM. Each test configuration was performed ten times and average statistics were calculated. The tests were performed using four Bayesian networks of varying sizes and complexity. Two of the networks were downloaded from a web-based repository [21]: stud farm (12 nodes) [13] and alarm (37 nodes) [22]. The other two networks, test71 (80 nodes) and test61 (200 nodes), were randomly generated to simulate complex networks. Table 1 shows statistics for the four networks. These statistics show the relative complexity of the networks and corresponding junction trees when one soft evidence finding is chosen.

Each network was tested with ten different test configurations consisting of one to ten soft evidence findings. Hard evidence was not used in our tests. Each test, randomly selects soft evidence variables accordingly to satisfy the test configuration chosen. The same set of soft evidence findings are applied to each of the three algorithms to compare their relative performance.

Table 1. Statistics for test networks

Network	Number of Nodes	Number of Cliques	Max Clique Size	Triangulation Weight
studfarm	12	9	16	116
alarm	37	27	144	1065
test71	80	65	2916	13793
test61	200	175	262144	347180

4   Results

We present here some of the experimental results obtained so far, without interpretation. Since we use the min-size heuristic, which is widely recognized as excellent [23], the cost to generate the junction tree is negligible. Accordingly, for all networks, we collect statistics only after the construction of the junction tree. Also, we found that, in our implementation, inference time corresponds closely to the number of elementary table operations performed, where we define number of elementary table operations as the sum of table multiplications, additions and divisions. As an example, compare Figure 1 with Figure 2. Therefore, the number of table operations provides a good measure of relative performance.

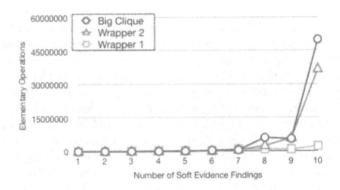

Fig. 1. Average number of elementary table operations for the alarm network

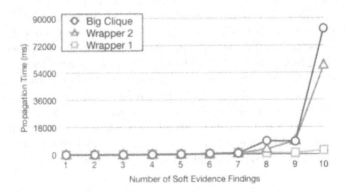

Fig. 2. Average propagation time for the alarm network

For all networks, it appears that wrapper 1 is slower than the other two methods when the number of soft evidence findings is small (less than 7 for the networks we consider). (We apologize to the reader for the fact that several of the graphs do not provide sufficient resolution to show this.) We conjecture that

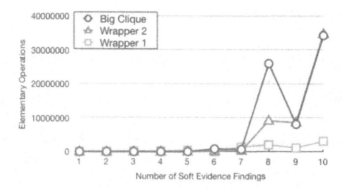

Fig. 3. Number of elementary table operations for test case 3 of the alarm network

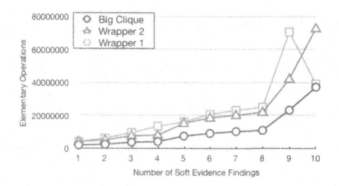

Fig. 4. Average number of elementary table operations for the test61 network

the reason is that the cost of propagation through the whole network dominates the cost of IPFP over a rather small joint probability. As a consequence, we also conjecture that this would not be the case for networks with large state spaces, for which the joint probability tables are large, even when they contain only a few nodes.

For all networks, wrapper 2 and big clique have similar run times. This is to be expected, because both methods need to compute the joint probability of the soft evidence variables, which requires, in a junction tree algorithm, the computation of the joint probability of variables in a clique that contains all the soft evidence variables. The big clique algorithm also performs IPFP on all variables in that clique, while the wrapper 2 method only performs IPFP on the soft evidence variables. On the other hand, the wrapper 2 method uses virtual evidence, which requires two full propagations, to compute posterior marginals, while the big clique method only needs one full propagation. When the cost of propagation is higher than the cost of IPFP on the big clique, the big clique algorithm will perform better, and vice versa.

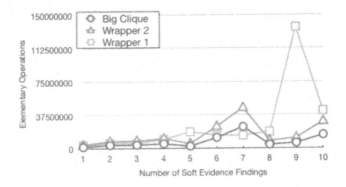

Fig. 5. Number of elementary table operations for test 6 of the test61 network

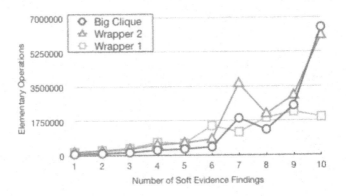

Fig. 6. Average number of elementary table operations for the test71 network

For the stud farm network (Figure 7), the cost of propagation in the very small junction tree is dominated by the cost of IPFP in the big clique and wrapper 2 algorithms. Use of IPFP requires the computation of the joint probability of the soft evidence variable(s), by first computing the joint probability of the variables in the cliques containing the soft evidence variable(s) and then marginalizing down to the soft evidence variable(s). On the other hand, the wrapper 1 method computes posterior marginal probabilities by updating with respect to each individual soft evidence variable in turn. This computation is very fast on the small junction tree of the stud farm network. Accordingly, the wrapper 1 method is the fastest for this network.

For the alarm network (Figure 1), the results are similar to those for stud farm. The relatively poor performance of big clique for eight soft evidence findings is explained by a particularly difficult evidence scenario, whose performance is reported in Figure 3. The resulting big clique for these soft evidence findings is very large resulting in an expensive IPFP computation. A similar situation occurs for ten soft evidence findings.

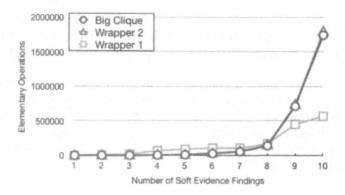

Fig. 7. Average number of elementary table operations for the stud farm network

For the test61 network (Figure 4), the state spaces of one of the cliques in the junction tree is very large, reflecting the fact that this is indeed a random network and not a typical, human-constructed, low-treewidth network [24]. The performance of the wrapper 1 algorithm is accordingly poor, because the cost of additional propagations required by this method overcomes the savings resulting from not performing IPFP on a joint distribution. Similarly, wrapper 2 is slower than the big clique algorithm, because it performs twice the number of propagations. The spike in the number of table operations for the wrapper 1 method with nine soft evidence findings is due mainly to one difficult evidence scenario, whose performance is reported in Figure 5, for which the number of IPFP iterations before convergence is very high.

For the test71 network (Figure 6), the number of operations for the wrapper 2 method is approximately double the number for big clique. This indicates that the contribution of IPFP is negligible, while the propagation cost for probability update after IPFP dominates the number of operations. Since wrapper 2 needs to perform two such propagations, as opposed to one for the big clique algorithm, the experimental result is explained. The junction tree constructed for the wrapper one method, which does not need to include all soft evidence variables in one clique, is much simpler than the one built for the other two methods, and this explains the comparatively better performance of wrapper one for seven evidence findings.

5   Conclusion

This paper only presents initial results. As discussed in the previous section, our initial tests indicate that the three algorithms for soft evidential update we have implemented have definite relative strengths and weaknesses. However, future work, such as improving the instrumentation of the implementation to collect better convergence data, designing experiments to test specific features of networks and evidence configurations that may include hard findings, and testing on a wider range of large networks, remains to be done in order to conclude under which conditions each algorithm is preferable.

Additional future work includes the analysis of several other proposed algorithms: the space-saving implementation of IPFP [18] and [19]; the soft updating algorithm of [10]; the approximate update algorithms by Peng and Ding [9]; and possibly more.

It will also be necessary to evaluate memory usage, which leads to a consideration of any-space algorithms such as recursive conditioning [13] instead of junction tree algorithms, and to evaluate the effect of performance tuning, such as the use of different query methods to calculate lazy messages and of different methods (e.g., variable passing [13] and query-based methods [17]) to calculate joint probabilities in BRUSE.

References

1. Valtorta, M., Kim, Y.G., Vomlel, J.: Soft evidential update for probabilistic multiagent systems. International Journal of Approximate Reasoning 29(1), 71–106 (2002)
2. Madsen, A.L., Jensen, F.V.: Lazy propagation: A junction tree inference algorithm based on lazy evaluation. Artificial Intelligence 113, 203–245 (1999)
3. Pan, R., Peng, Y., Ding, Z.: Belief update in Bayesian networks using uncertain evidence. In: ICTAI, pp. 441–444. IEEE Computer Society Press, Los Alamitos (2006)
4. Pearl, J.: Probabilistic Reasoning in Intelligent Systems: Networks of Plausible Inference. Morgan Kaufman, San Mateo (1988)
5. Chan, H., Darwiche, A.: On the revision of probabilistic beliefs using uncertain evidence. In: Proceedings of the Eighteenth International Joint Conference on Artificial Intelligence, Acapulco, Mexico, pp. 99–105 (2003)
6. Kim, Y.-G., Valtorta, M., Vomlel, J.: A prototypical system for soft evidential update. Applied Intelligence 21(1) (2004)
7. Vomlel, J.: Probabilistic reasoning with uncertain evidence. Neural Network World, International Journal on Neural and Mass-Parallel Computing and Information Systems 14(5), 453–456 (2004)
8. Chan, H., Darwiche, A.: On the revision of probabilistic beliefs using uncertain evidence. Artificial Intelligence 163, 67–90 (2005)
9. Peng, Y., Ding, Z.: Modifying Bayesian networks by probability constraints. In: Proceedings of the Twenty-first Annual Conference on Uncertainty in Artificial Intelligence (UAI 2005), Edinburgh, Scotland, July 2005, pp. 459–466 (2005)
10. Di Tomaso, E., Baldwin, J.: An approach to hybrid probabilistic models. International Journal of Approximate Reasoning 47, 202–218 (2008)
11. Madsen, A.L., Jensen, F., Kjaerulff, U.B., Lang, M.: The Hugin tool for probabilistic graphical models. Internationl Journal on Artificial Intelligence Tools 14, 507–543 (2005)
12. Lepar, V., Shenoy, P.P.: A comparison of Lauritzen-Spiegelhalter, Hugin, and Shenoy-Shafer architectures for computing marginals of probability distributions. In: Proceedings of the Fourteenth Annual Conference on Uncertainty in Artificial Intelligence (UAI 1998), Madison, WI, July 1998, pp. 328–337 (1998)
13. Jensen, F.V., Nielsen, T.D.: Bayesian Networks and Decision Graphs, 2nd edn. Springer, New York (2007)

14. Madsen, A.: Variations over the message computation algorithm of lazy propagation. IEEE Transactions on Systems, Man, and Cybernetics Part B 36, 636–648 (2006)
15. Csiszár, I.: *I*-divergence geometry of probability distributions and minimization problems. Ann. Prob. 3(1), 146–158 (1975)
16. Vomlel, J.: Methods of Probabilistic Knowledge Integration. PhD thesis, Department of Cybernetics, Faculty of Electrical Engineering, Czech Technical University (December 1999)
17. Bloemeke, M., Valtorta, M.: A hybrid algorithm to compute marginal and joint beliefs in Bayesian networks and its complexity. In: Proceedings of the Fourteenth Annual Conference on Uncertainty in Artificial Intelligence (UAI 1998), Madison, WI, July 1998, pp. 208–214 (1998)
18. Jiroušek, R.: Solution of the marginal problem and decomposable distributions. Kybernetika 27(5), 403–412 (1991)
19. Hajek, P., Havranek, T., Jirousek, R.: Uncertain Information Processing in Expert Systems. NRC Press, Boca Raton (1992)
20. Jiroušek, R., Přeučil, S.: On the effective implementation of the iterative proportional fitting procedure. Computational Statistics and Data Analysis 19, 177–189 (1995)
21. Elidan, G.: Bayesian network repository (2001) (accessed May 22, 2008), http://www.cs.huji.ac.il/labs/compbio/Repository/
22. Beinlich, I.A., Suermondt, H.J., Chavez, R.M., Cooper, G.F.: The ALARM monitoring system: A case study with two probabilistic inference techniques for belief networks. In: Proceedings of the Second European Conference on Artificial Intelligence in Medicine, London, pp. 247–256 (1989)
23. Kjaerulff, U.: Triangulation of graphs—algorithms giving small total state space, Technical Report R90-09. Technical report, Department of Computer Science, University of Aalborg (March 1990)
24. Boedlander, H.L.: Discovering treewidth. In: Vojtáš, P., Bieliková, M., Charron-Bost, B., Sýkora, O. (eds.) SOFSEM 2005. LNCS, vol. 3381, pp. 1–16. Springer, Heidelberg (2005)

Optimization of Queries over Interval Probabilistic Data

Matteo Magnani[1] and Danilo Montesi[2]

[1] University of Bologna, Italy
matteo.magnani@cs.unibo.it
[2] University of Bologna, Italy
danilo.montesi@unibo.it

Abstract. In this paper we deal with the logical and physical optimization of select-from-where queries over interval probabilistic data. We present a data model with algebraic equivalences, to be used to verify the equivalence of alternative query plans, and propose and compare different join algorithms over uncertain relations. We also provide a preliminary experimental evaluation of our contributions.

1 Introduction

The study of different aspects of imperfection in data management, like missing values [1,2], uncertain relational models [3,4,5,6,7,8], vagueness [9], imperfect non–relational data [10,11,12,13], system development [14,15,16,17,18,19], and applications [20,21,22,23], has always been of primary importance in database theory and practice. This paper concerns the optimization of select-from-where queries over interval probabilistic relational data. In particular, 1) we define a data model with algebraic equivalences to rewrite queries over relational data into equivalent expressions (logical optimization), and 2) introduce and compare different algorithms to perform joins over uncertain data (physical optimization). Although interesting, in this work we do not deal with uncertain data indexing.

To the best of our knowledge, existing systems for uncertain data use an underlying relational system to store the data structures defined in their uncertain data models, and translate queries over uncertain data into traditional relational queries. However, in general a query over uncertain data corresponds to *a sequence* of SQL operations manipulating groups of rows representing a single uncertain tuple. This has a *very relevant practical implication*: the underlying query optimizer may become less effective, because it believes it is working on a relational data model, while in fact it is working on an uncertain data model of which it is not aware.

With regard to the choice of using interval probabilities, this theory is one of many alternative approaches to manage imperfect data. Today, it is well recognized that these different approaches are not *competitors*. On the contrary, each one is best suited to tackle different problems — for a survey, see [24]. Interval probabilistic approaches have the following specific features: 1) they are more

S. Greco and T. Lukasiewicz (Eds.): SUM 2008, LNAI 5291, pp. 298–311, 2008.
© Springer-Verlag Berlin Heidelberg 2008

expressive than approaches based on simple probabilities, and reduce to them when singleton intervals are used, 2) can be used to represent both *uncertainty* (like in: John is probably 14 years old) and *non-specificity* (like in: John is between 13 and 16 years old), 3) and are useful when single probabilities are not known, or difficult to compute. In particular, in this paper we adopt Dempster's interval probabilistic model [25].

In the next section we introduce our data model and query algebra for interval probabilistic data, which are a relational application of the general structures and operators described in [26]. In addition, we show how our data structures are stored inside a traditional relational database management system. Then, in Section 3 we show an example of logical query rewriting. In Section 4 we present two join algorithms, with a preliminary experimental comparison that highlights their pros and cons. We conclude the paper with some final remarks.

2   Data Model and Query Algebra

An uncertain tuple is a distribution of probability over sets of alternative tuples, as usual. When probability 1 is assigned to a single tuple, it means we are certain that it describes the corresponding real world object, and the model reduces to the relational one. The meaning of the *compatibility flag* $\{T, F\}$ (true/false) will be clarified later, when we introduce the selection operator.

Definition 1 (Uncertain Tuple). *Let T^A be the set of all tuples over a set of attributes A. An uncertain tuple over A is a function $\bar{t}: \mathcal{P}(T^A \times \{T, F\}) \to [0, 1]$ ($\mathcal{P}$ indicates a powerset) such that:*

1. $\bar{t}(\emptyset) = 0$
2. $\sum_{B \subseteq T^A \times \{T,F\}} \bar{t}(B) = 1$.

From $\bar{t}$ we can compute the interval probability (upper and lower probability) of any tuple or set of alternative tuples, as follows:

$$LP(X) = \sum_{B \subseteq X} \bar{t}(B) \qquad UP(X) = \sum_{B \cap X \neq \emptyset} \bar{t}(B) .$$

To understand the meaning of these equations consider the following example, with two alternative tuples about Mr. X: #1) ⟨John, Ford⟩ and #2) ⟨Jack, Ford⟩ — we are not sure of his name. If we assign some probability to the expression *Mr. X's name is John*, this probability also supports the fact that Mr. X's surname is Ford — therefore, it increases the lower probability of tuple #1 and of the set of tuples {#1, #2} (LP equation). Now consider a probability assignment to the expression *Mr. X's surname is Ford*. This supports the fact that Mr. X's name is John or Jack, but does not directly support neither the first nor the second alternative. Therefore, it increases the upper probability of both tuples #1 and #2 (UP expression). As this is a well known mathematical theory, we do not further discuss these equations here — additional details and comprehensive examples are available in [27].

Definition 2 (Uncertain Relation). *An uncertain relation is a bag of uncertain tuples.*

p1(name starts with J) = p1(John, Jack) = .5
p1(name starts with R) = p1(Ron, Rick) = .5

U	T	C	Name	Surname
1	1	T	John	Ford
1	2	T	Jack	Ford
2	1	T	Robert	Morrison
2	2	T	Mitchell	Morrison
3	1	T	Tom	Mix

U	T	P
1	1	.6
1	2	.4
2	1	.3
2	1 2	.7
3	1	1

p(John) in [0, .5]   p(Ron) in [0, .5]
p(Jack) in [0, .5]   p(Rick) in [0, .5]

p2(name ends with N) = p2(John, Ron) = .5
p2(name ends with K) = p2(Jack, Rick) = .5

Fig. 1. An uncertain relation as we store it in a relational database management system. U is the uncertain tuple identifier, T represents the identifiers of each alternative tuple, C is the compatibility flag and P is the probability assigned to sets of alternative tuples. To the left, an example to show why we need two tables

In Figure 1 we have illustrated how we store uncertain relations inside an underlying relational database system. In each table there can be multiple rows representing different alternatives of the same uncertain tuple. In this case, these rows share an uncertain tuple identifier (U). Each alternative tuple has a local identifier, unique inside the uncertain tuple (T). Then, we store the compatibility flag and the actual values. Probabilities are stored inside a separate table, with the identifier of the uncertain tuple to which the assignment refers (column U), the set of local tuple identifiers (T), and the associated probability (P).

The fact that an interval of probability attached to the end of each tuple of the first table would not be sufficient to represent a complete interval probability distribution should be clear looking at the definition of uncertain tuple, where $\tilde{t}$ is defined over a powerset: for each n rows defining an uncertain tuple we may have up to 2^n different probability assignments. However, if we specify one interval for each row we will only have $2 \cdot n$ values. On the right hand side of Figure 1 we have provided an additional example: consider the two distributions of probability $p1$ and $p2$. It is easy to see that they correspond to the same intervals of probability, i.e., using four intervals we cannot distinguish the first distribution from the second. However, they are clearly different: if we add the information that the name is not John to $p1$, the probability of Jack becomes [.5, .5]. If we add the same information to $p2$, it is Ron's probability that changes!

Example 1 (Uncertain Relation). Figure 1 represents three uncertain tuples, with identifiers (U) 1, 2 and 3. The first uncertain tuple presents two alternatives, John Ford, with probability .6, and Jack Ford, with probability .4. The second uncertain tuple presents two alternatives, Robert Morrison and Mitchell Morrison, with probabilities respectively in the intervals [.3, 1] and [0, .7]. Finally, we have a certain tuple, Tom Mix, whose probability is 1.

2.1   Basic Operations on Uncertain Tuples

The mathematical theory of uncertainty that we use in our model provides some basic operations that we will use to define our manipulation operators. In this section we describe the two operations used in the paper: coarsening and combination.

Before providing a formal definition, we introduce the *coarsening* operation through an example. Consider the four alternative tuples represented in the center of Figure 2, and referring to an individual (Mr. X). Now assume we have three sources of evidence about the three facts listed in the figure. Now, we can show a coarsening: assume we make a projection on column *Name*. We will obtain two tuples, John and Jack, represented on the right hand side table of the figure. The first statement (Mr. X is called John Fard) supports the fact that Name is John, therefore p_1 will be reassigned to ⟨Name: John⟩. The second statement supports both names (John Ford and Jack Ford), therefore p_2 will be reassigned to both tuples. Finally the third statement supports the fact that the correct name is Jack (Jack Ford, Jack Fard), therefore p_3 will be assigned to Jack.

1. p(Mr. X is called John Fard) = p_1.
2. p(Mr. X's surname is Ford) = p_2.
3. p(Mr. X's name is Jack) = p_3.

	Name	Surname	p_1	p_2	p_3	Name
#1	John	Fard	×			
#2	John	Ford		×		John
#3	Jack	Ford		×	×	
#4	Jack	Fard			×	Jack

Fig. 2. An example to explain the semantics of the coarsening operator

From this example it should be intuitively clear that the new probability assignment is automatically defined by the *mapping* between input and output tuples. A coarsening is defined as follows:

Definition 3 (Coarsening). *Let $\bar{t}$ be an uncertain tuple over A, and* Map : $T^A \times \{T, F\} \to T^A \times \{T, F\}$. *$\bar{t}'$ is a Map–coarsening of $\bar{t}$, notated $\mathcal{C}_{\text{Map}}(\bar{t})$, if:*

$$\bar{t}'(X) = \sum_{\{B \subseteq T^A \times \{T,F\} | \text{Map}(B) = X\}} \bar{t}(B) \ . \tag{1}$$

The concept of coarsening can be generalized to n-ary functions — we do not include this generalization here because of space limitations.

The second important basic mathematical operation on uncertain tuples is *combination*:

Definition 4 (Combination). *For every subset X of $T^A \times \{T, F\}$, a combination of two uncertain tuples $\bar{t} = \bar{t}_1 \oplus \bar{t}_2$ is defined as:*

$$\bar{t}(X) = \begin{cases} 0 & \text{if } X = \emptyset \\ 0 & \text{if } \sum_{X_1 \cap X_2 = \emptyset} = 1 \\ \dfrac{\sum_{X_1 \cap X_2 = X} \bar{t}_1(X_1)\bar{t}_2(X_2)}{1 - \sum_{X_1 \cap X_2 = \emptyset} \bar{t}_1(X_1)\bar{t}_2(X_2)} & \text{o.w.} \end{cases} \tag{2}$$

In the previous definition, $X, X_1, X_2 \subseteq T^A \times \{T, F\}$. As you can see from Definition 4, when two uncertain tuples contradict each other (all probability assigned to disjoint sets, as in the second condition) they cannot be combined. In this case we will conventionally assign no probability at all, which is not a problem because these contradictory uncertain instances will always be removed from their collections.

2.2   Manipulation Algebra

Selection. Differently from traditional tuples, uncertain tuples may satisfy a selection predicate partially. If at least one alternative tuple with positive upper probability satisfies it, the uncertain tuple containing it will be selected. Inside it, the alternative tuples not satisfying the predicate will be marked using the *compatibility* flag (F), but not deleted.

In the following we will notate with $\mathrm{Comp}_{\bar{t}}$ the set $\{(t, b) \mid \mathrm{UP}(\{(t, b)\}) > 0 \wedge b = T\}$. As a consequence, the probability not assigned to $\mathrm{Comp}_{\bar{t}}$ corresponds to the fact that the uncertain tuple does not belong to its table. In addition, for the sake of simplicity we use a set notation without indicating the cardinality of each element — we remind the reader that the model is based on bags.

The reason for keeping these incompatible tuples is exemplified in Figure 3. Assume we have an uncertain tuple with the four alternatives illustrated in the figure, and equal probabilities (.5) associated to the two circled sets — as a consequence, all alternatives have a probability comprised between 0 and .5. If we want to select all tuples about male names, we will obviously retrieve this uncertain tuple because of the alternatives *John* and *Mark*. If then we get some evidence indicating that the name of this person is not *Jane*, we will obtain a modified probability distribution, with $P(Mark) \in [0, .5]$ and $P(John) = .5$, as indicated in the right hand side of the figure. Notice that to obtain this new probabilities we need to know that the probability associated to Jane was also associated to John and not to Mark.

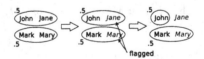

Fig. 3. Change of probabilities and selections

Moreover, in this way we can compute upper and lower probabilities for the new uncertain instance to belong to the resulting collection, because $\mathrm{Comp}_{\bar{t}}$ contains exactly the alternatives compatible with the new semantics. If $\mathrm{UP}(\mathrm{Comp}_{\bar{t}}) > 0$, then $\bar{t}$ is compatible with the new table, and is included in the result. Otherwise, it is not.

Definition 5 (Selection). *Let* $\mathrm{Map}_{A_i = c}$ *be a function defined as follows:*

$$\mathrm{Map}_{A_i = c}((t, b)) = \begin{cases} (t, F) & \text{if } b = F \vee t[A_i] \neq c \\ (t, T) & \text{if } b = T \wedge t[A_i] = c \end{cases} . \tag{3}$$

U	T	C	ID	Name	Surname	Age	P
1	1	T	0001	Mary	Sloan	30	[0,1]
1	2	T	0001	Mary	Sloan	50	[0,1]
2	1	T	0002	Mark	Shelley	18	[1,1]
3	1	T	0003	John	Smith	28	[0,1]
3	2	T	0003	John	Schmidt	28	[0,1]

U	T		P
1	1 2		1
2	1		1
3	1 2		1

U	T	C	Patient	Disease	P
1	1	T	0001	heart attack	[0,1]
1	2	T	0001	panic attack	[0,1]
2	1	T	0003	flu	[0,1]
2	2	T	0003	cold	[0,1]

U	T		P
1	1 2		1
2	1 2		1

Fig. 4. Uncertain tables PATIENT and DISEASE (we have also indicated the interval of probability associated to each tuple)

A selection operator on uncertain tables is defined as:

$$\sigma_{A_i=c}(T) = \{\bar{t}' \mid \bar{t} \in C \wedge \bar{t}' = C_{\text{Map}_{A_i=c}}(\bar{t}) \wedge \text{Comp}_{\bar{t}'} \neq \emptyset\} \ . \tag{4}$$

Similar definitions with other predicates, like the equality of two columns, are analogous. In Figure 5 we have represented the result of a selection of all patients whose surname is Smith — the input table is the one illustrated in Figure 4. The third uncertain tuple is selected, without changing its associated probabilities. However, the flag of the tuple with surname Schmidt has now been set to F, and the probability of this tuple to belong to this table is now comprised between 0 and 1 — in fact, if the real surname were Schmidt the result of the query would be the empty set.

U	T	C	ID	Name	Surname	Age	P
3	1	T	0003	John	Smith	28	[0,1]
3	2	F	0003	John	Schmidt	28	[0,1]

U	T		P
3	1 2		1

Fig. 5. $\sigma_{\text{SURNAME=Smith}}(\text{PATIENT})$

Projection. The principle at the basis of the projection operator is that if we have committed some belief to a tuple, the same belief will be committed to the fact that the projected tuple corresponds to the true result in the real world. Therefore, projections modify tuples, but do not directly alter probabilities. However, when two or more tuples are mapped to the same, their probabilities sum up. As an example, assume the two alternatives are that Mary is 18 years old or Mary is 17 years old. If we project on the name, we obtain a certain information: that the person is called Mary. Mathematically, this corresponds to a coarsening.

Definition 6 (Projection). *We define a function from* $T^A \times \{\mathrm{T},\mathrm{F}\}$ *to* $T^A \times \{\mathrm{T},\mathrm{F}\}$ *as follows:*

$$\mathrm{Map}_{A_1,\ldots,A_n}((t,b)) = (t[A_1,\ldots,A_n],b) \ . \tag{5}$$

A projection operator on uncertain tables is defined as:

$$\pi_{A_1,\ldots,A_n}(T) = \{\bar{t}' \mid \bar{t} \in T \wedge \bar{t}' = \mathcal{C}_{\mathrm{Map}_{A_1,\ldots,A_n}}(\bar{t})\} \ . \tag{6}$$

As an example, we project the table PATIENT on the attributes Id and Surname (Figure 6). The first uncertain tuple, which previously contained two alternative tuples, is now composed of only one alternative. According to our intuition, we obtain a certain tuple, because we are sure about Mary's Surname.

U	T	C	ID	Surname	P
1	1	T	0001	*Sloan*	[1,1]
2	1	T	0002	Shelley	[1,1]
3	1	T	0003	Smith	[0,1]
3	2	T	0003	Schmidt	[0,1]

U	T	P
1	1	1
2	1	1
3	1 2	1

Fig. 6. $\pi_{\mathrm{ID,SURNAME}}(\mathrm{PATIENT})$

Cross Product. Before defining the operator of cross product, which is quite complex in presence of probabilistic dependencies, we define a simplified version of it, using a strong independence assumption. Then, we will relax this assumption.

Definition 7 (Independent cross product). *We define a function* Map *as:*

$$\mathrm{Map}(t_1,b_1,t_2,b_2) = \begin{cases} (t_1 \cdot t_2, \mathrm{T}) & \text{if } b_1 = \mathrm{T} \wedge b_2 = \mathrm{T} \\ (t_1 \cdot t_2, \mathrm{F}) & \text{o.w.} \end{cases} \ . \tag{7}$$

In the previous definition, · *indicates a tuple concatenation operator. The independent cross product of two uncertain relations* T_1 *and* T_2 *over disjoint sets of attributes is defined as:*

$$T_1 \times T_2 = \{\bar{t} \mid \bar{t} = \mathcal{C}_{\mathrm{Map}}(\bar{t}_1, \bar{t}_2) \wedge \bar{t}_1 \in T_1 \wedge \bar{t}_2 \in T_2\} \tag{8}$$

The independence assumption can be relaxed using a probability assignment (i.e., an uncertain tuple) storing the information we have on dependencies, and combining it with the result of a cross product using the combination rule reported in Section 2.1. This information is usually expressed in form of predicates, without referencing single instances. For example, we can state that tuples with a gender attribute set to man should not be composed with job titles hostess and business woman, or that the probability of being old is increased by the fact one has children, and so on.

To express this probability distribution, we can use a list of mutually exclusive predicates $\mathrm{Pr} = \{\mathrm{Pr}_1, \ldots, \mathrm{Pr}_n\}$ and a probability assignment p over its powerset.

Then, we can define a probability assignment P_{Pr} corresponding to an assignment on the sets of tuples where the corresponding predicates are true. In particular:

$$P_{\mathrm{Pr}}(\{(t, \mathrm{T}), (t, \mathrm{F}) \mid \mathrm{Pr}_{x_1}(t) \vee \cdots \vee \mathrm{Pr}_{x_n}(t)\}) = p(\{\mathrm{Pr}_{x_1}, \ldots, \mathrm{Pr}_{x_n}\}) \ .$$

We will consider the combination as a separate operator $c_{\mathrm{Pr},p}$, and represent a generalized cross product as an independent cross product followed by a combination.

As an example, we show a cross product between PATIENT and DISEASE — together with a selection, to obtain a join. As in general there can be some information on the dependency between patients' personal data and the occurrence of diseases, in our example we will use the dependency information represented in Table 1 about the relationships between age, heart and panic attacks — this data has no scientific basis, it is only used to show how to compute dependencies. The result of the operation is illustrated in Figure 7.

U	T	C	ID	Name	Surname	Age	Patient	Disease	P
1	1	T	0001	Mary	Sloan	30	0001	heart attack	[.2,.2]
1	2	T	0001	Mary	Sloan	30	0001	panic attack	[.3,.3]
1	3	T	0001	Mary	Sloan	50	0001	heart attack	[.3,.3]
1	4	T	0001	Mary	Sloan	50	0001	panic attack	[.2,.2]
3	1	T	0003	John	Smith	28	0003	flu	[0,1]
3	2	T	0003	John	Smith	28	0003	cold	[0,1]
3	3	T	0003	John	Schmidt	28	0003	flu	[0,1]
3	4	T	0003	John	Schmidt	28	0003	cold	[0,1]

U	T	P
1	1	.2
1	2	.3
1	3	.3
1	4	.2
3	1 2 3 4	1

Fig. 7. $\sigma_{\mathrm{ID=PATIENT}}(c_{\mathrm{Pr},p}(\mathrm{PATIENT} \times \mathrm{DISEASE}))$

Table 1. Dependencies between age and diseases. The first column contains predicates about the Disease attribute, the header (first row) about Ages.

	< 30	∈ [30, 49]	∈ [50, 69]	> 70
∉ {Panic Attack, Heart Attack}		.6		.18
= Panic Attack	.05	.03	.02	.03
= Heart Attack	0	.02	.03	.04

3   Logical Optimization with Algebraic Equivalences

The query algebra introduced in this paper is very similar to the relational one, and shares with it many algebraic equivalences that can be used to transform a query into an equivalent but more efficient one[1]. We notate $\mathrm{attr}(P)$ the set of attributes (columns) involved in predicate P (for instance, $\mathrm{attr}(A = B) = \{A, B\}$), and with $\mathrm{sort}(T)$ the set of attributes of table T (for example, $\mathrm{sort}(\mathrm{PATIENT}) = \{\mathrm{Id, Name, Surname, Age}\}$). Here we indicate only the rules used in the following example.

---

[1] Similar rules have been applied to generic (non–relational) data in [26].

Theorem 1. *The following equivalences hold:*

$$c(\sigma_P(T)) \equiv \sigma_P(c(T)) \tag{9}$$

$$T_1 \times T_2 \equiv T_2 \times T_1 \tag{10}$$

$$\textit{if } \mathrm{attr}(P) \subseteq \mathrm{sort}(T_2) \textit{ then}$$

$$\sigma_P(T_1 \times T_2) \equiv T_1 \times \sigma_P(T_2) \tag{11}$$

In addition to these rules, we define the theta join operator ($\bowtie_P$) as a cross product followed by a selection, as usual. Rule 9 can be used to invert a selection with a conditioning. Rules (10) and (11) can be used to push a selection inside a cross product.

As an example of application of these rules, consider the logical query plan of Figure 8-1. This has been obtained through a direct translation of the query presented in the introduction. Now we can do the following:

- Invert the selection on the Surname (σ_b) with the conditioning, swap the arguments of the cross product and push the selection into it. This involves rules (9), (10) and (11).
- Invert the other selection with the conditioning and merge it with the cross product, obtaining a join. This involves rule (9) and the definition of join.

The logical query plan obtained through these transformations (Figure 8-2) is *equivalent* to the original one, i.e., it generates the same result. However, we can consider it as much more efficient, because: 1) we do not compute a cross product, but a join, 2) the join is not computed on all patients, but only on those whose surname is Smith, and 3) the computation of the new probabilities (conditioning) is performed only on tuples that have been filtered and that will be included in the result.

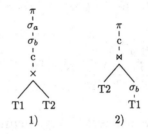

Fig. 8. Query plans: 1) logical 2) equivalent logical

4 Joining Uncertain Relations

The main difference between a traditional join and a join over relations representing interval probabilistic data is that when we compare two tuples we cannot know *locally* if they will be included in the result of the operation. In fact, even if they do not match (satisfy the join predicate), they could belong to uncertain tuples which match — because of other alternatives. As a consequence, we may follow two main approaches: the first is to compute traditional relational joins, followed by some additional work to recollect all tuples with the same uncertain tuple identifiers of matching rows. The second is the definition of an uncertainty-aware join over uncertain tuples.

Assume we want to join two uncertain relations T1 and T2 on attributes c1 and c2. Also, remember that the two relations are stored using four traditional tables: tT1 and tT2, with the actual data, and pT1 and pT2, containing the probability distributions. An *uncertain relational join* can be computed by evaluating the following expressions[2]:

- $(\pi_{tT1.U, tT2.U}(tT1 \bowtie_{c1=c2} tT2)) \bowtie tT1 \bowtie tT2$
- $(\pi_{tT1.U, tT2.U}(tT1 \bowtie_{c1=c2} tT2)) \bowtie_{tT1.U=pT1.U} pT1 \bowtie_{tT2.U=pT2.U} pT2$

The first part of the two queries extracts the pairs of uncertain tuple identifiers of matching rows. The next two joins of each equation recollect all rows belonging to these uncertain tuples.

The second approach is to explicitly consider each uncertain tuple as a whole, and extend a traditional join approach, such as a sort join algorithm. The main problem to define a sort join algorithm that works directly on uncertain tuples, i.e., an uncertainty-aware algorithm, is that while single tuples can be totally ordered, uncertain tuples only constitute a partially ordered set. Consider for example the following uncertain relations T1 and T2, with three uncertain tuples each:

T1 (**A**: 2 4 5 7), (**B**: 5 7 8), (**C**: 11 13 17 19)
T2 (**D**: 5 10), (**E**: 8 9), (**F**: 12 14 16)

If we consider uncertain tuples D and E, we can see that there is not a natural ordering, because D contains 5, which is less than 8, but also 10, which is greater than 9. The idea behind our algorithm is that each uncertain tuple can be considered as an interval, from its lower alternative tuple to its upper one. Therefore, we can represent A as [2, 7], B as [5, 8], and so on. This has two consequences: 1) two tuples potentially match only if their associated intervals have a non-empty intersection, and 2) this approach reduces to a traditional sort join when uncertain tuples are made by only one tuple — in fact, in this case intervals reduce to single points.

More specifically, uncertain tuples are ordered by their lower bound (**lb**). Then each uncertain tuple is compared only with those uncertain tuples whose lower bound is less than its upper bound (**ub**) — which corresponds to a non-empty intersection. This guarantees that all subsequent uncertain tuples will not match the uncertain tuple under consideration, and we can continue without considering it any longer, as it happens with a traditional sort join over non-uncertain relations.

---

[2] Some additional work is needed to construct the resulting uncertain tuples, but it has no relevant effect on the execution time if compared with the time needed to perform the joins. We do not discuss this less relevant aspect for space reasons.

As an example, our extended algorithm would work as follows on the uncertain relations listed above:

- A is the lower tuple. D.lb (lower bound) < A.up (upper bound), therefore they may match. The comparison confirms this, and A·D is computed.
- E.lb > A.up, therefore we are done with A, without considering any other uncertain tuple — A cannot match any tuple greater than E!
- Now we continue with D. D and B overlap, therefore they may match. After the comparison, we return B·D. D cannot match C, therefore we are also done with it.
- We continue in the same way: we will verify the matching of B and E, and of C and F. In the first case we will produce B·E, in the second we will find that there is no matching.

We have performed a preliminary experimental evaluation of the algorithm, which has been compared against a nested loop join over uncertain tuples. The evaluation is preliminary because to the best of our knowledge there are no existing benchmarks to test queries over interval probabilistic data. We have therefore generated synthetic sets of data as follows: first, we have produced pairs of identical tables with varying cardinality, and with a random string of 10 characters on the join attribute. Then, we have *perturbated* each table by adding an alternative tuple to each uncertain tuple. The alternative tuple contains the same string with a character randomly changed. This guarantees that each tuple will match at least one other tuple, and creates random intervals with an uniform probability distribution.

In the left hand side of Figure 9 we have illustrated the number of comparisons between uncertain tuples performed by a nested loop approach and by our extended sort join algorithm on this synthetic data. These results clearly suggest that the number of comparisons can be significantly reduced using this approach. However, they also show that the complexity of the extended sort join algorithm is not linear. This is due to the fact that all tuples in the input relations are uncertain (contain more than one alternative). In fact, as we will see shortly, the complexity of this algorithm depends on the *amount of uncertainty* it has to deal with.

The right hand side of the figure shows a comparison of the execution time of the extended sort join (continuous line) and uncertain relational join (dashed line) algorithms. The graph has been computed joining two relations with 100.000 simple tuples each, aggregated into uncertain tuples in different percentages. For example, the value 60% on the x axis means that 40.000 uncertain tuples are made of a single tuple, i.e., they are not uncertain, while the remaining have been aggregated two by two to build uncertain tuples. This highligths two important features of these algorithms. First, the extended sort join depends on the amount of uncertainty, while the uncertain relational join does not, as it is not aware of it and manipulates simple relational tuples — except while the uncertain result is aggregated, at the end of the computation. As a consequence, when there is **no** (or a few) **uncertainty**, the **extended sort join algorithm** is **more efficient**, because it

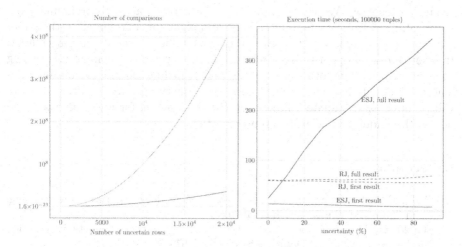

Fig. 9. Number of comparisons between uncertain tuples using a nested loop and an extended sort join approach (ESJ), and comparison of the execution times of an extended sort join and a relational uncertain join (RJ) — we have illustrated both the time to produce the full result and the time to output the first tuple). These experiments have been performed on a Linux 2.6 system — 1GHz CPU and 512MB RAM.

reduces to a simple sort join (compared with six joins needed to execute the uncertain relational join algorithm). Basically, there is an amount of uncertainty, to be better determined by further experiments, below which the extended sort join is more efficient, and **above which the uncertain relational join is better suited**.

The second important consideration is that in general relational systems do not compute all the result of a query, but start returning the first tuples as soon as they are ready. Usually, users must explicitly ask the system to load additional tuples, otherwise only a few are computed. Therefore, it is important to see how soon these algorithms start to produce their results.

When the extended sort join algorithm has finished to process one uncertain tuple, it knows if it will be included in the result or not. Therefore, after having sorted the two input relations it can start producing tuples at once. On the contrary, the uncertain relational join cannot output tuples until all the joins but the last have been completely computed — in case efficient secondary memory join algorithms are used. Therefore, the time to produce the first tuple is almost the same time needed to perform all the computation. In this case, the extended sort join algorithm is preferred.

5   Final Remarks

In this paper we have presented some advances towards the implementation of a query optimizer for interval probabilistic data. We have shown that both logical and physical optimizations are possible and can significantly affect the efficiency of query execution. We have supported our contributions with preliminary experimental results, showing that the two join algorithms presented in the paper are more or less efficient than the other depending on the execution context. In future work, we plan to build a benchmark to provide a comparable testing framework for our and other approaches, and to include the transformation rules holding in our data model inside a cost-based query optimizer, whose statistics will be obviously evaluated directly on the data model for uncertain data and not on the underlying relational representation.

References

1. Codd, E.F.: Extending the database relational model to capture more meaning. ACM Trans. Database Syst. 4(4) (1979)
2. Witold Lipski, J.: On semantic issues connected with incomplete information databases. ACM Trans. Database Syst. 4(3) (1979)
3. Barbara, D., Garcia-Molina, H., Porter, D.: The management of probabilistic data. IEEE Transactions on Knowledge and Data Engineering 4(5) (1992)
4. Lee, S.K.: An extended relational database model for uncertain and imprecise information. In: Yuan, L.Y. (ed.) VLDB Conference (1992)
5. Pittarelli, M.: An algebra for probabilistic databases. IEEE Transactions on Knowledge and Data Engineering 6(2) (1994)
6. Dey, D., Sarkar, S.: A probabilistic relational model and algebra. ACM Transactions on Database Systems 21(3) (1996)
7. Lakshmanan, L.V.S., Leone, N., Ross, R., Subrahmanian, V.S.: ProbView: a flexible probabilistic database system. ACM Trans. on Database Systems 22(3) (1997)
8. Fuhr, N., Rölleke, T.: A probabilistic relational algebra for the integration of information retrieval and database systems. ACM Transactions on Information Systems 15(1) (1997)
9. Bosc, P., Prade, H.: An introduction to the fuzzy set and possibility theory-based treatment of flexible queries and uncertain or imprecise databases. In: Uncertainty Management in Information Systems (1996)
10. Eiter, T., Lu, J.J., Lukasiewicz, T., Subrahmanian, V.S.: Probabilistic object bases. ACM Transactions on Database Systems 26(3), 264–312 (2001)
11. Nierman, A., Jagadish, H.V.: ProTDB: Probabilistic data in XML. In: VLDB Conference (2002)
12. Hung, E., Getoor, L., Subrahmanian, V.: PXML: A probabilistic semistructured data model and algebra. In: ICDE, Bangalore, India (2003)
13. Hung, E., Getoor, L., Subrahmanian, V.: Probabilistic interval XML. In: ICDT, Siena, Italy (2003)
14. Sarma, A.D., Benjelloun, O., Halevy, A.Y., Widom, J.: Working models for uncertain data. In: Proceedings of the 22nd International Conference on Data Engineering. IEEE Computer Society, Los Alamitos (2006)
15. Boulos, J., Dalvi, N.N., Mandhani, B., Mathur, S., Ré, C., Suciu, D.: Mystiq: a system for finding more answers by using probabilities. In: SIGMOD Conference (2005)
16. Cheng, R., Singh, S., Prabhakar, S.: U-dbms: A database system for managing constantly-evolving data. In: Proceedings of the 31st VLDB Conference. ACM Press, New York (2005)

17. Widom, J.: Trio: A system for integrated management of data, accuracy, and lineage. In: CIDR (2005)
18. Agrawal, P., Benjelloun, O., Sarma, A.D., Hayworth, C., Nabar, S.U., Sugihara, T., Widom, J.: Trio: A system for data, uncertainty, and lineage. In: Proceedings of the 32nd VLDB Conference. ACM Press, New York (2006)
19. Re, C., Dalvi, N.N., Suciu, D.: Efficient top-k query evaluation on probabilistic data. In: Proceedings of the 23rd ICDT Conference. IEEE, Los Alamitos (2007)
20. Magnani, M., Rizopoulos, N., McBrien, P., Montesi, D.: Schema integration based on uncertain semantic mappings. In: Delcambre, L.M.L., Kop, C., Mayr, H.C., Mylopoulos, J., Pastor, Ó. (eds.) ER 2005. LNCS, vol. 3716. Springer, Heidelberg (2005)
21. Gal, A., Anaby-Tavor, A., Trombetta, A., Montesi, D.: A framework for modeling and evaluating automatic semantic reconciliation. VLDB Journal 14(1) (2005)
22. van Keulen, M., de Keijzer, A., Alink, W.: A probabilistic XML approach to data integration. In: ICDE (2005)
23. Dong, X.L., Halevy, A.Y., Yu, C.: Data integration with uncertainty. In: Proceedings of the 33rd VLDB Conference. ACM Press, New York (2007)
24. Smets, P.: Probability, possibility, belief: Which and where? In: Handbook of Defeasible Reasoning and Uncertainty Management Systems, vol. 1. Kluwer Academic Publishers, Dordrecht (1998)
25. Dempster, A.P.: Upper and lower probabilities induced by a multivalued mapping. The Annals of Mathematical Statistics 38(2), 325–339 (1967)
26. Magnani, M., Montesi, D.: Management of interval probabilistic data. Acta Informatica 45(2) (2008)
27. Shafer, G.: A mathematical theory of evidence. Princeton University Press, Princeton (1976)

Polynomial Time Queries over Inconsistent Databases

Cristian Molinaro

DEIS, Universitá della Calabria, 87036 Rende, Italy
cmolinaro@deis.unical.it

Abstract. This paper investigates the problem of repairing and query-ing relational databases which may be inconsistent with respect to functional dependencies and foreign key constraints. Specifically, partic-ular sets of functional dependencies, called *canonical*, are considered. We present a repairing strategy whereby only tuple updates and insertions are allowed in order to restore consistency: when foreign key constraints are violated, new tuples (possibly containing *null values*) are inserted into the database; when functional dependency violations occur, tuple updates (possibly introducing *unknown values*) are performed. We pro-pose a semantics of constraint satisfaction for databases containing null and unknown values, since the repairing process can lead to such da-tabases. The proposed approach allows us to obtain a unique repaired database which can be computed in polynomial time. The result of the repairing technique is an incomplete database (in particular, an OR-database). The *consistent* query answers over an inconsistent database are the *certain* answers on the repaired database. Relying on the results in [17] on the complexity of query processing in OR-databases, we can identify conjunctive queries which can be evaluated in polynomial time.

1 Introduction

Inconsistent databases, namely databases which violate given integrity con-straints, may arise in several scenarios, such as database integration, data warehousing, automated reasoning systems and others. The problem of repairing and querying inconsistent database has been widely studied ([2,3,7,10,8,11,12,13,14,15,19]). Several works are based on the notion of *repair*, which is a consistent database obtained by modifying as little as possible the original (possibly inconsistent) one. Given a query, its *consistent* answers are those tuples which can be derived from every repair [3]. In most of the proposed approaches, only insertions and deletions of tuples are allowed in order to re-store the consistency of databases; only a few works have investigated the issue of repairing inconsistent databases by means of tuple updates ([22]).

In this paper we deal with the problem of repairing and querying databases in the presence of functional dependencies and foreign key constraints. Specifically, we consider particular sets of functional dependencies (called *canonical*) where attributes appearing in the right-hand side of functional dependencies cannot appear also in the left-hand side. We propose a repairing strategy which aims at

S. Greco and T. Lukasiewicz (Eds.): SUM 2008, LNAI 5291, pp. 312–325, 2008.
© Springer-Verlag Berlin Heidelberg 2008

preserving the information in the original database as much as possible: when foreign key constraints are violated new tuples are inserted into the database, whereas tuples updates are performed to make the database consistent w.r.t. functional dependencies; thus tuple deletions are never performed. Since tuple insertions and updates may introduce respectively null and unknown values in the database, we propose a semantics of constraint satisfaction for databases containing null and unknown values. Let us give the basic idea of our approach in the following example.

Example 1. Consider the following database:

Project	
$Name$	$Manager$
p1	john
p1	bob
p2	carl

Employee	
$Name$	$Phone$
john	123
bob	111

Suppose to have the following set of constraints (functional dependencies and foreign key constraints):

- fd_1 : $Name \rightarrow Manager$ defined over *Project*,
- fd_2 : $Name \rightarrow Phone$ defined over *Employee*,
- fk : $Project[Manager] \subseteq Employee[Name]$.

The database is inconsistent as it violates both fd_1 and fk: there are two different managers for the same project p1 and the manager *carl*, appearing in the project relation, is not in the employee relation. In this case, the repaired (consistent) database is as follows:

Project	
$Name$	$Manager$
p1	#1
p2	carl

Employee	
$Name$	$Phone$
john	123
bob	111
carl	$\perp_1$

where #1 is an *unknown value* whose domain is $\{john, bob\}$ whereas $\perp_1$ is a (labeled) *null value*. Therefore, in order to satisfy the functional dependency fd_1 we have introduced the unknown value #1 which expresses the fact that p1 has a unique manager that could be either *john* or *bob*. Observe that the first tuple in the project relation does not lead to a violation of fk because the manager of p1, whoever he may be, is in the employee relation too. The consistency of the original database w.r.t. fk has been restored by inserting the manager *carl* into the employee relation.   □

In the above example, observe that a labeled null value has been introduced for the phone number of *carl* since this information is missing. Specifically, we know neither if the telephone number of *carl* does not exist nor if the telephone number exists but is not known. Thus, neither the "nonexistent" (a value does not exist) nor the "unknown" (a value exists but it is not known) interpretation of the null is applicable in this situation. Here the null value is interpreted as "no information" ([23,24]), that is a placeholder for either a nonexistent or an unknown value. Thus, both unknown and null values express incomplete information, even though unknown values are "more informative than" null values.

As it will be shown in the paper, given an inconsistent database and a set of constraints consisting of functional dependencies and foreign key constraints, the proposed repairing strategy allows us to obtain a unique repaired database which can be computed in polynomial time.

It is worth noting that, the so obtained (incomplete) database represents a set of "possible worlds", namely the databases which are obtained by replacing every unknown value with a constant of its domain. The "certain answers" to a query over such a database are those tuples which can be derived from every possible world ([20,16]). Observe that, in our case, a possible world can contain labeled nulls; the evaluation of a query over such a database treats each labeled null like a standard constant. We propose a semantics of query answering over inconsistent databases which naturally follows from the previous observations: the *consistent answers* to a query over a possibly inconsistent database are the certain answers in the repaired database.

Example 2. Consider the database of Example 1. The consistent answer to the query asking for the manager of $p2$ is *carl*, because this answer can be obtained from every possible world of the repaired database. Clearly, there is no consistent answer to the query asking for the manager of $p1$. Observe that, the consistent answer to the query asking for the telephone number of $p2$'s manager is $\perp_1$, that means that we have no information about it.   □

Since repaired databases are OR-databases, relying on the result in [17], we can identify conjunctive queries that can be evaluated in polynomial time.

The rest of the paper is organized as follows. Section 2 introduces some preliminaries on relational databases and integrity constraints. Section 3 introduces a semantics of constraint satisfaction for databases containing null and unknown values, and a repairing strategy. The problem of querying inconsistent databases is tackled in Section 4. Finally, Section 5 contains concluding remarks and related work.

2   Preliminaries

This section introduces basic notions on relational databases and integrity constraints ([1,21]).

The existence of *alphabets* of *relation symbols* and *attribute symbols* is assumed. The *domain* of an attribute A is denoted by $Dom(A)$. The *database domain* is denoted by Dom. A *relation schema* is of the form $r(A_1, \ldots, A_m)$ where r is a relation symbol and the A_i's are attribute symbols (we denote the previous relation schema also as $r(U)$, where $U = \{A_1, \ldots, A_m\}$). A *relation instance* (or simply *relation*) R over $r(U)$ is a subset of $Dom(A_1) \times \ldots \times Dom(A_m)$. Each element of R is a *tuple*. Given a tuple $t \in R$ and a set $X \subseteq U$ of attributes (resp. a single attribute $A \in U$), we denote by $t[X]$ (resp. $t[A]$) the projection of t on X (resp. A). A *database schema* DS is a set $\{r_1(U_1), \ldots, r_n(U_n)\}$ of relation schemata. A *database instance* (or simply *database*) DB over DS is a set $\{R_1, \ldots, R_n\}$ where each R_i is a relation over $r_i(U_i)$, $i = 1..n$.

Integrity constraints express semantic information over data, i.e. relationships that should hold among data. They are mainly used to validate database transactions. In this paper we consider functional dependencies and foreign key constraints. The notation used hereafter is introduced below.

Given a relation schema $r(U)$, a *functional dependency* fd over $r(U)$ is of the form $X \rightarrow Y$, where $X, Y \subseteq U$. If Y is a single attribute, the functional dependency is in *standard form* whereas if $Y \subseteq X$ then fd is *trivial*. A relation R over $r(U)$ *satisfies* fd if $\forall t_1, t_2 \in R$ $t_1[X] = t_2[X]$ implies $t_1[Y] = t_2[Y]$ (we also say that R is *consistent* w.r.t. fd). Given a set FD of functional dependencies, a *key* of r is a minimal set K of attributes of r s.t. FD entails $K \rightarrow U$. A *primary key* of r is one designated key of r.

Given two relation schemata $r(U)$ and $s(V)$, a *foreign key constraint* fk is of the form $r(W) \subseteq s(Z)$, where $W \subseteq U, Z \subseteq V, |W| = |Z|$ and Z is a key of s (if Z is the primary key of s we call fk a *primary foreign key constraint*). Two relations R and S over $r(U)$ and $s(V)$ respectively, *satisfy* fk if for each tuple $t_1 \in R$ there is a tuple $t_2 \in S$ such that $t_1[W] = t_2[Z]$ (we also say that R and S are *consistent* w.r.t. fk).

A database satisfies (or is consistent w.r.t.) a set IC of constraints, if it satisfies every constraint in IC.

3   Repairing Inconsistent Databases

In this section we investigate the problem of repairing databases that are inconsistent w.r.t. functional dependencies and foreign key constraints. Specifically, in this paper we consider particular sets of functional dependencies, called *canonical*, which are introduced in the following definition.[1]

Definition 1. *Canonical sets of functional dependencies.* Let FD be a set of functional dependencies over the relation schema $r(U)$. FD is said to be in *canonical form* if for each functional dependency $X \rightarrow A \in FD$ does not exist a functional dependency $Y \rightarrow B \in FD$ such that $A \in Y$.   □

Thus, a set of functional dependencies is canonical if there is no attribute appearing in the right-hand side of a functional dependency and in the left-hand side of another one. When the database schema consists of more than one relation schema, each schema is associated with a canonical set of functional dependencies. It is easy to see that, given a canonical set FD of functional dependencies over a relation schema $r(U)$, there exists a unique key K of r and, moreover, every functional dependency $X \rightarrow A$ in FD is s.t. $X \subseteq K$. Thus, we observe that we deal with primary foreign key constraints.

---

[1] From now on, we assume that functional dependencies are nontrivial and in standard form.

Most of the proposed approaches for repairing inconsistent databases rely on tuple insertions and deletions; only a few works have investigated the computation of repairs by means of tuple updates ([22]). We propose a repairing strategy which aims at preserving the information in the original database as much as possible: when foreign key constraints are violated new tuples are inserted into the database whereas tuples updates are performed to make the database consistent w.r.t. functional dependencies; thus tuple deletions are never performed. As it has been shown in Example 1, null and unknown values can be introduced when repairing w.r.t. foreign key constraints and functional dependencies, respectively.

In the rest of this section, first we present a semantics of constraint satisfaction for databases containing null and unknown values, next we propose a repairing strategy.

3.1   Semantics of Constraint Satisfaction

First of all, let us introduce databases containing null and unknown values. We assume to have two infinite enumerable domains $D_{\#} = \{\#1, \ldots, \#n, \ldots\}$ and $D_{\perp} = \{\perp_1, \ldots, \perp_k, \ldots\}$ of distinct *unknown values* and distinct *labeled nulls*, respectively. The database domain, denoted as $Dom_{\#, \perp}$, contains, in addition to a set Dom of standard constants, the unknown values $D_{\#}$ and the null values $D_{\perp}$, i.e. $Dom_{\#, \perp} = Dom \cup D_{\#} \cup D_{\perp}$ (likewise, given an attribute A_i, its domain is $Dom_{\#, \perp}(A_i) = Dom(A_i) \cup D_{\#} \cup D_{\perp}$ where $Dom(A_i)$ is the set of constants for the attribute A_i). The sets of constants, null and unknown values are pairwise disjoint. A relation R over the schema $r(A_1, \ldots, A_n)$ is a subset of $Dom_{\#, \perp}(A_1) \times \cdots \times Dom_{\#, \perp}(A_n)$, where each unknown value $\#j$ appearing in R in correspondence of an attribute A_i is associated with a finite set of constants $dom(\#j) \subseteq Dom(A_i)$ (we call $dom(\#j)$ the domain of $\#j$). Given a tuple $t \in R$, we denote by $ground(t)$ the set of tuples obtained from t by replacing every unknown value occurring in t with a constant from its domain. We will call databases containing neither null nor unknown values *complete databases*. We point out that source databases are complete (and possibly inconsistent) and the proposed repairing strategy leads to consistent databases possibly containing null and unknown values.

We present first a semantics of constraint satisfaction for databases containing null and unknown values in the presence of foreign key constraints, and next a semantics for functional dependencies (in this paper we consider only canonical sets of functional dependencies, see Definition 1).

Definition 2. *Satisfaction of foreign key constraints.* Let R, S be two relations with schemata $r(U), s(V)$ respectively, and fk be a foreign key constraint of the form $r(X) \subseteq s(Y)$. R and S satisfy fk if for each tuple $t_R \in R$

- there exists X_i in X s.t. $t_R[X_i] = \perp_j$, or
- for each tuple $t'_R \in ground(t_R[X])$ there is a tuple $t_S \in S$ s.t. $t'_R = t_S[Y]$.

Clearly, a database DB satisfies a set FK of foreign key constraints if it satisfies every foreign key constraint in FK.   □

In the above definition, if a tuple $t \in R$ contains a null value on some attribute in X, then it does not violate the foreign key constraint fk. Observe that, if such a tuple could violate fk, a reasonable way (relying on tuple insertions) to repair the database would lead to the insertion in S of a new tuple containing null values on attributes belonging to the primary key, which is not desirable (we recall that we deal with primary foreign key constraints). If a tuple $t \in R$ does not contain any null value on X, intuitively, it could be any tuple in $ground(t_R)$ and, in order to consider the constraint not violated by t_R, we require that any tuple in $ground(t_R)$ does not violate the constraint (under the standard semantics). When complete databases are considered, the previous definition coincides with the classical semantics of foreign key constraint satisfaction.

Example 3. Consider the database schema of Example 1 and the following database.

Project	
Name	*Manager*
p1	$\perp_1$
p2	#1

Employee	
Name	*Phone*
john	123

where $dom(\#1) = \{john, bob\}$. The first tuple of the project relation does not lead to a violation of $Project[Manager] \subseteq Employee[Name]$ since it has a null value on the attribute $Manager$. With regard to the second tuple in the project relation, since the manager of p2 could possibly be *bob* and he is missing in the employee relation, the database is inconsistent.   □

Now we present the semantics of constraint satisfaction w.r.t. functional dependencies. As it has been observed before, given a canonical set FD of functional dependencies over a relation schema $r(U)$, every functional dependency $X \to Y$ in FD is s.t. each attribute $X_i \in X$ belongs to the primary key of r. Since null values cannot occur in correspondence of such attributes, in the following definition we assume that, given a relation R over $r(U)$, every tuple $t \in R$ contains constants or unknown values on attributes appearing in the left-hand side of some functional dependency. Moreover, for the sake of simplicity of presentation, we say that $dom(c) = \{c\}$ for every constant $c \in Dom$.

Definition 3. *Satisfaction of functional dependencies.* Given a relation R and a functional dependency $fd = X \to A$ over the schema $r(U)$, R satisfies fd if for every pair t_1, t_2 of tuples in R, $\bigwedge_{X_i \in X}(dom(t_1[X_i]) \cap dom(t_2[X_i]) \neq \emptyset)$ implies $t_1[A] = t_2[A]$. Clearly, R satisfies a set FD of functional dependencies if it satisfies every functional dependency in FD.   □

In the previous definition, similarly to the semantics for foreign key constraints, if two tuples in R could possibly have the same value on X, thus we require that they have same value on A in order to consider fd not violated. In the presence of complete databases the above definition coincides with the classical semantics of satisfaction of functional dependencies.

Example 4. Consider the database schema of Example 1 and the following database (the employee relation is empty and then omitted).

$Project$

$Name$	$Manager$
$p1$	$\perp_1$
$p1$	$\#1$
$p1$	$carl$

where $dom(\#1) = \{john, bob\}$. The tuples in the above relation are pairwise violating $fd_1 : Name \rightarrow Manager$ as they have the same information on $Name$ but different information on $Manager$.   □

3.2   Repairing

We now present how to repair inconsistent databases. Basically, we introduce a rule to be applied whenever functional dependency violations occur, and another rule to be applied when foreign key constraints are violated. Our repairing strategy consists in applying these rules in some arbitrary order as long as they are applicable. We show that this procedure always terminates and the final consistent database does not depend on the order the rules have been applied. Finally, we show that the repairing process is polynomial time.

Let DB be a database and FD, FK be sets of functional dependencies and foreign key constraints respectively. The aforementioned rules are the following:

- **FKC rule.** if there exist two relations R and S in DB with schemata $r(U)$ and $s(V)$ respectively, a foreign key constraint $fk : r(X) \subseteq s(Y)$ in FK and a tuple $t_R \in R$ which violate fk (according to Definition 2), then we say that the *FKC rule is applicable*. The rule is applied as follows: for each tuple $t \in ground(t_R[X])$ s.t. there is no tuple $t_S \in S$ s.t. $t_S[Y] = t$ insert a tuple t_{new} into S s.t. $t_{new}[Y] = t$ and $\forall A_i \in (V - Y)$ $t_{new}[A_i] = \perp_j$ where $\perp_j$ is a fresh labeled null.

- **FDC rule.** if there exist a functional dependency $fd : X \rightarrow A \in FD$ and a relation R over $r(U)$, and two tuples t_1, t_2 in R which violate fd (according to Definition 3), then we say that the *FDC rule is applicable*. For the sake of simplicity of presentation, we say that $dom(\perp_i) = \emptyset$ for every unknown value $\perp_i \in D_\perp$ and $dom(c) = \{c\}$ for every constant $c \in Dom$. The rule is applied as follows. Let $d = dom(t_1[A]) \cup dom(t_2[A])$. If $d = \{c\}$ then $t_1[A] := c, t_2[A] := c$. If $d = \emptyset$ then $t_1[A] := \perp_j$, $t_2[A] := \perp_j$, where $\perp_j$ is a fresh null value, and every occurrence of the old values $t_1[A]$ and $t_2[A]$ elsewhere is replaced with $\perp_j$. If both the previous cases do not hold then $t_1[A] := \#i$, $t_2[A] := \#i$, where $\#i$ is a fresh unknown value with domain $dom(\#i) = d$, and every occurrence of the old values $t_1[A]$ and $t_2[A]$ elsewhere, only if unknown values, is replaced with $\#i$.

Therefore, when a foreign key constraint is violated, the missing information is simply inserted into the database. By inserting a new tuple into the database, it may be the case that some information about the new tuple is missing and then we need to use null values. We adopt the no information interpretation of null values because, as it has been shown in Example 1, this interpretation allows us to model every kind of missing information, whereas adopting the unknown or the nonexistent interpretation non-factual information can be stored in the database.

Example 5. Consider the database of Example 3. By applying the FKC rule, the consistent database reported below is obtained.

Project	
Name	Manager
p1	$\perp_1$
p2	#1

Employee	
Name	Phone
john	123
bob	$\perp_2$

Thus, we have inserted *bob* into the employee relation as it could be *p2*'s manager.   □

The proposed rule for repairing w.r.t. functional dependencies stems from the observation that, if a relation contains two tuples t_1, t_2 which are equal on a set X of attributes, and a functional dependency $X \rightarrow A$ is defined, this means that $t_1[X]$ (equivalently, $t_2[X]$) should be associated with a unique A-value. When this is not the case, that is t_1 and t_2 violate $X \rightarrow A$, we modify both of them on the attribute A in such a way that they have the same information on this attribute. Specifically, when t_1, t_2 do not have a null value on A we "fix" them by assigning the same (unknown) value on A; the possible values for this unknown value come from the old values of t_1 and t_2 on A. Observe that the domain of an unknown value consists of constants which come from the original (complete) database, and, in particular, these values were in the original database in positions where the unknown value occurs.

Example 6. Consider the database schema of Example 1 and the following database (the employee relation is empty and then omitted).

Project	
Name	Manager
p1	#1
p1	carl

where $dom(\#1) = \{john, bob\}$. Clearly, the database violates $fd_1 : Name \rightarrow Manager$. By applying the FDC rule, we obtain the following consistent database:

Project	
Name	Manager
p1	#2

where $dom(\#2) = \{john, bob, carl\}$.   □

Let us consider the case where $t_1[A]$ and $t_2[A]$ contain null values. If $t_1[A] = \perp_i$ and $t_2[A] = \perp_j$, with $i \neq j$, then the same (fresh) labeled null is assigned to both $t_1[A]$ and $t_2[A]$ (every occurrence of $\perp_i$ and $\perp_j$ elsewhere is replaced with the new labeled null). Let us now consider the case where there is only one null values among $t_1[A]$ and $t_2[A]$. As we have stressed several times, a null value is interpreted as no information (the value either exists but it is not known or does not exist) whereas we can say more about unknown values (a value exists but it is not know and a finite set of possible values is known). In a sense, both constants and unknown values are more informative than null values. The proposed repairing strategy aims at exploiting functional dependencies to "infer" more precise information on null values: suppose that $t_1[A]$ is a null value whereas $t_2[A]$ is not, then we replace the null value with $t_2[A]$. We show this idea in the following example.

Example 7. Consider the database below.

Employee

Name	Dept	City
john	cs	rome
bob	cs	milan

Department

Name	City	Manager
cs	rome	carl

Suppose that the following constraints are defined.

- fd_1 : $Name \to Dept, City$ defined over *Employee*,
- fd_2 : $Name \to Manager$ defined over *Department*,
- fk : $Employee[Dept, City] \subseteq Department[Name, City]$.

Thus, a department can be located in different cities and has a unique manager. As the pair $cs, milan$ is missing in the department relation, the database violates fk. By applying the FKC rule we obtain the following database.

Employee

Name	Dept	City
john	cs	rome
bob	cs	milan

Department

Name	City	Manager
cs	rome	carl
cs	milan	$\perp_1$

The obtained database is inconsistent w.r.t. fd_2 since there are two tuples in the department relation regarding the same department cs and containing different information about its manager. As the first tuple states that the manager of cs is $carl$, whereas the second tuple does not say anything, it seems to be reasonable replacing the null value with a more precise information which comes from the first tuple, that is we exploit the functional dependency to "infer" missing information. By applying the FDC rule, the following consistent database is obtained.

Employee

Name	Dept	City
john	cs	rome
bob	cs	milan

Department

Name	City	Manager
cs	rome	carl
cs	milan	carl

Observe that unknown values are introduced only in correspondence of attributes appearing in the right-hand side of functional dependencies and, since we consider canonical sets of functional dependencies, unknown values never appear in correspondence of attributes in some left-hand side.

We point out that, since the original database is complete, every null value is introduced either by the FKC rule or by the FDC rule. As it has been discussed above, null values introduced by the FKC rule are no information nulls. Null values introduced by the FDC rule are used just for assigning the same label to different null values, and this does not change their no information interpretation. Thus, we deal only with no information nulls.

It is worth noting that the repairing strategy we propose consists in applying the FDC and FKC rules as long as they are applicable.

Definition 4. *Repairing sequence.* Let DB be a complete database, FD be a set of functional dependencies and FK be a set of foreign key constraints. A *repairing sequence* of DB w.r.t. FD and FK is a (possibly infinite) sequence $DB_0, \ldots, DB_j, \ldots$ s.t. $DB_0 = DB$ and for each $i > 0$ DB_i is the database obtained by applying the FDC or the FKC rule to DB_{i-1}. □

The following proposition states that the proposed repairing process always terminates.

Proposition 1. *Let DB be a complete database, FD be a set of functional dependencies and FK be a set of foreign key constraints. Each repairing sequence of DB w.r.t. FD and FK is finite.* □

Given a database DB, a set FD of functional dependency and a set FK of foreign key constraints, a repairing sequence $DB, \ldots, DB_n$ is *complete* if DB_n satisfies $FD \cup FK$ (we call DB_n *repaired database*). Clearly, Proposition 1 entails that a repaired database always exists.

Corollary 1. *Let DB be a complete database, FD be a set of functional dependencies and FK be a set of foreign key constraints. There exists a repaired database DB_n for DB w.r.t. FD and FK.* □

The following theorem states that, up to renaming of unknown and null values, the repaired database is unique.

Theorem 1. *Let DB be a complete database, FD be a set of functional dependencies and FK be a set of foreign key constraints. There exists a unique repaired database for DB w.r.t. FD and FK (up to renaming of unknown and null values).* □

As stated in the following theorem, the proposed repairing strategy is polynomial time.

Theorem 2. *Let DB be a complete database, FD be a set of functional dependencies and FK be a set of foreign key constraints. The repaired database of DB w.r.t. FD and FK can be computed in polynomial time.* □

4   Query Answering

In this section we present a semantics of query answering over possibly inconsistent databases. Relying on the results in [17], we show that there exists a class of conjunctive queries which can be evaluated in polynomial time.

In this section we consider only conjunctive queries. A conjunctive query Q is of the form $\exists y\, \Phi(x, y)$ where Φ is a conjunction of literals (a literal is of the form $p(t_1, \ldots, t_n)$ where p is a relation symbol and each t_i is a term, that is a constant or a variable) and x is the set of free variables of Q (x and y are sets of variables).

The proposed semantics of query answering stems form the following observations. The repairing strategy presented in the previous section lead to a consistent database possibly containing unknown and (labeled) null values. Specifically, the so obtained database is an OR-database [17] and thus it represents a set of "possible worlds", namely the databases which are obtained by replacing every unknown value with a constant of its domain (observe that we treat labeled nulls like standard constants). The "certain answers" to a query over an OR-database are those tuples which can be derived from every possible world of the database (we observe that, in our case, a possible world can contain labeled nulls; the evaluation of a query over a possible world treats such null values like standard constants). Then, it is natural to define the semantics of query answering over a possibly inconsistent database as the certain answers over its repaired database (Definition 5 below). Let DB be an OR-database. We denote by $pw(DB)$ the set of possible worlds of DB.

Definition 5. *Consistent Query Answers.* Let DB be a complete database, FD be a canonical set of functional dependencies, FK be a set of foreign key constraints and Q be a conjunctive query. Let $\overline{DB}$ be the repaired database for DB w.r.t. FD and FK. The *consistent answers* to Q on DB w.r.t. FD and FK are:

$$Q^c(DB, FD \cup FK) = \bigcap_{D \in pw(\overline{DB})} Q(D)$$

where $Q(D)$ denotes the result of applying Q over D.   □

Relying on the results in [17], we show that there exists a class of conjunctive queries whose consistent answers can be computed in polynomial time. The data complexity of queries is considered.

Let us briefly recall the results in [17]. Basically, *OR-Tables* are relations (as presented at the beginning of Section 3.1) which do not contain labeled null values. Unknown values are also called *OR-Objects*. Only in correspondence of certain attributes, OR-Tables are allowed to have variables and this is predesignated by a typing function α. Given a database schema DS, let Att be the set of attribute symbols in DS. The typing function α is defined as $\alpha : Att \rightarrow \{ATOMIC, OR\}$. Those attributes that are mapped to OR are called *OR-Attributes*.

Given a query Q and a literal l in Q, we denote by $VAR(l)$ the set of variables occurring in l.

Definition 6. Given a query Q, two literals l_1 and l_2 in Q are *connected* to each other if $VAR(l_1) \cap VAR(l_2) \neq \emptyset$ or, if there exists a literal l_3 in Q such that l_1 is *connected* to l_3 and $VAR(l_3) \cap VAR(l_2) \neq \emptyset$.   □

Given a database schema DS, a query Q and a literal $l = p(x_1, \ldots, x_n)$ in Q, then a variable x_i in l occurring in correspondence of an attribute A is said to *label* A. Moreover, x_i *occurs as OR in* l if it is in correspondence of an OR-Attribute (according to the typing function α for DS).

Definition 7. Let DS be a database schema, α be the corresponding typing function, Q be a query and l_1, l_2 be two different literals in Q. Then l_1 *marks* l_2 if there exists a variable $y \in VAR(l_1) \cap VAR(l_2)$, such that y occurs as OR in l_1 or, if there is another literal l_3 in Q such that l_1 *marks* l_3 and l_3 is connected to l_2.   □

Marking depends on both the typing function and the way the variables are shared in Q.

Definition 8. A query Q is an *acyclic query* if there are no two literals l_1 and l_2 in Q such that l_1 marks l_2 and l_2 marks l_1. A query which is not acyclic is called *cyclic query*.   □

Given a database schema DS, a typing function α for it and a query Q, we denote by $MODIFY(\alpha, Q)$ the typing function obtained by modifying α in such a way that every attribute labeled by a free variable in Q is $ATOMIC$. *Proper* conjunctive queries are those queries in which every pair of literals have different relation symbols.

Theorem 3. *[17] Let DS be a database schema, α be its typing function, Q be a proper conjunctive query and D be a database instance on DS. Let $\alpha' = MODIFY(\alpha, Q)$. Then, the data complexity of computing the certain answers of Q over D is in PTIME iff Q is acyclic with respect to α'.*   □

We recall that null values appearing in repaired databases are treated as constants in query evaluation. Consider a complete database DB, a canonical set FD of functional dependencies and a set FK of foreign key constraints. Let $\overline{DB}$ be the repaired database for DB w.r.t. FD and FK. According to the previous theorem, we can identify proper conjunctive queries which can be evaluated in polynomial time on $\overline{DB}$. As the certain answers computed on $\overline{DB}$ coincide with the consistent answers for DB w.r.t. FD and FK and $\overline{DB}$ can be computed in polynomial time, we can identify queries whose consistent answers over the original database can be computed in polynomial time.

5   Discussion

5.1   Summary of Results

This paper has proposed a framework for repairing and querying relational databases which may be inconsistent with respect to functional dependencies and foreign key constraints. Specifically, *canonical* sets of functional dependencies have been considered, that is sets of functional dependencies where attributes appearing in the right-hand side cannot appear also in the left-hand side. In order to restore the consistency of inconsistent databases, we have proposed a repairing strategy that performs tuple insertions when foreign key constraints are violated and tuple updates when functional dependency violations occur (tuple deletions are never performed). Since tuple insertions and updates may introduce, respectively, null and unknown values in the database, we have proposed a semantics of constraint satisfaction for databases containing null and unknown values. Our approach always allows us to obtain a unique (up to renaming of unknown and null values) repaired database which can be computed in polynomial time. The result of the repairing technique is an incomplete database (in particular, an OR-database). The consistent query answers over an inconsistent database are the certain answers on the repaired database. The results in [17] on the complexity of query processing in OR-databases allows us to identify conjunctive queries which can be evaluated in polynomial time.

5.2   Related Work

Several works have addressed the problem of repairing and querying inconsistent databases. Most of them are based on the notion of *repair* (a consistent database which minimally differs from the original one) and *consistent query answers* (query answers which can be obtained from every repair of an inconsistent database) [3]. An introduction to the central concepts of consistent query answering is [9], whereas surveys on this topic are [5,4]. We introduce below some approaches enabling the computation of repairs and consistent answers in possibly inconsistent databases.

In [18] a semantics of satisfaction of functional and inclusion dependencies in the presence of databases with null values is presented. Here the null value is interpreted as "unknown". The classical chase procedure is extended to incomplete relations and used to test whether a database satisfies a set of constraints. The axiomatization and the implication problem of functional and inclusion dependencies is studied. No repairing strategy is provided.

The issue of dealing with databases containing null values in the presence of integrity constraints has been considered also in [6]. In this work, null values are also used to repair the original database. The paper considers a wide class of integrity constraints which includes universal integrity constraints, denial constraints, cyclic sets of inclusion dependencies and others. The proposed semantics of constraint satisfaction takes into account *the relevance of the occurrence of a null value* in a relation and is compatible with the way null values are usually treated in commercial database management systems. The notion of repair is that one presented in [3], that is a consistent database instance which minimally differs from the original database.

References

1. Abiteboul, S., Hull, R., Vianu, V.: Foundations of Databases. Addison-Wesley, Reading (1994)
2. Agarwal, S., Keller, A.M., Wiederhold, G., Saraswat, K.: Flexible Relation: an Approach for Integrating Data from Multiple, Possibly Inconsistent Databases. In: ICDE (1995)
3. Arenas, M., Bertossi, L., Chomicki, J.: Consistent Query Answers in Inconsistent Databases. In: Proc. PODS 1999, pp. 68–79 (1999)
4. Bertossi, L.E.: Consistent query answering in databases. SIGMOD Record 35(2), 68–76 (2006)
5. Bertossi, L., Chomicki, J.: Query Answering in Inconsistent Databases. In: Logics for Emerging Applications of Databases, pp. 43–83 (2003)
6. Bravo, L., Bertossi, L.E.: Semantically Correct Query Answers in the Presence of Null Values. In: EDBT Workshops, pp. 336–357 (2006)
7. Bry, F.: Query Answering in Information System with Integrity Constraints. In: IICIS, pp. 113–130 (1997)
8. Cali, A., Calvanese, D., De Giacomo, G., Lenzerini, M.: Data Integration under Integrity Constraints. In: Pidduck, A.B., Mylopoulos, J., Woo, C.C., Ozsu, M.T. (eds.) CAiSE 2002. LNCS, vol. 2348, pp. 262–279. Springer, Heidelberg (2002)
9. Chomicki, J.: Consistent Query Answering: Five Easy Pieces. In: Schwentick, T., Suciu, D. (eds.) ICDT 2007. LNCS, vol. 4353, pp. 1–17. Springer, Heidelberg (2006)
10. Chomicki, J., Marcinkowski, J.: Minimal-change integrity maintenance using tuple deletions. Information & Computation 197(1/2), 90–121 (2005)
11. Dung, P.M.: Integrating Data from Possibly Inconsistent Databases. In: COOPIS, pp. 58–65 (1996)
12. Grant, J., Subrahmanian, V.S.: Reasoning in Inconsistent Knowledge Bases. IEEE-TKDE 7(1), 177–189 (1995)
13. Greco, S., Zumpano, E.: Querying Inconsistent Database LPAR, pp. 308-325 (2000)
14. Greco, G., Greco, S., Zumpano, E.: A Logic Programming Approach to the Integration, Repairing and Querying of Inconsistent Databases. In: Codognet, P. (ed.) ICLP 2001. LNCS, vol. 2237, pp. 348–364. Springer, Heidelberg (2001)
15. Greco, G., Greco, S., Zumpano, E.: A Logical Framework for Querying and Repairing Inconsistent Databases. TKDE 15(6), 1389–1408 (2003)
16. Imielinski, T., Lipski Jr., W.: Incomplete Information in Relational Databases. J. ACM 31(4), 761–791 (1984)
17. Imielinski, T., Vadaparty, K.: Complexity of Query Processing in Databases with OR-Objects. In: PODS, pp. 51–65 (1989)
18. Levene, M., Loizou, G.: Null Inclusion Dependencies in Relational Databases. Inf. Comput. 136(2), 67–108 (1997)
19. Lin, J.: A Semantics for Reasoning Consistently in the Presence of Inconsistency. AI 86(1), 75–95 (1996)
20. Lipski Jr., W.: On Semantic Issues Connected with Incomplete Information Databases. ACM Trans. Database Syst. 4(3), 262–296 (1979)
21. Ullman, J.D.: Principles of Database and Knowledge-Base Systems, vol. 1. Computer Science Pressingness (1998)
22. Wijsen, J.: Database repairing using updates. ACM Trans. Database Syst. 30(3), 722–768 (2005)
23. Zaniolo, C.: Database Relations with Null Values. J. Comput. Syst. Sci. 28(1), 142–166 (1984)
24. Zaniolo, C.: Database Relations with Null Values. In: PODS, pp. 27–33 (1982)

Using OBDDs for Efficient Query Evaluation on Probabilistic Databases

Dan Olteanu and Jiewen Huang

Oxford University Computing Laboratory, UK

Abstract. We consider the problem of query evaluation for tuple independent probabilistic databases and Boolean conjunctive queries with inequalities but without self-joins. We approach this problem as a construction problem for ordered binary decision diagrams (OBDDs): Given a query q and a probabilistic database D, we construct in polynomial time an OBDD such that the probability of $q(D)$ can be computed linearly in the size of that OBDD. This approach is applicable to a large class of queries, including the *hierarchical* queries, i.e., the Boolean conjunctive queries without self-joins that admit PTIME evaluation on any tuple-independent probabilistic database, hierarchical queries extended with inequalities, and non-hierarchical queries on restricted databases.

1 Introduction

Recently there has been renewed interest in probabilistic databases [2,10,20,5,6,1] due to important applications that systems for representing uncertain information have, such as data cleaning, data integration, and scientific databases.

In this paper we study the following evaluation problem: given a Boolean conjunctive query q without self-joins and with inequalities and a tuple-independent probabilistic databases D, compute the probability of $q(D)$.

Dalvi and Suciu's seminal work [5] on the evaluation of conjunctive queries without self-joins on tuple-independent probabilistic databases shows that the complexity of query evaluation is either PTIME or #P-hard. In case of PTIME queries, also called hierarchical [6], there exists an evaluation method that rewrites them into linear-size SQL queries (called safe plans) that compute the probability of the distinct answer tuples. Such SQL rewritings use aggregates to eagerly eliminate duplicates and compute the probability of distinct tuples in projections of the input and temporary tables. The addition of aggregates severely restricts the search space for good query plans to compute the answer tuples: In most cases it enforces unoptimal join orderings and each of these aggregates requires sorting. We also note that this rewriting approach cannot be naturally extended to cope with queries beyond the hierarchical ones.

In this paper we devise a new method for the aforementioned evaluation problem. Our method is rooted in the following two observations that relate query evaluation on probabilistic databases, #SAT procedures, and knowledge compilation. First, the probability of a query q on a probabilistic database D is

S. Greco and T. Lukasiewicz (Eds.): SUM 2008, LNAI 5291, pp. 326–340, 2008.
© Springer-Verlag Berlin Heidelberg 2008

the probability of the Boolean expression $\phi_{q,D}$ *associated* with q and D; such Boolean expressions encode the (provenance) information on which input tuples contribute to which answer tuples. Second, the probability of $\phi_{q,D}$ can be computed by compiling it into a propositional theory with PTIME model counting (and thus probability computation). Our approach is to compile $\phi_{q,D}$ into *reduced ordered binary decision diagrams* (OBDDs). Boolean expressions are commonly represented using OBDDs, as it is the case in hardware verification and model checking [4], program analysis [15], and probabilistic logic programming [18].

We show that OBDDs are effective in handling Boolean expressions of interest. In contrast to the approach of Dalvi and Suciu, our approach is more general as it covers the *orthogonal* tractable classes of both hierarchical queries and Boolean expressions of bounded treewidth, which are associated with probabilistic databases and non-hierarchical queries, and a large tractable class of conjunctive queries extended with inequalities.

The key technical challenge of our method is to efficiently find *good variable orders*, under which Boolean expressions associated with queries and probabilistic databases can be compiled into OBDDs in polynomial time.

The contributions of this article are as follows:

- We revisit the problem of query evaluation for conjunctive queries on tuple-independent probabilistic databases and connect it to the OBDD construction problem.
- We show that the expression $\phi_{q,D}$ associated with any hierarchical query q and tuple-independent probabilistic database D, can be brought into a special factored form, where each of its variables occurs exactly once. It then follows that such expressions can be efficiently compiled into OBDDs, whose sizes are linear in the number of their variables. This guarantees the robustness of our method.
- We define a large tractable class of queries with inequalities. Queries in this class can be represented as trees where nodes are hierarchical queries and each edge that connects two nodes for queries A and B represents one inequality on variables occuring in all subgoals of A and B, respectively.
- Within the #P-hard class of conjunctive queries, we identify one subclass that remains in PTIME under certain assumptions about the database. By relating the complexity of query evaluation to that of OBDD construction for arbitrary Boolean expressions, we are able to carry over results that bound the exponent of the evaluation time to the treewidth of such expressions.

To the best of our knowledge, this paper is the first to develop a robust framework based on OBDDs to efficiently evaluate queries on probabilistic databases. Similar in spirit to the approach of this paper, previous work [14] of the first author employs knowledge compilation techniques for probability computation of conjunctive queries on *arbitrary* probabilistic databases, but *without* polynomial-time guarantees. Follow-up work [17] of the same authors applies the results of this paper to implement in PostgreSQL a low-level query plan operator for probability computation, and shows experimentally that our method can outperform the method of Suciu and Dalvi by orders of magnitude.

R	A	B
x_1	a_1	b_1
x_2	a_2	b_1
x_3	a_2	b_2
x_4	a_3	b_3

S	A	C
y_1	a_1	c_1
y_2	a_1	c_2
y_3	a_2	c_1
y_4	a_4	c_2

T	D
z_1	c_1
z_2	c_2
z_3	c_3

Fig. 1. A tuple-independent probabilistic database over $\{R(A,B), S(A,C), T(D)\}$

2   Preliminaries

We next recall the notions of probabilistic databases, conjunctive queries, and ordered binary decision diagrams.

2.1   Tuple-Independent Probabilistic Databases

Let a finite set $\mathbf{X}$ of (independent) random Boolean variables and a probability distribution over their assignments given by a function P, i.e., $\forall x \in \mathbf{X} : P(x) + P(\overline{x}) = 1$. A *probabilistic relation* R over a schema and variable set $\mathbf{X}$ is a set of tuples over that schema, such that each tuple is associated with a distinct variable from $\mathbf{X}$. We denote by $Vars(R) \subseteq \mathbf{X}$ the set of variables of R. A *probabilistic database*, or database for short, is a set of probabilistic relations. Fig.1 gives such a database, where for instance $Vars(R) = \{x_1, x_2, x_3, x_4\}$.

The set of *possible worlds* is defined by the finite set of truth assignments of all variables from $\mathbf{X}$. There is a one-to-one correspondence between possible worlds and database instances. To obtain one instance, we fix a truth assignment f, and then process each relation R_i tuple by tuple. A tuple t with variable $\phi(t)$ is in R_i if $f(\phi(t))$ is true. For instance, the truth assignment that maps x_1, y_1, and z_1 to true and all remaining variables to false, defines the database instance where $R = \{(a_1, b_1)\}$, $S = \{(a_1, c_1)\}$, and $T = \{(c_1)\}$. The probability of this world is the product of the probabilities of x_1, y_1, and z_1 being true, and of the probabilities of the remaining variables being false.

2.2   Conjunctive Queries with Inequalities and without Self-joins

We consider Boolean conjunctive queries with negated equalities but without self-joins. We write queries using the Datalog notation: $q :\text{-} g_1, \ldots, g_n$ defines a query q where its body is a conjunction of n distinct positive relational predicates, called *subgoals*. A subgoal has the form $R(A_1, \ldots, A_k)$, where R is a relation name and A_1 to A_k are query variables. By $sg(A_i)$ we denote the set of subgoals of query variable A_i. An *eq-join variable* occurs in more than one subgoal. Inequality joins are expressed using inequality conditions, e.g., $B \neq C$ with query variables B and C occurring in some subgoals.

We partition the conjunctive queries into *hierarchical* and non-hierarchical [7]: The hierarchical queries admit polynomial-time evaluation, whereas the non-hierarchical ones are #P-hard in general [5].

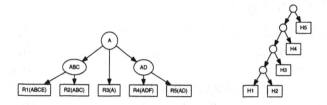

Fig. 2. (Left) Hierarchical query of Ex.1 and (right) IHQ$^{\neq}$ query of Ex.2

Definition 1 ([7]). *A conjunctive query is hierarchical if for any two variables, either their sets of subgoals are disjoint, or one set is contained in the other.*

Each connected component of a hierarchical query has at least one query variable that occurs in all subgoals. Following [7], we call such variables *maximal*. We represent hierarchical queries as trees, where the inner nodes are the join variables of the children and the leaves are query subgoals. The root is then the set of maximal variables in case of connected queries, or the empty set otherwise. Each inner node stands for a relation, which corresponds to the subquery of the tree rooted at that node, and can be realized as the natural join of the node's children followed by a projection on the node's join variables.

Example 1. The following query is hierarchical and the variable A is maximal:

$$h\text{:-}R_1(A, B, C, E), R_2(A, B, C), R_3(A), R_4(A, D, F), R_5(A, D).$$

Fig.2 gives its tree representation. If we remove A from either R_1 or R_2, we obtain a non-hierarchical query, because $sg(A) - sg(B) \neq \emptyset \neq sg(B) - sg(A)$. $\square$

We also consider a class of conjunctive queries with inequalities, which we show in Section 4 to be tractable.

Definition 2. *An IHQ$^{\neq}$ query is either hierarchical, or a join of two independent IHQ$^{\neq}$ queries using an inequality predicate on maximal query variables. Two queries are independent if they use disjoint sets of relations.*

IHQ$^{\neq}$ queries have no cycles containing inequalities. We use here a tree representation that cannot distinguish unconnected hierarchical queries from IHQ$^{\neq}$ queries. Consider a partial order on the hierarchical subqueries of a IHQ$^{\neq}$ query q such that if one subquery is joined with n others, then it occurs after all subqueries joined with at most $n - 1$ others (the acyclicity ensures the existence of such orders). We construct a binary left-deep tree representation of q by adding in the ordered subqueries from right to left. The leaves of such a tree represent the hierarchical subqueries and the inner nodes are labeled with empty sets. The leaves are then replaced by the tree representations of the subqueries.

Example 2. The IHQ$^{\neq}$ query

$$q:-R_1(A,B), R_2(A,C), \qquad\qquad (H_1)$$
$$U(H,I), \qquad\qquad (H_2)$$
$$T(F,G), \qquad\qquad (H_3)$$
$$S_1(C,D,E), S_2(C,D), D \neq A, C \neq F, \qquad\qquad (H_4)$$
$$V(J,K), J \neq I, K \neq C. \qquad\qquad (H_5)$$

consists of five hierarhical queries (denoted by H_1 to H_5 above). Fig.2 gives the tree representation of q corresponding to the order H_1, H_2, H_3, H_4, H_5. For space reasons, we do not replace the leaves H_i by their tree representations.   □

The query evaluation follows the standard semantics with the addition that each tuple t is associated with a Boolean expression over random variables [13], as shown below for product, selection, and projection:

$$Q_1 \times Q_2 = \{(t_1 \circ t_2, \phi_1\phi_2) \mid (t_1, \phi_1) \in Q_1, (t_2, \phi_2) \in Q_2\}$$
$$\sigma_{cond}(Q) = \{(t, \phi) \mid (t, \phi) \in Q, cond(t)\}$$
$$\pi_{\bar{A}}(Q) = \{(t.\bar{A}, \phi) \mid (t, \phi) \in Q\}$$

The expression associated with q and D, denoted by $\phi_{q,D}$, is the disjunction of the monotone expressions of the tuples in $q(D)$: $\phi_{q,D} := \sum_{(t_i,\phi_i) \in q(D)}(\phi_i)$. The *size* of an expression $\phi_{q,D}$, denoted by $|\phi_{q,D}|$, is the product of the number of its clauses (equal to the number of tuples in the answer $q(D)$) and the number of variables per clause (equal to the number the subgoals of q).

Proposition 1 ([5]). *For any query q and probabilistic database D, it holds that $P(q(D)) = P(\phi_{q,D})$.*

Example 3. Consider the Boolean queries

$$q_{eq}:-R(A,B), S(A,C) \qquad\qquad q_{neq}:-R(A,B), S(C,D), A \neq C$$

The expressions ϕ_{eq} and ϕ_{neq} are (in an easier to follow factored form)

$$\phi_{eq} = x_1(y_1 + y_2) + (x_2 + x_3)y_3$$
$$\phi_{neq} = x_1(y_3 + y_4) + (x_2 + x_3)(y_1 + y_2 + y_4) + x_4(y_1 + y_2 + y_3 + y_4)$$

2.3   Ordered Binary Decision Diagrams

Reduced ordered binary decision diagrams (OBDDs) are commonly used to represent compactly large Boolean expressions [16].

The idea behind OBDDs is to decompose Boolean expressions using variable elimination and to avoid redundancy in the representation. The decomposition step is normally based on exhaustive application of Shannon's expansion: Given a Boolean expression ϕ and one of its variables x, we have $\phi = x \cdot \phi\mid_x + \bar{x} \cdot \phi\mid_{\bar{x}}$, where $\phi\mid_x$ and $\phi\mid_{\bar{x}}$ are ϕ with x set to true and false, respectively. The order of

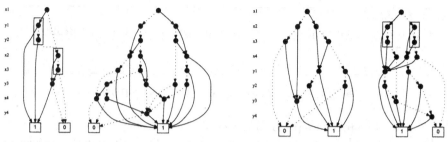

(a) Good variable order π_1 for eq-joins   (b) Good variable order π_2 for neq-joins
OBDDs: (a) left (ϕ_{eq}, π_1), (a) right (ϕ_{neq}, π_1), (b) left (ϕ_{eq}, π_2), (b) right (ϕ_{neq}, π_2).
The expressions ϕ_{eq} and ϕ_{neq} are given in Example 3.

Fig. 3. Eq-joins and neq-joins have different good variable orders

variable eliminations is a total order π on the set of variables of ϕ, called *variable order*. An OBDD for ϕ is uniquely identified by the pair (ϕ, π).

OBDDs are represented as directed acyclic graphs (DAG), with two terminal nodes representing the constants 0 (false) and 1 (true), and non-terminal nodes representing variables. Each node for a variable x has two outgoing edges corresponding to the two possible variable assignments: a high (solid) edge for $x = 1$ and a low (dashed) edge for $x = 0$. To evaluate the expression for a given set of variable assignments, we take the path from the root node to one of the terminal nodes, following the high edge of a node if the corresponding input variable is true, and the low edge otherwise. The terminal node gives the value of the expression. The non-redundancy is what makes OBDDs usually more compact than the textual representation of Boolean expressions: a node n is redundant if both its outgoing edges point to the same node, or if there is a node for the same decision variable and with the same children as n.

The choice of variable order can greatly influence the size of the OBDD.

Definition 3. *A variable order π is good for an expression ϕ if it can be computed from ϕ in PTIME and the OBBD (ϕ, π) has size polynomial in $|\phi|$.*

Some expressions do not admit good orders, either because they do not admit polynomial-size OBDDs, or because computing orders for such OBDDs is NP-hard [16]. In this paper, we nevertheless show that expressions associated with hierarchical queries and even with IHQ$^{\neq}$ queries admit good variable orders. Additionally, although not obvious in general, we are able to construct polynomial-size OBDDs in an *output-sensitive* manner and hence in PTIME.

Example 4. Fig. 3 depicts OBDDs for the expressions ϕ_{eq} and ϕ_{neq} of Example 3 under two distinct variable orders π_1 and π_2. The variable order π_1 is good for ϕ_{eq} as the size of the OBDD (ϕ_{eq}, π_1) is linear in the number of ϕ_{eq}'s variables. We show later that the variable order π_2 is good for ϕ_{neq}.   □

OBDDs can be maniputated efficiently. We exemplify here with linear-time probability computation, given a probability distribution over the OBDD variables.

```
prob (Node n)
    if (n.p = - 1) then n.p := P(n.v) * prob(n.high) + (1 - P(n.v)) * prob(n.low);
    return n.p;
end
```

Fig. 4. Computing the probability of an OBDD

Fig. 4 gives the procedure **prob** to this effect. We consider that for each OBDD node n, its variable is accessible by n.v, its probability by n.p, and its children by n.high and n.low. The probability value is initialized to 0 for terminal node 0, to 1 for terminal node 1, and to -1 for the remaining nodes. The probability of the OBDD is the probability of its root node, and the probability of any inner node n is the sum of the probabilities of their children weighted by the probabilities of the corresponding assignments of the decision variable n.v. Because we do a constant number of operations per node, we have that

Proposition 2. *The probability of the OBDD (ϕ, π) for an expression ϕ and a variable order π can be computed in time $O(|(\phi, \pi)|)$.*

From Query Evaluation to OBDD Construction. The problem of query evaluation on (not necessarily tuple-independent) probabilistic databases and the OBDD construction problem are closely connected. In particular, an efficient solution to the latter guarantees an efficient solution to the former. The connection follows in two steps: A reduction from the evaluation problem to probability computation of expressions over random Boolean variables, followed by a reduction from the latter problem to the problem of construction and probability computation of OBDDs.

Proposition 3. *For any query q, database D, and variable order π of $\phi_{q,D}$, it holds that $P(q(D)) = P((\phi_{q,D}, \pi))$.*

By Proposition 2, we can linearly reduce the query evaluation problem to the problem of OBDD construction.

Corollary 1. *Let query q and probabilistic database D. If there is a good variable order π such that the OBDD $(\phi_{q,D}, \pi)$ can be constructed in time polynomial in $|\phi_{q,D}|$, then $P(q(D))$ can be computed in PTIME.*

3   Hierarchical Queries

The hierarchical queries are the Boolean conjunctive queries without self-joins that admit PTIME evaluation on any tuple-independent probabilistic database [6]. The main result of this section is that

Theorem 1. *For any hierarchical query q and database D there is a good variable order π for $\phi_{q,D}$. In particular, π can be computed in time $O(|\phi_{q,D}| \log^2 |\phi_{q,D}|)$ and, given π, the OBDD $(\phi_{q,D}, \pi)$ can be computed in time $O(|Vars(\phi_{q,D})|)$.*

type (query q)	$= \tau(q, \emptyset)$
τ (inner node $\bar{A}(X_1, \ldots, X_n), L$)	$= \mathbf{ite}(L = \bar{A}, \tau(X_1, \bar{A}) \circ \ldots \circ \tau(X_n, \bar{A}))$
τ (leaf node $R(\bar{A}), L$)	$= \mathbf{ite}(L = \bar{A}, Vars(R))$
ite (Cond, t)	$= \mathbf{if}\ \text{Cond}\ \mathbf{then}\ t\ \mathbf{else}\ (t)^*$

Fig. 5. Deriving VO-types from queries represented in tree form

Example 5. Consider the eq-join query q_{eq} :- $R(A, B), S(A, C)$ of Example 3 and the database of Fig. 1, where R and S are partitioned according to the A-values. By the semantics of eq-join, the tuples of the a_1-partitions of R and S are paired independently of the a_2-partitions. We thus generate a disjunction of conjunctions representing *all* pairs of variables from the two partitions, i.e., x_1 is paired with y_1 and y_2, and x_2 and x_3 are paired with y_3. This information is made explicit in the factored form of ϕ_{eq} given in Example 3.

A good variable order makes use of the independence of conjunctions across partitions. We partition the set of variables of ϕ_{eq} in independent sets $\{x_1, y_1, y_2\}$ and $\{x_2, x_3, y_3\}$, and choose a total order on the sets. We also exploit the fact that, within any of these sets, all variables from the partition of R are combined with all variables from the corresponding partition of S. The good orders for ϕ_{eq} thus correspond to any permutation of elements within each (nesting or nested) set in $\{\{x_1, \{y_1, y_2\}\}, \{\{x_2, x_3\}, y_3\}\}$. Fig. 3 gives one of these good orders: $\pi_1 = x_1 y_1 y_2 x_2 x_3 y_3$, which induces an OBDD for ϕ_{eq} whose size is linear in the number of variables. The boxes surrounding the subgraphs for the expressions $y_1 + y_2$ and $x_2 + x_3$ highlight that under such good orders each of them can be treated as one variable (each box has one parent and two distinct children). $\square$

We next generalize our reasoning from Example 5. For a given hierarchical query q, we first derive a class of variable orders, or VO-type for short, that captures good variable orders, and then use the VO-type and the expression $\phi_{q,D}$ associated with q and D to create a good variable order.

Definition 4. *A VO-type is defined inductively as follows:*

- *A set* $\mathbf{X}$ *of variables is a VO-type that defines all variable orders consisting of one variable of* $\mathbf{X}$;
- *A reflexive transitive closure* α^* *of a VO-type* α *is a VO-type that defines all variable orders obtained by concatenating zero or more variable orders of* α;
- *A (unordered) concatenation* $\alpha\beta$ *of two VO-types* α *and* β *is a VO-type that defines all variable orders obtained by concatenating a variable order of* α *(β) and a variable order of* β *(resp.* α).

A set $\mathbf{X}$ *can only occur once in a VO-type.*

Example 6. Let $\mathbf{X} = \{x_1, x_2, x_3, x_4\}$ and $\mathbf{Y} = \{y_1, y_2, y_3, y_4\}$. The VO-types of the variable orders of Fig. 3 are $(\mathbf{X}^*\mathbf{Y}^*)^*$ and $\mathbf{X}^*\mathbf{Y}^*$, respectively. $\square$

Fig. 5 gives the function **type** that constructs a VO-type from the tree representation of a query q. While traversing the tree top-down, we keep the query

$$\begin{aligned}
\textbf{vo} \ (\alpha^*, \phi) &= \textbf{let} \ \phi_1, \ldots, \phi_n \ \text{be a maximal independent partitioning of } \phi \ \textbf{in} \\
&\quad \textbf{vo} \ (\alpha, \phi_1) \circ \ldots \circ \textbf{vo} \ (\alpha, \phi_n) \\
\textbf{vo} \ (\alpha\beta, \phi) &= \textbf{vo} \ (\alpha, \phi \ \text{restricted to } Vars(\alpha)) \circ \textbf{vo} \ (\beta, \phi \ \text{restricted to } Vars(\beta)) \\
\textbf{vo} \ (\mathbf{X}, \phi) &= \text{the only variable in } \phi
\end{aligned}$$

Fig. 6. Deriving good variable orders for Boolean expressions wrt given VO-types

variables of the parent node (which includes the variables of all the ancestors) in L; initially, $L = \emptyset$. For a query subgoal $R(\bar{A})$, we create a VO-type $Vars(R)$ or $(Vars(R))^*$. The former case occurs when $\bar{A}$ represents the parent variables L, and thus there is one tuple (and thus one variable) per distinct $\bar{A}$-value. Otherwise, there may be several tuples (variables) per distinct $\bar{A}$-value (due to the projection at the parent node on the proper subset L of $\bar{A}$), and hence the exponent (*). In case of an inner node, we recursively compute the VO-types for the children and then concatenate them in *any* order. Distinction on $\bar{A} = L$ applies here as well. Note that $\bar{A} = \emptyset$ covers the case of hierarchical subqueries that are unconnected or connected using inequalities (IHQ$^{\neq}$ queries discussed later). In both cases, we treat such subqueries independently.

Example 7. The query of Example 1 has the VO-type $((\mathbf{X}_1^*\mathbf{X}_2)^*\mathbf{X}_3(\mathbf{X}_4^*\mathbf{X}_5)^*)^*$, where $\mathbf{X}_i = Vars(R_i)$. The IHQ$^{\neq}$ query of Example 2 has the VO-type $(Vars(R_1)^* Vars(R_2)^*)^* Vars(U)^* Vars(T)^* \ (Vars(S_1)^* Vars(S_2))^* Vars(V)^*$.   □

The VO-type of a hierarchical query q is also useful for bringing the expression $\phi_{q,D}$ in a factored form where each variable of $\phi_{q,D}$ occurs exactly once.

Definition 5. *A DNF expression ϕ can be factored according to a VO-type*

- $\mathbf{X}$ *if ϕ is in one variable and that variable occurs in the set $\mathbf{X}$;*
- α^* *if there exist DNF expressions $\phi_1, \ldots, \phi_n$ that can be factored according to α, $\phi = \phi_1 + \ldots + \phi_n$ and $\forall 1 \leq i < j \leq n : Vars(\phi_i) \cap Vars(\phi_j) = \emptyset$;*
- $\alpha\beta$ *if there exist DNF expressions ϕ_1 and ϕ_2 that can be factored according to α and β, respectively, $\phi = (\phi_1)(\phi_2)$, and $Vars(\phi_1) \cap Vars(\phi_2) = \emptyset$.*

Example 8. As shown in Example 3, the expression ϕ_{eq} can be factored according to the VO-type $(Vars(R)^* Vars(S)^*)^*$ of q_{eq}: Some variables of $Vars(R)$ are paired with some variables of $Vars(S)$, and the same may apply to further independent sets of variables in $Vars(R)$ and $Vars(S)$.   □

Lemma 1. *For any hierarchical query q and database D, $\phi_{q,D}$ can be factored according to VO-type* $\textbf{type}(q)$.

Fig. 6 gives the function **vo** that computes good variable orders. This function uses pattern matching on the structure of VO-types.

In case of VO-types α^*, the variable order is a concatenation of variable orders for α. Because these variable orders use disjoint sets of variables, we compute the *maximally independent partitioning* of the input expression ϕ and continue on each partition independently. A partitioning $\phi_1, \ldots, \phi_n$ of $\phi_{q,D}$ is independent if $\phi_{q,D} = \phi_1 + \ldots + \phi_n$ and $\forall 1 \leq i \neq j \leq n : Vars(\phi_i) \cap Vars(\phi_j) = \emptyset$. An independent partitioning of $\phi_{q,D}$ is maximal if $\phi_{q,D}$ has no finer partitioning. For instance, consider again the expressions ϕ_{eq} and ϕ_{neq} of Example 3. A maximal independent partitioning of ϕ_{eq} is given by $x_1 y_1 + x_1 y_2$ and $x_2 y_3 + x_3 y_3$. The expression ϕ_{neq} has no maximal independent partitioning but itself.

In case of concatenated VO-types $\alpha\beta$, we recursively compute the variable order for α independently of β on the restrictions of ϕ computed by eliminating all occurrences of variables not in α and not in β, respectively. In case of a variable set $\mathbf{X}$, the (monotone) expression ϕ is necessarily in one variable.

Example 9. Let the VO-type $\theta = (Vars(R)^* Vars(S)^*)^*$ of q_{eq} of Example 3. The variable order $\mathbf{vo}(\theta, \phi_{eq})$ is obtained as follows. We first partition ϕ_{eq} in $\phi_1 = x_1 y_1 + x_1 y_2$ and $\phi_2 = x_2 y_3 + x_3 y_3$, each typed by $Vars(R)^* Vars(S)^*$. For ϕ_1, we obtain $x_1 + x_1$ with type $Vars(R)^*$, and $y_1 + y_2$ with type $Vars(S)^*$, then $x_1 + x_1$ with type $Vars(R)$ and y_1 and y_2 with type $Vars(S)$, and finally the variable order $x_1 y_1 y_2$. We proceed similarly with ϕ_2 and obtain $x_2 x_3 y_3$. We concatenate the two orders and return $x_1 y_1 y_2 x_2 x_3 y_3$. $\square$

Lemma 2. *For any query q and database D, $\mathbf{vo}(\mathbf{type}(q), \phi_{q,D})$ is a variable order, an instance of $\mathbf{type}(q)$, and can be computed in time $O(|\phi_{q,D}| \log^2 |\phi_{q,D}|)$.*

In case of hierarchical queries, the outcome of $\mathbf{vo}$ is a good variable order.

Lemma 3. *For any hierarchical query q and database D, $\pi = \mathbf{vo}(\mathbf{type}(q), \phi_{q,D})$ is a good variable order for $\phi_{q,D}$ and the OBDD $(\phi_{q,D}, \pi)$ can be computed in time $O(|Vars(\phi_{q,D})|)$.*

Theorem 1 follows immediately from Lemmata 2 and 3.

4   IHQ$^{\neq}$ Queries

We extend the PTIME result of Theorem 1 to the strictly more expressive IHQ$^{\neq}$. We consider IHQ$^{\neq}$ queries Q_n with n hierarchical subqueries. We assume these subqueries ordered as in the tree representation of Q_n and denote by v_i the number of variables occurring in both $\phi_{Q_n,D}$ and the relation produced by computing the hierarchical subquery i on a database D ($1 \leq i \leq n$). Then,

Theorem 2. *For any IHQ$^{\neq}$ query Q_n and database D there is a good variable order π for $\phi_{Q_n,D}$. In particular, π can be computed in time $O(|\phi_{Q_n,D}| \log^2 |\phi_{Q_n,D}|)$ and, given π, the OBDD $(\phi_{Q_n,D}, \pi)$ can be computed in time*

$$O\left(|\phi_{Q_n,D}| \cdot \left(\sum_{i=1}^{n-1} \left(\prod_{j=1}^{i} v_j\right) v_i + \prod_{i=1}^{n} v_i\right)\right).$$

The above time complexity for OBDD construction can be exponential in the size of the fixed query q.

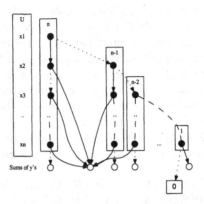

Fig. 7. Partial OBDD of quadratic size used in Lemma 4

Example 10. Consider the database of Fig. 1, the query q_{neq} :- $R(A, B), S(C, D)$, $A \neq C$, and the associated expression ϕ_{neq} of Example 3. Assume R and S are partitioned according to the A-values. The R-partition for a_i is paired with all S-partitions but for a_i. The factored form of ϕ_{neq} makes the relationship between the variables of partitions explicit (Example 3).

Fig. 3 shows the OBDD (ϕ_{neq}, π_2). Let $\pi_2 = U \circ L$, where $U = x_1 \ldots x_4$ and $L = y_1 \ldots y_4$. We partition horizontally this OBDD in the upper part for U and the lower part for L. Any edge crossing the border from U to L points to a subgraph that represents a possibly partial sum of y's and is thus representable linearly in the number of y's. Less obvious is that the number of these subgraphs is at most quadratic in the number of x's (see Lemma 4 below). In short, this is because by setting to true at most two variables from different R-partitions, we reduce ϕ_{neq} to a sum of some y's. For instance, we reach the leftmost node y_1 by any of the assignments $x_1 = x_2 = 1$, $x_1 = x_3 = 1$, and $x_4 = 1$, and each of these cases covers all possible (exponentially many) assignments for the remaining variables. It turns out that π_2 is a good variable order for ϕ_{neq}.   □

Like for hierarchical queries, we can derive VO-types for IHQ$^{\neq}$ queries and good variable orders using the functions **type** and **vo** described in Section 3.

We next discuss the base case of Theorem 2 with one inequality join on arbitrary relations, a generalization of q_{neq} from Example 10.

Lemma 4. *Let q :- $R(A_1, \ldots, A_k), S(B_1, \ldots, B_l), A_i \neq B_j$ for some $1 \leq i \leq k, 1 \leq j \leq l$, and database D. Then, $\pi = \textbf{vo}(type(q), \phi_{q,D})$ is a good variable order for $\phi_{q,D}$ and the OBDD $(\phi_{q,D}, \pi)$ can be computed in time $O(|\phi_{q,D}| \cdot (|Vars(R)|^2 + |Vars(R)| \cdot |Vars(S)|))$.*

Proof. Let $Vars(R) = \mathbf{X} = \{x_1, \ldots, x_n\}$ and $Vars(S) = \mathbf{Y} = \{y_1, \ldots, y_m\}$. The VO-type for q is $\mathbf{X^*Y^*}$ and the variable order $\pi = \textbf{vo}(type(q), \phi_{q,D}) = U \circ L$, where $U = x_1 \ldots x_n$ and $L = y_1 \ldots y_m$. We partition the OBDD $(\phi_{q,D}, \pi)$ into the upper part for U and the lower part for L.

We show that (1) the number of nodes in the upper part is at most quadratic in n and (2) the number of nodes in the lower part is at most linear in $n \cdot m$.

(1) A variable of $\mathbf{X}$, which is associated in R with an A_i-value a, is paired in $\phi_{q,D}$ with all variables of $\mathbf{Y}$ associated in S with a B_j value different from a. This also means that by setting to true at most two variables associated with different A_i-values, we reduce $\phi_{q,D}$ to a (possibly partial) sum of y's. Fig. 7 shows our OBDD under the assumption that there is one variable in $\mathbf{X}$ per distinct A_i-value. The number of nodes on path 1 is n, on path 2 is $n-1$, and on path n is 1. We thus have $n \cdot (n-1)/2$ nodes in the upper part, which can be computed as shown in the figure. In case there are several variables in $\mathbf{X}$ associated with the same A_i-values, then they behave like one variable. If any one of them is set to true, then the remaining ones become redundant ($x_1 + \ldots x_p = 1$ if at least one variable in the sum is 1); see the case of x_2 and x_3 in Fig. 3.

(2) Any edge crossing the border from the upper to the lower part points to a subgraph that represents a (possibly partial) sum of y's and thus linearly representable. This is because the expression $\phi_{q,D}$ is a bipartite monotone 2-DNF over $\mathbf{X}$ and $\mathbf{Y}$, and by crossing the border all variables of $\mathbf{X}$ are either set or irrelevant. The sum of all y's is reached from all upper part nodes having two variables of $\mathbf{X}$ set to true (depicted in Fig. 7 as the sum with most incoming edges). Regarding the partial sums, there is one such sum for each of the n clusters, namely when all or all but one variable in $\mathbf{X}$ are set to false (In case $n < m$ some of these sums are equal).

We create the quadratic-size OBDD as follows. We first choose an arbitrary order of $\mathbf{X}$-variables followed by an arbitrary order of $\mathbf{Y}$-variables. For the construction of each node, we have a variable v and an expression ϕ (initially, $\phi = \phi_{q,D}$). We compute $\phi|_v$ and $\phi|_{\bar{v}}$ in two scans over ϕ. To detect that two expressions without $\mathbf{X}$-variables are the same, we only need to check in time linear in $|\phi_{q,D}|$ that they were created by setting to true two $\mathbf{X}$-variables corresponding to different A_i-partitions. □

We next sketch the idea behind the proof of the general case of Theorem 2. We first simplify the input IHQ$^{\neq}$ query Q_n based on the observation that the hierarchical subqueries can be materialized to tuple-independent probabilistic relations. A good variable order π for $\phi_{Q_n,D}$ can then be obtained by concatenating the variables of the materialized relations, as given by the function **vo**.

If the tree of the simplified Q_n has under three leaves (corresponding to materialized hierarchical subqueries), then Theorem 1 or Lemma 4 applies. We otherwise construct the OBDD $(\phi_{Q_n,D}, \pi)$ by incrementally removing from Q_n hierarchical subqueries in the left-to-right order of their leaves in the tree. On removal, we create an OBDD fragment whose structure follows that of Fig.7.

Let H_1 and H_2 be the subquery to remove and a subquery that has an inequality with H_1, respectively. Let $\{x_1, \ldots, x_k\}$ and $\{y_1, \ldots, y_l\}$ be the sets of (independent) expressions that occur in $\phi_{Q_n,D}$ and are associated with the tuples of the materialized H_1 and H_2, respectively.

Due to the inequality joins between H_2 and H_1 on one hand, and of H_2 and some of the remaining subqueries on the other hand, the expression $\phi_{Q_n,D}$ can be factored as $y_1 f(y_1) g(y_1) + \ldots + y_l f(y_l) g(y_l)$, where for any expression y_j, the function g is a sum of x_i's and the function f defines the cofactors of $y_j g(y_j)$ in $\phi_{Q_n, D}$. We can now apply the OBDD construction from the proof of Lemma 4, where we replace y_j by $y_j f(y_j)$. After constructing the OBDD fragment for the variables $\{x_1, \ldots, x_k\}$, we continue with the $O(k)$ expressions representing sums S_y of some $y_j f(y_j)$ for $1 \leq j \leq l$. We consider each such sum in separation and proceed by removing the next hierarchical subquery H. Each expression S_y can be factored according to the expressions of the materialized H and of a further materialized subquery sharing an inequality with H (if any), because their co-occurrence in the same clauses is not influenced by the fact that some $y_j f(y_j)$ are missing - there is no join between H_1 and H and hence all their dependencies are through some other subqueries.

By induction, the upper bound on the OBDD construction time is $O(|\phi_{Q_n, D}| \cdot (k^2 + k * Rest))$, where $Rest$ is an upper bound for the size of sums S_y.

5   Hard Conjunctive Queries

We next discuss the case of general intractable conjunctive queries on restricted databases. The tractable classes of hierarchical queries and of queries with expressions $\phi_{q,D}$ of bounded treewidth are orthogonal, because the expressions $\phi_{q,D}$ do not admit in general bounded treewidth for hierarchical queries. Intuitively, this is because eq-joins lead in general to expressions $\phi_{q,D}$ consisting of clauses that pair an unbounded number of variables. We recall that the approach based on safe plans [5] cannot accommodate both aforementioned classes [6].

The #P-hard conjunctive queries have subqueries of the form [5]

$$R(\ldots, X, \ldots), S(\ldots, X, \ldots, Y, \ldots), T(\ldots, Y, \ldots).$$

Such queries are not hierarchical because the query variables X and Y have a common subgoal S and further distinct subgoals: R for X and T for Y. Intuitively, these queries are hard because they allow for arbitrary monotone DNF expressions (S can be constructed so as to allow arbitrary combinations of tuples of R and T), and some of them only admit exponential-size OBDDs [11].

Example 11. The expression $\phi_{q,D}$ for the hard query $q :- R(X, Z), S(X, Y), T(Y)$ and the database of Figure 1 is $x_1 y_1 z_1 + x_1 y_2 z_2 + (x_2 + x_3) y_3 z_1$. All clauses are transitively dependent on each other and do not adhere to the regular factored-form pattern as in the case of hierarchical queries.   □

Bounded Pathwidth. Our approach can benefit from existing significant work on tractable OBDD construction for Boolean expressions of bounded pathwidth or treewidth, e.g.,[12,8,9]. We use here the notion of pathwidth of the graph constructed from DNF formulas, where the nodes are variables and two nodes are directly connected if their variables occur in the same clause. The pathwidth of a graph measures how close the graph is to a path.

Definition 6 ([19]). *A path decomposition of a graph $G = (V, E)$ is a pair of path P with node set I and edge set F, and a family $L = \{L_i \mid i \in I\}$ of subsets of V such that: (1) $\bigcup_{i \in I} L_i = V$; (2) $\forall (v, w) \in E, \exists i \in I : \{v, w\} \subseteq L_i$; (3) $\forall i, j, k \in I$ if j is on the path from i to k in P, then $L_i \cap L_k \subseteq L_j$. The width of a path decomposition is $\max_{i \in I} |L_i| - 1$ and the pathwidth of a graph is the minimum width over all its possible path decompositions.*

The connection between pathwidth and treewidth follows by $pathwidth(G) = O(treewidth(G) \cdot \log n)$ for a graph G with n nodes. Using an argument similar to Theorem 2.1 of [9], we have that

Theorem 3. *For any query q and database D with $\phi_{q,D}$ of n variables and pathwidth p, $\phi_{q,D}$ has an OBDD of size $O(n2^p)$.*

In case p is bounded, $\phi_{q,D}$ admits a good variable order. The proof of Theorem 2.1 in [9] gives such an order: Let a path decomposition (P, L) for the graph of $\phi_{q,D}$ and define *First* and *Last* over the variables of $\phi_{q,D}$: $First(x) = \min\{n \in P \mid x \in L(n)\}$ and $Last(x) = \max\{n \in P \mid x \in L(n)\}$. A good variable order is the increasing lexicographic order of variables according to $(First(\cdot), Last(\cdot))$.

FD-induced Hierarchical Queries. We shortly mention a further important case of restricted databases that can ensure tractability of non-hierarchical queries. The idea is that under functional dependencies (FDs), non-hierarchical queries can sometimes admit equivalent hierarchical queries, and thus PTIME evaluation. Such equivalent hierarchical queries can be obtained by chasing the non-hierarchical query using FDs. Follow-up work [17] discusses this case in detail and shows that the conjunctive subqueries of most of the 22 TPC-H queries admit equivalent hierarchical rewritings under the TPC-H FDs.

References

1. Antova, L., Jansen, T., Koch, C., Olteanu, D.: Fast and Simple Relational Processing of Uncertain Data. In: Proc. ICDE (2008)
2. Benjelloun, O., Sarma, A.D., Halevy, A., Widom, J.: ULDBs: Databases with Uncertainty and Lineage. In: Proc. VLDB (2006)
3. Bryant, R.E.: Graph-based algorithms for boolean function manipulation. IEEE Trans. Computers 35(8), 677–691 (1986)
4. Burch, J.R., Clarke, E.M., McMillan, K.L., Dill, D.L., Hwang, L.J.: Symbolic model checking: 10^{20} states and beyond. Information and Computation : 98(2) (1992)
5. Dalvi, N., Suciu, D.: "Efficient query evaluation on probabilistic databases". VLDB Journal 16(4), 523–544 (2007)
6. Dalvi, N., Suciu, D.: Management of Probabilistic Data: Foundations and Challenges. In: Proc. PODS (2007)
7. Dalvi, N., Suciu, D.: The Dichotomy of Conjunctive Queries on Probabilistic Structures. In: Proc. PODS (2007)
8. Darwiche, A.: Decomposable negation normal form. Journal of the ACM 48(4) (2001)

9. Ferrara, A., Pan, G., Vardi, M.Y.: Treewidth in verification: Local vs. global. In: Sutcliffe, G., Voronkov, A. (eds.) LPAR 2005. LNCS (LNAI), vol. 3835. Springer, Heidelberg (2005)

10. Green, T.J., Tannen, V.: Models for Incomplete and Probabilistic Information. In: Proc. IIDB (2006)

11. Hayase, K., Imai, H.: OBDDs of a monotone function and of its prime implicants. In: Algorithms and Computation (1996)

12. Huang, J., Darwiche, A.: Using DPLL for efficient OBDD construction. In: H. Hoos, H., Mitchell, D.G. (eds.) SAT 2004. LNCS, vol. 3542. Springer, Heidelberg (2005)

13. Imielinski, T., Lipski, W.: Incomplete information in relational databases. Journal of ACM 31(4), 761–791 (1984)

14. Koch, C., Olteanu, D.: Conditioning Probabilistic Databases. In: JDMR (formerly Proc. VLDB), p. 1 (2008)

15. Lam, M.S., Whaley, J., Livshits, V.B., Martin, M.C., Avots, D., Carbin, M., Unkel, C.: Context-sensitive program analysis as database queries. In: PODS (2005)

16. Meinel, C., Theobald, T.: Algorithms and Data Structures in VLSI Design. Springer, Heidelberg (1998)

17. Olteanu, D., Huang, J., Koch, C.: Lazy versus Eager Query Plans for Tuple-Independent Probabilistic Databases. Technical report, Oxford University (2008)

18. Raedt, L.D., Kimmig, A., Toivonen, H.: ProbLog: A probabilistic Prolog and its application in link discovery. In: Proc. IJCAI (2007)

19. Robertson, N., Seymour, P.: Graph minors. ii. algorithmic aspects of treewidth. J. of Algorithms 7, 309–322 (1986)

20. Sen, P., Deshpande, A.: Representing and Querying Correlated Tuples in Probabilistic Databases. In: Proc. ICDE (2007)

A Logical Framework to Reinforcement Learning Using Hybrid Probabilistic Logic Programs

Emad Saad

College of Engineering and Computer Science
Abu Dhabi University
Abu Dhabi, UAE
emad.saad@adu.ac.ae

Abstract. Knowledge representation is an important issue in reinforcement learning. Although logic programming with answer set semantics is a standard in knowledge representation, it has not been exploited in reinforcement learning to resolve its knowledge representation issues. In this paper, we present a logic programming framework to reinforcement learning, by integrating reinforcement learning, in MDP environments, with normal hybrid probabilistic logic programs with probabilistic answer set semantics [29], that is capable of representing domain-specific knowledge. We show that any reinforcement learning problem, **MT**, can be translated into a normal hybrid probabilistic logic program whose probabilistic answer sets correspond to trajectories in **MT**. We formally prove the correctness of our approach. Moreover, we show that the complexity of finding a policy for a reinforcement learning problem in our approach is NP-complete. In addition, we show that any reinforcement learning problem, **MT**, can be encoded as a classical logic program with answer set semantics, whose answer sets corresponds to valid trajectories in **MT**. We also show that a reinforcement learning problem can be encoded as a SAT problem. In addition, we present a new high level action description language that allows the factored representation of MDP.

1   Introduction

Reinforcement learning is the problem of learning to act by trial and error interaction in dynamic environments. Under the assumption that a complete description of the environment is known, a reinforcement learning problem is modeled as a Markov Decision Process (MDP), in which an optimal policy can be found. Operation Research (OR) methods— mainly dynamic programming— have been extensively used to find the optimal policy for a reinforcement learning problem in MDP environment.

A limitation of OR methods to reinforcement learning is the inability to exploit domain-specific knowledge of the reinforcement learning problem domains to improve the efficiency of finding the optimal policy. In addition, these OR methods use primitive representation of states and actions as this representation does not capture the relationship between states [20] and makes it difficult

S. Greco and T. Lukasiewicz (Eds.): SUM 2008, LNAI 5291, pp. 341–355, 2008.
© Springer-Verlag Berlin Heidelberg 2008

to represent domain-specific knowledge. In addition, OR methods in general do not justify how policies are constructed which is vital in reasoning and decision making to convince the decision maker about the validity of the concluded policies. Moreover, it has been argued in [20] that using purely OR methods solve MDP with relatively small domain sizes. However, using richer knowledge representation frameworks for MDP allow to reason efficiently about policies in more complex stochastic domains and lead to develop methods to find optimal policies with larger domains sizes.

Logic programming with answer set semantics is a standard for knowledge representation and reasoning. In addition, it has been successfully applied to classical planning. A probabilistic extension to logic programming with answer set semantics— called normal hybrid probabilistic logic programs with probabilistic answer set semantics (NHPP)— has been introduced in [29] which is successfully applied to probabilistic planning [26]. It has been shown that NHPP subsumes logic programming with answer set semantics and inherits its knowledge representation and reasoning capabilities including the ability to represent and reason about domain-specific knowledge [29]. The probabilistic planning approach of [26] encodes in NHPP any probabilistic planning problem as an ordinary factored MDP without reward.

In this paper we integrate reinforcement learning with NHPP, providing a logical framework to reinforcement learning that overcomes the representational and reasoning limitations of OR methods to reinforcement learning. The proposed framework is capable of representing any reinforcement learning problem and its domain-specific knowledge as well as reasoning about policies. This is achieved by allowing the representation and reasoning about MDP using NHPP.

The choice of NHPP with probabilistic answer set semantics to represent and solve reinforcement learning problems in MDP environment is interesting for many reasons. NHPP with probabilistic answer set semantics is nonmonotonic, and hence, more suitable for knowledge representation and commonsense reasoning. It has been shown in [26] that NHPP can be easily and intuitively used to represent and reason about actions with probabilistic outcomes and change in stochastic domains. In addition, NHPP with probabilistic answer set semantics is a rich probabilistic logic programming framework that allows representing and reasoning about variety of fundamental probabilistic reasoning problems including probabilistic planning [26], probabilistic contingent planning, the most probable explanation in belief networks, and the most likely trajectory in probabilistic planning [27].

The contributions of this paper are as follows. We develop a new high level action language called $\mathcal{A}_{MD}$ that allows the factored representation and reasoning about MDP. We show that any reinforcement learning problem, **MT**, in the action language $\mathcal{A}_{MD}$, can be translated into a program in NHPP whose probabilistic answer sets correspond to trajectories in **MT**, with associated value function. We formally prove the correctness of the translation. We show that the complexity of finding a policy for a reinforcement learning problem in our approach is NP-complete. In addition, we show that any reinforcement learning problem in MDP environment, **MT**, can be encoded as a classical normal logic program, Π, with answer set semantics, where the answer sets of Π correspond to valid trajectories in **MT**. However, policy evaluation in classical normal logic programs is not as intuitive as in NHPP. Moreover, we show that any reinforcement learning problem in MDP environment can be encoded as a SAT problem. The importance of that is reinforcement learning problems can be now solved as SAT problems.

2 Syntax and Semantics of NHPP

This section describes a subclass of NHPP [29], called *atomic* NHPP, denoted by NHPP$_\mathcal{A}$, that is expressive enough and sufficient to represent and reason about MDP.

2.1 The Language of NHPP$_\mathcal{A}$

Let $\mathcal{L}$ be a first-order language with finitely many predicate symbols, function symbols, constants, and infinitely many variables. The Herbrand base of $\mathcal{L}$ is denoted by $\mathcal{B}_\mathcal{L}$. An annotation denotes a probability interval in $[0,1]$. Let $C[0,1]$ be the set of all closed intervals in $[0,1]$ and $[a_1, b_1], [a_2, b_2] \in C[0,1]$. Then we say that $[a_1, b_1] \leq_t [a_2, b_2]$ iff $a_1 \leq a_2$ and $b_1 \leq b_2$. A probabilistic logic program (*p-program*) in NHPP$_\mathcal{A}$ is a pair $P = \langle R, \tau \rangle$, where R is a finite set of normal probabilistic rules (p-rules) and τ is a mapping $\tau : \mathcal{B}_\mathcal{L} \rightarrow S_{disj}$, where S_{disj} is a set of disjunctive probabilistic strategies (p-strategies) whose composition functions, c, are mappings $c : C[0,1] \times C[0,1] \rightarrow C[0,1]$. A composition function of a disjunctive p-strategy returns the probability interval of a disjunction of two events given the probability intervals of its components. A p-rule is an expression of the form

$$A : \mu \leftarrow A_1 : \mu_1, \ldots, A_n : \mu_n, not\ (B_1 : \mu_{n+1}), \ldots, not\ (B_m : \mu_{n+m})$$

where $A, A_1, \ldots, A_n, B_1, \ldots, B_m$ are atoms and μ, μ_i $(1 \leq i \leq m + n)$ are annotations. Intuitively, the meaning of a p-rule is that if for each $A_i : \mu_i$, the probability interval of A_i is at least μ_i (w.r.t. $\leq_t$) and for each $not\ (B_j : \mu_j)$, it is not *believable* that the probability interval of B_j is at least μ_j, then the probability interval of A is μ. The mapping τ associates to each atom A a disjunctive p-strategy that will be employed to combine the probability intervals obtained from different p-rules having A in their heads. A p-program is ground if no variables appear in any of its p-rules.

2.2 Probabilistic Answer Set Semantics of NHPP$_\mathcal{A}$

A probabilistic interpretation (p-interpretation) is a mapping $h : \mathcal{B}_\mathcal{L} \rightarrow C[0,1]$. Let $P = \langle R, \tau \rangle$ be a ground p-program, h be a p-interpretation, and r be

$$A : \mu \leftarrow A_1 : \mu_1, \ldots, A_n : \mu_n, not\ (B_1 : \beta_1), \ldots, not\ (B_m : \beta_m) \in R.$$

Then, we say

- h satisfies $A_i : \mu_i$ (denoted by $h \models A_i : \mu_i$) iff $\mu_i \leq_t h(A_i)$.
- h satisfies $not\ (B_j : \beta_j)$ (denoted by $h \models not\ (B_j : \beta_j)$) iff $\beta_j \not\leq_t h(B_j)$.
- h satisfies $Body \equiv A_1 : \mu_1, \ldots, A_n : \mu_n, not\ (B_1 : \beta_1), \ldots, not\ (B_m : \beta_m)$ (denoted by $h \models Body$) iff $\forall (1 \leq i \leq n), h \models A_i : \mu_i$ and $\forall (1 \leq j \leq m), h \models not\ (B_j : \beta_j)$.
- h satisfies $A : \mu \leftarrow Body$ iff $h \models A : \mu$ or h does not satisfy $Body$.
- h satisfies P iff h satisfies every p-rule in R and for every atom $A \in \mathcal{B_L}$, we have

$$c_{\tau(A)} \{\!\!\{ \mu | A : \mu \leftarrow Body \in R \text{ such that } h \models Body \}\!\!\} \leq_t h(A).$$

The probabilistic reduct P^h of P w.r.t. h is a p-program $P^h = \langle R^h, \tau \rangle$ where:

$$R^h = \left\{ A : \mu \leftarrow A_1 : \mu_1, \ldots, A_n : \mu_n \left| \begin{array}{l} A : \mu \leftarrow A_1 : \mu_1, \ldots, A_n : \mu_n, \\ \quad not\ (B_1 : \beta_1), \ldots, not\ (B_m : \beta_m) \in R \text{ and} \\ \forall (1 \leq j \leq m), \beta_j \not\leq_t h(B_j) \end{array} \right. \right\}$$

Intuitively, for any $not\ (B_j : \beta_j)$ in the body of $r \in R$ with $\beta_j \not\leq_t h(B_j)$ is simply satisfied by h, and $not\ (B_j : \beta_j)$ is removed from the body of r. If $\beta_j \leq_t h(B_j)$ then the body of r is not satisfied and r is trivially ignored. A probabilistic model (p-model) of a p-program P is a p-interpretation of P that satisfies P. A p-interpretation h of a p-program P is said to be a probabilistic answer set of P if h is the minimal p-model of the probabilistic reduct of P w.r.t. h.

3   Markov Decision Processes (MDP)

In this section we review the definition of MDP. For simplicity, we consider finite-horizon MDP with stationary transition functions, stationary bounded reward functions, and stationary policies. MDP is a tuple of the form $\mathbf{M} = \langle S, S_0, A, T, \lambda, \mathcal{R} \rangle$ where: S is a finite set of states; S_0 is the initial state distribution; A is a finite set of stochastic actions; T is stationary transition function which is a mapping $T : S \times A \times S \rightarrow [0,1]$, where for any $s \in S$ and $a \in A$, $T(s, a, .)$ is the probability distribution over states resulting from executing a in s, given that a is executable in s, such that $\sum_{s' \in S} T(s, a, s') = 1$; $\lambda \in (0,1]$ is the discount factor; and $\mathcal{R} : S \times A \times S \rightarrow \mathbb{R}$ is a stationary bounded reward function, where $\mathcal{R}(s, a, s')$ is the reward received in state s' after executing the action a in a state s. A stationary policy is a mapping from states to actions of the form $\pi : S \rightarrow A$. The value of a policy π is determined by a value function V^π. The value function of a policy π with respect to an initial state $s_0 \in S_o$, with finite horizon of n steps remaining, denoted by $V_n^\pi(s_0)$, is given by

$$V_n^\pi(s_0) = \sum_{s_1 \in S} T(s_0, \pi(s_0), s_1) \left[\mathcal{R}(s_0, \pi(s_0), s_1) + \lambda V_{n-1}^\pi(s_1) \right]$$

The value function, V^π, of a policy, π, determines the expected sum of discounted rewards resulting from executing the policy π starting from s_0. A policy, π^*, is optimal for a given MDP, M, if π^* has the maximum value function, denoted by V_n^*, over all policies of M, which is given by

$$V_n^*(s_0) = \max_\pi V_n^\pi(s_0)$$

4   Markov Action Language $\mathcal{A}_{MD}$

In this section we develop a novel action language, called *Markov action language*, $\mathcal{A}_{MD}$, that allows the factored representation and reasoning about MDP. An action theory in $\mathcal{A}_{MD}$ is capable of representing the initial state distribution, the executability conditions of actions, the probabilistic transitions of actions, the discount factor, and the reward received from executing actions in states. The semantics of $\mathcal{A}_{MD}$ is based on a transition function that maps an action and a set of states to a set of states.

4.1   Language Syntax

A fluent is a predicate, which may contain variables, that describes a property of the environment. Let $\mathcal{F}$ be a set of fluents and $\mathcal{A}$ be a set of stochastic actions that can contain variables. A fluent literal is either a fluent $f \in \mathcal{F}$ or $\neg f$, the negation of f. A fluent formula is a formula formed from the set of fluent literals using the logical connectives $\wedge$, $\vee$, and $\neg$. Conjunctive fluent formula is a conjunction of fluent literals of the form $l_1 \wedge \ldots \wedge l_n$, where $l_1, \ldots, l_n$ are fluent literals. Sometimes we abuse the notation and refer to a conjunctive fluent formula as a set of fluent literals ($\emptyset$ denotes *true*). A Markov decision theory, **MT**, in $\mathcal{A}_{MD}$ is a tuple of the form $\mathbf{MT} = \langle S_0, \mathcal{AD}, \lambda \rangle$, where S_0 is a proposition of the form (1), $\mathcal{AD}$ is a set of propositions from (2-3), and $\lambda \in (0, 1]$ is a discount factor as follows:

$$\mathbf{initially} \begin{cases} \psi_1 \ : \ p_1 \\ \psi_2 \ : \ p_2 \\ \quad \ldots \\ \psi_n \ : \ p_n \end{cases} \tag{1}$$

$$\mathbf{executable}\ a\ \mathbf{if}\ \psi \tag{2}$$

$$a\ \mathbf{causes} \begin{cases} \phi_1 \ : \ p_1 \ : \ r_1\ \mathbf{if}\ \psi_1 \\ \phi_2 \ : \ p_2 \ : \ r_2\ \mathbf{if}\ \psi_2 \\ \quad \ldots \\ \phi_n \ : \ p_n \ : \ r_n\ \mathbf{if}\ \psi_n \end{cases} \tag{3}$$

where $\psi, \psi_1, \ldots, \psi_n, \phi_1, \ldots, \phi_n$ are conjunctive fluent formulas, $a \in \mathcal{A}$ is an action, and for all $1 \le i \le n$, we have $p_i \in [0, 1]$. The set of all ground ψ_i must be exhaustive and mutually exclusive, where $\forall i \ \sum_s p_i \ Pr(\psi_i|s) = 1$ and $\forall i, j, s, \ \psi_i \neq \psi_j \Rightarrow Pr(\psi_i \wedge \psi_j|s) = 0$ (given s is a state defined later).

Proposition (1) represents the *initial-state distribution*—a probability distribution over the possible initial states (see next section for the precise meaning of a state). It states that for all $1 \leq i \leq n$, the possible initial state ψ_i holds with probability p_i. *Executability condition* is represented by proposition (2)—where each variable that appears in a also appears in ψ— which states that an action a is executable in any state in which ψ holds. A proposition of the form (3) represents the probabilistic effects of an action a along with the rewards received in the states resulting from executing a in the states in which a is executable. For each $1 \leq i \leq n$, all variables that appear in ϕ_i also appear in a and ψ_i. Proposition (3) says that for all $1 \leq i \leq n$, a causes ϕ_i to hold with probability p_i and reward r_i is received in a successor state to a state in which a is executed and ψ_i holds. For each $1 \leq i \leq n$, ψ_i is called a precondition of an action a that corresponds to an effect ϕ_i, ϕ_i is called an effect of a, p_i is the probability that ϕ_i holds given that ψ_i holds, where $0 \leq p_i \leq 1$, and $r_i \in \mathbb{R}$ is the reward received in a state in which ϕ_i holds. For any proposition of the form (3), since the set of ground preconditions ψ_i are mutually exclusive and exhaustive, it will be more convenient for the subsequent results to represent an action a as a set of the form $a = \{a_1, \ldots, a_n\}$, where each a_i corresponds to ϕ_i, p_i, r_i, and ψ_i. Therefore, alternatively, for each $1 \leq i \leq n$, proposition (3) can be represented as

$$a_i \text{ causes } \phi_i \ : \ p_i : \ r_i \text{ if } \psi_i$$

A Markov decision theory is ground if it does not contain any variables.

Example 1. Consider the following simple blocks world domain example. Objects of the world are table and three blocks a, b, and c. Initially, the blocks a and b are on the table, the block c is on a, and the blocks b and c and the table are clear. A robot is trying to build a stack of blocks such that the block a is on table, b is on a, and c is on b. The robot using the action $move(X, Y)$ to move a block X on top of another block Y or on the table, given that both X and Y are clear. However, the moving operation is not always successful. The action move succeeds to move a block on top of another block or the table with 0.7 probability and r_1 reward, and cause no change in the world with 0.3 probability and r_2 reward. This block world domain is represented by the Markov decision theory $\mathbf{MT} = \langle S_0, \mathcal{AD}, \lambda \rangle$, where λ in any value in $(0, 1]$ and S_0 and $\mathcal{AD}$ are represented by (4) and (5)-(6)respectively as follows:

$$\textbf{initially} \left\{ \left\{ \begin{array}{l} on(a, table), on(b, table), on(c, a), \\ clear(b), clear(c), clear(table) \end{array} \right\} : 1 \right. \tag{4}$$

$$\textbf{executable } move(X, Y) \textbf{ if } \emptyset \qquad X \in \{a, b, c\}, Y \in \{a, b, c, table\}, X \neq Y \tag{5}$$

$$move(X, Y) \textbf{ causes} \left\{ \begin{array}{ll} \left\{ \begin{array}{l} on(X, Y), \neg\, clear(Y), \\ \neg\, on(X, Z), clear(Z) \end{array} \right\} : 0.7 : r_1 \textbf{ if } \left\{ \begin{array}{l} clear(X), clear(Y), \\ on(X, Z) \end{array} \right\} \\ \\ \emptyset \qquad\qquad\quad : 0.3 : r_2 \textbf{ if } \left\{ \begin{array}{l} clear(X), clear(Y), \\ on(X, Z) \end{array} \right\} \end{array} \right. \tag{6}$$

where $X \in \{a, b, c\}$ and $Y, Z \in \{a, b, c, table\}, X \neq Y \neq Z$.

4.2   Semantics

We say a set of ground literals ϕ is consistent if it does not contain a pair of complementary literals, i.e., l and $\neg l \notin \phi$. If a literal l belongs to a set of ground literals ϕ, then we say l is true (holds) in ϕ (denoted by $\phi \models l$), and l is false (does not hold) in ϕ if $\neg l$ is in ϕ (denoted by $\phi \models \neg l$). A set of literals σ is true (holds) in ϕ (denoted by $\phi \models \sigma$) if σ is contained in ϕ, otherwise, σ is false (does not hold) in ϕ (denoted by $\phi \nvDash \sigma$). A state s is a complete and consistent set of literals that describes the world at a certain time point.

Definition 1. *Let* $\mathbf{MT} = \langle S_0, \mathcal{AD}, \lambda \rangle$ *be a ground Markov decision theory, s be a state, a_i causes ϕ_i : p_i : r_i if ψ_i ($1 \leq i \leq n$) be a proposition in $\mathcal{AD}$, and $a = \{a_1, \ldots, a_n\}$ be an action, where each a_i corresponds to ϕ_i, p_i, r_i, and ψ_i for $1 \leq i \leq n$. Then, $\Phi(a_i, s)$ is the state resulting from executing a in s, given that a is executable in s, where:*

- *$l \in \Phi(a_i, s)$ and $\neg l \notin \Phi(a_i, s)$ if $l \in \phi_i$ and the precondition ψ_i holds in s.*
- *$\neg l \in \Phi(a_i, s)$ and $l \notin \Phi(a_i, s)$ if $\neg l \in \phi_i$ and the precondition ψ_i holds in s.*
- *Otherwise, $l \in \Phi(a_i, s)$ iff $l \in s$ and $\neg l \in \Phi(a_i, s)$ iff $\neg l \in s$.*

We call Φ a transition function.

Definition 2. *Let* $\mathbf{MT} = \langle S_0, \mathcal{AD}, \lambda \rangle$ *be a ground Markov decision theory, s be a state, and a_i causes ϕ_i : p_i : r_i if ψ_i ($1 \leq i \leq n$) be a proposition in $\mathcal{AD}$. Then, the probability distribution resulting from executing a in s is given by*

$$T(s, a, s') = \begin{cases} p_i & if s' = \Phi(a_i, s) \\ 0 & otherwise \end{cases}$$

In addition, the reward received in a state s' resulting from executing a in s is given by

$$\mathcal{R}(s, a, s') = \begin{cases} r_i & if s' = \Phi(a_i, s) \\ 0 & otherwise \end{cases}$$

Definition 3. *Let* $\mathbf{MT} = \langle S_0, \mathcal{AD}, \lambda \rangle$ *be a ground Markov decision theory, s_0 be an initial state, s, s' be states, and π be a policy for $\mathbf{MT}$. Then, the n-steps value function, V_n^π, of a policy π is given by*

$$V_n^\pi(s_0) = \sum_{s' \in S} T(s_0, \pi(s_0), s') \left[\mathcal{R}(s_0, \pi(s_0), s') + \lambda V_{n-1}^\pi(s') \right]$$

where after n steps, $V_0^\pi(s_n) = \mathcal{R}(s_{n-1}, \pi(s_{n-1}), s_n)$.

Given a policy π, $\pi(s) \in \mathcal{A}$ represents the action that is executed in a state s. Due to the stochastic nature of actions in $\mathcal{A}$, executing $\pi(s)$ in s causes a transition to a set of states. Let $\sigma = \{s'_1, s'_2, \ldots, s'_m\}$ be the set of states resulting from executing $\pi(s)$ in s. We abuse the notation and use $\pi(\sigma)$ to denote the set of actions $\pi(s'_1), \pi(s'_2), \ldots, \pi(s'_m)$ executed in the states $s'_1, s'_2, \ldots, s'_m$ respectively. Considering finite horizon policies with n steps and a set of stochastic actions $\mathcal{A}$, a policy $\pi : S \to \mathcal{A}$, can be represented as a set of ordered pairs starting from an initial state $\sigma_0 = s_0 \in S_0$ as $\pi = \{(\sigma_0, \pi(\sigma_0)), (\sigma_1, \pi(\sigma_1)), \dots, (\sigma_{n-1}, \pi(\sigma_{n-1}))\}$, where σ_i is the set of states resulting from executing $\pi(\sigma_{i-1})$ in σ_{i-1} for $1 \leq i \leq n$, and σ_n is the set of states resulting from executing $\pi(\sigma_{n-1})$ in σ_{n-1}. This set representation of finite horizon policies leads to view a policy as a set of trajectories, where each trajectory takes the form

$$s_0, \pi(s_0), s_1, \pi(s_1), \dots, s_{n-1}, \pi(s_{n-1}), s_n$$

where $\sigma_0 = s_0$, for all $1 \leq i \leq n$, $s_i \in \sigma_i$ and $\pi(s_i) \in \pi(\sigma_i)$, such that for any $1 \leq i \leq n$, $s_i = \Phi(s_{i-1}, \pi(s_{i-1}))$. Let π be a finite horizon policy of n steps and T_π be the set of trajectories representation of π.

Having the trajectory view of a policy π, the value function of π can be described by:

$$V_n^\pi(s_0) = \sum_{s_0, \pi(s_0), s_1, \pi(s_1), \dots, s_{n-1}, \pi(s_{n-1}), s_n \in T_\pi} \left[\sum_{t=0}^{n-1} \lambda^t \left[\prod_{i=0}^t T(s_i, \pi(s_i), s_{i+1}) \right] \mathcal{R}(s_t, \pi(s_t), s_{t+1}) \right]$$

Intuitively, the above formula accumulates the expected rewards of all trajectories of a policy π. Since the optimal policy V_n^* has the maximum value function among all policies, therefore, V_n^* is given by

$$V_n^*(s_0) = \max_\pi V_n^\pi(s_0)$$

5   Reinforcement Learning in NHPP

In this section we provide a translation from any Markov decision theory $\mathbf{MT} = \langle S_0, \mathcal{AD}, \lambda \rangle$, the representation of a reinforcement learning problem in MDP environment in the action language $\mathcal{A}_{MD}$, into a p-program, $\Pi_{\mathbf{MT}}$, in NHPP$_\mathcal{A}$, where the p-rules in $\Pi_{\mathbf{MT}}$ encode (1) the initial-state distribution S_0, (2) the transition function Φ, (3) the set of actions propositions $\mathcal{AD}$, (4) and the discount factor λ. The probabilistic answer sets of $\Pi_{\mathbf{MT}}$ correspond to valid trajectories in $\mathbf{MT}$, with associated value function. The p-program translation of Markov decision theories is mainly adapted from [26,30]. Since we consider only finite-horizon MDP, we assume that the length of the optimal policy that we are looking for is known and finite. We use the predicates; $holds(L, T)$ to represent the fact that a literal L holds at time moment T; $occ(AC, T)$ to describe that an action AC executes at time moment T; $state(T)$ to represent a possible state of the world at time moment T; $reward(T, r)$ to describe that the reward received at time moment T is r; $value(T, V)$ to represent that the value function of a state at time moment T is V; and $factor(T, \Lambda)$ to describe that the reward received at time moment T is discounted by Λ, where $\Lambda = \lambda^{T-1}$. We use lower case letters to represent constants and upper case letters to represent variables.

Let $\Pi_{\mathbf{MT}} = \langle R, \tau \rangle$ be the p-program translation of a Markov decision theory, $\mathbf{MT} = \langle S_0, \mathcal{AD}, \lambda \rangle$, where τ is any arbitrary assignment of disjunctive p-strategies and R is the set of p-rules described as follows. To simplify the presentation, any atom appearing in a p-rule in R with no annotation is assumed to be associated with the annotation $[1,1]$. In addition, given p is a predicate and $\psi = \{l_1, \ldots, l_n\}$, we use $p(\psi)$ to denote $p(l_1), \ldots, p(l_n)$.

– To represent each action $a = \{a_1, \ldots, a_n\} \in \mathcal{A}$, we add to R the set of facts

$$action(a_i) \leftarrow \qquad (7)$$

for each $1 \leq i \leq n$. States of the world are described by literals that are encoded in R by the p-rules

$$literal(A) \leftarrow atom(A) \qquad (8)$$
$$literal(\neg A) \leftarrow atom(A) \qquad (9)$$

where $atom(A)$ is a set of facts that describe the properties of the world. To specify that A and $\neg A$ are contrary literals the following p-rules are added to R.

$$contrary(A, \neg A) \leftarrow atom(A) \qquad (10)$$
$$contrary(\neg A, A) \leftarrow atom(A) \qquad (11)$$

– The initial-state distribution **initially** $\psi_i \; : \; p_i$ for $1 \leq i \leq n$ is represented in R as follows. Let $s_1, s_2, \ldots, s_n$ be the set of possible initial states, where for each $1 \leq i \leq n$, $s_i = \{l_1^i, \ldots, l_m^i\}$, and the initial probability distribution be $Pr(s_i) = p_i$. Moreover, let $s = s_1 \cup s_2 \cup \ldots \cup s_n$, $s' = s_1 \cap s_2 \cap \ldots \cap s_n$, $\widehat{s} = s - s'$, and $s'' = \{\, l \mid l \in \widehat{s} \vee \neg l \in \widehat{s}\}$. Intuitively, for any literal l in $\widehat{s}$, if l or $\neg l$ belongs to $\widehat{s}$, then s'' contains only l. The set of all possible initial states are generated by the following set of p-rules. For each literal $l \in s'$, the fact

$$holds(l, 0) \leftarrow \qquad (12)$$

is in R. This fact specifies that the literal l holds at time moment 0. This set of facts represents the set of literals that hold in every possible initial state. Moreover, for each literal $l \in s''$, we add to R the p-rules

$$holds(l, 0) \leftarrow not\ holds(\neg l, 0) \qquad (13)$$
$$holds(\neg l, 0) \leftarrow not\ holds(l, 0) \qquad (14)$$

The above p-rules say that the literal l (similarly $\neg l$) holds at time moment 0, if $\neg l$ (similarly l) does not hold at the time moment 0. The initial probability distribution over the initial states is represented in R by the following set of p-rules. For each possible initial state $s_i = \{l_1^i, \ldots, l_m^i\}$, the p-rule

$$state(0) : [p_i, p_i] \leftarrow holds(l_1^i, 0), \ldots, holds(l_m^i, 0) \qquad (15)$$

is in R. The above p-rule says that the probability of a state at time moment 0, s_i, is $[p_i, p_i]$ if the literals $l_1^i, \ldots, l_m^i$ hold at the time moment 0.

- Each executability condition proposition of an action $a = \{a_1, \ldots, a_n\}$ of the form (2) is encoded in R for each $1 \leq i \leq n$ as

$$exec(a_i, T) \leftarrow holds(\psi, T) \qquad (16)$$

- For each proposition of the form a_i **causes** $\phi_i : p_i : r_i$ **if** ψ_i ($1 \leq i \leq n$), in $\mathcal{AD}$, we proceed as follows. Let $\phi_i = \{l_i^1, \ldots, l_i^m\}$. Then, $\forall$ ($1 \leq i \leq n$), we have for each $1 \leq j \leq m$,

$$holds(l_i^j, T+1) \leftarrow occ(a_i, T), exec(a_i, T), holds(\psi_i, T) \qquad .(17)$$

belongs to R. This p-rule states that if the action a occurs at time moment T and the precondition ψ_i holds at the same time moment, then the literal l_i^j holds at the time moment $T+1$. The probability distribution over states resulting from executing the action a is represented in R using the p-rules:

$$state(T+1): [p_i \times U, p_i \times U] \leftarrow state(T):[U,U], occ(a_i, T), exec(a_i, T),$$
$$holds(\psi_i, T),$$
$$holds(\phi_i, T+1) \quad (18)$$

where U is an annotation variable ranging over $[0,1]$ acts as a place holder. This p-rule asserts that if the precondition ψ_i holds in a state of the world at time moment T, whose probability is $[U,U]$, and in which the action a is executable, then the probability of a successor state at time moment $T+1$, after executing an action a in the state at time T, is $[p_i \times U, p_i \times U]$, in which the effect ϕ_i holds. The reward r_i received at time moment $T+1$ resulting from executing the action a in a state at time moment T given that a is executable in the state at same time moment T is encoded in R by

$$reward(T+1, r_i) \leftarrow occ(a_i, T), exec(a_i, T) \qquad (19)$$

The following p-rule calculates the value of a state at time moment $T+1$ given the value of a state at time moment T in which an action a is executable.

$$value(T+1, V+F*U*r_i) \leftarrow value(T,V), factor(T,F), state(T+1):[U,U],$$
$$reward(T+1, r_i), occ(a_i, T), exec(a_i, T),$$
$$holds(\psi_i, T), holds(\phi_i, T+1)(20)$$

where the variables $V \in \mathbb{R}, F \in (0,1]$, and $U \in [0,1]$. The above p-rule says that the value of a state at time moment $T+1$ is equal to the value of a state at time moment T added to the product of the reward r_i received at time moment $T+1$ and the probability of a state at time moment $T+1$ discounted by $F = \lambda^{T+1}$, where the discount, $F = \lambda^{T+1}$, at time moment $T+1$ is calculated by the p-rules:

$$factor(0,1) \leftarrow \qquad (21)$$
$$factor(T+1, U*\lambda) \leftarrow factor(T,U) \qquad (22)$$

- The frame axioms are encoded in R as follows. For any literal L we have the p-rule

$$holds(L, T+1) \leftarrow holds(L, T), not\ holds(L', T+1), contrary(L, L') \quad (23)$$

in R. The above p-rule says that L holds at the time moment $T+1$ if it holds at the time moment T and its contrary does not hold at the time moment $T+1$.

- To describe the fact that a literal A and its negation $\neg A$ cannot hold at the same time, we add the following p-rule to R

$$inconsistent \leftarrow not\ inconsistent, holds(A, T), holds(\neg A, T) \quad (24)$$

where $inconsistent$ is a special literal that does not appear in **MT**.

- P-rules that generates actions are described by

$$occ(AC^i, T) \leftarrow action(AC^i), not\ abocc(AC^i, T) \quad (25)$$
$$abocc(AC^i, T) \leftarrow action(AC^i), action(AC^j), occ(AC^j, T), AC^i \neq AC^j \quad (26)$$

The above p-rules generate action occurrences once at a time, where AC^i and AC^j are variables representing actions.

- Let $\mathcal{G} = g_1 \wedge \ldots \wedge g_m$ be a goal expression, then $\mathcal{G}$ is encoded in R as

$$goal \leftarrow holds(g_1, T), \ldots, holds(g_m, T) \quad (27)$$

6   Correctness

In this section we show the correctness of our translation. We prove that the probabilistic answer sets of the p-program translation of a Markov decision theory, **MT**, correspond to trajectories in $\mathbf{MT} = \langle S_0, \mathcal{AD}, \lambda \rangle$, with associated values. In addition, we show that the complexity of finding a policy for **MT** in our approach is NP-complete. Let the domain of T be $\{0, \ldots, n\}$. Let Φ be a transition function associated with **MT**, s_0 is a possible initial state, and $a_0, \ldots, a_{n-1}$ be a set of actions in $\mathcal{A}$. Any action a_i can be represented as a set where $a_i = \{a_{1_i}, \ldots, a_{m_i}\}$. Therefore, a trajectory $s_0, \pi(s_0), s_1, \pi(s_1), \ldots, s_{n-1}, \pi(s_{n-1}), s_n$ in **MT** can be also represented as $s_0\ a_{j_0}\ s_1 \ldots a_{j_{n-1}}\ s_n$ for $(1 \leq j \leq m)$ and $(0 \leq i \leq n)$, such that $\forall (0 \leq i \leq n)$, s_i is a state, a_i is an action, $a_{j_i} \in a_i = \{a_{1_i}, \ldots, a_{m_i}\}$, $a_{j_i} = \pi(s_i)$, and $s_i = \Phi(a_{j_{i-1}}, s_{i-1})$.

Theorem 1. *Let **MT** be a Markov decision theory, π be a policy in **MT**, and T_π be the set of trajectories in π. Then, $s_0, \pi(s_0), s_1, \pi(s_1), \ldots, s_{n-1}, \pi(s_{n-1}), s_n$ is a trajectory in T_π iff $occ(\pi(s_0), 0), \ldots, occ(\pi(s_{n-1}), n-1)$ is true in a probabilistic answer set of $\Pi_{\mathbf{MT}}$.*

Theorem 1 states that any Markov decision theory, **MT**, can be translated into a p-program, $\Pi_{\mathbf{MT}}$, such that a trajectory in **MT** is equivalent to a probabilistic answer set of $\Pi_{\mathbf{MT}}$.

Theorem 2. *Let* **MT** *be a Markov decision theory, h be a probabilistic answer set of $\Pi_{\mathbf{MT}}$, π be a policy in* **MT**, *and T_π be the set of trajectories in π. Let $\mathcal{OCC}$ be a set that contains $occ(\pi(s_0), 0), \ldots, occ(\pi(s_{n-1}), n-1)$ iff $s_0, \pi(s_0), s_1, \pi(s_1), \ldots, s_{n-1}, \pi(s_{n-1}), s_n \in T_\pi$. Then,*

$$\sum_{h \models value(n,v) \text{ and } h \models occ(\pi(s_0),0),\ldots,occ(\pi(s_{n-1}),n-1) \in \mathcal{OCC}} v = V_n^\pi(s_0)$$

Theorem 2 asserts that the expected sum of discounted rewards after executing a policy π starting from a state s_0 is equivalent to the summation of the values v, appearing in $value(n,v)$ that is satisfied by a probabilistic answer set h in which $occ(\pi(s_0), 0), \ldots, occ(\pi(s_{n-1}), n-1)$ is satisfied.

NHPP$_\mathcal{A}$ with probabilistic answer set semantics finds policies for reinforcement learning problems in finite horizon MDP environments using the flat representation of the problem domains. Flat representation of a reinforcement learning problem domain is the explicit enumeration of world states [21]. Hence, Theorem 4 follows directly from Theorem 3.

Theorem 3 ([21]). *The stationary policy existence problem for finite-horizon MDP in the flat representation is NP-complete.*

Theorem 4. *The policy existence problem for a reinforcement learning problem in MDP environment using NHPP$_\mathcal{A}$ with probabilistic answer set semantics is NP-complete.*

7 Reinforcement Learning Using Answer Set Programming

In this section we show that any reinforcement learning problem in MDP environment can be encoded as a classical normal logic programs with classical answer set semantics. Excluding the p-rules (15), (18), (19), (20), (21), (22) from the p-program translation, $\Pi_{\mathbf{MT}}$, of a reinforcement learning problem, **MT**, results a p-program, denoted by $\Pi_{\mathbf{MT}}^{normal}$, with only annotations of the form $[1,1]$. As shown in [29], the syntax and semantics of this class of p-programs is equivalent to classical normal logic programs with answer set semantics.

Theorem 5. *Let* **MT** *be a Markov decision theory, π be a policy in* **MT**, *and T_π be the set of trajectories in π. Let $\Pi_{\mathbf{MT}}^{normal}$ be the normal logic program resulting after deleting the p-rules (15),(18), (19), (20), (21), (22) from $\Pi_{\mathbf{MT}}$. Then, $s_0, \pi(s_0), s_1, \pi(s_1), \ldots, s_{n-1}, \pi(s_{n-1}), s_n$ is a trajectory in T_π iff $occ(\pi(s_0), 0), \ldots, occ(\pi(s_{n-1}), n-1)$ is true in an answer set of $\Pi_{\mathbf{MT}}^{normal}$.*

Theorem 5 shows that classical normal logic programs with answer set semantics can be used to solve reinforcement learning problems in MDP environments in two steps. The first step is to translate a reinforcement learning problem, **MT**, into a classical normal logic program whose answer sets correspond to valid trajectories in **MT**. From the answer sets of the normal logic program translation of **MT**, we can determine the set of trajectories T_π for a policy π in **MT**. Then, as a second step, we calculate the value of the policy π using

$$\sum_{s_0,\pi(s_0),s_1,\pi(s_1),\ldots,s_{n-1},\pi(s_{n-1}),s_n \in T_\pi} \left[\sum_{t=0}^{n-1} \lambda^t \left[\prod_{i=0}^{t} T(s_i,\pi(s_i),s_{i+1}) \right] \mathcal{R}(s_t,\pi(s_t),s_{t+1}) \right]$$

In addition, we show that any reinforcement learning problem in MDP environment can be encoded as a SAT problem. Hence, state-of-the-art SAT solvers can be used to solve reinforcement learning problems. Any normal logic program, Π, can be translated into a SAT problem, S, where the models of S are equivalent to the answer sets of Π [18]. Hence, the normal logic program encoding of a reinforcement learning problem **MT** can be translated into an equivalent SAT problem, where the models of S correspond to valid trajectories in **MT**.

Theorem 6. *Let* **MT** *be a Markov decision theory and* $\Pi_{\mathbf{MT}}^{normal}$ *be the normal logic program encoding of* **MT**. *Then, the models of the SAT encoding of* $\Pi_{\mathbf{MT}}^{normal}$ *are equivalent to valid trajectories in* **MT**.

The transformation step from normal logic program encoding of a reinforcement learning problem to SAT can be avoided, by encoding a reinforcement learning problem directly to SAT. The following corollary shows any reinforcement learning problem can be encoded directly as SAT problem.

Corollary 1. *Let* **MT** *be a Markov decision theory. Then,* **MT** *can be directly encoded as a SAT formula* S *where the models of* S *are equivalent to valid trajectories in* **MT**.

However, encoding reinforcement learning problems in $\text{NHPP}_\mathcal{A}$ has advantages over normal logic program and SAT encoding. These include, the explicit representation of probabilities, the explicit assignment of probabilities to states, and the direct propagation of probabilities through states, which are naturally present in $\text{NHPP}_\mathcal{A}$ with probabilistic answer set semantics.

8   Conclusions and Related Work

We presented a new high level action language, $\mathcal{A}_{MD}$, that allows the specification of MDP, in addition, we introduced a new reinforcement learning framework by relating reinforcement learning, in MDP environment, to NHPP. The translation from a Markov decision theory, **MT**, into an NHPP program mainly relies on a similar translation from probabilistic planning into NHPP program [26]. The literature is rich with action languages that are capable of representing and reasoning about actions with probabilistic effects, which include [1,3,6,11,16]. In addition to $\mathcal{A}_{MD}$ is a high level language, the major difference between $\mathcal{A}_{MD}$ and these languages is that $\mathcal{A}_{MD}$ allows the factored specification of MDP through the representation of the initial state distribution, the executability conditions of actions, the probabilistic transitions of actions, discount factor, and the reward received from executing actions in states.

Moreover, many approaches for solving MDP to find the optimal policy have been presented. These approaches can be classified into two main categories of approaches; dynamic programming approaches and the search-based approaches (a detailed survey on these approaches can be found in [3]). However, dynamic programming approaches use primitive domain knowledge representation. On the other hand, the search-based approaches mainly rely on search heuristics which have limited knowledge representation capabilities to represent and use domain-specific knowledge.

A logic based approach for solving MDP, for probabilistic planning, has been presented in [19]. The approach of [19] converts a MDP specification of a probabilistic planing problem into a stochastic satisfiability problem and solving the stochastic satisfiability problem instead. Our approach is similar in spirit to [19] in the sense that both approaches are logic based approaches. However, it has been shown in [27] that NHPP is more expressive than stochastic satisfiability from the knowledge representation point of view. First-order logic representation of MDP has been described in [15] based on first-order logic programs without nonmonotonic negations. Similar to the first-order representation of MDP in [15], $\mathcal{A}_{MD}$ allows objects and relations. However, unlike $\mathcal{A}_{MD}$, [15] finds policies in the abstract level. In addition, NHPP allows objects and relations. A more expressive first-order representation of MDP than [15] has been presented in [4] that is a probabilistic extension to Reiter's situation calculus. Although more expressive, it is more complex than [15].

References

1. Baral, C., Tran, N., Tuan, L.C.: Reasoning about actions in a probabilistic setting. In: AAAI (2002)
2. Bagnell, J., Kakade, S., Ng, A., Schneider, J.: Policy search by dynamic programming. Neural Information Processing Systems 16 (2003)
3. Boutilier, C., Dean, T., Hanks, S.: Decision-theoretic planning: structural assumptions and computational leverage. Journal of AI Research 11, 1–94 (1999)
4. Boutilier, C., Reiter, R., Price, B.: Symbolic dynamic programming for first-order MDPs. In: 17th IJCAI (2001)
5. Dekhtyar, A., Subrahmanian, V.S.: Hybrid probabilistic program. Journal of Logic Programming 43(3), 187–250 (2000)
6. Eiter, T., Lukasiewicz, T.: Probabilistic reasoning about actions in nonmonotonic causal theories. In: 19th Conference on Uncertainty in Artificial Intelligence (2003)
7. Eiter, T., et al.: Declarative problem solving in dlv. In: Logic Based Artificial Intelligence (2000)
8. Gelfond, M., Lifschitz, V.: The stable model semantics for logic programming. In: ICSLP. MIT Press, Cambridge (1988)
9. Gelfond, M., Lifschitz, V.: Classical negation in logic programs and disjunctive databases. New Generation Computing 9(3-4), 363–385 (1991)

10. Gelfond, M., Lifschitz, V.: Representing action and change by logic programs. Journal of Logic Programming 17, 301–321 (1993)
11. Iocchi, L., Lukasiewicz, T., Nardi, D., Rosati, R.: Reasoning about actions with sensing under qualitative and probabilistic uncertainty. In: 16th European Conference on Artificial Intelligence (2004)
12. Kaelbling, L., Littman, M., Cassandra, A.: Planning and acting in partially observable stochastic domains. Artificial Intelligence 101, 99–134 (1998)
13. Kaelbling, L., Littman, M., Moore, A.: Reinforcement Learning: A Survey. Journal of Artificial Intelligence Research 4, 237–285 (1996)
14. Kautz, H., Selman, B.: Pushing the envelope: planning, propositional logic, and stochastic search. In: 13th National Conference on Artificial Intelligence (1996)
15. Kersting, K., De Raedt, L.: Logical Markov decision programs and the convergence of logical TD(λ). In: 14th International Conference on Inductive Logic Programming (2004)
16. Kushmerick, N., Hanks, S., Weld, D.: An algorithm for probabilistic planning. Artificial Intelligence 76(1-2), 239–286 (1995)
17. Lifschitz, V.: Answer set planning. In: ICLP (1999)
18. Lin, F., Zhao, Y.: ASSAT: Computing answer sets of a logic program by SAT solvers. Artificial Intelligence 157(1-2), 115–137 (2004)
19. Majercik, S., Littman, M.: MAXPLAN: A new approach to probabilistic planning. In: 4th International Conference on Artificial Intelligence Planning, pp. 86–93 (1998)
20. Majercik, S., Littman, M.: Contingent planning under uncertainty via stochastic satisfiability. Artificial Intelligence 147(1-2), 119–162 (2003)
21. Mundhenk, M., Goldsmith, J., Lusena, C., Allender, E.: Complexity of finite-horizon Markov decision process problems. Journal of the ACM (2000)
22. Niemela, I., Simons, P.: Efficient implementation of the well-founded and stable model semantics. In: Joint International Conference and Symposium on Logic Programming, pp. 289–303 (1996)
23. Saad, E.: Incomplete knowlege in hybrid probabilistic logic programs. In: 10th European Conference on Logics in Artificial Intelligence (2006)
24. Saad, E.: Towards the computation of the stable probabilistic model semantics. In: 29th Annual German Conference on Artificial Intelligence (June 2006)
25. Saad, E.: A logical approach to qualitative and quantitative reasoning. In: 9th European Conference on Symbolic and Quantitative Approaches to Reasoning with Uncertainty (2007)
26. Saad, E.: Probabilistic planning in hybrid probabilistic logic programs. In: 1st International Conference on Scalable Uncertainty Management (2007)
27. Saad, E.: On the relationship between hybrid probabilistic logic programs and stochastic satisfiability. In: 10th International Symposium on Artificial Intelligence and Mathematics (2008)
28. Saad, E., Pontelli, E.: Towards a more practical hybrid probabilistic logic programming framework. In: Practical Aspects of Declarative Languages (2005)
29. Saad, E., Pontelli, E.: A new approach to hybrid probabilistic logic programs. Annals of Mathematics and Artificial Intelligence Journal 48(3-4), 187–243 (2006)
30. Son, T., Baral, C., Nam, T., McIlraith, S.: Domain-dependent knowledge in answer set planning. ACM Transactions on Computational Logic 7(4), 613–657 (2006)
31. Subrahmanian, V.S., Zaniolo, C.: Relating stable models and AI planning domains. In: International Conference of Logic Programming, pp. 233–247 (1995)
32. Sutton, R., Barto, A.: Reinforcement Learning: An Introduction. MIT Press, Cambridge (1998)

On the Relationship between Hybrid Probabilistic Logic Programs and Stochastic Satisfiability

Emad Saad

College of Engineering and Computer Science
Abu Dhabi University
Abu Dhabi, UAE
emad.saad@adu.ac.ae

Abstract. In this paper we study the relationship between Stochastic Satisfiability (SSAT) [20,12] and Extended Hybrid Probabilistic Logic Programs (EHPP) with probabilistic answer set semantics [22]. We show that any instance of SSAT can be modularly translated into an EHPP program with probabilistic answer set semantics. In addition, we prove that there is no modular mapping from EHPP to SSAT. This shows that EHPP is more expressive than SSAT from the knowledge representation point of view. Moreover, we present that the translation in the other way around from a program in EHPP to SSAT is more involved. We show that not every program in EHPP can be translated into an SSAT instance, rather a restricted class of EHPP can be translated into SSAT.

1 Introduction

Hybrid Probabilistic Logic Programs (HPP) [25] modifies the original Hybrid Probabilistic Logic Programming framework of [5] and generalizes and modifies the *probabilistic annotated logic programming framework*, originally proposed in [16] and further extended in [17,18]. It was shown that the HPP [25] framework is more suitable for reasoning and decision making tasks, including those arising from probabilistic planning [24]. Furthermore, NHPP was extended to Extended Hybrid Probabilistic Logic Programs (EHPP) [22] to deal directly with classical negation as well as non-monotonic negation to allow reasoning in the presence of incomplete knowledge. It was shown that Baral et al's probabilistic logic programming approach for reasoning with causal Bayes networks (P-log) [1] is naturally subsumed by EHPP [22]. In addition, the semantics of EHPP is a natural extension to the answer set semantics of extended logic programs [7].

Stochastic Satisfiability (SSAT) was first introduced in [20] as an extension to SAT with random quantifiers, in addition to the existential quantifiers. The introduction of randomized quantifiers in SSAT brings uncertainty into the question of whether there is a satisfying assignment to a propositional formula. In [12], SSAT has been extended to allow existential, randomized, and universal quantifiers. Moreover, SSAT solver has been presented [12] that extends Davis-Putnam-Lognmann-Loveland (DPLL) algorithm [4] to solve SSAT instances.

S. Greco and T. Lukasiewicz (Eds.): SUM 2008, LNAI 5291, pp. 356–371, 2008.
© Springer-Verlag Berlin Heidelberg 2008

The extended DPLL algorithm [12] has been built by exploiting the existing work to solve SAT as efficiently as possible.

In this paper we study the relationship between Extended Hybrid Probabilistic Logic Programs (EHHP) and Stochastic Satisfiability (SSAT). We show that any SSAT formula can be easily reduced to an EHPP program, with probabilistic answer set semantics, using a local modular mapping. The importance of that is the application of SSAT to probabilistic planning, contingent probabilistic planning, the most probable explanation in belief networks, the most likely trajectory in probabilistic planning, and belief inference [14,15,12] carry over to EHPP. This shows that EHPP is applicable to a variety of *fundamental* probabilistic reasoning tasks including those solved by SSAT. Moreover, we show that there is no similar local and modular mapping from EHPP to SSAT implying that EHPP is more expressive than SSAT from the knowledge representation point of view.

Moreover, we show that, in general, any EHPP program cannot be translated into SSAT. However, there is a class of EHPP that can be translated into SSAT, called $EHPP_{SSAT}$. This class of EHPP is expressive enough to represent and reason with a *variety* of probabilistic reasoning tasks such as probabilistic planning and Bayes networks. The importance of this translation from $EHPP_{SSAT}$ to SSAT is that it provides a foundation for an implementation for computing probabilistic answer sets of EHPP by exploiting the existing work on SSAT with a selection from a variety of SSAT solvers.

This paper is organized as follows. Section 2 describes the syntax and the probabilistic answer set semantics of $EHPP_{SSAT}$. Section 3 reviews SSAT. Section 4 provides the translation from SSAT to $EHPP_{SSAT}$. In section 5, we introduce the translation from a restricted class of $EHPP_{SSAT}$ to SSAT. Conclusions and related work are presented in section 6.

2   Extended Hybrid Probabilistic Logic Programs ($EHPP_{SSAT}$)

In this section we quote the syntax and the probabilistic answer sets semantics of $EHPP_{SSAT}$. The syntax and semantics of the full version of EHPP is described in [22].

2.1   Language Syntax

Let $C[0,1]$ denotes the set of all closed intervals in $[0,1]$. In the context of $EHPP_{SSAT}$, probabilities are assigned to events (literals) as intervals in $C[0,1]$. Let $[\alpha_1,\beta_1],[\alpha_2,\beta_2] \in C[0,1]$. Then the *truth order* asserts that $[\alpha_1,\beta_1] \leq_t [\alpha_2,\beta_2]$ iff $\alpha_1 \leq \alpha_2$ and $\beta_1 \leq \beta_2$. Let $\mathcal{L}$ be an arbitrary first-order language with finitely many predicate symbols, constants, and infinitely many variables. The Herbrand base of $\mathcal{L}$ is denoted by $B_{\mathcal{L}}$. A literal is either an atom a or the negation of an atom $\neg a$, where $\neg$ is the classical negation. We denote the set of all literals in $\mathcal{L}$ by *Lit*. An *annotation* denotes a probability interval in $C[0,1]$.

An *annotated literal* is an expression of the form $l : \mu$, where l is a literal and μ is an annotation. An extended probabilistic rule (E-rule) is an expression of the form

$$l : \mu \leftarrow l_1 : \mu_1, \ldots, l_m : \mu_m, not\ (l_{m+1} : \mu_{m+1}), \ldots, not\ (l_n : \mu_n)$$

where l, l_i $(1 \le i \le n)$ are literals, and μ, μ_i $(1 \le i \le n)$ are annotations. The intuitive meaning of an E-rule is that, if for each $l_i : \mu_i$ $(1 \le i \le m)$, l_i is true with probability interval at least μ_i and for each $not\ (l_j : \mu_j)$ $(m+1 \le j \le n)$, it is not *known* that l_j is true with probability interval at least μ_j, then l is true with probability interval μ. An extended probabilistic logic program (*E-program*) is a pair $P = \langle R, \tau \rangle$, where R is a finite set of E-rules and τ is a mapping $\tau : Lit \rightarrow c_{pcd}$. c_{pcd} is the disjunctive positive correlation probabilistic composition function defined as $c_{pcd}([\alpha_1, \beta_1], [\alpha_2, \beta_2]) = [\max(\alpha_1, \alpha_2), \max(\beta_1, \beta_2)]$. The mapping τ in the above definition associates to each literal l the disjunctive positive correlation probabilistic composition function, c_{pcd}, that will be used to combine the probability intervals obtained from different E-rules having l in their heads. An E-program is ground if no variables appear in any of its rules.

2.2   The Probabilistic Answer Set Semantics of E-Programs

A probabilistic interpretation (p-interpretation) is a mapping $h : Lit \rightarrow C[0, 1]$. We say a set C, a subset of Lit, is a consistent set of literals if there is no pair of complementary literals a and $\neg a$ belonging to C. A partial or total p-interpretation h is a mapping from a consistent set of literals C to $C[0, 1]$. Let $P = \langle R, \tau \rangle$ be a ground E-program, h be a p-interpretation, and $r \equiv l : \mu \leftarrow l_1 : \mu_1, \ldots, l_m : \mu_m, not\ (l_{m+1} : \mu_{m+1}), \ldots, not\ (l_n : \mu_n)$. We say

- h satisfies $l_i : \mu_i$ (denoted by $h \models l_i : \mu_i$) iff $l_i \in dom(h)$ and $\mu_i \le_t h(l_i)$.
- h satisfies $not\ (l_j : \mu_j)$ (denoted by $h \models not\ (l_j : \mu_j)$) iff $l_j \in dom(h)$ and $\mu_j \not\le_t h(l_j)$ or $l_j \notin dom(h)$.
- h satisfies $Body \equiv l_1 : \mu_1, \ldots, l_m : \mu_m, not\ (l_{m+1} : \mu_{m+1}), \ldots, not\ (l_n : \mu_n)$ (denoted by $h \models Body$) iff $\forall (1 \le i \le m), h \models l_i : \mu_i$ and $\forall (m + 1 \le j \le n), h \models not\ (l_j : \mu_j)$.
- h satisfies $l : \mu \leftarrow Body$ iff $h \models l : \mu$ or h does not satisfy $Body$.
- h satisfies P iff h satisfies every E-rule in R and for every literal $l \in dom(h)$, $c_{pcd}\{\!\{\mu | l : \mu \leftarrow Body \in R\ and\ h \models Body\}\!\} \le_t h(l)$.

A probabilistic model (*p-model*) of an E-program P is a p-interpretation h of P that satisfies P. Given the p-models h_1 and h_2, we say $h_1 \le_o h_2$ if $dom(h_1) \subseteq dom(h_2)$ and $\forall l \in dom(h_1), h_1(l) \le_t h_2(l)$. We say that h is a minimal p-model of P (a probabilistic answer set of P) if there is no p-model h' of P such that $h' <_o h$. Let $P = \langle R, \tau \rangle$ be a ground E-program and h be a p-interpretation. The probabilistic reduct P^h of P w.r.t. h is $P^h = \langle R^h, \tau \rangle$ where:

$$R^h = \left\{ l : \mu \leftarrow l_1 : \mu_1, \ldots, l_m : \mu_m \ \middle| \ \begin{array}{l} l : \mu \leftarrow l_1 : \mu_1, \ldots, l_m : \mu_m, \\ not\ (l_{m+1} : \mu_{m+1}), \ldots, not\ (l_n : \mu_n) \in R\ and \\ \forall (m + 1 \le j \le n), \mu_j \not\le_t h(l_j)\ or\ l_j \notin dom(h) \end{array} \right\}$$

The probabilistic reduct P^h is an E-program without non-monotonic negation. Therefore, its probabilistic answer set is well-defined. For any $not\ (l_j : \mu_j)$ in the body of $r \in R$ with $\mu_j \not\leq_t h(l_j)$ means that it is not known that the probability interval of l_j is at least μ_j given the available knowledge, and $not\ (l_j : \mu_j)$ is removed from the body of r. In addition, if $l_j \notin dom(h)$, i.e., l_j is undefined in h, then it is completely $not\ known\ (undecidable)$ that the probability interval of l_j is at least μ_j. In this case, $not\ (l_j : \mu_j)$ is also removed from the body of r. A p-interpretation h is a probabilistic answer set of an E-program P if h is the probabilistic answer set of P^h.

3   Stochastic Satisfiability

In this section we review the definition of stochastic satisfiability presented in [20,12]. Stochastic satisfiability (SSAT) [20] extends deterministic satisfiability with random quantifiers. Let $\mathbf{x} = \{x_1, \ldots, x_n\}$ be a set of n propositional variables (1 for true and 0 for false) and $\phi(\mathbf{x})$ be a k-CNF propositional formula on the variables in $\mathbf{x}$, with the underlying ordering $x_1, \ldots, x_n$. An assignment $\mathbf{A}$ of propositional variables to values from $\{true, false\}$ is said to be a satisfying assignment (model) to a formula $\phi(\mathbf{x})$ if $\phi(\mathbf{A})$ evaluates to true, otherwise, $\mathbf{A}$ is said to be unsatisfying. Formally, an SSAT formula contains both existential and randomized quantifiers and takes the form

$$\exists x_1, \forall y_1, \ldots, \exists x_n, \forall y_n\ (E[\phi(\mathbf{x})] \geq \theta).$$

The SSAT decision problem determines that, given a formula $\phi(\mathbf{x})$, if there exists a value for x_1 such that for random values (true or false with equal probability) of $y_1, \ldots,$ there exists a value for x_n such that for random values of y_n, such that the expected probability of satisfying the formula $\phi(\mathbf{x})$ is at least a probability threshold θ, where $0 \leq \theta \leq 1$. An SSAT formula [12] can be represented as a triple $\langle \phi, \theta, Q \rangle$, where ϕ is a CNF formula over the variables $x_1, \ldots, x_n$, $0 \leq \theta \leq 1$, and Q is the mapping $Q : \mathbf{x} \to \{\exists, \forall\}$. The evaluation of an SSAT formula, $\langle \phi, \theta, Q \rangle$, is inductively defined on the number of quantifiers to determine the expected probability of satisfying the formula ϕ. Assume x_1 is the variable associated with the leftmost quantifier. The expected probability of satisfying ϕ, under Q, denoted by $val(\phi, Q)$, is inductively defined as:

- $val(\phi, Q) = 0.0$ if ϕ contains an empty clause.
- $val(\phi, Q) = 1.0$ if ϕ does not contain clauses.
- $val(\phi, Q) = \max(val(\phi\lceil_{x_1=0}, Q), val(\phi\lceil_{x_1=1}, Q))$ if $Q(x_1) = \exists$.
- $val(\phi, Q) = (val(\phi\lceil_{x_1=0}, Q) + val(\phi\lceil_{x_1=1}, Q))/2$ if $Q(x_1) = \forall$.

where $\phi\lceil_{x_i=b}$ is the (n-1)-variable CNF formula produced from the n-variable formula ϕ after assigning the variable x_i the value $b \in \{true, false\}$ and simplifying the outcome, in addition to, making any required variable renumbering. Given, an SSAT formula, $\langle \phi, \theta, Q \rangle$, we say $\exists x_1, \forall y_1, \ldots, \exists x_n, \forall y_n\ (E[\phi(\mathbf{x})] \geq \theta)$ is true (satisfied) if and only if $val(\phi, Q) \geq \theta$.

If $Q(x_1) = Ⅎ$, then the probability that x_1 evaluates to true leads to a satisfying formula ϕ is equally likely to the probability that x_1 evaluates to false leads to a satisfying ϕ, i.e., both have probability equal to 0.5. However, this is not necessary. A randomly quantified variable can take the value true or false with different probabilities. $Ⅎ^p x_1$ is used to represent that the random variable x_1 is true with probability p, which implies that the probability that x_1 is false is $1 - p$. Consequently, if $Q(x_1) = Ⅎ^p$, $val(\phi, Q)$ becomes $val(\phi, Q) = val(\phi\lceil_{x_1=0}, Q) \times (1 - p) + val(\phi\lceil_{x_1=1}, Q)) \times p$.

As pointed in [12], many decision problems can be reduced to special cases of SSAT. The satisfiability problem (SAT), can be expressed as an instance of SSAT by allowing only existential quantifiers and setting $\theta = 1$ as: $\exists x_1, \ldots, \exists x_n \ (E[\phi(\mathbf{x})] = 1)$. Another problem, MAJSAT, asks if the satisfying assignments of a CNF formula $\phi(\mathbf{x})$ is at least half of the possible assignments to $\phi(\mathbf{x})$. MAJSAT can be represented as an instance of SSAT of the form $Ⅎx_1, \ldots, Ⅎx_n \ (E[\phi(\mathbf{x})] \geq \frac{1}{2})$. SAT and MAJSAT can be combined together to form E-MAJSAT [12] which takes the form $\exists x_1, \ldots, \exists x_m, Ⅎx_{m+1}, \ldots, Ⅎx_n \ (E[\phi(\mathbf{x})] \geq \theta)$. E-MAJSAT asks wether there is an assignment to $x_1, \ldots, x_m$ so that the combined probability of a satisfying assignment of $\phi(\mathbf{x})$ with random variables $x_{m+1}, \ldots, x_n$ is at least θ.

4   Stochastic Satisfiability as $EHPP_{SSAT}$

In this section we show that any SSAT formula, $\langle\phi(\mathbf{x}), \theta, \mathbf{Q}\rangle$, can be modularly translated into an E-program in $EHPP_{SSAT}$ whose probabilistic answer sets correspond to the models of $\phi(\mathbf{x})$. Moreover, we show that SAT, MAJSAT, and E-MAJSAT can be mapped to $EHPP_{SSAT}$. These translations are mainly adapted from [19]. All probabilities used throughout the rest of the paper are point probabilities. Although probability intervals with the same bounds are used to represent point probabilities they are considered point probabilities. Therefore, all arithmetic operators used over probability intervals with the same bounds are also arithmetic operators over point probabilities.

4.1   SAT as $EHPP_{SSAT}$

Any SAT formula, $\exists x_1, \ldots, \exists x_n \ (E[\phi(\mathbf{x})] = 1)$, can be translated into an E-program, $P = \langle R, \tau \rangle$, where R is a set of E-rules consist of only atoms of the form

$$A : [1,1] \leftarrow A_1 : [1,1], \ldots, A_m : [1,1], not \ (A_{m+1} : [1,1]), \ldots, not \ (A_n : [1,1])$$

where $A, A_1, \ldots, A_n$ are atoms and $[1,1]$ represents the truth value $true$. The translation proceeds as follows:

1. For each existentially quantified variable x that appears in $\phi(\mathbf{x})$, we provide two atoms x and $\overline{x}$ and include in R the E-rules

$$x : [1,1] \leftarrow not(\overline{x} : [1,1]) \qquad \overline{x} : [1,1] \leftarrow not(x : [1,1])$$

where $x : [1,1]$ corresponds to the fact that x is true, however, $\overline{x} : [1,1]$ means that the negation of x ($\neg x$) is true or x is false.

2. For each clause c in $\phi(\mathbf{x})$ and for each variable l in c, if $l = x$, then $c : [1,1] \leftarrow x : [1,1]$ is included in R. Otherwise, if $l = \neg x$, then R includes $c : [1,1] \leftarrow \overline{x} : [1,1]$.

3. For each clause c in $\phi(\mathbf{x})$, we include in R

$$inconsistent : [1,1] \leftarrow not(inconsistent : [1,1]), not(c : [1,1])$$

where $inconsistent$ is a special atom that does not appear in $\phi(\mathbf{x})$.

Proposition 1. *Let S be a SAT formula and $P = \langle R, \tau \rangle$ be the E-program translation of S. Then, S has a model iff P has a probabilistic answer set.*

Example 1. Let S be a SAT formula of the form $\exists x, \exists y (E[(x \vee \neg y) \wedge (\neg x \vee y)] = 1)$. The E-program translation, $P = \langle R, \tau \rangle$, of S consists of the following E-rules, R,

$$x : [1,1] \leftarrow not\, (\overline{x} : [1,1]) \qquad \overline{x} : [1,1] \leftarrow not\, (x : [1,1])$$
$$y : [1,1] \leftarrow not\, (\overline{y} : [1,1]) \qquad \overline{y} : [1,1] \leftarrow not\, (y : [1,1])$$
$$c_1 : [1,1] \leftarrow x : [1,1] \qquad c_1 : [1,1] \leftarrow \overline{y} : [1,1]$$
$$c_2 : [1,1] \leftarrow \overline{x} : [1,1] \qquad c_2 : [1,1] \leftarrow y : [1,1]$$
$$inconsistent : [1,1] \leftarrow not(inconsistent : [1,1]), not(c_i : [1,1])$$

where $1 \leq i \leq 2$. P has two probabilistic answer sets h_1 and h_2, where $h_1(\overline{x}) = [1,1]$, $h_1(\overline{y}) = [1,1]$, $h_1(c_1) = [1,1]$, $h_1(c_2) = [1,1]$, and $h_2(x) = [1,1]$, $h_2(y) = [1,1]$, $h_2(c_1) = [1,1]$, $h_2(c_2) = [1,1]$. h_1 implies that $\neg x$ and $\neg y$, as well as, the clauses c_1 and c_2 are true in h_1. Furthermore, h_2 means that x, y, c_1, c_2 are true in h_2. Notice that S has two models $s_1 = \{\neg x, \neg y\}$, which implies that x and y are false in s_1, and $s_2 = \{x, y\}$, which means that x and y are true in s_2. This implies that there is a one-to-one correspondence between the probabilistic answer sets of P and the models of S, since s_1 corresponds to h_1 and s_2 corresponds to h_2.

4.2 MAJSAT as $EHPP_{SSAT}$

Let S be a MAJSAT formula of the form $\exists^{p_1} x_1, \ldots, \exists^{p_n} x_n$ $(E[\phi(\mathbf{x})] \geq \frac{1}{2})$, where all variables appear in $\phi(\mathbf{x})$ are randomly quantified. We say S is satisfied iff $val(\phi, Q) \geq \frac{1}{2}$. S can be translated into an E-program, $P = \langle R, \tau \rangle$, where R is a set of E-rules consist of only atoms. The translation proceeds as follows:

1. For each randomly quantified variable x that appears in $\phi(\mathbf{x})$, with $Q(x) = \exists^p$, we provide two atoms x and $\overline{x}$ and include in R the E-rules

$$x : [p,p] \leftarrow not(\overline{x} : [1-p, 1-p]) \qquad \overline{x} : [1-p, 1-p] \leftarrow not(x : [p,p])$$

where $x : [p,p]$ encodes the probability of x being true is p and $\overline{x} : [1-p, 1-p]$ represents the probability of x being false is $1 - p$. Obviously, if events are equally likely, then $p = 0.5$.

2. For each clause c in $\phi(\mathbf{x})$ and for each variable l in c, if $l = x$, then $c : [1,1] \leftarrow x : [p,p]$ is included in R. Otherwise, if $l = \neg x$, then R includes $c : [1,1] \leftarrow \overline{x} : [1-p, 1-p]$.

3. For each clause c in $\phi(\mathbf{x})$, we include in R

$$inconsistent : [1,1] \leftarrow not(inconsistent : [1,1]), not(c : [1,1])$$

where $inconsistent$ is a special atom that does not appear in $\phi(\mathbf{x})$.

Theorem 1. *Let* $S = \langle \phi(\mathbf{x}), \frac{1}{2}, \mathbf{Q} \rangle$ *be a MAJSAT formula,* $P = \langle R, \tau \rangle$ *be the E-program translation of* S, *and Ans be the set of all probabilistic answer sets of* P. *Then,* $\phi(\mathbf{x})$ *has a model iff* P *has a probabilistic answer set, and* S *is satisfied iff* $\sum_{h \in Ans} \prod_{x_i \in dom(h)} h(x_i) = val(\phi(\mathbf{x}), \mathbf{Q}) \geq \frac{1}{2}$.

Example 2. Let S be a MAJSAT formula of the form $\forall x, \forall y (E[(x \vee \neg y) \wedge (\neg x \vee y)] \geq \frac{1}{2})$. The E-program translation, $P = \langle R, \tau \rangle$, of S consists of the following E-rules, R,

$$
\begin{aligned}
x : \nu &\leftarrow not\,(\overline{x} : \nu) & \overline{x} : \nu &\leftarrow not\,(x : \nu) \\
y : \nu &\leftarrow not\,(\overline{y} : \nu) & \overline{y} : \nu &\leftarrow not\,(y : \nu) \\
c_1 : [1,1] &\leftarrow x : \nu & c_1 : [1,1] &\leftarrow \overline{y} : \nu \\
c_2 : [1,1] &\leftarrow \overline{x} : \nu & c_2 : [1,1] &\leftarrow y : \nu \\
inconsistent : [1,1] &\leftarrow not(inconsistent : [1,1]), not(c_i : [1,1])
\end{aligned}
$$

where $1 \leq i \leq 2$ and $\nu \equiv [0.5, 0.5]$. Clearly, S is satisfied, since $val(((x \vee \neg y) \wedge (\neg x \vee y)), Q) = \frac{1}{2} \geq \frac{1}{2}$. On the other hand, P has two probabilistic answer sets h_1 and h_2, where $h_1(\overline{x}) = [0.5, 0.5]$, $h_1(\overline{y}) = [0.5, 0.5]$, $h_1(c_1) = [1,1]$, $h_1(c_2) = [1,1]$, and $h_2(x) = [0.5, 0.5]$, $h_2(y) = [0.5, 0.5]$, $h_2(c_1) = [1,1]$, $h_2(c_2) = [1,1]$, and hence, $\sum_{h \in Ans} \prod_{x_i \in dom(h)} h(x_i) = h_1(\overline{x}) \times h_1(\overline{y}) + h_2(x) \times h_2(y) = 0.5 = val(\phi(\mathbf{x}), \mathbf{Q}) \geq \frac{1}{2}$. Moreover, $((x \vee \neg y) \wedge (\neg x \vee y))$ has two models $s_1 = \{\neg x, \neg y\}$ and $s_2 = \{x, y\}$. This implies that there is a one-to-one correspondence between the probabilistic answer sets of P and the models of $((x \vee \neg y) \wedge (\neg x \vee y))$, since s_1 corresponds to h_1 and s_2 corresponds to h_2.

4.3   E-MAJSAT as $EHPP_{SSAT}$

Let S be an E-MAJSAT formula of the form $\exists x_1, \ldots, \exists x_n, \forall^{p_1} y_1, \ldots, \forall^{p_n} y_n$ $(E[\phi(\mathbf{x})] \geq \theta)$, where a sequence of existentially quantified variables, x_i ($1 \leq i \leq n$), are followed by a sequence of randomly quantified variables, y_i ($1 \leq i \leq n$). Similarly, we say that an E-MAJSAT formula S is satisfied iff $val(\phi, Q) \geq \theta$. Since E-MAJSAT combines both SAT and MAJSAT together, a translation form E-MAJSAT to an E-program combines the SAT and MAJSAT translations to E-programs together. S can be translated into an E-program, $P = \langle R, \tau \rangle$, where R is a set of E-rules consist of only atoms. The translation proceeds as follows:

1. For each existentially quantified variable x that appears in $\phi(\mathbf{x})$, we provide two atoms x and $\overline{x}$ and include in R the E-rules

$$x : [1,1] \leftarrow not(\overline{x} : [1,1]) \qquad \overline{x} : [1,1] \leftarrow not(x : [1,1])$$

2. For each randomly quantified variable y that appears in $\phi(\mathbf{x})$, with $Q(y) = \forall^p$, we provide two atoms y and $\overline{y}$ and include in R the E-rules

$$y : [p,p] \leftarrow not(\overline{y} : [1-p, 1-p]) \qquad \overline{y} : [1-p, 1-p] \leftarrow not(y : [p,p])$$

3. For each clause c in $\phi(\mathbf{x})$ and for each variable l in c, if $l = x$, with $Q(x) = \exists$, then $c : [1,1] \leftarrow x : [1,1]$ is included in R. Otherwise, if $l = \neg x$, then R includes

$$c : [1,1] \leftarrow \overline{x} : [1,1].$$

4. For each clause c in $\phi(\mathbf{x})$ and for each variable l in c, if $l = y$, with $Q(y) = \exists^p$, then $c : [1,1] \leftarrow y : [p,p]$ is included in R. Otherwise, if $l = \neg y$, then R includes

$$c : [1,1] \leftarrow \overline{y} : [1-p, 1-p].$$

5. For each clause c in $\phi(\mathbf{x})$, we include in R

$$inconsistent : [1,1] \leftarrow not(inconsistent : [1,1]), not(c : [1,1])$$

where $inconsistent$ is a special atom that does not appear in $\phi(\mathbf{x})$.

Theorem 2. *Let $S = \langle \phi(\mathbf{x}), \theta, \mathbf{Q} \rangle$ be an E-MAJSAT formula, $P = \langle R, \tau \rangle$ be the E-program translation of S, Ans be the set of all probabilistic answer sets of P, and $h, h' \in Ans$ be probabilistic answer sets of P. Then, $\phi(\mathbf{x})$ has a model iff P has a probabilistic answer set, and S is satisfied iff*

$$\max\nolimits_{h \models \tilde{x}_1 : [1,1], \ldots, \tilde{x}_n : [1,1]} \left[h(\tilde{x}_n) \sum\nolimits_{h' \models D} \prod\nolimits_{i=1}^n h'(\tilde{y}_i) \right] \geq \theta. \text{ where } D \equiv \tilde{x}_1 : [1,1],$$
$$\ldots, \tilde{x}_n : [1,1], \tilde{y}_1 : [p_1, p_1], \ldots, \tilde{y}_n : [p_n, p_n] \text{ and } \tilde{x}_i = x_i \text{ or } \tilde{x}_i = \neg x_i \text{ and } \tilde{y}_i = y_i \text{ or }$$
$$\tilde{y}_i = \neg y_i.$$

Intuitively, in the expression of Theorem 2, the maximum is taken over all the possible assignments to the existentially quantified variables. For a given assignment to the existentially quantified variables, $\tilde{x}_1, \ldots, \tilde{x}_n$, a summation is taken over the product of probabilities associated with all randomly quantified variables in each satisfying assignment to $\phi(\mathbf{x})$, of the form $\tilde{x}_1, \ldots, \tilde{x}_n, \tilde{y}_1, \ldots, \tilde{y}_n$, that contains $\tilde{x}_1, \ldots, \tilde{x}_n$. This satisfying assignment corresponds to a probabilistic answer set h' of P.

Example 3. Let S be an E-MAJSAT formula of the form $\exists x, \forall y(E[(x \vee \neg y) \wedge (\neg x \vee y)] \geq 0.75)$. The E-program, $P = \langle R, \tau \rangle$, translation of S consists of the following E-rules, R,

$$
\begin{array}{ll}
x : [1,1] \leftarrow not\,(\overline{x} : [1,1]) & \overline{x} : [1,1] \leftarrow not\,(x : [1,1]) \\
y : \nu \leftarrow not\,(\overline{y} : \nu) & \overline{y} : \nu \leftarrow not\,(y : \nu) \\
c_1 : [1,1] \leftarrow x : [1,1] & c_1 : [1,1] \leftarrow \overline{y} : \nu \\
c_2 : [1,1] \leftarrow \overline{x} : [1,1] & c_2 : [1,1] \leftarrow y : \nu \\
inconsistent : [1,1] & \leftarrow not(inconsistent : [1,1]), not(c_i : [1,1])
\end{array}
$$

where $1 \leq i \leq 2$ and $\nu \equiv [0.5, 0.5]$. It can be easily verified that S is unsatisfied, since $val(((x \vee \neg y) \wedge (\neg x \vee y)), Q) = 0.5 \not\geq 0.75$. On the other hand, P has two probabilistic answer sets h_1 and h_2, where $h_1(\overline{x}) = [1,1], h_1(\tilde{y}) = [0.5, 0.5], h_1(c_1) = [1,1], h_1(c_2) = [1,1]$, and $h_2(x) = [1,1], h_2(y) = [0.5, 0.5], h_2(c_1) = [1,1], h_2(c_2) = [1,1]$, and hence, $\max_{h_1 \models \overline{x} : [1,1], h_2 \models x : [1,1]} [h_1(\overline{x}) \times h_1(y), h_2(x) \times h_2(\tilde{y})] = 0.5 = val(\phi(\mathbf{x}), Q) \not\geq 0.75$. Moreover, $((x \vee \neg y) \wedge (\neg x \vee y))$ has two models $s_1 = \{\neg x, \neg y\}$ and $s_2 = \{x, y\}$. This implies that there is a one-to-one correspondence between the probabilistic answer sets of P and the models of $((x \vee \neg y) \wedge (\neg x \vee y))$, since s_1 corresponds to h_1 and s_2 corresponds to h_2.

The translation from a general SSAT formula, where existentially quantified variables alternating with randomly quantified variables, is the same as the translation from an E-MAJSAT formula to an E-program. Then, the following proposition directly follows.

Proposition 2. *Let S be an SSAT formula of the form $\exists x_1, \forall y_1, \ldots, \exists x_n, \forall y_n$ $(E[\phi(\mathbf{x})] \geq \theta)$ and $P = \langle R, \tau \rangle$ be the E-program translation of S. Then, $\phi(\mathbf{x})$ has a model iff P has a probabilistic answer set.*

Observe that the translation from SSAT to $EHPP_{SSAT}$ is modular, since small local changes in the clauses in ϕ causes small local changes in the corresponding E-program translation. However, this is not the case in the reverse direction. There is no local modular mapping from $EHPP_{SSAT}$ to SSAT. This implies that $EHPP_{SSAT}$ is more expressive than SSAT from the knowledge representation point of view. Similar to [19], let, e.g., $\mathcal{M}(.)$ be a modular mapping from $EHPP_{SSAT}$ to SSAT. Let $P = \langle R, \tau \rangle$ be an E-program in $EHPP_{SSAT}$ that is modularly mapped to an SSAT formula $S = \langle \mathcal{M}(R), \theta, Q \rangle$, where $\mathcal{M}(R) = \phi(\mathbf{x})$. $\mathcal{M}(.)$ is said to be modular if for each set of facts $\mathcal{F}$ that is mapped to $\mathcal{M}(\mathcal{F})$, we have $P = \langle R \cup \mathcal{F}, \tau \rangle$ has a probabilistic answer set iff $\mathcal{M}(R) \cup \mathcal{M}(\mathcal{F})$ has a model. Intuitively, adding a fact to an E-program should make a local change in the translated SSAT formula, but not require translating the entire E-program.

Proposition 3. *There is no modular mapping from $EHPP_{SSAT}$ to SSAT.*

5 $EHPP_{SSAT}$ as SSAT

In general, it is not possible to translate any E-program in $EHPP_{SSAT}$ or EHPP [22] to SSAT, since $EHPP_{SSAT}$ allows probability intervals while SSAT deals with point probabilities. In addition, EHPP [22] allows conjunctions and disjunctions of literals to appear in the body of E-rules. However, we show that there is a class of $EHPP_{SSAT}$, namely *restricted $EHPP_{SSAT}$*, that can be translated into SSAT. An E-program in *restricted $EHPP_{SSAT}$* takes the form $P = \langle R \cup R_{neg}, \tau \rangle$, where $\tau : Lit \rightarrow c_{pcd}$ and $R \cup R_{neg}$ is a set of E-rules that satisfy the following conditions:

1. All events that appear in R are atomic events, represented as positive literals (atoms) in R.
2. All probabilities that appear in any E-rule in R are point probabilities of the form $[p, p]$.
3. If the probability of an event a is $[p, p]$, then the probability of all occurrences of a in R is $[p, p]$.
4. For any event a that appears in R, we have $Pr(a) + Pr(\neg a) = 1$.
5. For each event a that appears in R with probability $[p, p] < [1, 1]$, the E-rule

$$\bar{a} : [1 - p, 1 - p] \leftarrow not\ (a : [p, p])$$

belongs to R_{neg}. If the probability of a is $[1,1]$, then the above E-rule is simply written as

$$\bar{a} : [1,1] \leftarrow not\ (a : [1,1]).$$

This set of E-rules, R_{neg}, is not used in the translation from P to an SSAT formula. However, E-rules in R_{neg} are used to encode the default probabilities, i.e., to encode the fact that the probability of $\neg a$ is $1 - Pr(a)$.

Observe that an E-program in restricted $EHPP_{SSAT}$ contains E-rules that consist of only atoms of the form

$$r \equiv A : \mu \leftarrow A_1 : \mu_1, \ldots, A_m : \mu_m, not\ (A_{m+1} : \mu_{m+1}), \ldots, not\ (A_n : \mu_n)$$

where $A, A_i(1 \leq i \leq n)$ are atoms. Let $Head(r) = A$, $Pos(r) = \{A_1, \ldots, A_m\}$, and $Neg(r) = \{A_{m+1}, \ldots, A_n\}$. A positive dependency graph of an E-program, $P = \langle R \cup R_{neg}, \tau \rangle$ in restricted $EHPP_{SSAT}$, is a directed graph, G_P, such that (i) vertices of G_P are atoms appearing in R and (ii) for each E-rule r in R, there is an edge from $Head(r)$ to each atom in $Pos(r)$.

Definition 1. *An E-program P in restricted $EHPP_{SSAT}$ is tight E-program if the positive dependency graph of P is acyclic.*

5.1 Tight $EHPP_{SSAT}$ as SSAT

Any tight E-program, $P = \langle R \cup R_{neg}, \tau \rangle$ in restricted $EHPP_{SSAT}$, can be translated into an SSAT formula. The resulting SSAT formula can be viewed as SAT, MAJSAT, or E-MAJSAT, depending on the probability values that appear in R, and the type of quantifiers that we associate with each distinct variable in the resulting SSAT formula. If all probabilities that appear in R are $[1,1]$, then the resulting SSAT formula, $\mathcal{S}$, is SAT with existential quantifier associated with each variable appearing in $\mathcal{S}$. But, if all probabilities that appear in R are $[p,p] \neq [1,1]$, then the resulting formula, $\mathcal{S}$, is MAJSAT with randomized quantifier associated with each variable in $\mathcal{S}$. If the probabilities appearing in R are a combination of $[p,p]$ and $[1,1]$, then the resulting formula, $\mathcal{S}$, can be viewed as E-MAJSAT or MAJSAT, depending on how we want to view the formula. If $\mathcal{S}$ is viewed as E-MAJSAT, then an atom a in R, whose associated probability is $[1,1]$, corresponds to an existentially quantified variable in $\mathcal{S}$. However, if a is associated with probability $[p,p] \neq [1,1]$ in R, then a corresponds to a randomly quantified variable in $\mathcal{S}$ (given that all existentially quantified variables are followed by the randomly quantified ones). Let $atoms(P)$ denotes the set of atoms that appearing in R. The translation from an E-program, in restricted $EHPP_{SSAT}$, to SSAT is provided by defining the notion of *probabilistic completion* of $EHPP_{SSAT}$ adapted from [3]. The probabilistic completion of an E-program, $P = \langle R \cup R_{neg}, \tau \rangle$ in restricted $EHPP_{SSAT}$, is denoted by $Comp(P) = \langle \mathcal{R}, Q \rangle$, where:

- $\mathcal{R}$ is the set of propositional formulas formed from the E-rules in R as follows:
  - For each $A \in atoms(P)$, if

$$A : \mu \leftarrow A_1^i : \mu_1^i, \ldots, A_m^i : \mu_m^i, not\ (A_{m+1}^i : \mu_{m+1}^i), \ldots, not\ (A_n^i : \mu_n^i)$$

for $1 \leq i \leq k$, is the set of E-rules in R whose heads contain A, then $A \equiv Body_1 \vee \cdots \vee Body_k \in \mathcal{R}$ where $Body_i = A_1^i \wedge \ldots \wedge A_m^i \wedge \neg A_{m+1}^i \wedge \ldots \wedge \neg A_n^i$. If $k = 0$, i.e., there is no E-rule in R whose head contains A, then $\neg A \in \mathcal{R}$.
  - If R contains an E-rule of the form

$$inconsistent : [1,1] \leftarrow not(inconsistent : [1,1]), A_1 : \mu_1, \ldots, A_m : \mu_m,$$
$$not\ (A_{m+1} : \mu_{m+1}), \ldots, not\ (A_n : \mu_n)$$

then, $\neg Body \in \mathcal{R}$, where $Body = A_1 \wedge \ldots \wedge A_m \wedge \neg A_{m+1} \wedge \ldots \wedge \neg A_n$.

- Q is a mapping, where for each atom $A \in atoms(P)$, we have $Q(A) = \mho^p$, if $A : [p, p]$ appears in any E-rule r in R (either in the head of r or in its body). Similarly, $Q(A) = \exists$, if $A : [1,1]$ appears in any E-rule r in R (if the resulting SSAT is viewed as E-MAJSAT). In the mapping Q, $Q(A) = \mho^p$ says that, in the resulting SSAT formula, A is randomly quantified variable with the probability of A being true is p.

Theorem 3. *Let $P = \langle R \cup R_{neg}, \tau \rangle$ be a tight E-program in restricted $EHPP_{SSAT}$ and $Comp(P) = \langle \mathcal{R}, Q \rangle$ be the probabilistic completion of P. Then, $\mathcal{R}$ has a model iff P has a probabilistic answer set.*

Theorem 4. *Let $P = \langle R \cup R_{neg}, \tau \rangle$ be a tight E-program in restricted $EHPP_{SSAT}$ and $Comp(P) = \langle \mathcal{R}, Q \rangle$ be the probabilistic completion of P. Let Ans be the set of all probabilistic answer sets of P and $h, h' \in Ans$. Then, $\mathcal{S} = \langle \mathcal{R}, \theta, Q \rangle$ is satisfied iff $\sum_{h \in Ans} \prod_{A_i \in dom(h)} h(A_i) = val(\mathcal{R}, Q) \geq \theta$, viewing the SSAT formula, $\mathcal{S}$, as MAJSAT, where $\theta = \frac{1}{2}$, and $\max_{h \models \tilde{x}_1 : [1,1], \ldots, \tilde{x}_n : [1,1]} \left[h(\tilde{x}_n) \sum_{h' \models \mathcal{D}} \prod_{i=1}^n h'(\tilde{y}_i) \right] \geq \theta$. where $\mathcal{D} \equiv \tilde{x}_1 : [1,1], \ldots, \tilde{x}_n : [1,1], \tilde{y}_1 : [p_1, p_1], \ldots, \tilde{y}_n : [p_n, p_n]$ and $\tilde{x}_i = x_i$ or $\tilde{x}_i = \neg x_i$ and $\tilde{y}_i = y_i$ or $\tilde{y}_i = \neg y_i$, viewing the SSAT formula, $\mathcal{S}$, as E-MAJSAT.*

In the following examples, without loss of generality, we consider MAJSAT translation from E-programs.

Example 4. Consider the E-program, $P = \langle R \cup R_{neg}, \tau \rangle$ in restricted $EHPP_{SSAT}$, where $R \cup R_{neg}$ contains the E-rules

$$a : [0.9, 0.9] \leftarrow not\ (b : [0.2, 0.2]) \qquad b : [0.2, 0.2] \leftarrow not\ (a : [0.9, 0.9])$$
$$c : [1,1] \leftarrow a : [0.9, 0.9] \qquad\qquad c : [1,1] \leftarrow b : [0.2, 0.2]$$
$$\overline{a} : [0.1, 0.1] \leftarrow not\ (a : [0.9, 0.9]) \qquad \overline{b} : [0.8, 0.8] \leftarrow not\ (b : [0.2, 0.2])$$
$$\overline{c} : [1,1] \leftarrow not\ (c : [1,1])$$

The first four E-rules belong to R and the last three E-rules belong to R_{neg}. Clearly, P is tight. The probabilistic completion of P is $Comp(\mathcal{R}, Q)$, where $\mathcal{R} = \{a \equiv \neg b, b \equiv \neg a, c \equiv a \vee b\}$, and $Q(a) = \mho^{0.9}$, $Q(b) = \mho^{0.2}$, $Q(c) = \mho^1$. P

has two probabilistic answer sets h_1 and h_2, where $h_1(a) = [0.9, 0.9]$, $h_1(\bar{b}) = [0.8, 0.8]$, $h_1(c) = [1, 1]$, and $h_2(\bar{a}) = [0.1, 0.1]$, $h_2(b) = [0.2, 0.2]$, $h_2(c) = [1, 1]$. In addition, $\mathcal{R} = \{a \equiv \neg b, b \equiv \neg a, c \equiv a \vee b\}$ has two models $s_1 = \{a, \neg b, c\}$ and $s_2 = \{\neg a, b, c\}$. This implies that there is a one-to-one correspondence between the probabilistic answer sets of P and the models of $\mathcal{R}$, since s_1 corresponds to h_1 and s_2 corresponds to h_2. It can be easily verified that the SSAT formula, $\mathcal{S} = \langle \mathcal{R}, 0.5, Q \rangle$, is satisfied, since $val(\mathcal{R}, Q) = 0.74 \geq 0.5$, in addition, we have $\sum_{h \in Ans} \prod_{x_i \in dom(h)} h(x_i) = h_1(a) \times h_1(\bar{b}) \times h_1(c) + h_2(\bar{a}) \times h_2(b) \times h_2(c) = 0.74 = val(\mathcal{R}, Q) \geq 0.5$.

5.2   Non-tight $EHPP_{SSAT}$ as SSAT

Let $P = \langle R \cup R_{neg}, \tau \rangle$ be any E-program in restricted $EHPP_{SSAT}$ and $Comp(P) = \langle \mathcal{R}, Q \rangle$ be its probabilistic completion. It is possible to get a model of $\mathcal{R}$ that does not correspond to any probabilistic answer set of P, and hence, Theorems 3 and 4 do not apply for that E-program. This occurs for any E-program in restricted $EHPP_{SSAT}$ that is not tight. Consider the following E-program.

Example 5. Let $P = \langle R \cup R_{neg}, \tau \rangle$ be an E-program in restricted $EHPP_{SSAT}$, where $R \cup R_{neg}$ consists of the E-rules

$$a : [0.5, 0.5] \leftarrow b : [0.3, 0.3] \qquad b : [0.3, 0.3] \leftarrow a : [0.5, 0.5]$$
$$\bar{a} : [0.5, 0.5] \leftarrow not\ (a : [0.5, 0.5]) \qquad \bar{b} : [0.7, 0.7] \leftarrow not\ (b : [0.3, 0.3])$$

The probabilistic completion of P is $Comp(P) = \langle \mathcal{R}, Q \rangle$, where $\mathcal{R} = \{a \equiv b\}$ and $Q(a) = \mho^{0.5}$, $Q(b) = \mho^{0.3}$. This E-program, P, has only one probabilistic answer set, h, where $h(\bar{a}) = [0.5, 0.5]$ and $h(\bar{b}) = [0.7, 0.7]$ ($h(\bar{a})$ corresponds to $Pr(\neg a)$ and $h(\bar{b})$ corresponds to $Pr(\neg b)$). We have, $\sum_{h \in Ans} \prod_{A_i \in dom(h)} h(A_i) = \prod_{A_i \in dom(h)} h(A_i) = h(\bar{a}) \times h(\bar{b}) = [0.5, 0.5] \times [0.7, 0.7] = [0.35, 0.35]$. But, on the other hand, there are two models of $\mathcal{R}$ that contribute to $val(\mathcal{R}, Q)$. These models are $s_1 = \{\neg a, \neg b\}$ and $s_2 = \{a, b\}$. The probabilistic answer set h of P corresponds to the model $s_1 = \{\neg a, \neg b\}$ of $\mathcal{R}$. Given the models s_1 and s_2 of $\mathcal{R}$, it can be easily verified that $val(\mathcal{R}, Q) = [0.5, 0.5]$. This implies that $\sum_{h \in Ans} \prod_{A_i \in dom(h)} h(A_i) \neq val(\mathcal{R}, Q)$.

There is a one-to-one correspondence between the probabilistic answer sets of any tight E-program, P, in restricted $EHPP_{SSAT}$, and the models of $\mathcal{R}$ in $Comp(P) = \langle \mathcal{R}, Q \rangle$. But this is not the case for the E-program in Example 5. The reason is that this E-program, P, is not tight, since there is a cycle in the positive dependency graph of P. The set $\{a, b\}$ is a cycle (loop) in P because in the positive dependency graph of P, a depends on b from the first E-rule and b depends on a from the second E-rule. This loop does not allow us to conclude any knowledge about the probabilities of a and b using the probabilistic answer set semantics of $EHPP_{SSAT}$. However, in SSAT, assumptions can be made about the truth values and the probabilities of a and b in that loop. These loops are the reason for the existence of a model (or models) of $\mathcal{R}$ that does not correspond to any probabilistic answer set of P, and hence $\sum_{h \in Ans} \prod_{A_i \in dom(h)} h(A_i) \neq$

$val(\mathcal{R}, Q)$. In the rest of this section, we follow the approach of [11] adapted to deal with $EHPP_{SSAT}$.

Definition 2. Let $P = \langle R \cup R_{neg}, \tau \rangle$ be a (finite and non-tight) E-program in restricted $EHPP_{SSAT}$ and LP be a non-empty subset of atoms(P). Then, LP is a loop of P if for any $A, B \in LP$, there exists a path of length > 0 from A to B, in the positive dependency graph of P, such that all the vertices in the path are in LP.

Following [11], to allow Theorems 3 and 4 to be applied to non-tight E-programs $P = \langle R \cup R_{neg}, \tau \rangle$ in restricted $EHPP_{SSAT}$, we associate to each loop, LP, of P a formula, LF, called loop formula, and add this loop formula LF to $\mathcal{R}$ in the probabilistic completion, $Comp = \langle \mathcal{R}, Q \rangle$, of P. This obtains a one-to-one correspondence between the models of $\mathcal{R} \cup \mathcal{LF}$ and the probabilistic answer sets of P, and hence, Theorems 3 and 4 apply to non-tight E-programs (where $\mathcal{LF}$ is the set of all loop formulas of P). The loop means that non of the atoms involved in the loop can be defined in any probabilistic answer set, h, of P, and hence they do not exist in $dom(h)$. The added loop formulas associated with each loop of P to $\mathcal{R}$ in the probabilistic completion of P means that the atoms of the loops are not in any model of $\mathcal{R} \cup \mathcal{LF}$.

Definition 3. Let $P = \langle R \cup R_{neg}, \tau \rangle$ be an E-program in restricted $EHPP_{SSAT}$ and LP be a loop in P. We define

$$R_P^+(LP) = \left\{ \begin{array}{l} A : \mu \leftarrow A_1 : \mu_1, \ldots, A_m : \mu_m, \\ not\,(A_{m+1} : \mu_{m+1}), \ldots, not\,(A_n : \mu_n) \end{array} \middle| \begin{array}{l} A : \mu \leftarrow A_1 : \mu_1, \ldots, A_m : \mu_m, \\ not\,(A_{m+1} : \mu_{m+1}), \ldots, not\,(A_n : \mu_n) \in R, \\ and\ A \in LP, (\exists A').A' \in LP, A' \in \mathcal{B} \end{array} \right\}$$

$$R_P^-(LP) = \left\{ \begin{array}{l} A : \mu \leftarrow A_1 : \mu_1, \ldots, A_m : \mu_m, \\ not\,(A_{m+1} : \mu_{m+1}), \ldots, not\,(A_n : \mu_n) \end{array} \middle| \begin{array}{l} A : \mu \leftarrow A_1 : \mu_1, \ldots, A_m : \mu_m, \\ not\,(A_{m+1} : \mu_{m+1}), \ldots, not\,(A_n : \mu_n) \in R, \\ and\ A \in LP, \neg\,(\exists A').A' \in LP, A' \in \mathcal{B} \end{array} \right\}$$

where $\mathcal{B} = \{A_1, \ldots, A_m, A_{m+1}, \ldots, A_n\}$.

Intuitively, similar to [11], $R_P^+(LP)$ contains the E-rules in R that are involved in the loop LP. However, $R_P^-(LP)$ contains the E-rules in R that are not in the loop LP. Clearly, $R_P^+(LP)$ and $R_P^-(LP)$ are disjoint sets.

Definition 4. Let $P = \langle R \cup R_{neg}, \tau \rangle$ be an E-program in restricted $EHPP_{SSAT}$ and LP be a loop in P. Let $A^i : \mu^i \leftarrow A_1^{ij} : \mu_1^{ij}, \ldots, A_m^{ij} : \mu_m^{ij}, not\,(A_{m+1}^{ij} : \mu_{m+1}^{ij}), \ldots, not\,(A_n^{ij} : \mu_n^{ij})$ for $1 \leq j \leq k_n$, be the set of E-rules in $R_P^-(LP)$, for an atom A^i ($1 \leq i \leq n$). Then, the implication $\neg\,[Body_{11} \vee \cdots \vee Body_{1k_1} \vee \ldots \vee Body_{n1} \vee \ldots \vee Body_{nk_n}] \supset \bigwedge_{A \in LP} \neg A$ is called a probabilistic loop formula, denoted by $LF(LP)$, of LP, where $Body_{ij} = A_1^{ij} \wedge \ldots \wedge A_m^{ij} \wedge \neg A_{m+1}^{ij} \wedge \ldots \wedge \neg A_n^{ij}$.

Theorem 5. Let $P = \langle R \cup R_{neg}, \tau \rangle$ be any E-program in restricted $EHPP_{SSAT}$, $Comp(P) = \langle \mathcal{R}, Q \rangle$ be the probabilistic completion of P, Ans be the set of all probabilistic answer sets of P and $h \in$ Ans. Let $\mathcal{LF}$ be the set of all probabilistic loop *formulas associated with all loops of P. Then, $\mathcal{R} \cup \mathcal{LF}$ has a model iff P has a probabilistic answer set, and $S = \langle \mathcal{R} \cup \mathcal{LF}, \theta, Q \rangle$ is satisfied iff $\sum_{h \in Ans} \prod_{A_i \in dom(h)}$ $h(A_i) = val(\mathcal{R} \cup \mathcal{LF}, Q) \geq \theta$, viewing the SSAT formula, S, as $MAJSAT$, where $\theta = \frac{1}{2}$, and*

$$\max\nolimits_{h \models \tilde{x}_1 : [1,1], \dots, \tilde{x}_n : [1,1]} \left[h(\tilde{x}_n) \sum\nolimits_{h' \models \mathcal{D}} \prod\nolimits_{i=1}^{n} h'(\tilde{y}_i) \right] \geq \theta \text{ where } \mathcal{D} \equiv \tilde{x}_1 : [1,1], \dots,$$

$\tilde{x}_n : [1,1], \tilde{y}_1 : [p_1, p_1], \dots, \tilde{y}_n : [p_n, p_n]$ and $\tilde{x}_i = x_i$ or $\tilde{x}_i = \neg x_i$ and $\tilde{y}_i = y_i$ or $\tilde{y}_i = \neg y_i$, viewing the SSAT formula, S, as E-$MAJSAT$.

Example 6. Consider again the non-tight E-program, P, from Example 5. This E-program belongs to restricted $EHPP_{SSAT}$ and has one loop $LP = \{a, b\}$, where

$$R^+(LP) = \{a : [0.5, 0.5] \leftarrow b : [0.3, 0.3], b : [0.3, 0.3] \leftarrow a : [0.5, 0.5]\} \qquad R^-(LP) = \emptyset.$$

Thus, the loop formula $LF(LP)$ is $\neg false \supset (\neg a \wedge \neg b)$, which is equivalent to $(\neg a \wedge \neg b)$. Adding $LF(LP)$ to $\mathcal{R}$ outcomes the propositional formula $\mathcal{R} \cup LF(LP) = \{a \equiv b, (\neg a \wedge \neg b)\}$, which has only one model $\{\neg a, \neg b\}$. It can be easily verified that $val(\mathcal{R} \cup \{(\neg a \wedge \neg b)\}, Q) = 0.35$. This implies that the only probabilistic answer set h, where $h(\bar{a}) = [0.5, 0.5], h(\bar{b}) = [0.7, 0.7]$, of P corresponds to the only model of $\mathcal{R} \cup LF(LP)$. Moreover, the SSAT formula, $S = \langle \mathcal{R} \cup \{(\neg a \wedge \neg b)\}, 0.5, Q \rangle$, is unsatisfied, since $\sum_{h \in Ans} \prod_{A_i \in dom(h)} h(A_i) = 0.35 = val(\mathcal{R} \cup \{(\neg a \wedge \neg b)\}, Q) \not\geq 0.5$.

6 Related Work and Conclusions

We studied the relationship between EHPP and SSAT. EHPP is closely related to EDHPP presented in [23] that is similar to EHPP but allows disjunctions in the head of rules. We presented a modular translation from SSAT to EHPP. The translation is based on a corresponding local translation from SAT to normal logic programs described in [19]. Moreover, we proved that there is no modular mapping from EHPP to SSAT. This shows that EHPP is more expressive than SSAT from the knowledge representation point of view.

In addition, we presented a translation from $EHPP_{SSAT}$ to SSAT that relies on a corresponding translation from normal logic programs to SAT [3,11]. Two classes of $EHPP_{SSAT}$ are identified; tight and non-tight $EHPP_{SSAT}$. The translation form tight $EHPP_{SSAT}$ to SSAT is based on the translation from tight normal logic programs [6] to SAT, using Clark's completion [3]. In addition, the translation form non tight $EHPP_{SSAT}$ to SSAT relies on the translation from non tight normal logic programs to SAT, using loop formulas [11].

A similar relationship between SSAT and other probabilistic logic programming frameworks, e.g., [16,17,18,5,8,13,1,9,10,21,26], has not been studied. However, the relationship between the probabilistic logic programming frameworks [16,17,18,5,8,13] and a different extension to SAT, namely, Probabilistic SAT (PSAT) [2] has been studied. Given an assignment of probabilities to a collection of propositional formulas, PSAT asks if this assignment is consistent. The solution to PSAT is based on the possible world semantics. The possible world semantics solution to PSAT is achieved by compiling a linear program from the given probability assignments to a collection of propositional formulas, PSAT, and if this linear program has a solution, implies that the probability assignments to the set of propositional formulas is consistent. However, it is not clear how to translate PSAT to a probabilistic logic program in [16,17,18,5,8,13]. The probabilistic logic programming frameworks of [1,9,21,26] relate probabilistic logic programming to Bayesian networks, which is different from SSAT and PSAT.

References

1. Baral, C., Gelfond, M., Rushton, N.: Probabilistic reasoning with answer sets. In: 7th International Conference on Logic Programming and Nonmonotonic Reasoning. Springer, Heidelberg (2004)
2. Boole, G.: The laws of thought. Macmillan, London (1854)
3. Clark, K.: Negation as failure. In: Gallaire, H., Minker, J. (eds.) Logic and Data Bases, pp. 293–322. Plenum Press, New York (1978)
4. Davis, M., Logemann, G., Loveland, D.: A machine program for theorem-proving. Communications of the ACM 5(7), 394–397 (1962)
5. Dekhtyar, A., Subrahmanian, V.S.: Hybrid probabilistic program. Journal of Logic Programming 43(3), 187–250 (2000)
6. Fages, F.: Consistency of clark's completion and existence of stable models. Methods of Logic in Computer Science 1, 51–60 (1994)
7. Gelfond, M., Lifschitz, V.: Classical negation in logic programs and disjunctive databases. New Generation Computing 9(3-4), 363–385 (1991)
8. Kern-Isberner, G., Lukasiewicz, T.: Combining probabilistic logic programming with the power of maximum entropy. Artificial Intelligence 157(1-2), 139–202 (2004)
9. Kersting, K., De Raedt, L.: Bayesian logic programs. Inductive Logic Programming (2000)
10. Lakshmanan, L.V.S., Sadri, F.: On a theory of probabilistic deductive databases. Journal of Theory and Practice of Logic Programming 1(1), 5–42 (2001)
11. Lin, F., Zhao, Y.: Assat: Computing answer sets of a logic program by sat solvers. Artificial Intelligence 157(1-2), 115–137 (2004)
12. Littman, M., Majercik, S., Pitassi, T.: Stochastic boolean satisfiability. Journal of Automated Reasoning 27(3), 251–296 (2001)
13. Lukasiewicz, T.: Probabilistic logic programming. In: 13th European Conference on Artificial Intelligence, pp. 388–392 (1998)
14. Majercik, S., Littman, M.: Maxplan: A new approach to probabilistic planning. In: Fourth International Conference on Artificial Intelligence Planning, pp. 86–93 (1998)
15. Majercik, S., Littman, M.: Contingent planning under uncertainty via stochastic satisfiability. Artificial Intelligence 147(1-2), 119–162 (2003)
16. Ng, R.T., Subrahmanian, V.S.: Probabilistic logic programming. Information & Computation 101(2) (1992)
17. Ng, R.T., Subrahmanian, V.S.: A semantic framework for supporting subjective and conditional probabilities in deductive databases. Journal of Automated Reasoning 10(2) (1993)
18. Ng, R.T., Subrahmanian, V.S.: Stable semantics for probabilistic deductive databases. Information & Computation 110(1) (1994)

19. Niemela, I.: Logic programs with stable model semantics as a constraint programming paradigm. Annals of Mathematics and Artificial Intelligence 25(3-4), 241–273 (1999)
20. Papadimitriou, C.H.: Games against nature. Journal of Computer and System Sciences 31(2), 288–301 (1985)
21. Poole, D.: The independent choice logic for modelling multiple agents under uncertainty. Artificial Intelligence 94(1-2), 7–56 (1997)
22. Saad, E.: Incomplete knowledge in hybrid probabilistic logic programs. In: Tenth European Conference on Logics in Artificial Intelligence. Springer, Heidelberg (2006)
23. Saad, E.: A logical approach to qualitative and quantitative reasoning. In: 9th European Conference on Symbolic and Quantitative Approaches to Reasoning with Uncertainty (2007)
24. Saad, E.: Probabilistic planning in hybrid probabilistic logic programs. In: First International Conference on Scalable Uncertainty Management. Springer, Heidelberg (2007)
25. Saad, E., Pontelli, E.: A new approach to hybrid probabilistic logic programs. Annals of Mathematics and Artificial Intelligence 48(3-4), 187–243 (2006)
26. Vennekens, J., Verbaeten, S., Bruynooghe, M.: Logic programs with annotated disjunctions. In: International Conference on Logic Programming, pp. 431–445 (2004)

Scaling Most Probable World Computations in Probabilistic Logic Programs

Gerardo I. Simari, Maria Vanina Martinez, Amy Sliva, and V.S. Subrahmanian

University of Maryland College Park, College Park, MD 20742, USA
{gisimari,mvm,asliva,vs}@cs.umd.edu

Abstract. The "Most Probable World" (MPW) problem in probabilistic logic programming (PLPs) is that of finding a possible world with the highest probability. Past work has shown that this problem is computationally intractable and involves solving exponentially many linear programs, each of which is of exponential size. In this paper, we study what happens when the user focuses his interest on a set of atoms in such a PLP. We show that we can significantly reduce the number of worlds to be considered by defining a "reduced" linear program whose solution is in one-one correspondence with the exact solution to the MPW problem. However, the problem is still intractable. We develop a Monte Carlo sampling approach that enables us to build a quick approximation of the reduced linear program that allows us to estimate (inexactly) the exact solution to the MPW problem. We show experimentally that our approach works well in practice, scaling well to problems where the exact solution is intractable to compute.

1 Introduction

Action probabilistic logic programs (*ap*-programs for short) [5,4] provide a logic programming paradigm through which we can develop stochastic models of the behavior of real world organizations *without making any assumptions about independence* of events and/or conditions. Because no such assumptions are made, this paradigm is fundamentally different from others such as Bayesian Networks which are structured based on the knowledge that certain variables are only dependent on a specific subset of variables. *ap*-programs and their variants have been used extensively over the last couple of years to develop models of the behaviors of the various stakeholders in the Afghan drug trade [14] as well as terrorist groups such as Hezbollah [8] and Hamas [9]. These models, which are now available through a secure site to various law enforcement and military users [10], exist for over 36 groups ranging from Morocco to Afghanistan. The behavioral models themselves are expressed through a set of stochastic rules that are informally of the form "If condition C holds, then group g will take a given action a with a probability in the range $[\ell, u]$." Note that the use of *ap*-programs to model organizational behavior is not limited to organizations with suspicious activities - in theory, they could just as well be used to learn conditions about when an investment bank will buy or sell a certain stock, or when an insurance company will pay or deny a given claim, or when OPEC will raise oil prices. However, these latter applications have not been built to the best of our knowledge.

S. Greco and T. Lukasiewicz (Eds.): SUM 2008, LNAI 5291, pp. 372–385, 2008.
© Springer-Verlag Berlin Heidelberg 2008

A group's behavior is thus characterized by a set of such rules. Naturally, there is much interest in what a group will do in a given situation S (real or hypothetical) that may or may not have been encountered in the past. Past work by us has studied this problem in considerable detail. A "world" informally refers to a set of actions that the group might take in situation S. It is clear that the number of all possible worlds is exponential in the number of actions considered. The key question for decision makers is: what is the most (or k most) probable worlds in a given situation S for group g?

The naive approach to solving this problem as described in [5,4] is to derive a linear program from the ap-program and situation S, and to try to compute the probability of world w for each and every world w. This approach has two fundamental problems. First, the size of the linear program is exponential in the number of actions considered. Second, we need to solve an exponential number of such linear programs (one for each world) in order to determine the most probable world. [5,4] made three major improvements to alleviate these problems. First, they proposed a method to reduce the size of the linear program (sometimes but not always) from being exponential in the number of atoms, to being exponential in the number of rules. Second, they developed a "binary" heuristic that explores only a fixed number of worlds. Third, they developed a suite of parallel algorithms to solve the problem.

In this paper, we show that the approach of [5,4] can be significantly improved through the incorporation of yet another piece of knowledge. Under certain conditions, when we know what actions the user is interested in predicting (which is often the case and can be easily communicated by the user to a system implementation), we can reduce the size of the linear program significantly, while guaranteeing that an exact solution will be found, not an approximate solution. Furthermore, we develop a Monte Carlo sampling approach that, when used in conjunction with the reduced linear program, is enormously helpful in scaling the performance of the system. We describe these methods and provide experimental results showing that our system performs well even when a relatively large number of actions is considered.

2 Preliminaries

Action probabilistic logic programs (ap-programs) are a variant of the probabilistic logic programs introduced in [11,12]. We assume the existence of a logical alphabet that consists of a finite set $\mathcal{L}_{cons}$ of constant symbols, a finite set $\mathcal{L}_{pred}$ of predicate symbols (each with an associated arity) and an infinite set $\mathcal{V}$ of variable symbols: function symbols are not allowed in this language. Terms and atoms are defined in the usual way [6]. We assume that a subset $\mathcal{L}_{act}$ of $\mathcal{L}_{pred}$ is designated to be the set of *action symbols* (symbols that denote some action). Thus, if $t_1, \ldots, t_n$ are terms, and p is an n-ary action symbol, then $p(t_1, \ldots, t_n)$, is called an *action atom*. Ground terms and atoms are defined in the usual manner [6].

Definition 1. *A (ground) basic action formula is either a conjunction or a disjunction of (ground) atoms from $\mathcal{L}_{act}$.*

The set of all possible basic formulas is denoted by $bf(B_{\mathcal{L}_{act}})$, where $B_{\mathcal{L}_{act}}$ is the Herbrand base associated with $\mathcal{L}_{act}$ and $\mathcal{L}_{cons}$.

Definition 2. *If F is a basic action formula and $\mu = [\alpha, \beta] \subseteq [0, 1]$, then $F : \mu$ is called an* ap-*annotated action basic formula. μ is called the* ap-*annotation of F.*

Definition 3 (ap-rules). *If F is a basic action formula, $B_1, \ldots, B_n$ are non-action atoms, and $\mu, \mu_1, \ldots, \mu_m$ are ap-annotations, then $F : \mu \leftarrow B_1 \wedge \ldots B_m$ is called a basic ap-rule. If this rule is named c, then $Head(c)$ denotes $F : \mu$ and $Body(c)$ denotes $B_1 \wedge \ldots B_n$.*

Intuitively, the rule specified above says that if $B_1, \ldots, B_m$ are all true in a given situation, then there is a probability in the interval μ that F is true. Thus, if F is a basic action formula representing some actions that a given group might take, then this reflects the probability that the group will take the combination of atomic actions in F.

Definition 4 (ap-program). *A* basic *action probabilistic logic program (basic ap-program for short) is a finite set of basic ap-rules.*

In the following, we will refer to basic *ap*-programs simply as *ap*-programs when there is no ambiguity.

Definition 5 (world/state). *A* world *is any set of ground action atoms. A* state *is any finite set of ground non-action atoms.*

We use $\mathcal{W}$ to denote the set of all possible worlds. Note that both worlds and states are just ordinary Herbrand interpretations. As such, it is clear what it means for a state to satisfy the body of a rule [6].

Definition 6. *Let Π be an ap-program and s a state. The* reduction *of Π w.r.t. s, denoted by Π_s is $\{F : \mu \mid s$ satisfies Body and $F : \mu \leftarrow$ Body is a ground instance of a rule in $\Pi\}$.*

In the following, we assume that we have been provided with a distinguished set $\mathcal{Q}$ of *action atoms of interest* chosen from the set of all possible ground action atoms. For instance, when a user is reasoning about a given group, he might specify what actions he is interested in. The powerset of $\mathcal{Q}$ will be denoted by $\mathcal{W}^{\mathcal{Q}}$, and represents the *worlds of interest*; their importance in the reduction of the size of the resulting constraints when performing most probable world computations will be discussed below.

Definition 7. *Let $F \in bf(\mathcal{L}_{act})$ be a ground basic action formula, and $\mathcal{Q}$ be a set of ground action atoms. The* reduction *of F with respect to $\mathcal{Q}$, denoted by $red(F, \mathcal{Q})$ is defined as a new formula F', which is obtained by removing from F, the atoms that do not appear in $\mathcal{Q}$.*

We use $comp(F, \mathcal{Q})$ to denote the part of formula F that does contain the atoms in $\mathcal{Q}$ (this intuitively corresponds to the complement of $red(F, \mathcal{Q})$).

Definition 8. *Let $F \in bf(\mathcal{L}_{act})$ be a ground basic action formula, and $\mathcal{Q}$ be a set of ground action atoms. The* complement *of F with respect to $\mathcal{Q}$, denoted by $comp(F, \mathcal{Q})$ is defined as a new formula F', which is obtained by removing from F the atoms that do not appear in $red(F, \mathcal{Q})$.*

The example below illustrates these concepts.

Example 1. Let $F = a \vee b \vee c \vee d \vee e$, and $\mathcal{Q} = \{a, b, c\}$. In this case, $red(F, \mathcal{Q}) = a \vee b \vee c$, while $comp(F, \mathcal{Q}) = d \vee e$.

3 Exponential Speedup of Most Probable World Computations

Let Π be a basic *ap*-program, s be a state, $\mathcal{L}_{act}$ be the set of all possible action predicates, and $gr(\mathcal{L}_{act})$ be the set of all possible ground action atoms. Following the work of [2,13,3,1,12,7], [4] shows how we can associate a set of linear constraints with $\Pi, s, \mathcal{L}_{act}$. If $\mathcal{W}$ is the set of all possible worlds, and p_i is a variable denoting the (as yet unknown) probability of world $w_i \in \mathcal{W}$, then [4] creates the set of linear constraints defined by:

1. If $F_i : [\ell, u] \in \Pi_s$, then $\ell \leq \left(\sum_{w_j \mapsto F_i} p_j \right) \leq u$ is in $\mathrm{CONS}(\Pi, s)$.
2. $\Sigma_{w_i} p_i = 1$ is in $\mathrm{CONS}(\Pi, s)$.

Now suppose the user selects a set $\mathcal{Q}$ of ground action atoms that he considers to be of interest for his work. We can take advantage of $\mathcal{Q}$ to significantly reduce the size of the linear constraints specified in [4]. Given $\mathcal{Q}$, we define a set of linear constraints $\mathrm{CONS}_0(\Pi, s, \mathcal{Q})$. The intuition behind this set of constraints, as compared to that used in $\mathrm{CONS}(\Pi, s)$ [4] is that we now have a new set $\mathcal{W}^{\mathcal{Q}}$ that contains $2^{|\mathcal{Q}|}$ worlds, each of which is an *abstraction* of worlds in the old set $\mathcal{W}$ (each $w' \in \mathcal{W}'$ represents $2^{|\mathcal{W}| - |\mathcal{W}'|}$ worlds from the original set). The constraints are then defined over the set of all possible worlds of interest $\mathcal{W}^{\mathcal{Q}}$ as follows:

1. If $F_i : [\ell, u] \in \Pi_s$ and F_i is a conjunction, then $\ell \leq \left(\sum_{w_j \mapsto red(F, \mathcal{Q})} p_j \right) - q_0^i \leq u$ is in $\mathrm{CONS}_0(\Pi, s, \mathcal{Q})$.
2. If $F_i : [\ell, u] \in \Pi_s$ and F_i is a disjunction, then $\ell \leq \left(\sum_{w_j \mapsto red(F, \mathcal{Q})} p_j \right) + q_0^i \leq u$ is in $\mathrm{CONS}_0(\Pi, s, \mathcal{Q})$.
3. For each variable q_0^i introduced in the constraints of type (1) and (2), $\mathrm{CONS}_0(\Pi, s, \mathcal{Q})$ contains the constraint $q_0^i \geq 0$.
4. $\Sigma_{w_i} p_i = 1$ is in $\mathrm{CONS}_0(\Pi, s, \mathcal{Q})$.

The probability of each world in $\mathcal{W}^{\mathcal{Q}}$ represents the summation of probabilities of worlds in the original set of constraints. The q_0^i variables introduced in the constraints of type (1) and (2) (referred to as *auxiliary variables* from now on) serve the purpose of compensating for the loss of granularity of this new set of worlds; for conjunctions they appear as negative values, since the reduced formula has more satisfying worlds than the original, and for disjunctions the opposite holds. In the former case, the q_0^i values represent the summation

$$\sum_{w_i \models red(F_i, \mathcal{Q}) \wedge \neg comp(F_i, \mathcal{Q})} p_i \tag{1}$$

from the original constraints, while in the latter they represent the summation

$$\sum_{w_i \models comp(F_i, \mathcal{Q}) \wedge \neg red(F_i, \mathcal{Q})} p_i \tag{2}$$

$$
\begin{array}{ll}
1.\ a \vee b \vee c : [0.85, 0.95] & \leftarrow . \\
2.\ b \wedge c \quad\ : [0.4, 0.55] & \leftarrow . \\
3.\ a \vee b \vee d : [0.6, 0.78] & \leftarrow . \\
4.\ a \wedge c \wedge d : [0.15, 0.3] & \leftarrow . \\
\end{array}
$$

Fig. 1. A simple *ap*-program

In the following, we will abbreviate with $corr(v)$ (for *correction* formula) the formula associated with auxiliary variable v, which initially has the values just described. Now, this is only a first approximation towards obtaining a set of constraints that adequately reflects all the restrictions provided by the full set used in [4]. In order to clarify what we mean by this, we first present an example of how to obtain $CONS_0(\Pi, s, \mathcal{Q})$.

Example 2. Suppose we have the basic *ap*-program Π of Figure 1, and let $\mathcal{Q} = \{a, b\}$. While the original set of worlds $\mathcal{W}$ included 16 worlds, the reduced set $\mathcal{W}'$ contains only 4. As discussed, each of these worlds represents an abstraction of worlds from the original set; for instance, world $\{a\}$ represents worlds $\{a\}, \{a, c\}, \{a, d\}$, and $\{a, c, d\}$. This reflects the fact that the reasoning agent is only interested in the atoms in $\mathcal{Q}$, and therefore needs not differentiate among the worlds that only differ in atoms that are not in this set.

The following is the set of constraints $CONS(\Pi, s, \mathcal{Q})$, for which we use the enumeration of worlds $w_0 = \{\}, w_1 = \{a\}, w_2 = \{b\}$, and $w_3 = \{a, b\}$:

$$
\begin{array}{ll}
0.85 \leq p_1 + p_2 + p_3 + q_0^1 \leq 0.95 & \quad 0.4 \leq p_2 + p_3 - q_0^2 \leq 0.55 \\
0.6 \leq p_1 + p_2 + p_3 + q_0^3 \leq 0.78 & \quad 0.15 \leq p_1 + p_3 - q_0^4 \leq 0.3 \\
q_0^1, q_0^2, q_0^3, q_0^4 \geq 0 & \quad p_0 + p_1 + p_2 + p_3 = 1
\end{array}
$$

Here, for instance, $corr(q_0^2) = b \wedge \neg c$.

3.1 Refining the Set of Constraints

In Example 2, it can clearly be seen that the values of variables q_0^1 and q_0^3 are not independent of each other, since their corresponding formulas share models, *i.e.*, $(c \wedge \neg(a \vee b)) \wedge (d \wedge \neg(a \vee b)) \not\models \bot$. In this case, there is one world, $\{c, d\}$ that is a model of both correction formulas. This means that the initial set of constraints does not adequately represent the original restrictions on the probabilities that can be assigned to each world, and we should take this into account in order to refine the set of constraints. Figure 2 presents the RefineCONS algorithm which addresses this issue by replacing the variables that give rise to these situations with new variables, and setting their associated formulas accordingly. The *for* loop on line 11 states that each of the auxiliary variables must be bounded from above by the upper bounds that are associated with formulas in the head of rules in Π that are satisfied by their associated formulas. This process can add redundant constraints (since more than one formula could be satisfied, and then only the lowest upper bound would make a difference) but we do not include the simple checks to avoid this in order to keep the presentation clear. The following example shows the set of constraints from the previous example after applying this algorithm.

```
algorithm RefineCONS(Π, CONS)
1.  CONS' := copy of CONS; i := 1;
2.  while CONS' has two auxiliary variables u_{k_1}, v_{k_2} s.t.
              corr(u_{k_1}) ∧ corr(v_{k_2}) ⊭ ⊥ {
3.      replace u_{k_1} in CONS' with a new variable u_i;
4.      set corr(u_i) = corr(u_{k_1}) ∧ ¬corr(v_{k_2}); i := i+1;
5.      replace v_{k_2} in CONS' with a new variable v_i;
6.      set corr(v_i) = corr(v_{k_2}) ∧ ¬corr(u_{k_1}); i := i+1;
7.      introduce a new variable r_i in CONS' (coeff. +1)
              wherever u_{k_1} and v_{k_2} appeared;
8.      set corr(r_i) = (corr(u_{k_1}) ∧ corr(v_{k_2}));
9.      add constraint r_i ≥ 0 to CONS'; i := i+1;
10. }
11. for each aux variable v and formula F in Π s.t.
              corr(v) ∧ F ⊭ ⊥ and
              F : [L, U] is the head of a rule in Π {
12.     add constraint 0 ≤ v ≤ U to CONS'
13. }
14. return CONS';
```

Fig. 2. The RefineCONS algorithm

Example 3. When we apply the RefineCONS algorithm to the set of constraints obtained in Example 2, we obtain the following result.

(1). $0.85 \leq p_1 + p_2 + p_3 + q_1^1 + r_2 \leq 0.95$
(2). $0.4 \leq p_2 + p_3 - q_3^2 - r_4 \leq 0.55$
(3). $0.6 \leq p_1 + p_2 + p_3 + q_1^3 + r_2 \leq 0.78$
(4). $0.15 \leq p_1 + p_3 - q_3^4 - r_4 \leq 0.3$
(5). $q_1^1, q_3^2, q_1^3, q_3^4, r_2, r_4 \geq 0$
(6). $p_0 + p_1 + p_2 + p_3 = 1$
(7). $0 \leq q_1^1 \leq 0.95$;   (8). $0 \leq r_2 \leq 0.95$;   (9). $0 \leq r_2 \leq 0.78$
(10). $0 \leq q_3^2 \leq 0.95$;   (11). $0 \leq q_3^3 \leq 0.78$;   (12). $0 \leq r_4 \leq 0.95$
(13). $0 \leq r_4 \leq 0.78$;   (14). $0 \leq q_3^4 \leq 0.95$;   (15). $0 \leq q_3^4 \leq 0.55$
(16). $0 \leq q_3^4 \leq 0.78$

Here, for instance, $corr(q_3^2) = (b \wedge \neg c) \wedge \neg(a \wedge \neg(c \wedge d))$, constraint 11 states that, because $(a \vee b \vee d) \wedge corr(q_3^2) \not\models \bot$, the upper bound of rule 3 applies to q_3^2. As we discussed above, some of the constraints indicating upper bounds (constraints 7 to 16) are redundant and their insertion can be easily avoided by the algorithm. Such is the case of constraints 8, 10, 12, 14, and 16.

The following result links the results obtained from solving the output of RefineCONS with those obtained from solving the original set of constraints from [4] for the corresponding worlds. We use $Vars(C)$ to denote the set of variables occurring in a set C of constraints, and $val(V, S)$ to denote the value assigned to variable V by a solution S.

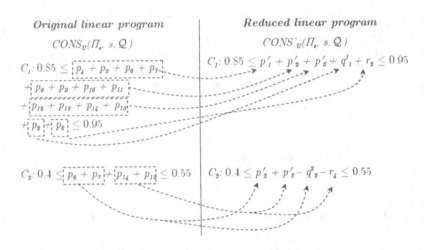

Fig. 3. Part of the set of constraints after applying the RefineCONS algorithm to the set of constraints obtained in Example 2. Here, we show one constraint arising from a rule whose head contains a disjunction and one arising from a rule containing a conjunction (C_1 and C_2, respectively) in order to demonstrate the two possible scenarios that come up.

Theorem 1. *Let Π be an* ap-*program, s be a state, $\mathcal{Q}$ be a subset of all possible action atoms, $C = CONS(\Pi, s)$ be the original set of constraints (obtained by considering the entire set of action atoms), and C^* be the set of constraints returned by RefineCONS(Π, C). Then, there exists a mapping $\mu : Vars(C^*) \rightarrow Vars(C)$ such that:*

1. If $V_1, V_2 \in Vars(C^*)$, $V_1 \neq V_2$, then $\mu(V_i) \cap \mu(V_2) = \emptyset$
2. For every solution S of C there exists a solution S^* of C^* such that for every $V_i^* \in S^*$, $val(V_i^*, S^*) = \sum_{V_j \in \mu(V_i^*)} val(V_j, S)$.

Proof sketch: We first establish how mapping μ is obtained. For any non-auxiliary variable p_j^* corresponding to a world of interest $w_j^* \mapsto red(F, Q)$, $\mu(p_j^*) = \{p_i \mid w_i = w_j^* \cup w_r$ where $w_r \in \mathcal{P}(\mathcal{W} - \mathcal{W}')\}$. For any auxiliary variable q_j^*, $\mu(q_j^*) = \{p_i \mid w_i \in \mathcal{W}$ and $w_i \mapsto corr(q_j^*)\}$. Note that this mapping is the by-product of how $CONS(\Pi, s, \mathcal{Q})$ is defined.

We must first prove that condition (1) holds. For non-auxiliary variables, it is clear from the definition of the mapping that no two images can intersect, since their elements are constructed from disjoint worlds in $\mathcal{W}'$. For auxiliary variables, the algorithm RefineCONS guarantees that the images of two different variables do not intersect, since the while loop in line 2 exits only when, for all pairs of auxiliary variables, their corresponding correction formulas do not share models.

   In order to prove condition 2, consider a solution S of C and an assignment of values S^* to variables of C^* satisfying the conditions in the theorem. We must now prove that S^* so defined is in fact a solution for C^*; in order to do this, we will consider constraints arising from disjunctions and conjunctions in turn:

- Let c_i^* be a constraint arising from a rule whose head is a *disjunction*. From the definition of $CONS(\Pi, s, \mathcal{Q})$ and the operations performed by the RefineCONS algorithm, all variables in the constraint appear with a coefficient of 1 (positive). Therefore, from condition (1) it follows that c_i^* is simply a rewriting of its corresponding constraint in C, where p_j^* replaces the block of variables $\mu(q_j^*)$.

- Let c_i^* be a constraint arising from a rule whose head is a *conjunction*. In this case we will have variables with a -1 coefficient. As before, it is possible to see c_i^* as a rewriting of its corresponding constraint in C. To see why, consider the set of non-auxiliary variables in c_i^*; the value assigned by S^* to the sum of all such variables can be separated into two positive values, $s_{i,1}^*$ and $s_{i,2}^*$, such that $s_{i,1}^* = \sum_{w_j \in W, w_j \mapsto red(F,\mathcal{Q}) \land \neg comp(F,\mathcal{Q})} p_j$ and $s_{i,2}^* = \sum_{w_j \in W, w_j \mapsto comp(F,\mathcal{Q}) \land \neg red(F,\mathcal{Q})} p_j$ (note that by definition $red(F, \mathcal{Q}) \land comp(F, \mathcal{Q}) \models \bot$). Therefore, $s_{i,2}^* = val(q_0^i)$ (as stated in Equation 1) and, since RefineCONS guarantees that q_0^i will be replaced by a set of variables whose correction formulas do not share models and with a union of models equal to that of q_0^i's correction formula, this means that the constraint is indeed a rewriting of its corresponding one in C, since $s_{i,2}^*$ is effectively added and then subtracted.   □

The following result is an immediate consequence of the above theorem and establishes the correctness of the RefineCons algorithm.

Corollary 1 (Correctness of RefineCONS). *Algorithm RefineCONS is correct, i.e., minimizing/maximizing w.r.t. a non-auxiliary variable q_i in $C^* = RefineCONS(\Pi, s, \mathcal{Q})$ yields the same value as that obtained by minimizing/maximizing the sum of variables associated with the set of worlds abstracted by world $w_i \in \mathcal{W}'$.*

3.2 Analysis of the RefineCONS Algorithm

The first aspect of the the algorithm that we will analyze is the number of times that the `while` loop in line 3 is executed. In the worst case, the auxiliary variables' sets of models are such that their *pairwise intersections* are all non-empty. This leads to a number of auxiliary variables that is exponential in the number of constraints. In Figure 4, we show how this situation can arise; on the left, we have two formulas whose sets of models intersect (shown in gray), while on the right we show the worst possible scenario when considering one more formula, *i.e.*, that the new formula's models intersects with all parts of the original diagram. This clearly leads to $2^c - 1$ auxiliary variables in the worst case, where c is the number of constraints in $CONS_0(\Pi, s, \mathcal{Q})$.

The second source of complexity is in evaluating whether the formulas associated with a given pair of auxiliary variables are consistent or not (i.e. whether their sets of models intersect or not). The alert reader may have noticed that correction formulas contain atoms from the *original* set, and therefore performing the satisfiability checks required to verify existence of common models will surely lead to intractable computations even for a moderate number of possible atoms. Even though we can leverage the

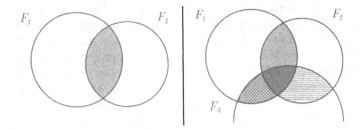

Fig. 4. A Venn diagram representation of the models of formulas. On the left, two formulas share at least one model; the set of shared models is shown in gray. On the right, a new formula is introduced, which shares models with all three sets from the left (*i.e.*, only F_1, only F_2, and both) generating a total of seven possible subsets.

fact that because rules only contain basic formulas, sets of models can be compactly represented using binary strings of length n, this property is lost once we perform a "cut" such as those performed in lines 5 and 7 of RefineCONS, since correction formulas are no longer basic. The best case running time, on the other hand, occurs when all pairs of formulas in rule heads are mutually inconsistent.

We can, however, perform a *single* step of refinement in polynomial time in the special case in which all formulas are conjunctions. In this case, non-emptiness of intersections of sets of models can be checked in time linear in the number of atoms in the original set. Therefore, the set of auxiliary variables after one step of refinement can be computed in time in $O(2^{|CONS(\Pi,s,\mathcal{Q})|})$.

3.3   A Monte Carlo Refinement Algorithm

In the previous section we saw that the applicability of the RefineCONS algorithm is limited due to the intensive computations that it must carry out in order to ensure that the constraints are fully refined. In this section, we will present a Monte Carlo algorithm that alleviates these computations, at the expense of not being able to guarantee full refinement.

The basic Monte Carlo refinement algorithm is described in Figure 5. The algorithm follows the same basic approach as RefineCONS, except that auxiliary variables are now refined based on randomly selected models instead of exhaustive verification of satisfiability of conjunctions of pairs of correction formulas. The `while` loop in line 3 uses a subroutine `terminationCond` as a condition; we assume that this subroutine is designed by the user to decide when enough refining attempts have been made (for instance, number of models tried, number of refinements made, time elapsed, etc). This basic algorithm can be enhanced by considering two heuristics, described next.

Small number of variables check. Before any sampling is done, we can perform checks for every pair of auxiliary variables to see if the total number of atoms occurring between them is small enough for an exhaustive verification, *i.e.*, a SAT check on their conjunction. This enhances the accuracy of the final result by identifying easy refinements that could otherwise be missed by the random generation of models.

```
algorithm MonteCarloRefineCONS(Π,CONS)
1. CONS' := copy of CONS;
2. i := 1; m := 0; VariableAssignment test;
3. while terminationCond(Π,CONS,i,m) = false {
4.      test = randomly generate a world wrt
5.              full set of atoms; m := m + 1
6.      for each pair of aux. variables v_{k_1} ≠ v_{k_2} s.t.
                test ⊨ corr(u_{k_1}) ∧ corr(v_{k_2})
7.          replace u_{k_1} in CONS' with a new variable u_i;
9.          set corr(u_i) = corr(u_{k_1}) ∧ ¬corr(v_{k_2}); i := i + 1;
10.         replace v_{k_2} in CONS' with a new variable v_i;
11.         set corr(v_i) = corr(v_{k_2}) ∧ ¬corr(u_{k_1}); i := i + 1;
12.         introduce a new variable r_i in CONS' (coeff. +1)
                wherever u_{k_1} and v_{k_2} appeared;
14.         add constraint r_i ≥ 0 to CONS'; i := i + 1;
15.     }
16. }
17. for each aux variable v and formula F in Π s.t.
        corr(v) ∧ F ⊭ ⊥ and
        F : [L,U] is the head of a rule in Π {
18.     add constraint 0 ≤ v ≤ U to CONS'
19. }
20. return CONS';
```

Fig. 5. The basic MonteCarloRefineCONS algorithm

Targeted sampling. A data structure can be maintained for storing the pairs of auxiliary variables that we have proved do not share models. Such a data structure can be an array of auxiliary variables, where each variable v_i has an associated set of auxiliary variables v_j such that $corr(v_i) \wedge corr(v_j) \models \bot$. These sets are all initially empty, and then can be updated either by the checks discussed above, or when a refinement is otherwise identified (such as when a randomly generated model satisfies two or more variables' correction formulas). When such an event occurs, the two variables involved are replaced by the new three, where the conjunction variable is associated with the union of the two other variables' sets.

When such a data structure is maintained, *targeted sampling* can be performed, *i.e.*, generation of models specifically geared towards certain pairs. This means that a certain pair of variables can be selected out of the possible ones remaining, and models can be generated involving only the atoms appearing in these variables' correction formulas, thus enhancing the chances of finding a model for their conjunction if one exists. If no model is found after a certain number of checks or time elapsed, the pair can be "declared" to be already refined. Another advantage of the use of such a data structure is in being able to determine how many pairs remain to be tested for refinement, and in particular if none remain.

```
algorithm FindMPW(Π, s, Q)
1.      let W_Q be the set of worlds according to Q;
2.      obtain CONS_0(Π, s, X, Q);
3.      CONS' = RefineCONS(CONS_0(Π, s, X, Q));
4.      let currlow = 0; currlowWorld = null;
5.      for each w_i^Q ∈ P(W^Q) {
6.          compute low(w_i^Q) w.r.t. CONS';
7.          if (low(w_i^Q) > currlow) {
8.              currlow:= low(w_i^Q);
9               currlowWorld:= w_i^Q;
10.         }
11.     }
12.     return currlowWorld;
```

Fig. 6. The FindMPW algorithm

4   Finding Most Probable Worlds of Interest

The FindMPW algorithm shown in Figure 6 correctly computes the most probable world as long as step 6 correctly computes the result of minimizing p_i subject to the constraints in $CONS_0(\Pi, s, Q)$. This can be done by minimizing this variable subject to the constraints computed by the RefineCONS algorithm, and in this case, the world returned by FindMPW is guaranteed to be the most probable world. However, if the Monte Carlo algorithm is used, then this is not guaranteed.

The FindMPW algorithm yields a significant improvement in performance. When $n = |\mathcal{W}|$, the savings in number of worlds (and number of LPs solved) when using algorithm FindMPW is given by a factor of $2^{n-|Q|}$. There is, however, an extra cost associated with this algorithm, since the RefineCONS subroutine incurs additional costs when trying to separate all the auxiliary variables into an adequate set.

5   Experimental Evaluation

We developed a prototype implementation of the FindMPW algorithm using both RefineCONS and MonteCarloRefineCONS constraint refinement methods described in this paper. The implementation consisted of about 2,500 lines of Java code run on a Linux computing cluster comprised of 64 8-core, 8-processor nodes with between 10GB and 20GB of RAM; the cluster was not used for parallel computations, but for concurrent independent runs. The linear constraints for finding the most probable world were solved using the QSopt linear programming solver library, and the logical formula manipulation code from the COBA belief revision system and SAT4J satisfaction library were used for the SAT checks in the refinement methods.

To test the FindMPW algorithm with both the full refinement approach and the Monte Carlo approximation, we conducted two experiments.

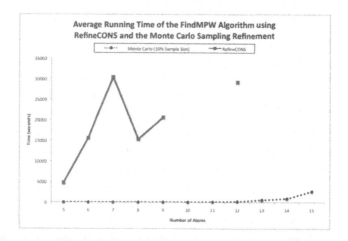

Fig. 7. Average running times for the FindMPW algorithm with both the full refinement and Monte Carlo refinement approaches

Experiment 1. In the first experiment, we compared the running time of the FindMPW algorithm using RefineCons to find an exact solution to using the Monte Carlo approach. The number of atoms was varied between 5 and 15 and the number of atoms of interest was set to 50% of the total for each run. For the Monte Carlo approach, we used a sample size that was 10% the number of possible worlds. Figure 7 below shows the running time results. The reader can readily see that the Monte Carlo algorithm works quite effectively, while the version of FindMPW that uses RefineCons is unable to perform when more than 12 atoms are present (and even for 10, 11 atoms, it can fail). The irregular shape of the curve for RefineCons is due to the fact that there is great variability in the running times depending on the specific programs that it is run on.

Experiment 2. As the previous experiment indicates, the FindMPW algorithm with Re-fineCONS can become intractable for a fairly small number of atoms. Experiment 2 focuses on the scalability of the FindMPW algorithm when used in conjunction with the Monte Carlo approach. Here we varied the number of atoms considered from 1,000 to 10,000 in steps of 1,000. In these experiments the sample size is fixed at 1,000 worlds and the number of interesting atoms is fixed at 10. Figure 8 shows the running times for FindMPW with Monte Carlo refinement for large numbers of atoms. Using the sampling refinement, FindMPW is able to find the most probable world of interest out of $2^{10,000}$ possible worlds in 97.7 minutes.

In past work, [4,5] have developed a method to determine the most probable world of an *ap*-program. However, in that work, an algorithm is presented in which a probability is associated with each subset X of rule heads of "applicable" rules in Π in state s [1]. Such a subset corresponds to the conjunction of rule heads in X with negations of applicable rule heads not in X. All worlds satisfying this conjunction have the same probability, but the timings reported in [4] do not include the time required to find this

---

[1] A rule in an *ap*-program Π is applicable in s iff s satisfies that rule's body.

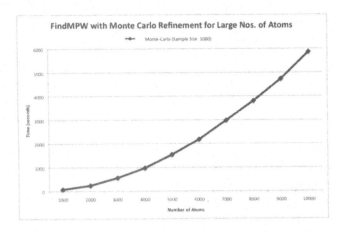

Fig. 8. Average running times for the FindMPW algorithm using the Monte Carlo approach for large numbers of atoms

probability. It should be noted that the algorithms presented here directly yield worlds of interest (along with their probabilities), without the need to take this extra step.

6 Conclusion

Though there has been extensive work on probabilistic logics and probabilistic logic programming, most of this work has focused on the entailment problem of checking whether an annotated formula $F : [\ell, u]$ is entailed by a PLP. This is done by solving up to two linear programs (minimizing and maximizing the same function expression subject to a given set of constraints). However, there are many applications in opponent modeling where we need to find the most probable set of actions that a given entity might take in a given situation. As a practical example of this, we have described our SOMA Terror Organization Portal [10] that contains *ap*-programs about 36 terror groups ranging from Morocco to Afghanistan. This system has registered users from several government agencies. Such users would like to experiment with "what if" scenarios. What is the most likely reaction from group g in a given situation? What set of actions are they most likely to take, and with what probability?

In this paper, we have developed methods to reduce the size of the linear programs involved by taking into account, the set of action atoms that a specific user might be interested in. By taking this into account, one can come up with a smaller linear program than that given in past work [4] that often, but not always, leads to a fast solution. The SemiHOP algorithm presented in [4] also proposes a reduction in number of variables in the resulting linear program by defining equivalence classes of worlds. However, that algorithm base the equivalence classes on co-occurrence of worlds in constraints, whereas the equivalence classes that arise here are purely a consequence of the input provided by the user through the set Q of actions that are interesting to him.

We have developed the RefineCons algorithm, and a Monte Carlo approach and conducted experiments showing that the latter works efficiently in practice. It remains to be seen what the accuracy of the Monte Carlo approach is, and whether it can be improved using the heuristics presented here.

Acknowledgements

The authors gratefully acknowledge funding support for this work provided by the Air Force Office of Scientific Research through the Laboratory for Computational Cultural Dynamics (LCCD) grants AFOSR grants FA95500610405 and FA95500510298, the Army Research Office under grant DAAD190310202, and the National Science Foundation under grant 0540216.

References

1. Fagin, R., Halpern, J.Y., Megiddo, N.: A logic for reasoning about probabilitie. Information and Computation 87(1/2), 78–128 (1990)
2. Hailperin, T.: Probability logic. Notre Dame J. of Formal Logic 25(3), 198–212 (1984)
3. Halpern, J.Y.: An analysis of first-order logics of probability. Artificial Intelligence 46(3), 311–350 (1990)
4. Khuller, S., Martinez, M.V., Nau, D., Simari, G., Sliva, A., Subrahmanian, V.: Computing Most Probable Worlds of Action Probabilistic Logic Programs: Scalable Estimation for $10^{30,000}$ Worlds. Annals of Mathematics and Artificial Intelligence 51(2-4), 295–331 (2007)
5. Khuller, S., Martinez, M.V., Nau, D., Simari, G., Sliva, A., Subrahmanian, V.: Finding most probable worlds of probabilistic logic programs. In: Prade, H., Subrahmanian, V.S. (eds.) SUM 2007. LNCS (LNAI), vol. 4772, pp. 45–59. Springer, Heidelberg (2007)
6. Lloyd, J.W.: Foundations of Logic Programming, 2nd edn. Springer, Heidelberg (1987)
7. Lukasiewicz, T.: Probabilistic logic programming. In: European Conference on Artificial Intelligence, pp. 388–392 (1998)
8. Mannes, A., Michael, M., Pate, A., Sliva, A., Subrahmanian, V., Wilkenfeld, J.: Stochastic opponent modelling agents: A case study with Hezbollah. In: Liu, H., Salerno, J. (eds.) Proc. 2008 First Intl. Workshop on Social Computing, Behavioral Modeling and Prediction (2008)
9. Mannes, A., Michel, M., Pate, A., Sliva, A., Subrahmanian, V., Wilkenfeld, J.: Stochastic opponent modeling agents: A case study with Hamas. In: Proceedings of ICCCD 2008 (2008)
10. Martinez, V., Simari, G., Sliva, A., Subrahmanian, V.: The soma terror organization portal (stop): Social network and analytic tools for the real-time analysis of terror groups. In: Liu, H., Salerno, J. (eds.) Proc. 2008 First Intl. Workshop on Social Computing, Behavioral Modeling and Prediction (2008)
11. Ng, R.T., Subrahmanian, V.S.: A semantic framework for supporting subjective and conditional probabilities in deductive databases. In: Furukawa, K. (ed.) Proceedings of the 8th International Conference on Logic Programming, pp. 565–580. The MIT Press, Cambridge (1991)
12. Ng, R.T., Subrahmanian, V.S.: Probabilistic logic programming. Probabilistic logic programming 102(2), 150–201 (1992)
13. Nilsson, N.: Probabilistic logic. Artificial Intelligence 28, 71–87 (1986)
14. Sliva, A., Martinez, V., Simari, G.I., Subrahmanian, V.: Soma models of the behaviors of stakeholders in the afghan drug economy: A preliminary report. In: First Int. Conference on Computational Cultural Dynamics (ICCCD 2007). ACM Press, New York (2007)

Measuring the Ignorance and Degree of Satisfaction for Answering Queries in Imprecise Probabilistic Logic Programs

Anbu Yue[1], Weiru Liu[1], and Anthony Hunter[2]

[1] School of Electronics, Electrical Engineering and Computer Science,
Queen's University Belfast, Belfast BT7 1NN, UK
{a.yue,w.liu}@qub.ac.uk
[2] Department of Computer Science, University College London,
Gower Street, London WC1E 6BT, UK
a.hunter@cs.ucl.ac.uk

Abstract. In probabilistic logic programming, given a query, either a probability interval or a precise probability obtained by using the maximum entropy principle is returned for the query. The former can be noninformative (e.g., interval $[0, 1]$) and the reliability of the latter is questionable when the priori knowledge is imprecise. To address this problem, in this paper, we propose some methods to quantitatively measure if a probability interval or a single probability is sufficient for answering a query. We first propose an approach to measuring the ignorance of a probabilistic logic program with respect to a query. The measure of ignorance (w.r.t. a query) reflects how reliable a precise probability for the query can be and a high value of ignorance suggests that a single probability is not suitable for the query. We then propose a method to measure the probability that the exact probability of a query falls in a given interval, e.g., a second order probability. We call it the degree of satisfaction. If the degree of satisfaction is high enough w.r.t. the query, then the given interval can be accepted as the answer to the query. We also provide properties of the two measures and use an example to demonstrate the significance of the measures.

1 Introduction

Probabilistic logic programming is a framework to represent and reason with imprecise (conditional) probabilistic knowledge. An agent's knowledge is represented by a *probabilistic logic program* (PLP) which is a set of (conditional) logical formulae with probability intervals. The impreciseness of the agent's knowledge is explicitly represented by assigning a probability interval to every logical formula (representing a conditional event) indicating that the probability of a formula shall be in the given interval.

Given a PLP and a query against the PLP, traditionally, a probability interval is returned as the answer. This interval implies that the true probability of the query shall be within the given interval. However, when this interval is too wide, it provides no useful information. For instance, if a PLP contains knowledge $\{(fly(X)|bird(X)[0.98, 1],$ $(bird(X)|magpie(X))[1, 1]\}$, then the answer to the query *Can a magpie fly?* (i.e., $?(fly(t)|magpie(t)))$ is a trivial bound $[0, 1]$.

S. Greco and T. Lukasiewicz (Eds.): SUM 2008, LNAI 5291, pp. 386–400, 2008.
© Springer-Verlag Berlin Heidelberg 2008

One way to enhance the reasoning power of a PLP is to apply the maximum entropy principle [1]. Based on this principle, a single probability distribution is selected and it is assumed to be the most acceptable one for the query among all possible probability distributions. As a consequence, a precise probability is given for a query even when the agent's original knowledge is imprecise. In the above example, by applying the maximum entropy principle, 0.98 is returned as the answer for the query. Intuitively, accepting a precise probability from (a prior) imprecise knowledge can be risky. When an agent's knowledge is rich enough then a single probability could be reliable, however, when an agent's knowledge is (very) imprecise, an interval is more appropriate than a single probability.

Therefore, in probabilistic logic programming as well as other conditional probabilistic logics, there is a question that has not been fully investigated, that is, how useful is a probabilistic logic program (PLP) to answering a given query? This question is important in two ways: first, it helps to analyze if a PLP is adequate to answer a query and second, if a PLP is sufficiently relevant to a query, then shall a single probability be obtained or shall a probability interval be more suitable? If it is an interval that is more suitable, then how can we get a more meaningful interval (which is satisfactory to certain extent), rather then a loose bound?

To answer the above questions, in this paper, we propose two concepts, *the measure of ignorance* and *the measure of the degree of satisfaction*, w.r.t. a PLP and a query. The former analyzes the impreciseness of the PLP w.r.t. the query, and the latter measures which (tighter) interval is sufficiently reliable to answer the query.

The main contributions of this paper are as follows. First, we propose a general framework which formally defines the measure of ignorance and the measure of the degree of satisfaction, and the postulates for these two measures. We also provide several consequence relations based on the degree of satisfaction. Second, by using the divergence of probabilistic distribution, we instantiate our framework, and show that the measure of ignorance and the measure of the degree of satisfaction have many desirable properties and provide much useful information about a PLP w.r.t. a query. Third, we prove that our framework is an extension of both reasoning on probabilistic logic program and reasoning under the maximum entropy principle. Fourth, we prove that these measures can be viewed as a second-order probability. More specifically, a high level of ignorance means a high probability about the given PLP (the agent's knowledge) is towards total absence of knowledge. The degree of satisfaction is the second-order probability about the actual probability for a conditional event given in the query falls in the given interval (provided in the query).

This paper is organized as follows. A brief review of probabilistic logic programming is given in Section 2. In Section 3, we formally analyze probabilistic logic programming and the maximum entropy principle, and provide our general framework. In Section 4, we give instantiations of the framework. We then use an example to demonstrate the significance of the measures in Section 5. Finally, we compare our approach with related work and conclude the paper in Section 6.

2 Probabilistic Logic Programming

We briefly review conditional probabilistic logic programming here [2,3].

We use Φ to denote the finite set of predicate symbols and constants symbols, $\mathcal{V}$ to denote the set of *object variables*, and $\mathcal{B}$ to denote the set of *bound constants* which describe the bound of probabilities and bound constants are in [0,1]. We use $a, b, \ldots$ to denote constants from Φ and $X, Y \ldots$ to denote object variables from $\mathcal{V}$. An *object term* t is a constant from Φ or an object variable from $\mathcal{V}$. An *atom* is of the form $p(t_1, \ldots, t_k)$, where p is a predicate symbol and $t_1, \ldots, t_k$ are object terms. We use Greek letters $\phi, \varphi, \psi, \ldots$ to denote *events* (or *formulae*) which are obtained from atoms by logic connectives $\wedge, \vee, \neg$ as usual. A *conditional event* is of the form $(\psi|\phi)$ where ψ and ϕ are events, and ϕ is called the *antecedent* and ψ is called the *consequent*. A *probabilistic formula*, denoted as $(\psi|\varphi)[l, u]$, means that the probability of conditional event $\psi|\varphi$ is between l and u, where l, u are bound constants. A set of probabilistic formulae is called a *conditional probabilistic logic program (PLP)*, a PLP is denoted as P in the rest of the paper.

A *ground* term, (resp. event, conditional event, probabilistic formula, or PLP) is a term, (resp. event, conditional event, probabilistic formula, or PLP) that does not contain any object variables in $\mathcal{V}$.

All the constants in Φ form the Herbrand universe, denoted as HU_Φ, and the Herbrand base, denoted as HB_Φ, is the finite nonempty set of all atoms constructed from the predicate symbols in Φ and constants in HU_Φ. A subset I of HB_Φ is called a *possible world* and $\mathcal{I}_\Phi$ is used to denote the set of all possible worlds over Φ. A function σ that maps each object variable to a constant is called an *assignment*. It is extended to object terms by $\sigma(c) = c$ for all constant symbols from Φ. An event φ satisfied by I under σ, denoted by $I \models_\sigma \varphi$, is defined inductively as:

- $I \models_\sigma p(t_1, \ldots, t_n)$ iff $p(\sigma(t_1), \ldots, \sigma(t_n)) \in I$;
- $I \models_\sigma \phi_1 \wedge \phi_2$ iff $I \models_\sigma \phi_1$ and $I \models_\sigma \phi_2$;
- $I \models_\sigma \phi_1 \vee \phi_2$ iff $I \models_\sigma \phi_1$ or $I \models_\sigma \phi_2$;
- $I \models_\sigma \neg\phi$ iff $I \not\models_\sigma \phi$

An event φ is satisfied by a possible world I, denoted by $I \models_{cl} \varphi$, iff $I \models_\sigma \varphi$ for all assignments σ. An event φ is a *logical consequence* of event ϕ, denoted as $\phi \models_{cl} \varphi$, iff all possible worlds that satisfy ϕ also satisfy φ.

In this paper, we use $\top$ to represent (ground) tautology, and we have that $I \models_{cl} \top$ for all I and all assignments σ. And we use $\bot$ to denote $\neg\top$.

If Pr is a function (or distribution) on $\mathcal{I}_\Phi$ (i.e., as $\mathcal{I}_\Phi$ is finite, Pr is a mapping from $\mathcal{I}_\Phi$ to the unit interval [0,1] such that $\sum_{I \in \mathcal{I}_\Phi} Pr(I) = 1$), then Pr is called a *probabilistic interpretation*. For an assignment σ, the probability assigned to an event φ by Pr, is denoted as $Pr_\sigma(\varphi)$ where $Pr_\sigma(\varphi) = \sum_{I \in \mathcal{I}_\Phi, I \models_\sigma \varphi} Pr(I)$. When φ is ground, we simply write it as $Pr(\varphi)$. When $Pr_\sigma(\phi) > 0$, the conditional probability, $Pr_\sigma(\psi|\phi)$, is defined as $Pr_\sigma(\psi|\phi) = Pr_\sigma(\psi \wedge \phi)/Pr_\sigma(\phi)$. When $Pr_\sigma(\phi) = 0$, $Pr_\sigma(\psi|\phi)$ is undefined. Also, when $(\psi|\phi)$ is ground, we simply written as $Pr(\psi|\phi)$.

A probabilistic interpretation Pr satisfies or is a *probabilistic model* of a probabilistic formula $(\psi|\phi)[l, u]$ under assignment σ, denoted as $Pr \models_\sigma (\psi|\phi)[l, u]$, iff $u \geq Pr_\sigma(\psi|\phi) \geq l$ or $Pr_\sigma(\phi) = 0$. A probabilistic interpretation Pr satisfies or is a *probabilistic model* of a probabilistic formula $(\psi|\phi)[l, u]$ iff Pr satisfies $(\psi|\phi)[l, u]$ under all assignments. A probabilistic interpretation Pr satisfies or is a *probabilistic model* of a PLP P iff for all assignment σ, $\forall(\psi|\phi)[l, u] \in P, Pr \models_\sigma (\psi|\phi)[l, u]$. A probabilistic formula $(\psi|\varphi)[l, u]$ is a *consequence* of the PLP P, denoted by $P \models (\psi|\varphi)[l, u]$, iff all probabilistic models of P satisfy $(\psi|\varphi)[l,u]$. A probabilistic formula $(\psi|\varphi)[l,u]$ is a *tight consequence* of P, denoted by $P \models_{tight} (\psi|\varphi)[l,u]$, iff $P \models (\psi|\varphi)[l,u]$, $P \not\models (\psi|\varphi)[l,u']$, $P \not\models (\psi|\varphi)[l',u]$ for all $l' > l$ and $u' < u$ ($l',u' \in [0,1]$). It is worth noting that if $P \models (\phi|\top)[0,0]$ then $P \models (\psi|\phi)[1,0]$ where $[1,0]$ stand for the empty set.

A query is of the form $?(\psi|\phi)$ or $?(\psi|\phi)[l,u]$, where ψ and ϕ are ground events and $l,u \in [0,1]$. For query $?(\psi|\phi)$, by the tight consequence relation, a bound $[l,u]$ is given as the answer, such that $P \models_{tight} (\psi|\phi)[l,u]$. For query $?(\psi|\phi)[l,u]$, a bound $[l,u]$ is given by the user. A PLP returns *True (or Yes)* if $P \models (\psi|\phi)[l,u]$ and *False (or No)* if $P \not\models (\psi|\phi)[l,u]$ [3].

The principle of maximum entropy is a well known techniques to represent probabilistic knowledge. Entropy quantifies the indeterminateness inherent to a distribution Pr by $H(Pr) = -\Sigma_{I \in \mathcal{I}_\Phi} Pr(I) \log Pr(I)$. Given a logic program P, the *principle of maximum entropy model* (or *me-model*), denoted by $me[P]$, is defined as: $H(me[P]) = \max H(Pr) = \max_{Pr \models P} -\Sigma_{I \in \mathcal{I}_\Phi} Pr(I) \log Pr(I)$.

$me[P]$ is the unique probabilistic interpretation Pr that is a probabilistic model of P and that has the greatest entropy among all the probabilistic models of P.

Let P be a ground PLP, we say that $(\psi|\varphi)[l,u]$ is a *me-consequent* of P, denoted by $P \models^{me} (\psi|\varphi)[l,u]$, iff P is unsatisfiable, or $me[P] \models (\psi|\varphi)[l,u]$.

We say that $(\psi|\varphi)[l,u]$ is a *tight me-consequent* of P, denoted by $P \models^{me}_{tight} (\psi|\varphi)[l,u]$, iff either P is unsatisfiable, $l = 1$, $u = 0$, or $P \models \bot \leftarrow \varphi$, $l = 1$, $u = 0$, or $me[P](\varphi) > 0$ and $me[P](\psi|\varphi) = l = u$.

3   General Framework

Example 1. Let P be a PLP:

$$P = \left\{ \begin{array}{l} (fly(X)|bird(X))[0.9,1], (bird(X)|magpie(X))[1,1] \\ (sickMagpie(X)|magpie(X))[0,0.1], (magpie(X)|sickMagpie(X))[1,1] \end{array} \right\}$$

From P, we can infer that $P \models_{tight} (fly(t)|magpie(t))[0,1]$, $P \models_{tight} (fly(t)|sickmagpie(t))[0,1]$, $P \models^{me}_{tight} (fly(t)|magpie(t))[0.9,0.9]$, and $P \models^{me}_{tight} (fly(t)|sickMagpie(t))[0.9,0.9]$.

In the above example, we get the same answers for queries on the proportions that magpies and sick magpies can fly. Since the proportion of sick magpies in birds is smaller than the proportion of magpies in birds, the knowledge about birds can fly should be more cautiously applied to sick magpies than magpies. In other words, the statement that more than 90% birds can fly is more about magpies than sick magpies. Therefore, to accept that 90% magpies can fly is more rational than to accept 90% sick magpies can fly. However, this analysis can not be obtained directly from comparing the bounds inferred from P.

In this section, we provide a framework to measure the ignorance of a PLP w.r.t. a conditional event and the degree of satisfaction for a conditional event with a user-given bound under a PLP.

Definition 1 (Ignorance). *Let* $\mathcal{PL}$ *be the set of all PLPs and* $\mathcal{E}$ *be a set of conditional events. Function* $\mathsf{IG} : \mathcal{PL} \times \mathcal{E} \mapsto [0,1]$ *is called a* measure[1] *of ignorance, iff for any PLP P and conditional event* $(\psi|\phi)$ *it satisfies the following postulates*

[Bounded] $\mathsf{IG}(P, \psi|\phi) \in [0,1]$.
[Preciseness] $\mathsf{IG}(P, \psi|\phi) = 0$ *iff* $P \models_{tight} (\psi|\phi)[u,u]$ *for some* $u \in [0,1]$ *or* $P \models \perp \leftarrow \phi$.
[Totally Ignorance] $\mathsf{IG}(\emptyset, \psi|\phi) = 1$, *if* $\not\models_{cl} \phi \rightarrow \psi$ *and* $\not\models_{cl} \phi \rightarrow \neg\psi$.
[Sound] *If* $\mathsf{IG}(P, \psi|\phi) = 1$ *then* $P \models (\psi|\phi)[l,u]$ *iff* $\emptyset \models (\psi|\phi)[l,u]$.
[Irrelevance] *If P and another PLP P' do not contain common syntaxes, i.e.* $\Phi \cap \Phi' = \emptyset$,
  then $\mathsf{IG}(P, \psi|\phi) = \mathsf{IG}(P \cup P', \psi|\phi)$, *where P and P' are defined over* Φ *and* Φ' *respectively.*

For simplicity, we use $\mathsf{IG}_P(\psi|\phi)$ *to denote* $\mathsf{IG}(P, \psi|\phi)$ *for a given PLP P and* $(\psi|\phi)$. *Value* $\mathsf{IG}_P(\psi|\phi)$ *defines the level of* ignorance *about* $(\psi|\phi)$ *from P.*

If $P = \emptyset$, only tautologies can be inferred from P. Therefore, from any PLP P, $\mathsf{IG}_P(\psi|\phi) \leq \mathsf{IG}_\emptyset(\psi|\phi)$, which means that an empty PLP has the biggest ignorance value for any conditional event. When $\mathsf{IG}_P(\psi|\phi) = 0$, event $(\psi|\phi)$ can be inferred precisely from P, since a single precise probability for $(\psi|\phi)$ can be obtained from P.

Definition 2 (Degree of Satisfaction). *Let* $\mathcal{PL}$ *be the set of all PLPs and* $\mathcal{F}$ *be a set of probabilistic formulae. Function* $\mathsf{SAT} : \mathcal{PL} \times \mathcal{F} \mapsto [0,1]$ *is called a measure of* degree *of satisfaction iff for any PLP P and ground probabilistic formula* $\mu = (\psi|\phi)[l,u]$, *it satisfies the following postulates:*

[Reflexive] $\mathsf{SAT}(P, \mu) = 1$, *iff* $P \models \mu$.
[Rational] $\mathsf{SAT}(P, \mu) = 0$ *if* $P \cup \{\mu\}$ *is unsatisfiable.*
[Monotonicity] $\mathsf{SAT}(P, \mu) \geq \mathsf{SAT}(P, (\psi|\phi)[l',u'])$, *if* $[l',u'] \subseteq [l,u]$.
  $\mathsf{SAT}(P, \mu) > \mathsf{SAT}(P, (\psi|\phi)[l',u'])$, *if* $[l',u'] \subset [l,u]$ *and* $\mathsf{SAT}(P, (\psi|\phi)[l',u']) < 1$.
[Cautious Monotonicity] *Let* $P' = P \cup \{(\psi|\phi)[l',u']\}$, *where* $P \models^{me} (\psi|\phi)[l',u']$
  Then $\mathsf{SAT}(P', \mu) \geq \mathsf{SAT}(P, \mu)$.

For simplicity, we use $\mathsf{SAT}_P(\mu)$ to denote $\mathsf{SAT}(P, \mu)$.

The reflexive property says that every consequence is totally satisfied. Rational says that 0 is given as the degree of satisfaction of an unsatisfiable probabilistic formula. Monotonicity says that if we expect a more precise interval for a query, then the chance that the exact probability of the query is *not* in the interval is getting bigger. Cautious monotonicity says that, if P and P' are equivalent except for the bound of $(\psi|\phi)$, and P' contains more knowledge about $(\psi|\phi)$, then the degree of satisfaction of $(\psi|\phi)[l,u]$ under P' should be bigger than that of $(\psi|\phi)[l,u]$ under P.

Proposition 1. *Function* SAT *is consistent with the maximum entropy principle, that is, it satisfies the following conditions for any PLP P and any conditional event* $(\psi|\phi)$ *with* $P \not\models \perp \leftarrow \phi$ *and* $l, u \in [0,1]$.

---

[1] In mathematical analysis, a measure $m : 2^S \mapsto [0, \infty]$ is a function, such that
1) $m(E_1) \geq 0$ for any $E \subseteq S$
2) $m(\emptyset) = 0$
3) If $E_1, E_2, E_3, \ldots$ is a countable sequence of pairwise disjoint subsets of S, the measure of the union of all the E_i's is equal to the sum of the measures of each E_i, that is,
$m(\bigcup_{i=1}^{\infty} E_i) = \sum_{i=1}^{\infty} m(E_i)$.

$$\text{SAT}_P((\psi|\phi)[l,u]) \begin{cases} = 0 \ if \ P \models^{me} (\psi|\phi)[l',l'], l' \notin [l,u] \\ > 0 \ if \ P \models^{me} (\psi|\phi)[l',l'], l' \in [l,u] \end{cases}$$

For a query $?(\psi|\phi)[l,u]$, when $\text{SAT}_P((\psi|\phi)[l,u]) < 1$ it means that the exact probability of $(\psi|\phi)$ in $[l,u]$ could be wrong based on the knowledge in P.

In our framework, given a PLP P, a conditional event $(\psi|\phi)$, and a probabilistic formula $(\psi|\phi)[l,u]$, the ignorance value $\text{IG}_P(\psi|\phi)$ and the degree of satisfaction $\text{SAT}_P(\mu)$ reveal different aspects of the impreciseness of the knowledge in P w.r.t. $(\psi|\phi)$ and $(\psi|\phi)[l,u]$. The former says how much this P can tell about $(\psi|\phi)$ and the latter says to what degree a user can be satisfied with the bound $[l,u]$ with $(\psi|\phi)$.

Proposition 2. *Let P be a PLP and $(\psi|\phi)$ be a conditional event. If $\text{IG}_P(\psi|\phi) = 0$ then $\text{SAT}_P((\psi|\phi)[l,l]) = 1$ for some $l \in [0,1]$.*

Definition 3. *Let $\text{SAT}_P(\mu)$ be the degree of satisfaction for a PLP P and $\mu = (\psi|\phi)[l,u]$ be a probabilistic formula. We define two consequence relations as*
$$P \models^{SAT \geq w} \mu \quad iff \quad \text{SAT}_P(\mu) \geq w,$$
$$P \models_{tight}^{SAT \geq w} \mu \quad iff \quad P \models^{SAT \geq w} \mu \ and \ P \not\models^{SAT \geq w} (\psi|\phi)[l',u'] \ for \ every \ [l',u'] \subset [l,u].$$

Proposition 3. *Let $\text{SAT}_P(\mu)$ be the degree of satisfaction for a PLP P and a probabilistic formula $\mu = (\psi|\phi)[l,u]$, then*

$$P \models \mu \ iff \ P \models^{SAT=1} \mu$$
$$P \models_{tight} \mu \ iff \ P \models_{tight}^{SAT=1} \mu$$

If SAT is also consistent with the maximum entropy principle, then
$$P \models_{tight}^{me} \mu \ iff \ \lim_{\epsilon \to 0+} P \models_{tight}^{SAT \geq \epsilon} \mu$$

In this proposition, we use $\text{SAT}_P(\mu) = 1$ instead of $\text{SAT}_P(\mu) \geq 1$, since the degree of satisfaction cannot be bigger than 1.

The above proposition says that our framework is a generalization of PLP under its original semantics as well as under the maximum entropy principle. That is, the classical consequence relations $\models$ and $\models_{tight}$ are too cautious - they are equivalent to requiring the degree of satisfaction of μ w.r.t P to be 1, which means that the true probability of $(\varphi|\phi)$ must fall in the bound $[l,u]$. On the other hand, the reasoning under the maximum entropy principle ($\models_{tight}^{me}$) is credulous – it excludes all the other possible probability distributions except for the most possible one.

Given a query $?(\varphi|\phi)[l,u]$ against a PLP P, the degree of satisfaction $\text{SAT}_P(\mu)$ tells the probability that $p(\varphi|\phi) \in [l,u]$. For a query $?(\varphi|\phi)$, the bound $[l,u]$ returned by $P \models_{tight} (\psi|\phi)[l,u]$ may be noninformative as discussed above. In our framework, we provide three ways to generate a more informative interval $[l',u']$ with $\text{SAT}_P((\varphi|\phi)[l',u']) \geq a$, where a is threshold given by the user. First, a user may want to know the highest acceptable lower bound, so the lower bound is increased from 0 to l' until $\text{SAT}_P((\varphi|\phi)[l',u]) \geq a$ holds. Second, a user may want to know the lowest upper bound, so u is decreased to be u' until $\text{SAT}_P((\varphi|\phi)[l,u']) \geq a$ is true. Third, a user may want to create an interval $[l',u']$ around $me[P]$, the precise probability given by the maximum entropy principle, where $\text{SAT}_P((\varphi|\phi)[l',u']) \geq a$ holds. To formalize these three scenarios, we define three consequence relations $\models_{maxLow}^{SAT \geq a}$, $\models_{minUp}^{SAT \geq a}$ and $\models_{aroundMe}^{SAT \geq a}$ for them respectively as

- $P \models_{maxLow}^{SAT \geq a} (\psi|\phi)[l', u]$ iff $P \models^{SAT \geq a} (\psi|\phi)[l', u]$ where $P \models_{tight} [l, u]$, and $l' > l$
- $P \models_{minUp}^{SAT \geq a} (\psi|\phi)[l, u']$ iff $P \models_{tight}^{SAT \geq a} (\psi|\phi)[l, u']$, where $P \models_{tight} [l, u]$ and $u > u'$
- $P \models_{aroundMe}^{SAT \geq a} (\psi|\phi)[l', u']$ iff $P \models_{tight}^{SAT \geq a} (\psi|\phi)[l', u']$ where $P \models_{tight} (\psi|\phi)[l, u]$, and $\exists b \geq 0, P \models_{tight}^{me} [m, m], l' = \max\{l, m - b\}, u' = \min\{u, m + b\}$

Example 2. Let $P = \{(fly(t)|bird(t))[0.90, 1], (bird(t)|magpie(t))[1, 1]\}$ be a PLP. From P, we can only infer that $P \models_{tight} (fly(t)|magpie(t))[0, 1]$, and $P \models_{tight}^{me} (fly(t)|magpie(t))[0.9, 0.9]$. As discussed above, the bound $[0, 1]$ is meaningless and there is not enough knowledge to infer that exactly 90% magpies can fly. In reality, taking $[0.9, 0.9]$ as the answer for this query is too risky, and there is no need to get a precise probability for the query. A more informative interval $[l, u]$ then $[0, 1]$ would be useful. Assume that a user is happy when there is a 80% (i.e. $a = 0.8$) chance that the actual probability of the query is in $[l, u]$, then we are able to use the above three consequence relations to get the following

$$P \models_{maxLow}^{SAT \geq 0.8} (fly(t)|magpie(t))[0.7, 1]$$

$$P \models_{minUp}^{SAT \geq 0.8} (fly(t)|magpie(t))[0, 0.96]$$

$$P \models_{aroundMe}^{SAT \geq 0.8} (fly(t)|magpie(t))[0.7, 1]$$

From the highest lower bound 0.7, the user can assume that a magpie very likely can fly. The user should not think that all magpies can fly either, since the lowest upper bound 0.96 is less than 1. The bound $[0.7, 1]$ gives an estimate for the probability of a magpie can fly.

In our framework, the user can calculate the degree of satisfaction for a query with a user-given bound, and the user can also calculate the tightest bound for a query s.t. the degree of satisfaction w.r.t. this bound is greater than a user-given threshold.

4   Instantiating the Framework

In this section, we provide an instantiation of our framework by defining a specific ignorance function and a satisfaction function. But first, we define a quasi-distance between probability distributions based on Kullback-Leibler divergence (KL-divergence) [4].

One of the most common measures of distance between probability distributions is the KL-divergence.

Definition 4. *Let Pr and Pr' be two probability distributions over the same set of interpretations $\mathcal{I}_\Phi$. The KL-divergence between Pr and Pr' is defined as:*

$$KL(Pr\|Pr') = -\Sigma_{I \in \mathcal{I}_\Phi} Pr(I) \log \frac{Pr'(I)}{Pr(I)}$$

KL-divergence is asymmetric and is also called *relative entropy*. It is worth noting that $KL(Pr, Pr')$ is undefined if $Pr'(I) = 0$ and $Pr(I) \neq 0$. This means that Pr has to be absolutely continuous w.r.t. Pr' for $KL(Pr\|Pr')$ to be defined.

4.1 Measurable Space

In this subsection, we first define a measurable space, in which we can measure how *wide* a set of probability distributions is.

Let $\mathbf{Pr}_\Phi$ be the set of all probability distributions on the set of interpretations $\mathcal{I}_\Phi$. Let $\mathbf{Pr}_1$ and $\mathbf{Pr}_2$ be two subsets of $\mathbf{Pr}_\Phi$, $\mathbf{Pr}_1$ and $\mathbf{Pr}_2$ are *separated* if each is disjoint from the other's *closure* [2]. A subset $\mathbf{Pr}$ of $\mathbf{Pr}_\Phi$ is called *inseparable* if it cannot be partitioned into two separated subsets. Empty set $\emptyset$ is defined as inseparable. For example, the intervals $[0, 0.3]$, $[0.4, 1]$ are separated and each of them is inseparable in the set of real numbers $\mathcal{R}$. Obviously, any subset $\mathbf{Pr}$ can be partitioned into a set of inseparable sets. Formally, there exists $\mathbf{Pr}_1, \mathbf{Pr}_2, \ldots$, such that every $\mathbf{Pr}_i$ is inseparable, $\mathbf{Pr}_i \cap \mathbf{Pr}_j = \emptyset$ $(i \neq j)$, and $\mathbf{Pr} = \bigcup_i \mathbf{Pr}_i$.

It is worth noting that, the set of all probabilistic models for a PLP is a convex set, which is an *inseparable set*. So, we only need to define a measurable space over all inseparable sets.

Definition 5. *Let $(\psi|\phi)$ be a conditional event and $\mathbf{Pr}$ be a subset of $\mathbf{Pr}_\Phi$. Suppose that $\mathbf{Pr}$ is inseparable, $l = \inf_{Pr \in \mathbf{Pr}} Pr(\psi|\phi)$, and $u = \sup_{Pr \in \mathbf{Pr}} Pr(\psi|\phi)$. We define $\delta^{ub} : 2^{\mathbf{Pr}_\Phi} \times \mathcal{F} \to [0, 1]$ and $\delta^{lb} : 2^{\mathbf{Pr}_\Phi} \times \mathcal{F} \to [0, 1]$ as*

$$\delta^{ub}(\mathbf{Pr}, (\psi|\phi)) = \min_{\substack{Pr \in \mathbf{Pr} \; Pr \models (\psi|\phi)[u, u]}} KL(Pr||Pr_{unif})$$

$$\delta^{lb}(\mathbf{Pr}, (\psi|\phi)) = \min_{\substack{Pr \in \mathbf{Pr} \; Pr \models (\psi|\phi)[l, l]}} KL(Pr||Pr_{unif})$$

where Pr_{unif} is the uniform distribution on $\mathcal{I}_\Phi$.
If $Pr(\phi) = 0$ for all $Pr \in \mathbf{Pr}$, we define $\delta^{ub}(\mathbf{Pr}, (\psi|\phi)) = \delta^{lb}(\mathbf{Pr}, (\psi|\phi)) = 0$.

For simplicity, we use $\delta_{\mathbf{Pr}}^{ub}(\psi|\phi)$ to denote $\delta^{ub}(\mathbf{Pr}, (\psi|\phi))$ and use $\delta_{\mathbf{Pr}}^{lb}(\psi|\phi)$ to denote $\delta^{lb}(\mathbf{Pr}, (\psi|\phi))$.

Value $\delta_{\mathbf{Pr}}^{ub}(\psi|\phi)$ (resp. $\delta_{\mathbf{Pr}}^{lb}(\psi|\phi)$) measures how much additional information needs to be added to the uniform distribution in order to infer the upper (resp. lower) bound of the conditional event $(\psi|\phi)$ given subset $\mathbf{Pr}$.

Definition 6. *Let $\mathbf{Pr}$ be an inseparable subset of $\mathbf{Pr}_\Phi$ and $(\psi|\phi)$ be a conditional event defined on Φ. Let $\mathbf{Pr}_{IS}$ contains all the inseparable subsets of $\mathbf{Pr}_\Phi$. We define $\vartheta_{\psi|\phi}$: $\mathbf{Pr}_{IS} \mapsto [0, 1]$ as $\vartheta_{\psi|\phi}(\mathbf{Pr}) = \text{sign}(p - u) * \delta_{\mathbf{Pr}}^{ub}(\psi|\phi) - \text{sign}(p - l) * \delta_{\mathbf{Pr}}^{lb}(\psi|\phi)$, where $p = Pr_{unif}(\psi|\phi)$, $l = \min_{Pr \in \mathbf{Pr}} Pr(\psi|\phi)$ and $u = \max_{Pr \in \mathbf{Pr}} Pr(\psi|\phi)$. Here, $\text{sign} : R \mapsto R$ is defined as $\text{sign}(x) = 1$ if $x \geq 0$ and $\text{sign}(x) = -1$ otherwise.*

In the above definition, if $Pr(\phi) = 0$ for all $Pr \in \mathbf{Pr}$, then we canonically define $\vartheta_{\psi|\phi}(\mathbf{Pr}) = 0$ since $\delta_{\mathbf{Pr}}^{ub}(\psi|\phi) = \delta_{\mathbf{Pr}}^{lb}(\psi|\phi) = 0$.

Let σ_Φ denote the smallest collection such that σ_Φ contains all the inseparable subsets of $\mathbf{Pr}_\Phi$ and it is closed under complement and countable unions of its members. Then, $\langle \mathbf{Pr}_\Phi, \sigma_\Phi \rangle$ is a *measurable space* over the set $\mathbf{Pr}_\Phi$. Obviously, $\mathbf{Pr}_\Phi \in \sigma_\Phi$, and if $\mathbf{Pr} = \{Pr \mid Pr \models P\}$ for any PLP P, then $\mathbf{Pr} \in \sigma_\Phi$.

We extend function $\vartheta_{\psi|\phi}$ to the members of σ_Φ.

---

[2] The closure of a set S is the smallest *closed* set containing S.

Definition 7. *Let* $\mathbf{Pr}$ *be a member of* σ_Φ *and* $(\psi|\phi)$ *be a conditional event. Define* $\vartheta_{\psi|\phi} : \sigma_\Phi \mapsto [0,1]$ *as* $\vartheta_{\psi|\phi}(\mathbf{Pr}) = \sum_{\mathbf{Pr_i} \in \mathfrak{P}} \vartheta_{(\psi|\phi)}\mathbf{Pr_i}$ *where* $\mathfrak{P}$ *is a partition of* $\mathbf{Pr}$ *such that each element of* $\mathfrak{P}$ *is inseparable.*

Informally, value $\vartheta_{(\psi|\phi)}(\mathbf{Pr})$ measures how *wide* the probability distributions in $\mathbf{Pr}$ is when inferring ψ given ϕ. For example, when all the distributions in $\mathbf{Pr}$ assign the same probability for the conditional event $(\psi|\phi)$, then the set $\mathbf{Pr}$ is acting like a single distribution when inferring ψ given ϕ, and $\mathbf{Pr}$ has *width* 0 for inferring ψ given ϕ.

From the definition, we know that function $\vartheta_{(\psi|\phi)}$ is a *measure*. Since it is a measure, we can define a probability distribution based on it, and we show that this probability distribution can be used as an instantiation of ignorance in the next subsection.

4.2   Instantiation of Ignorance

Definition 8. *Let* P *be a PLP and* $(\psi|\phi)$ *be a conditional event. Then a KL-divergence based ignorance, denoted* $\mathsf{IG}_P^{KL}(\psi|\phi)$, *is defined as* $\mathsf{IG}_P^{KL}(\psi|\phi) = \frac{\vartheta_{(\psi|\phi)}(\mathbf{Pr})}{\vartheta_{(\psi|\phi)}(\mathbf{Pr_\Phi})}$, *when* $\vartheta_{(\psi|\phi)}(\mathbf{Pr_\Phi}) > 0$, *where* $\mathbf{Pr} = \{Pr \mid Pr \models P\}$. *And we define* $\mathsf{IG}_P^{KL}(\psi|\phi) = 0$ *when* $\vartheta_{(\psi|\phi)}(\mathbf{Pr_\Phi}) = 0$.

Since $\vartheta_{\psi|\phi}$ is a measure, IG_P^{KL} is an uniform probability distribution. Therefore, $\mathsf{IG}_P^{KL}(\psi|\phi)$ is the probability that a randomly selected probability distribution from set $\mathbf{Pr_\Phi}$ assigns $\psi|\phi$ a probability value that is in the interval $[l, u]$, where $P \models_{tight} (\psi|\phi)[l, u]$. If this probability is close to 1, then reasoning on P is similar to reasoning on an empty PLP; when it is close to 0, it indicates that a tighter bound for $(\psi|\phi)$ can be inferred from P.

Proposition 4. *Let* P *be a PLP and* $(\psi|\phi)$ *be a conditional event. Suppose that* $P \models_{tight} (\psi|\phi)[l, u]$ *and* $pm = me[P](\psi|\phi)$. *Then* $IG_P^{KL}(\psi|\phi) = IG_{P_1}^{KL}(\psi|\phi) + IG_{P_2}^{KL}(\psi|\phi)$, *where* $P_1 = P \cup \{(\psi|\phi)[pm, u]\}$, $P_2 = P \cup \{(\psi|\phi)[l, pm]\}$.

This proposition says that the ignorance of a PLP about a conditional event is the sum of the ignorance of lacking knowledge supporting probability distributions above and below the maximum entropy probability. The ignorance can also be calculated according to maximum entropy as below.

Proposition 5. *Let* P *be a PLP and* $(\psi|\phi)$ *be a conditional event. Suppose that* $P \models_{tight} (\psi|\phi)[l, u]$, $\emptyset \models_{tight}^{me} (\psi|\phi)[p_{me}, p_{me}]$, *and* $\mathbf{Pr} = \{Pr \mid Pr \models P\}$, *then* $\vartheta_{(\psi|\phi)}(\mathbf{Pr}) = \text{sign}(u - p_{me}) * \max_{Pr \models P^u} H(Pr) - \text{sign}(l - p_{me}) * \max_{Pr \models P^l} H(Pr)$ *where* $P^u = P \cup \{(\psi|\phi)[u, u]\}$ *and* $P^l = P \cup \{(\psi|\phi)[l, l]\}$.

4.3   Instantiation of Satisfaction Function

Given a PLP P, a set of probability distributions can be induced such that $\mathbf{Pr} = \{Pr \mid Pr \models P\}$ and a unique probability distribution $me[P]$ in the set that has maximum entropy can be determined. In $\mathbf{Pr}$, some distribution is likely to be the actual probability distribution. Based on the maximum entropy principle, $me[P]$ is the most likely one, and the probability $me[P](\psi|\phi)$ is the most likely probability for the event $(\psi|\phi)$. Intuitively, the probability value that is closer to $me[P](\psi|\phi)$ is more likely to be the actual probability of $(\psi|\phi)$. Based on this, an interval that contains values closer to $me[P](\psi|\phi)$ are more likely to contain the actual probability of $(\psi|\phi)$. Of course, a loose interval is always more likely to contain the actual probability of $(\psi|\phi)$ than a tight interval.

From the KL-divergence, we can define how close a value is to $me[P]$ as:

$$\nu^{pos}_{P,(\psi|\phi)}(v) = \min_{Pr\models P, Pr(\psi|\phi)=v} KL(Pr||me), \text{ where } v \geq me[P]$$

$$\nu^{neg}_{P,(\psi|\phi)}(v) = \min_{Pr\models P, Pr(\psi|\phi)=v} KL(Pr||me), \text{ where } v \leq me[P]$$

$$dis^{pos}_{P,(\psi|\phi)}(u,v) = |\nu^{pos}_{P,(\psi|\phi)}(u) - \nu^{pos}_{P,(\psi|\phi)}(v)|$$

$$dis^{neg}_{P,(\psi|\phi)}(u,v) = |\nu^{neg}_{P,(\psi|\phi)}(u) - \nu^{neg}_{P,(\psi|\phi)}(v)|$$

Let dis be $dis^{pos}_{P,(\psi|\phi)}$ (resp. $dis^{neg}_{P,(\psi|\phi)}$). It is easy to see that dis is a distance function on $\mathcal{R}^{[pme,u]}$ (resp. $\mathcal{R}^{[l,pme]}$), where $P \models_{tight} (\psi|\phi)[l,u]$, $pme = me[P](\psi|\phi)$ and $\mathcal{R}^{[a,b]} = \{x \mid x \in [a,b], x \in \mathcal{R}\}$, i.e. dis satisfies the following:

- $dis(u,v) \geq 0$
- $dis(u,v) = 0$ iff $u = v$
- $dis(u,v) = dis(v,u)$
- $dis(u,v) \leq dis(u,x) + dis(x,v)$

Again, from the distance functions $dis^{pos}_{P,(\psi|\phi)}$ and $dis^{neg}_{P,(\psi|\phi)}$, a probability distribution can be defined. So, by KL-divergence, the possible probabilities of a conditional event $(\psi|\phi)$ are measurable. Consider every probability is equally possible, then the (second order) probability that the actual (first order) probability of $(\psi|\phi)$ falls in an interval $[a,b]$ is the *length* of $[a,b]$ divided by the *length* of $[l,u]$, where $P \models_{tight} (\psi|\phi)[l,u]$, according to the distance function $dis^{pos}_{P,(\psi|\phi)}$ and $dis^{neg}_{P,(\psi|\phi)}$. Formally, we define the degree of satisfaction as this second order probability:

Definition 9. *Let P be a PLP and $(\psi|\phi)$ be a conditional event. Suppose that $P \models_{tight} (\psi|\phi)[l,u]$ and $P \models^{me}_{tight} (\psi|\phi)[p_{me}, p_{me}]$, then we have that:*

$$\text{SAT}^{KL}_P((\psi|\phi)[a,b]) =$$
$$\begin{cases} 0.5(\dfrac{dis^{pos}_{P,(\psi|\phi)}(p_{me}, \min(u,b))}{dis^{pos}_{P,(\psi|\phi)}(p_{me}, u)} + \dfrac{dis^{neg}_{P,(\psi|\phi)}(p_{me}, \max(a,l))}{dis^{neg}_{P,(\psi|\phi)}(p_{me}, l)}), & if\ p_{me} \in [a,b] \\ 0, & otherwise \end{cases}$$

Proposition 6. *Let P be a PLP, then the function SAT^{KL}_P defined in Definition 9 satisfies all the postulates in Definition 2, and it is consistent with the maximum entropy principle, that is, it satisfies the conditions in Proposition 1.*

5 Examples

We illustrate the usefulness of our framework with two examples.

Example 3. Let P be a PLP as given in Example 1. In our framework, we calculate the KL-ignorance and KL-satisfaction for our queries. We have $\mathsf{IG}^{KL}_{(fly(t)|magpie(t))}(P) = 0.11$ and $\mathsf{IG}^{KL}_{(fly(t)|sickMagpie(t))}(P) = 0.0283$. This indicates that P is more useful to infer the proportion of magpies that can fly than to infer the proportion of sick magpies that can fly. We also have that $\mathsf{SAT}^{KL}_P((fly(t)|magpie(t))[0.8,1]) = 0.58$, $\mathsf{SAT}^{KL}_P((fly(t)|sickMagpie(t))[0.8,1]) = 0.53$. By comparing these KL degrees of satisfaction, we know that magpies are more likely to fly than sick magpies.

Example 4 (Route planning). [1]. Assume that John wants to pick up Mary after she stopped working. To do so, he must drive from his home to her office. Now, John has the following knowledge at hand: Given a road (ro) from R to S, the probability that he can reach (re) S from R without running into a traffic jam is greater than 0.7. Given a road in the south (so) of the town, this probability is even greater than 0.9. A friend just called him and gave him advice (ad) about some roads without any significant traffic. Clearly, if he can reach S from T and T from R, both without running into a traffic jam, then he can also reach S from R without running into a traffic jam. Furthermore, John has some concrete knowledge about the roads, the roads in the south of the town, and the roads that his friend was talking about. For example, he knows that there is a road from his home (h) to the university (u), from the university to the airport (a), and from the airport to Mary's office (o). Moreover, John believes that his friend was talking about the road from the university to the airport with a probability between 0.8 and 0.9 (he is not completely sure about it, though). The above and some other probabilistic knowledge is expressed by the following PLP P:

$$P = \left\{ \begin{array}{lll} ro(h,u)[1,1], & ro(u,a)[1,1], & ro(a,o)[1,1], \\ ad(h,u)[1,1], & ad(u,a)[0.8,0.9], & so(a,o)[1,1], \\ (re(R,S)|ro(R,S))[0.7,1], & (re(R,S)|ro(R,S) \wedge so(R,S))[0.9,1], \\ (re(R,S)|ro(R,S) \wedge ad(R,S))[1,1], \\ (re(R,S)|re(R,T) \wedge re(T,S))[1,1] \end{array} \right\}$$

John wants to know the probability of him running into a traffic jam, which can be expressed by the query: $Q_0 =?(re(h,o)|\top)$.

In [1], Q_0 can be answered by $P \models_{tight} (re(h,o)|\top)[0.7,1]$, and by $P \models^{me}_{tight} (re(h,o)|\top)[0.93,0.93]$. The user can either accept a noninformative bound $[0.7,1]$ or accept a unreliable precise probability 0.93, and no further reasoning can be done.

Using our method, we can get that $\mathsf{IG}^{KL}_P(re(h,o)|\top) = 0.066$. The ignorance value $\mathsf{IG}^{KL}_P(re(h,o)|\top)$ indicates that the knowledge is reliable about $(re(h,o)|\top)$. However, the actual probability of $(re(h,o)|\top)$ may be still different from 0.93, since $\mathsf{IG}^{KL}_P(re(h,o)|\top) > 0$.

John is wondering whether he can reach Mary's office from his home, such that the probability of him running into a traffic jam is smaller than 0.10. This can be expressed by the following probabilistic query: $Q_1 =?(re(h,o)|\top)[0.90,1]$. John is also wondering whether the probability of him running into a traffic jam is smaller than 0.10, if his friend was really talking about the road from the university to the airport. This can be expressed as a probabilistic query: $Q_2 =?(re(h,o)|ad(u,a))[0.90,1]$.

In [1], in the traditional probabilistic logic programming both Q_1 and Q_2 are given the answer "No"; by applying the maximum entropy principle Q_1 is given the answer "No" and Q_2 is given the answer "Yes". For Q_1 John will accept the answer "No",

Table 1. Degrees of satisfaction for queries Q_1 and Q_2

Bound	$(re(h, o)\vert\top)$	Bound	$(re(h, o)\vert ad(u, a))$
[0, 1]	1	[0, 1]	1
$\vdots$	$\vdots$	$\vdots$	$\vdots$
[0.70, 1]	1	[0.88, 1]	1
[0.75, 1]	0.785	[0.897, 1]	0.75
[0.80, 1]	0.658	[0.922, 1]	0.60
[0.86, 1]	0.500	[0.94, 1]	0.50
[0.90, 1]	0.000		

however, for Q_2, John may be confused and does not know which answer he should trust.

Using our method, we can calculate the degree of satisfaction of these two queries. For Q_1, $\mathrm{SAT}_P^{KL}(Q_1) = 0$, which means the bound $[0.9, 1]$ does not contain the probability given by applying the maximum entropy principle, and thus John has no confidence that he can reach Mary's office on time. For Q_2, $\mathrm{SAT}_P^{KL}(Q_2) = 0.724$, the relative high value "0.724" can help John to decide whether he should set off to pick up Mary.

Using our method, John can get an estimation of the probability that he can reach Mary's office from his home without running into a traffic jam. If it is a special day for him and Mary, he hopes that his estimation be more accurate, otherwise, he can tolerate a less accurate estimation. Formally, he needs to decide the threshold a for $\models_{maxLow}^{SAT \geq a}$. For example, for Q_2, he may set $a_N = 0.6$ for a normal day, and $a_I = 0.75$ for an important day. Therefore, he can infer that $P \models_{maxLow}^{SAT \geq 0.6} (re(h, o)\vert ad(u, a))[0.922, 1]$ and $P \models_{maxLow}^{SAT \geq 0.75} (re(h, o)\vert ad(u, a))[0.897, 1]$. If it is an ordinary day and the lowest probability is bigger than 0.90, then he can set off. On an important day, he will need to investigate more about the traffic (to decrease the ignorance of $(re(h, o)\vert ad(u, a))$) or he has to revise his plan, since $0.897 < 0.9$.

On the another hand, we can also analyze the usefulness of the advice from his friend. By analyzing his friend's knowledge, we have $\mathrm{IG}_P^{KL}(re(h, o)\vert ad(u, a)) = 0.0184$. This means that his friend's advice is indeed useful, since this ignorance value is significantly smaller than $\mathrm{IG}_P^{KL}(re(h, o)\vert\top)$. So, John needs to call his friend to make sure that his friend is really talking about the road from the university to the airport.

The degrees of satisfaction for various intervals are given in Table 1. From the table, we can see that, the degree of satisfaction decreases as the interval becomes tighter. This means that the second order probability that the actual probability of $(\psi\vert\phi)$ falls in $[l, u]$ is getting smaller.

6   Related Work and Conclusion

Related work. In recent years there have been a lot of research on integrating logical programming with probability theory. These probabilistic logic programs have been studied from different views and have different syntactic forms and semantics, including *conditional probabilistic logic programming* [5,3], *causal probabilistic logic programming* [6,7,8], *success probabilistic logic programming* [9,10], and some others [11].

In causal probabilistic logic programming [6,7], a rule $pr(a|\phi) = v$ is intuitively interpreted as *a is caused by factors determined by ϕ with probability v*. A causal probability statement implicitly represents a set of conditional independence assumptions: given its cause C, an effect E is probabilistically independent of all factors except the (direct or indirect) effects of E (see [6] for detail). Formally, if $pr(\psi|\phi_1) = y_1 \in P$ and $pr(\psi|\phi_2) = y_2 \in P$ where $y_1 \neq y_2$, then no possible world of P satisfies $\phi_1 \wedge \phi_2$.

In [9,10], the real number attached to a rule represents the probability that this rule is alliable (or satisfiable). In another word, a PLP in this view represents a set of (classical) logic programs, and the probability of each logic program is decided by all probabilities of all the rules. Then for any query, the answer is the probability of choosing a classical logic program from the set that can successfully infer the query. In this formalization, we can only query about the probability of ψ and cannot query about the probability of $(\psi|\phi)$, since $(\psi|\phi)$ is meaningless in classical logic programs.

In [11], the probabilities are attached to atoms, such as: $b[0.6, 0.7] \leftarrow a[0.2, 0.3]$, which means that if the probability of a is in between 0.2 and 0.3 then the probability of b is in between 0.6 and 0.7. Intuitively, the interpretation of rules is more close to casuality than conditioning. As a consequence, if we have another rule: $b[0.2, 0.3] \leftarrow c[0.5, 0.6]$, then $Pr(a) \in [0.2, 0.3]$ and $Pr(c) \in [0.5, 0.6]$ cannot be both true.

In this paper, we focus on the framework of conditional probabilistic logic programming for representing conditional events.

Because of its weakness in reasoning, subclasses cannot inherit the properties of its superclass in the basic semantics of PLP. For instance, subclass magpie can not inherit the attribute "can fly" from its superclass bird in Example 1, since $P \models_{tight} (fly(t)|magpie(t))[0, 1]$. In [12,13,14], Lukasiewicz provided another method to enhance the reasoning power mainly on the issue of inheritance. In this setting, *logic entailment strength* λ is introduced. With strength 1, subclasses can completely inherit the attributes of its superclass; with strength 0 subclasses cannot inherit the attributes of its superclass; with a strength between 0 and 1, subclasses can partially inherit the attributes of its superclass. Value strength appears to be similar to the degree of satisfaction in our framework, but they are totally different. First, λ is not a measurement for a query, but is given by a user to control the reasoning procedure, in other words, we cannot know beforehand the strength in order to infer a conclusion. Second, even if we can use a strength as a measurement, i.e. even if we can obtain the required strength to infer an expected conclusion, it is not an instance of degree of satisfaction, because the cautious monotonicity postulate in Definition 2 is not satisfied. Given a PLP P, assume that we can infer both $(\psi|\phi)[l_1, u_1]$ by strength $\lambda = \lambda_1$ and $(\psi|\phi)[l_2, u_2]$ by strength $\lambda = \lambda_2$. Now assume that $(\psi|\phi)[l_1, u_1]$ is added to P, however, in order to infer $(\psi|\phi)[l_2, u_2]$, we still need to have the strength $\lambda = \lambda_2$ given. That is, adding additional information to P does not avoid requiring the strength λ_2 if $(\psi|\phi)[l_2, u_2]$ is to be inferred. In contrast, if we have $(\psi|\phi)[l_1, u_1]$ added in the PLP, then the degree of satisfaction of $(\psi|\phi)[l_2, u_2]$ will increase.

In [15,16], the authors provided a second order uncertainty to measure the reliability of accepting the precise probability obtained by applying maximum entropy principle as the answer to a query in propositional probabilistic logic. The second order uncertainty for $(\psi|\phi)$ and PLP P is defined as $(-\log l - \log u)$ where $P \models_{tight} (\psi|\phi)[l, u]$. Similarly, we provided ignorance function to measure the usefulness of a PLP to answering a query. If a precise probability for a query is inferred from a PLP P then P contains full information about the query, and therefore accepting the probability is totally reliable. More precisely, their second order uncertainty is directly computed from the probability interval of the query inferred from P. In contrast, our ignorance is computed from the PLP, which provides more information than an interval. Therefore, our measure of ignorance is more accurate in reflecting the knowledge in a PLP.

Conclusion. In this paper, we investigated the issues surrounding how much we can *trust* a result for a query given a PLP with imprecise knowledge. We proposed a framework to measure both ignorance and the degree of satisfaction of an answer to a query under a given PLP. Using the consequence relations provided in this paper, we can get an informative and reliable interval as the answer for a query or alternatively we know how much we can trust a single probability. The proofs that our framework is an extension of both traditional probabilistic logic programming and the maximum entropy principle (in terms of consequence relations) show that our framework is theoretically sound.

References

1. Kern-Isberner, G., Lukasiewicz, T.: Combining probabilistic logic programming with the power of maximum entropy. Artificial Intelligence 157(1-2), 139–202 (2004)
2. Lukasiewicz, T.: Probabilistic logic programming. In: ECAI, pp. 388–392 (1998)
3. Lukasiewicz, T.: Probabilistic logic programming with conditional constraints. ACM Trans. Comput. Log. 2(3), 289–339 (2001)
4. Gray, R.M.: Entropy and information theory. Springer, New York (1990)
5. Costa, V.S., Page, D., Qazi, M., Cussens, J.: CLP($\mathcal{BN}$): Constraint logic programming for probabilistic knowledge. In: UAI, pp. 517–524 (2003)
6. Baral, C., Gelfond, M., Rushton, J.N.: Probabilistic reasoning with answer sets. In: Lifschitz, V., Niemelä, I. (eds.) LPNMR 2004. LNCS (LNAI), vol. 2923, pp. 21–33. Springer, Heidelberg (2003)
7. Baral, C., Hunsaker, M.: Using the probabilistic logic programming language p-log for causal and counterfactual reasoning and non-naive conditioning. In: IJCAI, pp. 243–249 (2007)
8. Saad, E.: Qualitative and quantitative reasoning in hybrid probabilistic logic programs. In: ISIPTA 2007 - Fifth International Symposium On Imprecise Probability: Theories And Applications (2007)
9. Raedt, L.D., Kimmig, A., Toivonen, H.: Problog: A probabilistic prolog and its application in link discovery. In: IJCAI, pp. 2462–2467 (2007)
10. Fuhr, N.: Probabilistic datalog: Implementing logical information retrieval for advanced applications. JASIS 51(2), 95–110 (2000)
11. Dekhtyar, A., Dekhtyar, M.I.: Possible worlds semantics for probabilistic logic programs. In: ICLP, pp. 137–148 (2004)
12. Lukasiewicz, T.: Probabilistic logic programming under inheritance with overriding. In: UAI, pp. 329–336 (2001)
13. Lukasiewicz, T.: Weak nonmonotonic probabilistic logics. Artif. Intell. 168(1-2), 119–161 (2005)

14. Lukasiewicz, T.: Nonmonotonic probabilistic logics under variable-strength inheritance with overriding: Complexity, algorithms, and implementation. Int. J. Approx. Reasoning 44(3), 301–321 (2007)
15. Rödder, W., Kern-Isberner, G.: From information to probability: An axiomatic approach - inference isinformation processing. Int. J. Intell. Syst. 18(4), 383–403 (2003)
16. Rödder, W.: On the measurability of knowledge acquisition, query processing. Int. J. Approx. Reasoning 33(2), 203–218 (2003)

Author Index